ON

CIVIL LIBERTY

AND

SELF-GOVERNMENT.

BY

FRANCIS LIEBER, LL.D.

CORRESPONDING MEMBER OF THE INSTITUTE OF FRANCE, ETC :

AUTHOR OF "POLITICAL ETHICS," "PRINCIPLES OF LEGAL AND POLITICAL INTERPRETATION," ETC. ETC.

ENLARGED EDITION IN ONE VOLUME.

THE LAWBOOK EXCHANGE, LTD.
Clark, New Jersey

ISBN 978-1-58477-070-1

Lawbook Exchange edition 2001, 2019

The quality of this reprint is equivalent to the quality of the original work.

THE LAWBOOK EXCHANGE, LTD.
33 Terminal Avenue
Clark, New Jersey 07066-1321

*Please see our website for a selection of our other publications
and fine facsimile reprints of classic works of legal history:*
www.lawbookexchange.com

Library of Congress Cataloging-in-Publication Data

Lieber, Francis, 1800-1872.
  On civil liberty and self-government / by Francis Lieber.— Enl. ed. in one
volume.
      p. cm.
  Originally published: Philadelphia: J.B. Lippincott and Co., 1859.
  Includes bibliogaphical references and index.
  ISBN 1-58477-070-8 (cloth: alk. paper)
  1. Political science. 2. Democracy. 3. Civil rights. I. Title.

JC212 . L72 2000
323—dc2l
                                   99-056928

Printed in the United States of America on acid-free paper

ON

CIVIL LIBERTY

AND

SELF-GOVERNMENT.

BY

FRANCIS LIEBER, LL.D.

CORRESPONDING MEMBER OF THE INSTITUTE OF FRANCE, ETC :

AUTHOR OF "POLITICAL ETHICS," "PRINCIPLES OF LEGAL AND POLITICAL INTERPRETATION," ETC. ETC.

ENLARGED EDITION IN ONE VOLUME.

PHILADELPHIA:

J. B. LIPPINCOTT AND CO.

LONDON: TRÜBNER AND CO.

MDCCCLIX.

TO

HIS FORMER PUPILS,

THIS VOLUME

IS

INSCRIBED

IN KIND REMEMBRANCE

BY THE AUTHOR.

TO MY FORMER PUPILS.

Gentlemen,

There are now in different portions of this country not far from a thousand citizens in the formation of whose minds I have had some share as a teacher. Many of you are in places of authority, and I consider myself more fortunate than the great founder of political science in this, that Aristotle taught a royal youth and future conqueror, and Athenians indeed, but at a period when the sun of Greece was setting, while my lot has been to instruct the future law-makers of a vast and growing commonwealth in the noblest branches that can be imparted to the minds of youths preparing themselves for the citizenship of a great republic. I have taught you in the early part of our history which God has destined to fill a fair page in the annals of man if we do our arduous duty. If not, our shame will be proportionate. He never holds out high rewards without corresponding penalties.

When you were members of this institution, I led you through the history of man, of rising and of ebbing civilization, of freedom, despotism and anarchy. I have taught you how men are destined to be producers and exchangers, how wealth is gathered and lost; and how without it, there can be no progress and no culture. I have studied with many of you, the ethics of states and of political man. You can bear me witness that I have endeavored to convince you of man's inextinguishable individuality and of the organic nature of society; that there is no right without a parallel duty, no honor without justice; no liberty without the supremacy of the law; no glory without freedom, and no high destiny without ear-

(v)

nest perseverance—that there can be no greatness of man and no grandeur of nations without self-denial.[1]

Through you my life and name are linked to the republic, and it seems natural that I should dedicate to you a work intended to complete that part of my Political Ethics which touches more especially on liberty. You will take it as the gift of a friend, and will allow it kindly to remind you of that room where you were accustomed to sit before your teacher with the busts of Washington, Socrates, Shakspeare, and other laborers in the vineyard of humanity, looking down upon us.

The suffrages of your fellow-citizens have carried many of you into the legislative halls of our confederated states; a few of you are clothed with their chief authority, or have risen to the bench; others have seats in our congress; some have become teachers of the young; some labor in the church. Many of you are at home, and near at hand; some are on the shores of the Pacific, or in foreign lands. Wherever this book may reach you, in whatever sphere of duty it may find you occupied, receive it as a work earnestly intended to draw increased attention to the great argument of our times.

Our age has added new and startling commentaries to many subjects discussed in the Political Ethics, and things there spoken of as probably past all recurrence have since burst upon an

---

[1] For other readers it may be mentioned that the writer is professor of History and of Political Philosophy and Economy in the State College of South Carolina.—So far the note, which was written in the year 1853. In the year 1857, he was appointed Professor of History and Political Science in Columbia College, in the city of New York, and the number of his former pupils, both in the South and the North, has increased much beyond the limits indicated at the beginning of these dedicatory pages. He affectionately includes in this address to his former pupils all those, who, since it was written, have passed from his tuition into the practical life of the citizen. Much has happened, in our own country and abroad, since the first writing of these pages, that makes the author address the sentiments contained in them and throughout the work with still warmer earnestness; and with an increased consciousness of their claim to an honest attention, and of their importance to the country whose welfare, in part, lies in the hands of the author's former pupils—the country for which they will have to give an account before that tribunal where acts and omissions are not judged of by the standard of party, passion, vanity or success, and where the *prava negligentia* stands recorded as a deed, as much so as the *prava deligentia*.

amazed world. We would never have supposed that socialism and despotism, the fatal negations of freedom, could have been boldly proclaimed in this century as the defence and refuge of humanity. We could never have believed possible such a waste of national zeal within so short a period, as we have witnessed in Italy and Germany—countries that are endeared to every civilized man.

A large part of Europe is in a state of violence, either convulsive action or enforced repose, and one of the greatest nations has apparently once more sought refuge in the reminiscences of the saddest times of Rome. History often reaches our shores from that portion of the globe by entire chapters. We are necessarily affected by new events and new ideas, as we in turn influence Europe; for we are of kindred blood, of one christian faith, of similar pursuits and civilization; we have one science and the same arts; we have one common treasure of knowledge and power; our alphabet and our numeric signs are the same; and we are members of one family of advanced nations. In such times it behooves us to keep a steady eye on all the signs of the times. Let us be attentive; let us understand. Goethe says truly that we must learn to read occasionally between the lines of books in order to understand them. It is a remark which applies with still greater force to the pages of history and those that record the changes of our own days.

You live in an energetic age. Men are intently bent on bold and comprehensive ends, and mischief is pursued with similar activity. The calling of our inter-oceanic country is a solemn one; the youngest nation shall bind the old to the oldest, and the Pacific shall unite, though the narrow Bosphorus has long divided. Your institutions come from the freest nation of ancient and venerable Europe—and your duties are proportionate to the blessings you are enjoying. The period we live in, our country's position and youth, our abundance of land and food, our descent and our freedom—all call upon us, and warn us.

If this work then aid, in ever so slight a degree, in the discharge of these high duties; if it help to show that the political and national Know Thyself is as important as the individual; if it impress more forcibly upon your minds the advice of Pliny : Habe ante oculos hanc esse terram quæ nobis miserit jura, and give it a meaning far wider than that which the Roman could give to it; if it prove an additional incentive to hold fast to our liberty and to cultivate it with fresh purity of purpose; if it increase our love of sterling action and disdain of self-praise; if it tend to confirm civil fortitude, that virtue which is acquired by the habit of at once obeying and insisting upon the laws of a free country, and shows itself most elevated when it resists alluring excitement; if, in some measure, it serve to restrain us from exaggeration and judging by plausibility—two faults that are rifer in our age than they have been almost at any other period; if it steady the reader against that enthusiasm which Wesley designates as "the looking to the end without the means;"[1] if it deepen our abhorrence of all abso-lutism, whether it be individual or collective, called by whatever name, monarchical or democratic, and founded upon whatever theory, whether on the jus divinum of a dynasty or the pretended universal suffrage of a Cæsar, or on the arrogance of a party and of its demagogue; and if it strengthen our conviction of the dignity of man, too feeble to wield unlimited power, and too noble to submit to it; if this book aid, in any degree, in the acknowledgment of St. Paul's great command: "Honor all men," in the wide sphere of political existence—then, indeed, I shall be richly rewarded, and shall not consider myself too bold if I point to you as Epaminondas, in his dying hour, pointed to Leuctra and Mantinea.[2]

COLUMBIA, S. C., July, 1853.   L.

---

[1] General Minutes, appended to his edition of the Book of Common Prayer, for the American Methodists.

[2] Diodor. Sic. L. xv. c. 87, 6.

CONTENTS.

(ix)

APPENDIX.

APPENDIX V.

APPENDIX VI.

APPENDIX VII.

APPENDIX VIII.

APPENDIX IX.

APPENDIX X.

APPENDIX XI.

APPENDIX XII.

APPENDIX XIII.

APPENDIX XIV.

CIVIL LIBERTY

AND

SELF-GOVERNMENT.

ON

CIVIL LIBERTY

AND

SELF-GOVERNMENT.

CHAPTER I.

INTRODUCTORY.

WE live at a period when it is the duty of reflecting men to ponder conscientiously these important questions: In what does civil liberty consist? How is it maintained? What are its means of self-diffusion, and under what forms do its chief dangers present themselves?

Our age, marked by restless activity in almost all departments of knowledge, and by struggles and aspirations before unknown, is stamped by no characteristic more deeply than by a desire to establish or extend freedom in the political societies of mankind. At no previous period, ancient or modern, has this impulse been felt at once so strongly and by such extensive numbers. The love of civil liberty is so leading a motive in our times, that no man who does not understand what civil liberty is, has acquired that self-knowledge without which we do not know where we stand, and are supernumeraries or instinctive followers, rather than conscious, working members of our race, in our day and generation.

The first half of our century has produced several hundred political constitutions, some few of substance and sterling worth, many transient like ephemeral beings, but all of them testifying to the endeavors of our age, and plainly pointing out the high problem that must be solved; many of them leaving roots in despite of their short existence, which some day

2

will sprout and prosper. It is in history as in nature. Of all the seeds that germinate, but few grow up to be trees, and of all the millions of blossoms, but thousands, or even hundreds ripen into fruit.

Changes, frequently far greater than are felt by those who stand in the midst of them, have taken place; violent convulsions have shaken large and small countries, and blood has been shed—that blood which has always flowed before great ideas could settle into actual institutions, or before the yearnings of humanity could become realities. Every marked struggle in the progress of civilization has its period of convulsion. Our race is in that period now, and thus our times resemble the epoch of the Reformation.

Many who unreservedly adhere to the past, or who fear its evils less than those of change, resist the present longings of our kind, and seem to forget that change is always going on, whether we will or not. States consist of living beings, and life is change. Others seem to claim a right of revolution for governments, under the name of *coup d'état*, but deny it to the people; and large portions of the people have overleaped civil liberty itself. They daringly disavow it, and pretend to believe that they find the solution of the great problem of our times either in an annihilation of individuality, or in an apotheosis of individual man, and preach communism, individual sovereignty, or the utmost concentration of all power and political action in one Cæsar. "Parliamentary liberty" is a term sneeringly used in whole countries to designate what they consider an obsolete encumbrance and decaying remnants of a political phase belonging to the past. The representative system is laughed at, and the idol of monarchical or popular absolutism is draped anew, and worshipped by thousands as if it were the latest avatar of their political god. What, but a lustre or two ago, would have been universally considered impossible, has come to pass; Rousseau's hatred of representative government is loudly and largely professed in France, not only by the army and the faction which holds power, but also by the French republican of extreme views, to whom nothing is more odious than decentralized self-government;

and the two seem perfectly to agree with the views lately proclaimed on an important occasion, that the essence of political civilization consists in universal suffrage and the code Napoleon, with which, and a moderately strong army, it would be easy to conquer Great Britain.[1]

There are not a few in our own country who, seeing the perversion of principles and political corruption, follow the besetting fallacy of men, and seek salvation from one evil in its opposite, as if the means of escaping death by fire were freezing to death.

We must find our way through all these mazes. This is one of our duties, because it has pleased Providence to cast our lot in the middle of the nineteenth century, and because an earnest man ought to understand, above all other social things, his own times.

Besides these general considerations, weighty as they are, there are others which press more immediately upon ourselves. Most of us descend in blood, and all of us politically, from that nation to which has been assigned, in common with ourselves, the high duty of developing modern civil liberty, and whose manliness and wisdom, combined with a certain historical good fortune, which enabled it to turn to advantage elements that proved sources of evil elsewhere, have saved it from the blight of absorbing centralization. England was the earliest country to put an end to feudal isolation, while still retaining independent institutions, and to unite the estates into a powerful general parliament, able to protect the nation

---

[1] These views were laid before the civilized world in a pamphlet, published in the summer of 1858, well known to be countenanced by the ruling party in France, and have been frequently stated before. The code Nopoleon flatters the vanity of the French people, and not being conscious of the fact that the most important element of political civilization is civil liberty, they take this code as the sum of political civilization, while it is peculiarly obtuse on all matters relating to political rights and man's protection as a freeman. How could it be otherwise with a code which proceeded from the civil law, and received, wherever it treats of personal rights, an impress from a man who, more perhaps than any other person on the stage of history, instinctively abhorred everything inclining toward liberty, even the first germs of freedom?

against the crown.[1] There, too, centuries ago, trials for high
treason were surrounded with peculiar safeguards, besides
those known in common criminal trials, in favor of the accused, an exception the very reverse of which we observe in
all other European countries down to the most recent times,
and in most countries to this day. In England, we first see
applied in practice, and on a grand scale, the idea which came
originally from the Netherlands, that liberty must not be a
boon of the government, but that government must derive its
rights from the people. Here, too, the people always clung
to the right to tax themselves; and here, from the earliest
times, the administration of justice has been separated from
the other functions of government, and devolved upon magistrates set apart for this end, a separation not yet found in all
countries.[2] In England, power of all kind, even of the crown,
has ever bowed, at least theoretically, to the supremacy of the
law,[3] and that country may claim the imperishable glory of

---

[1] The necessity of a union of the different courts and bodies of the state
was often perceived by those who felt called upon to resent the crown, and
the corresponding desire to defeat it, by the crown. An instance was furnished in France in 1648, when Mazarin strove to annul the *arrêt d'union*.

[2] I do not only allude to such bodies as the French parliaments, but to
the fact that down to this century the continental courts of justice conducted, in innumerable cases, what is now frequently called the administrative business, such as collecting taxes, letting crown domains, super-
intending roads and bridges. The early separation of the English judge—
I do not speak of his independence, which is of much later date—and the
early, comparatively speaking, independent position of the English church,
seem to me two of the most significant facts in English history, and answer in a great measure the question so often asked, Why is it that
France, constituted so much like England down to the twelfth or thirteenth century, lost her liberty, and England not? It partially accounts
for the still more surprising fact that the most advanced portions of Spain,
at one period, had a clearer perception of liberty than England had, and
is now immeasurably behind her.

[3] Even a Henry VIII. took care to have first the law changed when
it could not be bent to his tyrannical acts. Despots in other countries
did not take this trouble; and I do not know whether the history of any
other period impresses the student with that peculiar meaning which the
English word Law has acquired, more forcibly than this very reign of
tyranny and royal bloodshed.

having formed a national representative system of two houses, governed by a parliamentary law of their own, with that important element, at once conservative and progressive, of a lawful, loyal opposition. It is that country which alone saved judicial and political publicity, when secrecy prevailed everywhere else ;[1] which retained a self-developing common law and established the trial by jury. In England, the principles of self-government were not swept away, and all the chief principles and guarantees of her great charter and the petition of rights have passed over into our constitutions.

We belong to the Anglican race, which carries Anglican principles and liberty over the globe, because wherever it moves, liberal institutions and a common law full of manly rights and instinct with the principle of an expansive life, accompany it. We belong to that race whose obvious task it is, among other proud and sacred tasks, to rear and spread civil liberty over vast regions in every part of the earth, on continent and isle. We belong to that tribe which alone has the word Self-Government. We belong to that nation whose great lot it is to be placed, with the full inheritance of freedom, on the freshest soil in the noblest site between Europe and Asia, a nation young, whose kindred countries, powerful in wealth, armies, and intellect, are old. It is a period when a peaceful migration of nations, similar in the weight of numbers to the warlike migration of the early middle ages, pours its crowd into the lap of our more favored land, there to try and at times to test to the utmost, our institutions—institutions which are our foundations and buttresses, as the law which they embody and organize is our sole and sovereign master.

These are the reasons why it is incumbent upon every American again and again to present to his mind what his own liberty is, how he must guard and maintain it, and why, if he neglect it, he resembles the missionary that should proceed to convert the world without bible or prayer-book. These are

---

[1] Trials, especially criminal trials, remained public in several countries, for instance, in the Kingdom of Naples ; but judicial *and* political publicity vanished everywhere except in England ; nor was the publicity of such trials as those of Naples of much value.

the reasons why I feel called upon to write this work, in addition to what I have given long ago in another place on the subjects of Justice, Law, the State, Government and Sovereignty, on Liberty and Right,[1] and to which, therefore, I must refer my reader for many preliminary particulars; and these, too, are the reasons why I ask for an attention, corresponding to the sense of responsibility with which I approach the great theme of political vitality—the leading subject of Western history[2] and the characteristic stamp and feature of our race, our age, our own country and its calling.

[1] In my Political Ethics.

[2] I ask permission to draw the attention of the scholar to a subject which appears to me important. I have used the term Western history, yet it is so indistinct that I must explain what is meant by it. It ought not to be so. I mean by Western history, the history of all historically active, non-Asiatic nations and tribes—the history of the Europeans and their descendants in other parts of the world. In the grouping and division of comprehensive subjects, clearness depends in a great measure upon the distinctness of well-chosen terms. Many students of civilization have probably felt with me the desirableness of a concise term, which should comprehend within the bounds of one word, capable of furnishing us with an acceptable adjective, the whole of the Western Caucasian portion of mankind—the Europeans and all their descendants in whatever part of the world, in America, Australia, Africa, India, the Indian Archipelago and the Pacific Islands. It is an idea which constantly recurs, and makes the necessity of a proper and brief term daily felt. Bacon said that "the wise question is half the science;" and may we not add that a wise division and apt terminology is its completion? In my private papers I use the term Occidental in a sufficiently natural contradistinction to Oriental. But Occidental, like Western, indicates geographical position; nor did I feel otherwise authorized to use it here. Europides, would not be readily accepted either. Japhethian would comprehend more tribes than we wish to designate. That some term or other must soon be adopted seems to me clear, and I am ready to accept any expressive name formed in the spirit and according to the taste of our language. The chemist and natural historian are not the only ones that stand in need of distinct names for their subjects, but they are less exacting than scholars. As the whole race is called the Caucasian, shall we designate the group in question by the name of Cis-Caucasian? It is more important for the scholar of civilization to have a distinct name for the indicated group, than it was for the student of the natural history of our race to adopt the recently formal term of prognathous tribes, in order to group together all the tribes with projecting jaws.

CHAPTER II.

A DISTINGUISHED writer has said that every one desires liberty, but it is impossible to say what it is. If he meant by liberty, civil liberty, and that it is impossible to give a definition of it, using the term definition in its strictest sense, he was right; but he was mistaken if he intended to say that we cannot state and explain what is meant by civil liberty in certain periods, by certain tribes, and that we cannot collect something general from these different views. Civil liberty does not fare worse in this respect than all other terms which designate the collective amount of different applications of the same principle, such as Fine Arts, Religion, Property, Republic. The definitions of all these terms imply the use of others variable in their nature. The time, however, is passed when, as in the age of scholastic philosophy, it was believed that everything was strictly definable, and must be compressed within the narrow limits of an absolute definition before it could be entitled to the dignity of a thorough discussion. The hope of being able absolutely to define things that belong either to the commonest life[1] or the highest regions, betrays a misconception of human language, which itself is never absolute except in mathematics. It misleads. Bacon, so illustrious as a thinker, has two dicta which it will be well for us to remember throughout this discussion. He says: "Generalities

---

[1] Is it necessary to remind the reader of Dr. Johnson's definition of the Knife? or of the fact that the greater portion of all law business arises from the impossibility of giving absolute definitions for things that are not absolute themselves? A knife and a dagger are terms sufficiently clear in common life, but it has been found very difficult to define them, in many penal cases, when the law awards different punishments for wounds inflicted by the one or the other.

(23)

are barren, and the multiplicity of single facts present nothing but confusion. The middle principles alone are solid, orderly, and fruitful;" and in another part of his immortal works he states that "civil knowledge is of all others the most immersed in matter and the hardliest reduced to axioms." We may safely add, "And expressed in definitions." It would be easy, indeed, and correct, as far as it would go, to say: Civil liberty is the idea of liberty, which is untrammeled action, applied to the sphere of politics; but although this definition might be called "orderly," it would certainly neither be "solid" nor "fruitful," unless a long discussion should follow on what it means in reality and practice.

This does by no means, however, affect the importance of investigating the subject of civil liberty and of clearly presenting to our minds what we mean by it, and of what elements it consists. Disorders of great public inconvenience, even bloodshed and political crimes have often arisen from the fact that the two sacred words, Liberty and People, were freely and passionately used without a clear and definite meaning being attached to them. A people that loves liberty can do nothing better to promote the object of its love than deeply to study it, and in order to be able to do this, it is necessary to analyze it, and to know the threads which compose the valued texture.

In a general way, it may here be stated as an explanation—not offered as a definition—that when the term Civil Liberty is used, there is now always meant a high degree of mutually guaranteed protection against interference with the interests and rights, held dear and important by large classes of civilized men or by all the members of a state, together with an effectual share in the making and administration of the laws as the best apparatus to secure that protection, and constituting the most dignified government of men who are conscious of their rights and of the destiny of humanity. We understand by civil liberty not only the absence of individual restraint, but liberty within the social system and political organism—a combination of principles and laws which acknowledge, protect, and favor the dignity of man. But what are these guarantees, these interests and rights? Who are civilized men? In what does that share consist? Which are the men that are conscious of their rights? What is the destiny of humanity? Who are the large classes?

I mean by civil liberty that liberty which plainly results from the application of the general idea of freedom to the civil state of man, that is, to his relations as a political being—a being obliged by his nature and destined by his Creator to live in society. Civil liberty is the result of man's twofold character, as an individual and social being, so soon as both are equally respected.

All men desire freedom of action. We have this desire, in some degree, even in common with the animal, where it manifests itself at least as a desire for freedom of motion. The fiercest despot desires liberty as much as the most ardent republican; indeed, the difficulty is that he desires it too much—selfishly, exclusively.[1] He wants it for himself alone. He

---

[1] I believe that this has never been shown with greater and more truculent *naïveté*, than by the present King of Dahomey in the letter he wrote to the Queen of England in 1852. Every case in which an idea, bad or good, is carried to a point of extreme consistency is worth being noted; I shall give, therefore, a part of it.

The British government had sent an agent to that king, with presents, and the direction to prevent him from further trade in slaves; and the king's answer contains the following passage:—

"The King of Dahomey presents his compliments to the Queen of England. The presents which she has sent him are very acceptable and are good to his face. When Governor Winiett visited the king, the king told him that he must consult his people before he could give a final answer about the slave-trade. He cannot see that he and his people can do without it. It is from the slave-trade that he derives his principal revenue. This he has explained in a long palaver to Mr. Cruikshank. He begs the Queen of England to put a stop to the slave-trade everywhere else, and allow him to continue it."

In another passage he says:—

"The king begs the queen to make a law that no ships be allowed to

has not elevated himself to the idea of granting to his fellows the same liberty which he claims for himself, and of desiring to be limited in his own power of trenching on the same liberty of others. This is one of the greatest ideas to which man can rise. In this mutual grant and check lies the essence of civil liberty, as we shall presently see more fully, and in it lies its dignity. It is a grave error to suppose that the best government is absolutism with a wise and noble despot at the head of the state. As to consequences it is even worse than absolutism with a tyrant at its head. The tyrant may lead to reflection and resistance; the wisdom and brilliancy, however, of the government of a great despot or dictator deceives and unfits the people for a better civil state. This is at least true with reference to all tribes not utterly lost in despotism, as the Asiatics are. The periods succeeding those of great and brilliant despots have always been calamitous.[1] The noblest human work, nobler even than literature and science, is broad civil liberty, well secured and wisely handled. The highest ethical and social production of which man, with his inseparable moral, jural, æsthetic and religious attributes is capable, is the comprehensive and minutely organic self-government of a free people; and a people truly free at home, and dealing in fairness and justice with other nations, is the greatest, unfortunately also the rarest, subject offered in all the breadth and length of history.

In the definitions of civil liberty which philosophers or pub-

---

trade at any place near his domains lower down the coast than Wydah, as by means of trading vessels the people are getting rich and resisting his authority. He hopes the queen will send him some good tower guns and blunderbusses, and plenty of them, to enable him to make war," (which means razzias, in order to carry off captives for the barracu, or slave market.)

The claims of "undoubted sovereignty" and the "independent power" of kings, put forth by the Stuarts, by Louis XIV., and by all who looked upon kings, restricted in their power, as unworthy peers of the "real princes," must be classed under the same head with the aspirations of the principate of Dahomey, however they may differ in form.

[1] I have dwelt on this subject at length in my Political Ethics.

licists have, nevertheless, endeavored to give, they seem to have fallen into one or more of the following errors. Some have confounded liberty, the status of the freeman, as opposed to slavery, with civil liberty. But every one is aware, that while we speak of freemen in Asia, meaning only non-slaves, we would be very unwilling to speak of civil liberty in that part of the globe. The ancients knew this distinction perfectly well. There were the Spartans, constituting the ruling body of citizens, and enjoying what they would have called, in modern language, civil liberty, a full share in the government of the polity; there were Helots; and there were Lacedæmonian people, who were subject, indeed, to the sovereign body of the Spartans, but not slaves. They were freemen, compared to the Helots; but subjects, as distinguished from the Spartans. This distinction is very plain, but the confusion has not only frequently misled in times past, but is actually going on to this day in many countries.

Others have fallen into the error of substituting a different word for liberty, and believed that they had thus defined it; while others again have confounded the means by which liberty is secured in certain communities, with liberty itself. Some, again, have been led, unawares, to define an idea wholly different from civil liberty, while imagining that they were giving the generics and specifics of the subject.

The Roman lawyers say that liberty is the power (authority) of doing that which is not forbidden by the law. That the supremacy of the law and exclusion of arbitrary interference is a necessary element of all liberty, every one will readily admit; but if no additional characteristics be given, we have, indeed, no more than a definition of the status of a non-slave. It does not state whence the laws ought to come, or what spirit ought to pervade them. The same lawyers say: Whatever may please the ruler has the force of law.[1] They might have said with equal correctness: Freeman is he who is directly subject to the emperor; slave, he who is subject to the empe-

---

[1] Quod principi placuerit legis habet vigorem.—L. i. lib. i. tit. 4 Dig.

ror through an intermediate and individual master. It settles nothing as to what we call liberty, as little as the other dictum of the civil law, which divides all men into freemen and slaves. The meaning of freeman, in this case, is nothing more than non-slave; while our word freeman, when we use it in connection with civil liberty, means not merely a negation of slavery, but the enjoyment of positive and high civil privileges and rights.[1]

It is remarkable that an English writer of the last century, Dr. Price, makes the same simple division of slavery and liberty, although it leads him to very different results.[2] According to him, liberty is self-determination or self-government, and every interruption of self-determination is slavery. This is so extravagant, that it is hardly worth our while to show its fallacy. Civil liberty is liberty in a state of society; that is, in a state of union with equals; consequently limitation of self-determination is one of the necessary characteristics of civil liberty.

Cicero says: Liberty is the power of living as thou willest.[3] This does not apply to civil liberty. It would apply to savage insulation. If it was meant for political liberty, it would have been necessary to add: "So far as the same liberty of others does not limit your own living as you choose." But we always live in society, so that this definition can have a value only as a most general one, to serve as a starting-point, in order to explain liberty if applied to different spheres. Whether this was the probable intention of a practical Roman, I need not decide.

Libertas came to signify, in the course of time, and in republican Rome, simply republican government, abolition of royalty. We have advanced beyond this idea. The most

---

[1] Summa divisio de jure personarum haec est, quod omnes homines aut liberi sunt aut servi.—Inst. i. 3.

[2] Observations on the Nature of Civil Liberty, etc., by Richard Price, D.D., 3d ed.; Lond. 1776.

[3] Quid est libertas? Potestas vivendi ut velis.—Cic. Parad. 5, 1, 34.

sanguinary pages of history have taught us that a kingless government is not, on that account alone, a republic, if the term republic is intended to comprehend the idea of self-government in any degree. France had as absolute and as stringently concentrated a government under her so-called republics, as under any of her kings. To classify governments, with reference to liberty, into monarchies and republics, is an error in principle. An Englishman who lives under a monarchy, for such certainly his royal republic is called, enjoys an amount of self-government and individual liberty far greater than the Athenian ever possessed or is established in any republic of South America.

The Greeks likewise gave the meaning of a distinct form of government to their word for liberty. Eleutheria, they said, is that polity in which all are in turn rulers and ruled. It is plain that there is an inkling of what we now call self-government in this adaptation of the word, but it does not designate liberty as we understand it. For, it may happen, and indeed it has happened repeatedly, that although the rulers and ruled change, those that are rulers are arbitrary and oppressive whenever their turn arrives; and no political state of things is more efficient in preparing the people to pass over into despotism, by a sudden turn, than this alternation of arbitrary rule. If this definition really defined civil liberty, it would have been enjoyed in a high degree by those communities in the middle ages, in which constant changes of factions and persecutions of the weaker parties were taking place. Athens, when she had sunk so low that the lot decided the appointment to all important offices, would at that very period have been freest, while in fact her government had become plain democratic absolutism, one of the very worst of all governments, if, indeed, the term government can be properly used of that state of things which exhibits Athens after the times of Alexander, not like a bleeding and fallen hero, but rather like a dead body, on which birds and vermin make merry.

Not wholly dissimilar to this definition is the one we find in the French Political Dictionary, a work published in 1848, by leading republicans, as this term was understood in France. It says, under the word liberty: "Liberty is equality, equality is liberty." If both were the same, it would be surprising that there should be two distinct words. Why were both terms used in the famous device, "Liberty, Equality, Fraternity," if the first two are synonymous, yet an epigrammatic brevity was evidently desired? Napoleon distinguished between the two very pointedly, when he said to Las Cases, that he gave to the Frenchmen all the circumstances allowed, namely, equality, and that his son, had he succeeded him, would have added liberty. The dictum of Napoleon is mentioned here merely to show that he saw the difference between the two terms. Equality, of itself, without many other elements, has no intrinsic connection with liberty. All may be equally degraded, equally slavish, or equally tyrannical. Equality is one of the pervading features of Eastern despotism. A Turkish barber may be made vizier far more easily than an American hair-dresser can be made a commissioner of roads, but there is not on that account more liberty in Turkey.[1] Diversity is the law of life; absolute equality is that of stagnation and death.[2]

A German author of a work of mark begins it with this sentence: "Liberty—or justice, for where there is justice there is liberty, and liberty is nothing else than justice—has by no means been enjoyed by the ancients in a higher degree

---

[1] Since the publication of the first edition of this work, an article on "Mohametanism in Western Asia," has appeared in the "Edinburgh Review," October, 1853, in which the Eastern equality as an ingredient of despotism is illustrated by many striking instances from different spheres of life. The writer, who is plainly master of his subject, from personal knowledge, it would appear, agrees with us that liberty is based on individuality. Indeed, it may be said that in a great degree it consists in essential protection of individuality, of personal rights. The present Emperor of the French felt this when he wrote his chapter, De la Liberté individuelle en Angleterre. He was then an exile and could perceive liberty.

[2] More has been said on this subject in Political Ethics, and we shall return to it at a later period.

than by the moderns."[1] Either the author means by justice
something peculiar, which *ought* to be enjoyed by every one,
and which is not generally understood by the term, in which
case the whole sentence is nugatory, or it expresses a grave
error, since it makes equivalents of two things which have received two different names, simply because they are distinct
from one another. The two terms would not even be allowed
to explain each other in a dictionary.

Liberty has not unfrequently been defined as consisting in
the rule of the majority, or it has been said, Where the people
rule there is liberty. The rule of the majority, of itself, indicates the power of a certain body; but power is not liberty.
Suppose the majority bid you drink hemlock, is there liberty
for you? Or suppose the majority give away liberty, and
establish despotism? It has been done again and again:
Napoleon III. claims his crown by right of election by the
overwhelming majority of Frenchmen, and perpetuates his government by universal suffrage, as he says. Granting, for the
sake of argument that there was what we call a *bona fide* election, and that there is now existing an efficient universal suffrage, there is no man living who would vindicate liberty for
present France. Even the imperial government periodically
proclaims that it cannot yet establish liberty, because France
is distracted by factions, by "different nations," as an imperial dignitary lately expressed it in an official speech.

We might say with greater truth, that where the minority
is protected, although the majority rule, there, probably,
liberty exists. But in this latter case it is the protection, or
in other words, rights beyond the reach of the majority which
constitute liberty, not the power of the majority. There can
be no doubt that the majority ruled in the French massacres
of the Protestants; was there liberty in France on that account? All despotism, without a standing army, must be supported or acquiesced in by the majority. It could not stand

---

[1] Descriptions of the Grecian Polities, by F. W. Tittman; Leipsig,
1822.

otherwise. If the definition be urged, that where the people rule there is liberty, we must ask at once, what people, and how rule? These intended definitions, therefore, do not define.

Other writers have said: " Civil liberty consists in the responsibility of the rulers to the ruled." It is obvious that this is an element of all civil liberty; but the question, what responsibility is meant? is an essential one; nor does this responsibility alone suffice by any means to establish civil liberty. The Dey of Algiers used to be elected by the soldiery, who deposed him if he did not suit; but there was no liberty in Algiers, not even for the electing soldiery. The idea of the best government, repeatedly urged by a distinguished French publicist, Mr. Girardin, is, that all power should be centered in an elective chief magistrate, who by frequent election should be made responsible to the people—in fact, an elective despotism. Is there an American or Englishman living who would call such a political monstrosity freedom, even if the elected despot would allow himself to be voted upon a second time? This conception of civil liberty was the very one which Louis Napoleon published in his proclamation, issued after the *coup d'état*, and in which he tells the people that he leaves their fate in their own hands! Many Frenchmen voted for him and for these fundamental principles of a new government, but those who did so, voted for him for the very reason that they considered liberty dangerous and inadmissible. This definition, then, is peculiarly incorrect.

Again, it has been said, liberty is the power of doing all that we ought to be allowed to do. But who allows? What *ought* to be allowed? Even if these questions were answered, it would not define liberty. Is the imprisoned homicide free, although we allow him to do all that which he ought to be allowed to do? No despot, if not positively insane, would ask for more power. It is on the very ground that more freedom ought not to be allowed to the subject, for his own benefit and the welfare of the empire, that the greatest despots and even tyrants have asserted their power; nor does a father desire more power over his child, but he does not pretend to confound parental power with the establishment of liberty.

Bodinns, whom every scholar of political science remembers with respect, said that true liberty consists in nothing else than the undisturbed enjoyment of one's goods and the absence of apprehension that wrong be done to the honor and the life of one's self, of one's wife and family.[1] He who knows the times of French history when this jurist wrote his work on the republic, sees with compassion what led his mind to form this definition; nor is it denied that undisturbed enjoyment of property, as well as personal safety, constitute very important objects sought to be obtained by civil liberty; but it is the firmly-established guarantees of these enjoyments which constitute portions of civil liberty. Haroun Al Rashid may have allowed these enjoyments, but the Arabians had not civil liberty under him. It is very painful to observe that, in the middle of the nineteenth century, a writer could be reduced to declare before the Institute of France, in an elaborate essay, that this definition of liberty by Bodinns is the best ever given.[2]

Montesquieu says:[3] "Philosophical liberty consists in the exercise of one's will, or at least (if we must speak of all systems) in the opinion according to which one exercises his will. Political liberty consists in the security, or at least in the opinion which one has of one's security." He continues: "This security is never more attacked than in public and private accusations. It is therefore upon the excellence of the criminal laws that chiefly the liberty of the citizen depends."[4]

---

[1] De Republica, lib. xii. c. 6. I have mentioned in my Political Ethics that I studied, in the Congress library, the copy of Bodinns, which had belonged to President Jefferson, and in which many pencil marks and notes of the latter are found. It will interest many of my readers to hear that this relic has not perished in the fire which consumed the greater portion of the library.

[2] Mr. Parry, Séances et Travaux de l'Acad. des Sciences Politiques et Morales, July, 1855.

[3] Esprit des Lois, xii. 2; "Of the Liberty of the Citizen."

[4] He goes on treating liberty in a similar manner; for instance, at the beginning of chapter iv. of the same work.

That security is an element of liberty has been acknowledged; that just penal laws, and a carefully protected penal trial, are important ingredients of civil liberty, will be seen in the sequel; but it cannot be admitted that that great writer gives a definition of liberty in any way adequate to the subject. We ask at once, what security? Nations frequently rush into the arms of despotism for the avowed reason of finding security against anarchy. What else made the Romans so docile under Augustus? Those French who insist upon the "necessity" of Louis Napoleon, do it on the avowal that anarchy was impending; but no one of us will say that Augustus was the harbinger of freedom, or that the French emperor allows the people any enjoyment of liberty. If, however, Montesquieu meant the security of those liberties which Algernon Sidney meant when he said, "The liberties of nations are from God and nature, not from kings"—in that case he has not advanced the discussion, for he does not say in what they consist.

If, on the other hand, the penal law, in which it must be supposed Montesquieu included the penal trial, be made the chief test of liberty, we cannot help observing that a decent penal trial is a discovery in the science of government of the most recent date. The criminal trials of the Greeks and Romans, and of the middle ages, were deficient both in protecting the accused and society, and, without trespassing, we may say that in most cases they were scandalous, according to our ideas of justice. Must we then say, according to Montesquieu, that liberty never dwelt in those states?[1]

---

[1] That a writer of Montesquieu's sagacity and regard for liberty should have thus insufficiently defined so great a subject, is nothing more than what frequently happens. No man is always himself, and Bishop Berkeley, on Tar Water, represents a whole class of weak thoughts by strong minds. I do not only agree with what Sir James Mackintosh says in praise of Montesquieu, in his Discourse on the Study of the Law of Nature and Nations, but I would add, than no person can obtain a correct view of the history through which political liberty has been led in Europe, or can possess a clear insight into many of its details, without making himself acquainted with the Spirit of Laws. His work has doubtless been of great influence.

To pass from a great writer to one much his inferior, I shall give Dr. Paley's definition of civil liberty. He says, "Civil liberty is the not being restrained by any law but what conduces in a greater degree to the public welfare."[1] I should hardly have mentioned this definition, but that the work from which it is taken is still in the hands of thousands, and that the author has obviously shaped and framed it with attention. Who decides on what public welfare demands? Is that no important item of civil liberty? Who makes the law? Suffice it to say that the definition may pass for one of a good government in general, that is, one which befits the given circumstances; but it does not define civil liberty. A Titus, a benevolent Russian Czar, a wise dictator, a conscientious Sultan, a kind master of slaves, ordain no restraint but what they think is required by the general welfare; yet to say that the Romans under Titus, the Russian, the Asiatic, the slave is on that account in the enjoyment of civil liberty, is such a perversion of language that we need not dwell upon this definition, surprising even in one who does not generally distinguish himself by unexceptionable definitions.

The first (monarchical) French constitution of September 3, 1791,[2] says, "Liberty consists in the right to do everything that does not injure others. Therefore, the practice of the natural rights of each man has no other limits than those which secure the other members of society in the enjoyment of the same rights. These limits can only be determined by law." The last sentence makes all depend on the law; consequently we must ask again, who makes the law, and are there no limits necessary to the law itself?

Nothing is more striking in history, it seems to me, than a comparison of this declaration and of the "Rights of Men" with the British Petition of Right, whether we consider them as fruits or as seeds.

The second (republican) constitution of June 24, 1793, says:[3]

---

[1] Beginning of the fifth chapter of Paley's Political Philosophy.

[2] Paragraph four.

[3] Paragraph six of the Declaration of the Rights of Men.

Liberty is that faculty, according to which it belongs to man to do that which does not interfere with the rights of others; it has for its basis, nature; for its rule, justice; for its protection, the law; its moral limit is the maxim, Do not to another that which thou dost not wish him to do to thyself.

This definition sufficiently characterizes itself.

The Constitution of the United States has no definition of liberty. Its framers thought no more of defining it in that instrument, than people going to be married would stop to define what is love.

We almost feel tempted to close this list of definitions with the words with which Lord Russell begins his chapter on liberty. He curtly says, "Many definitions have been given of liberty. Most of these deserve no notice."[1]

Whatever the various definitions of civil liberty may be, we take the term in its usual adaptation among modern civilized nations, in which it always means liberty in the political sphere of man. We use it in that sense in which freemen, or those who strive to be free, love it; in which bureaucrats fear it and despots hate it; in a sense which comprehends what has been called public liberty and personal liberty; and in conformity with which all those who cherish and those who disrelish it distinctly feel that, whatever its details may be, it always means a high degree of untrammeled political action in the citizen, and an acknowledgment of his dignity and his important rights by the government which is subject to his positive and organic, not only to his roundabout and vague influence.

This has always been felt; but more is necessary. We ought to know our subject. We must answer, then, this question: In what does civil liberty truly consist?

---

[1] Lord John Russell's History of the English Government and Constitution, second ed., London, 1825. This prominent and long-tried statesman distinguishes, on page 15, between civil, personal, and political liberty; but even if he had been more successful in this distinction than he seems to me actually to have been, it would not be necessary to adopt it for our present purpose.

CHAPTER III.

THE MEANING OF CIVIL LIBERTY.

LIBERTY, in its absolute sense, means the faculty of willing and the power of doing what has been willed, without influence from any other source, or from without. It means self-determination; unrestrainedness of action.

In this absolute meaning, there is but one free being, because there is but one being whose will is absolutely independent of any influence but that which he wills himself, and whose power is adequate to his absolute will—who is almighty. Liberty, self-determination, unrestrainedness of action, ascribed to any other being, or applied to any other sphere of action, has necessarily a relative and limited, therefore an approximative sense only. With this modification, however, we may apply the idea of freedom to all spheres of action and reflection.[1]

---

[1] It will be observed that the terms Liberty and Freedom are used here as synonymes. Originally they meant the same. The German Freiheit (literally Freehood) is still the term for our Liberty and Freedom; but as it happened in so many cases in our language where a Saxon and Latin term existed for the same idea, each acquired in the course of time a different shade of the original meaning, either permanently so, or at least under certain circumstances. Liberty and Freedom are still used in many cases as synonymous. We speak of the freedom as well as the liberty of human agency. It cannot be otherwise, since we have but one adjective, namely Free, although we have two nouns. When these are used as distinctive terms, freedom means the general, liberty the specific. We say, the slave was restored to freedom; and we speak of the liberty of the press, of civil liberty. Still, no orator or poet would hesitate to say freedom of the press, if rhetorically or metrically it should suit better. As in almost all cases in which we have a Saxon and a Latin term for the same main idea, so in this, the first, because the older and origi-

If we apply the idea of self-determination to the sphere of politics, or to the state, and the relations which subsist between it and the individual, and between different states,

---

nal term, has a fuller, more compact, and more positive meaning; the latter a more pointed, abstract or scientific sense. This appears still more in the verbs, to free and to liberate. The German language has but one word for our Freedom and Liberty, namely Freiheit; and Freithum (literally freedom) means, in some portions of Germany, an estate of a Freiherr (baron.) In Dutch, the word Vryheid (literally freehood) is freedom, liberty; while Vrydom (literally freedom) means a privilege, an exemption from burdens. This shows still more that these words meant originally the same.

The subject of liberty will occupy us throughout this work, and is of itself a subject of such magnitude, that we may well allow ourselves the time of reflecting for a moment on the terms which man has employed to designate this great concept.

.The Greek word eleutheros, free, properly means, he who can walk where he likes. See Passow ad verbum, 'Ελεύθερος and 'Ερχομαι. The Latin liber is believed to be derived from the same root with the Gothic Lib, (in German Leib, body, connected with the Gothic Liban, our live, the German leben,) so that liber would have meant originally, he who has his own body, whose body does not belong to some one else. It is natural that freedom appeared to the ancients, first of all, as a contradistinction to slavery, or as its negation. This is not quite dissimilar to the fact that most languages designate the state of purity by an adjective, which indicates a negation of the state of guilt. We say innocent, the negation of nocent, guilty; as if we were calling light undarkness. The guilt, the crime, strikes first, and from it are abstracted the negations unguilt, innocence. If all were free, and if freedom had never been violated, we would probably have no word for freedom.

That Body is taken in this instance to designate independence, with which the ideas of individuality and humanity are closely connected, is in conformity with the history of all terms of abstraction. The sensuous world furnishes man with the original term and idea which the advancing intellect refines and distils. Nor can it surprise us who to this day say somebody, everybody, for some person, every man. Who does not think at once of Burns's lovely " Gif a body meet a body," where body is used for human individual? At the time of writing this note, I met with this question in a Scottish penal trial: Was that arsenic for a beast or a body?—Burton's Criminal Trials, vol. ii. page 59.

Here, then, body is taken so distinctly for man, that it is contradistinguished from beast. In the same natural manner, it may come to

we must remember that the following points are necessarily involved in the comprehensive idea of the state :—

The state is a society, or union of men—a sovereign society and a society of human beings, with an indelible character of individuality. The state is, moreover, an institution which acts through government, a contrivance which holds the power of the whole, opposite to the individual. Since the state then implies a society which acknowledges no superior, the idea of self-determination applied to it means that, as a unit and opposite to other states, it be independent, not dictated to by foreign governments, nor dependent upon them any more than itself has freely assented to be, by treaty and

---

signify man, not with reference to his intellect, but in connection with liberty, as contradistinguished from a man-thing, *i. e.* slave.

At a later period, the *soul* comes to designate individuals, as we say in statistical accounts, so many souls, for so many persons.

The word Free is one of the oldest words with which we are acquainted. We find free, fry, fryg, vry, in many languages, and Hesichius gives as a Lydian word βρίγα—το ἐλευθερόν, from which the name of the Phrygians was probably derived. It seems to be connected with several prepositions and verbs which we find in many languages ; but this is not the place to carry the etymological inquiry any farther. It may be added, however, that through all the ancient Teutonic languages there is running a root Fr and Pr, with words derived from it, which indicate protection, pax, fœdus. Frihals or Frijhals is the ancient High German for a protected man, a free man, a non-slave man. How this root again is connected with the Gothic frijan, frion, for loving, kissing, (hence our word friend,) and the Sanscrit pri, which means *exhilarare, amare,* cannot be settled here. I would refer the reader for more information on this sub-ject, to L. Difenbach's Comparative Dictionary of the Gothic Language, a German work, and to Grimm's German Dictionary, which, indeed, I have not yet been able to see; but the name of Grimm is so well known to the world as that of the undisputed highest authority on all questions of Teutonic etymology, that the author does not hesitate to direct his reader to a work which he himself has not yet examined.

It is a curious fact that the Armenians for liberty, a compound of *ink'n,* self, and *ishkhanootzoon,* dominion, sovereignty. So that the Armenians actually have our noble word, self-government. My learned friend, the Rev. J. W. Miles, of Charleston, to whom I owe this contri-bution and much information on the Asiatic terms for liberty, adds, "I think a word of similar composition is used in the Georgian for liberty."

upon the principles of common justice and morality, and that it be allowed to rule itself, or that it have what the Greeks chiefly meant by the word autonomy.[1] The term state, at the same time, means a society of men, that is, of beings with individual destinies and responsibilities from which arise individual rights,[2] that show themselves the clearer and become more important, as man advances in political civilization. Since, then, he is obliged and destined to live in society, it is necessary to prevent these rights from being encroached upon by his associates. Since, however, not only the individual rights of man become more distinctly developed with advancing civilization, but also his social character and all mutual dependence, this necessity of protecting each individual in his most important rights, or, which is the same, of checking each from interfering with each, becomes more important with every progress he makes.

Lastly, the idea of the state involving the idea of government, that is, of a certain contrivance with coercing power superior to the power of the individual, the idea of self-determination necessarily implies protection of the individual against encroaching power of the government, or checks against government interference. And again, society as a

---

[1] Autonomeia is literally translated Self-Government, and undoubtedly suggested the English word to our early divines. Donaldson, in his Greek Dictionary, gives Self-Government as the English equivalent for the Greek Autonomy, but, as it has been stated above, it meant in reality independence of other states, a non-colonial, non-provincial state of things. I beg the reader to remember this fact, for it is significant that the term autonomy retained with the Greeks this meaning, facing as it were foreign states, and that Self-Government, the same word, has acquired with ourselves, chiefly, or exclusively, a domestic meaning, facing the relations in which the individual and home institutions stand to the state which comprehends them.

[2] The fact that man is in his very essence at once a social being and an individual; that the two poles of sociality and individualism must forever determine his political being, and that he cannot give up either the one or the other, with the many relations flowing from this fundamental point, form the main subject of the first volume of my Political Ethics, to which I would refer the reader.

unit having its objects, ends, and duties, liberty includes a proper protection of government, as well as an efficient contrivance to coerce it to carry out the views of society, and to obtain its objects.

We come thus to the conclusion that liberty, applied to political man, practically means, in the main, protection or checks against undue interference, whether this be from individuals, from masses, or from government. The highest amount of liberty comes to signify the safest guarantees of undisturbed legitimate action, and the most efficient checks against undue interference.[1] Men, however, do not occupy themselves with that which is unnecessary. Breathing is unquestionably a right of each individual, proved by his existence; but, since no power has yet interfered with the undoubted right of respiration, no one has ever thought it necessary to guarantee this elementary right. We advance then a step farther in practically considering civil liberty, and find that it chiefly consists in guarantees (and corresponding checks) of those rights which experience has proved to be most exposed to interference, and which men hold dearest and most important.

This latter consideration adds a new element. Freemen protect their most important rights, or those rights and those

---

[1] It is interesting with reference to the above subject, that the Teutonic *frei* and *free* come from the same root *fr*, with *fridu* and *frida*, (in modern German *Friede*,) that is, *peace*, to which allusion has been made in the preceding note. *Fridon* in old Saxon meant to protect, to make secure. The old Norse has *frido*, (*fridho*,) which the lexicographer renders by *tutus, fortis, mansuetus, formosus*. In some parts of Germany and Switzerland *Friede* (*peace*) still means *fence*, that is, protection. In the middle ages *fredus* and *freda* meant the legal protection within a certain district. The word goes through the Franconian, Alemannian, Longobardian and other laws, and reminds us of the English term, the king's peace. Freiburg meant originally a town and district within which certain protection and security was to be found. Without multiplying the instances, which might be done ad infinitum, the fact that in the Teutonic languages the term freedom is of the same root with that for legal security and protection, or rather that the latter has passed over to that of liberty, is well established and full of meaning.

attributes of self-determination, which they hold to be most essential to their idea of humanity; and as this very idea of humanity comprehends partly some ideas common to men of all ages, when once conscious of their humanity, and partly other ideas, which differ according to the view of humanity itself which may prevail at different periods, we shall find, in examining the great subject of civil freedom, that there are certain permanent principles met with wherever we discover any aspiration to liberty; and that, on the other hand, it is rational to speak of ancient, medieval, or modern liberty, of Greek or Roman, Anglican and Gallican, Pagan and Christian, American and English liberty. Certain tribes or nations, moreover, may actually aim at the same objects of liberty, but may have been led, in the course of their history, and accord- to the variety of circumstances produced in its long course, to different means to obtain similar ends. So that this fact, likewise, would evolve different systems of civil liberty, either necessarily or only incidentally so. Politics are like archi- tecture, which is determined by the objects the builder has in view, the materials at his disposal, and the desire he feels of manifesting and revealing ideas and aspirations in the material before him. Civil liberty is the idea of liberty in connection with politics, and must necessarily partake of the character or intertwine itself with the whole system of politics of a given nation.

This view, however correct, has, nevertheless, misled many nations. It is true, that the system of politics must adapt itself to the materials and destinies of a nation; but this very truth is frequently perverted by rulers who wish to withhold liberty from the people, and do it on the plea that the destiny of the nation is conquest, or concentrated action in different spheres of civilization, with which liberty would interfere. In the same manner are, sometimes, whole portions of a people, or even large majorities, misled. They seem to think that there is a fate written somewhere beyond the nation itself, and independent of its own morality, to which everything, even justice and liberty, must be sacrificed. It is at least a very large portion of the French that thus believes the highest destiny of France to consist in ruling as the first power in Europe, and who openly say, that everything must bend to this great destiny. So are many among us, who seem to believe that the highest destiny of the United States consists in the extension of her territory—a task in which, at best, we can only be imitators, while, on the contrary, our destiny is one of its own, and of a substantive character.

At the present stage of our inquiry, however, we have not time to occupy ourselves with these aberrations.

All that is necessary to vindicate at present is, that it is sound and logical to speak of eternal principles of liberty, and at the same time of ancient and modern liberty, and that there may be, and often must be, various systems of civil liberty, though they need not, on that account, differ as to the intensity of liberty which they guarantee.

That Civil Liberty, or simply Liberty, as it is often called, naturally comes to signify certain measures, institutions, guarantees or forms of government, by which people secure or hope to secure liberty, or an unimpeded action in those civil matters, or those spheres of activity which they hold most important, appears even from ancient writers. When Aristotle, in his work on politics speaks of liberty, he means certain peculiar forms of government, and he uses these as tests, to decide whether liberty does or does not exist in a polity, which he contemplates at the time. In the Latin language Libertas came to signify what we call republic, or a non-regal government. Respublica did not necessarily mean the same as our word Republic, as our term Commonwealth may mean a republic—a commonwealth man meant a republican in the English revolution[1]—

---

[1] The republic—if, indeed, we can say that an actual and *bona fide* republic ever existed in England—was called *the State*, in contradistinction to the regal government. During the Restoration under Charles II., men would say, "In the times of the State," meaning the interval between the death of the first Charles and the resumption of government by the second. The term State acquired first this peculiar meaning under the Presbyterian government.

but it does not necessarily do so. When we find in Quintilian the expression, *Asserere libertatem reipublicæ*, we clearly see that respublica does not necessarily mean republic, but only when the commonwealth, the system of public affairs, was what we now call a republic. Since this, however, actually was the case during the best times of Roman history, it was natural that respublica received the meaning of our word republic in most cases.

The term liberty had the same meaning in the middle ages, wherever popular governments supplanted monarchical, often where they superseded aristocratic polities. Liberty and republic became in these cases synonymous.[1]

---

[1] It is in a similar sense that Freiligrath, a modern German poet, begins one of his most fervent songs with the line, Die Freiheit ist die Republik; that is, Freedom is the Republic. On the other hand, I found that Prussia, at the time of Frederic the Great, was called, on a few occasions, the Republic, manifestly without any reference to the form of government, and meaning simply the common or public weal or concern.

CHAPTER IV.

THAT which the ancients understood by liberty differed essentially from what we moderns call civil liberty. Man appeared to the ancients in his highest and noblest character, when they considered him as a member of the state or as a political being. Man could rise no higher in their view. Citizenship was in their eyes the highest phase of humanity. Aristotle says in this sense, the state is before the individual. With us the state, and consequently the citizenship, remain means—all-important ones, indeed, but still means—to obtain still higher objects, the fullest possible development of humanity in this world and for the world to come. There was no sacrifice of individuality to the state too great for the ancients. The greatest political philosophers of antiquity unite in holding up Sparta as the best regulated commonwealth—a communism in which the individual was sacrificed in such a degree, that to the most brilliant pages of all history she has contributed little more than deeds of bravery and saliant anecdotes of stoic heroism. Greece has rekindled modern civilization, in the restoration of letters. The degenerate keepers of Greek literature and art, who fled from Constantinople when it was conquered by the Turks, and settled in Western Europe, were nevertheless the harbingers of a new era. So great was Grecian knowledge and civilization even in this weakened and crippled state! Yet in all that intellectuality of Greece which lighted our torch in the fifteenth and sixteenth centuries, there is hardly a single Lacedæmonian element.

Plato, when he endeavors to depict a model republic, ends

(45)

with giving us a communism, in which even individual marriage is destroyed for his higher classes.[1]

We, on the other hand, acknowledge individual and primordial rights, and seek one of the highest aims of civil liberty in the most efficient protection of individual action, endeavor, and rights. I have dwelt upon this striking and instructive difference at length in my work on Political Ethics,[2] where I have endeavored to support the opinion here stated by historical facts and passages of the ancients. I must refer the reader, therefore, to that part of the work; but there is a passage which seems to me so important for the present inquiry, as well as for another which will soon occupy our attention, that, unable to express myself better than I have done in the mentioned work, I must beg leave to insert it here. It is this:—

"We consider the protection of the individual as one of the chief subjects of the whole science of politics. The $\pi o\lambda\iota\tau\iota\varkappa\tilde{\eta}$ $\dot{\epsilon}\pi\iota\sigma\tau\dot{\eta}\mu\eta$, or political science of the ancients, does not occupy itself with the rights of the individual. The ancient science of politics is what we would term the art of government, that is, 'the art of regulating the state, and the means of preserving and directing it.' The ancients set out from the idea of the state, and deduce every relation of the individual to it from this first position. The moderns acknowledge that the state, however important and indispensable to mankind, however natural, and though of absolute necessity, still is but a means to obtain certain objects, both for the individual and for society collectively, in which the individual is bound to live by his nature. The ancients had not that which the moderns understand by jus naturale, or the law which flows from the

---

[1] It is a striking fact that nearly all political writers who have indulged in creating Utopias—I believe all without exception—have followed so closely the ancient writers, that they rose no higher than to communism. It may be owing in part to the fact that these writers composed their works soon after the restoration of letters, when the ancients naturally ruled the minds of men.

[2] Chapter xiii. of the second book.

individual rights of man as man, and serves to ascertain how, by means of the state, those objects are obtained which justice demands for every one. On what supreme power rests, what the extent and limitation of supreme power ought to be, according to the fundamental idea of the state,—these questions have never occupied the ancient votaries of political science.

"Aristotle, Plato, Cicero, do not begin with this question. Their works are mainly occupied with the discussion of the question, Who shall govern? The safety of the state is their principal problem; the safety of the individual is one of our greatest. No ancient, therefore, doubted the extent of supreme power. If the people possessed it, no one ever hesitated in allowing to them absolute power over every one and everything. If it passed from the people to a few, or was usurped by one, they considered, in many cases, the acquisition of power unlawful, but never doubted its unlimited extent. Hence, in Greece and Rome the apparently inconsistent, yet, in reality, natural sudden transitions from entirely or partially popular governments to absolute monarchies; while, in modern states, even in the absolute monarchies, there exists a certain acknowledgment of a public law of individual rights, of the idea that the state, after all, is for the protection of the individual, however ill-conceived the means to obtain this object may be.

"The idea that the Roman people gave to themselves, or had a right to give to themselves, their emperors, was never entirely abandoned, though the soldiery arrogated to themselves the power of electing the masters. * * *. Yet the moment that the emperor was established on his throne, no one doubted his right to the absolute supreme power, with whatever violence it was used.[1]

---

[1] This was written in the year 1837. Since then, events have occurred in France which may well cause the reader to reflect whether, after all, the author was entirely correct in drawing this peculiar line between antiquity and modern times. All I can say in this place is, that the political movements in France resemble the dire imperial times of Rome

"Liberty, with the ancients, consisted materially in the degree of participation in government, 'where all are in turn the ruled and the rulers.' Liberty, with the moderns, consists less in the forms of authority, which are with them but means to obtain the protection of the individual and the undisturbed action of society in its minor and larger circles. Ἐλευθερία, indeed, frequently signifies with the Greek political writers, equality; that is, absolute equality, and ἰσότης, equality as well as ἐλευθερία, are terms actually used for democracy,[1] by which was understood what we term democratic absolutism, or unlimited despotic power in the demos, which, practically, can only mean the majority, without any guarantee of any rights. It was, therefore, perfectly consistent that the Greeks aimed at perfect liberty in perfect equality, as Aristotle states, not even allowing a difference on account of talent and virtue; so that they give the πάλος, the lot, as the true characteristic of democracy. They were consistently led to the lot; in seeking for liberty, that is, the highest enjoyment and manifestation of reason and will, or self-determination, they were led to its very negation and annihilation—to the lot, that is, to chance. Not only were magistrates, but even generals and orators determined by lot."[2]

Had the ancients possessed other free states than city-states, they would have been forced out of this position; but there were no states in antiquity, if we take the term in the adaptation in which we use it, when we mean sovereign political societies spreading over extensive territories and forming an organic legal whole. Even the vast monarchies of ancient Asia were conglomerated conquests with much of what has just been called a city-state. Nineveh, Babylon, were mighty

---

just so far as the French, or rather the Napoleonists among them, step out of the broad path of modern political civilization, actually courting a comparison with imperial Rome, and that this renewed imperial period will be nothing but a phase in the long chain of political revulsions and ruptures of France. The phase will not be of long duration, and after it will have passed, it will serve as an additional proof of our position.

[1] Plato, Gorg. 39.

[2] For the evidence and proof I must refer to the original.

cities that swayed over vast dominions as mistresses, but did not form part of a common State in the modern term.

In the middle ages liberty appears in a different phase. The Teutonic spirit of individual independence was one of the causes which led to the feudal system, and frequently prospered under it in rank disorder. There was no state proper in the middle ages; the feudal system is justly called a mere system. It was no state; and medieval liberty appears in the shape of liberties, of franchises, singly chartered, separately conquered, individually arrogated—each society, party, or person obtaining as much as possible, unmindful of others, and each denying to others as much as might be conveniently done. The term freedom, therefore, came distinctly to signify, in the middle ages, not exactly the amount of free action allowed to the citizen or guaranteed to the person who enjoyed it, but the exemption from burdens and duties imposed upon others, or exacted in former times. Liberty had not yet acquired a substantive meaning, although it need not be mentioned that then as well as in ancient times, the principle which made noble hearts throb for liberty and independence, was the same that has made the modern martyrs of liberty mount the scaffold with confidence and reliance on the truth of their cause.

I am here again obliged to refer to the Political Ethics, where I have treated of this peculiarity of the middle ages in the chapter on the duties of the modern representative, contradistinguished from the medieval deputy.

The nearer we approach to modern times the more clearly we perceive two movements, which, at first glance, would appear to be destructive the one to the other. On the one hand states, in the present sense of the term, are formed. There is a distinct period in the history of our race, which may be aptly called the period of nationalization. Tribes, fragments, separate political societies, are united into nations, and politically they appear more and more as states. It is one of the many fortunate occurrences which have fallen to England in the course of her history, that she became nationalized at a comparatively very early period. The feudal system was

4

introduced at a late period, and as a royal measure. The
king made the Norman-English nobility. The nobility did
not make the king. The English nobility, therefore, could
not resist the national movement and consolidation of the
people into a nation, as it did on the continent, and, the
crown thus not being obliged to gather all possible strength,
in order to be able to subdue the baronial power, had not the
opportunity to pass over into the concentrated principate,
which was one of the political phases in every other part of
Europe.[1]

On the other hand we observe that the priceless individual
worth and value which Christianity gives to each human being,
by making him an individually responsible being, with the
highest duties and the highest privileges, together with advancing civilization, in a great measure produced by itself—
the Teutonic spirit of personal independence, connected not a
little with the less impressionable, and therefore more tenacious, and sometimes dogged character of the Teutonic—all
these combinedly, developed more and more the idea of individual rights, and the desire of protecting them.

These two facts have materially influenced the development

----

[1] The history of no nation reminds the student so frequently of the fact
that " His ways are not our ways," as that of England. Many events which
have brought ruin elsewhere, served there, in the end, to obtain greater
liberty and a higher nationality. The fact that the Norman nobility in
England was the creature of the king—for this, doubtless, it was, although
they came as Norman noblemen to the field of Hastings—is one of these
remarkable circumstances. The English civil wars ; the fact that most
of England's monarchs have been indifferent persons, and that after
Alfred the Great, but one truly great man has been among her kings;
the inhospitable climate, which was treated by the people like a gauntlet
thrown down by nature ; and they developed that whole world of domestic
comfort and well-being, known nowhere else, and of such important influence upon all her political life ; her limited territory ; her repeated
change of language ; her early conquests,—these are some items of a list
which might easily be extended.

Since this note was originally written, a work in praise of Henry VIII.
has attracted sufficient attention to make it necessary for me to state that
the author means William III. as the great monarch after Alfred.

of modern liberty, that liberty which we call our own. The progress we value so much was greatly retarded on the continent by an historical process which was universal among the nations of Europe, excepting those of Sclavonic origin, because they had not yet entered the lists of civilization.

The feudal system, of far greater power on the continent than in England, interfered with the process of nationalization and the formation of states proper. The people gradually rose to a higher position, a higher consciousness of rights, and the inhabitants of the cities generally found the baronial element hostile to them. The consequence was, that the crowns and the people united to break the power of the baron. But in the same degree as the struggle was tenacious, and the crown had used stronger power to subdue the feudal lord, it found itself unshackled when the struggle was over, and easily domineered over both the people and the lords. Then came the time of absorbing regal power, of centralization and monarchical absolutism, of government-states, as Niebuhr calls them. The liberties of the middle ages were gone; the principles of self-government were allowed to exist nowhere; and we find, at the present period only, the whole of the European continent, with the exception of Russia, as a matter of course, engaged in an arduous struggle to regain liberty, or rather to establish modern freedom. Everywhere the first ideas of the new liberty were taken from England, and, later, from the United States. The desire of possessing a well-guaranteed political liberty and enjoyment of free action, was kindled on the European continent by the example of England. The course which we observe in France, from Montesquieu, who, in his brilliant work on the Spirit of Laws, has chiefly England in view as a model, to the question at the beginning of the first French Revolution, whether the principles of British liberty should be adopted, was virtually repeated everywhere. The representative principle, the trial by jury, the liberty of the press, taxation and appropriations by the people's representatives, the division of power, the habeas corpus principle, publicity, and whatever else was prominent in that liberty peculiar to the Anglican race, whether it had originated with it, or had been retained by it when elsewhere it had been lost in the general shipwreck of freedom, was longed for by the continental people, insisted on, or struggled for.

It is well, then, to ask ourselves, in what does this Anglican liberty consist? The answer is important, in a general point of view, as well as because it is the broad foundation and frame-work of our own American liberty.

CHAPTER V.

ANGLICAN LIBERTY.

In order to ascertain in what this peculiar system of civil liberty consists, we must examine those charters of the whole Anglican race, which belong to "the times when governments chartered liberty," and to those "when the people charter governments." We must observe what principles, measures, and guarantees were most insisted upon in periods most distinguished by an active spirit of liberty, of opposition to encroaching power, or of a desire to prune public power so as to make it in future better harmonize with the claims of individual liberty. We must see what it is that the people of England and the people of America in great political periods have solemnly declared their rights and obligations. We must study the periods of a vigorous development of liberty, and we must weigh Magna Charta, the Petition of Right, and the Bill of Rights—the three statutes which Lord Chatham called the Bible of the English Constitution. We must inquire into the public common law of England, and the common law as it has developed itself on this side of the Atlantic; and especially into the leading cases of political and constitutional importance that have been decided in England and the United States.[1] We must ponder our great federal pact, with the contemporaneous writers on this constitution, and the debates which led to its adoption after the failure of the original articles

---

[1] A chronological table of the leading cases in England and the United States, by which great constitutional principles or essential individual rights have been settled and sown like a spreading, self-increasing plant, would be highly instructive, and show how much we owe to the *growth* of liberty, and how much this growth is owing to the husbanding of practical cases in the spirit of freedom.

(53)

of confederation, as well as the special charters which were considered peculiarly favorable to liberty, such as many of the colonies possessed, out of which the United States arose. We must attentively study the struggles in which the people waged their all to preserve their liberties, or to obtain new ones, and those periods which, with reference to civil liberty, may be called classical. We must analyze the British and our own revolutions, and compare them with the political revolutions of other nations, and we must study not only the outward events, or the ultimate measures, but we must trace their genesis, and ascertain how and why these things came about, and what the principles were for which the chief men engaged in the arduous task contended. We must mark what it is that those nations wish to introduce among themselves, that are longing for freedom similar to that which we enjoy. We must test which of the many institutions peculiar to our tribe have proved, in the course of time, as real props of freedom, or most prolific in shooting forth new branches. We must read the best writers on law, history, and political philosophy with reference to these subjects, and observe the process of spreading liberty. We must note which are the most fruitful principles of Anglican self-government in the widening colonies, north and south of the equator ; and examine our own lives as citizens of the freest land, as well as the great process of expansion of liberty with ourselves. We ought clearly to bring before our minds those guarantees, which invariably are the main points of assault when the attempt is made to batter the ramparts of civil liberty and bring the gallant garrison to surrender. And lastly, we ought to study the course of despotism ; for the physiologist learns as much from pathology as from a body in vigorous health.

We call this liberty Anglican freedom, not because we think that it ought to be restricted to the Anglican race, or will or can be so ; but simply because it has been evolved first and chiefly by this race, and because we must contradistinguish it from Gallican liberty as the sequel will show.[1] Nor is it

---

[1] In the year 1848 I published, in an American journal, a paper headed Anglican and Gallican Liberty, in which I indicated several views which

maintained that all that is included in Anglican liberty is of especial Anglican origin.   Liberty is one of the wreaths of humanity, and in all liberty there must be a large fund of universal humanity, as all cultivated languages must agree in embodying the most important principles of intellectual analysis and combination ; and as Grecian architecture does not contain exclusively what the Greeks originated, and is not, on account of its very humanity, restricted to Greece, still, we call it Greek architecture, and we do so with propriety; for it was in Greece that that column and capital were developed which are found everywhere with civilized man, have passed over from a pagan world into Christian civilization, and are seen wherever the bible is carried.

have been further developed in the present work.   A distinguished German criminalist and publicist did me the honor of publishing a German translation of this paper, in which, however, he says that what I have called Anglican liberty is more generally called Germanic liberty.   This is an error.   I allow that the original Teutonic spirit of individual independence, distinguished as it is from the Celtic disposition of being swayed by masses, and from the consequent proclivity toward centralization in politics, religion, and literature, and a certain inability to remain long in the opposition, or to stand aloof of a party,—I allow that this original Teutonic spirit largely enters into what I have termed Anglican liberty ; but this is a system of civil liberty which has developed itself independent of all other Teutonic nations, has been increasing while nearly all the other Teutonic nations lost their liberty, and of which, unfortunately, the Germans, who ought to be supposed the most Germanic of the Germanic tribes, have nothing, except what may remain of the late attempts at engrafting anew principles or guarantees of liberty on their polities, which had become more and more a copy of French centralization.   This is not the place to discuss the subject of so-called Germanic liberty.   All that is necessary here to state is, that what is called Anglican liberty consists, as was said before, in a body of guarantees which, as an entire system, has been elaborated by the Anglican race, and is peculiar to them unless imitated by others.   Many a detail of Anglican liberty existed long ago in other parts of Europe, and was enjoyed at times in a higher degree than by the English at that period.   But it withered or ran wild, and never became a part of a constitutional organism.   What has become of the Arragonese *Justicia* or chief justice ?   What of the Hungarian excessive self-government of the county ?

Now, what we call Anglican liberty, are the guarantees
which our race has élaborated, as guarantees of those rights
which experience has shown to be most exposed to the danger
of attack by the strongest power in the state, namely, the
executive, or as most important to a frame of government
which will be least liable to generate these dangers, and also
most important to the essential yet weaker branches of government. It consists in the civil guarantees of those principles
which are most favorable to a manly individual independence
and ungrudged enjoyment of individual humanity ; and those
guarantees which insure the people, meaning the totality of the
individuals as a unit, or the nation, against being driven from
the pursuit of those high aims which have been assigned to it
by Providence as a nation, or as a united people. Where the
one or the other is omitted, or exclusively pursued, there is no
full liberty. If the word people be taken as never meaning
anything else than a unit, a widely extended and vigorous
action of that unit may exist indeed—blinding ambition may
be enjoyed, but it is no liberty; if, on the other hand, the
term people is never taken in any other sense than a mere
term of brevity, and for the impossible enumeration of all individuals, without inherent connection, the consequence must
be a sejunctive egotism which loses the very power of protecting the individual rights and liberties.

What is guarantee for one is check to the other, and if
liberty consists in mutual guaranteeing of certain rights of
actions and endeavors, it is clear that, correspondingly, it
consists in certain mutual checking, which, again, cannot exist
without corresponding mutual toleration. We find therefore,
in history, that no people who have not fairly learned to bear
with one another, can enjoy liberty. The absence of toleration is the stigma of absolutisms, the establishment of " the
opposition" is the glory of freedom. Freedom allows of
variety ; the tyrant, whether one or a multitude, calls heretic
at every one who thinks or feels differently.[1]

---

[1] Bunsen, in his Signs of the Times, calls mutual toleration the true

These guarantees, then, as we acknowledge them in the period of civil development in which we live, and as far as they are common to the whole Anglican race, and, if of a more general character, are still inseparably interwoven with what is peculiar to the race, we call Anglican liberty. These guarantees and checks I now proceed to enumerate.

---

evidence of a firm Christian faith and the only valid evidence before God and men.

He speaks of religion, but the remark, with proper modification, is applicable in all spheres. Strong conviction of right and truth and reality early rises to respectful toleration—a generous acknowledgment of the rights, as well as the opinions of others. Feebleness of conviction or consciousness of feebleness makes tyrannical and vindictive. And, let us add, this is one of the many points where true liberty and gentlemanliness meet in requirements and effects.

CHAPTER VI.

NATIONAL INDEPENDENCE. PERSONAL LIBERTY.

1. It is impossible to imagine liberty in its fulness, if the people as a totality, the country, the nation, whatever name may be preferred, or its government, is not independent of foreign interference. The country must have what the Greeks called autonomy. This implies that the country must have the right, and, of course, the power, of establishing that government which it considers best, unexposed to interference from without or pressure from above. No foreigner must dictate; no extra-governmental principle, no divine right or " principle of legitimacy" must act in the choice and foundation of the government ; no claim superior to that of the people's, that is, superior to national sovereignty, must be allowed.[1] This independence or national self-government further implies that, the civil government of free choice or free acquiescence being established, no influence from without, besides that of freely acknowledged justice, fairness, and morality, must be admitted. There must then be the requisite strength to resist when necessary. While the author is setting down these remarks, the news is reaching us of the manly declaration made in the British Commons, by the minister of foreign affairs, Lord Palmerston, that the united calls of all the continental powers would be utterly insufficient to give up or to drive from the British territory those political exiles who have sought an asylum on English soil, and of the ready support given by the press to the spokesman of the nation. Even the French, so far as they are allowed at the present untoward conjunction to express themselves, applaud this declaration as a proof of British freedom.

---

[1] Political Ethics, chapter on Sovereignty.

The Helvetic Cantons, on the other hand, are forced to yield to the demands even of an Austrian government; and the worried Republic of Switzerland, so far as this goes, cannot be said to be free. The history of the nineteenth century, but especially that of our own age, is full of instances of the interference with the autonomy of nations or states. Italy, Germany, especially Hessia; Spain, Hungary, furnish numerous instances. Cases may occur, indeed, in which foreign interference becomes imperative. All we can then say is, that the people's liberty so far is gone, and must be recovered. No one will maintain that interference with Turkish affairs at the present time is wrong in those powers who resist Russian influence in that quarter, but no one will say either that Turkey enjoys full autonomy. The very existence of Turkey depends upon foreign sufferance.

Since the preceding paragraph was written, historical illustrations have occurred, too important to be appended in a note. The same statesman who, as minister of foreign affairs in the year 1853, made the manly declaration concerning political fugitives, allowed himself, as prime minister, in the year 1858, to propose a law in the House of Commons, at the instigation of the emperor of the French, by which the fomenting of conspiracies, in England, against foreign princes, should be visited with a higher punishment, or be made punishable, if it was not already so. The English Commons indignantly rejected such a bill proposed at that very time; the premier lost his place, and from that historical jury-box of Middlesex proceeded a verdict of not guilty when a Frenchman, residing in England, was tried for having been an accessory before the fact, of Orsini, who had attempted to assassinate Napoleon III. The verdict was plainly on the ground that Englishmen would not be dictated to in their legislation by a despotic foreign government, and as such was hailed with joy by every man on the European continent, who wishes well to liberty.[1] It was a similar spirit no doubt, which lately caused many Americans to

---

[1] The case is the Queen vs. Bernard.

take so warm a part against the reported attempts of English vessels to search American traders.

On the other hand, it must be remembered that this unstinted autonomy is greatly endangered at home by interfering with the domestic affairs of foreigners. The opinion, therefore, urged by Washington, that we should keep ourselves aloof from foreign politics, is of far greater weight than those believe who take it merely with reference to foreign alliances and ensuing wars. The interference need not necessarily proceed from government. Petitions, affecting foreign public measures or institutions, and coming from large bodies, or even committees sent to express the approval of a foreign government, of which we have had a recent and most remarkable instance,[1] are reprehensible on the same ground.

It is one of the reasons why a broadcast liberty and national development was so difficult in the middle ages, that the pope, in the times of his highest power, could interfere with the

---

[1] The address and declaration of four thousand British merchants, presented in the month of April, 1853, to the emperor of the French, will forever remain a striking proof of British liberty; for in every other European country the government would have imprisoned every signer, if, indeed, the police had not nipped the petition in the bud; and it will also forever remain a testimony how far people can forget themselves and their national character when funds are believed to be endangered, or capital is desired to be placed advantageously. But I have alluded to it in the text as an instance only of popular interference with foreign governments, doubtless the most remarkable instance of the kind on record. Whether the whole proceeding was "not far short of high treason," as Lord Campbell stigmatized it in the House of Lords, may be left undecided. It certainly would have been treated as such during some periods of English history, and must be treated by all right-minded men of the present period as a most unworthy procedure.

To this must now be added the record of the tone which pervaded the address of the lord mayor and aldermen of London to Count Walewski, French Ambassador, in the early part of the year 1858, and the manner in which it was received, when Orsini had attempted to assassinate the count's master and cousin, having obtained his explosive weapons in England. The reply of the ambassador was submitted to, although rising to such a degree of impertinence that it was necessary, at a later period, diplomatically to explain and partially to unsay it.

autonomy of states. I do not discuss here whether this was not salutary at times. Gregory VII. was a great, and, possibly, a necessary man; but where civil liberty is the object, as it is now with civilized nations, this medieval interference of the pope would be an abridgment of it, just as much as the Austrian or French influence in the States of the Church is an abridgment of their independence at present.

It is a remarkable feature in the history of England, that even in her most catholic times the people were more jealous of papal interference by legates or other means, than any other nation, unless we except the Germans, when their emperors were in open war with the popes. This was, however, transitory, while in England intercourse with the papal see was legally restricted and actually made penal.

2. Civil liberty requires firm guarantees of individual liberty, and among these there is none more important than the guarantee of personal liberty, or the great habeas corpus principle, and the prohibition of "general warrants" of arrest of persons.

To protect the individual against the interference with personal liberty by the power-holder is one of the elementary requisites of all freedom, and one of the most difficult problems to be solved in practical politics. If any one could doubt the difficulty, history would soon convince him of the fact. The English and Americans safely guard themselves against illegal arrest; but a long and ardent struggle in England was necessary to obtain this simple element, and the ramparts around personal liberty, now happily existing, would soon be disregarded, should the people, by a real prava negligentia malorum, ever lose sight of this primary requisite.

The means by which Anglican liberty secures personal liberty are threefold: the principle that every man's house is his castle, the prohibition of general warrants, and the habeas corpus act.

Every man's house is his castle. It is a principle evolved by the common law of the land itself, and is exhibited in a yet stronger light in the Latin version, which is, Domus sua cuique

est tutissimum refugium, and Nemo de domo sua extrahi debet,
which led the great Chatham, when speaking on general warrants, to pronounce that passage with which now every English
and American schoolboy has become familiar through his
Reader. "Every man's house," he said, "is called his castle.
Why? Because it is surrounded by a moat, or defended by a
wall? No. It may be a straw-built hut; the wind may whistle
around it, the rain may enter it, but the king cannot."[1]

Accordingly, no man's house can be forcibly opened, or he
or his goods be carried away after it has thus been forced, except in cases of felony, and then the sheriff must be furnished
with a warrant, and take great care lest he commit a trespass.
This principle is jealously insisted upon. It has been but
recently decided in England, that although a house may have
been unlawfully erected on a common, and every injured commoner may pull it down, he is nevertheless not justified in
doing so if there are actually people in it.

There have been nations, indeed, enjoying a high degree of
liberty, without this law maxim; but the question in this place
is even less about the decided advantages, arising to freemen
from the existence of this principle, than about the sturdiness
of the law and its independent development, that could evolve
and establish this bold maxim. It must be a manly race of
freedom-loving people, whose own common law could deposit
such fruitful soil. For, let it be observed, that this sterling

---

[1] In many countries, and even among hardly civilized tribes, it has
been a rule that no one should enter a man's house without the consent
of the owner. Missionaries tell us that the Yarriba people in Central
Africa do not allow their king to enter a house, even to arrest a
criminal, without the consent of the head of the family. So we are very
often told that the trial by jury was known before England had its present name; but the question of importance is, how far a principle is
developed, how securely it is guaranteed, how essential a part of a
general system it is, and how strong it is to resist when public power
should choose to interfere with it. The Chinese have censorship, but
this absence of censorship is not liberty of the press. The Romans
cared very little about the religion of their subjects, (so that they were
not Christians,) but this was not constitutional toleration or freedom of
worship.

maxim was not established, and is not maintained, by a disjunctive or a law-defying race. The Mainots considered their Lacedæmonian mountain fastnesses as their castles too, during the whole Turkish reign in Greece; the feudal baron braved authority and law in his castle; the Mino-tze[1] have never been subdued by the Tartar dynasty of China, and defy the government in their mountain fastnesses to this day, much as the Highlanders of Scotland did before the battle of Culloden; but the English maxim was settled by a highly conjunctive, a nationalized people, and at the same time when law and general government was extending more and more over the land. It is insisted on in the most crowded city the world has ever seen, with the same jealousy as in a lonely mountain dwelling; it is carried out, not by retainers and in a state of war made permanent, as Essex tried to do when he was arrested, but by the law, which itself has given birth to it. The law itself says: Be a man, thou shalt be sovereign in thy house. It is this spirit which brought forth the maxim, and the spirit which it necessarily nourishes, that makes it important.

It is its direct antagonism to a mere police government, its bold acknowledgment of individual security opposite to government, it is its close relationship to self-government, which give so much dignity to this guarantee. To see its value, we need only throw a glance at the continental police, how it enters at night or in the day, any house or room, breaks open any drawer, seizes papers or anything it deems fit, without any other warrant than the police hat, coat and button.

Nor must we believe that the maxim is preserved as a piece of constitutional virtu. As late as the month of June, 1853, a bill was before the House of Commons, proposing some guarantee against property of nuns and monks being too easily withdrawn from relations, and that certain officers should have the right to enter nunneries, from eight A.M. to eight o'clock P.M., provided there was strong suspicion that an inmate was retained against her will. The leading minis-

---

[1] In the province of Konang-Si, containing mountainous regions.

ter of the crown in the Commons, Lord John Russell, opposed the bill, and said: "Pass this bill, and where will be
the boasted safety of our houses? It would establish general
tyranny."

The prohibition of "general warrants." The warrant is
the paper which justifies the arresting person to commit so
grave an act as depriving a citizen, or alien, of personal liberty.
It is important, therefore, to know who has the right to issue
such warrants, against whom it may be done, and how it must
be done, in order to protect the individual against arbitrary
police measures. The Anglican race has been so exact and
minute regarding this subject, that the whole theory of the
warrant may be said to be peculiarly Anglican, and a great
self-grown institution. "A warrant," the books say, "to deprive a citizen of his personal liberty should be in writing,
and ought to show the authority of the person who makes it,
the act which is authorized to be done, the name or description of the party who is authorized to execute it, and of the
party against whom it is made; and, in criminal cases, the
grounds upon which it is made." The warrant should name
the person against whom it is directed; if it does not, it is
called a general warrant, and Anglican liberty does not
allow it.[1] Where it is allowed there is police government, but
not the government for freemen. It is necessary that the
person who executes the warrant be named in it. Otherwise
the injured citizen, in case of illegal arrest, would not know
whom he should make responsible; but if the person be named,
he is answerable, according to the Anglican principle that
every officer remains answerable for the legality of all his
acts, no matter who directed them to be done. Indeed, we

---

[1] A warrant to apprehend all persons suspected, or all persons guilty,
etc. etc. is illegal. The person against whom the warrant runs, ought
to be pointed out. The law on this momentous subject was laid down
by Lord Mansfield in the case of Money *vs.* Leach, 3 Bur. 1742, where the
"general warrant" which had been in use since the revolution, directing
the officers to apprehend the "authors, printers, and publishers" of the
famous No. 45 of the North Briton, was held to be illegal and void.

may say the special warrant is a death-blow to police government.

The Constitution of the United States demands that "no warrants shall issue but upon probable cause, supported by oath or affirmation, and particularly describing the place to be searched, and the persons or things to be seized, etc."[1]

The warrant is held to be so important an element of civil liberty, that a defective warrant is considered by the common law of England and America one of the reasons which reduce the killing of an officer from murder to manslaughter. The reader will see this from the following passage, which I copy from a work of authority both here and in England. I give the passage entire, because it relates wholly to individual liberty, and I shall have to recur to it.[2] The learned jurist says:

"Though the killing of an officer of justice, while in the regular execution of his duty, knowing him to be an officer, and with intent to resist him in such exercise of duty, is murder, the law in that case implying malice, yet where the process is defective or illegal, or is executed in an illegal manner, the killing is only manslaughter, unless circumstances appear, to show express malice; and then it is murder. Thus, the killing will be reduced to manslaughter, if it be shown in evidence that it was done in the act of protecting the slayer against an arrest by an officer acting beyond the limits of his precinct; or, by an assistant, not in the presence of the officer; or, by virtue of a warrant essentially defective in describing either the person accused, or the offence; or, where the party had no notice, either expressly, or from the circumstances of the case, that a lawful arrest was intended; but,

---

[1] The reader will find a copy of the Constitution of the United States in the appendix.

[2] This is section 123 of vol. iii. of Dr. Greenleaf on Evidence, which I have copied by the permission of my esteemed and distinguished friend. I have left out all the legal references. The professional lawyer is acquainted with the book, and the references would be important to him alone.

on the contrary, honestly believed that his liberty was assailed without any pretence of legal authority; or, where the arrest attempted, though for a felony, was not only without warrant, but without hue and cry, or fresh pursuit; or, being for a misdemeanor only, was not made flagrante delicto; or, where the party was on any other ground, not legally liable to be arrested or imprisoned. So, if the arrest, though the party were legally liable, was made in violation of law, as, by breaking open the outer door or window of the party's dwelling-house, on civil process; for such process does not justify the breaking of the dwelling-house, to make an original arrest; or, by breaking the outer door or window, on criminal process, without previous notice given of his business, with demand of admission, or something equivalent thereto, and a refusal."

The Habeas Corpus Act. This famous act of parliament was passed under Charles II., and is intended to insure to an arrested person, whether by warrant or on the spot, that at his demand he be brought, by the person detaining him, before a judge, who may liberate him, bail him, or remand him, no matter at whose command or for what reasons the prisoner is detained. It allows of no "administrative arrests," as extra-judicial arrests are called in France, or imprisonment for reasons of state. The habeas corpus act further insures a speedy trial,[1] a trial by the law of the land and by the lawful court—three points of the last importance. It, moreover, guarantees that the prisoner know for what he is arrested, and may properly prepare for trial. The habeas corpus act did by no means first establish all these principles, but numberless attempts to secure them had failed, and the act may be considered as the ultimate result of a long struggle between law and the individual on the one hand, and power on the

---

[1] Long imprisonments before trial are customary means resorted to on the continent of Europe in order to harass the subjects. Guerrazzi and other liberals were sentenced, in Tuscany, on the first of July, 1853, after having been imprisoned for fifty months before ever being brought to trial. It is useless to mention more instances; for, long imprisonment before trial is the rule in absolute governments whenever it suits them.

other. The history of this act is interesting and sympto-matic.[1]

The Constitution of the United States prohibits the sus-pension of the habeas corpus act, "unless when, in cases of rebellion or invasion, the public safety may require it;" and Alexander Hamilton says, in the "Federalist":[2] "The esta-blishment of the writ of habeas corpus, the prohibition of ex post facto laws and of titles of nobility, to which we have no corresponding provisions in our constitution," (therefore per-sonal liberty, or protection and safety, supremacy of the law and equality,) "are perhaps greater securities to liberty than any it contains;" and, with reference to the first two, he justly adds the words of "the judicious Blackstone."[3]

All our state constitutions have adopted these important principles. The very opposite of this guarantee was the "lettre de cachet," or is the arbitrary imprisonment at pre-sent in France.

A witness of singular weight, as to the essential importance of Anglican personal liberty, must not be omitted here. The Emperor Napoleon III. who, after Orsini's attempt to assassi-nate him, obtained the "law of suspects" according to which the French police, or administration, (not the courts of justice,) may transport a "suspect" for seven years, wrote, in earlier days, with admiration of English individual liberty.[4]

---

[1] The appendix contains the habeas corpus act.

[2] Paper, No. lxxxiv.

[3] Blackstone's Commentaries, vol. i. page 136. Note, in the "Fede-ralist."

[4] In 1854 a complete edition of the emperor's works was published. In that edition was a chapter headed De la Liberté individuelle en Angle-terre. In it are the following passages:

"No inhabitant of Great Britain (excepting convicts) can be expelled from the United Kingdom. Any infraction of this clause (the habeas corpus act) would be visited with the severest penalties." He remarks that we have no public prosecutor, the attorney-general interfering only on extraordinary occasions; and if criminals sometimes escape justice, personal liberty is the less endangered. "In England, authority is never influenced by passion; its proceedings are always moderate, always legal;" there is "no violation of the citizen's domicile, so common in

There was in England, until within a recent date, a remarkable deviation from the principles of personal liberty—the impressment. The crown assumed the right to force any able-bodied man on board a man-of-war, to serve there as sailor. There has always been much doubt about this arrogated privilege of the crown, and, generally, sailors only were taken, chiefly in times of war and when no hands would freely enlist. Every friend of liberty will rejoice that the present administration has taken in hand a new plan of manning the navy, by which this blemish will be removed.[1]

France ;" family correspondence is inviolate, and no passports bar the most perfect freedom of traffic,—" passports, the oppressive invention of the Committee of Public Safety, which are an embarrassment and an obstacle to the peaceable citizen, but which are utterly powerless against those who wish to deceive the vigilance of authority." A law deprived of the general support of public opinion would be a mere scrap of paper.

" It suffices for us to note this fact, that in France, where such jealousy is shown of everything which touches equality and national honor, people do not attach themselves so religiously to personal liberty. The tranquillity of the citizen may be disturbed, his domicile may be violated, he may be made to undergo for whole months a preventive imprisonment personal guarantees may be despised, and a few generous men shall raise their voices ; but public opinion will remain calm and impassible as long as no political passion is awakened. There lies the greatest reason for the violence of authority ; it can be arbitrary because there is no curb to check it. In England, on the contrary, political passions cease the moment a violation of common right is committed ; and this, because England is a country of legality, and France has not yet become so ; because England is a country solidly constituted, while France struggles by turns for forty years between revolutions and counter-revolutions, and the sanctity of principle has yet to be created there."

[1] The plan has not yet been published, but one of the ministers, Sir James Graham, said in the Commons, in April, 1853 :

" The first point on which all the authorities consulted were agreed is, that whatever measures are taken, must rely for success on the voluntary acceptance of them by the seamen, and that any attempt to introduce a coercive mode of enlistment would be followed by mischievous consequences and failure." The difficult question does not yet seem to be wholly settled (1859.) It seems difficult to obtain a sufficient number of seamen to man the fleet in emergencies. In France seamen are drafted, as soldiers are for the army.

CHAPTER VII.

BAIL. PENAL TRIAL.

3. CONNECTED with the guarantees of personal liberty, treated of in the foregoing chapter, is the bail.

The law of all nations not wholly depraved in a political point of view, adopts the principle that a man shall be held innocent until proved by process of law to be otherwise. In fact, the very idea of a trial implies as much. Theoretically, at least, this is acknowledged by all civilized nations, although often the way in which judicial affairs are conducted, and in many countries the very mode of trying itself, are practical denials of the principle. But even in the freest country there is this painful yet unavoidable contradiction, that while we hold every person innocent until by lawful trial proved to be guilty, we must arrest a person in order to bring him to a penal trial; and, although by the law he is still considered innocent, he must be deprived of personal liberty until his trial can take place, which cannot always follow instantly upon the arrest. To mitigate this harshness as much as possible, free nations guarantee the principle of bailing in all cases in which the loss of the bailed sum may be considered as a more serious evil than the possible punishment. The amount of bail must depend upon the seriousness of the charge, and also upon the means of the charged person. If judges were allowed to demand exorbitant bail, they might defeat the action of this principle in every practical case. It was enacted, therefore, in the first year of William and Mary,[1] and has been adopted in all our constitutions, that no "excessive bail"

---

[1] William and Mary, stat. ii. c. 2.

shall be required.   The nature of the case admits of no more exact term; but, with an impeachment hanging over the judges, should the principle thus solemnly pronounced be disregarded, it has worked well for the arrested person.   Indeed, there are frequent cases in the United States in which this principle is abused and society is endangered, because persons are bailed who are under the heaviest charges, and have thus an opportunity of escape if they know themselves guilty.   As this can take place only with persons who have large sums at their disposal, either in their own possession or in that of their friends, and as liberty demands first of all the foundation of justice, it is evident that this abuse of bail works as much against essential liberty as the proper use of bail guarantees it.   We ought, everywhere, to return to the principle of distinguishing transgressions of the law into bailable offences and offences for the suspected commission of which the judge can take no bail. These are especially those offences for the punishment of which no equivalent in money can be imagined; for instance, death or imprisonment for life, and those offences which put the offender into the possession of the sum required for the bail.

It has been objected to the bail that it works unjustly.   It temporarily deals with so precious a thing as personal liberty according to possession of wealth: but it must be remembered that the whole arrest before trial is an evil of absolute necessity, and the more we can limit it the better.

Liberty requires bail, and that it be extended as far as possible; and it requires likewise that it be not extended to all offences, and that substantial bail only be accepted.

4. Another guarantee, of the last importance, is a well-secured penal trial, hedged in with an efficient protection of the indicted person, the certainty of his defence, a distinct indictment charging a distinct act, the duty of proving this act on the part of government, and not the duty of proving innocence on the part of the prisoner, the fairness of the trial by peers of the prisoner, the soundness of the rules of evidence, the publicity of the trial, the accusatorial (and not the inquisitorial) process, the certainty of the law which is to be applied,

together with speed and utter impartiality, and an absolute verdict. It is moreover necessary that the preparatory process be as little vexatious as possible.

When a person is penally indicted, he individually forms one party, and society, the state, the government, forms the other. It is evident that unless very strong and distinct guarantees of protection are given to the former, that he be subjected to a fair trial, and that nothing be adjudged to him but what the law already existing demands and allows, there can be no security against oppression. For government is a power, and, like every power in existence, it is desirous of carrying its point—a desire which increases in intensity the greater the difficulties are which it finds in its way.

Hence it is that modern free nations ascribe so great an importance to well regulated and carefully elaborated penal trials. Montesquieu, after having given his definitions of what he calls philosophical liberty, and of political liberty, which, as we have seen, he says, consists in security, continues thus: "This security is never more attacked than in public and private accusations. It is, therefore, upon the excellence of the criminal laws that chiefly the liberty of the citizen depends."[1] Although we consider this opinion far too general, it nevertheless shows how great a value Montesquieu set on a well-guarded penal trial, and he bears us out in considering it an essential element of modern liberty. The concluding words of Mr. Mittermaier's work on the Penal Process of England, Scotland, and the United States, are: "It will be more and more acknowledged how true it is that the penal legislation is the key-stone of a nation's public law."[2]

This passage of the German criminalist expresses the truth more accurately than the quoted dictum of Montesquieu. For, although we consider the penal trial and penal law in general intimately connected with civil liberty, it is nevertheless a fact that a sound penal trial is invariably one of the last fruits of

---

[1] Esprit des Lois, xii. 2; "Of the Liberty of the Citizen."

[2] This comprehensive and excellent work was published in Germany, Erlangen, 1851.

political civilization, partly because it is one of the most difficult subjects to elaborate, and because it requires long experience to find the proper mean between a due protection of
the indicted person and an equally due protection of society ;
partly because it is one of the most difficult things in all
spheres of action to induce irritated power to limit itself, as
well as to give to an indicted person the full practical benefit
of the theoretic sentence, easily pronounced like all theory,
that the law holds every one innocent until proved not to be
so. The Roman and Athenian penal trials were sadly deficient. The English have allowed counsel to the penally indicted person, only within our memory, while they had been
long allowed in the United States.[1] The penal trial in the
Netherlands was imperfect, when, nevertheless, the Netherlanders are allowed on all hands to have enjoyed a high degree of civil liberty. It is one of the most common facts in
history that a nation is more or less advancing in nearly all
the branches of civilization, while the penal trial and the
whole penal law remains almost stationary in its barbarous
inconsistency. The penal trial of France, up to the first
revolution, remained equally shocking to the feelings of humanity and to the laws of logic.

---

[1] It must not be forgotten, however, that deficient as the penal trial of
England, without counsel for the defendant was, it contained many guarantees of protection, especially publicity, a fixed law of evidence, with the
exclusion of hearsay evidence, the jury and the neutral position of the
judge in consequence of the trial by jury ; and the strictly accusatorial
character of the trial, with the most rigid adhesion to the principle of
trying a person upon the indictment alone, so that the judge could be,
and in later times really had been, the protector of the prisoner. Had
the trial been inquisitorial instead of accusatorial, the absence of counsel
for defence would have been an enormity. To this enormity Austria has
actually returned since the beginning of this century. The code promulgated by Joseph gave counsel, or a "defensor," to the prisoner ; but,
although the process remained inquisitorial, the defensor was again dis-
allowed. The late revolution re-established him, but whether he has been
discontinued again of late I do not know. Nor can it be of very great
importance in a country in which the "state of siege" and martial law
seem to be almost permanent.

The reason of this apparent inconsistency is that, in most cases, penal trials affect individuals who do not belong to the classes which have the greatest influence upon legislation. This point is especially important in countries where the penal trial is not public. People never learn what is going on in the houses of justice. Another and great reason is that generally lawyers by profession are far less interested in the penal branch of the law than in the civil. This, again, arises from the fact that the civil law is far more varied and complicated, consequently more attractive to a judicial mind, that the civil cases are far more remunerative, and form the large bulk of the administration of justice. How much the difficulty to be solved constitutes the attraction for the lawyer, we may see from the fact that very few professional lawyers take an interest in the punishment itself. A penal case has attraction for them so long as it is undecided, but what imprisonment follows, if imprisonment has been awarded, interests them little. Very few lawyers have taken a lead in the reform of criminal law and in prison discipline, Sir Samuel Romilly always excepted.

Among the points which characterize a fair and sound penal trial according to our advancement in political civilization, we would designate the following : The person to be tried must be present, (and of course, living ;)[1] no intimidation before the trial, or attempts by artifice to induce the prisoner to confess ; a contrivance which protects the citizen even against being placed too easily into a state of accusation ; the fullest possible realization of the principle that every man is held innocent

---

[1] Penal trials of absent persons are common in countries where the principles of the Roman law prevail. They are common in France; and the church has even tried deceased persons for heresy, found them guilty, and confiscated the property which had belonged to the heretic. The presence of the indicted person at his trial, is a principle plain to every one so soon as once pronounced, but power acknowledges it at a late period only, and always has a tendency to return to it, whether this power be a monarch or his government, or an impassioned populace. Several of the almost solemn procedures of lynch law which have occurred of late in some of our western states, and according to which absent persons were warned never to return to their domicile, are instances in point.

until proved to be otherwise, and bail; a total discarding of
the principle that the more heinous the imputed crime is, the
less ought to be the protection of the prisoner, but, on the contrary, the adoption of the reverse; a distinct indictment, and
the acquaintance of the prisoner with it, sufficiently long before the trial, to give him time for preparing the defence ; that
no one be held to incriminate himself ; the accusatorial process, with jury and publicity, therefore an oral trial and not a
process in writing; counsel or defensors of the prisoner; a
distinct theory or law of evidence, and no hearsay testimony;
a verdict upon evidence alone and pronouncing guilty or not
guilty ; a punishment in proportion to the offence and in accordance with common sense and justice;[1] especially no punitory
imprisonment of a sort that necessarily must make the prisoner
worse than he was when he fell into the hands of government,
nor cautionary imprisonment before trial, which by contami-
nation must advance the prisoner in his criminality ; and that
the punishment adapt itself as much as possible to the crime
and criminality of the offender;[2] that nothing but what the
law demands or allows be inflicted,[3] and that all that the law de-

---

[1] The idea expressed by Dr. Paley regarding this point is revolting.
He says, in his Political Philosophy, that we may choose between two
systems, the one with fair punishments always applied, the other with
very severe punishments occasionally applied. He thus degrades penal
law, from a law founded above all upon strict principles of justice, to a
mere matter of prudential expediency, putting it on a level with military
decimation.

[2] Lieber's Popular Essay on Subjects of Penal Law, and on Uninterrupted Solitary Confinement at Labor, etc.; Philadelphia, 1838. I have
there treated of this all-important subject at some length.

[3] Tiberius Gracchus erected a temple in honor of Liberty, with a sum
obtained for fines. If the fines were just, there was no inconsistency in
thus making penal justice build a temple of freedom, for liberty demands
security and order, and, therefore, penal justice.

On the other hand, what does a citizen reared in Anglican liberty feel
when he reads in a simple newspaper article in a French provincial paper, in 1853, the following ? "The minister of general police has just
decided that Chapitel, sentenced by the court to six months' imprisonment for having been connected with a secret society, and Brayet, sen-

mands be inflicted—no arbitrary injudicious pardoning, which is a direct interference with the true government of law.

The subject of pardoning is so important, especially in our country, that I have deemed it advisable to add a paper on pardoning, which the reader will find in the appendix.

Perhaps there are no points so important in the penal trial in a free country, as the principle that no one shall be held to incriminate himself, that the indictment as well as the verdict

tenced for the same offence, to two months' imprisonment, shall be transported to Cayenne for ten years, after the expiration of their sentence !"

The decree of the eighth of December, 1851, not a law, but a mere dictatorial order, upon which ten years' transportation are added by way of "rider" to a few months' imprisonment adjudged by the courts of law, is this :

"Article 1. Every individual placed under the surveillance of the high police, who shall be found having broken his assigned limits of residence, may be transported, by way of general safety, to one of the penitentiary colonies, at Cayenne or in Algeria.

"The duration of transportation shall be five years or less, and ten years or more." (We translate literally and correctly, whatever the reader may think of this sentence, which would be very droll, were it not very sad.)

"Article 2. The same measure shall be applicable to individuals found to be guilty of having formed part of a secret society."

The French of the last sentence is, *individus reconnus coupable d'avoir fait partie d'une société secrète.* This *reconnus* (found, acknowledged,) is of a sinister import. For the question is, Found by whom? Of course not only by the courts, for finding a man guilty by process of law is in French *convaincre.* The rêconnaitre, therefore, was used in order to include the police or any one else in authority. So that we arrive at this striking fact: The despot may add an enormous punishment to a legal sentence, as in the cited case, or he may award it, or rather the minister of police under him may do it, without trial, upon mere police information. Two hundred years ago, the English declared executive transportation beyond the seas, or deportation, to be an unwarranted grievance ; and here we have it again, no doubt in imitation of the Roman imperial times, (the saddest in all history,) in the middle of the nineteenth century.

So far the note as written in 1853. In 1858 Orsini made his attempt of assassinating the Emperor of the French, when a far more stringent law was passed, and the principle of "suspicion," so flourishing as an element of criminality in the first French revolution, was revived.

must be definite and clear, and that no hearsay evidence be admitted. Certainly none are more essential.

A great lawyer and excellent man, Sir Samuel Romilly, justly says, that if the ascertaining of truth and meting out of justice is the object of the trial, no possible objection can be taken against it on principle. But there is this difficulty, that if judges themselves question, they become deeply interested in the success of their own cross-examinations, they become biased against the prisoner, should he thwart them, or turn questions into ridicule. Romilly makes this remark after having actually seen this result in France, where it is always done, (witness Mad. Lafarge's trial, or any French trial of importance,) and certainly often with success.[1] Or let us observe English prosecutions some centuries back.

In the inquisitorial process, it is not only done, but the process depends upon the questioning of the prisoner.

There are other dangers connected with it. An accused man cannot feel that perfect equanimity of mind which alone might secure his answers against suspicion. I know from personal experience how galling it is to see your most candid answers rewarded with suspicions and renewed questions, if the subject is such that you cannot possibly at once clear up all doubts. It ought never to be forgotten that the accused person labors under considerable disadvantages, merely by the fact that he is accused. Bullying and oppressive judges were common in England when the principle was not yet settled that no one shall be held to incriminate himself. The times of the Stuarts furnish us with many instances of altercations in the court, between the judge and the prisoner, and of judicial brow-beating, to the detriment of all justice.

The trial of Elizabeth Grant, the aged and deaf Baptist woman, who had given a night's rest under her roof to a soldier of Monmouth's dispersed army, under Chief-Justice Jones,[2] may serve as an instance.

---

[1] Sir Samuel Romilly's Memoirs, vol. i. p. 315, 2d ed.; London, 1840.

[2] Philipps's State Trials, vol. ii. 214, et seq., and, indeed, in many parts of the work.

It is, among other reasons, for this very fact of prisoners on trial being asked by the French judge about the fact at issue, his whereabouts at the time, his previous life, and a number of things which throw suspicion on the prisoner, although unconnected with the question at issue, that Mr. Béranger says, in a work of just repute: "We," that is, the French, "have contented ourselves to place a magnificent frontispiece before the ruins of despotism; a deceiving monument, whose aspect seduces, but which makes one freeze with horror when entered. Under liberal appearances, with pompous words of juries, public debates, judicial independence, individual liberty, we are slowly led to the abuse of all these things, and the disregard of all rights; an iron rod is used with us, instead of the staff of justice."[1]

There are peculiar reasons against examining the prisoner in public trials, and many peculiar to the secret trial. Although it cannot be denied, that often the questioning of the prisoner may shorten the trial and lead to condign conviction, which otherwise may not be the result, it is nevertheless right that most, perhaps all our state constitutions have adopted this principle. It is just; it is dignified; it is fair. The government prosecutes; then let it prove what it charges. So soon as this principle is discarded, we fall into the dire error of throwing the burden of proving innocence wholly or partially on the prisoner; while, on the contrary, all the burden ought to lie on the government, with all its power, to prove the charged facts. Proving an offence and fastening it on the offender, is one important point in the penal trial; but the method *how* it is done is of equal importance. The Turkish cadi acknowledges the first point only; yet what I have stated is not only true with reference to the jural society, it is even true in the family and the school.

It is an interesting fact for the political philosopher that, while the Anglican race thus insists on the principle of non-self-incrimination, the whole Chinese code for that people

---

[1] Béranger, De la Justice Criminelle de France; Paris, 1818, page 2.

under a systematic mandarinism is pervaded even by the principle of self-accusation for all, but especially for the mandarins.

The principle that on government lies the burden of proving the guilt, leads consistently to the other principle, that the verdict must be definite and absolute. Hence these two important facts : The verdict must be guilty or not guilty, and no absolutio ab instantia, as it is called in some countries of the European continent; that is to say, no verdict or decision which says, According to the present trial we cannot find you guilty, but there is strong suspicion, and we may take you up another time;[1] nor any "not proven," as the Scottish trial admits of, ought to be permitted. " Not proven," does not indeed allow a second trial, but it expresses : You are free, although we have very strong suspicion. Secondly, the main principle leads to the fact that no man ought to be tried twice for the same offence. This is logical, and is necessary for the security of the individual. A person might otherwise be harassed by the government until ruined. Repeated trials for charges, which the government knows very well to be unfounded, are a common means resorted to by despotic executives. Frequently such procedures have led the persecuted individual to compound with government rather than lose all his substance.

The Anglican race, therefore, justly makes it an elementary principle of its constitutional law, that " no man shall be tried twice for the same offence."

I have said that a fair trial for freemen requires that the preparatory steps for the trial be as little vexatious as possible. They must also acknowledge the principle of non-incrimination. This is disregarded on the whole of the European continent. The free range of police power, the mean tricks resorted to by the " instructing" judge or officer, before the trial, in order to

---

[1] The reader will find in the appendix a paper on the subject of some continental trials, and the admission of half and quarter proof and proportional punishment.

bring the prisoner to confession, are almost inconceivable,[1] and they are the worse, because applied before the trial, when the prisoner is not surrounded by those protections which the trial itself grants. With reference to this point, and in order to modify what I have stated regarding Greek penal trials, I wish to mention the interesting fact that "the prosecutor, in Athens, who failed to make good his charge, incurred certain penalties, unless he obtained at least one-fifth of the votes in his favor. In public suits, he forfeited one thousand drachmæ to the state, and could never again institute a similar suit. The same punishment was incurred if he declined to proceed with the case. In private suits, he paid the defendant one-sixth of the amount of the disputed property, as a compensation for the inconvenience he had suffered in person or character."[2]

Sir Samuel Romilly had the intention of proposing in a similar spirit, a bill by which an acquitted prisoner, having been prosecuted for felony, should be compensated by the county, at the discretion of the court, for loss of time and the many evils endured. Indeed, he thought that far more ought to be done.[3] Leave was given to bring in the compensation bill, but it was afterwards withdrawn. It is evident that the great difficulty would lie in the fact that the discretion of the judge would establish at once a distinction between the verdicts, similar to that produced by the Scottish "not guilty" and "not proven." To compensate, however, all acquitted persons

---

[1] This may be amply seen in the reports on French trials, and, among other works, in Feuerbach's Collection of German Criminal Trials.

[2] Herman, Political Antiquit. of Greece; Oxon. 1836, sec. 144, where more, and all the necessary authorities can be found.

[3] Memoirs of the Life of Sir Samuel Romilly, 2d ed.; London, 1840, vol. ii. p. 235. Strange enough, there is an English law, 25 George II., ch. 36, according to which prosecutors are to have the expenses of their prosecution reimbursed, and a compensation afforded them for their trouble and loss of time. This is evidently to induce people freely to prosecute; but no guarantee is given on the other hand against undue prosecution, and a compensation for the trouble and loss of time of the acquitted person.

would be very mischievous if we consider how many persons are acquitted who nevertheless are guilty. Indeed, it might well be asked whether the fear of burdening the county with the payment of the compensation would not, in some cases, induce the jury to find more easily a verdict of guilty.

The professional reader may think that I have not sufficiently dwelt upon some essential points of a sound penal trial, for instance, on publicity, or the independence of counsel. He will find, however, that these subjects are treated of in other parts of this work, to which it was necessary to refer them.

CHAPTER VIII.

HIGH TREASON.

5. THAT penal trial which is the most important with reference to civil liberty, and in which the accused individual stands most in need of peculiar protection by the law, is the trial for treason. The English law does not know the term "political offence," of which the trial for treason is, commonly, the highest in importance. Political Offence is a term belonging to the modern law of some countries of the European continent,[1] and it was doubtless trials for offences of this character, which those jurists and publicists had partly in view, who, the reader will recollect, point out a well-guarded penal trial, almost as the sole characteristic of civil liberty.

If a well-guarded penal trial in general forms an important element of our liberty, because the individual is placed opposite to public power, a carefully organized trial for treason is emphatically so. In the trial for treason the government is no longer theoretically the prosecuting party, as it may be said it is in the case of theft or assault, but government is the really offended, irritated party, endowed at the same time with all the force of the government, to annoy, persecute, and often

---

[1] The American reader ought to keep in mind that the term political offence is now a well-established term on the continent of Europe. It is used in legislation; thus the late French republic abolished capital punishment for political offenders, and in the treaty of extradition between France and Spain, "political offenders" are excepted, and not subject to extradition. It would, nevertheless, be difficult to give a definition of the term Political Offence sufficiently clear to be acceptable to a law-abiding administration of justice. Indeed, we may say, that it was natural this term should have presented itself, in the course of things on the continent of Europe, and it is equally natural, and is full of meaning, that the English law does not know it.

6 (81)

to crush. Governments have, therefore, been most tenacious in retaining whatever power they could in the trial for treason; and, on the other hand, it is most important for the free citizen that in the trial for treason, he should not only enjoy the common protection of a sound penal trial, but far greater protection. In despotic countries we always find that the little protection granted in common criminal trials, is withheld in trials for treason; in free countries, at least in England and the United States, greater protection is granted, and more caution demanded, in trials for treason than in the common penal process. The trial for treason is a gauge of liberty. Tell us how they try people for treason, and we will tell you whether they are free. It redounds to the glory of England that attention was directed to this subject from early times, and that guarantees were granted to the prisoner indicted for treason, centuries before they were allowed to the person suspected of a common offence; and to that of the United States, that they plainly defined the crime of treason, and restricted it to narrow limits, in their very constitution. This great charter says, Section III.:

1. "Treason against the United States shall consist only in levying war against them, or in adhering to their enemies, giving them aid and comfort. No person shall be convicted of treason, unless on the testimony of two witnesses to the same overt act, or confession in open court.

2. "Congress shall have power to declare the punishment of treason; but no attainder of treason shall work corruption of blood or forfeiture, except during the life of the person attainted."

Whether political societies, not so fortunately situated as ourselves, yet equally prizing civil liberty, might safely restrict the crime of treason to such narrow limits as the wise and bold framers of our constitution have done, is a subject which belongs to a branch of political science that does not occupy us here; but it may be asserted that several cases have actually occurred in the United States, in which all nations except the American would have considered the provisions of our constitution insufficient, and in which nevertheless they have been found adequate.

We may consider the American law of high treason as the purest in existence, and it shows how closely the law of treason is connected with civil liberty. Chief Justice Marshall said: "As there is no crime which can more excite and agitate the passions of men than treason, no charge demands more from the tribunal before which it is made a deliberate and temperate inquiry. Whether the inquiry be directed to the fact or to the law, none can be more solemn, none more important to the citizen or to the government; none can more affect the safety of both."[1]

All constitutions of the different American states, which mention treason, have the same provision. Those that say nothing special about it, have the same by law, and in conformity with the principles which the respective constitutions lay down regarding penal trials.[2] None admit of retrospective laws, of legislative condemnations of individuals, or of attainders.

The course which the development of the law of treason takes in history is this: At first there exists no law of treason, because the crime is not yet separated from other offences, as indeed the penal and civil laws are not separated in the earliest periods. The Chinese code, so minute in many respects, mixes the two branches, and debtors are treated as criminal offenders, reminding us, in this particular, of the early Roman law. When

[1] The Writings of John Marshall, p. 42. Ex parte Bollman and Swartwout. The rebellion of the Mormons in 1858, has occurred since the remarks in the text were written. It would seem sound reasoning and statesmanship, that the narrower the limits are to which the public law restricts treason, the more necessary it becomes to execute the law fully within those limits.

[2] Judge Story says: "A state cannot take cognizance, or punish the offence (i.e. treason against the United States,) whatever it may do in relation to the offence of treason, committed exclusively against itself, if indeed any case can, under the constitution, exist, which is not at the same time treason against the United States." Chap. 28, vol. iii. of Commentaries on the Constitution of the United States.

first treason comes to be separated from the other offences, it
is for the twofold purpose of inflicting more excruciating pains,
and of withholding from the trial the poor protection which is
granted to persons indicted for common offences. The dire
idea of a crimen exceptum gains ground. The reasoning, or
rather unreasoning, is that the crime is so enormous that the
criminal ought not to have the same chances of escape, thus
assuming that the accused, yet to be proved to be a criminal,
is in fact a criminal, and forgetting, as has been indicated
before, that the graver the accusation is, and the severer
therefore the punishment, in case of established guilt, may be,
the safer and more guarded ought to be the trial. It is a
fearful inconsistency, very plain when thus stated, yet we find
that men continually fall into the same error, even in our
own days. How often is lynch law resorted to in our country,
on the very plea that the crime, still a suspected one, is so infamous that the regular course of law is too slow or too doubtful! The same error prevailed regarding witchcraft. The
pope declared it a crimen exceptum—too abominable to be
tried by common process. Protestant governments followed
the example.[1]

At the same time we find that, at the period of which we
are now speaking, the law of treason is vastly extending, and
all sorts of offences, either because considered peculiarly
heinous, or because peculiarly displeasing to the public power,
are drawn within the meaning of treason. A list of all the
offences which at some time or other have been considered to

---

[1] I seize upon this opportunity of advising every young reader of this
work to study with earnest attention the history of the witch-trials, forming, possibly, with the African slave-trade, the greatest aberrations of
our Cis-Caucasian race. Such works as Soldan's History of the Witch-
Trials exhibit the psychology of public and private passion, of crime and
criminal law, in so impressive and instructive a manner, that the sad
course of crime and error having been ran through, it ought not to stand
on record in vain for us. We learn, in history and in psychology, as in nature, to understand the principles, motives, and laws of minor actions, by
the changes and convulsions on a large scale ; and the vast changes and
revulsions by the microscopic observation of the minute reality around us.

amount to treason, from the crime of "offended divine majesty," (crimen læsæ majestatis divinæ,) in which stealing from a church was included, to the most trivial common offences, and which I have made out for my own use, would astound the reader, if this were the place to exhibit it.

When political civilization advances, and people come to understand more clearly the object and use of government, as well as the dangers which threaten society and the individual, the very opposite course takes place. More protection is granted to the person indicted for treason, than in common penal trials, and the meaning of treason is more and more narrowed. The definition of treason is made more distinct, and constructive treason is less and less allowed, until we arrive at our own clear and definite law of treason.

It is thus that the law of treason becomes, as I stated before, a symptomatic fact, and is in politics what roads, the position of woman, public amusements, the tenure of land, architecture, habits of cleanliness, are in other spheres. They are gauges of social advancement. The more I studied this subject, the more I became convinced of the instruction to be derived from the history of the law of treason in ancient times, the middle ages, and modern periods, and it was my intention to append a paper to this work, which should give a survey of the whole. When, however, I came to arrange my long collected materials, I found, although firmly resolved to disregard an author's partiality for materials of interest once collected, and to restrict the paper to the merest outlines, that it would be impossible to do any justice to the subject without allowing to it a disproportionally large place. I decided, therefore, to leave the subject for a separate work.

In conclusion I would repeat, experience proves that not only are all the guarantees of a fair penal trial peculiarly necessary for a fair trial for treason, but that it requires additional safeguards; and, of the one or the other, the following seem to me the most important:

The indictment must be clear as to facts and time, when the indicted act has been committed;

The prisoner must have the indictment a sufficient time before the trial, so as to be able to prepare for it;

He must have a list of the witnesses against him, an equal time beforehand;

A sufficient time for the trial must be allowed; and the prisoner must not be seized, tried, and executed, as Cornish was, in 1685, in a week;

Counsel must be allowed, as a matter of course;

The judges must be impartial and independent, and ample challenges must be allowed; peers must judge. Consequently, judges must not be asked by the executive, before the trial, what their judgment would be if such or such a case should be brought before them, as was repeatedly done by the Stuarts;

Of all trials, hearsay must be excluded from the trial for treason;

Facts, not tendencies; acts, not words or papers written by the indicted person, and which have never been allowed to leave his desk, must be charged;

Perfect publicity must take place from beginning to end, and reporters must not be excluded; for it is no publicity in a populous country that allows only some twenty or forty by-standers;[1]

The trial must be in presence of the prisoner;

Several witnesses must be required to testify to the same fact, and the witnesses for the prisoner must be as much upon oath as those for the government;

Confession, if unconditionally admitted at all, must at least be in open court;

There must be no physical nor psychical torture or coercion;

There must be good witnesses, not known villains or acknowledged liars, as Titus Oates, or Lord Howard against Lord Russell;

The judges must not depend upon the executive;

---

[1] When, in 1858, Count Montalembert was tried in Paris for having written a pamphlet in praise of England, a peculiarly small court-room was selected, only a few persons were admitted, by tickets, and no notes were allowed to be taken.

No evidence must be admitted which is not admitted in other trials;

There must be a fixed punishment;

There must be no constructive treason;

And the judges must not be political bodies.

These guarantees have been elaborated by statute and common law, through periods of freedom and tyranny, by the Anglican race. The English law grants these safeguards, except indeed the last to lords, because, according to the principle that every one must be tried by his peers, a lord is tried by the house of lords. It showed great wisdom that the framers of our constitution did not assign the trial for treason to the senate,[1] as the former French constitution appointed the house of peers to be the court for high treason. American impeachments are tried indeed by the senate, but it will be observed that the American trial of impeachment is not a penal trial for offences, but a political institution, trying for political capacity. The senate, when sitting as a court to try impeachments, can only remove from office, whatever the crime may have been; and the impeached person can be penally tried after the senate has removed him from office. In its political character, then, but in no other point, the American impeachment resembles the Athenian ostracism, which was likewise a political, and not a penal institution. The English impeachment is a penal trial.

The trials for treason going on in many countries of the European continent, especially in Naples and the Austrian dominions, are, by way of opposite, fair illustrations of what has been stated here.[2]

The trial for treason has been treated of in this place because naturally connected with the subject of the penal trial in general. Otherwise it would have been more properly

---

[1] The American trials for treason are collected in Francis Wharton's State Trials of the United States; Philadelphia, 1846.

[2] The reader may be acquainted with the Right Hon. Mr. Gladstone's pamphlet on Neapolitan trials for treason, published in 1851. It is but a sample.

enumerated among the guarantees connected more especially with the general government of a free country. We return, therefore, once more to the guarantees of individual rights.[1]

---

[1] I would mention for the younger student, that when I study pervading institutions, or laws and principles which form running threads through the whole web of history, I find it useful to make chronological tables of their chief advancements and reverses. Such tables are very suggestive, and strikingly show what we owe to the continuity of human society. None of these tables has been more instructive to me than that on the history of the law of treason.

CHAPTER IX.

COMMUNION. LOCOMOTION, EMIGRATION.

6. The freedom of communion is one of the most precious and necessary rights of the individual, and one of the indispensable elements of all advancing humanity—so much so, indeed, that it is one of those elements of liberty, which would have never been singled out, had not experience shown that it forms invariably one of the first objects of attack, when arbitrary power wishes to establish itself, and one of the first objects of conquest, when an unfree people declares itself free.

I have dwelt on the primordial right of communion in the Political Ethics at great length, and endeavored to show that the question is not whether free communion or a fettered press be conducive to more good, but that everything in the individual and in nations depends in a great measure upon communion, and that free communion is a pre-existing condition. The only question is, how to select the best government with it, and how best to shield it, unless, indeed, we were speaking of tribes in a state of tutelage, ruled over by some highly advanced nation.

In this place we only enumerate freedom of communion as one of the primary elements of civil liberty. It is an element of all civil liberty. No one can imagine himself free if his communion with his fellows is interrupted or submitted to surveillance; but it is the Anglican race which first established it on a large scale, broadly and nationally acknowledged.[1]

Free nations demand and guarantee free communion of speech, the right of assembling and publicly speaking, for it is communion of speech in this form which is peculiarly exposed

---

[1] The first fair play was given to a free press in the Netherlands.

to abridgment or suppression by the public power; they guarantee the liberty of the press, and, lastly, the sacredness of epistolary communion.

It is a very striking fact that, although the Constitution of the United States distinctly declares that the government of the United States shall only have the power and authority positively granted in that instrument, so that, in a certain respect, it was unnecessary to say what the government should not have the right to do, still, in the very first article of the Additions and Amendments of the Constitution, congress is forbidden to make any "law respecting an establishment of religion, or prohibiting the free exercise thereof; or abridging the freedom of speech, or of the press, or the right of the people peaceably to assemble, and to petition the government for a redress of grievances."

The reader will keep in mind that the framers of our constitution went out of their way and preferred to appear inconsistent, rather than omit the enumeration of those important liberties, that of conscience, as it is generally called, that of communion, and of petitioning; and the reader will remember, moreover, that these rights were added as amendments. They must then have appeared very important to those who made our constitution, both on account of their intrinsic importance, and because so often attacked by the power-holders. Let the reader also remember that, if it be thus important to abridge the power of government to interfere with free communion, it is at least equally important that no person or number of men interfere, in any manner, with this sacred right. Oppression does not come from government or official bodies alone. The worst oppression is of a social character, or by a multitude.

The English have established the right of communion, as so many other precious rights by common law, by decisions, by struggles, by revolution. All the guarantee they have for the unstinted enjoyment of the right lies in the fact that the whole nation says with one accord, as it were: Let them try to take it away.

It is the same with our epistolary communion. The right

of freely corresponding is unquestionably one of the dearest as well as most necessary of civilized man; yet, our forefathers were so little acquainted with a police government, that no one thought of enumerating the sacredness of letters along with the freedom of speech and the liberty of the press. The liberty of correspondence stands between the two; free word, free letter, free print. The framers did not think of it, as the first law-makers of Rome are said to have omitted the punishment of parricide.

The sacredness of the letter appears the more important when it is considered that in almost all civilized countries the government is the carrier of letters and actually forbids any individual to carry sealed letters.[1] So soon as the letter, therefore, is dropped into the box, where, as it has just been stated, the government itself obliges the correspondent to deposit it, it is exclusively entrusted to the good faith and honorable dealing of government. If spies, informers, and mouchards are odious to every freeman and gentleman, the prying into letters, carried on in France and other countries, with bureaucratic system, is tenfold so, for it strikes humanity in one of its vital points, and had the mail acquired as great an importance in the seventeenth century as in ours, as an agent of civilization, and had Charles I. threatened this agent as he invaded the right of personal liberty, the Petition of Right would have mentioned the sacredness of letters as surely, as it pointed out the billeting of soldiers, as one of the four great grievances of which the English would be freed, before they would grant any supplies to the government.[2]

---

[1] The law of the United States prohibits any private person periodically and regularly to carry letters, and also to carry letters in mail ships.

[2] The American states in which slavery exists, have not considered the laws or principles relating to letters to apply to public journals, when suspicion exists that they contain articles hostile to slavery. In some cases people have broken into the post-office and seized the obnoxious papers; in other cases the state legislature have decreed punishments for propagating abolition papers. Thus we read in the *National Intelligencer*, Washington, October 6, 1853, that "Mr. Herndon, postmaster at Glenville, informs the editor of the *Religious Telescope*, at Circleville, Ohio,

In all the late struggles for liberty on the continent of Europe, the sacredness of letters was insisted upon, not from abstract notions, but for the very practical reason that governments had been in the habit of disregarding it. Of course, they now do so again. The English parliament took umbrage, a few years ago, at the liberty a minister had taken of ordering the opening of letters of certain political exiles residing in England, and although he stated that it had been the habit of all administrations to order it under certain circumstances, he promised to abstain in future. In the United States there is no process or means known to us, not even by writ of a court, we believe, by which a letter could be extracted from the post-office, except by him to whom it is addressed; and, as to the executive unduly opening letters, it would be cause for instant impeachment.

Quite recently, in the month of April, 1853, it appeared in the prosecution of several persons of distinction at Paris, for giving wrong and injurious news to foreign papers, that their letters had not only been opened at the post-office, but that the originals had been kept back, and copies had been sent to the recipients, with a postcript, written by the government officer, for the purpose of fraudulently explaining the different handwriting. It stated that the correspondent had a sore hand. When the counsel for the accused said that the falsifying officer ought to be on the bench of the accused, the court justified the prefect of the police, on the ground of

---

that having, according to the laws of Virginia, opened and inspected his papers, and found them to contain abolition sentiments, he has refused to deliver them as addressed, and has publicly burnt them in presence of a magistrate. It appears by his letter that the penalty for circulating such papers, is imprisonment in the penitentiary for not less than one, nor more than five years."

Such is the law, and its lawfulness, wisdom, and dignity must be judged of by the laws and principles by which other measures are judged; but it cannot be denied that a freeman feels himself circumscribed so far as he is denied to read what he chooses. If a government or a set of men were to forbid a man to read an atheistic paper, though he might be a fervent christian, his liberty would be undoubtedly circumscribed *pro tanto*.

That the seizure of English papers on the continent, is of frequent occurrence, is well known by every reader of the daily papers.

"reasons of state." No commentary is necessary on such self-vilification of governments; but this may be added, that these outrages were committed even without a formal warrant from any one, but on the sole command of the police. Are we, then, wrong in calling such governments police governments? It is not from a desire to stigmatize these governments. It is on account of the prevailing principle, and the stigma is a natural consequence of this principle.[1]

---

[1] In the decision of the appellate court in the same case we find this to be the chief argument, that government establishes post-offices, and cannot be expected to lend its hand to the promotion of mischief, by carrying letters of evil-doers. This is totally fallacious. Government does not establish post-offices, but society establishes them for itself, though it may be through government. The mail is no boon granted by government.

If it did, it is not a benefit done by a second party, as when A makes a present to B, but government is simply and purely an agent; and, what is more, the right of establishing post-offices is not an inherent attribute of government, such as the administration of justice or making war. Government merely becomes the public carrier, for the sake of general convenience. There are many private posts, and governments without government post-offices, for instance, the republic of Hamburg.

The opening of letters without proper warrant is a frightful perversion of power, and though government should be able to get at secret machinations, the secret of letters is a primordial condition. Government might, undoubtedly, know many useful things, if the sacredness of catholic confession were broken into; but that is considered a primordial and pre-political condition. So, many codes do not force a son to testify against a father; the family affection is considered a primordial condition. The very state of society, for which it is worth living, is invaded, if the correspondence is exposed to this sort of government burglary.

The argument is simply this. Man is destined to live in society, united by converse and intercommunion; this is a basis of humanity. If you open letters, you seriously invade this primary condition. Men are individuals, and social beings, destined for civilization and united progress, and the question is not whether they may be dispensed with, but how to govern with them. Governments too frequently act as though the government were the primary condition, and the remaining question only was, how much may be spared by government to be left for society or individuals. The opposite is the truth.

After this note had been published, the French court of cassation, "all chambers united," decided in the last resort, that in the case of Coëtlogon, Flandin, and others, no illegal act had been committed by the prefect of

England, as may be supposed, has not always enjoyed liberty of the press. It is a conquest of high civilization.[1] It is, however, a remarkable fact, that England owed its transitory but most stringent law of a censorship to her republican government.

On September 20, 1647,[2] it was decreed by the republican government in England that no book henceforth be printed without previously being read and permitted by the public censor, all privileges to the contrary notwithstanding. House searches for prohibited books and presses should be made, and the post-office would dispatch innocent books only. All places where printing-presses may exist should be indicated by authority. Printers, publishers, and authors were obliged to give caution-money for their names. No one was permitted to harbor a printer without permission, and no one permitted to sell foreign books without permission. Book-itinerants and ballad-singers were imprisoned and whipped. We are all acquainted with Milton's beautiful and searching essay on the liberty of the press against this censorship.

The reader who pays attention to the events of his own days, will remember the law against the press, issued immediately after the *coup d'état* of Louis Napoleon, which puts the sale of printing and lithographic presses, copying machines, as well as types, under police supervision, and which, in one word, intercepts all public communion.

I suppose it will be hardly necessary to treat, in connection with the liberty of communion, of the " liberty of silence," as a French paper headed an article, when, soon after the *coup d'état*, it was intimated to a Paris paper, by the police, that its total silence on political matters would not be looked upon by government with favor, should the paper insist on continuing it.

It would be, however, a great mistake to suppose that govern-

---

the police, in opening letters, etc. etc. The decision is given in full in the *Courrier des Etats Unis*, New York, December 12, 1853.

[1] See Lieber's Letter to Hon. W. C. Preston, on International Copyright.

[2] The same year, therefore, in which Charles I. was executed.

ments alone interfere with correspondence and free communion. Governments are bodies of men, and all bodies of men
act similarly under similar circumstances, if the power is
allowed them. All absolutism is the same. I have ever observed, in all countries in which I have lived, that, if party
struggle rises to factious passion, the different parties endeavor to get hold of the letters of their adversaries. It is,
therefore, of the last importance, both that the secret of letters and the freedom of all communion be legally protected as
much as possible, and that every true friend of liberty present
the importance of this right in the clearest possible manner
to his own mind.

7. The right of locomotion, or of free egress and regress,
as well as free motion within the country, is another important
individual right and element of liberty.

The strength of governments was generally considered, in
the last century, to consist in a large population, large amount
of money, that is, specie, within the country, and a large
army founded upon both. It was consistent, therefore, that
in countries in which individual rights went for little, and the
people were considered the mere substratum upon which the
state, that is, the government, was erected, emigration was
considered with a jealous eye, or wholly prohibited. Nor can
it be denied that emigration may present itself in a serious
aspect. So many people are leaving Ireland, that it is now
common, and not inappropriate, to speak of the Irish exodus;
and it has been calculated, upon authentic data, both in Germany and the United States, that for the last few years the
German emigrants have carried not far from fifteen millions
of Prussian dollars annually into the United States.[1] The

---

[1] On the other hand, an immense amount of capital annually returns, from successful emigrants in the United States, to Ireland and
Germany. Persons who have not paid attention to the subject, cannot
have any conception how many hard yet gladly earned pounds and tha-
lers are sent from our country to aged parents or toiling sisters and brothers in Europe. A wide-spread and blessed process of affection is thus
all the time going on—silent, gladdening, and full of beauty, like the
secret and beautifying process of spring. It is curious to observe, in

amount of emigrating capital may become greater even; but freemen believe that governments are for them, not they for governments, and that it is a precious right of every one to seek that spot on earth where he can best pursue the ends of life, physical and mental, religious, political, and cultural.[1]

If, under peculiar circumstances, a country should find itself forced to prohibit emigration, the measure would, at any rate, so far as this right goes, be an abridgment of liberty. We can imagine many cases in which emigration should be stopped by changing those circumstances which cause it, but none in which it ought to be simply prohibited. The universal principle of adhesiveness, so strong in all spheres of action, thought, and affection, and which forms one of the elementary principles of society and continuity of civilization, is sufficiently strong to keep people where they are, if they can remain; and if they leave an over-peopled country, or one in which they cannot find work or a fair living, they become active producers in the new country, and, consequently proportionate consumers in the great market of the world, so that the old country will reap its proportionate benefit, provided free exchange be allowed by the latter.

The same applies with the capital removed along with emigration. It becomes more productive, and mankind at large are benefited by it.

Besides, it is but a part of the general question, shall or shall not governments prohibit the efflux of money? It was formerly considered one of the highest problems of statesmanship, even by rulers so wise as Frederic II. of Prussia, to prevent money from flowing out of the country; for wealth

---

connection with this emigration of coin from Europe, (for, a large portion of the emigrating capital consists in European specie,) how the coins are first carried to the distant west in the pouches of the emigrants, and then are sent in large boxes from the western banks, into which they naturally flow, to the New York banks, to be sold to the specie broker, who sells them for shipment back to France, Germany, or England. The Banks of New York, by T. S. Gibbons; New York, 1859.

[1] In the Prussian constitution of 1850, Tit. ii. Art. ii., it is said, "The right to emigrate cannot be restricted by the state, except with respect to the duty of military service."

was believed to consist in money. Experience has made us wiser. We know that the freest action in this, as in so many other cases, is also the most conducive to general prosperity. It was stated in the journals of the day that Miss Jenny Lind remitted five hundred thousand dollars from the United States to Europe. Suppose this to be true, would we have been benefited had she been forced to leave that sum in this country?[1] Or would we, upon the whole, profit by preventing five million dollars, which, according to the statement of our secretary of state, are now annually sent by our Irish emigrants to Ireland, from leaving our shores?[2] Unquestionably not. But this is not the place for further pursuing a question of political economy.

The English provided for a free egress and regress as early as in Magna Charta. As to the freest possible locomotion within the country, I am aware that many persons accustomed to Anglican liberty may consider my mentioning it as part of civil liberty too minute. If they will direct their attention to countries in which this liberty is not enjoyed in its fullest extent, they will agree that I have good reason

---

[1] The papers of September, 1853, reported that "the Silby estate, belonging to the Hon. Mrs. Petre, has been sold to Lord Londesborough for £270,000. Mrs. Petre, whose property was left by her husband entirely at her own disposal, has taken the veil in a nunnery in France, which will of course receive the whole of her fortune."

This emigration of more than a million of dollars, and serving for the purpose of a religious community not favored by the country whence it emigrates, (not to speak of the actual *droit d'Anbaine* in France before the revolution,) indicates a great advance of civilization, and would not be allowed in several countries.

[2] Hon. Edward Everett's dispatch to Mr. Crampton, on the Island of Cuba, December 1, 1852. The London *Spectator* of December 17, 1853, said :—

"Not less than £2,972,000 was remitted from Irish emigrants in America to their friends and relatives at home, in 1848, 1849, 1850, and 1851. It is estimated that if the remittances have continued at the same rate, upwards of four millions must have been remitted in the last six years."

for enumerating it.   Passports are odious things to Americans
and Englishmen, and may they always be so.[1]

---

[1] The primordial right of locomotion and emigration has been discussed by me in Political Ethics, at considerable length.   The state of
Mississippi declares in its bill of rights, that the right of emigration shall
never be infringed by law or authority.   The English distaste of passports was severely tried when, after Orsini's attempt to assassinate Napoleon III., stringent passport regulations were adopted in France; but
the English found them too irksome, (and the money they spend is so
acceptable to the continent,) that those police regulations were soon
relaxed in a very great degree.   Napoleon III., when an exile, wrote on
the individual liberty in England, and called passports "that invention
of the Committee of Public Safety."   See his works.   The modern passport was, doubtless, greatly *developed* in the first French revolution, but
not invented.   The history of the passport, from the Roman Empire to
the modern railroad, which naturally interferes with its stringency, is an
interesting portion of the history of our race, but it belongs to what the
Germans have carved out as a separate branch under the name of Police
Science, (Polizei-Wissenschaft.)

CHAPTER X.

8. LIBERTY of conscience, or, as it ought to be called more properly,[1] the liberty of worship, is one of the primordial rights of man,[2] and no system of liberty can be considered comprehensive which does not include guarantees for the free exercise of this right. It belongs to American liberty to separate entirely the institution which has for its object the support and diffusion of religion from the political government. We have seen already what our constitution says on this point. All state constitutions have similar provisions. They prohibit government from founding or endowing churches, and from demanding a religious qualification for any office or the exercise of any right. They are not hostile to religion, for we see that all the state governments direct or allow the bible to be read in the public schools; but they adhere strictly to these two points: No worship shall be interfered with, either directly by persecution, or indirectly by disqualifying members of certain sects, or by favoring one sect above the others; and no church shall be declared the church of the state, or "established church;" nor shall the people be taxed by government to support the clergy of all the churches, as is the case in France.

---

[1] Conscience lies beyond the reach of government. "Thoughts are free," is an old German saying. The same must be said of feelings and conscience. That which government, even the most despotic, can alone interfere with, is the profession of religion, worship, and church government.

[2] See Primordial Rights in Political Ethics.

(99)

In England there is an established church, and religious qualifications are required for certain offices and places, at least in an indirect way. A member of parliament cannot take his seat without taking a certain oath "upon the faith of a christian;" which, of course, excludes Jews. There is no doubt, however, that this disqualification will soon be removed.[1]

---

[1] This disqualification has at length been removed, in 1858. The words "upon the faith of a christian" may be left out of the qualifying oath by a non-christian. There are now, 1859, three Jews in the house of commons.

Since the text, to which this note is appended, was written, the case of the Madiai family has attracted the attention of all civilized nations in the old and new world. The Madiai family, natives of Tuscany, had become protestants, and used to read the bible. No offence has ever been charged to them, except that they read the bible in the vernacular. Their imprisonment and prosecution caused the formation of a Society for Protecting the Rights of Conscience, in England, in July, 1857. Archbishop Whately presided at the first meeting, and in giving the scope of society, spoke of the topic in hand, with a degree of discrimination which entitles his remarks to be reproduced here. He said :

"We are entirely unconnected with conversion, except so far as converts may be exposed to persecutions, for conscience sake. We enter into no connection with any society for diffusing religious knowledge of any kind. By rights, we understand not necessarily that every one is right in the religion that he adopts, but that his neighbors have no right to interfere with him. We merely maintain that a man has a right, not necessarily a moral right, nor a right in point of judgment, but a civil right, to worship God according to his own conscience, without suffering any hardships at the hands of his neighbors for so doing. We limit ourselves entirely to those descriptions of persecution in which the law can give no relief. As for assaults and violence of any kind, where the law provides and holds out a remedy, we leave all persons to seek that remedy for themselves ; and we do not undertake to guard, or to remunerate, or to compensate any persons who are exposed to obloquy, to curses, denunciations of Divine vengeance uttered by men, to ridicule, or to any sort of annoyance of that kind. They should be taught to bear it and to support it with joy and satisfaction through Divine help, and rejoicing that they are counted worthy to suffer in the good cause. But when attempts are made to compel men to conform to what they do not conscientiously believe, by the fear of starvation, by turning them out of employment when they are honest and industrious laborers, by refusing to buy and sell, or hold any intercourse with them, then I think it is, and then only, that a society like this ought to come forward, and that all

Whether it will be done or not, we are nevertheless authorized to say that liberty of conscience forms one of the elements of Anglican liberty. It has not yet arrived at full maturity in some portions of the Anglican race, but we can discern it in the whole race, in whose modern history we find religious toleration at an earlier date than in that of any other large portion of mankind. Venice, and some minor states, found the economical and commercial benefit of toleration at an early period, but England was the earliest country of any magnitude where toleration, which precedes real religious liberty, was established. While Louis XIV. of France, called the Great, "dragonaded" the protestants on no other ground than that they would not become catholics, a greater king, William III., declared, in England, that "conscience is God's province." The catholics were long treated with severity in England, but it was more on a political ground, because the pope supported for a long time the opponents to the ruling dynasty, than on purely religious grounds.

There is a new religious zeal manifesting itself in all branches of the christian church. The catholic church seems to be animated by a renewed spirit of activity, not dissimilar to that which inspired it in the seventeenth century, by which it regained much of the ground lost by the reformation, and which has been so well described by Mr. Ranke. The protestants are not idle; they study, probe, preach, and act with great zeal. May Providence grant that the Anglican tribe, and all the members of the civilized race, may more and more distinctly act upon the principle of religious liberty, and not swerve from it, even under the most galling circumstances. Calamitous consequences, of which very few may have any conception at this moment, might easily follow.

As to that unhappy and most remarkable sect called the Mormons, who have sprung up and consolidated themselves

---

persons, whatever religion they may be of, or whether they are of any religion at all or not, in a feeling of humanity and justice, ought to look with a favorable eye on such a society as yours, provided it keep itself within its own proper bounds."

within our country, and who doubtless may become troublesome when sufficiently numerous to call on us for admission
into the Union, I take it that the political trouble they may
give cannot arise from religious grounds. Whether they have
fallen back into Buddhism, making their god a perfectible
being, with parts and local dwelling, cannot become a direct
political question, however it may indirectly affect society in
all its parts. The potent questions which will offer great
difficulty will be, whether a Mormon state, with its "theo-
democratic" government, as they term it, can be called a
republic, in the sense in which our constitution guarantees it
to every member of the Union. It will then, probably for the
first time in history, become necessary legally to define what
a republic is. The other difficulty will arise out of the question which every honest man will put to himself, can we admit
as a state a society of men who deny the very first principle,
not of our common law, not of christian politics, not of modern
progress, but of our whole western civilization, as contradistinguished from oriental life—of that whole civilization in
which we have our being, and which is the precious joint product of christianity and antiquity—who disavow monogamy.

No one will now deny that the English parliament followed
too tardily the advice of those great statesmen who urged
long ago to abolish test oaths, and other religious impedi-
ments; but to judge impartially, we must not forget that the
removal of disqualifications in countries enjoying a high
degree of liberty, is more difficult than in despotic countries,
where all beneath the despot live in one waste equality.
Liberty implies the enjoyment of important rights and high
privileges. To share them freely with others who until then
have not enjoyed them appears like losing part of them. It
is a universal psychologic law. Neither religion nor color
constitutes half the difference in many Asiatic states, which
they establish in many free countries. It must likewise be
remembered that liberty implies power, the authority of acting; consequently, an admission to equality in a free country
implies admission to power, and it is this which frequently

creates, justly or unjustly, the difficulty of perfect religious equality in certain states of society.

The end, however, which is to be reached, and toward which all liberty and political civilization tends, is perfect liberty of conscience.

9. One of the staunchest principles of civil liberty is the firmest possible protection of individual property[1]—acquired or acquiring, produced and accumulated, or producing and accumulating. We include, therefore, unrestrained action in producing and exchanging, the prohibition of all unfair monopolies, commercial freedom, and the guarantee that no property shall be taken except in the course of law; and the principle that, in particular, the constant taking away of part of property, called taxation, shall not take place, except by the direct or indirect consent of the owner—the tax-payer— and, moreover, that the power of government to take part of the property, even with the consent of the payer, be granted for short periods only, so that the taxes must be renewed, and may be revised at brief intervals. The true protection of individual property demands likewise the exclusion of confiscation. For, although confiscation as a punishment is to be rejected on account of the undefined character of the punishment, depending not upon itself but upon the fact whether the punished person has any property, and how much, it is likewise inadmissible on the ground that individual property implies individual transmission,[2] which confiscation totally destroys. It would perhaps not be wholly unjust to deprive an individual of his property as a punishment for certain crimes,

---

[1] It has been one of the main objects in my Essays on Labor and Property, to show the necessity and justice of individual property, and its direct connection with man's individuality, of which it is but the reflex in the material world around him. Man suffers in individuality, therefore in liberty, in the degree in which absolutism, which is always of a communistic nature, deprives him of the possession, enjoyment, production, and exchange of individual property. The Essays treat of property in a political, psychologic, and economical point of view.

[2] The subject of individual inheritance has also been treated at length in the Essays mentioned in the preceding note.

if we were to allow it to pass to his heirs. We do it in fact when we imprison a man for life, and submit him to the regular prison discipline, disallowing him any benefit of the property he may possess; but it is unjust to deprive his children or other heirs of the individual property, not to speak of the appetizing effect which confiscation of property has often produced upon governments.

The English attainder and corruption of blood, so far as it affects property, is hostile to this great principle of the utmost protection of individual property, and has come down to the present times from a period of semi-communism, when the king was considered the primary owner of all land. Corruption of blood is distinctly abolished by our constitution.

Individual property is coexistent with government. Indeed, if by government be understood not only the existence of any authority, but rather the more regular and clearly established governments of states, property exists long before government, and is not its creature; as values exist long before money, and money long before coin, and coin before government coin. We find, therefore, that the rightful and peaceful enjoyment of individual property is not mentioned as a particular item of civil liberty, as little as the institution of the family, except when communistic[1] ideas have endangered it, or, in particular

---

[1] I shall not have room to give a whole chapter to the subject of communism, or rather a single chapter would be wholly insufficient on this interesting subject, which, moreover, belongs to general political philosophy, rather than to our branch. I shall mention, therefore, this only, that I use in these pages the word communism in its common adaptation, meaning a state of society in which individual property is abolished, or in which it is the futile endeavor of the lawgiver to abolish it, such as hundreds of attempts in ancient times, in the middle ages, and in modern epochs, in Asia and in Europe have been made—among the Spartans, the anabaptists, and French communists. I do not take here the term communism in that philosophical sense, according to which every state, indeed every society whatever, necessarily consists of the two elements, of individualism and socialism. The grave error of the socialist is that he extends the principle of socialism, correct in itself, to the sphere where individualism or separatism, equally correct, ought to determine our actions. The socialist is as mistaken an enthusiast as the individualist would be,

cases, when private property must be given up for the public benefit,[1] and laws or constitutions settle that it shall not be done except for equivalents given by the public through government.[2]

Our constitution goes farther. It distinctly enacts that "no state shall pass any law impairing the obligation of contracts," which includes contracts with governments, and not only common contracts, but rights conferred for equivalents.[3]

The right of self-taxation has been mentioned as a guarantee of private property, for, no matter what form taxation may assume, it must always consist in the appropriation of private property for public ends. Taxation has, however, another, purely political and highly important meaning, and we shall consider it under this aspect in another part of this work.

who, forgetting the element of socialism, should carry his principle to the extreme of disjunctive egotism, and insist upon a dissolution of government and a disavowal of the sovereignty of society in political matters. It is instructive to observe how, also, in this case, the extremes meet; for works have been actually published by socialists which wind up with an entire denial of government, and an avowal of "individual sovereignty."

[1] See the constitution of the French Republic of 1848, in the appendix. It contains a paragraph acknowledging private property, the family, etc. It was right to insert it, under the circumstances. If the Spartans had ever reformed their government, and passed from their socialism to individualism, they would have been justified in proclaiming the sanctity of the family and the acknowledgment of private cookery, however ludicrous this might be under other circumstances.

[2] Points belonging to this subject and its primordial character, were pronounced with clearness in the late pleadings in the French courts, when it was endeavored to show, unfortunately in vain, that Louis Napoleon had no right, even as a dictator, to confiscate the private property of the Orleans family, and that the courts were competent to restore it to the lawful owners.

[3] See Judge Story, in his Commentaries on the Constitution of the United States, and his Opinion, as well as Chief Justice Marshall's in the celebrated Dartmouth Case, 4 Wheaton R. 518, and also Mr. Webster's Works for his argument in that case.

The English go much farther than ourselves, not indeed in principle, but because they consider many rights, places, and privileges, as vested property which we by no means consider as such.

Every single subject here mentioned, monopolies,[1] freedom of trading, freedom of home production, freedom of exchange, possession of property, taxation and confiscation—each one has a long history, full of struggle against error and government interference, running through many centuries and even a thousand years. On each a separate and instructive history might be written. Each shows the continued course of gradually, though very slowly, expanding freedom. Nor has this history of development reached its close, although it has attained to that period in which we acknowledge the highest protection of individual property as an element of our freedom.

That the so-called repudiation—it is always unfortunate and suspicious when offences that have long received their proper name, are stamped with a new and apparently innocent one; still worse it is when the error is elevated into a commendable act; and Bacon is right when he says, Pessima enim res est errorum apotheosis—that repudiation is a violation of the sacred principle we treat of, no one now will have the hardihood to deny. Still it is true, that abroad it is almost universally treated erroneously, as well in regard to its causes as to its extent, the inferences drawn from it regarding republican government, and the supposed novelty of the case. We could give a long list of monarchical repudiation. But we do not claim this as an excuse. The worst of all arguments is, although in constant use, from the school-boy to princes, presidents, and writers on national affairs, that things are equally bad or worse with others. Right and truth, wrong and falsehood remain forever what they are; and Mr. Webster pointedly said at the time of repudiation, in the senate of the United States: "You may repudiate, but that does not pay your debts." Repudiation was, and remains, a serious wrong, but its immorality does not authorize to draw wrong conclusions,

---

[1] An act of parliament, under James I. (21 James I. i. 3) prohibited all monopolies granted by the crown, after the courts had repeatedly, even under Elizabeth, declared certain monopolies null and void.

and we totally deny the correctness of the assumed facts and
inferences drawn from them by Sir A. Alison.[1]

---

[1] Paragraph fifty-nine, chap. i. vol. i. of History of Europe from the
fall of Napoleon to the accession of Louis Philippe. Possibly an opportunity may offer itself some day to treat of this melancholy subject at
length and in all its details.

I cannot forbear, however, to copy a passage of Sir A. Alison, viz.: "The
principal states of the Union have, by common consent, repudiated their
state debts as soon as the storms of adversity blew; and they have in
some instances resumed the payment of their interest only when the sale
of lands they had wrested from the Indians afforded them the means of
doing so, without recurring to the dreaded horrors of direct taxation"—
and to add that there is not one fact in this whole passage. The principal states did not repudiate; the repudiation was not by common consent; no land has been wrested from the Indians and sold for the benefit
of the states, and direct taxation exists in most states; perhaps in all the
states to some extent. Many of those readers who have been my pupils
will remember that for a number of years I was in the habit of delivering
a course of lectures on Repudiation, in which, I trust, I showed no disposition to mince matters, but to repudiate the representative principle as
Sir Archibald does when treating of Repudiation; and to present the
latter as a natural consequence of republicanism, transcends the bounds
of reason. What element in the English polity, we would ask, is it that
makes English credit so firm? Is it the monarchical? This cannot well
be, for many monarchs have more than loosely dealt with credit, public
funds, and even private property. I believe, on the contrary, that the
credit of England mainly rests on her representative, her republican principle. I do not mean to say that people lend their money just because
she has a parliament. What I mean is that the reliance of the world on
the good faith of England in money matters, has been built up by her
parliamentary government, and would not have been built up without it.

The Republic of the United States of the Netherlands enjoyed great
credit, while the Regent of France, and his council of state, seriously debated whether the "new government" was obliged to acknowledge the
debts of the defunct Louis XIV. One of the worst cases of repudiation
was exhibited in England long before the unhappy laxity became manifest in our land. The Prince of Wales (George IV.) and two of his
brothers, the Dukes of York and Clarence, desired to escape paying a
loan of 3,600,000 guilders which they had made in Holland, through
the banker, Thomas Hammersly. When the bond holders came to
England to enforce payment, Sir Arthur Pigott, attorney-general of
the Duchy of Cornwall, acting for the Prince of Wales, stated in the

10. There can be no individual liberty where every citizen is not subject to the law, and where he is subject to aught else than the law—that is public opinion organically passed into public will.[1] This we call the supremacy of the law.[2] All subjective arbitrariness is contrary to freedom. The law of a freeman is a general rule of action, having grown out of the custom of the people, or having been laid down by the authority empowered by the people to do so. A law must be a rule which does not violate a superior law or civil principle, it must be made before the case to which it is applied has

---

court that he had never heard of the bonds, which was absolutely untrue. All London, and indeed all England, knew of it. The arguments were worthy of any Mississippi repudiator, such as, the present bond holders are not the original lenders ; war has broken out. Ultimately the Dutch bond holders who were in England were arrested under the alien law and put on board a vessel, where, English writers say, I cannot say with what degree of truth, they perished, though none of the crew died.

Sir A. Alison says somewhere in his writings, that the richest men in the city of New York do not dare to have stately fronts for their houses, however costly the interior may be, from fear of displeasing the democracy. Truth and essential progress are never promoted by wrong or false argument.

[1] We shall presently say more on the all-important word Law ; but for an extensive discussion of the subject I must refer the reader to the Political Ethics.

[2] It will hardly be necessary to state that the term supremacy of the law, has a meaning only when by law we understand general and pre-existing rules of action expressing public will. Whether the name of law be given to personal decrees and arbitrary decisions, is not of the smallest importance. Napoleon, at St. Helena, expressed his surprise at having been called a despot, " I," said he, " who have always acted by law !" This forcibly reminds us of a prominent French paper, *The Univers*, which lately stated that it was decidedly in favor of representative government, and that it was only necessary to know what is understood by representative government. *The Univers*—so said the paper itself—understands by this term a legislative corps, which represents the government. I have known, in an official capacity, a patient in a hospital for the insane, who perseveringly maintained that the difference between him and me consisted solely in the name. " Suppose," he used to say, " we patients vote that we are sane, and the out-door party is crazy?" " Don't you see ?" he would add with a knowing look.

occurred (without which it cannot be mens sine affectu, as the ancients called the law,) and it must be truly as well as plainly published.

The citizen, therefore, ought not to be subject to ex post facto laws,[1] to a "government by commissions," nor to extraordinary courts[2] of justice, to a dispensing power in the executive (so much insisted on by the Stuarts, and, indeed, by all rulers who claim to rule by a higher law than the law of the land,) or to mere "proclamations" of the crown or executive, nor to the dictation of mobs, nor any people who claim to be *the* people; indeed, to no dictates of the people except in its political, that is, in its organized and organic capacity.

All the modern constitutions by which it is endeavored to transplant Anglican liberty, declare that the citizen shall be subject to his "natural courts" only. The charter of Louis XVIII. prohibited cours prevolates.[3] It had become very necessary to point out in the charter that every one should be judged by his "natural court," because the extraordinary courts had been a great grievance in former times, and because Napoleon had introduced le jugement adminis-

---

[1] Our constitution prohibits them.

[2] By extraordinary courts of justice are meant, in this connection, courts of an extraordinary composition, not those that are simply directed to sit at an unusual time. The difference between justice, that is, right distributed among men by lawful and regularly appointed judges on the one hand, and the trials by commissioners on the other hand, is well pointed out by an anecdote, such as Plutarch would not have disdained to give in his writings. Montaign, grand-master of the household of Charles VI., was tried, tortured, and executed by Commissioners. He was buried in the church of the Celestines, and when Francis I. came to see his tomb, the king said, "This Montaign has been condemned by justice." "No, sire," answered the simple monk, who guided the king, "he was condemned by Commissioners." Histoire du Parlement de Paris, Amsterdam, 1769, ch. 4. Commissioners as judges form a "packed" court, do not feel lasting responsibility, and, in cases of importance to the executive, act on the foregone conclusion almost as distinctly as the "judges" of the Duke d'Enghien did. In this consists the danger of courts-martial, when established for the ordinary courts.

[3] See the French charter in the appendix.

tratif, although lettres de cachet remained abolished in his reign.
An administrative or executive judgment simply meant decisions, imprisonment or other punishments, although the courts
had absolved the prisoner, or taking effect without the action of
any court. It is nothing less than plain police government.

The American Declaration of Independence has a passage
referring to the subject of "natural courts." It enumerates as
one of the grounds of justification for separating from
England, that the government has "transported us beyond
the seas to be tried for pretended offences."

All continental governments which were bent on defeating
the action of the new constitutions, even while they existed,
resorted to declaring large cities and entire districts in "a
state of siege," thus subjecting them to martial law. All
absolute governments, whether monarchical or democratic,
have ever found the regular course of justice inconvenient,
and made war upon the organic action of the law, which
proves its necessity as a guarantee of liberty.

It is obvious that, whatever wise provisions a constitution
may contain, nothing is gained if the power of declaring
martial law be left in the hands of the executive ; for declaring martial law, or proclaiming a place or district in a state of
siege, simply means the suspension of the due course of law,
of the right of habeas corpus, of the common law, and of the
action of courts. The military commander places the prisoners
whom he chooses to withdraw from the ordinary courts before
courts-martial. There were many French departments in "a
state of siege" before the coup d'état. After it, all France
may be said to have been so.

In England, when there is a rebellion or wide-spread disorder, threatening life and property, a regular act of parliament is passed, suspending the habeas corpus. The act states
the necessity or reasons, and the time of its duration. This
last point is of great importance.[1]

---

[1] The act by which martial law was declared in Ireland, during the
rebellion in 1798, can be seen in Tytler's Essay on Military Law, appendix, No. 6. I copy this reference from an article, Martial Law, in Political Dictionary; London, 1846.

We have seen already under what circumstances our constitution permits the suspension of the habeas corpus, and that this cannot be done by the president alone, but by congress only, need hardly be mentioned.

It has been necessary to mention here the supremacy of the law as a peculiar guarantee of personal liberty. We shall return to the subject, and consider it in its wider relations.

11. The preceding guarantee of the supremacy of the law leads to a principle, which, so far as I know, it has never been attempted to transplant from the soil inhabited by Anglican people, and which nevertheless has been in our system of liberty the natural production of a thorough government of law, as distinguished from a government of functionaries. It is so natural to the Anglican race that few think of it as essentially important to civil liberty, and it is of such vital importance that none who have studied the acts of government elsewhere, can help recognizing it as an indispensable element of civil liberty.

It is this, that, on the one hand, every officer, however high or low, remains personally answerable to the affected person for the legality of the act he executes, no matter whether his lawful superior has ordered it or not, and, even, whether the executive officer had it in his power to judge of the legality of the act he is ordered to do, or not; and that, on the other hand, every individual is authorized to resist an unlawful act, whether executed by an otherwise lawfully appointed officer or not. The resistance is made at the resister's peril. In all other countries, obedience to the officer is demanded in all cases, and redress can only take place after previous obedience.[1] Occasionally, this principle acts harshly upon the officer; but we prefer this inconvenience to the inroad which its abandonment would make in the government of law. We will not submit to individual men, but only to men who are, and when they are, the organs of the law.[2] A coup d'état, such as we have lately seen in

---

[1] Extreme cases, as a matter of course, would be allowed to form exceptions.

[2] I must again refer to the Political Ethics, chapter on Obedience to the Law.

France, would not be feasible in a nation accustomed to this principle. All the answer which the police officers gave to men like General Cavaignac, who asked them whether they were aware that they committed a high crime in arresting a representative of the people, was, that they had orders from their superior, and had nothing to do with the question of legality. It is obvious how much this peculiar Anglican principle heightens the importance of obedience to the officer, representing the law, and the law alone. Lawlessness in this, as in all other cases, is peculiarly incompatible with the spirit of Anglican freedom.

As an instance of the opposite to the French principle of that huge institution called *gendarmerie*, the following simple case may be taken :

A sheriff, provided with the proper warrant, has the right, after request and denial, to open the house door, forcibly to open it, if a third party has taken refuge in it, or sent his goods there. "Every man's house is his castle," will not protect any one but the bona fide dweller in it. Nevertheless, the sheriff, provided with his legal warrant, does it at his own peril; for, if he break open the house, however well his suspicion may be grounded, and neither the party nor the goods sought for be there, the sheriff is a trespasser, and as such answerable to the inhabitant of the house before the courts of the land. This may be inconvenient in single cases. It may be that the maxim which has been quoted has "been carried as far as the true principles of political practice will warrant— perhaps beyond what in the scale of sound reason and good policy they will warrant."[1] I doubt it, whatever the inconvenience in single cases may be. All law is inconvenient in some cases; but even if this opinion were founded, how august, on the other hand, appears the law—I do not mean a single statute, but the whole self-evolving system of a common law of the land—that errs on the side of individual liberty against the public power and the united weight of government !

---

[1] Sir M. Foster, Discourse of Homicide, p. 319. I quote from Broom's Legal Maxims.

This Anglican principle might be supposed by those who are not familiar with it, that fear of resolute action in the officer would be the consequence. But this is not the case, as experience in England and the United States sufficiently proves. When magistrates and officers, who according to their sphere of action ought not to be elective, are made elective, timidity or time-serving encroach indeed upon the resolute performance of the officer's duty; but this has nothing to do with the principle here treated. Nor is it denied that exceptions may take place. A police officer lately stated in open court in London, when asked why he had not performed a certain act clearly lying within the sphere of his duty, that it was so difficult for him to know what was lawful for him to do, according to the opinion of the magistrate, that he had preferred not to act. No machinery works without occasional friction. Compare with this the ruthless European continental police, and chose. The reader will find at the end of the foot-note appended to this page, an amusing illustration of the fact that monarchical absolutism does not necessarily give freedom or boldness of action to officers.[1]

[1] The very opposite to the Anglican principle, that each officer remains responsible for the legality of his own acts, prevails in China and Japan, and probably in all thoroughly systematized Asiatic despotisms. The superior officer is punished for the offence and even for the misfortune of the inferior, or for the accident which may have befallen the latter. The blows with the bamboo, which in China go down from the superior through many grades to the inferior, are well known. Before the late opening of the Japanese ports to the Americans and Europeans, a christian vessel was driven on the shores of Japan. The governor ripped open his belly, and the viceroy, in whose province the wreck had happened, was imprisoned for one hundred days, although he was at the time a hundred miles from the place of the disaster. There is also, however, in these cases, to be taken into consideration the confusion of moral laws, and physical laws, and fate, which pervades the whole Chinese code, the ethics of Japan, the moral code of all early nations, and which we find in the early mythology of all nations. The earliest period of Greek history and mythology furnishes us with many illustrations.

Mr. King, in his Notes of the Voyage of the Morrison, New York, 1839, gives the following anecdote: "We had inquired of the Japanese how their officers were to be distinguished; whether they wore any

The reader has seen from the passage on warrants, which I gave in a preceding part of this work, how far this principle is carried in the case of resisting an officer, even to the killing him, if his warrant be not wholly correct. Another proof of the uniform acknowledgment of this principle and essential pillar of civil liberty, is this, that when a British minister obtains an act of indemnity, which is an act of impunity for certain illegal acts, which, nevertheless, necessity demanded, the act of indemnity is never for him alone, but it expresses that the act shall also cover what the inferior officers have done by the direction of the minister in the premises.[1]

In conclusion, I would remark that it is wholly indifferent

---

badges besides the ever-famous 'two sabres.' The answer was, If you see a man come on board that trembles very much, he is a mandarine."

The student must take care not to consider the fining of companies for want of caution, skill, or honesty in the persons or officers employed by them, (now so common in consequence of railway accidents,) as invalidating the principle laid down in the text.

[1] For instance, in the scarcity of grain in the year 1766, Chatham prohibited exportation of grain. When parliament met, he read a passage from Locke, to show that what he had done was not legal yet right. Indemnity was passed for him and those who had acted under him. In 1818, ministers asked and obtained indemnity for the suspension of habeas corpus, for themselves and magistrates under them. Many other instances might be given. See Lieber's Legal and Political Hermeneutics, note to page 79. Acts of indemnity cannot be passed with us, because we have a constitution of which the legislature itself is but the creature, and we cannot pass ex post facto laws. All that remains for us to do in cases of absolute necessity or transcendent utility is to pass over the occurrence in silence ; or congress may show its concurrence by aiding in the act. This was the case when Mr. Jefferson purchased the mouth of the Mississippi, *i.e.* the territory of Louisiana. Still, congress cannot make the act constitutional; though the silence of congress, or the countenance given by it to an act, give it such apparent legality, that we find in the present time (1859) many men calling themselves adherents to the strictest interpretation of the constitution, and insisting on liberal interpretation, urging the purchase of the island of Cuba, as if the constitution, which itself declares that it permits nothing but what it distinctly and positively grants, had allowed the purchase of foreign territory.

who gives the order. If it be illegal, the person who executes it remains responsible for the act, although the president or the king should have ordered it, or the offending person should be a soldier obeying his commander. It is a stern law, but it is a sacred principle, a strict government of law cannot dispense with it, and it has worked well.

CHAPTER XI.

12. Governments, if not very closely hedged in, have it in their power to worry citizens into submission by many indirect methods. One of these, frequently resorted to since the introduction of standing armies, is, that soldiers are billeted with the disaffected citizens. An insolent soldiery, supported by the executive, find a thousand ways of annoying, insult ng, and ruining the family with whom they are quartered. It has been deemed necessary, therefore, specially to prohibit the quartering of soldiers with citizens, as an important guarantee of civil liberty. The English bill of rights, "declaring the rights and liberties of the subject," of 1688, enumerates in the preamble, as one of the proofs that James II. " did endeavor to subvert and extirpate" . . . "the laws and liberties of this kingdom," his "raising and keeping a standing army within the kingdom in time of peace, without consent of parliament, and quartering soldiers contrary to law." It is, in England, therefore, a high offence to quarter soldiers without consent of parliament; and the Constitution of the United States ordains that "no soldier shall in time of peace be quartered in any house without the consent of the owner, nor in time of war, but in a manner to be prescribed by law." The framers of the constitution, it will be observed, were very exact in drawing up this paragraph.

Persons not versed in the history of civil liberty and of progressive absolutism, might be surprised at this singling out of quartering soldiers in documents of such elevated character and condensed national demands as the Bill of Rights and the American Constitution are; but the "dragonades" of

(116)

Louis XIV. in France, of James II. in Scotland, and those of more recent and present date in certain countries, furnish sufficient justification for this specific guarantee.

13. The preceding safeguard, although justly pointed out separately, is still only part of the general one that the forces must be strictly submitted to the law. The navy cannot be, in its nature, so formidable an instrument in the hands of the executive as the army. It cannot be brought to bear upon the people; it is not centralized in its character, and it cannot surround the ruler. There are many other reasons why the navy, the floating bulwarks of a nation, has always shown an inherent affinity with the popular element, and why free nations only can have efficient navies or merchant fleets, as a distinguished statesman of the United States[1] has observed.

It is far different with the land forces. Ever since standing armies have been established, it has been necessary, in various ways, to prevent the army from becoming independent of the legislature. There is no liberty, for one who is bred in the Anglican school, where there is not a perfect submission of the army to the legislature of the people. We hold it to be necessary, therefore, to make but brief appropriations for the army. The King of England cannot raise an army, or any part of it, without act of parliament;[2] the army-estimates are passed for one year only, so that, were parliament to refuse appropriations, after a twelvemonth the army would be dissolved. The mutiny-bill, by which power is given to the king to hold courts-martial for certain offences in the army, is likewise passed for a year only; so that, without repassing it, the crown would have no power even to keep up military discipline.

---

[1] Mr. Poinsett.

[2] The guards of Charles II. were declared anti-constitutional, and the army of James II. was one of the evidences by which he was presumed to have abdicated; that is, in other words, one of his breaches of the fundamental law of the land. A new sanction was given to this principle in the sixth article of the Bill of Rights, which runs thus : A standing army, without the consent of parliament, is against law.

The Constitution of the United States makes the president, indeed, commander-in-chief, but he cannot enlist a man, or pay a dollar for his support, without the previous appropriation by congress, to which the constitution gives "power to make rules for the government and regulation of the land and naval forces," and to which it denies the authority of making any appropriation for the support of the national forces for a longer term than two years.

The importance of this dependence of the army upon the civil power has been felt by all parties. While the people are bent on submitting the army to the legislature, the governments, which in the late struggles were anxious to grant as little liberty as possible, always endeavored to exclude the army from the obligation of taking the constitutional oath. Constitutional oaths, like other political oaths, are indeed no firm guarantee in times of civil disturbance; but where circumstances are such that people must start in the career of freedom with an enacted constitution, it is natural and necessary that the army should take the oath of fidelity to the fundamental law, like any other persons employed in public service, especially where the oath of allegiance to the monarch continues. The oath, when taken, we have already admitted, does not furnish any great security; but in this, as in so many other cases, the negative assumes a very great and distinct importance, although the positive may be destitute of any direct weight. The refusal of this oath shows distinctly that the executive does not intend frankly to enter on the path of civil freedom. This was lately the case in Prussia, when it was the endeavor of the people to establish constitutional liberty.

The Declaration of Independence says: "He has kept among us in times of peace standing armies without the consent of our legislatures" It is enumerated as a radical grievance, plain and palpable to every Anglican mind. Immediately after, the declaration significantly adds: "He has affected to render the military independent of, and superior to, the civil power." This "affected" is striking. The attempt of doing it, though the term affected indicates the want of success, is counted as a grievance sufficient to warrant, among others, an extinction of allegiance. Of the twenty-seven grievances enumerated in the declaration as justification for a revolution, three relate to the army.[1]

Dr. Samuel Johnson, not biased, as the reader well knows, in favor of popular liberties, nevertheless showed that he was bred in England, when he speaks of "the greatest of political evils—the necessity of ruling by immediate force."[2] There is, however, a greater evil still—the ruling by immediate force when it is not necessary or against the people.

Standing armies are not only dangerous to civil liberty because directly depending upon the executive. They have the additional evil effect that they infuse into the whole nation—especially when they are national armies, so that the old soldiers return continually to the people—a spirit directly opposite to that which ought to be the general spirit of a free people devoted to self-government. A nation of freemen stands in need of a pervading spirit of obedience to the laws; an army teaches and must teach a spirit of prompt obedience to orders. Habits of disobedience and of contempt for the citizen are produced, and a view of government is induced which is contrary to liberty, self-reliance, self-government. Command ought to rule in an army; self-development of law and self-sustaining order ought to pervade a free people. A German king, in one of his throne speeches, when a liberal spirit had already manifested itself in that country, said: "The will of one must ultimately rule in the government, even as it is in the camp." This shows exactly what we mean. The entire state, with its jural and civic character, is compared to a camp, and ruinous inferences are drawn from the comparison.

---

[1] A remarkable debate took place in the British commons, in April, 1856, when Mr. Cowan brought under the notice of the house the billeting system pursued in Scotland, according to which "militia and troops of the line are billeted upon private houses in Scotland." "It is an intolerable grievance." Redress was obtained.

[2] Considerations on the Corn Laws, by Dr. Samuel Johnson.

The officers of a large army are in the habit of contemptu-
ously speaking of the "babbling lawyers." Les légistes have
always been spoken of by the French officers in the same tone
as "those lawyers" were talked of by Strafford and Laud.
Where the people worship the army an opinion is engendered
as if really courage in battle were the highest phase of
humanity; and the army, in turn, more than aught else, leads
to the worship of one man—so detrimental to liberty. All
debate is in common times odious to the soldiers. They
habitually ridicule parliamentary debates of long duration.
Act, act, is their cry, which in that case means: Command
and obey are the two poles round which public life ought to
turn. A man who has been a soldier himself, and has seen
the inspiring and rallying effect which a distinctive uniform
may have in battle—the desire not to disgrace the coat, is not
likely to fall in with the sweeping denunciations of the uniform,
now frequently uttered by the "peacemen;" but it is true
that the uniform, if constantly worn, and if the army is large,
as on the continent of Europe, greatly aids in separating the
army from the people, and in increasing that alienating esprit
de corps which ought not to exist where the people value their
liberty. Modern despotism carefully fosters this spirit of
separation, because it relies mainly on the standing army.
The insolence of the officers of Napoleon I. rose to a frightful
degree, even in France itself; and many startling events have
lately occurred in that country, showing how far Napoleon III.
indulges his officers in insulting and maltreating the citizen.[1]
No security whatever arises from the fact that the army is
"democratic" in its character. On the contrary, the danger is
only the greater, because it makes the army apparently a part
of the people; the people themselves look to it for one of the
careers in which they may expect promotion, (not quite unlike
the church in the middle ages,) while, in spite of all this, the
army becomes a secluded caste, essentially opposed to the
aspirations of the people. No better illustration is afforded

---

[1] I write at the beginning of 1859.

in history, of this important fact, than by the present state of things in France.

Nor is the case better, when the army is the ruling body, and its officers belong exclusively to the country nobility, in a country where every son of a nobleman is likewise noble, and a large, poor nobility is the consequence. A numerous and poor nobility is one of the most injurious and ruinous things in a state. It leads infallibly to that spirit which tries to make up by arrogance what it does not possess in wealth or substance, which considers the state as an institution made for the provision of the poor noblemen, and disregards the true and the high interests of the nation—a state of things which revealed itself, for Prussia, in the terrible disaster at Jena, in 1806, and which has received in that and other German countries, of late, the distinct appellation of *Junkerthum*.

Standing armies, therefore, wherever necessary—and they are necessary at present, as well as far preferable to the medieval militia—ought to be as small as possible, and completely dependent on the legislature for their existence. Such standing armies as we see in the different countries of the European continent are wholly incompatible with civil liberty, by their spirit, number and cost.

A perfect dependence of the forces, however, requires more than short appropriations, and limited authority of the executive over them. It is further necessary—because they are under strict discipline, and therefore under a strong influence of the executive—that these forces, and especially the army, be not allowed to become deliberative bodies, and that they be not allowed to vote as military bodies. Wherever these guarantees have been disregarded, liberty has fallen. These are rules of importance at all times, but especially in countries where, unfortunately, very large standing armies exist. In France, the army consists of half a million, yet universal suffrage gave it the right to vote, and the army as well as the navy did vote to justify the second of December, as well as to make Louis Napoleon Bonaparte emperor. This may be in harmony with French "equality;" it may be democratic, if this term be taken in the sense in which it is wholly unconnected with liberty; all that we—people with whom liberty is more than a theory, or something æsthetically longed for, and who learn liberty as the artisan learns his craft, by handling it—all that we know is, that it is not liberty; that it is directly destructive of it.[1]

It was formerly the belief that standing armies were incompatible with liberty, and a very small one was granted to the King of England with much reluctance; and in France we have a gigantic standing army, itself incompatible with liberty, for whom in addition the right of voting is claimed.

The Bill of Rights, and our own Declaration of Independence, show how large a place the army occupied in the minds of the patriotic citizens and statesmen who drew up those historic documents, the reasons they had to mention it repeatedly, and of erecting fences against it.

Military bodies ought not to be allowed even the right of petitioning, as bodies. History fully proves the danger, that must be guarded against.[2] English history, as well as that of other nations, furnishes us with instructive instances.

A wise medium is necessary; for an army without thorough

---

[1] The French soldiers vote at present, whenever universal suffrage is appealed to—not with the citizens, but for themselves, and the way in which this military voting generally takes place is very remarkable.

[2] I do not feel authorized to say that the Anglicans consider it an elementary guarantee of liberty not to be subjected to the obligation of serving in the army, but certain it is that as matters now stand, and as our feelings now are, we should not consider it compatible with individual liberty ; indeed, it would be considered as intolerable oppression, if we were forced to spend part of our lives in the standing army. It would not be tolerated. The feeling would be as strong against the French system of conscription, which drafts by lot a certain number of young men for the army, and permits those who have been drafted to furnish substitutes, as against the Prussian system, which obliges every one, from the highest to the lowest, to serve a certain time in the standing army, with the exception only of a few " mediatized princes." The Anglicans, therefore, may be said to be at present unequivocally in favor of enlisted standing armies, where standing armies are necessary.

unity is useless; indeed, worse than useless. It produces a thousand evils without any good; while it must always be considered as a distinct command of Civil Liberty, that a well-organized army is of itself a subject of great danger. To make an efficient army, in modern times, harmonize with all the demands of substantial civil liberty is doubtless one of the problems of our race and age, and one most difficult to solve—forming, perhaps, with the problem of carrying out a high degree of individual liberty in large and densely peopled cities, the two most difficult problems of high, patriotic and substantial statesmanship.

14. Akin to the last-mentioned guarantee, is that which secures to every citizen the right of possessing and bearing arms. Our constitution says: " The right of the people to keep and bear arms shall not be infringed upon;" and the Bill of Rights secured this right to every protestant. It extends now to every English subject. It will hardly be necessary to add, that laws prohibiting secret weapons, or those which necessarily endanger the lives of the citizens, are no infringement of liberty; on the contrary, liberty resting necessarily on law, and a lawful, that is, peaceful state of the citizens, liberty itself requires the suppression of a return to force and violence among the citizens—a fact by no means sufficiently weighed in recent times in America.

Whenever attempts at establishing liberty have lately been made on the continent of Europe, a general military organization of the people, or "national guards," has been deemed necessary, but we cannot point them out as characteristics of Anglican liberty.

CHAPTER XII.

PETITION. ASSOCIATION.

15. WE pass over to the great right of petitioning, so jealously suppressed wherever absolute power rules or desires to establish itself, so distinctly contended for by the English in their revolution, and so positively acknowledged by our constitution.

An American statesman of great mark has spoken lightly of the right of petition in a country in which the citizens are so fully represented as with us;[1] but this is an error. It is a right which can be abused, like any other right, and which in the United States is so far abused as to deprive the petition of weight and importance. It is nevertheless a sacred right which in difficult times shows itself in its full magnitude, frequently serves as a safety-valve, if judiciously treated by the recipients,[2] and may give to the representatives or other bodies the most valuable information. It may right many a wrong, and the privation of it would at once be felt by every freeman as a degradation. The right of petitioning is indeed a necessary consequence of the right of free speech and deliberation, a simple, primitive and natural right. As a privilege it is not even denied the creature in addressing the deity. It is so

---

[1] It was stated by him that the right of petition was of essential value only in a monarchy, against the encroachments of the crown. But this whole view was unquestionably a confined one, and caused by irritation against a peculiar class of persevering petitioners.

[2] There is no more striking instance on record, so far as our knowledge goes, than the formidable petition of the chartists in 1848, and the calm respect with which this threatening document was received by the commons, after a speech full of dignity and manly acknowledgment of the people by Lord Morpeth, now Earl of Carlisle.

natural a right, in all spheres where there are superiors and inferiors, that its special acknowledgment in charters or by-laws would be surprising, had not ample experience shown the necessity of expressing it.[1]

Where the government is founded on the parental principle, or where the despot appears as an earthly providence, the petition of individuals plays, naturally, an important part, so

---

[1] The discussion of petitions in the house of commons seems to have undergone a marked change, as will appear from the following remarks of Lord Brougham, which he made in the house of lords, in June 1853, when the extension of the time of the income tax was under debate. Lord Brougham said that he did not expect that the income tax would expire in 1860. He recalled the circumstances under which the old income tax was repealed, in defiance of the government of that day; through the instrumentality of nightly discussions on petitions—*a popular privilege no longer allowed in the house of commons.*

"In 1806, when the income tax was 10 per cent., it was imposed till the end of the war, and no longer. The war ended in 1814, but it broke out again in 1815; and after its final termination a great fight against the continuance of the tax took place in the house of commons. It had been said that the present income tax would not be abandoned in 1860; and he believed that the campaign which took place in parliament in 1816 could not be fought again. How was that campaign conducted? By means of petitions. For five or six weeks, from four o'clock in the afternoon till two or three o'clock in the morning, petition after petition was presented, and each petition was debated. If an account was given of the proceedings of the five or six weeks during which that campaign against the income tax was fought, it would describe one of the most extraordinary scenes ever witnessed within the walls of the house of commons, and a resistance which was perfectly successful. He might mention one incident which occurred during those discussions. After the fight had continued some three weeks or more, one night about eleven or twelve o'clock, a question was put from the chair about bringing up the petitions; and all the members on one bench—who might have been supposed to be exhausted by the long sitting—rose in competition with each other to catch, as it was called, the speaker's eye; and the gallantry of those men in standing by their colors under such circumstances so struck the house that they were hailed with a general cheer of applause. He did not think, however, that in 1860, unless a great change took place elsewhere, the same campaign and stand against the income tax would be possible."

long as it does not become either dangerous or troublesome, or unwelcome to the officers near the person of the monarch.

The Emperor Nicholas of Russia, was often spoken to in the streets by petitioners; while, on the other hand, we remember a royal decree in Prussia, published about thirty years ago, which directed that petitions must no longer be thrust upon the monarch personally. Under Frederic the Great, again, it was a common thing for petitioners to attract the king's attention by holding the petition above the heads of the crowd, when he would send an aid to take it. In China the right of petitioning the monarch is symbolically acknowledged, by the drum or gong at the palace gate, which the petitioner beats when he drops the petition into the receiving box. But the Chinese doubtless think and feel what the Russians express in the significant saying: " God lives high, and the emperor far." The missionary Huc informs us that popular meetings, where petitions are adopted or dismissed, are not rare in China.[1]

The political philosopher in treating of this subject must distinguish between petitions to the executive, (and as to petitions for pardon, which have become a most serious evil in the United States, the reader is referred to the paper on pardons in the appendix ;) petitions of the army, which history amply teaches, must be absolutely interdicted ; we need only remind the reader of the English history, and that of France; and, lastly, petitions to the legislature. As to the latter, it is all-important for the cause of civil liberty, that is, the freedom of the people in earnest and in reality, that the petition, whatever demonstration of moral power or public opinion it may be, be unaccompanied by physical demonstration of crowds, armed or unarmed, in the legislative halls or outside. Indeed, they cease to be petitions and become physical threats

---

[1] It would be a grave error indeed, to conclude, from this fact, or from the general democratic character of the Chinese system, that there is liberty in China—a conclusion as hasty as it would be to infer that freedom exists in France because the empire declares itself to be founded on universal suffrage.

or coercion. The history of the French revolution is almost one continued commentary on this position. The whole meaning of a legislature, as a necessary element of liberty, is that it be free, and it ceases to be free, so soon as crowds threaten it.

We maintain that the right of petitioning is important, and for this very reason it must neither be treated lightly, on the part of the petitioners, nor wrenched from its meaning and be changed into coercing threat. The petition in free states is an institution, and not an incident as in the despotic government. Resorted to as one of the civil agents by a free people, its distinct uses lie in its direct effect, in inciting and awakening public attention; in keeping alive an important idea, although it may not lead to immediate action; in countenancing those who desire to act and to be supported; in showing public opinion concerning some distinct point; in serving as a safety-valve in times of public excitement, and in being a substitute for unorganized and unreasoning crowds. Its dangers are the dangers of all agents whatever—its abuses, and in the wide-spread weakness of men, which induces them inconsiderately to put down their names, rather than refuse the signature.

16. Closely connected with the right just mentioned is the right of citizens peaceably to meet and to take public matters into consideration, and

17. To organize themselves into associations, whether for political, religious, social, scientific, industrial, commercial or cultural purposes. That this right can become dangerous, and that laws are frequently necessary to protect society against abuse, every one knows perfectly well who has the least knowledge of the French clubs in the first revolution. But it is with rights, in our political relations, as with the principles of our physical and mental organization—the more elementary and indispensable they are, the more dangerous they become, if not guided by reason. Attempts to suppress their action lead to mischief and misery. What has been more abused than private and traditional judgment in all the spheres of

thought and taste ?   Yet both are necessary.   What principle of our nature has led, and is daily leading, to more vice and crime than that on which the propagation of our species and the formation of the family depend,[1] or that which indicates by thirst, the necessity of refreshing the exhausted body? Shall the free sale of cutlery be interfered with, because murders are committed with knives and hatchets ?

The associative principle is an element of progress, protection, and efficient activity.   The freer a nation, the more developed we find it in larger or smaller spheres ; and the more despotic a government is, the more actively it suppresses all associations. The Roman emperors did not even look with favor upon the associations of handicrafts.   In modern times no instances of the power which associations may wield, and of the full extent which a free country may safely allow to their operations, seem to be more striking than those of the Anti-Corn-Law League in England, which, by gigantic exertions, ultimately carried free trade in corn against the strongest and most privileged body of land-owners that has probably ever existed, either in modern or ancient times ;[2] and, in our own country, the Colonization Society, a private society, planting a new state which will be of great influence in the spreading cause of civilization—a society which, according to the Liberian declaration of independence, " has nobly and in perfect faith redeemed its pledges."   In every country, except in the United States and in England, the cry would have been, Im-

---

[1] The so-called Shakers endeavor to extirpate this principle, and furnish us with an illustration of the evils arising from the endeavor.

[2] A careful study of the whole history of this remarkable association, which in no state of the European continent would have been allowed to rise and expand, is recommended to every student of civil liberty.   It is instructive as an instance of perseverance ; of an activity the most multifarious, and an organization the most extensive ; of combined talent and shrewd adaptation of the means to the end ; and, which is always of equal importance, of a proper conception of the end according to the means at our disposal, without which it is impossible to do that which Cicero so highly praised in Brutus, when he said, Quid vult valde vult.

perium in imperio, and both would have been speedily put down.

We may also mention our extensive churches, or the Law Amendment Association in England—a society, which, so far as we can judge at this distance, has already produced most beneficial effects upon English legislation, and which in every other country, occupied by our race, except in the United States, would be stigmatized as an imperium in imperio full of assumption. There is nothing that more forcibly strikes a person arriving for the first time from the European continent, either in the United States or in England, than the thousandfold evidences of an all-pervading associative spirit in all moral and practical spheres, from the almost universal commercial co-partnerships and associations, the "exchanges" of artisans, and banks, to those unofficial yet national associations which rise to real grandeur. Strike out from England or America this feature and principle, and they are no longer the same self-relying, energetic, indomitably active people. The spirit of self-government would be gone. In France, an opposite spirit prevails. Not only does the government believe that it must control everything, but the people themselves seem hardly ever to believe in success until the government has made the undertaking its own.[1]

---

[1] I cannot forbear mentioning here one of those occurrences, which, although apparently trivial, nevertheless show the constant action of a great principle, as the leaf of a tree reveals to the philosopher, the operation of the vastest elements in nature. At a meeting of the Royal Academy at London in 1852, at which the ministers were present, the premier, Lord Aberdeen, said that "as a fact full of hope, he remarked that for several years the public, in the appreciation of art, had outstripped the government and the parliament itself."

The chief executive officer considers it a fact full of hope that the people have outstripped, in interest and action, the government and parliament. How different would a similar case have presented itself in any of the continental countries!

CHAPTER XIII.

18. WE now approach those guarantees of liberty which relate more especially to the government of a free country, and the character of its polity. The first of all we have to mention under this head is publicity of public business. This implies the publicity of legislatures and judicial courts, as well as of all minor transactions that can in their nature be transacted publicly, and also the publication of all important documents and reports, treaties, and whatever else can interest the people at large. It further implies the perfect freedom with which reporters may publish the transactions of public bodies.[1] Without the latter, the admission of the public would hardly amount in our days to any publicity at all. We do not assem-

---

[1] In the year 1857 the following case was decided in the court of common pleas at Columbia, S. C., in favor of the plaintiff. The city council held, in 1855, a public meeting. The editor of one of the city papers being present, was asked by the mayor whether he had come to take notes. The mayor being answered in the affirmative, ordered the chief police officer to turn the editor out of the room, declaring at the time that he acted on the strength of a resolution of the city council. At a later period this procedure was defended on the ground that the city appoints a paper to give, officially, all the transactions of the board. Robert W. Gibbes vs. Edward J. Arthur and John Burdell. This novel case was reported with great care, and published with all the arguments, at Columbia, S. C., in 1857, under the title, Rights of Corporations and Reporters. The public owes thanks to the plaintiff for having perseveringly pursued this surprising case, the first of the kind, it would appear. The pamphlet contains letters of nearly thirty American mayors, testifying that reporters cannot be denied admission to the deliberations of the councils of their cities, although there be an appointed printer to the board.

(130)

ble in the markets as the people of antiquity did. The millions depending upon public information, in our national states, could not meet in the market, as was possible in the ancient city-states, even if we had not a representative government. The public journals are in some respects to modern freemen what the agora was to the Athenian, the forum to the Roman. A modern free city-state can be imagined without a public press; a modern free country cannot; although we must never forget the gigantic, and therefore dangerous power which, under certain circumstances, a single public journal may obtain, and, consequently, ought to be counteracted by the means which lie in the publicity and freedom of the press itself.

Publicity, in connection with civil liberty, means publicity in the transaction of the business of the public, in all branches— publicity in the great process by which public opinion passes over into public will, which is legislation; and publicity in the elaboration of the opinion of the public, as well as in the process of ascertaining or enouncing it by elections. Hence the radical error of secret political societies in free countries. They are intrinsically hostile to liberty.

Important as the printing of transactions, reports, and documents is, it is nevertheless true that oral discussions are a most important feature of Anglican publicity of legislative, judicial, and of many of the common administrative transactions. Modern centralized absolutism has developed a system of writing and secrecy, and consequent formalism, abhorrent to free citizens who exist and feed upon the living word of liberty.[1] Bureaucracy is founded upon writing, liberty on the

---

[1] The following passage is given here for a twofold purpose. Everything in it applies to the government of the pen on the continent of Europe, and it shows how similar causes have produced similar results in India and under Englishmen, who at home are so adverse to government writing and to bureaucracy. In the Notes on the Northwestern Provinces of India, by Charles Raikes, Magistrate and Collector of Mynpoorie, London, 1853, we find this passage :

"Action, however, and energy, are what we now lay most stress upon, because in days of peace and outward tranquillity these qualities are not always valued at their true price, and their absence is not so palpably

breathing word. Extensive writing, pervading the minutest branches of the administration, is the most active assistant of modern centralization. It systematizes a police government in a degree, which no one can conceive of, that does not know it from personal observation and experience, and forms one of the greatest obstacles, perhaps the most serious difficulty, when nations, long accustomed to this all-penetrative agent of centralism, desire to establish liberty. I do not hesitate to point out orality, especially in the administration of justice, in legislation and local self-government, as an important element of our civil liberty. I do not believe that a high degree of liberty can be imagined without widely pervading orality; but oral transaction alone is no indication of liberty. The patriarchal and tribal governments of Asia, the chieftain government of our Indians, indeed all primitive governments are carried on by oral transaction without any civil liberty.

---

mischievous as in more stirring times. There is more danger now of men becoming plodding, methodical, mere office functionaries, than of their stepping with too hasty a zeal beyond the limits of the law. There is truth, too, in Jacquemont's sneer—India *is* governed by stationery, to a more than sufficient extent; and one of the commonest errors of our magistrates, which they imbibe from constant and early Indian associations, is to mistake *writing* for *action*, to fancy that *dictation* will supply the place of *exertion*. In no other country are so many written orders issued with so much confidence, received with such respect, and broken with such complacency. In fact, as for writing, we believe the infection of the 'cacoethes scribendi' must first have grown up in the East. It pervades everything, but is more rampant and more out of place in a police office than anywhere else. It was not the magistrate who originated this passion for scribbling; but they have never succeeded in repressing it, nor while the law requires that every discontented old woman's story shall be taken down in writing, is it to be expected they ever will. The Khayeths worship their pen and ink on certain festivals, and there is a sort of 'religio' attaching to written forms and statements, which is not confined to official life, but pervades the whole social polity of the writing tribes. An Indian scribe, whose domestic expenditure may average a sixpence a day, will keep an account-book with as many columns, headings, and totals, as would serve for the budget of a chancellor of the exchequer. To Tudor Mul and such worthies we owe, no doubt, a great deal for the method and order which they infused into

Publicus, originally Populicus, meant that which relates to the Populus, to the state, and it is significant that the term gradually acquired the meaning of public, as we take it—as significant, as it is that a great French philosopher, honored throughout our whole country, lately wrote to a friend: "Political matters here are no longer public matters."[1]

In free countries political matters relate to the people, and therefore ought to be public. Publicity informs of public matters; it teaches, and educates, and it binds together. There is no patriotism without publicity, and though publicity can not always prevent mischief, it is at all events an alarm bell, which calls the public attention to the spot of danger. In former times secrecy was considered indispensable in public matters; it is still so where cabinet policy is pursued, or monarchical absolutism sways; but these governments, also, have been obliged somewhat to yield to a better spirit, and the Russian government now publishes occasionally government reports.

That there are certain transactions which the public service requires to be withdrawn for a time from publicity, is evident. We need point only to diplomatic transactions when not yet brought to a close. But even with reference to these, it will be observed that a great change has been wrought in modern times, and comparatively a great degree of publicity now prevails in the foreign intercourse of nations—a change of which the United States have set the example. A state secret was formerly a potent word; while one of our first statesmen wrote to the author, many years ago, "I would not give a

_____

public records; but we have also to thank these knights of the pen for the plaguiest long-figured statements, and the greatest number of such statements, which the world ever saw." Well may the continental European, reading this, exclaim, C'est tout comme chez nous! In 1858, one of the most distinguished statesmen of France, universally known as a publicist, a former member, cabinet minister, and orator in the house of representatives, wrote from Germany, "I observe that the writing which I have always considered so injurious to our affairs in France, is carried, if possible, to a still greater degree in this country."

[1] This observation followed a request to write henceforth with caution, because, said he, choses politiques ne sont plus ici choses publiques.

dime for all the secrets that people may imagine to be locked up in the United States archives."

It is a remarkable fact that no law insures the publicity of the courts of justice, either in England or the United States. Our constitution secures neither the publicity of courts nor that of Congress, and in England the admission of the public to the commons or the lords is merely by sufferance. The public may at any time be excluded merely by a member observing to the presiding officer that strangers are present, while we all know that the candid publication of the debates was not permitted in the time of Dr. Johnson. Yet so thoroughly is publicity now ingrained in the American and Englishman that a suppression of this precious principle cannot even be conceived of. If any serious attempt should be made to carry out the existing law in England, and the public were really excluded from the house of commons, a revolution would be unquestionably the consequence, and publicity would be added to the declaration of rights. We can no more imagine England or the United States without the reporting newspapers, than nature without the principle of vegetation.

Publicity pervaded the system of American politics so generally, that the framers of our constitution probably never thought of it, or if they did, they did not think it worth while to provide for it in the constitution, since no one had doubted it. It is part and parcel of our common law of political existence. They did not trouble themselves with unnecessaries, or things which would have had a value only as possibly completing a certain symmetry of theory.

It is, however, interesting to note that the first distinctly authorized publicity of a legislative body in modern times, was that of the Massachusetts house of representatives, which adopted it in 1766.[1]

---

[1] I follow the opinion of Mr. Robert C. Winthrop, late speaker of the house of representatives of the United States, and believe him to be correct, when, in an address before the Maine Historical Society, (Boston, 1849,) he says: "The earliest instance of authorized publicity being given to the deliberations of a legislative body in modern days, was in this same

Publicity of speaking has its dangers, and occasionally exposes to grave inconveniences, as all guarantees do, and necessarily in a greater degree, as they are of a more elementary
character.   It is the price at which we enjoy all excellence in
this world.   The science of politics and political ethics must
point out the dangers as well as the formal and moral checks
which may avert or mitigate the evils arising from publicity
in general, and public oral transaction of affairs in particular.   It is not our business here.   We treat of it in this place as
a guarantee of liberty, and have to show its indispensable-
ness.   Those who know liberty as a practical and traditional
reality and as a true business of life, as we do, know that the
question is not whether it be better to have publicity or not,
but, being obliged to have it, how we can best manage to avoid
its dangers while we enjoy its fullest benefit and blessing.   It
is the same as with the air we breathe.   The question is not
whether we ought to dispense with a free respiration of all-
surrounding air, but how, with free inhalation, we may best
guard ourselves against colds and other distempers caused by
the elementary requisite of physical life, that we must live in
the atmosphere.[1]

---

house of representatives of Massachusetts, on the 3d day of June, 1766,
when, upon motion of James Otis, and during the debates which arose
on the question of the repeal of the stamp act, and of compensation to
the sufferers by the riots in Boston, to which that act had given occasion,
a resolution was carried 'for opening a gallery for such as wished to hear
the debates.' The influence of this measure in preparing the public mind
for the great revolutionary events which were soon to follow, can hardly
be exaggerated." The American reader is referred to the note at the
end of this chapter for an account of the introduction of publicity into
the senate of the United States.

[1] Great as the inconvenience is which arises from the abuse of public
speaking, and of that sort of prolixity which in our country is familiarly
called by a term understood by every one, Speaking for Buncombe, yet
it must be remembered that the freest possible, and, therefore, often
abused latitude of speaking, is frequently a safety-valve, in times of
public danger, for which nothing else can be substituted. The debates
in congress, when lately the Union itself was in danger, lasted for entire
months, and words seemed fairly to weary out the nation when every one

Liberty, I said, is coupled with the public word, and however frequently the public word may be abused, it is nevertheless true that out of it arises oratory—the æsthetics of liberty. What would Greece and Rome be to us without their Demosthenes and Cicero? And what would their other writers have been, had not their languages been coined out by the orator? What would England be without her host of manly and masterly speakers? Who of us could wish to see the treasures of our own civilization robbed of the words contributed by our speakers, from Patrick Henry to Webster? The speeches of great orators are a fund of wealth for a free people, from which the school-boy begins to draw when he declaims from his Reader, and which enriches, elevates, and nourishes the souls of the old.

Publicity is indispensable to eloquence. No one speaks well in secret before a few. Orators are in this respect like poets—their kin, of whom Goethe, "one of the craft," says that they cannot sing unless they are heard.

The abuse of public speaking has been alluded to. It is a frequent theme of blame and ridicule, frequently dwelt upon by those who disrelish "parliamentarism," but it is necessary to observe that if civil liberty demands representative legislative bodies, which it assuredly does, these bodies have no

---

called for action. There was no citizen capable of following closely all those lengthy and occasionally empty debates, with all their lateral issues. Still, now that the whole is over, it may well be asked whether there is a single attentive and experienced American who doubts that, had it not been for that flood of debate, we must have been exposed to civil disturbances, perhaps to the rending of the Union.

Nevertheless, it is a fact that the more popular an assembly is, the more liable it is to suffer from verbose discussions, and thus to see its action impeded. This is especially the case in a country in which, as in ours, a personal facility of public speaking is almost universal, and where an elocutional laxity coexists with a patient tenacity of hearing, and a love of listening which can never be surfeited. It has its ruinous effect upon oratory, literature, the standard of thought, upon vigorous action, on public business, and gives a wide field to dull mediocrity. This anti-Pythagorean evil has led to the adoption of the "one hour rule" in the house of representatives, in congress, and (in 1847) in the supreme

meaning without exchange and mutual modification of ideas, without debate, and actual debate requires the spoken word. I consider it an evil hour not only for eloquence, but for liberty itself, when our senate first permitted one of its members to read his speeches, on account of some infirmity. The true principle has now been abandoned, and written speeches are almost as common in congress as they were in the former house of representatives of France, where, however, I may

---

court of the United States. The one hour rule was first proposed by Mr. Holmes, of Charleston, in imitation of the Athenian one hour clepsydra—yes, the prince of orators had that dropping monitor by his side!—and is now renewed by every new house. The English have begun to feel the same evil, and the adoption of the same rule was proposed in the commons, in February, 1849. But the debate concluded adversely to it, after Sir Robert Peel had adverted to Burke's glorious eloquence. Our one hour rule, however, is not entirely new in modern times. In the year 1562 (on the 21st of July) the Council of Trent adopted the rule that the fathers in delivering their opinions should be restricted to half an hour, which having elapsed, the master of ceremonies was to give them a sign to leave off. Yet, on the same day, an exception was made in favor of Salmeron, the pope's first divine, who occupied the whole sitting, (History of the Life of Reginald Pole, by T. Phillips, Oxf. 1764, p. 397,) very much as in February, 1849, the whole American house called "go on" when Governor McDowel had spoken an hour. He continued for several hours.

Having mentioned the inconvenience of prolix speaking, it may not be improper to add another passage of the address of Mr. Winthrop, already mentioned. It will be recollected that this gentleman has been speaker. He knows, therefore, the inconvenience in its whole magnitude. "Doubtless," he says, "when debates were conducted with closed doors, there were no speeches for Buncombe, no claptrap for the galleries, no flourishes for the ladies, and it required no hour rule, perhaps, to keep men within some bounds of relevancy. But one of the great sources of instruction and information, in regard both to the general measures of government and to the particular conduct of their own representatives, was then shut out from the people, and words which might have roused them to the vindication of justice, or to the overthrow of tyranny, were lost in the utterance. The perfect publicity of legislative proceedings is hardly second to the freedom of the press, in its influence upon the progress and perpetuity of human liberty, though, like the freedom of the press, it may be attended with inconveniences and abuses."

state on authority, they became rarer as constitutional liberty increased and developed its energy.

All governments hostile to liberty are hostile to publicity, and parliamentary eloquence is odious to them, because it is a great power which the executive can neither create nor control. There is in imperial France a positive hatred against the "*tribune.*" Mr. Cousin, desirous of leading his readers to compare the imperial system with that of the past governments, since the restoration, says of the Bourbons that, whatever it may be the fashion of saying of them, "they gave us at any rate the tribune," (the public word,) while Mr. de Morney, brother of Napoleon III., issued a circular to the prefects, when minister of the interior, in 1852, in which the publicity of parliamentary government is called theatricals. It is remarkable that this declaration should have come from a government which, above all others, seems, in a great measure, to rely on military and other shows.

Publicity begets confidence, and confidence is indispensable for the government of free countries—it is the soul of loyalty in jealous freemen. This necessary influence is twofold—confidence in the government, and confidence of society in itself. It is with reference to the latter that secret political societies in free countries are essentially injurious to all liberty, in addition, that they prevent the growth and development of manly character, and promote vanity ; that they are, as all secret societies must inherently be, submissive to secret superior will and decision,—a great danger in politics,—and unjust to the rest of fellow-citizens, by deciding on public measures and men without the trial of public discussion, and by bringing to bear a secretly united body on the decision or election. Secret societies in free countries are cancers against which history teaches us that men who value their freedom ought to guard themselves most attentively. It would lead us too far from our topic were we to discuss the important fact that mysterious and secret societies belong to paganism rather than to christianity, and we conclude these remarks by observing that those societies which may be called doubly secret, that is to

say, societies which not only foster certain secrets and have
secret transactions, but the members of which are bound to
deny either the existence of the society or their membership,
are schools of untruth ; and that parents as well as teachers,
in the United States, would do no more than perform a solemn
duty, if they were using every means in their power to exhibit to those whose welfare is entrusted to them, the despicable
character of the thousand juvenile secret societies which
flourish in our land and which are the preparatory schools for
secret political societies.[1]

---

[1] The following note consists of an article by Mr. James C. Welling,
of the *National Intelligencer*, Washington city. It appeared on the
30th of October, 1858, in consequence of some questions I had put regarding a previous article on my remarks on Publicity in the United
States. Mr. Welling had doubtless free access to the ample stores of
personal recollections possessed by the founders of that public journal.
The student of history will find it an instructive document, and I have
preferred to give the whole, even with the introduction on the early intercourse between congress and the President of the United States, partly
on account of antiquarian interest, partly because it is not unconnected
with the publicity of debate in the senate.

Mr. Welling says that it has been remarked that the principle of publicity seems to have so thoroughly pervaded all the politics of the United
States that the framers of our constitution never thought of it, or if they
did, they thought it hardly worth while to make special provision for it,
since none doubted its observance. While this statement has a deep
foundation in much of our civil history during the period of the revolution and the formation of our present constitution, it should not be forgotten that the sessions of our continental congress were held in secret,
and even after the formation of our present constitution, one branch of
the national legislature, for more than five years, *sat with closed doors.*
We allude to the senate, whose deliberations, unlike those of the house
of representatives, were conducted in secret during the whole of the first
and second congresses, and also during a part of the third. As the particulars connected with this fact in our parliamentary history are perhaps
not familiarly known to every reader, we have thought it might not be
without interest to recall some of the reminiscences corroborative of a
statement which, at the present day, and with our established notions,
must seem not a little extraordinary and anomalous. In doing so, we
may take occasion to allude incidentally, by way of preface, to a few
subsidiary topics relating to the forms of official intercourse existing

between the executive and legislative departments of the government during the earlier days of the republic.

The first session of the first congress of the United States held under the constitution framed and submitted by the federal convention in Philadelphia, was begun in the city of New York on the 4th of March, 1789. Neither house, however, could at once proceed to the transaction of business from the want of a quorum, which was secured in the popular branch only, on the 1st of April following, and in the senate on the 6th of the same month. On that day the latter body, having elected a president *pro tem.*, proceeded, in the presence of the house of representatives, assembled in the senate chamber by invitation, to count the votes of the electors of the several states for President and Vice-President of the United States, when it was found that George Washington was unanimously elected to the former office by the voice of the eleven states then composing the Union, (Rhode Island and North Carolina not having yet adopted the constitution,) and that John Adams was chosen vice-president by a majority of the votes cast for that office. The senate thereupon appointed Mr. Charles Thomson (long the clerk of the continental congress) to notify Gen. Washington, and Mr. Sylvanus Bourne to notify John Adams of their election to the offices for which they had been respectively designated.

Mr. Adams took his chair as president of the senate on the 21st of the same month, and on the 30th Gen. Washington received the oath of office, as President of the United States, in the senate chamber, in the presence of both houses of congress, assembled on the occasion to witness the ceremonial. The oath was administered by the chancellor of the State of New York, who proclaimed, as the same was accepted by the president, "Long live George Washington, President of the United States." The president then resumed the seat from which he had risen to take the oath, and, after a short pause, rose and delivered before the senate and house of representatives his inaugural address. On its conclusion, the president, the vice-president, the senate, and the house of representatives proceeded to St. Paul's Chapel, in New York, where divine service was performed by the chaplain of congress, after which the president was reconducted to his house by a committee appointed for that purpose.

After the celebration of these religious exercises the senate reassembled and appointed a committee to prepare an "answer to the president's speech." In the house of representatives a similar committee was appointed on the following day. The reply of the senate was read and adopted in that body on the 7th of May, and agreeably to previous arrangement was delivered to the president at his own house on the 18th following, the senate waiting upon the president for this purpose with the vice-president, their presiding officer, at their head. The president, on receiving the address, made a brief and appropriate response. The reply of the house of representatives was read and adopted on the 5th of May, and, by a similar pre-concert, was delivered to the president on the 8th of the same month, in a room adjoining the representatives' chamber, where the speaker, attended by the members of the house, placed in the president's hands a copy of the address, for which the president returned his thanks in a few appropriate remarks.

Such was the nature of the ceremonial observed in the official communications interchanged between the president and the two houses of congress at the opening of every session of congress during the administration of Washington and John Adams. On the accession of Mr. Jefferson, the practice of delivering the annual presidential speech in person before both houses of congress at its opening was superseded by the present custom of sending a written message. And with this change the habit of preparing a formal reply on the part of both houses to the recommendations of the president fell into similar desuetude. Mr. Jefferson, it is well known, was subsequently accustomed to point to this change as one of the " reforms" he had effected in what he called the " Anglican tendencies" and "royal usages" of our government under the administration of the federalists.*

To resume the principal topic of remark in the present article, we repeat that the senate, in the earlier days of the government, sat *with closed doors*, as well during its legislative as in its executive sessions. Its debates, therefore, unlike those of the house of representatives, were for a time held in secret; but it was provided by a resolution passed on the 19th of May, 1789, that one hundred and twenty copies of the journal of the legislative proceedings of the senate should be printed

---

* It may not be uninteresting to add that President Jefferson, at the time when this change was made, attributed it to other causes. His first annual address to both houses of congress was sent in on the 8th of December, 1801, and was accompanied with the subjoined letter, addressed to the presiding officer of each body:

DECEMBER 8, 1801.

SIR: The circumstances under which we find ourselves at this place [Washington] rendering inconvenient the mode heretofore practised, of making by personal address the first communications between the legislative and executive branches, I have adopted that by message, as used on all subsequent occasions through the session. In doing this I have had principal regard to the convenience of the legislature, to the economy of their time, to their relief from the embarrassment of immediate answers on subjects not yet fully before them, and to the benefits thence resulting to the public affairs. Trusting that a procedure founded in these motives will meet their approbation, I beg leave, through you, sir, to communicate the enclosed message, with the documents accompanying it, to the honorable the senate, and pray you to accept, for yourself and them, the homage of my high respect and consideration.

The Hon. the President of the senate.   TH. JEFFERSON.

once a month for distribution among the members of the body, and, we suppose, for partial dissemination among the public, since it was pro-vided that each member should be furnished with but a single copy on his own account.

At this distance of time we may not perhaps be able to understand or state the reasons which determined the senate to sit with closed doors in all their deliberations, as still in those which pertain to executive business. It is probable that the habit grew out of the fact that the senate, in the original theory of its constitution, was regarded primarily as a confidential and advisory council to the executive ; and, as is well known, its earlier sessions were pre-eminently occupied in executive business. In relation to measures of legislation it seems to have been conceived that its function was mainly revisory and deliberative ; and hence the greater prominence of the house in initiating and debating not only " revenue bills," which it was provided by the constitution should be originated only by the Representatives, but also other measures of federal legislation. In evidence of this fact we may state that the se-nate was wholly without standing committees until the year 1816, when during the second session of the fourteenth congress it was determined to provide for their appointment. In the house they had been raised by a standing rule as early as the year 1799, although at first their num-ber was restricted to five—a committee respectively on elections, claims, commerce, ways and means, and on revisal and on unfinished business.

The first executive business of the senate was transacted on the 25th of May, 1789, when the president communicated for the advice and con-sent of the senate certain treaties made with the northern and north-western Indians. At subsequent sessions he sent in by letter his nomi-nations for various offices appointed to be filled with the advice and consent of the same body. The senate having refused to ratify the no-mination of Mr. Benjamin Fishbourn as naval officer for the port of Sa-vannah, President Washington, on the 7th of August, addressed a mes-sage to the body vindicating his reasons for nominating that gentleman, and suggesting to the senate the expediency of communicating to him their views on occasions where the propriety of his nominations appeared questionable to them.

Moved by this intimation of the president, the senate appointed a committee to wait on him for the purpose of concerting a mode of com-munication proper to be pursued between both parties in the formation of treaties and making appointments to office. Accordingly it was re-solved that, in conformity with the president's pleasure, he might make his nominations to the senate either in writing or in person ; and it was further provided that for this purpose he might wait on the senate in their own chamber, (in which case he should occupy the chair of the president of the senate,) or might summon the president of the senate and the senators to meet him at such place as he should designate. It was provided, however, that all questions, whether in the presence or absence of the President of the United States, should be put by the president of the senate, and " that the senators should signify their assent or dissent by answering, *viva voce*, aye or no." On the day following the adoption of this minute, that is, on the 22d of August, 1789, it appears from the journal that the President of the United States came into the senate chamber, attended by General Knox, and laid before the senate a statement of facts in reference to the negotiation of certain treaties with various Indian tribes. Desiring to fix certain principles on which the negotiations should be conducted, he reported to the senate a series of questions, to each of which he requested a categorical answer, to guide him in giving instructions to the commissioners appointed to treat with the Indians. The questions were seven in number, and were considered throughout two daily sessions, in the presence of the president, and, as appears from the journal, of General Knox.

How long the relations between the president and the senate remained on this footing we are unable to say with any accuracy, though the practice of his personal attendance during their sessions in executive business seems to have been abandoned after a time ; and authentic tradition records that its disuse was hastened by the blunt speeches of certain senators, who intimated that the presence of the president operated as a restraint on them in canvassing the merits of the candidates submitted for their advice and consent. It soon became habitual for the president to communicate all his nominations to the senate in writing.

As has been already stated, the proceedings of the senate, as well legislative as executive, were conducted during the first session with closed doors. During the second session of the first congress, which was begun in New York on the 4th of January, 1790, the same custom was retained, though, as appears from the journal, not without protest and dissent on the part of some senators. For it appears that on the 29th of April following it was moved " that the doors of the senate chamber shall be open when the senate is sitting in their legislative capacity, to the end that such of the citizens of the United States as may choose to hear the debates of this house may have an opportunity of so doing." This resolution, being postponed for consideration on the following day, was then taken up, and, after debate, rejected.

At a third session of the first congress, begun in Philadelphia on the 6th of December, 1790, it was again proposed, on the 23d of February following, "that it be a standing rule that the doors of the senate chamber remain open whilst the senate shall be sitting in a legislative capacity, except on such occasions as, in their judgment, may require secrecy ; and that this rule shall commence and be in force on the first day of the next session of congress." And to this end it was proposed " that the

secretary of the senate request the commissioners of the city and county
of Philadelphia to cause a proper gallery to be erected for the accommodation of the audience." After debate, extending through two days,
the proposition was rejected by a vote of 9 yeas to 17 nays. The names
of those voting in the affirmative are Messrs. Butler, Foster, Gunn, Hawkins, King, Lee, Maclay, Monroe, and Schuyler. Those voting in the
negative were Messrs. Bassett, Carroll, Dalton, Dickinson, Ellsworth,
Elmer, Few, Henry, Johnson, Johnston, Izard, Langdon, Morris, Read,
Stanton, Strong, and Wingate.

The first session of the second congress was begun at Philadelphia on
the 24th of October, 1791. On the 26th of March following—a few
weeks before the adjournment of congress at that session—a resolution
identical in terms with that rejected at the last session of the first congress was moved by Mr. Monroe and seconded by Mr. Lee, both of Virginia. The proposition met with the same fate, receiving fewer votes
than at the former session. Some days after the rejection of 'this resolution it was moved "that when the senate are sitting in their legislative capacity the members of the house of representatives may be
admitted to attend the debates, and each member of the senate may
also admit a number not exceeding two persons; provided the operation
of this resolution be suspended until the senate chamber is sufficiently
enlarged." This proposition also failed to be adopted, receiving only
six votes.

We have recited these several and ineffectual attempts to procure the
abrogation of this established rule of the senate for the purpose of
showing that it did not grow up as an unregarded usage, but was founded
on considerations satisfactory to a majority of the senate at that day.
Nor does it appear to have been a question of party politics, since we
find federalists voting with republicans for its abolition, and republicans voting with federalists for its retention.

The first session of the third congress of the United States, which
commenced at Philadelphia on the 2d of December, 1793, was destined
to witness the overthrow of the rule which had previously obtained on
this point. The senate was called at this session to consider and decide
a question which elicited a large share of public interest, because of the
political susceptibilities which had been awakened by its discussion. We
allude to the contest raised respecting the eligibility of Mr. Albert Gallatin as a member of the senate from the state of Pennsylvania. On
the first day of the session of that year a petition was presented by
Conrad Laub and others, representing that Mr. G. at the date of his
election had not been, as the constitution requires, "nine years a citizen
of the United States." The committee to which the whole subject was
referred, reported adversely to the claims of Mr. Gallatin on the 31st of
December, and the report, after being read and ordered to lie over for

future consideration, was taken up, on the 9th of January following, and discussed through several successive days, when, on the 13th of the same month, the matter was re-committed to a special committee of elections appointed for the purpose of hearing both parties to the contest. Before this committee reported, and on the 16th of January, 1794, Mr. Martin, of North Carolina, moved the adoption of the following formal resolutions against the principles and policy of the existing regulations of the senate in regard to the secrecy of its deliberations :

"*Resolved*, That in all representative governments, the representatives are responsible for their conduct to their constituents, who are entitled to such information, that a discrimination and just estimate be made thereof.

"*Resolved*, That the senate of the United States, being the representatives of the sovereignties of the individual states, whose basis is the people, owe equal responsibility to the powers by which they are appointed, as if that body were derived immediately from the people, and that all questions and debates arising thereupon in their legislative and judiciary capacity, ought to be public.

"*Resolved*, That the mode adopted by the senate of publishing their journals, and extracts from them, in newspapers, is not adequate to the purpose of circulating satisfactory information. While the principles and designs of the individual members are withheld from public view, responsibility is destroyed, which, on the publicity of their deliberations, would be restored; the constitutional powers of the senate become more important, in being more influential over the other branch of the legislature ; abuse of power, mal-administration of office, more easily detected and corrected ; jealousies, rising in the public mind from secret legislation, prevented ; and greater confidence placed by our fellow-citizens in the national government, by which their lives, liberties, and properties are to be secured and protected.

"*Resolved, therefore*, That it be a standing rule that the doors of the senate chamber remain open while the senate shall be sitting in a legislative and judiciary capacity, except on such occasions as in their judgment may require secrecy ; and that this rule commence on the —— day of ——."

These resolutions, being called up on the morrow, were postponed successively from day to day, when, on the 10th day of February, the committee which had Mr. Gallatin's case in charge, made their report to the senate, and a day was fixed for its consideration. Immediately on the presentation of the report, it was moved by a member " that the doors of the senate be opened and continued open during the discussion upon the contested election of Albert Gallatin," *which resolution was adopted on the 11th of February*, 1794. Meanwhile the series of resolutions abolishing the whole system of secrecy during legislative proceedings, was still pending, and came up for consideration on the 19th of February, when each resolution was finally rejected, and a substitute offered in the following terms :

"*Resolved*, That after the end of the present session of congress, and so soon as suitable galleries shall be provided for the senate chamber, the said galleries shall be permitted to be opened every morning, so long as the senate shall be engaged in their legislative capacity, unless in such cases as may, in the opinion of the senate, require secrecy, after which the said galleries shall be closed."

This resolution was passed on the following day by a vote of nineteen yeas to eight nays. Those who voted in the affirmative were Messrs. Bradley, Brown, Butler, Edwards, Ellsworth, Foster, Gallatin, Gunn, Hawkins, Jackson, King, Langdon, Livermore, Martin, Monroe, Potts, Taylor, and Vining. Those who voted in the negative were Messrs. Bradford, Cabot, Frelinghuysen, Izard, Mitchell, Morris, Rutherfurd, and Strong.

So this regulation of the senate was prospectively repealed and declared inoperative "after the présent session," as by a previous resolution it had been expressly suspended during the debate on the case of Mr. Gallatin. Yet this step was not taken without reservation and caution, as is apparent from the fact that on the same day with the passage of the prospective resolution, it was unanimously resolved "That, on a motion made and seconded to shut the doors of the senate, on the discussion *of any business* which may, in the opinion of a member, require secrecy, the president shall direct the gallery to be cleared ; and that during the discussion of such motion the doors shall remain shut."

It only remains for us to add, in conclusion, that on the day following the passage of these resolutions, the case of Mr. Gallatin was debated in open senate. The discussion extended through several days, and was conducted in the form of a trial, Mr. Gallatin affirming his right to the character of a citizen of the United States, and Mr. Lewis, a member of the Pennsylvania bar, attended by Mr. Schmyser, a member of the state senate of Pennsylvania, appearing as managers of the prosecution on the part of the petitioners. The pleadings, opened on the 21st of February, were closed on the 28th of the same month, when the senate decided that the election of Mr. Gallatin was void, in consequence of his not having been a citizen of the United States during the term of years required by the constitution as a qualification for membership in the United States senate. This case being settled, the doors of the senate were closed against the public during the residue of the session; but since that period, so far as we can recall, the legislative deliberations of the body have been uniformly conducted in public, without any interruption other than that which has sometimes arisen from the inadvertence of the senate, in resuming its legislative discussions after a secret session, and without thinking for a time to re-open the doors which had been closed during the transaction of executive business.

We need hardly say that it has been frequently proposed to abolish the secrecy of the senate even when called to sit in judgment on the treaties formed, or the nominations submitted by the executive branch of the government. But the propriety of such a reservation, made in behalf of diplomatic negotiations not yet brought to a close, is too manifest to need remark, while the freedom and independence which the senator should enjoy in canvassing the propriety and character of the official appointments made with his advice and consent, plead perhaps with equal force in favor of retaining the rule so far as it relates to this other branch of executive business. The injunction of secrecy is from time to time removed by resolution of the senate from all subjects of popular concern, whose publication can no longer frustrate the ends of prudent legislation.

CHAPTER XIV.

19. THE supremacy of the law, in the sense in which it has already been mentioned, or the protection against the absolutism of one, of several, or the people, (which, practically, and for common transactions, means of course, the majority,) requires other guarantees or checks of great importance.

It is necessary that the public funds be under close and efficient popular control, chiefly, therefore, under the supervision of the popular branch of the legislature, which is likewise the most important branch in granting the supplies, and the one in which, according to the English and American fundamental laws, all money bills must originate. The English are so jealous of this principle, that the commons will not even allow the lords to propose amendments affecting money grants or taxation.[1]

If the power over the public treasury, and that of imposing taxes, be left to the executive, there is an end to public liberty. Hampden knew it when he made the trifling sum of a pound of unlawfully imposed ship-money a great national issue, and our Declaration of Independence enumerates, as one of the gravest grievances against the mother country, that England " has imposed taxes without our consent."

One of the most serious mistakes of those who are not versed in liberty is to imagine that liberty consists in withhold-

---

[1] While these sheets were passing through the press, (March, 1859,) the house of representatives, at Washington, refused to consider certain amendments, passed in the senate, for the purpose of raising the postage on letters, the house declaring by resolution that these amendments interfered with the constitutional and exclusive right of the house to originate bills affecting the revenue.

ing the necessary power from government. Liberty is not of a negative character. It does not consist in merely denying power to government. Government must have power to perform its functions, and if no provision is made for an orderly and organic grant of power, it will, in cases of necessity, arrogate it. A liberty thus merely hedging in, would resemble embankments of our Mississippi, without an outlet for freshets. No one believes that there would be sufficient time to repair the *crevasse*. This applies to all subjects of government, and especially to appropriations of money. Merely denying money to government, or, still worse, not creating a proper organism for granting it, must lead either to inanity or to executive plundering; but it is equally true that the strictest possible limitation and hedging in by law, of the money grants, are as requisite for the cause of liberty as the avoidance of the error I have just pointed out. This subject is well treated in our "Federalist,"[1] and the insufficiency of our ancient articles of confederation was one of the prominent causes which led our forefathers to the adoption of the federal constitution. Lord Nugent truly calls the power of granting or refusing supplies, vested in parliament, but especially in the house of commons, or, as he says, "the entire and independent control of parliament over the supplies," "the stoutest buttress of the English constitution."[2]

It is the Anglican rule to make but short appropriations, and to make appropriations for distinct purposes. We insist still more on this principle than the English, and justly demand that appropriations be made as distinct and specific as possible, and that no transfer of appropriations by the executive take place; that is to say, that the executive be not authorized to use a certain appropriation, if not wholly spent, partially for purposes for which another appropriated sum has proved to be insufficient. It is not only necessary for vigorous civil liberty that the legislature, and chiefly the popu-

---

[1] "Federalist," No. xxx. and sequel, Concerning Taxation, and other parts of that sage book.

[2] "Memorials of John Hampden," vol. i. p. 212; London, 1832.

lar branch of it, keep the purse-strings of the public treasury;
but also that the same principle be acted upon in all minor circles of the vast public fabric.   The money of the people must
be under the control of the trustees of the people, and not at
the disposal of officials unconnected with the people, or at the
disposal of an irresponsible multitude, which, itself without
property, readily countenances those malappropriations of
money which we meet with in every democratic absolutism,
from the later times of Athens to the worst-governed large
cities of our own country.

The French imperial constitution decrees, indeed, that the
budgets of the different ministers must be voted by the deputies, but they must be voted each as a whole; no amendments
can be made either in the sums thus voted in the lump, or in
anything else proposed by the government, the government
alone having the initiative.   All the deputies can do is to send
back a bill to the government, with remarks.   The French
provision, therefore, is founded on a principle the very opposite to that which we consider essential regarding money appropriations.

The history of the control over the public funds, in granting, specifying and spending them, may well be said to be
a continuous index of the growth of English liberty.   It
is this principle which has essentially aided in establishing
self-government in England; and which has made the house
of commons the real seat of the national government as we
now find it.   Every one knows that the "supplies" are the
means by which the English effect in a regular and easy way
that which the Roman populus occasionally and not regularly
effected against the senate, by a refusal to enlist in the army
when war was at the gates of the city.[1]

---

[1] Chatham, when minister of the crown in 1759, and while Lord Clive
was making his great conquests in the East, said that neither the East
India Company nor the crown ought to have that immense revenue.   If
the latter had it, it would endanger all liberty.   Chatham's Correspondence, vol. i.   In the year 1858, however, the government of the East Indies was taken from the company and given to the crown.   It would

The history of the British civil list, or the personal revenue granted to the monarch at the beginning of his reign, is also instructive in regard to this subject. In the middle ages the monarch was the chief nobleman, and had, like every other nobleman, his domains, from which he drew his revenue. Taxes were considered extraordinary gifts. As the monarch, however, wanted more money, either for just or unjust purposes, loans were made, which were never redeemed. Mr. Francis correctly observes, that it is absurd to charge William III. with having created a public debt, as Hume and so many others have done. William III., on the contrary, was the first monarch who treated loans really as loans, and provided either for their repayment or the payment of interest.[1]

As civil liberty advanced, all revenue of the monarch, independent of the people, was more and more withdrawn from him, and crown domains were more and more made public domains, until we see George III. giving up all extra-parliamentary revenue. The monarch was made dependent on the civil list exclusively.

20. It is further necessary that the power of making war essentially reside with the people, and not with the executive. In England, it is true, the privilege of making war and concluding peace is called a royal prerogative, but as no war can be carried on without the nervus rerum gerendarum, it is the commons who decide whether the war shall be carried on or not. They can grant or decline the authority of enlisting men, and the money to support them and to provide for the war. The Constitution of the United States decrees that congress shall have power to make war,[2] and an American declaration

---

seem that the commons felt so secure, in the middle of the nineteenth century, that they did not fear to have that vast eastern empire ruled over, theoretically, by the monarch, in reality, by a minister responsible to parliament.

[1] Francis, Chronicles and Characters of the Stock Exchange.

[2] It may as well be observed here that congress means the senate and house of representatives. The president is not included in the term. Parliament, on the other hand, means commons, lords, and king. Practically speaking, the difference is not great; for, the president has

of war must be passed by congress, like any other law. A declaration of war by the United States is a law.

Where the executive has not only the nominal, but the real power of declaring war, we cannot speak of civil liberty or of self-government; for that which most essentially affects the people in all their relations, is in that case beyond their control. Even with the best contrived safeguards, and a deeply rooted tradition, it seems impossible to guard against occasional high-handed assumption of power by the executive in this particular. Whatever our late Mexican war ultimately became in its character, there is probably now no person who will deny that, in its beginning, it was what is called a cabinet war. It was commenced by the cabinet, which, after hostilities had begun, called on congress to ratify its measures.

It has already been stated (paragraph 13) that a perfect dependence of the forces upon the civil power is an indispensable requisite and element of civil liberty.

21. The supremacy of the law and that unstinted protection of the individual as well as of society, in which civil liberty essentially consists, require on the one hand the fullest possible protection of the minority, and, on the other hand, the security of the majority that no factious minority or cabal shall rule over it.

The protection of the minority leads to that great institution, as it has been boldly but not inappropriately called—the opposition. A well organized and fully protected opposition, in and out of the legislature—a loyal opposition, by which is meant a party which opposes, on principle, the administration or the set of men who have, for the time being, the government in their hands, but does so under and within the common fundamental law, is so important an element of civil liberty, whether considered as a protecting fence or as a creative

---

the veto power, of which he makes occasional use, while the King of England has not made any use of it for about a century. The English administration would resign before it would become necessary in their eyes to veto a bill. But the King of England has the greatest of all veto powers—he can dissolve parliament, which our executive cannot do.

power, that it would be impossible here to give to the subject that space which its full treatment would require. I have attempted to do so, and to sketch its history, in my Political Ethics.

The elaboration of that which we call an opposition, is an honor which belongs to the English, and seems to me as great and as noble a contribution to the treasures of civil freedom, as the development of the power of our supreme courts (of the United States and of the different states) to declare, upon trial of specific cases, a law passed by the legislature unconstitutional and void. They are two of the noblest acquisitions in the cause of liberty, order and civilization.

22. The majority, and through it the people at large, are protected by the principle that the administration is founded upon party principles, or, as it has been called, by a government by party, if by party we mean men who agree on certain "leading general principles in government"[1] in opposition to others, and act in unison accordingly. If by party be understood a despicable union of men, to turn out a certain set of office-holders merely to obtain the lucrative places, and, when they are obtained, a union to keep them, it becomes an odious faction of placemen or office-hunters, the last of those citizens to whom the government ought to be entrusted. The ruinous and rapidly degrading effect of such a state of things is directly contrary to sound liberty, and serves as a fearful encouragemet to those, who, politically speaking, are the most worthless. But freedom of thought and action produces contention in all spheres, and, where great tasks are to be performed and where weighty interests are at stake, those who agree on the most important principles, will unite and must do so in order to be sufficiently strong to do their work. Without party administration, and party action, it is impossible that the majority should rule, or that a vigorous opposition can rise to a majority and rule in turn. Liberty requires a parliamentary government, and no truly parliamentary government can be conceived of without the principle of party administration.

---

[1] Burke.

It became fully developed under George I., or we should rather say under Sir Robert Walpole. Under the previous governments mixed cabinets of whigs and tories were common, when court intrigues and individual royal likings and dislikes had necessarily often a greater effect than national views and interests, to which it is the object of party administration to give the sway. We have to deal with parties, in this place, only as connected with civil liberty.

For their dangers, their affinity to faction as well as their existence in the arts, sciences, religion and even in trades—in fact, wherever free action is allowed; for the public inconvenience, and indeed danger in having more than two parties ; the necessity that political parties should be founded upon broad, comprehensive and political principles, for the galling insolence to which parties in power frequently rise, even in countries as ours, and for the fact that, in England at least, there is a manifest disposition to treat measures and politics in general, as far as possible without reference to mere party politics, as well as for many other important matters connected with the subject of parties, I must refer to other places.[1]

23. A principle and guarantee of liberty, so acknowledged and common with the Anglican people, that few think of its magnitude, yet of really organic and fundamental importance, is the division of government into three distinct functions, or rather the keeping of these functions clearly apart.

It is, as has been mentioned, one of the greatest political blessings of England, that from a very early period her courts of justice were not occupied with " administrative business," for instance, the collection of taxes, and that her parliament became the exclusive legislature, while the parliaments of France united a judicial, legislative and administrative character. The union of these functions is absolutism, or despotism on the one hand, and slavery on the other, no matter in whom

---

[1] These subjects have been considered at length in the Political Ethics. The reader will peruse with advantage the chapter on Party in Lord John Russell's Essay on the History of the English Government and Constitution, 2d edit. London, 1823.

they are united, whether in one despot or in many, or in the multitude, as in Athens after the time of Cleon the tanner. The English political philosophers have pointed out long ago[1] the necessity of keeping the three powers separate in a "constitutional" government. Those, however, who have no other definition of liberty than that it is equality, discard this division, except, indeed, so far as the mere convenience of transacting business would require.

We have seen already that a distinguished French publicist, Mr. Girardin, declares himself for an undivided public power.[2] Unité du pouvoir is the watchword of the French republicans, and it is the very principle with which Louis Napoleon checkmated them. It belongs to what may well be called Rousseauism. Rousseau is distinctly against division of power. His Social Contract became the political bible of the convention-men, and it has ever since kept a firm hold on the mind of a very large part of the French people, probably of the largest portion. Indeed we may say that the two great types of government now existing among the civilized and striving portion of mankind are representive (or, as the French choose to

---

[1] For instance, Locke. Montesquieu, at a later period, is generally considered the political philosopher who first distinctly conceived the necessity of the division of power. The English practised it earliest and established it most clearly; and the French have again given it up, for a time at least, ever since the revolution of 1848, nor has it ever been properly carried out by them, their principle of centralization preventing it. See Pol. Ethics, book ii. c. xxiii.

[2] He has repeatedly given his views, but especially in an elaborate and brilliantly written, but, according to our opinion, superficial paper on the question, why the republic (of 1848) came to a fall. Mr. Girardin and all the French who believe that liberty exists in the right of choosing the ruler, although once elected he be absolute, seem entirely to forget that all the generals of the monastic orders are elective; that, in many orders, even in those of nuns, for instance in the Ursuline order, the superiors are elected by universal suffrage, but that no person has ever claimed the possession of liberty for the monks or nuns. Indeed their very vow is against it. But "republicanism" has actually been vindicated for the monastic orders. In the same way Rome might be considered a republic because the pope is elective.

call it, parliamentary) government, which is essentially of a co-operative character — it is the government of Anglican liberty; and unity of power, the Gallican type. The French people themselves are divided according to these two types. Mr. Guizot may perhaps be considered as the French representative of the first type. A pamphlet, on the other hand, on government, and generally ascribed to Louis Napoleon, published not long before the explosion of the republic, for which it was evidently intended to prepare the public mind, advocates the unity of power in the last extreme, and as a truly French principle.

It may be granted that when French publicists and historians speak with undisguised praise of the introduction of centralization and unity of power as one of the greatest blessings, they may at times mean an organized and uniform government, as opposed to merely specific protection in antiquity and the middle ages, where tribunes, jurats and other officers were appointed to protect certain interests or classes, somewhat like foreign ministers or consuls of the portions of society, in times of peace—it is possible that they occasionally mean something of this sort, without being quite conscious of the difference; but, as matters stand, we who love Anglican liberty, believe what is now and emphatically called unity of power, is unvarnished absolutism. It is indifferent who wields it. We insist upon the supremacy, not the absolutism, of the legislature. We require the harmonious union of the co-operative whole, but abhor the unity of power.

What the French republicans demand in the name of the democracy, kings insist upon in the name of divine right. Both loudly protest against the " division of sovereignty,'' which can only mean a clear division of power ; for what in a philosophical sense can truly be called sovereignty, can never be divided, and its division need not, therefore, be guarded against. Sovereignty is the self-sufficient source of all power from which all specific powers are derived. It can dwell, therefore, according to the views of freemen, with society, the nation only; but sovereignty is not absolutism. It is remarkable how all absolutists, monarchical or democratic, agree on the unity of power.[1]

Power, according to its inherent nature, goes on increasing until checked. The reason is not that power is necessarily of an evil tendency, but because without it, it would not be power.[2] Montesquieu says: "It is a lasting experience that every man who has power is brought to the abuse of it. He goes on until he finds its limits."[3] And it is so with "every man," because it lies in the very nature of power itself. The reader is invited to reperuse the "Federalist" on this weighty subject.[4]

The unity of power doubtless dazzles, and thus is the more dangerous. The French ought to listen to their own great countryman. He says: "A despotic government (and all unity of power is despotic) strikes the eye, (saute pour ainsi dire aux yeux ;) it is uniform throughout : as it requires nothing but passions to establish it, all sorts of people are sufficiently good for it."[5]

Our own Webster, in his speech on the presidential protest, delivered the following admirable passage on the subject of

---

[1] Innumerable official instances might be cited. The King of Prussia, when, in May, 1847, he delivered his first throne speech to the united committees of the provincial estates, which were to serve as a substitute for the expected estates general, "appealed in advance to his people," against everything we are accustomed to call constitutional. "My people does not want a participation of representatives in ruling. . . . . nor the division of sovereignty, nor the breaking up of the plenitude of royal power," etc. General Bonaparte wrote to the Directory, May 14, 1796 : "One bad general is even better than two good ones. War is like government, it is a matter of tact"—words which Mr. Girardin quotes with approval, and as an authority for his theory of the best government consisting in a succession of perfectly absolute single rulers to be appointed, and at pleasure recalled by universal suffrage.

[2] This I have endeavored plainly to show in the Political Ethics.

[3] Esprit des Loix, xi. 5.

[4] Mr. Madison's paper on The Meaning of the Maxim, which requires a Separation of the Departments of Power, examined and ascertained. Federalist, No. xlvii. and sequ.

[5] Esprit des Loix, book v. c. 14.

which we treat, and on liberty in general—a passage which I give entire, in spite of its length, because I cannot find the courage to mutilate it. I have tried to select some sentences, but it seemed to me like attempting to break off some limbs of a master-work of sculpture which has happily come down to us entire.[1]

Mr. Webster said: " The first object of a free people is the preservation of their liberty, and liberty is only to be preserved by maintaining constitutional restraints and just divisions of political power. Nothing is more deceptive or more dangerous than the pretence of a desire to simplify government.

The simplest governments are despotisms ; the next simplest limited monarchies ; but all republics, all governments of law, must impose numerous limitations and qualifications of authority, and give many positive and many qualified rights. In other words, they must be subject to rule and regulation. This is the very essence of free political institutions.

" The spirit of liberty is, indeed, a bold and fearless spirit ; but it is also a sharp-sighted spirit ; it is a cautious, sagacious, discriminating, far-seeing intelligence ; it is jealous of encroachment, jealous of power, jealous of man. It demands checks ; it seeks for guards ; it insists on securities ; it entrenches itself behind strong defences, and fortifies itself with all possible care against the assaults of ambition and passion.

---

[1] The speech was delivered in the Senate of the United States on the 7th of May, 1834. If I might place myself by the side of these men I would refer the reader to the Political Ethics, where I stated that despotism is simple and coarse. It is like a block of granite, and may last in its unchanging coarseness a long time ; but liberty is organic with all the delicate vitality of organic bodies, with development, growth and expansion. Despotism may have accretion, but liberty widens by its own vital power, and gains in intensity as it expands. The long duration of some despotisms decides nothing. Longevity of states is indeed a requisite of modern civilization, but if we must choose, who would not prefer a few hundred years of Roman liberty to the thousands of Chinese dreary mandarinism and despotism ? Besides, we must not forget that a shoe once trodden down to a slipper, will always serve longer in its slipshod capacity than it did as a shoe.

It does not trust the amiable weaknesses of human nature, and therefore it will not permit power to overstep its prescribed limits, though benevolence, good intent and patriotic purpose come along with it. Neither does it satisfy itself with flashy and temporary resistance to its legal authority. Far otherwise. It seeks for duration and permanence. It looks before and after; and, building on the experience of ages which are past, it labors diligently for the benefit of ages to come. This is the nature of constitutional liberty; and this is *our* liberty, if we will rightly understand and preserve it. Every free government is necessarily complicated, because all such governments establish restraints, as well on the power of government itself as on that of individuals. If we will abolish the distinction of branches, and have but one branch; if we will abolish jury trials, and leave all to the judge; if we will then ordain that the legislator shall himself be that judge; and if we place the executive power in the same hands, we may readily simplify government. We may easily bring it to the simplest of all possible forms, a pure despotism. But a separation of departments, so far as practicable, and the preservation of clear lines of division between them, is the fundamental idea in the creation of all our constitutions; and, doubtless, the continuance of regulated liberty depends on maintaining these boundaries."[1]

Unity of power, if sought for in wide-spread democracy, must always lead to monarchical absolutism. Virtually it is such; for it is indifferent what the appearance or name may be, the democracy is not a unit in reality; yet actual absolutism existing, it must be wielded by one man. All absolutism is therefore essentially a one-man government. The ruler may

---

[1] Page 122, vol. iv. of the Works of Daniel Webster. I have not transcribed this long passage without the permission of those who have the right to give it.

To my mind it appears the most Demosthenian passage of that orator. Perhaps I am biased, because the extract maintains what I have always asserted on the nature of liberty, and what has shown itself with such remarkable clearness and undraped nakedness in the late French affairs.

not immediately take the crown; the pear may not yet be ripe, as Nopoleon said to Sieyes ; but it soon ripens, and then the avowed absolute ruler has far more power than the king whose absolute power is traditional, because the tradition itself brings along with it some limitations by popular opinion. Of all absolute monarchs, however, it is true that " it is the vice of a pure (absolute) monarchy to raise the power so high and to surround it with so much grandeur that the head is turned of him who possesses it, and that those who are beneath him scarcely dare to look at him. The sovereign believes himself a god, the people fall into idolatry. People may then write on the duties of kings and the rights of subjects ; they may even constantly preach upon them, but the situations have greater power than the words, and when the inequality is immense, the one easily forgets his duties, the others their rights."[1] Change

---

[1] Guizot, Essais, sur l'Histoire de France, p. 359.

General Rapp, first aid of Napoleon, gives a good picture of the false position of an absolute monarch, in his Memoirs, Paris, 1832, ch. 2. He says that "whenever Napoleon was angry, his confidants, far from ap- peasing him, increased his anger by their representations. 'Your majesty is right,' they would say : 'such a person has merited to be shot, or disgraced, or discarded. . . . I have long known him to be your enemy. Examples are necessary; they are necessary for the maintenance of tranquillity.' When it was required to levy contributions from the enemies' country and Napoleon would perhaps ask for twenty thousand, he was advised to demand ten more. If it was the question to levy two hundred thousand men, he was persuaded to ask for three hundred thousand ; in liquidating a debt which was indisputable, they would insinuate doubts on its legitimacy, and would often cause him to reduce to a half, or a third, and sometimes entirely, the amount of the demand. If he spoke of making war, they would applaud the noble resolution : war alone would enrich France ; it was necessary to astonish the world in a manner suitable to the power of the great nation. Thus it was that in provoking and encouraging expectations, and uncertain enterprises, he was precipitated into continual wars. Thus it is that they succeeded in giving to his reign a character of violence which did not belong to him. His disposition and habits were altogether good-natured. Never a man was more inclined to indulgence and more awake to the voice of humanity. I could cite thousands of examples."

Whether Napoleon was good-natured or not need not be discussed

the terms, and nearly every word applies to absolute democracies with equal truth. Aristotle says that the perfected democracy (what we would call democratic absolutism) is equal to the tyrannis (monarchical absolutism.)[1] This is true, yet we must add these modifications : The power of the absolute monarch, though centered in one man, according to theory is lent to him by those over whom he rules; he may be brought to an account; but the power of an absolute democracy is fearful reality, with which there is no reckoning. It strikes, and the strikers vanish. Where shall they be impeached? Even he who led them is shielded by the inorganic multitude that followed him. It is felt to be heroic to oppose the absolute monarch; it is considered unpatriotic or treasonous to oppose the absolute democracy, or those people who call themselves *the* people.

Absolute monarchs, indeed, often allow free words. The philosopher Kant uttered remarkable political sentiments under Frederic the Great, and Montesquieu published his Spirit of Laws under the auspices of Madame de Tincin, the chanoiness mistress of the Duke of Orleans, regent of France, and successively mistress of many others. Montesquieu was favored by these persons; for nothing is more common than that sprightly people have a sentimental love for the theory of liberty. But neither Kant nor Montesquieu would have been suffered to utter their sentiments had there been any fear whatever that they might pass into reality. There is an immense difference between admiring liberty as a philosophical speculation, loving her like an imaginary beauty by sonnet and madrigal, and uniting with her in real wedlock for better and for worse. Liberty is the loved wife and honored companion, through this earthly life, of every true American and Englishman, and no mistress for sentimental sport or the gratification of spasmodic

---

here, nor is it important to state that he was not so weak as represented by Rapp; but it is instructive to see how a man like Rapp, an uncompromising absolutist, unawares lays bare his own opinion of the character of an absolute monarch, because he is absolute.

[1] Pol. v. 9, § 6; vi. 2, § 12.

passion, nor is she for them a misty nymph with whom a mortal falls in consuming love, nor is she the antiquated portrait of an ancestor, looked upon with respect, perhaps even with factitious reverence, but without life-imparting actuality.[1]

---

[1] Since the foregoing chapter was originally written, history has furnished us with many additional and impressive illustrations of some of its contents. Numerous French writers, anxious to vindicate for France the leadership in the race of civilization, yet sadly aware that liberty exists no more in France, have declared that the essence of liberty exists simply in universal suffrage, or, if they abandon even the name of liberty, that the height of political civilization consists in two things—universal suffrage and the code Napoleon, with the proclamation of which it has been stoutly maintained a French army would find the conquest of England and the regeneration of Italy an easy matter. Once the principle of universal suffrage established, the French statesmen of the imperial school demand that everything flowing from it, by what they term severe or uncompromising logic, must be accepted. This peculiar demand of severe logic is, nevertheless, wholly illogical, for politics are a means to obtain a high object, and the application to certain given circumstances is of paramount importance. We do not build houses, cure or sustain our bodies, by logic ; and a bill of rights is infinitely more important and intrinsically true, than the most symmetrically logical rights of men. The "severe logic" leads, moreover, different men to entirely different results, as, for instance, Mr. Louis Blanc on the one hand, and the imperial absolutists on the other ; and, if universal suffrage, without guaranteeing institutions, is the only principle of importance, the question presents itself immediately, Why appeal to it on rare occasions only, perhaps only once in order to transfer power, and what does universal suffrage mean if not the ascertaining of the opinion of the majority ? If this be the object, then we must further ask, Why is discussion necessary to form the opinion suppressed, and how could Mr. de Montalembert be charged with, and tried for, having attacked the principle of universal suffrage in a pamphlet, the whole object of which could not be anything else than influencing those who, under universal suffrage, have to give their votes. This is not "severe logic."

If much has happened and been written since the original penning of this chapter to illustrate the utter falsity of universal suffrage, naked and pure, we must not omit to mention, on the other hand, works of merit which have been written in a very opposite train of thought, by men of great mark, of whom Mr. de Tocqueville deserves particular mention on account of his Ancien Régime.

CHAPTER XV.

24. It is not only necessary that every officer remain individually answerable for his acts, but it is equally important that
no act be done for which some one is not responsible.   This
applies in particular, so far as liberty is to be protected, to that
branch of government which directs the military.   It is important, therefore, that no decree of government go forth without
the name of a responsible person; and that the officers, or single
acts of theirs, shall be tried, when trial becomes necessary, by
regular action at law, or by impeachment; and that no positive
order by the supreme executive, even though this be a king, as
in England, be allowed as a plea for impunity.   A long time
elapsed before this principle came clearly to be established in
England.   Charles I. reproved the commons for proffering their
loyalty to his own person, while they opposed his ministers, and
measures which he had personally ordered.   England in this, as
in almost all else that relates to constitutional liberty, had the
start of the continent by two hundred years and more.   The
same complaints were heard on the continent of Europe when
lately attempts were made to establish liberty in monarchies;
and more will be heard when the time of new attempts shall
have arrived.   Responsible ministers, and a cabinet dependent
upon a parliamentary majority, were the objects of peculiar
distaste to the present emperor of the French, as they have
been to all absolute monarchs.   His own proclamations distinctly express it, and his newspapers continue to decry the
servile position of government when ministers are "in the ser-

(163)

vice of a house of representatives,"[1] which means dependent on a parliamentary majority.

In unfree countries, the principle prevails that complaints against the act of an officer, relating to his public duty, must be laid before his own superiors. An overcharge of duty on imported goods cannot there be tried before a common court, as is the case with us.

25. As a general rule, it may be said that the principle prevails in Anglican liberty, that the executive may do that which is positively allowed either by the fundamental or other law, and not all that which is not prohibited. The royal prerogatives of the English crown doubtless made the evolution of this principle difficult, and may occasionally make clear action upon it still so; but the modern development of liberty has unquestionably tended more and more distinctly to establish the principle that for everything the executive does there must be the warrant of the law. The principle is of high importance, and it need hardly to be added that it forms one of the prominent elements of American liberty. Our presidents, indeed, have done that for which many citizens believed they had no warrant in law, for instance, when General Jackson removed the public deposits from the bank of the United States; but the doubt consisted in the question whether the law warranted the

---

[1] It is sufficiently remarkable to be mentioned here, that Napoleon III., when the sanguinary *coup d'état* had been perpetrated, supported his demand of a cabinet exclusively dependent upon the chief of the state, by the example of the American president, not seeing or not mentioning that congress has a controlling power.

The following extract of a letter, written by Lord Liverpool to Lord Castlereagh, (October 23, 1818,) and taken from Correspondence, Despatches, and other Papers of Viscount Castlereagh, second Marquis of Londonderry, 12 vols., London, 1853, is interesting, if we consider how thorough a tory minister Lord Liverpool was :

" Bathurst's despatch and letter of Tuesday, and my letter of to-day, will put you entirely in possession of our sentiments upon the present state of the negotiations. The Russians must be made to feel that we have a parliament and a public to which we are responsible, and that we cannot permit ourselves to be drawn into views of policy which are wholly incompatible with the spirit of our government.

" Ever sincerely yours,   LIVERPOOL."

measure or not. It was not claimed that he could do it because it was nowhere prohibited. The Constitution of the United States declares that "the powers not delegated to the United States by the constitution, nor prohibited by it to the states, are reserved to the states, respectively, or to the people;" and the principle which I have mentioned may be considered as involved in it; but in the different states, where the legislature certainly has the right, as a general rule, to do all that seems necessary for the common welfare and is not specifically prohibited, the mentioned principle prevails regarding the executive.[1]

---

[1] I have already mentioned the judgment given by the French court, with reference to the opening of letters by the police, in order to find out the traces of offences. I now give an extract, and shall italicize those passages which bear upon the subject above :

"Considering that if, by the terms of existing legislation, and particularly by art. 187 of the penal code, functionaries and agents of the government, and of the post-office administration, are forbidden either to suppress or to open letters confided to the said administration, this disposition cannot reach the prefect of police, acting by virtue of powers conferred upon him by art. 10 of the Code of Criminal Instruction :

"Considering that the law, in giving to him the mission to investigate offences, to collect evidence in support of them, and to hand their authors over to the tribunals charged with punishing them, *has not limited the means placed at his disposition for attaining that end :**

"That, in fact, the right of perquisition in aid of judicial instructions is solemnly affirmed by numerous legal dispositions, and that it is of common law in this matter :

"That the seizure in question *was made in order to follow the trace of an offence ; that it resulted in the discovery of useful and important facts ;* that, finally, the authors of the said letters have been prosecuted in a court of justice :

"Considering, moreover, that the court *is not called upon to inquire into the origin of documents submitted to its appreciation; that its mission is merely to establish their authenticity* or their sincerity ; that, in fact, the letters in question are not denied by their authors :

---

* Does not this argument, from the absence of restriction, remind the reader of that Baron Viereck, who consented to his daughter's marrying the King of Denmark, the undivorced queen living, and who replied to an expostulating friend that he could find no passage in the bible prohibiting kings of Denmark from having two wives?

26. The supremacy of the law requires that where enacted constitutions[1] form the fundamental law there be some authority which can pronounce whether the legislature itself has or

---

" For these reasons the letters are declared admissible as evidence," etc.

It is pleasing to read by the side of this remarkable judgment so simple a passage as the following, which was contained in an English paper at the same time that the French judgment was given. It relates to a London police regulation concerning cabmen :

" Now, we have no wish to palliate the bad conduct of a class who at least furnish amusing topics to contemporaries. By all means let the evils be remedied, but let the remedy come within the limits of law. It will be an evil day for England when irresponsible legislation and police law, even for cabmen, are recognized and applauded by a certain public because in a given example it happens to be convenient to them. If the ordinary law is not sufficient, let it be reformed ; but do not leave the making of penal laws to the police, and the execution of those laws to the correctional tribunal of the same authority."—*Spectator*, April 2, 1853.

[1] They are generally called written constitutions ; but it is evident that the essential distinction of constitutions, derived from their origin, is not whether they are written or unwritten, which is incidental, but whether they are enacted or cumulative. The English constitution, that is the aggregate of those laws and rules which are considered of fundamental importance, and essential in giving to the state and its government those features which characterize them, or those laws and institutions which give to England her peculiar political organic being, consist in cumulated usages and branches of the common law, in decisions of fundamental importance, in self-grown and in enacted institutions, in compacts, and in statutes embodying principles of political magnitude. From these the Americans have extracted what has appeared important or applicable to our circumstances; we have added, expanded and systematized, and then enacted this aggregate as a whole, calling it a constitution— enacted, not by the legislature, which is a creature of this very constitution, but by the people. Whether the constitution is written, printed, carved in stone, or remembered only, as laws were of old, is not the distinctive feature. It is the positive enactment of the whole at one time, and by distinct authority, which marks the difference between the origin of our constitutions and those of England or ancient Rome. Although the term written constitution does not express the distinctive principle, it was nevertheless natural that it should have been adopted, for it is analogous to the term lex scripta, by which the enacted or statute law is distinguished from the unenacted, grown and cumulative common law.

has not transgressed it in the passing of some law, or whether a specific law conflicts with the superior law, the constitution. If a separate body of men were established to pronounce upon the constitutionality of a law, nothing would be gained. It would be as much the creature of the constitution as the legislature, and might err as much as the latter. Quis custodet custodes? Tribunes or ephori? They are apt to transgress their powers as other mortals. But there exists a body of men in all well-organized polities, who, in the regular course of business assigned to them, must decide upon clashing interests, and do so exclusively by the force of reason, according to law, without the power of armies, the weight of patronage or imposing pomp, and who, moreover, do not decide upon principles in the abstract, but upon practical cases which involve them—the middle men between the pure philosophers and the pure men of government. These are the judges—courts of law.

When laws conflict in actual cases, they must decide which is the superior law and which must yield; and as we have seen that according to our principles every officer remains answerable for what he officially does, a citizen, believing that the law he enforces is incompatible with the superior law, the constitution, simply sues the officer before the proper court as having unlawfully aggrieved him in the particular case. The court, bound to do justice to every one, is bound also to decide this case as a simple case of conflicting laws. The court does not decide directly upon the doings of the legislature. It simply decides, for the case in hand, whether there actually are conflicting laws, and if so, which is the higher law that demands obedience, when both may not be obeyed at the same time. As, however, this decision becomes the leading decision for all future cases of the same import, until, indeed, proper and legitimate authority should reverse it, the question of constitutionality is virtually decided, and it is decided in a natural, easy, legitimate and safe manner, according to the principle of the supremacy of the law and the independence of justice. It is one of the most interesting and important evolutions of the government of law, and one of the greatest protections of the citizen. It may well be called a very jewel of Anglican liberty, one of the best fruits of our political civilization.[1]

27. Of all the guarantees of liberty there is none more important, and none which in its ample and manifold development is more peculiarly Anglican, than the representative government. Every one who possesses a slight acquaintance with history, knows that a government by assembled estates was common to all nations arising out of the conquests of the Teutonic race; but the members of the estates were deputies or attorneys sent with specific powers of attorney to remedy specific grievances. They became nowhere, out of England and her colonies, general representatives—that is, representatives for the state at large, and with the general power of legislation. This constitutes one of the most essential differences between the deputative medieval estates, and the modern representative legislatures—a government prized by us as one of the highest political blessings, and sneered at by the enemies of liberty on the continent, at this moment, as "the unwieldy parliamentary government." I have endeavored thoroughly to treat of this important difference; of the fact that the representative is not a substitute for something which would be better were it practicable, but has its own substantive value; of political instruction and mandates to the representatives, and of the duties of the representative, in the Political Ethics, to which I must necessarily refer the reader.

With reference to the great subject of civil liberty, and as one of the main guarantees of freedom, the representative government has its value as an institution by which public opinion organically passes over into public will, that is law;

---

[1] The ancient justicia of Aragon had the power of declaring laws unlawful or unconstitutional, as we call it, against the king and estates, but it was done without the trial of a specific case and specific persons. He was therefore simply in these cases above king and estates, that is, king himself, and it became necessary in course of time to suppress this feature. See Pol. Ethics, vol. ii. p. 281.

as one of the chief bars against absolutism of the executive on the one, and of the masses on the other hand ; as the only contrivance by which it is possible to induce at the same time an essentially popular government and the supremacy of the law, or the union of liberty and order; as an invaluable high school to teach the handling and the protection, and to instil the love of liberty ; as the organism by which the average justice, on which all fair laws must be based, can be ascertained ; as that sun which throws the rays of publicity on the whole government with a more penetrating light the more perfect it becomes; and as one of the most efficacious preventives of the growth of centralization and a bureaucratic[1] government—as that institution without which no clear division of the functions of government can exist.

Before we consider the most prominent points of a representative government, so far as it is a guarantee of liberty, it may be proper to revert to two subjects just mentioned.

There was a time when, it seems, it was universally believed, and many persons believe still, that a representative

---

[1] The term bureaucracy is called by many barbarous, nor has it, so far as I know, been introduced into dictionaries of great authority. Be it so ; but while we have innumerable words, compounded of elements which belong to different languages, a term for that distinct idea which is designated by the word Bureaucracy has become indispensable in the progress of political science, because the thing which must be named has distinctly developed itself in the progress of centralization combined with writing. In spite, therefore, of the want of lexical authority, it is almost universally used; for necessity presses. I am under this necessity, and shall use it until a better and more acceptable term be proposed. Mandarinism would not be preferable. Mandarinism would express indeed a government by mandarins, by officials, but it would not designate the characteristics which it is intended to point out by the term bureaucracy, namely, a government carried on, not only by a hierarchy of officials, but also by scribbling bureaus. All bureaucracies must be mandarinisms, I take it ; but every mandarinism need not be a bureaucracy. I observe that the French, from whom indeed the term has been received, freely use it, even in their best writings. It is to be regretted that we Americans frequently use the French term Bureau for the old term Board. There are different associations of ideas connected with each of these words.

government is indeed a very acceptable substitute, yet only a substitute, for a state of things which would be the perfect one, but which it is physically impossible to obtain at present, namely, the meeting of the people themselves, instead of an assembly of their representatives. A secondary value only is thus allowed to the representative system. This is a grave error. Even were it physically or locally possible to assemble the entire American people, and rule by the Athenian pebble or procheironia, (the show of hands,) we must still cling to the representative system as a substantive institution. The market government belongs to antiquity—the period of city-states—not to our period of national states ; and national states have not only a meaning relating to physical extent of country.

It has been observed that the period of nationalization of tribes toward the close of the middle ages, is one of the most important in the progress of civilization and modern political development, as a period of medieval disintegration and division would be the necessary effect of denationalization. Rome perished of a political bankruptcy, because the ancient city-state was incompatible with an extensive empire. A representative government could alone have saved it ; for its recollections and forms of liberty prevented a full-blown centralization, the only other form which could have given it a Russian stability. Constantine, indeed, established a centralized court government ; but it was then too late. The decree had gone forth that the vessel should part amidst the breakers.

The market democracy is irreconcilable with liberty as we love it. It is absolutism which exists wherever power, unmitigated, undivided and unchecked, is in the hands of any one or any body of men. It is the opposite of liberty. The people, which means nothing more than an aggregate of men, require fundamental laws of restraint, as much as each component individual does. Unless we divide the power into two parts—into the electing power, which periodically appoints and recalls, and into the power of elected trustees appointed to legislate, and, as trustees, are limited in their power, absolutism is unavoidable. Absolutism is the negation of protection; protection in its highest sense is an essential element of liberty.[1] It is the trusteeship that gives so high a value to the representative government. When the Athenians, trying the unfortunate generals after the battle of Argenusæ, were reminded that they acted in direct contradiction to the laws, they exclaimed that they were the people; they made the laws, why should they not have the privilege of disregarding them?

Every one feels his responsibility far more distinctly as trustee than otherwise. Let a man in an excited crowd be suddenly singled out, and made a member of a committee to reflect and resolve for that crowd, and he will feel the difference in an instant. How easy it would be to receive the most lavish and most dangerous money grants from an undivided and absolute multitude! Is it necessary to remind the reader that liberty has been lost quite as often from false gratitude toward a personally popular man as from any other reason? Trustees, carefully looking around them, and conscious that they have to give an account of themselves, are not so easily swayed by ravishing gratitude. The trusteeship in the representative government is the only means yet discovered to temper the rashness of the democracy and to overcome the obstinacy of monarchs.

How necessary for modern liberty a national[2] representa-

---

[1] To refer to books on such a subject is very difficult; for it almost comprehends the whole history of modern liberty.

I have treated on many points connected with the representative system, in the Political Ethics. The reader will peruse with interest M. Guizot's Histoire des Origines du Gouvernement Représentatif en Europe, Paris, 1851. It is interesting to learn the views of a Frenchman of such celebrity on a subject of vital interest to us. Regarding the deputative principle, the Histoire de la Formation et des Progres du Tiers Etat, by Augustin Thierry, Paris, 1853, is instructive. I am sorry that I have not been able to read Mr. George Harris's True Theory of Representation in a State, London, 1852.

[2] I take here the term National in the sense of relating to an entire society spread over the territory of an extensive state; and as contradistinguished from what belongs to a city-state, or from the system of the middle ages, which was deputative, on the one hand, (see my Political Ethics on Representative System,) and a system of juxtaposition rather than of pervading organization, like the Chinese language compared to our

tive government is—a representative system comprehending the whole state, and throwing liberty over it broadcast—will appear at once, if we remember that local self-government exists in a very high degree in many Asiatic countries, where, however, there is no union of these many insulated self-governments, and no state self-government, and therefore no liberty. We shall also presently see that where there is only a national representative government without local self-government, there is no liberty as we understand it.

Nor must we forget two facts, which furnish us with an important lesson on this subject. Wherever estates or other bodies have existed, no matter how great their privileges were or how zealously they defended their liberties, civil liberty has not been firmly established; on the contrary, it has been lost in the course of time, unless the estates have become united into some national or state representative system. Where are the liberties of Aragon, and where is the freedom of the many Germanic polities? It was one of the greatest political blessings of England that favorable circumstances promoted an early national fusion of the estates into two houses. On the other hand, we find that those governments which can no longer resist the demand of liberty by the people, yet are bent on yielding as little as possible, always have tried as long as was feasible to grant provincial estates only. Some monarchs of this century have shown a real horror of national representation, and would rather have periled their crown than granted it; yet some of these monarchs have readily granted an urban self-government of considerable extent. Their ministers and servants have frequently gone so far as to extol local self-government and to proclaim the idea that liberty consists far more in the "administration" being left to the people, than in any general representative government. In doing so,

---

grammatical languages. In this sense, then, the government of Virginia or New York would be national, although we use the word in America as synonymous with federal. It were well if we could adopt a distinct term for national in the first sense. See the note at the end of this chapter.

they pointed to countries in which the latter, existing alone, had brought no real liberty. Asia, as was before stated, furnishes us with innumerable instances of local self-government, which are there neither a source nor a test of liberty.[1] True liberty stands in need of both, and of a bona fide representative government largely and minutely carried out.[2]

---

[1] A curious picture of Asiatic local self-government, without any liberty, has lately been given to the public, in Lieutenant-colonel C. G. Dixon's Sketch of Maiwara, giving a brief Account of the Origin and Habits of the Mairs, etc., London, 1851.

[2] National representation is closely connected with the idea of *country*, indispensable for high modern civilization. *Nations* and *Countries* appear to me so much elements of modern civilization and of modern liberty that I may be permitted to give an extract relating to this topic, from my Inaugural Speech in 1858:

"Our government is a federal union. We loyally adhere to it and turn our faces from centralization, however brilliant, for a time, the lustre of its focus may appear, however imposingly centred power, that saps self-government, may hide for a day the inherent weakness of military concentrated polities. But truths are truths. It is a truth that modern civilization stands in need of entire countries; and it is a truth that every government, as indeed every institution whatever, is, by its nature, exposed to the danger of gradually increased and, at last, excessive action of its vital principle. One-sidedness is a universal effect of man's state of sin. Confederacies are exposed to the danger of sejunction as unitary governments are exposed to absorbing central power— centrifugal power in the one case, centripetal power in the other. That illustrious predecessor of ours, from whom we borrowed our very name, the United States of the Netherlands, ailed long with the paralyzing poison of sejunction in her limbs, and was brought to an early grave by it, after having added to the stock of humanity the worshipful names of William of Orange, and de Witt, Grotius, de Ruyter and William III.* There is no German among you that does not sadly remember

---

* Every historian knows that William of Orange, the founder of the Netherlands' republic, had much at heart to induce the cities of the new union to admit representatives of the *country;* but the "sovereign" cities would allow no representatives to the farmers and landowners, unless noblemen, who, nevertheless, were taking their full share in the longest and most sanguinary struggle for independence and liberty; but the following detail, probably, is not known to many. The estates of Holland and West Friesland were displeased with the public prayers for the Prince of Orange, which some high-calvanistic ministers were gradually introducing, in the latter half of the seventeenth century, and in 1663 a decree was issued ordaining

that his country, too, furnishes us with bitter commentaries on this truth; and we are not exempt from the dangers common to mortals. Yet as was indicated just now, the patria of us moderns ought to consist in a wide land covered by a nation, and not in a city or a little colony. Mankind have outgrown the ancient city-state. *Countries* are the orchards and the broad acres where modern civilization gathers her grain and nutritious fruits. The narrow garden-beds of antiquity suffice for our widened humanity no more than the short existence of ancient states. Moderns stand in need of nations and of national longevity, for their literatures and law, their industry, liberty and patriotism; we want countries to work and write and glow for, to live and to die for. The sphere of humanity has steadily widened, and nations alone can now-a-days acquire the membership of that great commonwealth of our race which extends over Europe and America. Has it ever been sufficiently impressed on our minds how slender the threads are that unite us in a mere political system of states, if we are not tied together by the far stronger cords of those feelings which arise from the consciousness of having a country to cling to and to pray for, and unimpeded land and water roads to move on?

Should we, then, not avail ourselves of so well proved a cultural means of fostering and promoting a generous nationality, as a comprehensive university is known to be? Shall we never have this noble pledge of our nationality? All Athens, the choicest city-state of antiquity, may well be said to have been one great university, where masters daily met with masters; and shall we not have even one for our whole empire, which does not extend from bay to bay like little Attica, but from sea to sea, and is destined one day to link ancient Europe to still older Asia, and thus to help completing the zone of civilization around the globe? All that has been said of countries and nations and a national university would retain its full force even if the threatened cleaving of this broad land should come upon us. But let me not enter on that topic of lowering political reality, however near to every citizen's heart, when I am bidden by you to discourse on political philosophy, and it is meet for me not to leave the sphere of inaugural generalities.

---

to pray first of all "for their noble high mightinesses, the estates of Holland and West Friesland, as the true sovereign, and only sovereign power after God, in this province; next, for the estates of the other provinces, their allies, and for all the deputies in the assembly of the States General, and of the Council of State."

"Separatismus," as German historians have called the tendency of the German princes to make themselves as independent of the empire as possible, until their treason against the country reached "sovereignty," has made the political history of Germany resemble the river Rhine, whose glorious water runs out in a number of shallow and muddy streamlets, having lost its imperial identity long before reaching the broad ocean.

CHAPTER XVI.

28. THE prominent points of a national representative
government, considered as a guarantee of liberty, consist in
the representative principle, that is, the basis of representation
and the right of voting for the representative, in the election
laws, in the fact that those who have the right to vote do vote,
(hence the importance, and, I believe, the necessity of regis-
tration laws,) and in the organization of the representative
legislature, with its own protection and liberties.

All that we can say regarding the requirements of Anglican
liberty with reference to the principle of representation, is that
it be a broad or popular one. Universal suffrage cannot be
said to be an Anglican principle, whatever the American view,
of which we shall treat by and by, may be. The application
of the principle of a wide popular representation, however, or
an extensive right of voting, has constantly though slowly expanded in England, and continues to be expanding.[1]

The English, not allowing universal suffrage or indeed a
representation based upon numbers alone, require some limit
beyond which the right of voting shall not go. This limit is,
as a general rule, which has however its exceptions, indicated
either by property or by a certain annual expense which
usually designates the amount of income over which man may
dispose, namely, house-rent. Hence it is often said that property is the basis of representation in England. This is not
correct. Property, or the enjoyment of a certain revenue

---

[1] For the historic development of the English representative government it will hardly be necessary to refer the reader to Hallam's History
of the English Constitution.

either from acquired property or from an industrial occupation, gives the right of voting, but it is not the basis of representation.

When it is maintained in modern times that property ought
to be the basis of representation, or it is asserted that the
English constitution is founded on property, an inappropriate
term is used, which carries along with it erroneous associations,
in almost all discussions on this subject. When we say that
population is the basis of representation, we mean indeed that
one representative is chosen for a distinct number of represented citizens, and that therefore a large population should
have more representatives than a small one; but when it is
said that property is or ought to be the basis of representation, we mean in almost all cases nothing more than that a
certain amount of property or revenue is required to entitle a
man to vote. The Roman constitution ascribed to Servius
Tullius was really founded upon property, because the six
classes of citizens actually took a share in the government of
the state in proportion to the property they held. Thus likewise there is a partial representation of property prescribed
by the constitution of South Carolina, for the composition of
the state senate, inasmuch as the small but wealthy divisions
of the lower part of the state elect a number of senators
disproportionately large compared to the number of senators
sent from the upper districts of the state, which are very
populous and possessed of proportionately less property. This
was at least the case when the constitution was adopted.[1]

What is really meant when it is said that a constitution
ought to be founded on property, is this: that a minimum
amount of property ought to be adopted as the last line beyond which no suffrage ought to be granted, but not that a
capital of a million or the possession of a thousand acres of
land ought to be entitled to a greater share in government
than the possession of a few thousand dollars. It is meant

---

[1] Those votes which are given in England, according to rate-paying, in
local matters, are indeed votes founded on property and industrial pursuits.

that we seek for a criterion which will enable us to distinguish those who have a fair stake in the welfare of the state from those who have not. But here occurs at once the question: Is this criterion in our age any longer safe, just, and natural, which it may be supposed to have been in former ages? Are there not thousands of men without property who have quite as great a stake in the public welfare as those who may possess a house or enjoy a certain amount of revenue? This criterion becomes an actual absurdity when by property landed property only is understood. It was indeed in the middle ages almost the exclusive property of lasting and extensive value; but nothing has since changed its character more than property itself. This whole question is one of vastest extent, and emphatically belongs to the science of politics and real statesmanship. In regard to the subject immediately in hand, we have only to repeat that an extensive basis of representation is doubtless a characteristic element of Anglican liberty.

29. As important as the basis of representation—indeed, in many cases more important—is the question whether there shall be direct elections by the people, or whether there shall be double elections; that is to say, elections of electors by the constituents, which electors elect the representative. It may be safely asserted that the Anglican people are distinctly in favor of simple elections. Elections by electing middle men deprive the representation of its directness in responsibility and temper; the first electors lose their interest, because they do not know what their action may end in; no distinct candidates can be before the constituents, and be canvassed by them, and, inasmuch as the number of electors is a small one, intrigue is made easy.

The fact that a double or mediate election foils in a great degree the very object of a representative government, is so well known by the enemies of liberty, that despotic governments, unable to hold their absolute power any longer, have frequently struggled hard to establish universal suffrage with double election. An intention to deceive, or a want of acquaintance with the operation of the principle must explain

12

the measure.[1] I believe that neither American nor Englishman would think the franchise worth having were double
elections introduced, and so decidedly is the simple election
ingrained in the Anglican character, that in the only notable
case in which a mediate election is prescribed in America,
namely, the election of the President of the United States,
the whole has naturally and of itself become a direct election.
The constitution is obeyed, and electors are elected, but it is
well known for which candidate the elector is going to vote,
before the people elect him.   There is but one case of old
date in which an elector, elected to vote for a certain candidate for the presidency, voted for another, and his political
character was gone for life; while in the month of November,
1856, the legislature of South Carolina, the only legislature
in the United States which has retained for itself the election
of presidential electors, actually "instructed" the electors to
vote for Mr. Buchanan, and in the state of Pennsylvania
committees belonging to different parties or sections of parties
agreed upon certain "Union Electoral Tickets" for the election of electors, to satisfy the claims of the different voters.
These instances, and many more might be given, show how
the principle of a double election has been wholly abandoned
in the election for the president, although the form still exists.

    Civil liberty demands a fair representative system; the
latter requires that the representatives really represent the
people, which is by no means necessarily obtained by simple
universal suffrage.   Indeed it is one of the highest problems
of political philosophy on the one hand and of genuine statesmanship on the other, to establish, combine, and, as circumstances may require, to change the basis of representation.
In England we find that a large number of persons lately
urged an additional "representation of education."   Essential
representation requires a fair representation of the minority,[2]

---

    [1] According to the present constitution of Prussia (1859) there is
universal suffrage for the election of a certain number of electors, and
in addition a graduated property qualification for the election of other
electors, who with the former elect representatives.

    [2] See Political Ethics on Opposition and Representatives.

which, until now, has been obtained, in the system of Anglican liberty, by making election districts sufficiently small, so that persons of different political opinions would be elected, and by discountenancing "general tickets." It might be supposed that the most consistent method, opposite to the "general ticket," would be to make election districts so small that each elects but one person, as the present constitution of the state of New York prescribes;[1] but practice, it seems, does not bear out this supposition in the mentioned state. When election districts are very small, many citizens whom it is most desirable to see in the legislature decline contending with paltry local interests and jealousies. And here it may be mentioned, that a marked difference between England and America consists in the fact, that in the first-mentioned country voters may take their representative from any portion of the country, while in America the principle prevails, we believe universally, that the representative must be a resident in his constituency, which is an additional reason that election districts ought not to be too narrow.

But the idea of representing the minority in a more direct manner, than by a minority in the house of representatives, has been much discussed of late in England, and, to judge from the journals of the day, there seem to be many persons, who believe that this could best be obtained, by obliging each voter to vote for a number of representatives, less than the whole number, to be sent to parliament, for instance, for two members, if three are to be sent three, or for three, if five are to be sent. This novel feature seems to have been actually adopted in some colonial constitutions. No one is able to say how such a principle may operate in certain conditions of the voters, but, as a general principle, it would seem injudicious, inoperative toward the desired object, and not Anglican.[2] Another

---

[1] 1859.

[2] This principle has been adopted in our country for the purpose of electing election managers, where the very purpose is to elect two men of opposite parties. The Pennsylvania election law of 1839 decrees: Section 4: Each of such qualified citizens shall vote for one person as judge, and also for one person as inspector of elections, and the person

method was adopted to secure the representation of the minority, in the so-called Ruatan Warrant, in 1856. In this instrument every voter received the right to give, if four representatives are to be elected, all four votes to one person, or three to one and one to another, or to cast his four votes in equal halves for two persons.[1] This is legalizing, and indeed intensifying, the voting of " plumpers,"[2] as it is vulgarly called

---

having the greatest number of votes for judge shall be publicly declared to be elected judge ; and the two persons having the greatest number of votes for inspectors shall, in like manner, be declared to be elected inspectors of elections.

[1] The queen's warrant for erecting the island of Ruatan and certain other islands in the bay of Honduras into a colony, under the name of Bay Islands has this provision :

"Every elector, qualified as aforesaid, shall be entitled to give three votes, and shall be entitled at his discretion to give such three votes to three separate candidates, or to give two of such votes, or all of them, to one candidate." This, an English writer continues, "provides for a full representation of a respectable minority in the colony." It seems, on the contrary, that the effect would soon be of electing only one instead of several representatives.

[2] A plumper is a ballot with a less number of names, than places to be filled. A relative and great advantage is thus given to the persons voted for. As to the Ruatan principle, it can be easily shown that two out of three representatives might be elected by the minority. Suppose there are eleven voters, of whom 2 give "plumpers" for O (opposition,) 2 the same for M (also opposition,) 6 regular tickets for 3 administration members each, and one voting 2 votes for *O* and one for *M*, we would have

O   .   .   .   .   .   .   8 votes.
M   .   ·   .   .   .   .   7 votes.

each majority member 6 votes. .

The constitution proposed by the British ministers for Australia in 1858, has also the provision that in districts entitled to three members, the elector shall vote for two candidates only ; if entitled to five members, for three only ; and if entitled to seven members, for four only. An uneven number of representatives is assigned to each district, for this purpose. I cannot say whether this constitution has been adopted. Two members might be elected by half a dozen of votes, in districts all but unanimous.

The constitution proposed by the British ministers for Australia in
This principle will probably attract much attention for some time to come, and it may be sufficiently interesting, therefore, to record that, in

in this country, a kind of voting generally considered unfair and dishonest, and which it would be just and right to provide against by our constitutions. Each ballot ought to contain as many names as representatives are to be voted for; if not, it ought to be thrown out.

It does not seem to be the Anglican principle to elect with the representative, his substitute, in case of absence of the former from the legislature. If a representative resigns or dies, another is elected; if he absents himself, the constituents lose his vote. It seems that representation is considered too direct a relation to admit of a substitute beforehand. Yet for conventions it is customary in America to elect substitutes. They do not allow of sufficient time for a new election. On the continent of Europe, *suppléans* are immediately elected.[1]

As a matter of historical curiosity I would direct attention to the circuitous ways and multiplied elections by which it was frequently attempted in the middle ages, to insure an impartial or pure election. The master of the Knights of Malta was elected by no less than seventeen consecutive elections of electors, each election connected with oaths;[2] and the Doge of Venice was elected by nine different acts, namely, five

England, it is ascribed to M. G. L. Craik, professor of history in Queen's College, Belfast. He published his plan in 1836, in the Companion to the Newspaper. Soon after he learned from Mr. Coleridge that Mr. Praed had suggested a similar idea. The subject has since been discussed in the periodicals. In 1854 Mr. Craik published an interesting Letter in the Belfast Mercury on the same subject.

It may be mentioned here that at this period (February, 1859,) when a new Reform Bill is much discussed in England, some reformers propose as an enlargement of the franchise and an avoidance of universal suffrage, of which they see such uninviting consequences in France, a franchise on the rate-paying principle, which would give to some voters, by way of franchise, more votes than to another—a principle adopted in the English town government.

[1] We elect substitutes for executive officers. The Roman custom was to take, in case of need, the predecessor of the failing incumbent, a principle adopted, at least in former times, in Geneva and other cities.

[2] Vertot's History of the Knights of Malta, folio edition, London, 1728; vol. ii. Old and New Statutes.

elections alternating with four acts of drawing lots,[1] with the addition of collateral votings.

30. The representative principle farther requires that the management of the elections be in the hands of the voters, or of a popular character; that especially the government do not interfere with them, either in the election *bureau* itself, or by indecently proposing and urging certain candidates; that the house for which the candidates are elected be the sole judge of the validity of the election, and that the opening of the poll do not depend upon the executive, which by mere omission might prevent the entire election in order to exclude a distasteful citizen from the house.

The beginning of an election, the appointment of managers, the protection of the minority in this matter, and the conscientious counting of votes, where the ballot exists, are always matters of much interest and of great practical difficulty, to all those who have not traditionally learned it. Collections of election laws are therefore very instructive; and the labor of giving birth to an election with nations unaccustomed to liberty is very great. Mr. Dumont gives some instructive and amusing anecdotes, relating to the first French elections, in his Memoirs of Mirabeau.

The English law is that all the military must leave the place where an election is going on, and can only enter it when called in by the town authorities or the justices of the peace, in case of riot.

The British house of commons is the sole judge of the validity of elections; and the same is declared for the house of representatives by the American constitution.[2]

One of the gravest charges against the Duke of Polignac and his fellow-members of the cabinet, when they were tried for their lives after the revolution of 1830, was that they had

---

[1] Daru, Histoire de Venise; Paris, 1821, vol. i.

[2] A full statement of all the laws relating to these guarantees in England will be found in Stephens's De Lolme, Rise and Progress of the British Constitution; and Story's Commentaries on the Constitution of the United States gives our constitutional law on these subjects.

allowed or induced Charles X. to influence certain electors, by letter, to elect government candidates; while the government under the late so-called republic openly supported certain persons as government candidates, and bishops wrote then, and have since sent solemn pastoral letters, calling on their flocks to elect men of certain political color. It is wholly indifferent to decide here whether peculiar circumstances made this interference necessary. I simply maintain that it is not liberty.

31. Representative bodies must be free. This implies that they must be freely chosen, neither under the threat or violence of the executive, nor of the rabble or whatever portion of the people;[1] that when met, they are independent of the threat or seduction of the executive, or of the mob, armed or not armed; that they are protected by the law as a representative body; and that a wise parliamentary law and usage protect, within the body, the rights of each representative and the elaboration of the law.

Representative legislatures cannot be truly the organisms through which public opinion passes into public will, nor can they be really considered representative bodies, if the members, or at least the members of the popular branch, be not elected for a moderately short period only; if the legislature does not sit frequently; if the elections for the popular branch are not for an entire renewal of the house; and if the member is made answerable for what he says in the house to any one or any power besides the house to which he belongs.

---

[1] Fearful cases to the contrary have happened in France and our own country. In the former country a court of justice decided against a person, because not being the government candidate he had dared to print and distribute his own ticket. Mr. de Montalembert made a speech against the abuse, whereupon the minister of the Interior, Mr. Billault, formerly a socialist, issued a circular to the prefects, instructing them, April, 1857, how to conduct themselves regarding the distribution of election tickets. In our country sanguinary troubles have occurred in New Orleans and Baltimore, in October, 1857, which called forth proclamations of the governors that revealed a frightful state of things. And these crimes at elections were not restricted to the two mentioned cities.

What a moderately short period, or the frequency of sessions means, cannot, as a matter of course, be absolutely stated. Fairness and practice, as well as the character of the times, must necessarily settle these points. England had a law that, from the year 1696, each parliament should not last longer than three years, but in 1716, the septennial bill was carried, under a whig administration, forced to do it by the intrigues of the tories, who were for bringing back the Stuarts. This law has ever since prevailed, but even Pitt called it, in 1783, one of the greatest defects in the system of popular representation. Chatham, his father, had expressed himself against it[1] before him, and it would really seem that England will return, at no distant time, to a shorter period of parliaments.[2]

When Count Villêle, in 1824, was desirous of diminishing the liberal spirit of the French charter, he introduced and carried a septennial bill, which was, however, abolished in 1830 by the "July Revolution." Parliaments for too short a period would lead to a discontinuous action of government, and unsettle instead of settling; hence, they would be as much against liberty as too long ones. In America, two years has become a pretty generally adopted time for the duration of legislatures. It is a remarkable fact that the people in America feel so perfectly safe from attacks of the executive that, in several states, where the constitutions have been revised, a fundamental law has been enacted that the legislature shall not meet more often than every two years. This is to avoid expense and over-legislation. The general principle remains true that "parliaments ought to be held frequently," as the British Declaration of Rights and Liberties enacts it. The Constitution of the United States makes the meeting and dissolution of congress entirely independent of the executive,

---

[1] Volume ii. page 174, of Correspondence of William Pitt, Earl of Chatham.

[2] I have given a sufficiently long account of the Septennial Bill, under this head, in the Encyclopædia Americana.

and enacts that congress shall meet at least once in every year, on the first Monday in December, and that the house of representatives shall be entirely renewed every second year.

As to the irresponsibility of members for their remarks in parliament, the declaration of rights enacts " that the freedom of speech, and debates or proceedings in parliament, ought not to be impeached or questioned in any court or place out of parliament." This was adopted by the framers of our constitution, in the words that " for any speech or debate in either house, they (senators and representatives) shall not be questioned in any other place."[1]

32. A farther and peculiar protection is granted to the members of the legislature, both in the United States and in England, by protecting them against arrest during session, except for certain specified crimes. The English house of commons " for the first time took upon themselves to avenge their own injury, in 1543,"[2] when they ordered George Ferrers, a burgess who had been arrested in going to parliament, to be released, and carried their point. "But the first legislative recognition of the privilege was under James I."[3] The Constitution of the United States enacts that senators and representatives shall "in all cases, except treason, felony, and breach of the peace, be privileged from arrest during their attendance at the session of their respective houses, and in going and returning from the same."

---

[1] Free discussion on all things, appearing important to the representatives, is a right which was obtained after hard struggles, and only in comparatively recent times. Elizabeth repeatedly warned the commons in no gentle terms, not to meddle with high matters of state, which they could not understand. James I. and Charles I. did the same.

A similar spirit is now visible on the continent of Europe in unfree or half-free countries. In the bed of justice, held in 1602, Louis XIV. then fourteen years old, forbade his parliament to deliberate on government and finances or upon the conduct of the ministers of his choice, and forbade its members to assume too sumptuous habits in the palaces of the great. Chevenix, on Nat. Charact., vol. ii. p. 510.

[2] Hallam, Hist. of English Constitution, 5th edit. vol. i. p. 268.

[3] Ibidem, vol. i. p. 303,

33. It is farther necessary that every member possess the initiative, or right to propose any measure or resolution.   This is universally acknowledged and established where Anglican liberty exists, not by enactment, but by absence of prohibition, and as arising out of the character of a member of the legislature itself.   In most countries, not under the ægis of Anglican liberty, this right of the initiative has been denied the members, and government, that is, the executive, has reserved it to itself.   So has the so-called legislative corps of the present French empire no initiative.   Napoleon III. took it to himself exclusively, immediately after the coup d'état. The French legislative corps has indeed not even the privilege of amendment; it has not the right of voting on the ministerial estimates, except on the whole estimate of one ministry at once.[1]   In some countries, as in France under the charter of the July revolution, the initiative is vested in the houses and in government ; that is to say, the government, as government, can propose a measure through a minister, who is not a member of the house.   In England no bill can be proposed by the executive as such, but as every cabinet minister is either a peer or must contrive to be elected into the commons, the ministers have of course the right of the initiative as members of their respective houses.   The Constitution of the United States prohibits any officer of the United States from being a member of either house, and the law does not allow the members of the administration a seat and the right to speak in the houses.   Some think that a law to that effect ought to be passed.   The representatives of our territories are in this position ; they have a seat in the house of representatives, and may speak, but have no vote.   A minister had the right to speak in either house, under the former French charters, in his capacity of cabinet minister, whether he was a member of the house or not.   Whenever the executive of the United States is desirous to have a law passed, the bill must

---

[1] Why, indeed, it is called legislative corps does not appear.   Legislative corpse would be intelligible.

be proposed by some friend of the administration who is a member of one or the other house.

It has been mentioned already that the initiative of money bills belongs exclusively to the popular branch of the legislature, both in the United States and in England, by the constitution in the one, and by ancient usage, which has become a fundamental principle, in the other.

CHAPTER XVII.

PARLIAMENTARY LAW AND USAGE. THE SPEAKER. TWO HOUSES. THE VETO.

34. IT is not only necessary that the legislature be the sole judge of the right each member may have to his seat, but that the whole internal management and the rules of proceeding with the business belong to itself. It is indispensable that the legislature possess that power and those privileges which are necessary to protect itself and its own dignity, taking care, however, that this power may not, in turn, become an aggressive one.

In this respect are peculiarly important the presiding officer of the popular branch or speaker, the parliamentary law, and the rules of the houses.

The speaker of the English commons was in former times very dependent on the crown. Since the revolution of 1688, his election may be said to have become wholly independent. It is true, that the form of obtaining the consent of the monarch is still gone through, but it is a form only, and a change of the administration would unquestionably take place, were the ministers to advise the crown to withhold its consent.

Were the refusal insisted on, disturbances would doubtless follow, which would end in a positive declaration and distinct acknowledgment on all hands, that the choice of the speaker "belongs, and of right ought to belong," to the house of commons. There is no danger on that score in England, so long as a parliamentary government exists there at all. The growth of the commons' independence in this respect is as interesting a study as it is historically to trace step by step any other expanding branch of British liberty.

(188)

The Constitution of the United States says that "the house of representatives shall choose their speaker and other officers," and so chosen, he is speaker, without any other sanction.

The charter granted by Louis XVIII. of France, prescribed that "the president of the chamber of deputies is nominated by the king from a list of five members presented by the chamber." This was altered by the revolution of 1830, and the charter then adopted decreed that "the president of the chamber of deputies is to be elected by the chamber itself at the opening of each session." It need not be added that, according to the " constitution of the empire," the emperor of the French simply appoints the president of the "legislative corps." In all the states of the Union the speakers are within the exclusive appointment of the houses. In the British colonial legislatures, the speaker must be confirmed by the governor, but, as was observed of the speaker of the commons, if consent be refused it would be a case of disagreement between the administration and the legislature, which must be remedied either by a new administration or a new house—that is, new elections.

The presiding officer of the upper house is not made thus dependent upon it. In England, the chief officer of the law, the lord chancellor or keeper of the seals,[1] presides over the

---

[1] A keeper of the seals, whom usage does not require to be a peer, is now appointed as the chief officer of the law, only when for some reason or other no lord chancellor is appointed. The keeper of the seals, nevertheless, presides in the house of lords, or "sits on the woolsack." The chancellor is now always made a peer if he is not already a member of the house of lords, and he is always a member of the cabinet. This mixture of a judicial and political character is inadmissible according to American views; yet it ought to be remembered as an honorable fact, that no complaint of partiality has been made in modern times against any lord chancellor in his judicial capacity, although he is so deeply mixed up with politics. Lord Eldon was probably as uncompromising, and, perhaps, as bigoted a politician as has ever been connected with public affairs, but I am not aware that any suspicion has existed on this ground against his judicial impartiality. There is at present a traditional

house of peers.   There seems to be a growing desire in England wholly to separate the lord chancellor from the cabinet and politics.   At present he is always a member of the administration, and, of course, leaves his office when the cabinet to which he belongs goes out.   It will be an interesting subject to determine who shall preside over the lords, if the change thus desired by many should take place.

The United States senate is presided over by the Vice-President of the United States, who is elected by the Union at large, as the president is.   It must be observed, however, that neither the chancellor on the woolsack, nor the Vice-President of the United States, as president of the senate, exercises any influence over their respective legislative bodies, that can in any degree be compared to that of the speakers over their houses.   The American senate and the British house of lords allow but very little power in regulating and appointing, to the presiding officer, who interferes only when called upon to do so.[1]

The power of the houses of parliament over persons that are not members, or the privileges of parliament, or of either house, so far as they affect the liberty of individuals and the support of their own power, constitute what is called parliamentary law—an important branch of the common law.   Like all common law, it consists in usage and decisions ; there are

---

fund of uncompromising judicial rectitude in England which has never been so great at any other period of her own history, or excelled in any other country.

[1] This difference in the position of the presiding officers appears, among other things, from the fact that the members of the house of lords address " My lords," and not the chancellor, while usage and positive rules demand that the member of the other house who wishes to speak, shall address " Mr. Speaker," and receive " the floor" from him.   The chancellor would only give the floor if appealed to in case of doubt.   In the United States senate, the president of the senate is, indeed, directly addressed, although occasionally "senators" have been addressed in the course of a speech.   That body, however, appoints its committees, and leaves little influence to the presiding officer, who, it will be remembered, is not a member of the senate, and has a casting vote only.

doubtful points as well as many firmly settled ones. It must be learned from works such as Hatsell's Precedents, etc., Townsend's History of the House of Commons, and others.

As a general remark, it may be stated that, with the rise of liberty in England, the jealousy of the house of commons also rose, and continued during the period of its struggle with the executive; and that, as the power of the house has become confirmed and acknowledged, the jealousy of the house has naturally abated. I very much doubt whether at any earlier period the committee of privileges would have made the same declaration which it made after Lord Cochrane, in 1815, had been arrested by the marshal of the king's bench, while sitting on the privy councillor's bench in the house of commons, prayers not yet having been read. The committee declared that "the privileges of parliament did not appear to have been violated so as to call for the interposition of the house."[1]

The two American houses naturally claim the "power of sending for persons and papers and of examining upon oath," and they have also exercised the power of punishing disturbances of their debates by intruders, and libellers of members or whole houses. But no power to do so is explicitly conferred by the Constitution of the United States.[2]

---

[1] I would refer the general reader, on this and kindred subjects, to the article Parliament, in the Political Dictionary; London, 1846.

[2] This is not the place for discussing the doubts which some have entertained regarding the power of the houses of congress to do that which is possessed by every court of justice, though the lowest, namely, to arrest and punish disturbers. The doubt is simply on the ground that it has not been conferred. But there are certain rights which flow directly from the existence of a thing itself, and some that are the necessary consequence of action and life, and without which neither can manifest itself. A legislative body without the power of sending for persons to be examined by committees, would be forced to legislate, in many cases, in the dark. It is true, that legislative bodies have become tyrannical; but it must not be forgotten that wherever, in the wide range of history, any struggle for liberty has taken place, we find that a struggle to establish the habeas corpus principle has always accompanied it, and that this struggle for securing personal liberty is always against the execu-

Of far greater importance is the body of the rules of procedure and that usage which has gradually grown up as a part of common law, by which the dispatch of parliamentary business and its protection against impassioned hurry are secured, and by which the order and freedom of debate, fairness, and an organic gestation of the laws are intended to be obtained. The development of parliamentary practice, or rules of proceeding and debate, such as it has been developed by England, independently of the executive, and like the rest of the common law, been carried over to our soil, form a most essential part of our Anglican constitutional, parliamentary liberty. This practice, as we will call it for brevity's sake, is not only one of the highest importance for legislatures themselves, but serves as an element of freedom all over the country, in every meeting, small or large, primary or not. It is an important guarantee of liberty, because it serves, like the well-worn and banked bed of a river, which receives the waters that, without it, would either lose their force and use, by spreading over plains, or become ruinous by their impetuosity when meeting with obstruction. Every other nation of antiquity and modern times has severely suffered from not having a parliamentary practice such as the Anglican race possesses, and no one familiar with history and the many attempts to establish liberty on the continent of Europe or in South America, can help observing how essentially important that practice is to us, and how it serves to ease liberty, if we may say so.[1]

---

tive. I do not remember a single case of an established and separate guarantee of personal liberty against parliamentary violence.

The reader is referred to Mr. Justice Story's Comm. on the Const. U. S., chap. xii., and to Chancellor Kent's Commentaries.

[1] The ancients had no parliamentary law and usage. The Greek agora could of course not have it. Mass meetings cannot debate; they can only ratify or refuse proposed measures. It is the same in the democratic Swiss cantons, where the people meet in primary assemblage. See Political Ethics. In the Roman senate was no debating proper. There was rather a succession of set speeches, and I may be permitted to state here that in debating oratory, in replying on the spot, vigorously and

It is not a French "reglement," prescribed by the executive with but little room for self-action; nor does it permit legislative disorder or internal anarchy. It has been often observed that the want of parliamentary practice created infinite mischief in the first French revolution. Dumont mentions that there was not even always a distinct proposition before the convention; and the stormiest sessions, which frequently ended by the worst decrees—the *décrets d'acclamation*—were those in which there were speeches and harangues without propositions. Sir Samuel Romilly[1] says: "If one single rule had been adopted, namely, that every motion should be reduced into writing in the form of a proposition before it was put from the chair, instead of proceeding, as was their constant course, by first resolving the principle as they called it (décreter le principe,) and leaving the drawing up of what they had so resolved (or, as they called it, la redaction) for a subsequent

clearly to an adversary, the best orators of the last and present centuries are greatly superior to the ancients.

Since the publication of the first edition, an American senator, Mr. Edward Everett, has added his testimony to the vital importance of Anglican parliamentary rules. On December 8, 1853, when resolutions with reference to the late Vice-President of the United States, (and, therefore, presiding officer of the senate,) W. Rufus King, were under discussion, Mr. Everett observed, in the course of his remarks :

"In fact, sir, he was highly endowed with what Cicero beautifully commends as the *boni Senatoris prudentia*, the 'wisdom of a good senator;' and in his accurate study and ready application of the rules of parliamentary law, he rendered a service to the country, not perhaps of the most brilliant kind, but assuredly of no secondary importance. There is nothing which so distinguishes the great national race to which we belong, as its aptitude for government by deliberative assemblies ; its willingness, while it asserts the largest liberty of parliamentary right, to respect what the senator from Virginia, in another connection, has called the self-imposed restrictions of parliamentary order ; and I do not think it an exaggeration to say that there is no trait in their character which has proved more conducive to the dispatch of the public business, to the freedom of debate, to the honor of the country—I will say even which has done more to establish and perpetuate constitutional liberty."

[1] He was himself of unmixed French descent, as Lord Brougham observes, although his family had resided for generations in England.

operation, it is astonishing how great an influence it would have had in their debates and on their measures."[1]

The great importance of the subject and the general superiority of the English parliamentary practice have been acknowledged by French writers, practically acquainted with it; especially by the author of a work the full title of which I shall give in a note, because it shows its interesting contents.[2]

Foreigners frequently express their surprise at the ease with which, in our country, meetings, societies, bodies, communities, and even territories[3] self-constitute and organize themselves; and transact business without violence, and without any force in the hands of the majority to coerce the minority, or in the hands of the minority to protect itself against the majority. One of the chief reasons of this phenomenon is the universal familiarity of our people with parliamentary practice, which may be observed on board of any steamboat where a number of persons, entire strangers to one another, proceed to pass some resolution or other, and which they learn even as chil-

---

[1] Memoirs of the Life of Sir Samuel Romilly, etc., 2d edit. vol. i. p. 103.

[2] A Treatise on the Formation of Laws, (Traité de la Confection des Lois,) or an Inquiry into the Rules (Réglements) of the French Legislative Assemblies, compared with the Parliamentary Forms of England, the United States, Belgium, Spain, Switzerland, etc., by Ph. Vallette, Advocate, etc., and Secretary of the Presidency of the Chamber of Deputies, and by Benat Saint-Martin, Advocate, etc., 2d edit., Paris, 1839; with the words of Mr. Dupin, who long presided over the chamber, as motto, "The excellence of laws depends especially upon the care taken in the elaboration of the bills. The drawing up of laws constitutes a large share of their efficiency."

[3] As a striking instance may be mentioned the whole procedure of the people of Oregon, when congress omitted to organize the territory, and ultimately "Organic Laws" were adopted "until such time as the United States of America extend their jurisdiction over us." They were printed by the senate, May 21, 1846, and, although consisting of a few pages only, form a document of great interest to the political philosopher in more than one respect. A French statesman of mark wrote to the author, years ago, from Algeria: "I wish your way of organizing distant territories, or of allowing themselves to organize, could be transplanted to this colony." Justice requires to add now (1859) that our Kansas troubles had not then occurred.

dren. There are few schools the members of which have not formed some debating society, in which parliamentary forms are observed, and in which the rigorously enforced fine impresses upon the boy of ten or eleven years the rules which the man of forty follows as naturally as he bows to an acquaintance.[1]

The Constitution of the United States says that "each house may determine the rules of its proceedings, punish its members for disorderly behavior, and, with the concurrence of two-thirds, expel a member." If, however, the parliamentary practice had not already been spread over the colonies, like the common law itself, this power, justly and necessarily conferred on each house, would have been of comparatively little advantage. Parliamentary practice—that *ars obstetrix animarum*, as Mr. Bentham calls it, although it ought to be called the obstetric art of united bodies of men, for in this lies the difficulty—is not a thing to be invented nor to be decreed, but must be developed.[2]

---

[1] An excellent book of its kind is the small work of Judge L. S. Cushing, Rules of Proceeding and Debate in Deliberative Assemblies, Boston, Mass. It has gone through many editions. The same author published in 1855, Law and Practice of Legislative Assemblies in the United States.

[2] Mr. Jeremy Bentham's Tactique des Assemblées Legislative, edited by E. Dumont, Geneva, 1816, is no pure invention, and could have been written by an Englishman or American only.

See also Mr. Jefferson's Manual of Parliamentary Practice for the use of the senate of the United States.

There is a very curious book, Parliamentary Logic, etc., by Right Hon. W. Gerard Hamilton, (called in his time Single-Speech Hamilton,) with considerations on the Corn Laws, by Dr. Samuel Johnson; London, 1808. The copy which I own belonged to Dr. Thomas Cooper. That distinguished man has written the following remark on the fly-leaf: "This book contains the theory of deception in parliamentary debate; how to get the better of your opponent, and how to make the *worse* appear the *better* reason. It is the well-written work of a hackneyed politician. . . . . . The counterpart to it is the admirable tract of Mr. Jeremy Bentham on Parliamentary Logic, the book of *Fallacies*. No politician ought to be ignorant of the one book or the other. They are *well* worth (not perusing, but) studying. T. C."

It is not only a guarantee of the free share of every representative in the legislation of his country, but it is also, as has been indicated, a guarantee, for the people, that its legislature remain in its proper bounds, and that the laws be not decreed as the effects of mere impulse or passion.

It is a psychological fact that whatever interests or excites a number of separate individuals will interest or excite them still more when brought together. They countenance one another; and that psychical reduplication which, for bad or good, produces so great an effect wherever individuals of the same mind or acting under the same impulse come in close contact, must be guarded against in representative assemblies. Parliamentary practice, as we possess it, is as efficient a means to calm and to regulate these excitements, as the laws of evidence and the procedure of courts are in tempering exciting trials and impassioned pleadings.

These remarks may fitly conclude with the words of Judge Story, which he uttered when he left the speaker's chair of the Massachusetts house of representatives, to take his seat on the bench of the supreme court of the United States. They ought to be remembered by every one on both sides of the Atlantic that prizes practical and practicable liberty:

" Cheered, indeed, by your kindness, I have been able, in controversies, marked with peculiar political zeal, to appreciate the excellence of those established rules which invite liberal discussions, but define the boundary of right, and check the intemperance of debate. I have learned that the rigid enforcement of these rules, while it enables the majority to mature their measures with wisdom and dignity, is the only barrier of the rights of the minority against the encroachments of power and ambition. If anything can restrain the impetuosity of triumph, or the vehemence of opposition—if anything can awaken the glow of oratory, and the spirit of virtue—if anything can preserve the courtesy of generous minds amidst the rivalries and jealousies of contending parties, it will be found in the protection with which these rules encircle and shield every member of the legislative body. Permit me, therefore, with the sincerity of a parting friend, earnestly to recommend to your attention a steady adherence to these venerable usages."[1]

35. If parliamentary practice is a guarantee of liberty by excluding, in a high degree, impassioned legislation, and aiding in embodying, in the law, the collective mind of the legislature, the principle of two houses, or the bicameral system, as Mr. Bentham has called it, is another and no less efficient guarantee.

Practical knowledge alone can show the whole advantage of this Anglican principle, according to which we equally discard the idea of three and four estates, and of one house only. Both are equally and essentially un-Anglican.   Although, however, practice alone can show the whole advantage that may be derived from the system of two houses, it must appear, nevertheless, as a striking fact to every inquirer in distant countries, that not only has the system of two houses historically developed itself in England, but it has been adopted by the United States, and all the states as well as by the single territories, and by all the British colonies, where local legislatures exist. We may mention even the African state of Liberia. The bicameral system accompanies the Anglican race like the common law,[2] and everywhere it succeeds; while no one attempt at introducing the unicameral system, in larger countries, has so far succeeded. France, Spain, Naples, Portugal,—in all these countries it has been tried, and everywhere it has failed.   The idea of one house flows from that of the unity of power, so popular in France. The bicameral system is called by the advocates of democratic unity of power an aristocratic institution. This is an utter mistake. In reality it is a truly popular principle to insist on

---

[1] Life and Letters of Joseph Story; Boston, Mass., 1851, vol. i. p. 203.

[2] No instance illustrating this fact is perhaps more striking than the meeting of settlers in Oregon territory, when congress had neglected to provide for them, as has been mentioned in a previous note. The people met for the purpose of establishing some legislature for themselves, and at once adopted the principle of two houses. It is to us as natural as the jury.

the protection of a legislature divided into two houses; and as to the historical view of the question, it is sufficient to state that two houses have been insisted upon and rejected by all parties, aristocratic and popular, according to the circumstances of the times. In this the principle resembles the instruction of the representative by his constituents. This too has been insisted on and rejected by all parties at different periods.

Attempts were made in our earlier times to establish a single house, for instance in Pennsylvania,[1] but the practical and sober sense of the Anglican people led them back to the two houses. The danger was perhaps not trifling. " During the American revolution, there grew up a party in every state who, ignorant of this great political truth, opposed the notion that our state constitutions should be conformed to the English model. No less a person than Dr. Franklin was of this party. And through his influence, in a great measure, Pennsylvania adopted a government of a single legislative assembly. When he went to Paris, he took with him the different American constitutions. Mr. Turgot, to whom he showed them, disregarding, as Dr. Franklin had done, the voice of history, approved that of Pennsylvania, and condemned those framed after the English constitution. In a letter to Dr. Price of England, Mr. Turgot says: ' I am not satisfied with the constitutions which have hitherto been formed for the different states of America. By most of them, the customs of England are imitated without any particular motive. Instead of collecting all authority into one centre, that of the nation, they established different bodies, a body of representatives, a council, and a governor, because there is in England, a house of commons, a house of lords, and a king. They endeavored to balance three different·powers, as if this equilibrium, which in

---

[1] It was at the period when Dr. Franklin asked why people would put horses not only before, but also behind the wagon, pulling in opposite directions? The true answer would have been, that whenever a vehicle is pulled down an inclined plane we actually do employ an impeding force to prevent its being dashed to pieces.

England may be a necessary check to the enormous influence of royalty, could be of any use in republics founded upon the equality of all the citizens, and as if establishing different orders of men was not a source of divisions and disputes.' This notion of a single national assembly began to gain ground so rapidly in America, that the elder Adams, in order to counteract it, in the beginning of the year 1787 published his Defence of the American Constitutions. In the September of the same year, the national convention changed the federal constitution from the single assembly of the confederacy, to a government formed after the English model. Pennsylvania changed her government also; and all the states and territories of this vast confederacy have now governments framed on the plan of the English."[1]

Mr. de Lamartine pronounced the true reason why we ought to hold fast to the bicameral system, although he spoke against it. When in the last French constituent assembly Mr. Odillon Barrot had urged with ability the adoption of two houses, Mr. de Lamartine replied that the great principle of unity (he meant, no doubt, of centralization) required the establishment of one house, and that, unless the legislature was vested in one house alone, it would be too difficult to make it pass over from a simple legislature to an assembly with

---

[1] I have quoted this long passage from the First Report of the Commissioners, appointed by the General Assembly of Maryland, to revise, simplify and abridge the Rules of Practice, Pleadings, etc. in the courts of the State, Frederic City, Md., 1855 — a work important also with reference to the subject of codification. This first report is believed to have been written by Mr. Samuel Tyler, one of the commissioners, a gentleman alike distinguished as advocate and writer on philosophy. His last work on the Progress of Philosophy in the Past and the Future, entitles him to a place among the profoundest writers on philosophy. His friend, the late Sir William Hamilton, acknowledged his great merits.

The reader is referred to de Tocqueville's Ancien Régime for numerous passages, showing how general the error of Turgot was in France, and how sincerely the Anglican diversity, necessarily accompanying self-government, was disrelished by the French, profoundly worshipping, not only unity of power, but also uniformity of action.

dictatorial power.   This is precisely the danger to be avoided.[1]
Parliamentary practice and the two-house system are subjects
of such magnitude that it is impossible here, where they are
mentioned as gurantees, to enter upon details; but I cannot
dismiss them without recommending them to the serious and
repeated attention of every one who may have looked upon
them as accidents rather than essentials.   The French acknowledge as the first thing to be obtained, power, force; and their
philosophical writers, such as Rousseau, seek, almost exclusively, a philosophical or legitimate source of that power.
Hence their view of universal suffrage, and the power, be that
of an all-powerful Cæsar, or of a concentrated single cham-

---

[1] The speech was delivered on the 27th September, 1848.   Mr. de Lamartine speaks of a division of the sovereignty into two parts, by two
houses !   Poor sovereignty !   What strange things have been imagined
under that word !   If the reader can find access to that speech, I advise
him to peruse it, for it is curious from beginning to end, especially as
coming from a person who for a time was one of the rulers of France.
His exact words are these.   Speaking of domestic dangers, he says : "To
such a danger you must not think of opposing two or three powers.
That which ought to oppose it, is a direct dictatorship, uniting within its
hand all the powers of the state."   He adds more of the kind, but this
extract will suffice.

Mr. Lamartine committed another grave error.   He said that two
houses in the United States were natural, because we are a confederacy,
and the senate was established to represent the states as such.   But he
seems not to have been aware that all our states, in their unitary character, have established the same system, and that it is as natural to
the men on the shores of the Pacific as to those in Maine, or to the
settlers on the Swan River.

I ought in justice to add, however, that in 1850 Mr. de Lamartine
said, in his Counsellor of the People, that he was now for two houses,
and that he had been for one house in 1848 because he wanted a dictatorial power ; and, added he, La dictature ne se divise pas.   But how
can a dictatorship be called undivided, when it belongs to a house composed of eight hundred members ?   And must not, in the nature of
things, a division of execution always take place ?   It is surprising that
something temporarily desired for a dictatorship should have been insisted upon by Mr. Lamartine with so much vehemence as an integral
part of the fundamental law, or was peradventure the constitution of
1848 intended not to last ?

ber, all-providing and all-penetrating, when once established, arising out of it. Hence the prosecution of Mr. de Montalembert, as having attacked the legitimate power of the emperor, when he had written against the French view of universal suffrage. The Anglicans seek, first of all, for freedom, for self-government; and then for guarantees of these.

Experience has proved to the English and Americans that to have a measure discussed entirely de novo by a different set of men, with equal powers, and combined upon a different basis—that this, and the three readings, with notice and leave of bringing in, and the going into committee before the third reading, have a wonderful effect in sifting, moderating, discovering, and in enlightening the country. Take the history of any great act of parliament or congress, and test what has been asserted. This effect of two houses, and the rules of procedure just mentioned, are indeed like so many pillars to the fabric of liberty.

The question has been asked, why should there be two chambers? What philosophical principle is there enshrined in this number? All we would answer is, that it has been found that more than one house is necessary, and more than two is too many. Three and even four houses belong to the medieval estates and to the deputative, not to the modern national representative system. The mischief of three houses is as great as that of three parties. The weakest becomes the deciding one by a casting vote. And one house only belongs to centralization. It is incompatible with a government of a co-operative or concurrent character, which we hold to be the government of freedom.

I cannot agree with the opinion expressed by Lord Brougham in his work on Political Philosophy, that it is essentially necessary that the composition of the two houses should be based upon entirely different principles, meaning that the one ought not to be elective, and that it ought to represent entirely different interests. A thorough discussion of this subject belongs to the province of politics proper, but I ask the reader's indulgence for a few moments.

If the two houses were elected for the same period, and by the same electors, they would amount in practice to little more than two committees of the same house; but we want two bona fide different houses, representing the impulse as well as the continuity, the progress and the conservatism, the onward zeal and the retentive element, innovation and adhesion, which must ever form integral elements of all civilization. One house, therefore, ought to be large; the other, comparatively small, and elected or appointed for a longer time. Now, as to the right of sitting in the smaller or upper house, of longer duration, there are different modes of bestowing it. It may be hereditary, as the English peers proper are hereditary; or the members may have seats for life, and in their personal capacity, as the French peers had under the charter. This is probably the worst of all these methods. It gives great power to the crown and keeps the house of peers in a state of submission, which hereditary peers generally do not know. Or, again, the members may be elected for life by a class, as Scottish representative peers are elected by the Scottish nobility for the British house of peers; or the members may be similarly elected for one parliament alone, as the Irish peers are that sit in parliament; or the people may elect senators for life, or for a shorter time, as the senators of Belgium, and all the senators in our state, are; or, lastly, the members of the house we are speaking of may be elected, not by the people in their primary capacity, but by different bodies, such as our senators of congress are. The senators of the United States are elected by the states, as states, consequently an equal number of representing senators is given to each state irrespective of its size or population.

It would be very difficult to pronounce the one or the other principle absolutely the best, without references to circumstances, and we are sure that Lord Brougham would be the last man that would maintain the absolute necessity of having a hereditary peerage wherever two houses exist. As to the different classes, or interests, however, which ought to be represented, I would only state that the idea belongs to the middle ages, and, if adopted, would lead at once to several estates again. It is hostile to the idea of two houses only. Why represent the different interests of the nation in two houses? Are there not more broad, national interests? It would be difficult indeed to understand why the land-owner in present England should have his house and not the manufacturer, the merchant, the wide educational interest, the sanitary interest, the artisan, the literary interest, with the journalism. The excellence of the bicameral system in our representative (and not deputative) government does not rest on the representation of different interests, but on the different modes of composing the houses and their different duration.

On the other hand, we may observe that, when in 1848 the French established a legislature of one house, they found themselves obliged to establish, by the constitution, a council of state, as the Athenians established the council (boule) to aid the general assembly (ecclesia.) The French know, instinctively if not otherwise, that a single house of French representatives would be exposed to the rashest legislation. The council of state, however, is not public, the members are appointed by the executive; in one word, what was gained? Much indeed was lost.

Whether the representative is the representative of his immediate constituents or of the nation at large, whether he ought to obey instructions sent him by his constituents—on these and other subjects connected with them I have treated at great length in my Political Ethics. I shall simply mention here the fact that civil liberty distinctly requires that the representative be the representative of his political society at large, and not of his election district. The idea that he merely represents his immediate constituents is an idea which belongs to the middle ages and their deputative system,—not to our far nobler representative system. The representative is not a deputy sent with simple powers of attorney, as the deputy of the middle ages was.

36. I hesitate whether I ought to enumerate the Veto as an Anglican guarantee of liberty. I hold it to be in our political system a check upon the legislature, and therefore a protec-

tion of the citizen; one that can be abused, and probably has been abused; but everything intrusted to the hands of man may be abused. The question concerns its probable average operation.

Although the veto is thus acknowledged to be an important part of our polity, it may be said no longer to exist in England. It has been mentioned before, that should parliament pass a bill from which the ministers believe the royal assent ought to be withheld, they would not, according to the present usage, expose the king to an open disagreement with the lords and commons, but they would resign, upon which an administration would be formed which would agree with parliament; or parliament would be dissolved, and an " appeal to the country" would be made.

Yet we have received the veto from England, and it is all these considerations which make me hesitate, as I said before, to call the veto an Anglican guarantee.

The use of the veto can become very galling, and at such times we often find the party whose favorite measure has been vetoed vehemently attacking the principle itself. It was thus the whigs in the United States that earnestly spoke and wrote against the principle, when General Jackson declined giving his assent to some measures they considered of great importance, and the democrats were loud in favor of the veto power because it had been used by a president of their own party.

In treating this whole subject much confusion has arisen from the ill-chosen word veto, after the term used by the Roman tribune. The veto of the Roman tribune and the so-called modern veto are not the same. The tribune could veto indeed. When a law was passed he could wholly or partially stop its operation, by the tribunitial *auxilium*, the personal prevention of the action of magistrates in particular cases. To this was added, at a later period, the *intercessio*, by which the tribune could prevent a decree of the senate or a rogation before the comitia from becoming a law. The dispensatory power claimed by the Stuarts would have been the full veto power. The chief of the state in the United States or England, however, has no such power. The law, so soon as it is law, says to every one: Hands off. What we call the veto power, is in reality a power of an abnuent character, and ought to have been called the declinative. But this declinative is possessed in a much greater degree by each house against the other. To make a bill a law the concurrence of three parties is required—that of the two houses and the executive, and this concurrence may be withheld as a matter of course, otherwise it would not be concurrence.

It is a wise provision in our constitution which directs that a bill not having received the president's approval, nevertheless passes into a law if two-thirds of congress adhere to the bill. Many of our state constitutions do not require the concurrence of the executive. This is not felt in many cases as an evil, because the action of the states is limited, but in my opinion it would be an evil day when the veto should be taken from the President of the United States. It would be the beginning of a state of things such as we daily observe with our South American neighbors. The American conditional veto is in a great measure a conciliatory principle with us, as the refusal of supplies is of an eminently conciliatory character in the British polity.

The only case in which our executives have a real vetitive power, is the case of pardon, and most unfortunately it is used in an alarming degree, against the supremacy of the law and the stability of right—both essential to civil liberty. I consider the indiscriminate pardoning, so frequent in many parts of the United States, one of the most hostile things, now at work in our country, to a perfect government of law. In the only case, therefore, in which we have a full veto power, we ought greatly to modify it.[1]

---

[1] I shall append a paper on pardoning—a subject which has become all-important in the United States.

CHAPTER XVIII.

INDEPENDENCE OF THE JUDICIARY. THE LAW, JUS, COMMON LAW.

37. ONE of the main stays of civil liberty, and quite as important as the representative principle, is that of which the independence of the judiciary forms a part, and which we shall call the independence or the freedom of the law—of jus and justice.[1] It is a great element of civil liberty and part of a real government of law, which in its totality has been developed by the Anglican tribe alone. It is this portion of freemen only, on the face of the earth, which enjoys it in its entirety.

In the present case I do not take the term law in the sense in which it was used when we treated of the supremacy of the law. I apply it now to everything that may be said to belong to the wide department of justice. I use it in the sense in which the Anglican lawyer takes it when he says that an opinion, or decision, or act is or is not law, or good law—an adaptation of the word peculiar to the English language. It is not the author's fault that Law must be taken in one and the same essay, in which philosophical accuracy may be expected, in two different meanings.

The word law has obtained this peculiar meaning in our language, otherwise so discriminating in terms appertaining to politics and public matters, chiefly from two reasons. The

---

[1] The lack of a proper word for *jus*, in the English language, induced me to use it on a few occasions in the Political Ethics. The Rev. Dr. W. Whewell, some years later, seems to have felt the same want, adopting in his work on the Elements of Morality, including Polity, London, 1845, the word *jural*, first used in the Political Ethics, where a note explains why I was compelled to form the word.

(206)

first is the serious inconvenience, arising from the fact that our tongue has not two terms for the two very distinct ideas which in Latin are designated by Lex and Jus, in French by Lois and Droit, in German by Gesez and Recht; the second is the fact, of which every Anglican may be proud, that the English jus has developed itself as an independent organism, and continues to do so with undiminished vitality. It is based upon a common law, acknowledged to be above the crown in England, and to be the broad basis of all our own constitutions—a body of law and " practice," in the administration of justice, which has never been deadened by the superinduction of a foreign and closed law, as was the case with the common law of those nations that received the civil law in a body as authority for all unsettled cases. The superinduction of the Latin language extinguished, in a manner not wholly dissimilar, the living common languages of many tribes, or dried up the sources of expansive and formative life contained in them.

The independence of the judges is a term happily of old standing with all political philosophers who have written in our language; but it will be seen that the independence of the judiciary, by which is meant generally a position of the judge independent of the executive or legislative, and chiefly, his appointment for life, or immovability by the executive, and frequently, the prohibition of a decrease or increase of his salary after his appointment has taken place—that this independence of the judiciary forms but a part of what I have been obliged to call the far more comprehensive Independence of the Law.[1]

---

[1] When therefore I published a small work on this subject, during my visit to Germany, in 1848, I called it *Die Unabhängigkeit der Justiz oder die Freiheit des Rechts*, Heidelberg, 1848. Literally translated, this would be The Independence of Justice and Freedom of the Law. *Justiz* in German, however, does not mean the virtue justice, but the administration of justice; and *Recht* means, in this connection, *jus*, not a single *jus*, but the body of rights and usages, laws and legal practice of a people.

The independence of the law, or the freedom of the jus, in the fullest and widest sense, requires a living common law, a clear division of the judiciary from other powers, the public accusatorial process, the independence of the judge, the trial by jury, and an independent position of the advocate, These subjects will be treated in the order in which they have .been enumerated here.

A living common law is, as has been indicated, like a living common language, like a living common architecture, like a living common literature. It has the principle of its own organic vitality, and of formative as well as assimilative expansion within itself. It consists in the customs and usages of the people, the decisions which have been made accordingly in the course of administering justice itself, the principles which reason demands and practice applies to ever-varying circumstances, and the administration of justice which has developed itself gradually and steadily. It requires, therefore, self-interpretation or interpretation by the judiciary itself, the principle of the precedent and "practice" acknowledged as of an authoritative character, and not merely winked at; and, in general, it requires the non-interference of other branches of the government or any dictating power. The Roman law itself consisted of these elements and was developed in this manner so long as it was a living thing.

The common law acknowledges statute or enacted law in the broadest sense, but it retains its own vitality even with reference to the lex scripta in this, that it decides by its own organism and upon its own principles, on the interpretation of the statute when applied to concrete and complex cases. All that is pronounced in human language requires constant interpretation, except mathematics.[1] Even if the English law should be codified, as at this moment the question of codification has been brought before parliament, the living

---

[1] Hence the peculiar power and the peculiar narrowness of the branch. I have treated of this subject, and the unceasing necessity of interpretation, at the beginning of my Principles of Interpretation and Construction in Law and Politics, Boston, 1839.

common law would lose as little of its own inherent vigor and expansiveness, as it has lost in Massachusetts or New York by the "Revised Statutes" of those states. The difference between such a code in England and the codes which have been promulgated on the continent of Europe, would always consist in this, that the English digest would have a retrospective character. It would be the garnering of a crop; but the living orchard is expected to bear new fruits, while it was the pronounced intention of the promulgators of continental codices to prevent interpretation, for which end it was ordained analogously to the rule of the civil law, that recourse should be had in all doubtful cases to the legislator, that is, to the emperor or king, or to the officer appointed by the monarch for that purpose.[1]

---

[1] I cannot avoid referring again to my work on the Principles of Interpretation and Construction in Law and Politics, where this subject is repeatedly treated of, as it forms one of vital importance in all law, liberty, politics and self-government. I have given there instances of prohibited commenting and even lecturing, in the universities, on the codes. This is the pervading spirit of the civil law as it was adopted by modern nations. It is a necessary and combined consequence of the principle contained in the Justinian code itself, namely, that the emperor is the executive, legislator and all; that, therefore, no self-development of the law, such as had indeed produced the Roman jus, could any longer be allowed; and of the fact that the Roman law was adopted as a finished system from abroad. The principle of non-interpretation by the courts prevails for the same reasons in the canon law. I give the following as an interesting instance:

The bull of Pope Pius IV., 26 January, 1564, sanctioning and proclaiming the canons and decrees of the Council of Trent, contains also the prohibition to publish interpretations and dissertations on these canons and decrees. The words of the bull, which correspond exactly to the authority reserved by government concerning the understanding of the law, where codes have been introduced, and the common law principle is not acknowledged, are these:

"Ad vitandam præterea perversionem et confusionem, quæ oriri posset, si unicuique liceret, prout ei liberet, in decreta Concilii commentarios et interpretationes suas edere, Apostolica auctoritate inhibemus omnibus—ne quis sine auctoritate nostra audeat ullos commentarios, glossas, admonitiones, scholia, ullumve interpretationis genus super

14

Judge Story has very clearly expressed what a code, with reference to the English law, ought to be. He says : "Not-withstanding all that is said to the contrary, I am a decided friend to codification, so as to fix in a text the law as it is, and ought to be, as far as it has gone, and leave new cases to furnish new doctrines as they arise and reduce these again at distant intervals into the text."[1]

Locke, on the other hand, expresses the view which is almost

ipsius Concilii decretis, quocunque modo, edere, aut quidquam quocun-que nomine, etiam sub prætexta majoris decretorum corroberationis, aut executionis, aliove quæestio colore, statuere."

The papal bull goes on declaring that if there be any obscurity in the decrees the doubter shall ascend to the place which the Lord has ap-pointed, viz., the apostolic see, and that the pope will solve the doubts.

[1] Life and Letters of Judge Story, vol. i. p. 448. The necessity of proper codification has appeared more and more clearly to the English mind, since the work was first published, and many preparatory steps have been taken. In the month of August Lord Chancellor Cranworth presented a report to the lords of which he said, that in the first place, a list had been prepared of all the statutes not obsolete, nor for tem-porary and local but for general purposes, which have been passed since Magna Charta. The number is 16,000; but, taking away 5300 repealed or virtually repealed, a number besides those which relate to Scotland or Ireland exclusively, and 3900 which the commissioners have not determined on, there remain, say 2500 acts for consolidation ; and these have been analyzed. As there is some difference of opinion as to the best mode of consolidation, specimens on different principles had been prepared ; and one of these, a digest of the law of distress for rent, was in the re port. Mr. Coode, he says, has completed a digest of the poor-laws. What Lord Cranworth then proposed was to see whether the whole of the provisions relating to one subject might not be put into one statute. Each of the commissioners had been requested to take a subject and frame a scheme of consolidation with that view.

A very interesting speech on this and cognate topics, was made in February, 1856, in the house of commons, by Mr. Napier, attorney-general of Ireland, on the introduction of his motion:

"That, in the opinion of this house, as a measure of administrative reform, provision should be made for an efficient and responsible depart-ment of public justice, with a view to secure the skilful preparation and proper structure of parliamentary bills, and promote the progressive amendment of the laws of the United Kingdom."

always taken by philosophers who stop short with theory and do not add the necessary considerations of the statesman and friend of practical liberty, when he proposed the following passage in the constitution he drew up for South Carolina: "Since multiplicity of comments as well as of laws have great inconvenience, and serve only to obscure and perplex, all manner of comments and expositions, on any part of these fundamental constitutions, or on any part of the common or statute laws of Carolina, are absolutely prohibited."[1]

This is quite as strong as the Bavarian code or the pope's decree, mentioned in a previous note. The fact is simply this: on the one hand analyzing and systematizing are attributes of humanity, and development, growth, assimilation and adaptation are the very elements of life. Man has to lay out his road between the two, and will, naturally, incline more to the one or the other according to the bias of his mind or the general course of reasoning common to his peculiar science or profession.

If interpretation, which takes place when the general rule is applied to a real case, is not left to the law itself, the law ceases to have its own life, and the citizen ceases strictly to live under the law. He lives under the dictating or interfering power, because each practical case, that is, each time that the rule passes over from an abstraction into a reality, is subject to that power, be it, as it generally is, the executive or the legislative. This does not exclude what is called authentic interpretation, or interpretation by the legislature itself, for future cases. Accurately speaking, authentic interpretation is no interpretation, but rather additional legislation. We would distinctly exclude, however, retrospective authentic interpretation; for this amounts, indeed, to an application of the law by the legislature, and is incompatible with a true government of law. It is obvious that the same holds with reference to all power, whether monarchical or popular. The

---

[1] Locke's Constitution for South Carolina, 1669, paragraph 80.

law must be the lord and our "earthly god," and not a man, a set of men, or the multitude.

As to the principle of the precedent, it is one of the elements of all development, contradistinguished from dictation and mere command. Everything that is a progressive continuum requires the precedent. A precedent in law is an ascertained principle applied to a new class of cases, which in the variety of practical life has offered itself. It rests on law and reason, which is law itself. It is not absolute. It does not possess binding power merely as a fact, or as an occurrence. If that were the case, Anaximander would have been right when he said that Themis was standing by the throne of Alexander to stamp with right and justice whatever he did. Nor is it unchangeable. A precedent can be overruled. But again, it must be done by the law itself, and that which upsets the precedent cannot otherwise than become, in the independent life of the law, precedent in turn.[1]

The continental lawyers have a great fear of the precedent, but they forget that their almost worshipped Roman law itself was built up by precedent. Indeed, they do not comprehend the nature of the precedent, its origin and its power, as an element of a free jus. They frequently point to the fact that the most tyrannical acts of the Stuarts were founded upon real or presumed precedents, and that crown lawyers helped in the nefarious work ; but they forget that British liberty was also rescued from despotism in a great measure by lawyers resting on the common law. Nothing gave to the popular party more strength than the precedent. On this particular subject, and on the nature of the precedent and the distinction of the legal from the executive precedent, as well as the eminent danger of regarding a mere fact as a precedent, I have

---

[1] Dr. Greenleaf published, in Portland, Maine, 1821, A Collection of Cases overruled, doubted, or limited in their application, taken from American and English Reports. Several subsequent editions have been published, with additions, for which Dr. Greenleaf, however, has declared himself irresponsible.

fully treated in two other works.[1] The present work does not
permit me to enter more fully on the subject, or to repeat what
I have there said. A truth of the weightiest importance it
remains, that liberty and steady progression require the principle of the precedent in all spheres. It is one of the roots
with which the tree of liberty fastens in the soil of real life,
and through which it receives the sap of fresh existence. It
is the weapon by which interference is warded of. The principle of the precedent is eminently philosophical. The English
constitution would not have developed itself without it. What
is called the English constitution consists of the fundamentals
of the British polity laid down in custom, precedent, decisions, and statutes; and the common law in it is a far greater
portion than the statute law. The English constitution is
chiefly a common law constitution, and this reflex of a continuous society in a continuous law is more truly "philosophical," than the theoretic and systematic but lifeless constitutions
of recent France.

Every idea has its caricature, and the more unfailingly so,
the more actively and practically the idea is working in real
life. It is, therefore, natural that we should meet with caricatures of the precedent especially in England, as the English
have been obliged to build up slowly and gradually that system
of liberty and the independence of the law, which we have
carried over to this country in a body, and which we have farther developed. When we read that at every opening of a new
parliament a committee of the commons proceeds—lantern in
hand—to the cellar under the house, to see whether no modern
Guy Fawkes has collected combustibles there for the purpose of
exploding parliament, because the thing had been done under
James I., we must acknowledge the procedure more pitiful,
though far more innocent, than Alexander's dragging the body
of the gallant Betis at the wheels of his chariot round the
walls of Gaza, in order to follow the precedent of his progeni-
tor Achilles. But this *is* caricature, and it is unphilosophical

[1] In my Ethics, and especially in my Princ.ples of Legal and Political Interpretation and Construction.

to point at the case, in order to prove the futility or mischief of the precedent. It is a proper subject for Punch to exterminate such farces, not for us to discuss them, any more than seriously treating the French publicist, who, speaking of the intrigues of the legitimists, lately said that the elder Bourbons should remember that Louis Napoleon had *created for himself* a formidable precedent, in the spoliation of the Orleans branch. Nero's fiddle might at this rate legalize the sentimental burning of any capital.

The precedent has been called judge-made law, and as such deprecated. A more correct term would be court-evolved law. If the precedent is bad, let it be overruled by all means, or let the legislature regulate the matter by statute. Bacon's dictum, already quoted, that the worst of things is the apotheosis of error, applies to the bad precedent as forcibly as to any other error, but the difficulty is not avoided by simply disavowing the precedent. Some one must decide. Now is it better that government or a "minister of justice" shall lay down a rule in the style of the civil law, or that the principle shall be decided in court by the whole organism established to give reality and practical life to justice, and in the natural course of things?

Continental jurists, when they compare the civil law with the common law, always commit this error, that they merely compare the contents of the two great systems of law, on which I shall presently say a few words; whilst they invariably forget to add to the comparisons this difference, that the civil law, where it now exists, has been introduced as a dead and foreign law; it is a matter of learned study, of antiquity; whereas the common law is a living, vigorous law of a living people. It is this that constitutes more than half its excellence; and though we should have brought from England all else, our liberty, had we adopted the civil law, would have had a very precarious existence. Judge Story relates " as perfectly well authenticated, that President (John) Adams, when he was Vice-President of the United States, and Blount's conspiracy was before the senate, and the question whether the common law was to be adopted was discussed before that body, emphatically exclaimed, when all looked at him for his opinion as that of a great lawyer, that if he had ever imagined that the common law had not by the revolution become the law of the United States under the new government, he never would have drawn his sword in the contest. So dear to him were the great privileges which that law recognized and enforced."[1]

A common law, to be a real advantage to the people, must be a general law, and the judicial organism must contain that organic arrangement by which confusion and consequent insecurity is prevented. Without it the common law, as any other system of law, ceases proportionately to be a protection of the citizen; while the gradual generalization of the law, in the respective countries occupied by our race, as well as the steady extension and internal growth of international law, form one of the most important topics of that portion of our history which, for want of better terms, may be called the nationalization and uniformation of our race, in governments, languages, literature and law systems.

The civil law excels the common law in some points. Where the relations of property are concerned, it reasons clearly and its language is admirable, but as to personal rights, the freedom of the citizen, the trial, the independence of the law, the principles of self-government, and the supremacy of the law, the common law is incomparably superior.[2]

---

[1] Page 299, vol. i., Life and Letters of Joseph Story.

[2] The civil law, a law of wisdom but of servitude ; the law of a great commercial empire, digested in the days of Justinian, and containing all the principles of justice and equity suited to the relations of men in society with each other; but a law under which the head of government was "Imperator Augustus, legibus solutus."—John Quincy Adams, seventh President of the United States, in a letter to Judge Story, page 20, vol. ii., Life and Letters of Judge Story.

The young American reader is recommended to peruse a letter to a young friend, by Mr. Legaré, first published in the National Intelligencer, in which he urges the study of the Civil Law as one of the best means of mental legal training. That distinguished advocate told the author that whenever he was peculiarly complimented on an argument in civil suits

Nor has the civil law remained without its influence, but it never superseded the common law. The common law remained a living system, and it assimilated to itself parts of the civil law as it assimilates any other element. For instance, Judge Story, in one of his essays, says: The doctrine of bailments, too, was almost struck out at a single beat by Lord Holt,[1] who had the good sense to incorporate into the English code that system which the text and the commentaries of the civil law had already built up on the continent of Europe.[2]

The common law is all the time expanding and improving. I have given a very interesting instance of this fact, in the law of whalers, which has developed itself among the hardy hunters of the Pacific,[3] and has been acknowledged, when the proper occasion offered itself, in the courts of Massachusetts.[4]

---

or had gained a very difficult case, he could trace the reason to his having thoroughly studied the civil law in his younger days in Europe. Mr. Legaré also wrote an extensive article on Roman Law and Legislation in the Southern Review.

[1] The case of Coggs vs. Bernard, 2 ed. Raym. R. 909—note by Judge Story.

[2] Story's Miscellaneous Writings, p. 224.

[3] In a similar, though in a far less interesting way, I observe that a whole code has established itself for the extensive sale of books at auction in London. It is a real specimen of the genius of one part of common law.

[4] See Article Common Law, in the Encyclopædia Americana. It was written, as many others on subjects of law, by my lamented friend, Judge Story. An opportunity has never offered itself to me publicly to acknowledge the great obligation under which I am to that distinguished jurist, for the assistance he most readily and cheerfully gave me in editing the Americana. I shall never forget the offer he made to contribute some articles when I complained of my embarrassment as to getting proper articles on the main subjects of law, for my work intended for the general reader. Many of them were sent from Washington, while he was fully occupied with the important business of the supreme court. He himself made out the list of articles to be contributed by him, and I do not remember ever having been obliged to wait for one. The only condition this kind-hearted man made was that I should not publish the fact that he had contributed the articles in the work until some period subsequent to their appearance. They have met with much approbation, and I hope I am not guilty of indiscretion, if I state here that

The idea of a common law, with its own inherent vitality and independence is, as a matter of course, wholly disavowed by those who follow the French views, and who, as we have seen, strive above all for union of force, and who consider the essence of democracy to consist in absolute equality concentrated in absolute dominion, whether of the majority, or of one to whom the majority has transferred the absolute power—the democratic Cæsar. Those American writers, therefore, who take this Gallican or Rousseau's view of democracy, share with the French this hostility to the common law. It was rifest at the time of the French revolution, since which time I believe it may be affirmed that it has greatly subsided. Yet it subsists still, and is occasionally uttered with an energy which surprises those who believe that the severest lesson taught by the first half of the nineteenth century, is, perhaps, that absolute democracy has no connection with liberty.[1]

another friend, a distinguished orator and lawyer, the Hon. William C. Preston, has repeatedly expressed his admiration of them.

The contributions of Judge Story to the Americana " comprise more than 120 pages, closely printed in double columns. But a higher interest than that growing out of their intrinsic worth belongs to them. They were labors dedicated purely to friendship, and illustrate a generosity which is as beautiful as it is rare." To these words, copied from p. 27, vol. ii. of Life and Letters of Joseph Story, where a list of all his contributions may be found, I may add that Judge Story made his offer at a time when he to whom it was made was known to very few persons in this country, and had but lately arrived here; and that Judge Story took at once the liveliest and most active interest in the whole enterprise, and contributed much to cheer on the stranger in his arduous task.

[1] Theory of Politics: An Inquiry into the Foundations of Governments, and the Causes and Progress of Political Revolutions. By Richard Hildreth, author of "The History of the United States of America," etc.; New York, 1853. In this work the reader will find the opinion maintained that the practical working of a democratic government in our own country is obstructed by several disturbing causes, of which the greatest is the common law—"a scheme directly hostile to the spirit of democracy," and therefore, "under an enlightened democratical government, entirely out of place."

CHAPTER XIX.

INDEPENDENCE OF JUS, SELF-DEVELOPMENT OF LAW CON-
TINUED.   ACCUSATORIAL AND INQUISITORIAL TRIALS.   IN-
DEPENDENCE OF THE JUDGE.

38. THE practice or usage of the administration of justice belongs of right to the development of that administration itself,—avowedly so, and not merely by indulgence or connivance.[1]

In countries in which this important principle is not acknowledged, certain changes, produced by "practice," were and are, nevertheless, winked at, and happily so, because legislation has neglected to make the necessary changes, and humanity will not be outraged.   Thus, in German countries, practice had abolished the application of the torture and fearful punishments, demanded by positive law, long before they were abolished by law.   But it was an exception only demanded by common sense and by a general feeling of humanity.

The common law of the Anglican race, however, assigns the right of development to the courts.   It is part and parcel of the common law.   Innumerable instances and of almost daily occurrence might be given.

The following instance is given here simply because the writer happens to think of it, and because it seems to be an apt illustration.

---

[1] Lord Mansfield, in a note to a Scottish judge, who had asked his advice as to the introduction of trial by jury in civil cases into Scotland, has this remark : "Great alterations in the course of the administration of justice ought to be sparingly made and by degrees, and rather by the court than by the legislature." Lord Campbell's Chief Justices of England, vol. ii. p. 554.

When a court is directed to sit two weeks, and a jury, being summoned to act for the first week of the term, and having retired to consider of their verdict before midnight of Saturday, in the first week, return into court after midnight, and before daylight of Sunday; shall or shall not their verdict be received and published? Shall it be rejected on the ground that Sunday is a dies nonjuridicus? This question was lately decided in South Carolina, not by applying for information to a "minister of justice," or "the emperor," as the civil law directs, but by itself, upon the principle of vital self-sufficiency, by inquiry into its own principles, and an examination of precedents in the whole range of English law, and of statute laws, if there were any exactly applying to the case under consideration.[1]

This principle of self-development is important likewise with reference to a clear division of the judiciary from other branches of the public power. The law is not independent, and consequently the citizen not free, where aught else than the administration of justice belongs to the court, and where anything that belongs to the administration of justice is decided by any one but the courts; where things are decided by aught else than the natural course of law, and where, as has been stated, interpretation or application belongs to any one else than to the judiciary.[2] Hence there ought to be no pressure from without, either by a Stuart sending for the judges to tamper

---

[1] The learned "opinion" of the court of errors was delivered by Judge Wardlaw, Hiller *vs.* English, 4 Strokhart's Reports, Columbia, S. C. 1850. While I was writing this, the supreme court of Massachusetts decided that the "squeeze of the hand" of a dying person, unable to speak, but having been made aware of the fact that the pressure would be taken as an affirmative, may be taken as "a dying declaration," though with caution.—*National Intelligencer*, Washington, May 21, 1853.

[2] Even the Constitution of the French Republic of 1848 said, article 89 :

"Conflicts of privileges and duties between the administrative and judicial authority shall be regulated by a special tribunal composed of members of the court of cassation and of counsellors of state, to be appointed, every three years, in equal number, by the respective bodies to which they belong. This tribunal shall be presided over by the minister of justice."

with them, or to ask them how they would decide a certain case if brought before them, or by a multitude assuming the name of the people. No judge ought to give his opinion before the practical case has come on and been discussed according to law, either to monarch, political party, or suitor. He is an integral part of the law, but only a part, which must not be disconnected from the law. There must not be what are called in France *jugements administratifs*, nor any exraordinary or exceptional courts, as has been mentioned; no judgments by extraordinary commissions, nor any decisions by the executive regarding the application of the law. The following instance is here given, not because the case is of itself important, but because it exhibits the principle with perfect clearness, and because it refers to a royal proclamation—an executive act. The English government had published in 1852 a proclamation against the public appearance of Roman catholics in their religious vestments; and the well-known father Newman asked the secretary for the home department whether this royal proclamation must be considered as directed also against the wearing of "cassocks and cloaks" in the streets of Birmingham, where the Roman catholics had been in the habit of appearing thus "under legal advice" for full four years. The answer of secretary Walpole, one of the ministers, was this:

"I am to inform you, that her majesty's proclamation is directed against all violations of the 26th section of the statute 10th George IV. c. 7, and that if you feel any difficulty in the construction of the enactment, your proper course will be to consult your legal adviser. The secretary of state would not be justified in pronouncing an opinion on the question submitted to him; for if any doubt exists on the point, the decision of it must rest with the courts of law, and not with the government."[1]

There is no country except ours and England where a similar answer would, or indeed could, have been given. Everywhere else it would have been called a destruction of the prin-

---

[1] The letter is dated June 24, 1852.—London *Spectator*, July 3, 1852.

ciple of unity in the government. We call it a small but choice cabinet specimen of a most noble principle, forming an element of our very polities. Nor must it be forgotten that it was a tory government which made this exclusively Anglican reply. The reader will remember the directly opposite principle declared in the bull of Pope Pius IV., quoted before, as well as Locke's provision in his constitution of South Carolina.

39. The public accusatorial[1] trial is another element of the independence of the law, as it is one of the efficient protections of the citizen. By accusatorial process is understood here, not what is generally understood by the term of trial by accusation, (that is, individual accusation,)[2] but that penal trial which places the court wholly above the two parties in criminal matters, as the judge is everywhere placed, at least theoretically so, in civil cases; although the two parties be the prosecuting state or government on the one hand, and the indicted person on the other. The accusatorial trial is thus contradistinguished from the inquisitorial trial, which came into use through the canon law, and especially through the unhallowed witch-trials. In it, the judge inquires, investigates, in one word, is the prosecuting party as well as the judging, and in some cases he is even expected to be likewise the protecting party of the indicted prisoner, thus uniting a triad of functions within himself which amounts to a psychological incongruity.[3]

It may be said that the public accusatorial trial has prevailed or been aimed at by all free nations, modern and ancient. We,

[1] The trial by accusation has a distinct meaning in the English law; still I have adopted the term Accusatorial Trial, in conformity to continental lawyers. A distinct term in contradistinction to the Inquisitorial Trial is necessary, and I prefer Accusatorial to Litigious Trial, which I observe Mr. Stephen uses in an interesting paper on English Criminal Law in the collection of articles published from time to time by former students of the two English universities, Oxford and Cambridge respectively.

[2] There was no public prosecutor in Rome. An individual appeared as accuser, and formed throughout the trial, the prosecuting party. See article Criminal Law, in the Encyclop. Americ.

[3] See Feuerbach on the Jury.

the English, the Netherlanders, the Norwegians, the Swedes, the French, since the first revolution,[1] the Germans in the earlier times, the Greeks and Romans—all have or had it, but it has nowhere been carried out with that consistency which we find in the Anglican penal trial.

The penal trial or procedure is quite as important as the criminal law itself, and with reference to protection, to liberty, to a pervading consciousness of manly rights, it is even more so. This is the chief reason which explains why the English, the freest nation of Europe, endured so long one of the worst and most unphilosophical bodies of criminal laws—so sanguinary in its character that the monstrosity came to pass, of calling all punishments not capital, secondary punishments, as if death were the current penal coin, and the rest of punishments merely the copper to make small "change." The English public accusatorial process, since the expulsion of the Stuarts, contained great guarantees of public security, even while those deficiencies yet existed which have been remedied of late, thanks to Sir Samuel Romilly and Sir Robert Peel. For a long time the English judge was the short bridge of fairness, such as even that was in earlier times, between the cruel treatment of prisoners before and after the trial, for it was only in 1774 that, at the earnest solicitation of Howard, parliament passed an act according to which jailors should be paid from public funds, and not, as theretofore, by fees of the prisoners, so that persons found not guilty should no longer be returned to prison, there to be kept until they could pay the jailor.[2]

We consider that the accusatorial procedure, carried out with consistency and good faith, requires that the accusation itself be not made by the executive, but upon information, by whom-

---

[1] Under the present absolutism, the trial is of course at the mercy of the executive, if the government has any interest in the matter; that is, punishments are inflicted without trial, and certain offences are punished summarily, although punishable with severe visitation of the law.

[2] Such fearful inconsistencies are almost bewildering, but Woe to the penally indicted, was the word of the law on the whole continent. There are similarly glaring and cruel inconsistencies still existing in our proud race.

soever made, through an act, which itself includes a guarantee against frivolous or oppressive accusation; for, as has been stated, trial itself, though followed by acquittal, is a hardship. Hence the importance of a grand jury. The Constitution of the United States ordains that "no person shall be held to answer for a capital or otherwise infamous crime unless on a presentment or indictment of a grand jury." The French penal trial contains no such guarantee, but it has passed over into the fundamental laws of all our states. It is farther necessary that the whole trial be bona fide public and remain bona fide accusatorial. Hence there ought to be no secret examinations of the prisoner by the public prosecutor before the trial, the results of which are to be used at the trial, as this actually forms part of the French penal trial. On the other hand, the judge should remain, during the trial, mere judge, and never become inquirer or part of the prosecution, as this is likewise the case in France. Nor must the prisoner be asked to incriminate himself. All this belongs to the inquisitorial trial. The indictment must be clear, and the prosecuting officer must not be allowed to influence the jury by an address before the witnesses are examined, nor be allowed to bring in irrelevant matter. Lastly, full scope must be given to counsel for prisoner. In all these details most of the accusatorial trials, except the Anglican, are more or less, and some sadly deficient.

40. The independence of the law or administration of justice requires the independence of the judge. All the guarantees we have mentioned support the judge in his independence, and are requisite for it. He cannot be so without a distinct separation of the judiciary from the other branches of the government, without a living, self-sustaining jus, or without the accusatorial procedure. But more is necessary.

The appointment, the duration in office and the removal, must be so that the judge feels no dependence upon any one or anything, except the law itself. This ought to be the case at least in as high a degree as it is possible for human wisdom to make it, or for human frailty to carry out.[1] Where there

---

[1] See "Federalist," No. lxxviii. and sequ.

is a pervading publicity in the political life, an independent bar and self-sustaining jus and administration of justice, with responsible ministers of the executive or a responsible chief magistrate, carefully limited in his power, there is probably as little danger of having bad judges, in giving the appointing power to the executive, especially if, as is the case with us, the senate must confirm the appointment, as in any other mode of appointing—indeed, far less danger than in those other modes which so far have been adopted in most of our states. Where peculiar fitness, peculiar skill and learning, and peculiar aptitude are requisite, it is for many psychological reasons the best to throw the responsibility of appointing, on a few or one, so that it be concentrated, provided these few or the one are made to feel by a proper organization that they are responsible to the public. It is unwise to give such appointments to irresponsible bodies, or to numerous bodies, which, according to the universal deception of a divided responsibility, are not apt to feel the requisite pressure of responsibility, and necessarily must act by groups or parties. If it be done, that hallowed character—a wise and upright judge, a type of humanity, which antiquity and modern times, paganism, mohametanism, the old and new testaments, and the most revered passages of civil history, have ever held as one of the highest and most worthy, soon fades away in the forgetfulness of one of the most important elements of all that is right, honorable, and civilized.[1]

---

[1] Hard as the task of recording the following occurrence may be, it is better that the distemper be known, so that its cure may become possible. In the year 1857, after the Police Law had long been resisted by the mayor of the city of New York, and after the supreme court of the state had declared it constitutional, a convention of one of the largest parties was held in that state, in order to nominate proper candidates for the various offices to be filled by the approaching election. When the judge of the supreme court, who belonged to the same party, and who, on the bench, had decided for the constitutionality of the Police Law, came to be nominated, the nomination was opposed by the person who had been mayor of New York, in a public speech, on the avowed ground that judges had been made elective by the party, although he himself had been adverse to it; that therefore the judges had been drawn into the sphere of party poli-

Laws ought to be the result of mutually modifying compromise; many appointments ought not. Election in such cases, by a large body, would lead to few efficient and truly serviceable ambassadors, and it has long been settled by that nation, which probably knows most about efficient appointment of university professors, the Germans, that their appointment by election, either by a numerous corporation or by the professors of a university themselves, ought to be discarded.[1]

If the appointment of judges ought not to be vested in legislatures, far less ought the people at large to burden themselves with the election of judges. The election of judges by the people themselves, which has now been established in many of the United States, is founded, in my opinion, on a radical error— the confusion of mistaking popular power alone for liberty, and the idea that the more the one is increased, in so much a higher degree will the other be enjoyed. As if all power, no matter what name be given to it, if it sways as power alone,

---

tics. The party had voted against the Police Law, and the judge had declared it constitutional, therefore he ought not to be nominated for re-election. The worst of the Stuarts never said anything worse concerning judges, and the painful account has been given here to show to the younger students of this work how fearfully rapid the decline of national sentiment is. Not more than ten years ago, such sentiments, publicly avowed, would have created universal abhorrence. May my younger readers remember that the curses pronounced on unjust judges extend to those who appoint judges known to be unjust, or adopt a system which must make them so; be they monarchs or the people—execrations and blessings make no distinction between them. That judges ought to judge by the law alone, has been often felt even by absolute monarchs. Frederic II. of Prussia, wrote a letter to the supreme court of his kingdom, enjoining the members to be faithful to their oath, and to do justice in spite of royal demand. The court ordered the letter to be framed and hung up in its hall. Louis XII. of France, in his edict of 1499, concerning the parliaments or high courts of justice, ordained that the law should always be followed, in spite of royal orders, which, as the ordinance says, Importunity may have wrung from the monarch.

[1] The remarks of that wise philosopher, Sir William Hamilton, on the election of professors, in his minor works, apply, so far as I remember them now, with equal force, and probably even with greater strength, to the election of judges.

were not absolutism, and had not the inherent tendency, natural to all power whatever, to increase in absorbing strength! All despotic governments, whether the absolutism rests with an individual or the people, (meaning of course the majority,) strive to make the judiciary dependent upon themselves. Louis XIV. did it, Napoleon did it, and every absolute democracy has done it. All essential, practical liberty, like all sterling law itself, loves the light of common sense and plain experience. All absolutism, if indeed we except the mere brutal despotism of the sword, which despises every question of right, loves mysticism —the mysticism of some divine right. The monarchical absolutists wrap themselves in it, and the popular absolutists do the same. But there is no mystery about the word People. People means an aggregate of individuals to each of whom we deny any divine right, and to each of whom—I, you, and every one included—we justly ascribe frailties, failings, and the possibility of subordinating our judgment and virtue to passion and vice. Each one of them separately stands in need of moderating and protecting laws and constitutions, and all of them unitedly as much as the individual. Where the people are the first and chiefest source of all power, as is the case with us, the electing of judges, and especially their election for a limited time, is nothing less than an invasion of the necessary division of power, and the submission of the judiciary to the influence of the power-holder. It is therefore a diminution of liberty, for it is of the last importance to place the judge between the chief power and the party, and to protect him as the independent, not indeed as the despotic organ of the law.

It has been repeated by some who, not long ago, urged an elective judiciary, that an independent judiciary may be necessary in order to stand between the crown and the people, but that these two parties do not exist with us, and that therefore the judges ought to be dependent on the people, whose simple servants they are. Not to mention that the word people is used in this fallacious argument, as it is often in other cases, for a mysterious unit, which exists nowhere, it may suffice to say that the English judge does not stand between the crown and the people. The crown, opposite the people, is sufficiently weak. The English judge stands between the crown and the accused individual, while with us the judge stands between the people and the individual, which creates a far greater difficulty. To resist the crown is considered patriotic, heroic; to resist the people (and frequently, nay in most excited cases, this means only a loud or impassioned portion of them,) is considered unpatriotic, mean, and even treasonable.

An independent judiciary is one of the most indispensable elements of self-government, for self-government always implies mutual restraint. It is one of the wisest acts in a perfectly free people to establish the highest possible degree of judicial independence, while they only act as all common power acts, if they wish to retain absolute power.[1]

Those of our states, which have of late given the appointment of judges to popular elections, labor under a surprising inconsistency; for all those states, I believe, exclude judges from the legislature. They fear "political judges," yet make them elective. Now, everything electional within the state becomes necessarily, in time, political. If the physician of a hospital, the captain of a vessel, or the watchmaker to repair our timepieces, were elected by the people, they would, to a certainty, in most cases, be elected not according to their medical, nautical, or horological skill and trustworthiness, but on political grounds. There is nothing reproachful in this to the people at large. It is the natural course of things. Even members of the French Academy have been elected on political grounds, when the government has taken a deep interest in the election.

The question whether judges ought to sit in the house of commons was recently before parliament.[2] There are many

---

[1] In 1774 parliament passed an act making the justices of the supreme court of Massachusetts independent of the people for their salaries. The grand jurors refused to serve. Paul Revere was one of the grand jury.

[2] See Mr. Macaulay's speech in the commons, June 1, 1853, on a bill to exclude judges from the house of commons. The chief question was to exclude the vice-chancellor from a seat in the commons. Mr. Macaulay is decidedly in favor of letting judges sit in the commons.

English authorities on the American side of the question, at least so far as the house of commons is concerned. Lords Brougham and Langdale, Sir Samuel Romilly and Mr. Curran may be mentioned as such. On the other hand, Mr. Bentham was of opinion that there was so little legislative talent in the world that no place fits so well for legislative business as the bench, and that it was suicidal to exclude the judges. The questions we have to answer are these: Does experience teach us that judges, having a seat in the legislature, where they needs must belong to one or the other party, allow themselves to be influenced on the bench? In England, there are striking instances that, in modern times, they may resist their own political bias, in Eldon, Thurlow, Mansfield, and Hardwicke. But this remark extends to common cases only. Were they, or would they have been utterly unbiased in all those trials that may be called political? The pervading character of self-government and independence of the law has certainly given to the English bench a traditional independence. But how long has this existed, and what times may not possibly recur? It appears, throughout the Life and Correspondence of Justice Story, that so soon as he was elevated to the bench he not only avoided being mixed up with politics in any degree whatsoever, but even the mere semblance of it. He seems to have been peculiarly scrupulous on this point.

The second question we must answer is this: How does the judge get into the legislature? Can he do so without electioneering? The more popular a representative government is, the more necessary the immediate contact between the candidate and the constituents becomes. And who wishes to see the judge, that ought to be the independent oracle of the law, in this position?

Mr. Bentham's observation regarding the general unfitness of the world at large for legislative business, and the peculiar fitness of judges for it, requires also some modification. How is it with sanitary laws? Few physicians sit in legislatures, and those that have a seat are not placed there because they are at the head of their profession. We must necessarily trust to the general influence under which a legislature legislates. As to the fitting of the bench for legislative business, it is undoubtedly true with regard to a large class of that business; but we must not forget that the judge is and ought to be a peculiar representative of conservatism; which nevertheless unfits him, in a measure, for all that business which is of a peculiarly progressive character. Almost all law reforms have originally been resisted by the bench. It is not in all cases to be regretted. The judges are the breaks which prevent the vehicle from descending too fast on an inclined plane; but the retarding force must be overcome in many cases, however serviceable it may be that the action of overcoming the difficulty may have been modified by the very process.

I cannot help believing, then, that upon the whole judges ought to be excluded from the legislature; they certainly ought to be so with us. To allow them a seat in concentrated governments as in France would be calamitous. But this reason is, à fortiori, one why judges ought not to be elected by the people.

We are frequently asked whether the elective judiciary works badly? The answer is, that a ball rolls awhile from the first impulse given to it. So far old judges have generally been elected under the new system; and we would ask on the other hand: Has the former system worked badly? I believe, then, that elective judges are a departure from substantial civil liberty, because it is a departure from the all-important independence of the law.

The foregoing paragraph was written in 1853; and I have now to add, in 1859, that a judiciary elected by the people seems to be, universally and unqualifiedly, considered a serious failure. I state this, conscientiously to record facts concerning so important a topic. The most attentive observation, extensive perusal of public journals, consultation of lawyers and statesmen, have not brought to my knowledge a single opinion in favor of an elective judiciary. Everywhere it seems to be acknowledged that it was introduced into our constitutions from no dissatisfaction with the existing system, or with the judges, but simply to satisfy the desire of increasing the power of the power-holder—to be subservient to the sovereign; that in reality it does not increase the power of the people, since persons, if appointed by popular vote, are nominated by a small number of so-called leading politicians, and the people at large can discuss the matter as little as the ecclesia in the agora could discuss; that the confidence of the people in the judiciary has been lessened, and through it the confidence even in the jury system; that if a possible increase of salary is believed to be capable of influencing the judges, for which reason it is prohibited by all our constitutions, it follows, à fortiori, that a re-election by the people, or the losing it, must influence the judge far more; that instances of want of independence have occurred in various states, and the lack of independence has especially and sadly interfered with our penal trials and the salutary operation of the law; that it has in many cases elevated individuals to the bench who had no standing among their fellow lawyers, and whom no governor would have dared to appoint, feeling his responsibility as a trustee, while the electing people are irresponsible, and that in several states it has actually occurred that candidates for judicial seats have been asked in the public journals how they mean to decide if certain questions (e. g. the constitutionality of the New York liquor law) should come before them, in the same way in which certain political questions are put to candidates for the legislature.[1]

It is necessary to appoint judges for a long period, and the best is probably for life, with a proper provision which prevents incapacity from old age.[2] The experience which is required, and the authority he must have, although unsupported by any

---

[1] The report of the Reform Committee of the New York legislature reveals a state of things which reminds us of the worst state of Athens, while the Louisiana papers copied the most important portions, with strengthening commentaries and illustrations from their state. Numerous individuals, judges, and lawyers, have publicly expressed their disapprobation. We trust so great an evil will soon be redressed.

[2] See Political Ethics, under the heads of *Judge, Independence of the Judiciary.*

material power, make this equally desirable, as well as the fact
that the best legal talents cannot be obtained for the bench if
the tenure amounts to a mere interruption of the business of
the lawyer.[1] The constitution of the French republic of 1848,
so democratic in its character, decreed the tenure of judicial
office to be for life.[2]

It is for a similar reason of public importance that the salary
of the judges be liberal, which means that, combined with the
honor attached to a seat on the bench, it be capable of commanding the fairest legal talents. The judge must enjoy, as
has been stated, proper independence; but he is dependent, and
in the worst degree so, if he is conscious that the best lawyers
before him are superior to him in talent, experience, learning and
character. None but such inferior men can be obtained for an
illiberal salary, according to the universal law that the laborer
is worthy of his hire, and that he will seek to obtain this hire
in the great market of labor and talent. Even the common
consideration that every private individual expects that his
affairs will be served best by an efficient clerk for a liberal
hire, and not by a poorly paid hireling whose incapacity can
command no higher wages, should induce us to pay judges, as
indeed every one who must be paid, and is worthy of being
paid at all, with a liberality which equally avoids lavishness
and penury. Liberal salaries are essential to a popular
government.

To make judges independent or remove from them the possible suspicion of dependence, it has been ordered in the Constitution of the United States that the "judges of the supreme
and inferior courts shall hold their offices during good behavior,
and shall at stated times receive for their services a compensation which shall not be diminished during their continuance
in office." This principle has been adopted in most, if not in
all our constitutions; many have added that it shall not be

---

[1] I would refer the reader, on all these subjects, to Judge Chambers's
Speech on the Judicial Tenure, in the Maryland convention, Baltimore,
1851.

[2] This constitution will be found in the appendix.

increased either, during continuance in office.[1]   But what is
the possible dependence feared from an increase or decrease of
salary compared to that unavoidable dependence which must
be the consequence of short terms of office, and of appointment by election?   It will hardly be necessary to mention
that a fixed salary, independent of fees and fines, is indispensable for the independence of the judge and the protection of
the citizen.   Even common decency requires it.   Don Miguel
of Portugal made the judges who tried political offenders
depend upon part of the fines and confiscations they decreed,
and we know what was done under James II. and Lord Jeffreys.   The hounds receiving part of the hunted game suggest themselves at once.

With a view of making the judiciary independent, the
removal of judges from office has been justly taken out of the
hands of the executive.   The immovability of judges is an
essential element of civil liberty.   Neither the executive nor
the sovereign himself ought to have the power of removing a
judge.   He can therefore be removed by impeachment only,
and this requires, according to the Constitution of the United
States, two-thirds of the votes of the senate.   In some states
they can be removed by two-thirds of the whole legislature.[2]

Although the principle of arbitration cannot be called a characteristic of liberty, for as a characteristic it belongs rather
to the patriarchal government, and courts of arbitration may
flourish in despotic states, it will be necessary to consider this
topic in the present place.   It is very possible that our people
would more readily give up an elective judiciary, where it has
been established, if the law or the state constitutions directed
or admitted of regular courts of arbitration.   Wherever they

---

[1] When it has become necessary to increase the salary of judges, the
difficulty has sometimes been avoided by the judges resigning, upon the
understanding that, after the legislature shall have increased the salary,
they should be re-appointed.

[2] It seems to me a strange anomaly that, as it would seem by a late
resolution of the United States senate, the president has authority to remove judges in the "territories."

have been tried in modern times, they have been found of the greatest benefit to the people, for instance, in Prussia and Denmark. Great efforts are made in England, by such leading men as Lord Brougham, to introduce them in that country of law. In England as well as in the United States the law admits indeed of arbitration, but a single arbitration though acknowledged by law, if certain prescribed conditions have been fulfilled, differs in effect, and the advantage resulting from it, from a court of arbitration.

Where these courts now exist, the following are, I believe, their characteristics:

The country is divided into certain arbitration districts, in each of which the people elect several judges of arbitration, so that the people may have a choice, because the whole business transacted by them is an affair of confidence;

Parties must agree to go to arbitration, and select the judge:

They must commence business by handing in a written declaration that they will abide by the decision of the judge, without any appeal, and the decision of the judge has full force in all courts;

Going to arbitration is a purely voluntary matter;

Parties must state their own cases, and no pleaders for others, no lawyers are admitted;

There is no jury;

The arbitration extends to civil cases only, as a matter of course;

The judges of arbitration are elected for a limited time;

The judge decides on the common principles of fairness;

Great care is taken to establish, as the first step, that the parties come into court, truly and verily, of their own accord and free will.

The chief objections to Lord Brougham's repeated propositions to introduce courts of arbitration have been made by professional lawyers, namely, that parties ignorant of their full rights would expose themselves to great losses. The statistics of those countries where these peculiar courts exist seem to prove the contrary. The number of cases decided by them has been increasing from year to year, and is now, as well as the amount of property upon which they have decided, surprisingly large. Cases in which the disputed property amounted to several hundred thousand dollars have been taken before these courts, and it has repeatedly happened in Prussia, that in a suit before the regular courts of law, the settlement of portions of the suit have been taken, by common consent, to arbitration, and the suit at law has proceeded with the decision of the court of arbitration. It is remarkable that the amount of property at stake, thus taken out of the court of law to the court of arbitration, has sometimes been very large.

The establishment of courts of arbitration has produced a signal decrease of litigation and diminution of expenses.

Finally, it may be observed, that the fundamental idea of courts of arbitration somewhat resembles, in one point, the principle upon which, originally at least,[1] the house of lords, decided as the last court of appeal,—a principle which many of our states had imitated, by giving the last appeal to the state senates, and which, so far as my inquiry has led me to conclude, produced beneficial results. The introduction of courts of arbitration, along with the abolition of elective judges, and especially of judges elected for a short term, would produce the best effects in our country.[2]

---

[1] At present, when the house of lords sits as a court of appeal, none but the law lords are generally present.

[2] In some manufacturing districts on the continent of Europe, for instance in Rhenish Prussia, so called Manufactory Courts exist. They consist of elected employers and employed, and judge of all the minor difficulties which may arise between the employers and the employed out of their immediate relation to one another. The common question, for instance, whether the woven piece, returned by the weaver, contains all the material given to him, or whether it be returned in a perfect state, is adjudged by them. General satisfaction seems to prevail with these courts, whose German name is Fabrik-Gerichte.

CHAPTER XX.

INDEPENDENCE OF JUS, CONTINUED. TRIAL BY JURY. THE ADVOCATE.

41. THE judge cannot occupy a sufficiently independent position between the parties by the accusatorial proceeding alone. If there is not what may be called a division of the judicial labor, separating the finding of guilt or innocence, or of the facts, from the presiding over the whole trial and the application as well as the pronouncing and expounding of the law, the judge must still be exposed to taking sides in the trial. This division of judicial labor is obtained by the institution of the jury. This, it seems to me, is one of the most essential advantages of this comprehensive, self-grown institution. It is likewise a guarantee of liberty in giving the people a participation in the administration of justice, without the ruin and horrors of an administration of justice by a multitude, as it was in Athens. The jury is moreover the best school of the citizen, both for teaching him his rights and how to protect them, and for practically teaching him the necessity of law and government. The jury, in this respect, is eminently conservative. In this, as in many other respects, it is necessary that the institution of the jury exist for the civil trial as well as for the penal, and not, as in many countries, for the latter only. The necessity of the jury does not militate against the arbitration courts, which have proved, as has been stated, a great blessing in all countries in which they have been properly established, or against certain courts of minor importance which may be advantageously conducted without a jury.[1]

---

[1] For the history of this institution in general, the reader is referred to William Forsyth, History of the Trial by Jury; London, 1852.

The results of trial by jury have occasionally been such that even in England and here, voices have been raised against it. Men feel the existing evil only; they do not see those evils that would result a hundredfold from an opposite state of things. Nor are those, who feel irritated at some results of the trial by jury, acquainted with the operation of trials without jury. So is occasionally the publicity of trials highly inconvenient; yet should we desire secret trials? Liberty, as we conceive it, can no more exist without the trial by jury— that "buttress of liberty," as Chatham called it,[1] and as our ancestors worshipped it—than without the representative system. But we must remember that in all spheres the exception is patent; the continuous operation of the rule is latent.[2]

The Declaration of Independence specifies, as one of the reasons why this country was justified in severing itself from the mother country, that Americans have been "deprived in many cases of the benefits of trial by jury."

---

[1] Lord Erskine, when he was raised to the peerage, adopted the words Trial by Jury, as the scroll of his coat of arms.

[2] The laxity now, unfortunately so common, in the administration and execution of the laws; the crying evil that in our large cities numerous idlers, of a low character, make their living, during court time, by being ready to serve as jurymen when called upon, of which they are now very sure, owing to the facility with which judges excuse citizens from serving; the frequency of non-agreement and consequent new trials; the length to which the doctrine is carried that juries are judges of law as well as fact; and many other things, have induced several persons loudly to call for the abolition of the jury. They do not seem to know much of history, or they would know that courts without juries are, indeed, not exempt from falling into abuses, or from becoming actual nuisances. Let us imagine our present elective judges without jury, would that mend matters? The opposite is hardly ever the cure of an evil. A glutton would not take the right step of amendment by the resolution of starving himself to death. Our jury trials exhibit many deplorable facts, in the present time, owing to the general spirit of disorder; but the administration of justice, it would seem, suffers far more from want of energy in the judges. Let us fervently hope that the recuperative power which has been shown by modern nations, and by modern nations alone, will manifest itself also with us. At any rate, no good is done, when the ship of state is in danger, by cutting away the very ribs of the ship.

It may not be improper here to enumerate briefly all the advantages of so great an institution, whether they are directly connected with liberty or not.

The trial by jury, then, if properly and intelligently administered, divides the labor of the administration of justice, and permits each part quietly to find the truth in the sphere assigned to it;

It allows the judge to stand, as the independent organ of the law, not only above the parties, hostilely arraigned against each other, but also above the whole practical case before the court;

It enables plain, common, and practical sense properly to admix itself with keen professional and scientific distinction, in each single case, and thus prevents the effect of that disposition to sacrifice reality to attenuated theory, to which every individual is liable in his own profession and peculiar pursuit— the worship of the means, forgetting the end;[1]

---

[1] And this is the reason that nearly all great reforms have worked their way from without, and from the non-professional to the professional, or from below upward.

I beg to arrest the reader's attention for a moment on this topic.

In all civilized countries it is acknowledged that there are some important cases, which on the one hand it is necessary to decide, for Mine and Thine are involved, and which, on the other hand, are not of a character that the lines of demarcation can be drawn with absolute distinctness, in a manner which would make it easy to apply the law; e.g. the cases which relate to the imitation of a part of a work of art, of a pattern, or the question of a bona fide extract from an author's work, which, according to the Prussian copyright law, was decided by a jury of "experts," long before the general introduction of the jury in that country. A similar case is presented when an officer is accused of unofficer-like and ungentlemanly conduct. Now the question becomes: Are not these cases far more frequent than it is supposed in the countries where the trial by jury does not exist? Are not almost all complex cases, such as require in a high degree good strong common sense, the tact of practical life, together with the law, to be justly decided? Are not, perhaps, the greater part of civil cases such? The English and Americans seem to believe they are. They believe that close logical reasoning is indeed necessary in the application of the law, and they assign this to the law-officers, but they believe also that a high degree of plain good common

It makes a participation of the people in the administration of justice possible without having the serious evil of courts, consisting of multitudes or mobs, or the confusion of the branches of the administration of justice, of judges and triers;

It obtains the great advantage of a mean of views of facts, regarding which Aristotle said that many persons are more just than one, although each of the many were less so than

---

sense, unshackled by technicalities, is necessary to decide whether, "upon the whole," "taken all in all," the individual case in hand is such as to bring it within the province of the specific law, with reference to which it is brought before the court, and they assign this part of the trial to the jury, that is, to non-professional citizens. The English, and the people of some American states, do not only follow this view in the first stage of a case, but, in order to avoid the evil of letting technicalities get the better of essential justice, of letting the minds of professional lawyers, whose very duty it is to train themselves in strict, uncompromising logic, decide complicated and important cases in the last resort, they allow an appeal from all the judges to the house of lords, or to the senate.

It appears to me an important fact, which ought always to be remembered when the subject of trial by jury in general is discussed, that by the trial by jury, the Anglican race endeavors, among other things, to insure the continuous and necessary admixture of common sense, in the decision of cases; and who can deny that in all practical cases, in all controversies, in all disputes, and in all questions which require the application of general rules or principles to concrete cases, common sense is indispensable, that is, sound judgment, which avoids the Nimium? Who will deny that every one is liable to have this tact and plain soundness of judgment impaired in that very line or sphere in which his calling has made it his duty to settle general principles, to find general rules, to defend general points? The grammarian, by profession, frequently, perhaps generally, writes pedantically and stiffly; the religious controversialist goes to extremes; the philosopher, by profession, is apt to divide, distinguish, and classify beyond what reality warrants; the soldier, by profession, is apt to sacrifice advantages to his science. Dr. Sangrado is the caricature of the truth here maintained.

The denial of the necessity of profound study and professional occupation would be as fanatical as the disregard of common sense would be supercilious and unphilosophical. Truth stands, in all spheres, emphatically in need of both.

the one; without incurring the disadvantages and the injustice of vague multitudes;

It brings, in most cases, a degree of personal acquaintance with the parties, and frequently with the witnesses, to aid in deciding;

It gives the people opportunities to ward off the inadmissible and strained demands of the government;[1]

It is necessary for a complete accusatorial procedure;

It makes the administration of justice a matter of the people, and awakens confidence;

It binds the citizen with increased public spirit to the government of his commonwealth, and gives him a constant and renewed share in one of the highest public affairs, the application of the abstract law to the reality of life—the administration of justice;

It teaches law and liberty, order and rights, justice and government, and carries this knowledge over the land;[2] it is the greatest practical school of free citizenship;

It throws a great part of the responsibility upon the people, and thus elevates the citizen while it legitimately strengthens the government;

It does not only elevate the judge, but makes him a popular

---

[1] The whole history of the libel down to Charles Fox's immortal bill may serve as an illustration.

[2] Lord Chancellor Cranworth said, in February, 1853, in the house of lords:

"There were many other subjects to be considered. Trial by judge instead of by jury had been eminently successful in the county courts; but in attempting to extend this to cases tried in other courts, we must not lose sight of the fact that we should be taking a step towards unfitting for their duties those who are to send representatives to the other house of parliament, who are to perform municipal functions in towns, and who are to exercise a variety of those local jurisdictions which constitute in some sort in this country a system of self-government. It may be very dangerous to withdraw from them that duty of assisting in the administration of justice. Mechanics' schools may afford valuable instruction, but I doubt if there is any school that reads such practical lessons of wisdom, and tends so much to strengthen the mind, as assisting as jurymen in the administration of justice."

magistrate, looked up to with confidence and favor ; which is nowhere else the case in the same degree, and yet is of great importance, especially for liberty;

It is the great bulwark of liberty in monarchies against the crown;

It stands, in republics, as a committee of the people, between the accused and the people themselves, a more exacting king when excited than one that wears a crown ;

It alone makes it possible to decide to the satisfaction of the public those cases which must be decided, and which, nevertheless, do not lie within the strict limits of the positive law ;

It alone makes it possible to reconcile, in some degree, old and cruel laws, if the legislature omits to abolish them, with a spirit of humanity, which the judge could never do without undermining the ground on which alone he can have a firm footing ;

It is hardly possible to imagine a living, vigorous, and expanding common law without it;

It is with the representative system one of the greatest institutions which develop the love of the law, and without this love there can be no sovereignty of the law in the true sense ;

It is part and parcel of the Anglican self-government;

It gives to the advocate that independent and honored position which the accusatorial process as well as liberty requires, and it is a school for those great advocates without which broad popular liberty does not exist.

Mr. Hallam, speaking in his work on the Middle Ages of "the grand principle of the Saxon polity, the trial of facts by the country," says, "from this principle (except as to that preposterous relic of barbarism, the requirement of unanimity,) may we never swerve—may we never be compelled in wish to swerve—by a contempt of their oaths in jurors, a disregard of the just limits of their trusts." To these latter words I shall only add, that the fact of the jury's being called by the law, the country, and of the indicted person's saying that he will be tried by God and his country, are facts full of meaning, and expressive of a great part of the beauty and the

advantages of the trial by jury.[1] There is, however, no
mysterious efficacy inherent in this or any other institution,
nor any peculiar property in the name. Juries must be well
organized, and must conscientiously do their duty. They become, like all other guarantees of liberty, very dangerous in
the hands of the government, when nothing but the form is
left, and the spirit of loyalty and of liberty is gone. A corrupt or facile jury is the most convenient agent for despotism,
or a sure road to anarchy.

The jury trial has been mentioned here as one of the guarantees of liberty, and it might not be improper to add some
remarks on the question whether the unanimous verdict ought
to be retained, or whether a verdict as the result of two-thirds
or a simple majority of jurors agreeing, ought to be adopted.
This is an important subject, occupying the serious attention
of many persons. But, however important the subject may
be, and connected as I believe it to be with the very continuance of the trial by jury as a wholesome institution, and with
the supremacy of the law, it is one still so much debated that
a proper discussion would far exceed the limits to which this
work is restricted; and the mere avowal that it is my firm
conviction, after long observation and study, that the unanimity principle ought to be given up, would be of no value.[2]

---

[1] On all these subjects connected with the jury I must refer to the
Political Ethics.

[2] My conviction has been much strengthened since the original writing of this work. The Scottish jury (consisting of fifteen members)
decides by majority. Our continued failures of verdicts would cease.
Whenever the jury is out more than half an hour, it is a pretty sure sign
that the unanimity is, after all, only one in form and not in truth. Perhaps most professional men adhere to the unanimity principle, but
reforms very rarely proceed from the profession, in any sphere. It was
not the theologians of the pope from whom the reformation proceeded.
We can add, however, high authority in favor of our opinion. In
January, 1859, Lord Campbell, chief justice of England, declared in
court, after the jury had pronounced an absurd verdict, which he declined
accepting, that he intended to propose a bill, in parliament, for the purpose of adopting the majority principle in civil cases; and while I was

I beg, however, to add as a fact, at all events of interest to the student, that Locke was against the unanimity principle. His constitution for South Carolina has this provision: "Every jury shall consist of twelve men; and it shall not be necessary they should all agree, but the verdict shall be according to the consent of the majority."

The "duke's laws" in New York, generally ascribed to the Lord Chancellor Clarendon, the father-in-law of the Duke of York, demanded seven jurors, and unanimity only in capital cases.[1]

It is, besides, well-known that our number of twelve jurymen, and the principle of their unanimity, arose from the circumstance that in ancient times *at least* twelve of the compurgators were obliged to agree before a verdict could be given, and that compurgators were added until twelve of them agreed one way or the other.[2]

I conclude here my remarks on the institution of the jury, and pass over to the last element of the independence of the law—the independent position of the advocate.

42. Where the inquisitorial trial exists, where the judiciary in general is not independent, and where the judges more or less feel themselves, and are universally considered, as government officers, it is in vain to look for independent advocates, as a class of men. Their whole position, especially where the trial is not public, prevents the development of this independence, and the consideration they have to take of their future career would soon check it where it might occasionally happen to spring forth.[3]

---

revising these pages, a very respectable petition, urged even by judges, to allow judges to decide in civil cases by the majority of jurymen, when they cannot agree on a unanimous verdict, was presented to the Massachusetts legislature. I consider, however, the principle of verdicts by two-thirds in penal cases even more important than in civil cases.

[1] Judge Daly's Historical Sketch of the Judicial Tribunals of New York; New York, 1855, page 53.

[2] Forsyth, History of the Trial by Jury.

[3] Feuerbach, in his Manual of the Common German Penal Law, 10th edition, § 623, says that in the inquisitorial proceeding we have to re-

The independence of the advocate is important in many respects. The prisoner, in penal trials, ought to have counsel. Even Lord Jeffreys, who, among judges, is what Alexander VI. was among popes, declared it, as far back as the seventeenth century, a cruel anomaly that counsel were permitted in a case of a few shillings, but not in a case of life and death. But counsel of the prisoner can be of no avail, if they do not feel themselves independent in a very high degree. This independence is necessary for the daily protection of the citizen's rights. It is important for a proper and sound development of the law; for it is not only the decisions of the judges which frequently settle the most weighty points and rights, but also the masterly arguments of the advocates; and lastly, it is important in all so-called political trials.

May we never have reason to wish it otherwise! The limits of the advocate, especially as counsel in criminal cases, and which doubtless form a subject connected with liberty itself,

---

present the judge to our minds as the representative of the offended state, inasmuch as it is his duty to see justice done for it according to the penal law; as representative of the accused, inasmuch as he is bound at the same time to find out everything on which innocence or a less degree of criminality can be founded; and finally, as judge, inasmuch as he must decide upon the given facts. Why not add to this fearful triad, the jailer, the executioner?

Although a "defensor" is appointed, it is difficult for him to do his work properly; for in the German inquisitorial process the defence begins when the inquiring judge has finished, or the "acta" are closed, that is, when the written report of the judge is made. Now, a lawyer does not feel very free to attack the writing of a judge, upon whom his advancement probably depends, even if any latitude were given to the advocate. Mr. Mittermaier, note d, § 14, of his Art of Defending, 2d edition, speaks openly of the great difficulty encountered by the "defensor," in unveiling the imperfections of the *acta* which have been sent him, because he thereby offends his superior, upon whom his whole career may depend; and Mr. Voget, the defensor of the woman Gottfried, in Bremen, who had poisoned some thirty persons, fully indorses these remarks of Mr. Mittermaier, in his work, The Poisoner, G. M. Gottfried, Bremen, 1830, (first division, pp. 17 and 18.) He concludes his remarks with these words: "Who does not occasionally think of the passage, 1 Sam. 29: 6—Non inveni in te quidquam mali, sed satrapis non places," (or, as our version of the bible has it: Nevertheless, the lords favor thee not.)

nevertheless belong more properly to political and especially to legal ethics. As such I have treated of them in the Political Ethics. I own, however, that, when writing the work, the topic had not acquired in my mind all the importance and distinctness which its farther pursuit, and the perusal of works on this important chapter of practical ethics, have produced. I am sorry to say that very few of these works or essays seem manfully to grapple with it, and to put it upon solid ground. It is desirable that this should be done thoroughly and philosophically. This is the more necessary, as the loosest and vaguest notions on the rights of the advocate are entertained by many respectable men, and the most untenable opinions have been uttered by high authorities.[1]

In this work, however, all that I am permitted to do is to indicate the true position of the advocate in our Anglican system of justice, and to allude to the duties flowing from it.

Most writers discuss "the time-honored usage of the profession in advocating one side," and of saying all that can be said in defence of the prisoner. No one at all conversant with the subject has ever had any doubt upon this point. It is a necessary effect of the accusatorial procedure. Indeed, it forms an essential part of it. But the writers go on maintaining that, therefore, the advocate may, and indeed must, do and say for his client all that the latter would do and say for himself, had he the requisite talent and knowledge. And here lies the error, moral as well as legal.[2]

---

[1] For instance, Lord Brougham's well-known assertion uttered at the trial of Queen Caroline—often commented upon, but never taken back or modified by the speaker; p. 91, Legal and Political Hermeneutics. See also an article on License of Counsel in the January number, 1841, of Westminster Review. The case of Sir Arthur Pigott, attorney-general of the Duchy of Cornwall, stating in court, for the Prince of Wales, that he had never heard of bonds of the Dutch loan, which the prince and some of his brokers had made, has been referred to before. The list of shameful tricks—actual tricks—to which counsel have occasionally resorted in our courts, would require a large space.

[2] Consult Hortensius: an Historical View of the Office and Duties of an Advocate, by William Forsyth; London, 1853.

No man is allowed to do wrong, for instance to tell an untruth, or to asperse the character of an innocent person, either in his own behalf or for another. The prisoner would do wrong in lying, and no one has a right to do it for him. The lawyer is no more freed from the moral law or the obligation of truth than any other mortal, nor can he divest himself of his individuality any more than other men. If he lies, he lies as every other man, at his own individual peril. If, as Lord Brougham stated it, the only object of counsel is to free the prisoner, at whatever risk, why, then, not also do certain things for the prisoner which he would do, were he free? Many an indicted murderer would make away with a dangerous witness, if the prison did not prevent him. Why, then, ought not the lawyer to do this for him? Because it would be murder? And why not? If the advocate is to say and do all the prisoner would do and say for himself, irrespective of morality, the supposed case is more glaring, indeed, but in principle the same with many actual ones. The fact is, the rights of the advocate, or the defence of his speaking on one side, cannot be put on a worse foundation than by thus making him a part of the prisoner's individuality, or a substitute. Nor would there be a more degrading position than that of letting one's talent or knowledge for hire, no matter whether for just or unjust, moral or immoral purposes. Indeed, why should this knowledge for hire begin its appropriate operation during the trial only, if escape is the only object? Why not try to foil the endeavors of the detective police? Is it only because the retaining fee has not yet been paid, and that, so soon as it is in the advocate's hand, he has a right to say, with the ancient poet: I deem no speaking evil that results in gain?[1] This cannot be. All of us have learned to venerate Socrates, whom Lord Mansfield calls the greatest of lawyers, for having made victorious war on the sophists, and having established ethics on pure and dignified principles; and now we are called upon to sanction everything, without reference to morality and truth, in an en-

---

[1] Δοκῶ μὲν οὐδὲν ῥῆμα σὺν κερδεῖ κάκον.

tire and highly privileged classs, and in the performance of the most sacred business of which political man has any knowledge. If lawyers insist upon this revolting exemption from the eternal laws of truth and rectitude, they ought to consider that this will serve in the end as a suggestion to the people of returning to the Athenian court of the people.

The true position of the advocate in the Anglican accusatorial trial, and in a free and orderly country, is not one which would almost assimilate him to the "receiver." It is a far different one. Nearly in all free countries, but especially in all modern free countries, has the advocate assumed a prominent position. He is an important person as advocate, and as belonging to that profession from which the people necessarily must always take many of their most efficient law-makers, from which arise many of the greatest statesmen, whatever the English prejudice, even of such men as Chatham, to the contrary may long have been, and which has formed in free states many of their immortal orators.[1]

---

[1] There was a time when diplomacy and dishonest subtlety were nearly synonymous—when it was discussed how signatures might be written so that after a number of years they would vanish. Since that time, diplomacy has signally improved. We are now living in an age in which a corresponding improvement is manifestly going on in legal ethics. We discuss the pertinent topics at least, and public attention is alive. The following article, taken from the London Spectator, Sept. 3, 1853, may find an appropriate place in a note:

"However little the Smyth case can have answered the purpose of the man who claimed the property, it will not be entirely without beneficial result, since it has put in a very strong light a moral which has not escaped the legal profession. Some time ago it was argued, that a barrister becomes completely the agent and advocate of his client, engaged solely to present all that may be said on the side of that client, and disengaged from any moral responsibility as to the merits of the case. This doctrine, however, although it was convenient for the consciences of professional men less sensitive than Romilly, could not be sustained entirely; and barristers have gone to the equally erroneous opposite extreme—that of throwing up a brief as soon as a grossly fraudulent character was exposed in their case. Mr. Bovill threw up his brief in the Smyth case, and in doing so, we think, violated the true principle upon which a barrister should act; a principle which has not

The advocate is part and parcel of the whole machinery of administering justice, as much so as the jury, the judge, or the prosecutor. He forms an integral part of the whole contrivance called the trial; and the only object of the trial is to find out legal truth, so that justice may be administered. In this trial, it has been found most desirable to place the judge beyond the parties, to let both parties appear before him, and to let both parties say all they can say in their favor, so that the truth may be ascertained without the judge's taking part in the inquiry, and thus becoming personally interested in the conviction, or in either party. The advocate is essentially an amicus curæ; he helps to find the truth, and for this purpose it is necessary that all that can be said in favor of his client or in mitigation of the law, be stated; because the opposite

---

been unrecognized by the profession. It is, that the barrister is engaged for the purpose of seeing that his client be treated according to law and in no other way; that he have all the evidence that can be procured and set forth for him; that the evidence be taken according to rule and practice; that the judge charge the jury according to law and rule; in short, that the whole proceedings be regular and complete in all that is required on the part of the client. Acting on this principle, the barrister can retain his brief to the last, as well as on the principle of absolute agency; but he is not required to be an accomplice in suborning false evidence, or in setting forth pleas that he knows to be fraudulent; nor is he bound to anticipate the judgment by a declaration of the verdict in the act of throwing up his brief.

"This principle has been recognized so far that there is a prospect of its becoming more generally adopted as the rule of the profession. But the Smyth case suggests to us, that it may very properly be extended to the other half of the profession—the attorneys. They are bound to exercise discretion in their conduct with their clients, otherwise they become parties to conspiracy and fraud. Considering all the opportunities that a man in the profession has of discriminating, it is difficult to find him thus placed and to acquit him either of an extraordinary degree of dulness or of culpable knowledge. It is, for example, excessively difficult to understand how any professional man could see Smyth, hear him tell his lies—nay, take them down in writing in order to insert them in the brief—and not understand the whole character of the fraud. Now no attorney would put himself into this position, however fraudulent his client might be, if he confined himself to the principle which we have mentioned as adopted by barristers."

party does the opposite, and because the case as well as the law ought to be viewed from all sides, before a decision be made. The advocate ought not only to say all that his client might say, had he the necessary skill and knowledge, but even more; but the client or prisoner has no right to speak the untruth in his own behalf, nor has the lawyer the right to do it for him.

Chief Justice Hale severely reproves the misstating authorities and thus misleading the court; but why should this be wrong, and the misstating of facts not? Many prisoners would certainly misstate authorities if they could. Trials are not established for lawyers to show their skill or to get their fees, nor for arraigned persons to escape. They are established as a means of ascertaining truth and dispensing justice; not to promote or aid injustice or immorality. The advocate's duty is, then, to say everything that possibly can be said in favor of his case or client, even if he does not feel any strong reliance on his argument, because what appears to himself weak may not appear as such to other minds, or may contain some truth which will modify the result of the whole. But he is not allowed to use falsehood, nor to injure others. Allowing this to him would not be independence, but an arbitrarily privileged position, tyrannical toward the rest of society.[1] To allow tricks to a whole profession, or to claim them by law, seems monstrous. There is no separate decalogue for lawyers any more than for king, partisan or beadle.

The lawyer is obliged, as was stated before, to find out everything that can be found in favor of the person who has intrusted himself to his protecting care, because the opposite

---

[1] The famous case of Mr. Philips, now on the bench, when defending Courvoisier, is treated at considerable length in Townsend's Modern State Trials, under the trial of Courvoisier. It must be allowed that the defence is not successful, though ingenious. On page 312 of vol. i. of that work, the reader will also find the titles of numerous writings bearing on the moral obligations of the advocate, to which may be added those I have mentioned in the notes appended to my remarks on the advocate in the 2d vol. of the Political Ethics. I also refer to pp. 59 and sequ. in my Character of the Gentleman; Charleston, S. C. 1847.

will be done by the opposite party. He has no right to decline the defence of a person, which means the finding out for him all that fairly can be said in his favor, except indeed in very peculiar cases. Declining the defence beforehand would amount to a prejudging of the case, and in the division of judicial labor every one ought to be defended.[1] The defence of possible innocence, not the defeat of justice, is the aim of counsel.

Great advocates, such as Romilly,[2] have very distinctly pronounced themselves against that view which still seems the prevailing one among the lawyers; and Dr. Thomas Arnold was so deeply impressed with the moral danger to which the profession of the law, at present, exposes its votary, that he used to persuade his pupils not to become lawyers, while

---

[1] At the very moment that these pages are passing through the press, (in 1853,) a case has occurred in an English court, of a young man indicted for burglariously entering the room of some young woman. His counsel in the defence suggested that probably the young lady had given an appointment to the prisoner. "That is not in the brief," cried the prisoner himself, and the court justly reprimanded the barrister. It ought to be added that in this case the barrister wrote a letter of submission to the court. This has not been done in other cases quite as bad in principle. Thus, another publicly reproved barrister insisted that he had done what the profession required, when he had resorted to the following trick. He had subpœnaed the chief witness against his client, so that he could not appear, and then argued that the prosecutor must know his client to be innocent, else he would certainly have produced his witness, etc.

Since this was written, the following case has occurred (in Cincinnati, 1853.) When the defence came on, 300 witnesses were sworn. The prosecution of course did not believe that its turn would come for a long time. But the defence only examined some four witnesses, and then declared it had done. The prosecution was not prepared to proceed, and asked for delay, but the court decided that the case could not be stopped. Thus the whole trial was upset, and a verdict of not guilty was found. Now, are such atrocities to be borne with? Does freedom consist in giving all possible protection to trickery?

[2] There is a very excellent passage on this topic in the reflections of Sir Samuel Romilly, on himself and the good he might do, should he be appointed lord chancellor, page 384 and sequ. of vol. iii. of his Memoirs; 2d ed. London, 1840.

Mr. Bentham openly declared that no person could escape, and that even Romilly had not remained wholly untainted.

It ought to be observed, however, that a more correct opinion on the obligations of the advocate seems to be fast gaining ground in England. At present it seems to be restricted to the public, but the time will come when this opinion will reach the profession itself. Like almost all reforms, it comes from without, and will ultimately force an entrance into the courts and the inns. We are thus earnest in our desire of seeing correct views on this subject prevail, because we have so high an opinion of the importance of the advocate in a modern free polity.[1]

---

[1] This was written in 1853.

CHAPTER XXI.

SELF-GOVERNMENT.

THE last constituent of our liberty that I shall mention is local and institutional self-government.[1] Many of the guaran-

[1] The history of this proud word is this : It was doubtless made in imitation of the Greek autonomy, and seems originally to have been used in a moral sense only. It is of frequent occurrence in the works of the divines who flourished in the sixteenth and seventeenth centuries. After that period it appears to have been dropped for a time. We find it in none of the English dictionaries, although a long list of words is given compounded with self, and among them many which are now wholly out of use ; for instance, Shakspeare's Self-sovereignty. In Dr. Worcester's Universal and Crit. Dictionary, the word is marked with a star, which denotes that he has added it to Dr. Johnson's, and the authority given is Paley, who, to my certain knowledge, does not use it in his Political Philosophy, nor have several of my friends succeeded in finding it in any other part of his works, although diligent search has been made.

Whether the term was first used for political self-government in England or America I have not been able to ascertain. Richard Price, D.D., used it in a political sense in his Observations on the Nature of Civil Liberty, etc., 3d edition, London, 1776, although it does not clearly appear whether he means what we now designate by independence, or internal (domestic) self-government. Jefferson said, in 1798, that "the residuary rights are reserved to their (the American states) own *self-government.*" The term is now freely used both in England and America. In the former country we find a book on Local Self-government ; in ours, Daniel Webster said, on May the 22d, 1852, in his Faneuil Hall speech : "But I say to you and to our whole country, and to all the crowned heads and aristocratic powers and feudal systems that exist, that it is to self-government, the great principle of popular representation and administration—the system that lets in all to participate in the counsels that are to assign the good or evil to all—that we may owe what we are and what we hope to be."

Earl Derby, when premier, said, in the house of lords, that the officers

tees of individual liberty which have been mentioned receive their true import in a pervading system of self-government, and on the other hand are its refreshing springs. Individual liberty consists, in a great measure, in politically acknowledged self-reliance, and self-government is the sanction of self-reliance and self-determination in the various minor and larger circles in which government acts and of which it consists.

---

sent from abroad to assist in the funeral of the Duke of Wellington, would " bear witness back to their own country how safely and to what extent a people might be relied upon in whom the strongest hold of their government was their own reverence and respect for the free institutions of their country, and the principles of popular self-government controlled and modified by constitutional monarchy."

In one word, self-government is now largely used on both sides of the Atlantic, in a political sense.

This modern use of the word is no innovation, as it was no innovation when St. Paul used the old Greek word πίστις in the vastly expanded sense of christian faith. Ideas must be designated. The innovation was christianity itself, not the use of the word to designate an idea greater than Pistis could have signified before.

That self-government in politics is always applied by the English-speaking race for the self-government of the people or of an institution, in other words, that *self* has in this sense a reflective meaning, is as natural as the fact itself that the word has come, in course of time, to be applied to political government, simply because we must express the idea of a people or a part of a people who govern themselves and are not governed by some one else.

Self-government belongs to the Anglican race, and the English word is used even by foreigners. A German and a French statesman, both distinguished in literature and politics, used not long ago the English word in conversations in their own languages with me.

Donaldson's Greek Dictionary renders ἀυτονομια with self-government.

The word self, or its corresponding term in other languages, may have a reflective sense, as in self-murder, or it may have a merely emphatic or exclusive meaning, *ipse*, he himself. Hence the fact that the Emperor of Russia calls himself autocrat of all the Russias, (self-ruler, himself and alone the ruler,) and we use the corresponding word self-government for the opposite, the government in which the ruling is left to the ruled. The old English self-sovereign is the exact rendering of autocrat. The Germans use the word Selbst-Verlag, *i.e.* sale of the book by the author himself. German wine-shops in New York have frequently on their signs in English, the ludicrous words, Self-Imported Wines.

Without local self-government, in other words, self-government consistently carried out and applied to the realities of life, and not remaining a mere general theory, there is no real self-government according to Anglican views and feelings. Self-government is founded on the willingness of the people to take care of their own affairs, and the absence of that disposition which looks to the general government for everything; as well as on the willingness in each to let others take care of their own affairs. It cannot exist where the general principle of interference prevails, that is, the general disposition in the executive and administration, to do all it possibly can do, and to substitute its action for individual or minor activity and for self-reliance. Self-government is the corollary of liberty.

So far we have chiefly spoken of that part of liberty which consists in checks, except indeed when we treated of representative legislatures; self-government may be said to be liberty in action. It requires a pervading conviction throughout the whole community that government, and especially the executive and administrative branch, should do nothing but what it necessarily must do, and which cannot, or ought not, or will not be done by self-action; and that, moreover, it should allow matters to grow and develop themselves. Self-government implies self-institution, not only at the first setting out of government, but as a permanent principle of political life. In a pervading self-government, the formative action of the citizens is the rule; the general action of the government is the exception, and only an aid. The common action of government in this system is not originative, but regulative and moderative, or conciliative and adjusting. Self-government, therefore, transacts by far the greater bulk of all public business through citizens, who, even while clad with authority, remain essentially and strictly citizens, and parts of the people. It does not create nor tolerate a vast hierarchy of officers, forming a class of mandarins for themselves, and acting as though they formed and were the state, and the people only the substratum on which the state is founded, similar to the former view that the church consists of the hierarchy of priests and that the laity are only the ground on which it stands.

A pervading self-government, in the Anglican sense, is organic. It does not consist in the mere negation of power, which would be absurd, for all government implies power, authority on the one hand and obedience on the other; nor does it consist in mere absence of action, as little as the mere absence of censorship in China is liberty of the press. It consists in organs of combined self-action, in institutions, and in a systematic connection of these institutions. It is therefore the opposite at once of a disintegration of society into individual, dismembered and disjunctive independencies, and of despotism, whether this consists in the satrap despotism of the east, (in which the pacha or satrap embodies indeed the general principle of unfreedom in relation to his superior, but is a miniature despot or sultan to all below him,) or whether it consist in the centralized despotism resting on a dense and thoroughly systematized hierarchy of officials, as in China, or in the European despotic countries. Anglican self-government differs in principle from the sejunction into which ultimately the government of the Netherlands lapsed; and it is equally far from popular absolutism, in which the majority is the absolute despot. The majority may shift, indeed, in popular absolutism, but the principle does not, and the whole can only be called a mutually tyrannizing society, not a self-government. An American orator of note has lately called self-government, a people sitting in committee of the whole. It is a happy expression of what he conceives self-government to be. We understand at once what he means; but what he means is the Athenian market democracy, in its worst time, or as a French writer has expressed it, Le peuple-empereur, the people-despot. It is, in fact, one of the opposites of self-government, as much so as the one expressed in the favorite saying of Napoleon I.: "Everything for the people, nothing by the people." Self-government means Everything for the people, and by the people, considered as the totality of organic institutions, constantly evolving in their character, as all organic life is, but not a dictatorial multitude. Dictating is the rule of the army, not of liberty; it is the destruction of individuality. But liberty, as we have seen, consists in a great measure in protection of individuality.

While Napoleon I. thus epigrammatically expressed the essence of French centralization,[1] his chief antagonist, William Pitt, even the tory premier, could not help becoming the organ of Anglican self-government, as appears from the anecdote, which I relate in full as it was lately given to the public, because the indorsement by the uncompromising soldier gives it additional meaning:

" A day or two before the death of the Duke of Wellington, referring to the subject of civic feasts, he told an incident in the life of Pitt which is worth recording. The last public dinner which Pitt attended was at the Mansion house; when his health was proposed as the savior of his country. The duke expressed his admiration of Pitt's speech in reply; which was in substance, that the country had saved herself by her own exertions, and that every other country might do the same by following her example."[2]

Self-government is in its nature the opposite to political apathy and that moral torpidity or social indifference which is sure to give free play to absolutism, or else to dissolve the whole polity. We have a fearful instance in the later Roman empire. It draws its strength from self-reliance, as has been stated, and it promotes it in turn; it cannot exist where

---

[1] As to the first part of this imperial dictum—tout pour le peuple—we know very well how difficult it is to know what is for the people, without institutional indexes of public opinion, and how easy it is, even for the wisest and the best, to mistake and substitute individual, family and class interests, and passions, for the wants of the people. This, indeed, constitutes one of the inherent and greatest difficulties of monarchical despotism. A benevolent eastern despot could not have said it, for there is no people, politically speaking, in Asia; and for a European ruler it was either hypocritical, or showing that Napoleon was ignorant of the drift of modern civilization, of which political development forms so large a portion.

[2] London Spectator of September 18, 1852.

there is not in each a disposition and manliness of character willing and able to acknowledge it in others.   Nothing strikes an observer, accustomed to Anglican self-government, more strongly in France than the constant desire and tendency even in the French democracy to interfere with all things and actions, and to leave nothing to self-development.   Self-government requires politically, in bodies, that self-rule which moral self-government requires of the individual—the readiness of resigning the use of power which we may possess, quite as often as using it.   Yet it would be a great mistake to suppose that self-government implies weakness.   Absolutism is weak.   It can summon great strength upon certain occasions, as all concentration can ;   but it is no school of strength or character; nor is a certain concentration by any means foreign to self-government, but it is not left in the hands of the executive, to use it arbitrarily.   Nor is it maintained that self-government necessarily leads in each single case soonest and most directly to a desired end, especially when this belongs to the physical welfare of the people ; nor that absolute and centralized governments may not occasionally perform brilliant deeds, or carry out sudden improvements on a vast scale which it may not be in the power of self-governments so rapidly to execute.   But the main question for the freeman is which is the most befitting to man in his nobler state ; which produces the best and most lasting results upon the whole and in the long run ; which effects the greatest stability and continuity of development; in which is more action of sound and healthful life and not of feverish paroxysms; which possesses the greatest tenacity ?   Is it the brilliant exploits which constitute the grandeur of nations if surveyed in history, and are there not many brilliant actions peculiar to self-government and denied to centralized absolutism?

In history at large, we observe that the material and brilliant influence of states is frequently in accordance with their size and the concentration of their governments; but that the lasting and essential influence exercised by states is in propor-

tion to their vigorous self-government. This influence, however, is less visible, and requires analyzing investigation, to be
discovered and laid open. The influence of England on the
whole progress of our race has been far greater than that of
France, but far less brilliant than that of the period of Louis
XIV. A similar observation may be made in all spheres.
The influence which the mind of Aristotle has had on our race
far surpasses the effects of all the brilliant exploits of his imperial pupil, yet thousands learn the name of Alexander the
Great, even in our primary schools, who never hear of Aristotle. Nature herself furnishes man with illustrations of this
fact. The organic life which silently pervades the whole with
a creative power, is not readily seen, while convulsions, erup-
tions and startling phenomena attract the attention, or cause
at least the wonder of the least observing.

Where self-government does not exist, the people are always
exposed to the danger that the end of government is lost
sight of, and that governments assume themselves as their
own ends, sometimes under the name of the country, sometimes under the name of the ruling house. Where self-
government exists, a somewhat similar danger presents itself
in political parties. They frequently assume that they
themselves are the end and object, and forget that they can
stand on defensible ground only if they subserve the country.
Man is always exposed to the danger of substituting the means
for the ends. The variations we might make on the ancient
Propter vitam vivendi perdere causas, with perfect justice, are
indeed endless.[1]

Napoleon I., who well knew the character of absolute
government and pursued it as the great end of his life, nevertheless speaks of the "impuissance de la force"—the impotency

---

[1] Do not all the following, and many more, find their daily or historical
applications: Propter imperium imperandi perdere causas; Propter
ecclesiam ecclesiæ perdere causas; Propter legem legis perdere causas;
Propter argumentationem argumenti perdere causas; Propter dictionem
dicendi perdere causas?

17

of power.[1] He felt, on his imperial throne, which on another
and public occasion he called wood and velvet unless occupied
by him, and which was but another wording of Louis XIV.'s
l'état c'est moi, that which all sultans have felt when their
janizaries deposed them—he felt, that of all governments the
czar-government is the most precarious.   He felt what, with
other important truths, Mr. de Tocqueville had the boldness to
tell the national assembly, in a carefully considered report of
a committee, in 1851, when he said:

"That people, of all nations in the whole world, which has
indeed overthrown its government more frequently than any
other, has, nevertheless, the habit, and feels more than any
other the necessity of being ruled.

"The nations which have a federal existence, even those
which, without having divided the sovereignty, possess an
aristocracy, or who enjoy provincial liberties deeply rooted in
their traditions—these nations are able to exist a long time
with a feeble government, and even to support, for a certain
period, the complete absence of a government.   Each part of
the people has its own life, which permits society to support
itself for some time when the general life is suspended.   But
are we one of those nations?   Have we not centralized all
matters, and thus created of all governments that which, indeed, it is the easiest to upset, but with which it is at the same
time the most difficult to dispense for a moment?"[2]

---

[1] The Memoirs of Count Miot, the first volumes of which have lately
been published, show more in detail, than any other work, with what
eagerness, consistency and boldness, Napoleon I. endeavored, step by
step, to break down every guarantee of liberty which the French people had established.   He did this so soon as he had been made consul
for life, and succeeded, through the newly-established senate and council
of state, in nearly all cases.   When he attempted to abolish the trial by
jury, supported as he was by his high law-officers, the institution was
saved by a few men, showing, on that occasion, a degree of resolution
which had become rare, even at so early a period.

[2] Mr. de Tocqueville made this report on the 8th of July, in the name
of the majority of that committee, to which had been referred several
propositions relating to a revision of the constitution.   It was the time

With this extract I conclude, for the present, my remarks on self-government, and with them the enumeration of the guarantees and institutions which characterize, and in their aggregate constitute Anglican liberty.

---

when the constitutional term of the president drew to its end, and the desire of annulling the ineligibility for a second term became manifest. It was the feverish time that preceded the second of December, destined to become another of the many commentaries on the facility with which governments founded upon centralization are upset, by able conspiracies or by a terror-striking surprise, such as the revolution of February had been, when the Orleans dynasty was expelled, and another proof how easy it is in such states to obtain an acquiescent majority or its semblance.

In connection with the foregoing, I must ask leave to add the concluding remarks of the Ancien Régime, published since the first edition of Civil Liberty was issued. I know of no passage in modern literature which reminds the reader so directly of the energy and gloom of Tacitus. I quote from Mr. Bonner's translation, New York, 1856, and wish to say that the whole work of Mr. de Tocqueville is a continued historical commentary of all that is said in the present work on Gallican political tendencies.

"When I examine that nation (the French) in itself, I cannot help thinking it is more extraordinary than any of the events of its history. Did there ever appear on the earth another nation so fertile in contrasts, so extreme in its acts—more under the dominion of feeling, less ruled by principle; always better or worse than was anticipated—now below the level of humanity, now far above; a people so unchangeable in its leading features, that it may be recognized by portraits drawn two or three thousand years ago, and yet so fickle in its daily opinions and tastes that it becomes at last a mystery to itself, and is as much astonished as strangers at the sight of what it has done; naturally fond of home and routine, yet once driven forth, and forced to adopt new customs, ready to carry principles to any lengths, and to dare anything; indocile by disposition, but better pleased with the arbitrary and even violent rule of a sovereign, than with a free and regular government under its chief citizens; now fixed in hostility to subjection of any kind, now so passionately wedded to servitude that nations made to serve can not vie with it; led by a thread so long as no word of resistance is spoken, wholly ungovernable when the standard of revolt has been raised—thus always deceiving its masters, who fear it too much or too little; never so free that it can not be subjugated, nor so kept down that it can not break the yoke; qualified for every pursuit, but excelling in nothing but war; more prone to worship chance, force, success, eclat, noise, than real glory; endowed

They prevail more or less developed wherever the Anglican race has spread and formed governments, or established distinct polities. Yet, as each of them may be carried out with peculiar consistency, or is subject to be developed under the influence of additional circumstances, or as a peculiar character may be given to the expansion of the one or the other element, it is a natural consequence that the system of guarantees which we have called Anglican, presents itself in various forms. All the broad Anglican principles, as they have been stated, are necessary to us, but there is, nevertheless, that which we can call American liberty—a development of Anglican liberty peculiar to ourselves. Those features which may, perhaps, be called the most characteristic, are given in the following chapter.

---

with more heroism than virtue, more genius than common sense; better adapted for the conception of grand designs than the accomplishment of great enterprises; the most brilliant and the most dangerous nation of Europe, and the one that is surest to inspire admiration, hatred, terror, or pity, but never indifference ?

"No nation but such a one as this could give birth to a revolution so sudden, so radical, so impetuous in its course, and yet so full of missteps, contradictory facts, and conflicting examples. The French could not have done it but for the reasons I have alleged; but it must be admitted even these reasons would not suffice to explain such a revolution in any country but France."

CHAPTER XXII.

AMERICAN LIBERTY.

AMERICAN liberty belongs to the great division of Anglican liberty. It is founded upon the checks, guarantees and self-government of the Anglican race.[1] The trial by jury, the representative government, the common law, self-taxation, the supremacy of the law, publicity, the submission of the army to the legislature, and whatever else has been enumerated, form part and parcel of our liberty. There are, however, features and guarantees, which are peculiar to ourselves, and which, therefore, we may say constitute American liberty. They may be summed up, perhaps, under these heads : republican federalism, strict separation of the state from the church, greater equality and acknowledgment of abstract rights in the citizen, and a more popular or democratic cast of the whole polity.

The Americans do not say that there can be no liberty without republicanism, nor do they, indeed, believe that wherever a republican or kingless government exists, there is liberty. The founders of our own independence acknowledged that freedom can exist under a monarchical government, in the very act of their declaration of independence. Throughout

---

[1] We have discussed the trial by jury and even the grand jury, as elements of Anglican liberty. I am now obliged to add, that when this page was correcting for the press, the author learned that the state of Michigan had passed a law by which, after the 12th day of April, 1859, the grand jury is to be dispensed with as an ordinary instrument of criminal proceeding, though power is reserved to the judges to resort to it in certain special cases. The people of Michigan have thus shown an inclination toward the French system: French, and continental European lawyers in general have an aversion to the grand jury.

that instrument the Americans are spoken of as freemen whose rights and liberties England had unwarrantably invaded. It rests all its assertions and all the claimed rights on the liberty that had been enjoyed, and after a long recital of deeds of misrule ascribed to the king, it says: "A prince, whose character is thus marked by every act which may define a tyrant, is unfit to be the ruler of a free people." It broadly admits, therefore, that a free people may have a monarch, and that the Americans were, and considered themselves a free people before they claimed to form a separate nation.

Nevertheless it will be denied by no one that the Americans believe that to be the happiest political state of things in which a republican government is the fittest; nor that republicanism has thoroughly infused itself into all their institutions and views. This republicanism, though openly pronounced at the time of the revolution only, had been long, and historically prepared, by nearly all the institutions and the peculiarly fortunate situation of the colonies, or, it may be said, that the republican elements of British self-government found a peculiarly favorable soil in America from the first settlements.

A fault of England, to speak from an English point of view, was of great service to American republicanism. England never created a colonial aristocracy. Had she sprinkled this country with a colonial peerage and put this peerage in some vital connection with the peerage of Great Britain; for instance, had she allowed the colonial peers to elect representative peers to sit in the British house of lords, as is the case with Scottish peers, and had she given some proportionate precedence to American noblemen, e.g. had she allowed an American duke to take precedence with a British earl, she would have had a strong support in this country at the time of the revolution. Possibly, we would have had not only a simple war of independence, but a civil war, and our so-called revolution, which was no revolution in the sense in which we take the word when we apply it to the revolutions of England and France, and which in German is called an Abfall (severance,) must have had a far different character. It was one of our great blessings that we were not obliged to pass through an internal convulsion in order to establish independence and republican freedom. It was a blessing, a fortune, vouchsafed us, not made by us—a fact which we must never forget when we compare our struggle, or that of the Netherlands, with the real revolutions of other countries, if we desire to be just.

But it is not only republicanism that forms one of the prominent features of American liberty, it is representative republicanism and the principle of confederation or federalism,[1] which must be added, in order to express this principle correctly. We do not only consider the representative principle necessary in all our states in their unitary character, but the framers of our constitution boldly conceived a federal republic, or the application of the representative principle with its two houses to a confederacy. It was the first instance in history. The Netherlands, which served our forefathers as models in many respects, even in the name bestowed on our confederacy, furnished them with no example for this great conception. It is the chief American contribution to the common treasures of political civilization. It is that by which America will influence other parts of the world more than by any other political institution or principle. Already are voices heard in Australia for a representative federal republic like ours. Switzerland, so far as she has of late reformed her federal constitution, has done so in avowed imitation of the federal pact of our Union. I consider the mixture of wisdom and daring, shown in the framing of our constitution, as one of the most remarkable facts in all history. Our frame of government, then, is justly called a federal republic, with one chief magistrate elected by what the Greeks called, in politics, the Koinon, the Whole, with a complete representative government for that whole, a common army, a judiciary of the Union, and with the authority of taxing the whole. It is called by no one a league.

---

[1] Federalism is taken here, of course, in its philosophical, and not in its party sense.

Of the strict separation of the church from the state, in all the federated states, I have spoken already. The Americans consider it as a legitimate consequence of the liberty of conscience. They believe that the contrary would lead to disastrous results with reference to religion itself, and it is undeniable that another state of things could not by possibility have been established here. We believe, moreover, that the great mission which this country has to perform, with reference to Europe, requires this total divorce of state and church (not religion.)[1] Doubtless, this unstinted liberty leads to occasional inconvenience ; even the multiplicity of sects itself is not free from evils; but how would it be if this divorce did not exist ? The Americans cling with peculiar fervor to this very principle.

We carry the principle of political equality much farther than any free nation. We had no colonial nobility, although some idea of establishing it was entertained in England when the revolution broke out, and the framers of the constitution took care to forbid every state, and the United States collectively, from establishing any nobility. Even the establishment of the innocent Cincinnati Society gave umbrage to

---

[1] I lately saw a pamphlet written by an American minister, in which the Constitution of the United States was called atheistical—an expression I have seen before. I do not pretend exactly to understand its meaning. I suppose, however, that the word atheistical is taken in this case as purely negative, and as equivalent to non-mentioning God, not, of course, as equivalent to reviling the deity. Even in this more moderate sense, however, the expression seems to me surprising. There was a time when every treaty, nay every bill of lading began with the words, In the name of the Holy Trinity, and every physician put the alpha and omega at the top of his recipe. Whatever the sources may have been from which these usages sprang, I believe it will be admitted that the modern usage is preferable, and that it does not necessarily indicate a diminished zeal. The most religious among the framers may not have thought of placing the name of God at the head of our constitution, for the very reason that God was before their eyes, and that this occasion did not suggest to them the idea of specially expressing their belief. Nec deus intersit nisi dignus vindice nodus.

many.[1] We have no right of primogeniture.[2] This equality has more and more developed itself, and all states I believe have adopted the principle of universal suffrage. Property qualification for voting does not exist any longer, and for being elected, it exists in very few states. The Constitution of the United States provides for representation in the lower house, according to numbers, except that slave property is represented.

But here it must be observed that, however unqualifiedly the principle of political equality is adopted throughout the whole country with reference to the white population, it stops short with the race. Property is not allowed to establish any difference, but color is. Socially the colored man is denied equality in all states, and politically he is so in those states in which the free colored man is denied the right of voting, and where slavery exists. I believe I may state as a fact that the stanchest abolitionist, who insists upon immediate manumission of all slaves, does not likewise insist upon an immediate admission of the whole manumitted population to a perfect political equality. In this, however, I may be mistaken.

Two elements constitute all human progress, historical development and abstract reasoning. It results from the very nature of man, whom God has made an individual and a social

---

[1] In Europe, where an accurate knowledge of the American state of things did not exist, it was, I believe, universally considered as the beginning of a new nobility, and pointed out as a glaring inconsistency.

[2] We can do entirely without it as to property in land. Our abundance of land does not require it; but there are countries in which the constant parcelling of land led to such a ruinous subdivision, that the governments were obliged to establish a minimum beyond which land shall not be allowed to be divided, and which, thus undivided, goes either to the oldest or the youngest of the sons. The late president von Vincke, one of the most distinguished Prussian statesmen, mentioned in an elaborate report on the extreme division of land, that there had been a lawsuit in the Rhenish province about a square foot or two of vineyard land. Such cases, probably, are of frequent occurrence in China. What would be said in those densely-peopled countries, of our Virginia or worm-fences, which waste a strip of land five feet wide throughout the south and west?

being. His historical development results from the continuity of society.[1] Without it, without traditional knowledge and institutions, without education, man would no longer be man; without individual reasoning, without bold abstraction, there would be no advancement either. Now, single men, entire societies, whole periods will incline more to the one or to the other element, and both present themselves occasionally in individuals and entire epochs as caricatures. One-sidedness is to be shunned in this as in all other cases; perfection, wisdom, results from the well-balanced conjunction of both, and I do not know any nobler instance of this wisdom than that which is presented by the men of our revolution. They were bold men, as I have stated already; they went fearlessly to work, and launched upon a sea that had as yet been little navigated, when they proposed to themselves the establishment of a republic for a large country. Yet they changed only what imperatively required change; what they retained constituted an infinitely greater portion than that which they changed. It does not require an extraordinary power of abstraction, nor very profound knowledge, to imagine what must have been the consequence, had they upset the whole system in which they lived, and allowed their ill-will toward England, or a puerile vanity, to induce them to attempt an entirely new state of things.

They, on the contrary, adopted every principle and institution of liberty that had been elaborated by the English. They acted like the legislators of antiquity. Had they acted otherwise, their constitution must have proved a still-born child, as so many other constitutions proclaimed since their days, have done. Their absence of all conceit, and their manly calmness, will forever redound to their honor.

It seems to me that while the English incline occasionally too much to the historical element, we, in turn, incline occasionally too much toward abstraction.

However this may be, it is certain that we conceive of the rights of the citizen more in the abstract and more as attri-

---

[1] This is treated more fully in the Political Ethics.

butes of his humanity, so long as this means our own white race. Beyond it the abstraction ceases, so much so that the supreme court lately decided that people of color (although they were unquestionably subjects to the King of England before the independence of the United States) are not citizens in the sense of the constitution,[1] and that several free states have enacted laws against the ingress of people of color, which seem to be founded exclusively on the power which the white race possesses over the colored, and which elicit little examination because the first basis of all justice, sympathy, is wanting between the two races.

From this conception of the citizenship—this carrying of the ancient jus ante omnia jura natum, so long as it relates to our own race, much farther than the English do—arises the fact that in nearly all states universal suffrage has been established, while in England the idea of class representation much more prevails. The Americans do not know, I believe, in a single case the English rate-paying suffrage; but it must be recorded that the serious misrule of American cities has induced the opinion of many reflecting men that populous cities can not be ruled by bare universal suffrage; since universal suffrage, applied to city governments, gives to the great majority, that do not own houses or land, the right to raise and dispose of the taxes solely levied on real property.

On the other hand, it appears to Americans a flagrant act to disfranchise entire corporate constituencies for gross pervading bribery, as has been repeatedly done in English history. Indeed the right of voting has been often pronounced in England a vested right of property.

I have also stated that our whole government has a more popular cast than that of England, and with reference to this fact, as well as to the one mentioned immediately before it, I would point out the following farther characteristics of American liberty.

---

[1] The Dred Scott case, already so famous, but which will become far more famous still in the course of our history.

We have established everywhere voting by ballot. There
is an annually increasing number of members voting in the
English commons for the ballot. It is desired there to prevent intimidation. Probably it would have that effect in England, but certainly not in such a degree as the English seem
to expect. The ballot does not necessarily prevent the vote
of a person from being known.[1] Although the ballot is so
strongly insisted upon in America, it is occasionally entirely
lost sight of.

"Tickets" printed on paper whose color indicates the party
which has issued it, are the most common things; and, in the
place of my former residence, it happened some years ago that
party feeling ran to such a height, that, in order to prevent
melancholy consequences, the leaders came to an agreement.
It consisted in this : that alternate hours should be assigned
to the two parties, during which the members of one party only
should vote. This open defeat of the ballot was carried out
readily and in good faith.

The Constitution of the United States, and those of all the
states, provide that the houses of the legislatures shall keep
their journals, and that on the demand of a certain, not very
large, number of members, the ayes and noes shall be recorded. The ayes and noes have sometimes a remarkable effect.
It is recorded of Philip IV. of Spain,[2] that he asked the
opinion of his council on a certain subject. The opinion was
unanimously adverse, whereupon the monarch ordered every
counsellor to send in his vote signed with his name, and every

---

[1] There is an instructive article on voting in the Edinburgh Review,
of October, 1852, on Representative Reform. The writer, who justly
thinks it all-important that every one who has the right to vote for a
member of parliament should vote, proposes written votes to be left at
the house of every voter, the blanks to be filled by him, as is now
actually done for parish elections. There existed written votes in the
early times of New England, and people were fined for not sending them.
It was not necessary to carry them personally to the poll. These written
votes prevailed in the middle ages. For this and other subjects connected with elections, see the paper on elections in the appendix.

[2] Coxe's Memoirs of the Bourbons in Spain.

vote turned out to be in favor of the proposed measure. The ayes and noes have unfortunately sometimes a similar effect with us. Still, this peculiar voting may operate upon the timid as often beneficially as otherwise; at any rate, the Americans believe that it is proper thus to oblige members to make their vote known to their constituents.

We never give the executive the right of dissolving the legislature, nor to prorogue it.

We have never closed the list of the states composing the Union, in which we differ from most other confederacies, ancient or modern; we admit freely to our citizenship those who are foreigners by birth, and we do not believe in inalienable allegiance.[1]

We allow, as it has been seen, no attainder of blood.

We allow no ex post facto laws.

---

[1] The character of the English, and of our allegiance, is treated at length in the Political Ethics. I there took the ground that even English allegiance is a national one, whatever the language of the law books may be to the contrary. The following may serve as a farther proof that English allegiance, after all, *is* dissoluble. It appears from the New England charter, granted by James I., that he claimed, or had the right "to put a person out of his allegiance and protection." Page 16, Compact, with the Charter and Laws of the Colony of New Plymouth, etc.; Boston, 1836.

Had we any nobility, or had we closed our confederacy, we must have been exposed to the troubles to which the ancient republics were exposed, and which form a leading feature through the whole history of Rome. We acquired Louisiana, and, with her French population she is fairly assimilated with our great polity. She would have been a dangerous cancer had we treated her as Rome treated her acquisitions, and a war of the *Socii*, as the Romans had it, must ultimately have broken out. In this then we differ in a marked way from the English. When Scotland was united to England, by establishing one legislature for both, and when a similar process took place with reference to Ireland, a perfect assimilation was not the consequence as had been the case with Wales. The non-assimilation is still more marked in the case of the colonies. English readers may possibly believe that a foreign author passes his proper boundary if he ventures to discuss a subject of the highest statesmanship peculiarly domestic in its character, but "the by-stander often sees the faults of the men in the ring." How could we write on foreign his-

American liberty contains, as one of its characteristic elements, the enacted or written constitution. This feature distinguishes it especially from the English polity with its accumulative constitution.

We do not allow, therefore, our legislatures to be politically "omnipotent," as, theoretically at least, the British parliament is.[1] This characteristic, again, naturally led to the right and duty of our supreme courts in the states, and of the supreme court of the United States, to decide whether a law passed, by

---

tory, were we not allowed to judge of foreign subjects? Nor is this subject wholly foreign to an American, because he naturally knows more of Canada than most English do, and he knows his own colonial history. Thus justified, and making full allowance for the difficulties that may exist, we cannot help feeling surprised that England, in many other respects the only power that has shown true liberality toward colonies—so different from Spain!—and with our war of independence before her eyes, should not think of tying the distant empires she creates in all the portions of the globe, by a representation in her parliament, making it, so far as the colonies are concerned, the imperial congress. Though each distinct colony with a colonial self-government should have but two or three representatives in the commons, representing the colony as such, it seems that the effect upon the consistency of the whole gigantic empire would be distinct, and that such a measure is the only one that would promise continued cohesiveness.

[1] For the English reader I would add that the following works ought to be studied, or consulted on this subject: The Constitution of the United States, and the constitutions of the different states, which are published from time to time, collected in one volume; the Debates on the Federal Constitution; The Federalist, by Hamilton, Madison, and Jay; the Writings of Chief Justice Marshall, Boston, 1839; the History of the Constitution of the United States, by G. T. Curtis, a work of mark; Mr. Justice Story's Commentaries on the Constitution of the United States; Mr. Calhoun's and Mr. Webster's Works; Mr. Rawle's work on the Constitution, and Mr. Frederic Grimke's Considerations upon the Nature and Tendency of Free Institutions, Cincinnati, 1848. To these may be added the Course of Lectures on the Constitutional Jurisprudence of the United States, by W. A. Duer, Boston, 1856. An entire literature of its own has accumulated, by this time, on the constitution, jurisprudence and constitutional history of the United States. The chief of the enumerated works will suffice to lead the student to the more detailed works of this department.

the legislature or by congress, is in conformity with the superior law—the constitution, or not, in other words, on the constitutionality of a law. It has been stated already that the courts have no power to decide on the law in general; but they decide, incidentally, on the whole law, when a specific case of conflict between a certain law and the constitution is brought before them.

I may add as a feature of American liberty, that the American impeachment is, as I have stated before, a political, and not a penal institution. It seems to me that I am borne out in this view by the Federalist.[1]

In conclusion, I would state as one of the characteristics of American liberty, the freedom of our rivers. The unimpeded navigation of rivers belongs to the right of free locomotion and intercommunication, of which we have treated; yet there is no topic of greater interest to the historian, the economist, and the statesman, than the navigation of rivers, because though the rivers are nature's own highways, and ought to be as efficient agents of civilization as the Road, or the Mail, their agency has been thwarted by the oppressive force of man, in almost all periods of our history. The Roman empire, doing little indeed for commerce, by comprehensive statesmanships, effected at least a general freedom of the rivers, within its territory, as a natural consequence of its unity. The Danube became free, from the interior of Germany to the Black Sea. But the barbarous times which succeeded reduced, once more, the rivers to the state of insecurity in which they had been before the imperial arm had warded off intrusion and interruption. Free navigation had not even been re-established in

---

[1] No. lxv.

As to the parties in America, they may fairly be said to have little to do with civil liberty, which will be readily seen by the so-called National Platforms, resolved upon as the true indexes of the parties by the conventions held preparatory to the presidential elections. Nor do the names of the parties indicate anything with reference to Liberty. The term Democratic has wholly lost its original meaning, as used to designate the party which has taken it. Among others, the Resolutions published by the different conventions in the year 1853, previous to Mr. Pierce's election, and which were drawn up with great care, fully prove this.

all the larger empires of the European continent, when the first
French revolution broke out.   It was one of the most important
provisions of the act of confederation, agreed upon at Vienna,
in 1815, between the Germanic states, that immediate steps
should be taken, to make the river navigation in Germany free,
but the desired object had not been obtained as late as in 1848.[1]
The long dispute about the navigation of the river Scheldt has
become famous in the history of law and of human progress. In
this case, however, a foreign power, the Netherlands, denied
free navigation to those in whose country the river rises and becomes navigable.[2] Magna Charta declares, indeed, what has
been called " the freedom of the rivers," but, on the one hand,
English rivers are, comparatively speaking, of little importance
to navigation, and, on the other hand, England had not to overcome the difficulty which arises out of the same river passing
through different states.   It was therefore a signal step in the
progress of our species, when the wise framers of our constitution
enacted, that vessels bound to, or from one state, shall not be
obliged to enter, clear or pay duties in another,[3] and every one
who cherishes his country and the essential interests of our
species must be grateful that subsequent legislation, and decisions by courts have firmly established[4] the inestimable right of
free navigation in a country, endowed with a system of rivers
more magnificent and more benign, if left free and open, than

---

[1] I owe to the friendship of Mr. Kapp, (author of the Life of Baron
Steuben,) a book of remarkable interest, in many respects : Gottlieb Mit-
telberger's Journey to Pennsylvania in the year 1750 and Return to
Germany in 1754; Frankfurt, 1756.   Mittelberger was organist and
schoolmaster. He was seven weeks on his way from Wurtemberg to
Rotterdam, chiefly on the Rhine. The Journal of Albert Durer, the
great painter, gives the same lamentable account of his journey on the
Main and Rhine.

[2] A time may come—I believe it will—when the international law of
our family of nations, will acknowledge that those who border on a
navigable river, have a right, by nature, to sail down that river to the
sea without hindrance, toll or inconvenience.

[3] Constitution of the United States, section 9.

[4] See, among others, Duer's Lectures on the Constitutional Jurisprudence of the United States, 2d edition, page 258 and sequ.

that of any other country. An able writer and comprehensive statesman says:

"It was under the salutary instruction thus afforded by the Scheldt, and just before the French revolution broke its shackles, that our thirteen confederated states acquired the Mississippi.

"In March, 1785, Rufus King, then a delegate from Massachusetts in the congress of the confederation, received from Timothy Pickering a letter containing these emphatic and memorable words:

"'The water communications in that country will always be in the highest degree interesting to the inhabitants. It seems very necessary to secure the *freedom of navigating* these to *all the inhabitants of all the states.* I hope we shall have no *Scheldts* in that country.'[1]

"The high duty of carrying into effect that great suggestion, immediately occupied the attention of Mr. King and his associates. The honor of framing the clause—which secures, 'not for a day, but for all time,' freedom of commerce over an unbroken net-work of navigable water spread out for more than sixteen thousand miles—was shared between Massachusetts and Virginia, then standing shoulder to shoulder, where they had stood throughout the Revolution.

"The clause was formally introduced into the Congress by Mr. Grayson, of Virginia, and seconded by Mr. King, of Massachusetts. Listen to its words, so broadly national, so purely American:

"'The navigable waters leading into the Mississippi and St. Lawrence, and the carrying places between the same, shall be *common property*, and FOREVER FREE, as well to the inhabitants of the said country, as to the citizens of the United States, and those of any other states that may be admitted into the confederacy—WITHOUT ANY TAX, DUTY, OR IMPOST THEREFOR.'"

---

[1] The original is in the possession of Dr. Charles King, president of Columbia College, New York.

"The clause was immediately incorporated into the ordinance, and passed by the congress on the 13th day of July, 1787.

"Here, then, we behold the Magna Charta of the internal navigation of America,"[1] which we enjoy, and have first enjoyed, of all confederacies, ancient or modern. It gives the absolutely free use of the noblest river system extending over a continent.

---

[1] This passage is copied from a Defence of the Right and the Duty of the American Union to improve the Navigable Waters, by Samuel B. Ruggles, a speech delivered in October, 1852. The speaker has given his views on this and kindred topics, more extensively in a state paper of rare excellence, whether the contents, the historical survey and statistic knowledge, or the transparency of the style and language be considered. The paper bears the title, Memorial of the Canal Board and Canal Commissioners of the State of New York, asking for the Improvement of the Lake Harbors by the General Government, Albany, N. Y., 1858, and was, as such, adopted by the legislature of New York and presented to congress.

CHAPTER XXIII.

IN WHAT CIVIL LIBERTY CONSISTS, PROVED BY CONTRARIES.

I HAVE endeavored to give a sketch of Anglican liberty. It is the liberty we prize and love for a hundred reasons, and which we would love if there were no other reason than that it *is* liberty. We know that it is the political state most befitting to conscious man. History as well as our own pregnant times prove to us the value of those guarantees; their necessity, if we wish to see our political dignity secure, and their effect upon the stability of government, as well as on the energies of the people. We are proud of our self-government and our love of the law as our master, and we cling the faster to all these ancient and modern guarantees, the more we observe that, wherever the task which men have proposed to themselves is the suppression of liberty, these guarantees are sure to be the first objects of determined and persevering attack. It is instructive for the friend of freedom to observe how uniformly and instinctively the despots of all ages and countries have assailed the different guarantees enumerated in the preceding pages. We can learn much in all practical matters by the rule of contraries. As the arithmetician proves his multiplication by division, and his subtraction by addition, so may we learn what those who love liberty ought to prize, by observing what those who hate freedom suppress or war against. This process is made peculiarly easy as well as interesting at this very period, when the government of a large nation is avowedly engaged in suppressing all liberty and in establishing the most uncompromising monarchical absolutism.

I do not know a single guarantee contained in the foregoing pages, which might not be accompanied by a long historical commentary showing how necessary it is, from the fact that it has been attacked by those who are plainly and universally acknowledged as having oppressed liberty or as having been, at least, guilty of the inchoate crime. It is a useful way to turn the study of history to account, especially for the youth of free nations. It turns their general ardor to distinct realities, and furnishes the student with confirmations by facts. We ought always to remember that one of the most efficient modes of learning the healthful state of our body and the normal operation of its various organs, consists in the study of their diseased states and abnormal conditions. The pathologic method is an indispensable one in all philosophy and in politics. The imperial time of Rome is as replete with pathetic lessons for the statesman as the republican epoch.

It would lead me far beyond the proper limits of this work, were I to select all the most noted periods of usurpation, or those times in which absolutism, whether monarchical or democratic, has assumed the sway over liberty, and thus to try the gage of our guarantees. It may be well, however, to select a few instances.

In doing so I shall restrict myself to instances taken from the transactions of modern nations of our own race; but the student will do well to compare the bulk of our liberty with the characteristics of ancient and modern despotism in Asia, and see how the absence of our safeguards has there always prevented the development of humanity which we prize so highly. He ought then to compare this our own modern liberty with what is more particularly called antiquity, and see in what we excel the ancients or fall behind them, and in what that which they revered as liberty differed from ours. He ought to keep in mind our guarantees in reading the history of former free states, and of the processes by which they lost their liberty, or of the means to which the enemies of liberty have resorted, from those so masterly delineated by Aristotle, down to Dr. Francia and those of the present time, and he ought again to compare our broadcast national liberty with the liberties of the feudal age. He ought lastly to present clearly to his mind the psychologic processes by which liberty has been lost—by gratitude, hero-worship, impatience, indolence, permitting great personal popularity to overshadow institutions and laws, hatred against opposite parties or classes, denial of proper power to government, the arrogation of more and more power, and the gradual transition into absolutism; by local jealousies, by love of glory and conquest, by passing unwise laws against a magnified and irritating evil—laws which afterwards serve to oppress all, by recoiling oppression of a part, by poverty and by worthless use of wealth, by sensuality and that indifference which always follows in its train.

Liberty of communion is one of the first requisites of freedom. Wherever, therefore, a government struggles against liberty, this communion forms a subject of peculiar attention. Not only is liberty of the press abolished, but all communion is watched over by the power-holder, or suppressed as far as possible. The spy, the mouchard, the dilator, the informer, the sycophant, are sure accompaniments of absolutism.[1] The British administration under Charles II. and James II. looked with a jealous eye on the "coffee-houses," and occasionally suppressed them. One of the first things done by the French minister of police, after the second of December, was to close a number of "cabarets" at Paris, and to put all France under surveillance. This may become necessary for a time under pressing circumstances, which may place a government in the position of a general in a beleaguered city, but it is not liberty; it is the contrary, and if the measure is adopted as a permanent one, it becomes sheer despotism. So soon as Louis Napoleon had placed himself at the head of an absolute government, he not only abolished the liberty of the press, but he went much farther, as we have seen; he placed the printing-presses themselves and the sale of type under the police, and ordered that no press with the necessary

---

[1] Much that relates to the history of the spy and informer, in ancient and modern times, may be found in the second volume of Political Ethics, where the citizen's duty of informing is discussed.

printing materials should be sold or change hands without previous information being given to the police.

While it is a characteristic of our liberty that the public funds are under the peculiar guardianship of the popular house of the legislature, and that short appropriations are made for distinct purposes, especially for the army and navy, all governments hostile to liberty endeavor to rule without appropriations, or, if this is not feasible, by having the appropriations made for a long term, and not for detailed purposes. The last decree of Napoleon III., relating to this subject, is that the legislative corps must vote the budget of each department *en bloc*, that is, in a lump, and either wholly reject or adopt it, without amendment. English history furnishes a long commentary on this point of appropriations. Charles I. lost his head in his struggle for a government without parliament, which then meant, in a great measure, without regular appropriations, or the assumption of ruling by taxation on royal authority. Wherever on the European continent it has been the endeavor to establish a constitutional government, the absolutists have complained of the "indecency" of making governments annually "beg" for supplies.

Liberty requires the supremacy of the law; the supremacy of the law requires the subordination of the army to the legislature and the whole civil government. The Declaration of Rights enumerates the raising and keeping a standing army without consent of parliament, as one of the proofs that James II. had endeavored "to subvert and extirpate the laws and liberties" of England; while all governments reluctantly yielding to the demands of liberty have struggled to prevent at least the obligation of the army to take the oath of fidelity to the constitution. The army is studiously separated from the people, and courted as peculiarly allied to the prince. Napoleon I. treated the army as the church was often treated in the middle ages—the main body in the state; and Napoleon III. lately said in a solemn speech that he desired to present the new empress to the people and the army, as if it formed at least one-half of the state and were a body, separate from the people. When he gave eagles to the whole army at what is called the fête of the eagles, in 1852, he said: "The history of nations is in a great measure the history of armies," and continued in a strain sounding as if it belonged to the times of the migration of nations.[1]

But English and American freemen will never forget that the highest glory of a great people, and that by which it most signally performs the task assigned to it in the furtherance of our race, are its literature and its law, if this consists in a wise system founded on justice, humanity and freedom.

The supremacy of the law is an elementary requisite of liberty. All absolutism spurns, and has a peculiar dislike of, the idea of fundamental laws. Aristotle enumerates as the fourth species of government that in which the multitude and not the law is the supreme master; James II. claimed the dispensing power, and Louis Napoleon affirmed, when yet president under the republican constitution, which prohibited his re-election, that if the people wanted him to continue in office, he should do it nevertheless, and all his adherents declared that the people being the masters could do as they liked,

---

[1] I quote the whole passage of this stupendous allocution, which no historian or political philosopher, had he discovered it, as Cuvier found and construed remains of animals, would have assigned to the middle of the nineteenth century. What becomes of England and the United States if the essence of history does not lie in the development of the nation and especially of its institutions? The following are the exact words:

"Soldiers, the history of nations is in great part the history of armies. On their success, or on their reverses, depends the fate of civilization and of the country. When they are vanquished, there is either invasion or anarchy; when victorious, glory or order.

"In consequence, nations, like armies, pay a religious veneration to the emblems of military honor, which sum up in themselves a whole past existence of struggles and of triumphs.

"The Roman eagle, adopted by the Emperor Napoleon at the commencement of the present century, was the most striking signification of the regeneration and grandeur of France;" and so on.

When the democratic Cæsar reviewed the guards, before they started for the Crimea, in 1855, he called the army the nobility of the French nation.

which reminds us of the Athenians who impatiently exclaimed: "Can we not do what we list?" when told that there was a law forbidding what they intended to do.

The division of power, which was already observed as an important point in government by "the master of all that know," is invariably broken down as far as possible by the absolutists. The judiciary is interfered with whenever its slow procedure or its probable results irritate the power-holder. The history of all nations from the earliest times to Napoleon III.'s taking the trial on the legality of the Orleans spoliation out of the hands of the judiciary, proves it on every page.

Self-government, general as well as local, is indispensable to our liberty, but interference and dictation are the essence of absolutism. Monarchical absolutisms presume to do everything and to provide for everything, and Robespierre, in his "great speech" for the restoration of the Supreme Being, said: The function of government is to direct the moral and physical forces of the nation. For this purpose the aim of a constitutional government is the republic.[1]

Liberty requires that every one should be judged by his common court. All despots insist on extraordinary courts, courts of commission, and an easy application of martial law.

Forcible expatriation or deportation "beyond the seas" by the executive is looked upon with peculiar horror by all freemen. The English were roused by it to resistance; Napoleon III. began his absolute reign with exile and deportation. So did the Greek factions banish their opponents when they had the power of doing so, because no "opposition" in the modern sense was known to them. With them it was the blundering business of factions; moderns know better, and if they return to it, it is because despotism is a thing full of fear and love of show.

How great an offence it is to deprive a man of his lawful

---

[1] The words of Robespierre are sufficiently clear, if taken as an illustration of what has been stated in the text; otherwise, I own, the sense is not perfectly apparent.

court and to judge him by aught else than by the laws of the land, now in the middle of the nineteenth century, will appear the more forcibly, if the reader will bring to his mind that passage of Magna Charta which appeared to Chatham worth all the classics, and if he will remember the year when the Great Charter was carried. The passage, so pregnant to the mind of Chatham, is this:

"No freeman shall be taken, or imprisoned, or be disseised of his freehold or liberties, or free customs, or be outlawed or exiled, or any otherwise destroyed; nor will we (the king) pass upon him, nor condemn him, but by lawful judgment of his peers, or by the law of the land. We will sell to no man, we will not deny or defer to any man, justice or right."

Publicity is a condition without which liberty cannot live. The moment it had been concluded by the present government of France to root out civil freedom, it was ordained that neither the remarks of the members of the legislative corps, nor the pleadings in the courts of justice, should be reported in the papers. Modern political publicity, however, consists chiefly in publication through the journals. We acknowledge this practically by the fact that, although our courts are never closed,[1] yet, for particular reasons arising out of the case under consideration, the publication of the proceedings is sometimes prohibited by the judge until the close of the trial, but never beyond it.

Liberty stands in need of the legal precedent, and Charles I. pursued Cotton because he furnished Pym and other patriots with precedents, while the present French government has excluded instruction in history from the plan of general education. History, in a certain point of view, may be called the great precedent. History is of all branches the most nourishing for public life and liberty. It furnishes a strong pabulum and incites by great examples removed beyond all party or selfish views. The favorite book of Chatham was Plutarch, and his son educated himself upon Thucydides.[2] The best

---

[1] Very scandalous judicial cases, offensive to public morals, are, in France, conducted with closed doors.

[2] So Bishop Tomlinson tells us in the Life of his pupil.

historians have been produced by liberty, and the despot is consistent when he wishes to shackle the noble muse.

Sincere civil liberty requires that the legislature should have the initiative. All governments reluctant to grant full liberty have withheld it, and one of the first things decreed by Louis Napoleon after the second of December was that the "legislative corps" should discuss such propositions of laws only as the council of state should send to it. The council of state, however, is a mere body of officers appointed and discharged at the will of the ruler.

Liberty requires that government do not form a body permanently and essentially separated from the people; all modern absolute rulers have resorted to a number of distinctions— titles, ribbons, orders, peacock feathers and buttons, uniforms, or whatever other means of separating individuals from the people at large may seem expedient.

Liberty requires the trial by jury. Consequently one of the first attacks which arbitrary power makes upon freedom is regularly directed against that trial. There is now a law in preparation in France, of which the outlines have been published, and which will place the jurors under the almost exclusive influence of the government.

Liberty requires, as we have seen, a candid and well-guaranteed trial for treason; all despotic governments, on the contrary, endeavor to break down these guarantees in particular. They arrogate the power of condemning political offenders without trial, or strip the trial for treason of its best guarantees.

But we might go through the whole list of safeguards and principles of liberty, and find that in each case absolutism does the opposite.

If the American peruses the Declaration of Independence, he will find there, in the complaints of our forefathers, almost a complete list of those rights, privileges, and guarantees which they held dearest and most essential to liberty; for they believed that nearly every guarantee had been assailed.

CHAPTER XXIV.

HAVING considered Anglican liberty, it will be proper for us to examine the French type of civil freedom, or Gallican liberty.

In speaking here of Gallican liberty, we mean, of course, that liberty which is characteristically French, either in reality, if we shall find that at any period it has taken actual root, or in theory, if it have remained such, and never practically developed itself. Liberty has sprouted in France as in other countries. People have felt there, as all over Europe, that the administration of justice ought to be independent of the other branches of government. The separation of the three great functions of government was proclaimed by the first constituent assembly. But the question here is, whether any of these or other endeavors to establish liberty have been consolidated into permanent institutions, whether they have been allowed to develop themselves, and whether they were or are peculiar to the French, or were adopted from another system of developed civil liberty, as we adopt the whole or parts of an order of architecture or a philosophical system; and, if we find no such institutions or guarantees peculiar to the French, whether there be a general idea and conception of liberty which pervades all France and is peculiar to that country.

In viewing the French institutions, which have been intended for the protection of individual rights or the preservation of liberty, I can discover none which has had a permanent existence, except the court of cassation or quashing. It is the highest court of France, possessing the power of annulling or

breaking[1] the judgments of all other courts of justice, whether
in civil or criminal matters, on account of faults and flaws in
the judicial forms and procedure, or of misapplications of the
existing law. It has no power to examine the verdict. It
resembles, therefore, the court of Westminster, in England,
when the assembled judges hear questions of law, or our supreme court of the United States on similar occasions, and the
supreme courts or courts of appeal or error in the different
states. The court of cassation must necessarily sometimes
judge of certain procedures of the government against individuals, and declare whether individual rights, publicly guaranteed, have been invaded. Thus it showed its power to
some extent when Paris was declared in a state of siege, and
the whole city was under martial law. But the high attribute
of pronouncing upon the constitutionality of the laws themselves, which we cherish in our supreme courts, does not
belong to it, nor can its power be vigorously and broadly
exercised in a conflict with the supreme power, since this
power bears down everything in a country so vast and yet
so centralized as France, and in which the principle of development, independent of the executive or central power, is
not acknowledged in the different institutions. The court of
cassation has at the same time a supervisory authority over
the judges of other courts, and can send them before the
keeper of the seals (the minister of justice) to give an account
of their conduct. It is likewise an object of the court of
cassation to keep the application of the law uniform in the
different portions of the country. This is a necessary effect
of its power to quash judgments.

The institution of the justice of the peace ought to be
mentioned here, although it can only be considered as indirectly connected with liberty. The French justice of the
peace differs from the English officer of the same name in this,
that his function is exclusively of a conciliatory character.
Courts of conciliation have existed in many countries, and

---

[1] Casser is the French for breaking; hence the name of the court.

long before the present justices of the peace were established
in France by the first constituent assembly; but as we see
them now there, they must be called a French institution.   It
has proved itself in France, as well as in other countries, of
the highest value in preventing litigation, with all the evils
which necessarily attach themselves to it. [1]

No one, I suppose, would expect the senate, first established
by Napoleon I. and then called conservative senate, that is, the
senate whose nominal duty it was to conserve the constitution,
and now re-established by Napoleon III., to be enumerated as
an institution for the support of liberty.   It has no more
connection with liberty than the Roman senate had under
the emperors.   Its very origin would lead no one to expect
in it a guarantee of liberty.   On the contrary, the French
senate has been a great aid to imperial absolutism, by giving
to comprehensive measures of monarchical despotism the
semblance of not having originated with the absolute monarch
or of having received the countenance of a high and numerous
political body.   In this respect the French senate seems to me
worse than that of Russia.   The Russian senate is nothing
but a council, leaving all power and responsibility with the
czar, in appearance as well as in reality.

That which after careful examination must be pronounced
to be Gallican liberty, is, I take it, the idea of equality
founded upon or acting through universal suffrage, or, as it is
frequently called by the French, " the undivided sovereignty
of the people" with an uncompromising centralism.   As it is
necessarily felt by many, that the rule of universal suffrage
can, practically, mean only the rule of the majority, liberty

---

[1] We have seen that courts of conciliation have attracted renewed
attention in England since Lord Brougham's proposition of an act for
the Farther Cheapening of Justice, in May, 1851.   An instructive article
on this important subject, and the excellent effects these courts have
produced in many countries, shown by official statistics, can be found
in the German Staats-Lexicon, ad verbum Friedensgericht.

is believed in France, as has been said, to consist in the absolute rule of the majority.[1]

Every one who has steadily followed the discussions of the
late constituent and national assemblies, who has resolutely
gone through the debates of the first *constituente*, and studied
the history of the revolution, and who is fairly acquainted with
French literature, will agree, I trust, that the idea of Gallican
liberty has been correctly stated.   There are many Frenchmen, indeed, who know that this is not liberty, that at most
it can only be a means to obtain it, but we now speak of the
conception of liberty peculiar to the French school.

Institutions, such as we conceive their necessary character
to be, that is, establishments with the important element of
self-government, and of a system of guarantees beyond the
reach of daily change, do not enter as necessary elements into
the idea of Gallican liberty.   Self-government is sought for in
the least impeded rule of the majority.   It has been seen,
however, that, according to the Anglican view, the question
who shall rule is an important question of liberty indeed, but
only one about the means ; for if the ruler, whoever he be,
deprives the ruled of liberty, there is of course no liberty.   A
suicide does not the less cease to live because he kills himself ;
and two game fowls nearly matched, as the parties in a nation
may be, do not symbolize liberty, because at one time the one
may be uppermost, and at another time the other.

There seems to be in France a constant confusion of equality
and democracy on the one hand, and of democracy and liberty
on the other ; now, although equality largely enters as an
element in all liberty, and no liberty can be imagined without
a democratic element, equality and democracy of themselves
are far from constituting liberty.   They may be the worst of
despotisms : the one by annihilating individuality, as the com-

---

[1] I have given my views on the subject of the nature of sovereignty
and the way it acts, at length in the first volume of the Political Ethics.
If I have not succeeded there in mastering the subject, I should not be
able to do it here ; if I have succeeded, I cannot in fairness repeat a long
discussion.

munist strives to do; the other—if it means democratic absolutism—by being real sweeping power itself—not power lent as that of the monarch always must be—power without personal responsibility. It acts; but where is the actor, who is responsible, who can be made responsible, who will judge?

It is with reference to this rule, and this mistaken view of liberty, that one of their wisest, best, and most liberty loving men, Mr. Royer Collard, has said:[1] "It is nothing but a sovereignty of brute force, and a most absolute form of absolute power. Before this sovereignty, without rule, without limit, without duty, and without conscience, there is neither constitution nor law, neither good nor evil, nor past nor future. The will of to-day annuls that of yesterday, without engaging that of to-morrow. The pretensions of the most capricious and most extravagant tyranny do not go so far, because they are not in the same degree disengaged from all responsibility."

Where any one, or any two, or any three, or any thousand, or any million can do what they have the mere power to do, there is no liberty. Arbitrary power does not become less arbitrary because it is the united power of many.

Napoleon said: "The French love equality; they care little for liberty."[2] Napoleon certainly mistook the French, and mankind in general, very seriously in some points, as all men of his stamp are liable to do; there are some entire instincts wanting in them; but we fear that he was right in this saying with reference to a large part of the French people. Present events seem to prove it.[3]

---

[1] Royer Collard's Opinion, of October 4, 1831.

[2] Words spoken to Lord Ebrington, in his exile on the island of Elba.

[3] Rousseau expressed the political idea of equality, the aversion to representative governments and institutional polities, and the disapproval of private property, boldly and clearly in his Social Contract, a masterly written work, which has exercised an incalculable effect on French affairs. It was the favorite book of the leading men of the first revolution, and continues largely to influence the French. Yet Rousseau only pronounced more clearly, and boldly carried farther, the ideas of unity, concentration and equality, that had been gradually growing stronger in the French mind long before him. They can be traced, not only in politics but in all spheres.

This equality is again very generally mistaken for uniformity, so that it would naturally lead of itself to centralization, even if the French had not contracted a real passion for centralization ever since the reigns of Richelieu and Louis XIV. It has increased with almost every change of government. It is the love of power carried into every detail, and therefore the opposite of what we call self-government;[1] it is the exceeding partiality of the French for logical neatness and consistency

---

[1] I have given some remarkable instances of interference on the part of modern absolute governments, in the Political Ethics. I shall add the following recent instance: I am sure that no one accustomed to Anglican self-government considers such details trivial, however well he may be acquainted with the fact in general, that government in those countries tries to guide, direct, manage, initiate, and complete everything that seems of any importance. Some years ago a German king ironically called, in a throne speech, constitutions Paper Providences. The expression was every way most unfortunate. It seems to me that it is these very governments of centralized mandarinism that play at providence, in which they closely resemble the communists, as indeed all absolutism contains a strong element of communism.

The following is taken from the Paris Moniteur, the French official paper, or organ of government, in October, 1852. I do not give the entire decree, but the principal articles:

There will be published, under the care of the minister of public instruction, a general collection of the popular poetry of France, either to be found in manuscript in the libraries, or transmitted by the successive memories of generations.

The collection of the popular poetry of France will consist of

Religious and warlike songs;

Festive songs and ballads;

Historical recitals, legends, tales, satirical songs.

The committee of language, history, and the arts of France, connected with the ministry of public instruction, is charged with the selection of all pieces sent for inspection, and to determine which are to be received, to regulate them, and give the necessary commentaries.

A medal is to be given to those persons who, by their discoveries and researches, particularly contribute to enrich the collection, which will be called Récueil des Poésies Populaires.

It is unnecessary to remind the reader that if this undertaking has been dictated by any desire of promoting literature, a political motive has been at least equally strong, according to the old saying: Give me the ballad making, and I will rule the people.

of form, strikingly manifested in the fact that the word logical is now universally used in French for consistency of action or natural sequence of changes—it is this mathematical enthusiasm, if the expression be permitted, applied to the vast field of political practice.

It seems that we can explain the cry of République democratique et sociale, so often repeated by the most advanced of the democrats during the late government without a king, only on the ground of equality being considered the foundation of all liberty. Indeed it is considered by many a requisite which lies beyond liberty, and the banners of socialists bore the motto Equality and Fraternity, or Equality, Fraternity, Industry, the word Liberty having been altogether dropped from that once worshipped legend: Liberty, Fraternity, Equality. I have never been able to find an explanation of the watchword, Democratic and Social Republic, given by those who use it, but it seems to bear no other interpretation than this: Democratic republic signifies that republic which is founded upon the total political equality of its members, carried to its last degree, and social republic must mean a republic based on equality of social condition. Whether this be possible, or desirable if it were possible, cannot occupy us at present. The frequent use of this term by a very large part of the French nation has been mentioned here as one of the evidences showing the prevailing love of mere equality among the French.

Still, it is not easy to say what the French exactly mean by equality, or what Napoleon meant by it, when, at St. Helena, he said that he had given equality to the French, and that this was all he could give them, but that his son would have given them liberty. How he knew that his son would have done it, we certainly do not know; but how did he give them equality, when it was he who re-established the ancient orders of nobility? So there are, in spite of all the love of equality, no people who more universally love uniforms and an order with a ribbon, than the French. This inconsistency is a political misfortune. In theory, equality and democracy, carried to

19

the utmost, are demanded, while the habits, tendencies, and desires of the people have a different bent. There is in this respect, it seems, an intellectual and psychical dualism with antagonistic elements in France, similar to that which we frequently observe in individuals in regard to liberty and despotism.[1]

It is evident how nearly allied this desired equality and uniformity, together with universal but uninstitutional suffrage, and that kind of sovereignty which is in addition confounded with absolute power, are to those political extravagances which strike our eyes in present France.

They are the natural effects of the one or the other, strictly carried out, however inconsistent they may appear with one another. Equality absolutely carried out leads to communism; the idea of undivided sovereignty leads to Mr. Girardin's conception of having no legislature, no division of power—nothing but a succession of popular sultans; the idea of seeking all liberty in universal suffrage alone leads with the greatest ease to a Napoleon—a transfer of everything to one man, and of all future generations to his descendants, thus actually realizing the fearful theory of Hobbes; and the absence of a love of institutions leads to a remarkable tendency to worship one man, to centralization, or, in some cases, to the very opposite —a desire to abolish all government, and establish the "sovereignty of the individual." All extremes in politics meet.

There is no greater error than the idea of making the vote

---

[1] Nothing is more common than men with a decided intellectual bent towards freedom, and an equally decided psychical inclination towards absolutism. Their intellect admires the grandeur of liberty, their reason acknowledges the principles of justice; their desires are for free action, and yet their souls resent every opposition. They appear, therefore, often as hypocrites, without being such in reality. There is a dualism within them whose two elements are at war, very similar to that which, without hypocrisy, makes many persons sincerely preach peace and charity abroad, but act at home as domestic tyrants.

History is full of such characters, and we have had an exhibition of it in one of our presidents. Happily our institutional system did not allow a very wide play of such a disposition.

or election the sole basis of liberty—of believing that, with the establishment of an extensive or universal suffrage, we found liberty, however true it is that liberty stands in need of election. Absolutism may rest on this as on any other basis. The deys of Algiers were elective, but once elected they were unbounded masters, in the oriental sense of the term. The generals of nearly all, I believe of all, the monastic orders are elective, but, once elected, the vow of obedience of every monk and the distinct renunciation of liberty, make the general master. No order, no human association, has carried the doctrine of absolute obedience to a more frightful extent than the Jesuits, whose founder demands that the inferior shall be in the hands of the superior ut baculum, like a mere staff, and whose distinctly expressed principle it is, that every command of the superior shall be like a commandment from on high, even though sin be commanded. Yet the government of the order is founded on election. Mr. Guizot, in speaking of the monastic orders,[1] says: "As regards the political code of the monasteries, the rule of St. Benedict offers a singular mixture of despotism and liberty. Passive obedience is its fundamental principle; at the same time the government is elective; the abbot is always chosen by the brothers. When once the choice is made, they lose all liberty, they fall under the absolute domination of their superior. Moreover, in imposing obedience on the monks, the rule orders that the abbot consult them. Chap. iii. expressly says, 'Whenever anything of importance is to take place in the monastery, let the abbot convoke the whole congregation, and say what the question is; and after having heard the advice of the brothers, he shall think of it apart, and shall do as appears to him most suitable.' Thus, in this singular government, election, deliberation, and absolute power, were coexistent."

The pope is an elective monarch over the States of the Church. No one has ever maintained that on this account liberty has a home in that country. Nor would the case be altered if the pope were elected, not by the college of cardinals, but by a more nu-

---

[1] History of Civilization, chapter xiv.

merous body of electors, or by all male adults, or even by the
whole population, male and female.   The high priest or president in the polity of that stupendous outrage called Mormonism, is elective, and the Mormons themselves call their government a theo-democracy ;[1] yet a greater absolutism has never
existed, indeed, we may fairly say, none equal to it.   It unites
democracy and communism, which is absolutism, with continuous and permanent revelations of the deity, not only on dog-
matic points, but on every measure of weight.   It is a jus
divinum such as the ancients did not even dream of when they
derived their kings from the loins of the gods, and it is a communism such as Mohammed never dared to embody in his
politico-religious system.

The unicameral system must be mentioned here as a feature of Gallican liberty, because it is held by all those
persons who seem to be the most distinct enunciators of this
species of liberty, a necessary requisite if they allow the
principle of representation at all.   They consider that the
bicameral system of representatives is aristocratic, or else, as
one of their writers expresses it, that two houses can never be
reconciled except by money or by blood.   The partiality for
a legislature of one house is a necessary consequence of the
French idea of unity in the government or the unity of the
state, and actual abhorrence of confederacies.

The Anglican wants union in his general government; the

---

[1] Theo-democracy does not contain a contradiction, however novel,
and, at first sight, startling the term may appear to us.   If democracy
necessarily expressed the idea of liberty, then, indeed, the name theo-
democracy would be senseless, for all theocracy or sacerdotal rule is a
negation of civil liberty.   It immures in dogma.

In a similar manner, and with equal justice, the Rev. Mr. Payne says
of the Grebo tribe, at Cape Palmas, that their constitution is patriarchal,
with a purely democratic government.   His account is contained in "The
Report of the Rev. R. R. Gurley, who was recently sent out by the government to obtain information in respect to Liberia," published by the
senate of the United States, in 1850, thirty-first congress, first session,
executive document No. 75.   The political philosopher can hardly read
a more interesting paper than this.

Gallican, unity. He wants his government to be a solid unit.[1] He wishes to deprive every institution, as much as possible, of the principle of self-government and independence, and the only question which remains is, who shall be the ruler and receive that power which government gives? To this subject, as to many others on which I have touched, we shall return when I shall treat more fully of the institutional government and its opposite.

It is not likely that people who speak with derision of parliamentary government, by which nothing is meant but a government in which a deliberative and representative legislature forms an integral part, and of *parlementarism*, as the new phrase is, would treat the legislature as an institution with self-government and a necessary degree of independence. According to their idea, the safeguards which we believe are found in a mutually moderative contrivance ought to be done away with. Speedy energy, absence of opposition and of results

---

[1] The extent to which this idea is occasionally carried out is almost inconceivable to us, accustomed as we are to so essentially different a system and train of political thoughts. A few years ago the minister of the interior had given some new directions regarding the quarantine regulations. They were more in conformity with the opinions of scientific men on the contagiousness of the plague. The people of Marseilles, who still keep the terrible plague of the last century in vivid remembrance, disapproved of these orders from the central government, and a meeting of certain persons was called together. Whereupon most newspapers took part with the government, and charged the citizens, with whom this little germ of self-government had shown itself, with the hideous sin of *federalism*, the crime for which many had lost their heads in the first revolution. This was in the times of the so-called republic before the second of December, and the few papers which took side with the citizens were legitimist papers, thus furnishing, by the way, another instance of the fact that all sorts of things are possible under peculiar circumstances. It was the tories who resisted the septennial bill abolishing triennial parliaments; it was the Jesuits who first enunciated the doctrine of the sovereignty of the people, in order to get a fulcrum against heretical monarchs; it was a Spanish Jesuit who defended regicide under Philip II.; and here we have legitimists, working for a descendant of Louis XIV., who took side for a principle of self-action against the central government!

which are the products of mutual modification and mutual toleration, unity of ideas, not consisting in collective effects but in
a merely logical carrying out of some abstract principle; these
are the main objects, according to Gallican views.   The United
States are far from being favorably looked upon by the French
people, and they are viewed with real ill-will by the Red Republicans on account of our *decentralization*.   Rosseau seems
to have harbored a positive ill-will toward the representative
system, and his followers have a still stronger antipathy
against federal governments, and self-government which may
be said, in one point of view, to be a minute application of
the federative principle.

The Spaniards, the Portuguese, the Neapolitans have made
the trial of copying the French, but have succeeded with the
system of one house no better than the French themselves,
and have passed over to the bicameral legislature, or abolished
representation altogether.

There are governments in which the medieval principle of
estates still exists.   But it may be fairly maintained that this
is a remnant of the middle ages, at variance with the changed
state of modern society.   Nowhere do they present themselves
as a system of civil liberty—it is rather a system (and rarely
even this) of privileges or *liberties*.   In Sweden the estates
still exist, namely the clergy, nobility, citizens, and peasants,
and a high degree of liberty is enjoyed.   But in examining
the constitution of Sweden we cannot fail to observe that
modern liberty is rather superinduced or engrafted on the system of states, than evolved out of it.   The constitution of
Norway, on the other hand, is clearly of the character of that
liberty which we have designated as Anglican.

Frenchmen would probably point out their national guards
as an element or guarantee of Gallican liberty.   They were
established during the first revolution, and have always been
diminished in number and restricted in power, in those periods in which the government made war·upon liberty.   They
cannot, however, be considered a valid guarantee in so concentrated a government as the French, and in a country in

which the army is so gigantic. It was chiefly as a popular force against the king, that the national guards appeared as an important element of liberty in the first French revolution; but they cannot be called a real guarantee of civil liberty, especially when no institutional guarantees of self-government exist.

It must have plainly appeared that liberty seems to me efficiently secured only by the Anglican system. Other attempts in modern times have been but very partially successful, and of these there are only a few. The question arises at once, are those persons in the main correct who roundly assert that no people are fit for liberty except the Anglo-Saxons? For thus they call the English nation, and those who have descended from it. Or is it correct to say that whoever wishes to enjoy liberty must copy the main institutions of Anglican liberty? On these and some cognate subjects so many startling errors exist, that the remarks on the different types of liberty may be appropriately concluded by some observations on these misconceptions. They have a practical bearing, and influence large masses.

It is doubtless true that the greatest amount of liberty is at present enjoyed by the Anglican race, whose institutions and guarantees seem to form the only extensive and consistent, as well as practical system of civil liberty, the only one in which liberty and law have become firmly interlocked, and by which it has thus become possible to establish, as a practical reality, what Tacitus held to be impossible—the union of libertas and imperium. It is true also that the Anglican division has had a greater influence than any other tribe on the whole white race, and that other nations seem to have enjoyed liberty or advanced on the path of freedom, in recent times, in the same proportion only in which they have adopted the main principles and chief institutions elaborated by this portion of our race; and it is equally true that we enjoy so great an amount of freedom because we are accustomed to liberty and a government of law, and because our race has perseveringly developed it for centuries. But it must not be forgotten, on the one hand, that other nations and races may possibly develop certain principles in a manner peculiar to their character and circumstances; and, on the other hand, that it is the rule of all spreading advancement of humanity that the full amount of what has been gained by patience, blood, or fortunate combinations, is transferred to other regions and distant tribes.

The missionary—from St. Paul, when he went to Rome, to those who now embark for the Pacific—does not demand the neophyte to pass through the dispensations of the old testament, and all the experience of the early church, before he begins to teach the dispensation of the new testament, and to establish churches according to the government and the theology which exist at his home.

There are many persons who pretend to admire liberty, but withhold it from the people on the plea that they are not prepared for it. Unquestionably, all races are not prepared for the same amount of liberty, and many are not yet fit for any real liberty at all. But two things are certain, that all nations, and especially those belonging to our own civilized family, prove that they are prepared for the beginning of liberty, by desiring it and insisting upon it, and that you cannot otherwise prepare nations for enjoying liberty than by beginning to establish it, as you best prepare nations for a high christianity by beginning to preach it.

There are persons even among ourselves who, observing how many and sad failures have taken place with other nations, bluntly assert that none but the Anglo-Saxons are fit for liberty, and that it cannot be enjoyed by others. That some nations are fitter for the elaboration or peaceful enjoyment of liberty than others, according to their character, which makes them perhaps less fit to excel in some other branches of civilization, cannot be denied. So was the Greek more fit for the fine arts than the Roman. That some tribes appear on the stage of history, act their part, and vanish again without having made any progress in civil liberty, or ever having become conscious of it as an element of advancing civilization, is equally true. But do we hold any nation, once fairly entered upon the path of civilization, unfit for science or the arts, or a stable government, or a literature, or for christianity? That in which man rises highest, and manifests himself most intellectually—christianity, is believed to be meet for all, but should liberty be restricted to a tribe or a single nation? It is not likely. I have admitted that some nations are fitter for the one or the other. All will not equally cultivate all branches; each cannot originate every branch; but all will partake of every element of civilization; and while it may be proper for the historian to say such a nation has not been able to act with originality in this or another branch, it is not becoming to the philosopher to say that such a portion of our race *will* not be able to do so. When the Greek scholars were driven from Constantinople, and carried the last embers of Grecian civilization and intellectuality over the west; when Providence made them the missionaries of a renewed civilization, and the restoration of letters prepared the way for still higher achievements, no one said that the English, or French, or Germans were unfit to partake in the humanizing blessing, although the Italian soil, still bearing the effects of former culture, was the first to bring forth delectable fruit. When Gothic architecture had been elaborated by some, it was not believed that other nations could not raise cathedrals in the same style, and enjoy it and develop it in their own way.

On the other hand, we meet with the very reverse. Anglican liberty is opposed on the ground that it is not indigenous, and that it is both inexpedient and unworthy to adopt it. Large numbers in France, both communists and imperialists, treat "parliamentarism" in this manner; and the emperor said, when he had assembled the senate and the legislative corps, soon after the restoration of the empire, that France for "the first time enjoyed the happiness of possessing institutions, exclusively French and original."[1] As to the

---

[1] This idea has been, since, carried much farther. A large number of persons, and it would seem, all imperialists, love to dwell upon the idea that imperialism represents Latin civilization, opposite to Teutonic unwieldly, uncentralized, barbaric freedom. When thus Latinism is taken as a distinctive mark, Roman imperialism is meant, not of course Repub-

originality, we would only observe that they are fac-similes
of what Napoleon I. had established, and that he copied
the senate, as he did the eagle, the title and idea of emperor,
the name of legion, of prefect, from Rome, unfortunately
at her worst period, for the Roman senate during the better
time was part of the proud Senatus Populusque Romanus;
and the corps legislatif, if there be any element of a representative legislature in it, is not of French origin; if it be
a mute body, however, there is no originality in it either.
Even if it were as the emperor proclaimed it, there would be
nothing in it to be rejoiced at.   The law of all spreading civilization is emigration, transmission, and addition.   Ought the
French to reject the Grecian orders of architecture because
they are not French, or ought our medical students not to go
to Paris because the French science of medicine is not ours?
Has modern music been rejected by all the nations except the
Italians and the Germans because it is of native growth with
these nations?   Ought the French to reject saving banks because they were first established and developed in England,
and ought the English to discard Jacquard's loom because
invented in France?

The son of Sirach said, that wisdom was hovering like
the clouds until it "took root in an honorable people"[1]—
the Israelites.   It is thus with all wisdom, all great ideas and
comprehensive systems.   They take root with "an honorable people," that develops them.   After that come the winds
of heaven and carry the seeds far and about.   Patriotism
and national vanity are not the same.   Patriotism is excellent so long as it is the love of its own to such a degree
that it is ready to make any sacrifice, and to do all for its
benefit; it is not a virtue when it consists in being enamored

---

lican Roman self-government.   The French in trying to renovate Latinism, seem to fall, as to principle, into an anachronism not dissimilar to that
into which the Germans fell as to language when they officially called
their empire, down to its dissolution, the Holy Roman Empire of the
Germans.

[1] Ecclesiasticus, 24.

with itself. Narcissus is not the symbol of patriotism, but Lycurgus and Solon are, travelling far in order to gather knowledge for their own country.

At all great and distinct periods of modern history, there are a general idea and certain adequate forms pervading the whole. Such was the papal period at the beginning of the middle ages; such was the universal feudal system; such the period of universities springing up everywhere; such the periods of art; such the periods of Abelard and scholastic philosophy; such the rising of free cities in all active parts of Europe; such the ardor of maritime discovery and enthusiasm for "cosmography;" such the period of monasteries; such protestantism; and such is, I believe, the present period of civil liberty, which, for centuries to come, will be essentially of the Anglican type. To learn liberty, I believe that nations must go to America and England, as we go to Italy to study music and to have the vast world of the fine arts opened to us, or as we go to France to study science, or to Germany that we may learn how to instruct and spread education. It was a peculiar feature of antiquity that law, religion, dress, the arts and customs, that everything in fact was localized. Modern civilization extends over regions, tends to make uniform, and eradicates even the physical differences of tribes and races.[1] Thus made uniform, nations receive and

---

[1] The mutual influence of different literatures is daily extending. Take as an instance the literature of England, France, Germany, and the United States, and add the mutual influence of the journals of these nations. Then consider how many of the elements of civilization are not national, but common to all—the alphabet, the numeric signs, with the decimal system, musical notation and music itself, commercial usages and bookkeeping, international law, social intercourse and laws of politeness; the visiting card, the railway, the steamboat, the post-office, the institution of money, the bill of exchange, insurance—indeed it is impossible to enumerate all the agreements of nations belonging to our race. I shall only add the dress, the furniture and even cookery.

The most recent and a choice illustration of progressive uniformity of our race and its civilization, is the adoption of Commander Maury's, U. S. N., plan of a uniform maritime observation and record, adopted

give more freely.   If it has pleased God to appoint the Anglican race as the first workmen to rear the temple of liberty,
shall others find fault with Providence?   The all-pervading
law of civilization is physical and mental mutual dependence,
and not isolation.

Many governments deny liberty to the people on the ground
that it is not national; yet they copy foreign absolutism.
There is doubtless something essential in the idea of national
development, but let us never forget two facts: Men, however
different, are far more uniform than different; and most of
the noblest nations have arisen from the mixture of others.

---

by many governments in consequence of the naval congress at Brussels,
in 1853. May a uniform standard of value soon follow. The wide-
spread dollar or scudo has prepared the way for it.

CHAPTER XXV.

THE INSTITUTION. ITS DEFINITION. ITS POWER FOR GOOD
AND EVIL.

It has been shown that civil liberty, as we understand and cherish it, consists in a large amount of individual rights, checks of power and guarantees of self-government. We have more or less fully indicated that self-government, in the sense in which we take it, and in connection with liberty, consists in the independence of the whole political society, in a national representative government and local self-government, which implies that even general laws and impulses are carried out and realized, as far as possible, by citizens who, in receiving an office, be it by election or appointment, essentially remain citizens, and do not become members of a hierarchy of placemen.[1] We have seen that self-government, in general, requires

---

[1] At a sumptuous ball, which the city of Paris gave, in the year 1851, to the commissioners of the London Exhibition, I was sitting in a corner and reflecting on the police officers in their uniforms and the actual patrols of the military pompiers in the very midst of the festive and crowded assemblage, when I was introduced to one of the first statesmen of France and a liberal member of the national assembly. He had been at London, to view the exhibition. It was the first time he had visited England. "Do you know," said he, "what struck me most—far more than the exhibition of works of art and industry? It was the exhibition of the *civism anglais* (this was the term he used) in the London police." It may be readily supposed that an American citizen turned his face toward the speaker, to hear more, when the Frenchman continued: "I am in earnest. The large number of policemen, with their citizen appearance, although in uniform, seeming to be there for no other purpose than to assist the people—and the people ever ready to assist them —this is what has most attracted my attention. Liberty and the govern-

(301)

that there be an organism to elaborate and ascertain public
opinion, and that, when known, it shall pass into law, and,
plainly, rule the rulers; that government interfere as an exception, and not as the rule; and that, on the other hand,
self-government neither means self-absolutism, nor absence of
rule, but that, on the contrary, liberty requires a true government.   A weak government is a negation of liberty; it cannot
furnish us with a guaranteeing power, nor can it procure
supremacy for public will.   In other spheres it may be true
that license is exaggerated liberty, but in politics there can be
nothing more unlike liberty than anarchy.

We have still to ascertain how this system of civil liberty
is to be realized.   Liberty cannot flourish, nor can freedom
become a permanent business of actual life, without a permanent love and a habit of liberty.   How is the one to be engendered, and the other to be acquired ?

There is no mathematical formula by which liberty can be

---

ment of law are even depicted in their police, where we should seek it
least.   What is it that strikes you most in coming here?"

"The American," I replied, "in visiting the continent of Europe, is
most impressed by the fact that the whole population, from Moscow to
Lisbon, seems to be divided into two wholly distinct parts—the round
hats, the people, and the cocked hats, the visible government.   The two
layers are as distinct as the hats, and the traveller sees almost as many
of the one form as of the other."

There are large police establishments in all European states.   Densely
peopled countries require them.   The different spirit and organization, however, of these establishments are most characteristic.   Nothing, perhaps, shows more the character of a citizen-government in
England than the wide-spread institution of the police, which has
developed itself, under Sir Robert Peel, out of the ancient constable.
It has great power; it has preventive, detective and custodial authority;
yet it is supported by the citizens, and no one fears that it ever will be
used as an institution of political espionage and denunciation—as dela-
tores of old and mouchards of modern times.   It is strictly under the
public law, and that implies under publicity.   There is a whole literature
on this subject, but I know of no brief paper exhibiting so well its essential character as the seventh paragraph of Mittermaier's English, Scottish and American Penal Processes.

solved, nor are there laws by which liberty can be decreed, without other aids. We gain no more by throwing power unchecked into the hands of the people. It remains power, and is not liberty, and people still remain men. Flattery does not change us, for we are all

> " Obnoxious, first and last,
> To basest things,"[1]

and thus flattery is no foundation for liberty. Each one of us may be declared a sovereign, as every Frenchman was designated in a solemn circular,[2] by the provisional government; or the people may be called almighty—le peuple tout-puissant—as in the midst of loathsome political obscenity they were termed by the dictatorial government when they were expected and led to vote for a new emperor, and thus by an act of omnipotence to extinguish every vestige of their power. They were asked to divest themselves of this very omnipotence, which nevertheless is exclusively claimed for the nation as inherent in its own nature, and to submit their omnipotence to a still greater power of one man. Nothing of all this is liberty. Self-immolation, even where it is an actual and not a theoretical act of free agency, is not life.

Enthusiasm is necessary for liberty as for every great and noble work, but enthusiasm comes and goes like the breezes of the ocean. How shall they be used for the positive interests of the navigator? Enthusiasm is not liberty, nor does the reality of liberty consist in an æsthetical love of freedom. The

---

[1] Paradise Lost, book 9, line 170.

[2] In a circular, sent by the provisional government all over France before the general election for the national constituent assembly, in 1848, was this sentence: "Every Frenchman of the age of manhood is a political citizen; every citizen is an elector; every elector is a sovereign. There is no one citizen who can say to another: 'You are more of a sovereign than I.' Contemplate your power, prepare to execute it, and be worthy of entering on the possession of your kingdom." The author of these phrases is Mr. de Lamartine, who says, in his Revolution of 1848: "The reign of the people is called the republic."

poet may be as much the priest of liberty as he is the seer of love, but poetry is no more the thing it sings than theory is the deed, or ethics the character of man.

Education has been considered by many as the true basis of popular liberty. It is unquestionably true, and proudly acknowledged by every lover of modern popular liberty, that a wide-spread and sound education is indispensable to liberty. But it is not liberty itself, nor does it necessarily lead to it. Prussia is one of the best educated of countries, but liberty has not yet found a dwelling-place there. The Chinese government is avowedly based upon general education and democratic equality in the hierarchy of officers, but China has never made a step in the path of liberty. Education is almost like the alphabet it teaches. It depends upon what we use it for. Many despotic governments have found it their interest to promote popular education, and the schoolmaster alone cannot establish or maintain liberty, although he will ever be acknowledged as an efficient and indispensable assistant in the cause of modern freedom. Liberty stands in need of character.

How then is real and essential self-government, in the service of liberty, to be obtained and to be perpetuated? There is no other means than a vast system of institutions, whose number supports the whole, as the many pillars support the rotunda of our capitol. They may be modest in their appearance, and even unseen by the passer-by, as those pillars are, but they are nevertheless the real support.

Let us then consider the nature of institutional liberty more closely. In order to appreciate this subject, it will be desirable to inquire first into the nature of institutions in general.

According to the highest meaning which the term has gradually acquired, an institution is a system or body of usages, laws, or regulations of extensive and recurring operation, containing within itself an organism by which it effects its own independent action, continuance, and generally its own farther development. Its object is to generate, effect, regulate or sanction a succession of acts, transactions or productions of a peculiar kind or class. The idea of an institution implies a degree of self-government. Laws act through human agents, and these are, in the case of institutions, their officers or members.

We are likewise in the habit of calling single laws or usages (which are laws of spontaneous growth) institutions, if their operation is of vital importance and vast scope, and if their continuance is in a high degree independent of any interfering power. These two characteristics establish a close affinity between such laws and institutions proper as they have been just defined. Thus we call marriage an institution in consideration of its pervading importance, its extensive operation, the innumerable relations it affects, and the security which its continuance enjoys in the conviction of almost all men, against any attempts at its abolition. Indeed, we generally mean by the term Institution of Marriage, pretty much the institution of the family, that is, the family as a community sanctioned and fostered by the law, by authoritative usages, and by religion—the cluster of laws and usages, social, political, and religious, which relate to this well-defined community.

It always forms a prominent element in the idea of an institution, whether the term be taken in the strictest sense or not, that it is a group of laws, usages and operations standing in close relation to one another, and forming an independent whole with a united and distinguishing character of its own.

A system of laws very often consists of a variety of systems, each enjoying a proportionate degree of self-government, as a general organism is composed of many organs with distinct and peculiar functions of their own, although working in unison and according to the principles and regulative laws of the general organism. We have many institutions which consist of a number of institutions either of the first mentioned or second sort, and as institutions may exist in all the great spheres of human action, it naturally results that there are institutions of the greatest variety in character and extent. A bank, parliament, a court of justice, the bar, the church, the mail, a state are institutions, as well as the lord's supper, a university, the inquisition, all the laws relating to property,

the sabbath, the feudal system.   The Roman triumph, the
Hindoo castes, the bill of exchange, the French Institute, our
presidency, the New York tract society, the Areopagus or
the Olympic games, an insurance company, the janizaries,
the English common law, the episcopate, the tribunate, the
"captainship" of a fishing fleet on the banks, "the crown,"
the German book trade, the Goldsmith's Company at London,
our senate, our representatives, our congress, our state legislatures, courts of conciliation, the justiceship of the peace, the
priesthood, a confederacy, the patent, the copyright, hospitals
for lunatics, estates, the East India Company—all these and
thousands more are or were institutions in the one or the other
adaptation of the term.   Whether they are good or bad, expedient or unwise, human or divine, has nothing to do with the
distinctive character of an institution as such.

" The School," that is to say, the whole school system, as
well as the modern national army, in Prussia, have been called
institutions, when it was desired to express the idea that they
are establishments of vast importance and that they enjoy a
supposed degree of independent vitality.   Baron Bunsen, in
his Hyppolitus, calls the book of common prayer a "national
institution." [1]

The noun Institution is, indeed, formed of the verb to Institute, but it does not, on that account, express, as noun, the
action or the effect of that which constitutes the meaning of
the verb.   The sense of the noun frequently diverges from
that of the verb, in all languages, and especially so in the
English. [2]   We institute an inquiry; but an inquiry is not an

----

[1] Vol. iii. 293.—A member of the late French national assembly,
speaking of the enormous California lottery, which was then in its full
ruinous operation in France, used the expression: "This is not a
lottery; it is a series of lotteries; I ought to say an institution of lotteries."

The exaggeration was carried farthest when an English newspaper
called the Duke of Wellington an institution.   We see, however,
through the exaggeration, the original sense universally attributed to
the term.

[2] The word is a finished and a given thing; the idea is in a constant

institution; and on the other hand, there are many institutions which have never been instituted. They have grown.

This class of institutions forms in a certain point of view the most important, as will be admitted when we consider that the jury, systems of common law, the British parliament and our bicameral systems of the legislature, most governments and the states themselves, are grown institutions.

The English language has but one term for both, the crescive institutions, as they might be termed, and the instituted or enacted institutions, such as a corporation, congress or our legislatures; whose institutors are the people enacting the constitutions. Grown or spontaneous institutions are not ill-defined or loosely distinguished from one another on that account; they may be as individualized as a shady tree in the forest; and enacted or contrived institutions are not confined and narrow on that account. They may be as extensive in action as an Atlantic steamship. The speakership is a well-defined crescive institution; the supreme court of the United States is a vast enacted institution.

Most of the institutions which owe their origin to spontaneous growth have become in course of time mixed institutions.

---

state of expansion or contraction, far exceeding the formative powers even of the most perfect language, so that frequently a whole class of words derived from the same root retains nothing in common but a vague association of ideas, and even this often vanishes. The history of the changing meaning of man's words is instructive, and equally so the history of the changing word. I need only allude to such remarkable words as *Stare*, Status, Statute, Stand, Establishment, Stabilis, Estate, and the whole history through which the meaning of the word State has passed and is still passing on the one hand, and the many branches such as Stable, Staple, Staff, Station, Statistics; or we may take *Civis*, Civitas, Civilis, Civilitas, Civility, Civil (in its two distinct terms,) Civilization, Citizen; Nascor, Nation, National; Populus, Publicus (for populicus,) Public, People, Popular and Popularii; Gignere, Genus, Gens, Gentile, Gentle, Genteel, Gentleman, with the different meanings through which this last word has passed from the time when it meant a man of gentle, that is, not vulgar, not common blood or extraction, to its present import, which relates exclusively to character and breeding. Breeding itself might be mentioned here.

Positive legislation has become mingled with self-grown usage, as is the case with the institution of property, the jury, the bill of exchange, the Hindoo castes, money.

It is for the purpose of comprehending the grown as well as the established institutions, that the words "usages, laws or regulations," have been employed in the definition at the head of this discussion.

Dr. Thomas Arnold, whose name few mention without veneration, says, at the beginning of his Lectures on History: " I would first say that by institution I wish to understand such officers, orders of men, public bodies, settlements of property, customs or regulations, concerning matters of general usage, as do not owe their existence to any express law or laws, but having originated in various ways, at a period of remote antiquity, are already parts of the national system, at the very beginning of our historical view of it, and are recognized by all actual laws, as being themselves a kind of primary condition on which all recorded legislation proceeds. And I would confine the term laws to the enactments of a known legislative power at a certain known period."

It will be seen that this writer restricts the meaning of the term institution to what has been called grown institutions ; nor does he do this with philosophical cogency. He enumerates instances rather than gives a definition ; and it seems arbitrary to bestow the term on grown institutions only. It is contrary to universal usage, as well as to the necessity of the case. What is an instituted legislature of Wisconsin, an incorporated bank, an orphan asylum, or a chartered city government, if it be not an institution ? According to Dr. Arnold, scarcely a pure institution exists, for in all, or nearly all institutions positive enactments have become mixed up with the unenacted usage, as has been mentioned before.

Nor is it accurate to call certain "officers or orders of men" institutions. What unites the individual officers into an institution ? or how can the institution outlast the individual officers existing at any given period ? How could the house of representatives of congress be an institution, which every one calls it, and which assuredly it is, when its members cease to be such every two years ? They are but temporary members of the perpetual institution. The institution itself is the organic law in the Constitution of the United States which provides for the organization and periodical renewal of the house. The same is true with reference to the state and its citizens, living at any given time. Citizens are born and die, but the state is a continuum. The jury of the common law is an institution now spreading over the territory of at least sixty-eight millions of people, but the jurors form only very transitory, although continually repeated representations or embodiments of the institution.[1]

It is this very fact, passed over by Dr. Arnold, that constitutes one of the most important practical features of the institution. It spreads the framework of the same system of laws over sets of men periodically renewed, prescribing their line of action, so that it becomes a consistent continuation of that which their predecessors have done, or, to express it in other words, it breathes the same leading principles into different aggregates of men and different generations as the same principles in varying matter produce and reproduce the same seasons. The institution thus insures perpetuity, and

---

[1] The term Institute seems to differ from Institution, according to present usuage, in this, that the first, when it does not mean the initiatory knowledge of a wide system of science (as the institutes of the pandects, of medicine,) is chiefly used as a noun proper for an institution of learning or the diffusion of knowledge, for instance French Institute, Mechanics' Institute. It may be used as a generic term for institutions of diffusion of knowledge of a higher character; but it is frequently abused in these cases. Schools of some pretence are called institutes, with that deplorable extravagance with which common schools are called academies, common colleges universities, auction rooms auction marts, a single and simple person a party, every chairman a president, and which has so sadly invaded our manly language that many superlative words, such as splendid, magnificent, giantlike, transcendent, illustrious, and hundreds of others can hardly be any longer used by a sober and vigorous writer, and have become worth little more than old coins, once good but now clipped, punched, and sweated by unlawful usage.

renders development possible, while without it there is little more than subjective impulsiveness, which may be good and noble, or ruinous and purely passionate, but always lacks continuity, and consequently development and safe assimilating growth. A market assembly, convened at stated intervals, without institutions, can produce little more than a succession of instinctive or impulsive actions—the more impulsive the more exciting the subject is on which the uninstitutional multitude acts. The same applies to larger communities, if they act without institutions, and in this resemble the Indians of the pampas, who meet and act on each question by simple majority, unguided, unmoulded, unrestrained by permanent laws and usages, or without a maturing organism.

There is nothing so void of lasting good as that history which consists of a mere succession of acts through which there runs no connecting idea, and which show neither growth nor expansion. It sinks to mere anecdotical chronology. All that is deeply good or truly great, and not only vast, in the sense of Attila's conquest, requires development and progress. Impulsiveness without institutions, enthusiasm without an organism, may produce a brilliant period indeed, but it is generally like the light of a meteor. That period of Portuguese history which is inscribed with the names of Prince Henry the Navigator, Camoens and Albuquerque, is radiant with brilliant deeds, but how short a day between long and dreary nights! Portugal had no institutions to perpetuate her glory, and that splendor was but the accidental effect of fortunate circumstances happening to combine at that period. Noble national impulses, without institutions, are at best happy accidents.

When it is said that one of the requisites of the institution is that it shall contain within itself an organism by which it effects its own independent action and continuance, it is obvious that this must be taken in a comparative sense, because every institution ought to stand in connection with others, and is frequently a minor organism of a more comprehensive one; or an institution may be actually the creature of the legislature, and the legislature itself may be the creature of the constitution, which may have emanated from the sovereign will of the people. Yet we call a body of laws or usages an institution only when we unite the idea of an independent individuality with it. It must have its own distinct character, its own peculiar action, and it must not owe its continuance to the arbitrary mandate of a will foreign to it. Independence does not mean disjunction or isolation.

If this were not so, we would not stand in need of the term institution, and the simple term of Law or Ordinance would suffice.

Neither the Romans nor the Greeks had a separate term for institution;[1] indeed the Greeks had not even distinct words for the Latin jus and lex, a paucity of language which we share with them; and if the Romans had no word for institution, although they had many real institutions, we have many important separate systems of law, such as the law of insurance, of bailment, the maritime law, without having an appropriate term for separate bodies of laws and rules. Nor did the Roman probably feel the want of a word for Institution, for the same reason that he expressed time by saying: "Two hundred years after *the founded city.*" The thing itself, the city, was in his mind. We would say: Two hundred years after the *foundation of the city.* The foundation of the city, an abstraction, is in our mind. The Roman said Respublica, the Public Thing, and upon this raft of words, strong but

---

[1] The Latin Institutum does not exactly correspond to our word institution. It means a purpose, object, plan or design, and, finally, a settled procedure, by which it is intended to obtain a certain object; hence a uniform method of action, to be observed when similar cases occur. *Institutum* is very frequently used in conjunction with *consuetudo,* and often means nothing more than settled usage with reference to certain cases. *Institutum* thus designates one of the elements of our Institution, but it does not include the idea of a distinctly limited system of laws or usages with a considerable degree of autonomy, nor does it comprehend the idea of our enacted institutions. *Institutum* retains the idea of usage throughout. Still, it is readily seen how the Roman word *institutum* was naturally changed and expanded into the modern word Institution.

coarse, his own political progress and civic life forced him
to put a heavy freight of meaning, until it came to designate
the vast idea Commonwealth. The Roman was adverse to abstract terms.[1]   Abstracting was a process at which he was no
good hand.[2]   The Greeks, however, may have lacked a proper
term for the idea institution, although so ready to abstract,
and possessed of a plastic language, which offered peculiar facilities for the formation of abstract terms, while yet the people were characterized by an eminently political temperament,
simply because the Greeks were, comparatively speaking, not
a tribe of a strongly institutional bias.   They were not prone to
establish political institutions, and, with the exception of the
Dorians, preferred to bring everything under the more or less
direct will of the mass.   But, although the Greeks abstracted
well, and had a language in which they could readily cast any
abstraction, it must not be forgotten that they rather re-

---

[1] The Roman shunned abstraction even though he should become
illogical.   He said : In medias res, into the middle things, instead of
into the middle of things, and we moderns abstract even against all
sense.   I read but yesterday in large letters over a shop this word—
Carpetings.   Here we have first an unmeaning abstraction of a simple
and sound word, carpet, and then a plural is made of the more abstract
term.   The Americans, altogether inclined to use pompous and grandi-
loquent words, are also given to use abstract terms or those that
approach abstraction, far more than the English.   The sign of the
smallest baker's shop will not be John Smith, Baker, but Bakery by
John Smith, perhaps even American Bakery, or, should it happen to
be near the sea, Ocean Bakery.   A common shop of a green grocer
in the second largest city of the United States, calls itself United
States Market.   The negroes have caught the fever.   Not long ago
I saw a common *shanty* erected in a southern forest, to accommo-
date travellers with coffee while their luggage was ferried over a
river, adorned with the following words on a pine board : Jenny Lind
and Sontag Hotel.   The railway bridge had been carried away, and this
café was erected for a few days only.

[2] The best grammarians tell us that Latin nouns ending in *io*, and
adjectives ending in *ilis*, (that is, abstract terms,) must be used with
circumspection, and not without good authority, since they are comparatively rare in the best writers.   It speaks volumes concerning the
Roman character and mental constitution.

stricted their terms of abstraction to philosophical speculation, and in all the other spheres of life and action they manifested the true antique spirit, that of positive reality. Their style and expressions accorded with this bias. They might as easily as ourselves have said the Union or the League of the Achaeans, but their word for our union was simply "the whole," (τὸ κοίνον.)

Few nations have evinced a greater and more constant tendency to build up institutions, or to cluster together usages and laws relating to cognate subjects into one system, and to allow it its own vitality, than the Romans in their better period. The Greeks, as has been observed, were far less an institutional people There is a degree of adhesiveness and tenacity —a willingness to accumulate and to develop precedents, and a political patience to abide by them—necessary for the growth of strong and enduring institutions, which little agreed with the brilliant, excitable, and therefore changeable Greeks. This was at least the case with the Athenians and all their kindred, and to them belongs the main part of all that we honor and cherish as Grecian.

The London Times has called the Queen of England an institution. This is rhetorically putting the representative for the thing—the queen for the crown, which, itself, is a figurative expression for the kingly element of the British polity. Nevertheless, the meaning of the position that the Queen of England is an institution, is correct and British. It originated from a conviction, that the monarch of Great Britain is not such by his own individuality, that he is not appointed by a superior power or divine right, but that he enjoys his power by the law of the land, which confines and regulates it. It means that he is the chief office-bearer, or, it may be, the chief emblem-bearer, of a vast institution which forms an integral part of the still more comprehensive institution called the British government or the state.[1] In the same way are

---

[1] The reader who desires to become acquainted with the opposite view, must turn to the Christian Politics, by Rev. Wm. Sewell, Fellow and Subrector of Exeter College, London, 1848 ; a book which carries

the lord chancellor, the justice of the peace, the coroner, institutions; not indeed the individuals who happen to be invested with the office, but those systems of laws and usages which they represent at the time.

It is likewise obvious why very old usages or offices of large influence are often called institutions. The fact of their being old proves a degree of independent action or existence. No change of things around them has swept them away; no power

---

out the views of Filmer to an extent which that apologist of absolutism never contemplated. It may be fairly considered to occupy the point opposite to that of the most rabid socialist of France; and, according to the rule that we ought to dwell on works which carry their principles to the fullest length, no matter what those principles may be, it is worth the student's while to make himself acquainted with it. If he can get through the whole, however, he is more patient than I found it possible to be. According to Mr. Sewell, there is but one true government, absolute monarchy, demanding absolute obedience; the king makes the state, and the view I have endeavored to prove in my Ethics, that the state, despite of its comprehensive importance, still remains a means to obtain certain ends, is attacked as the opinion of mere "philosophers." The king, the house of lords, and that of the commons, as they ought to be considered, indicate, according to this writer, the relation in which possibly the three persons of the one deity stand. Filmer stopped short at least with Adam. To counteract the revolting effect which may have just been produced, I refer the reader to page 146, where he will find, in a passage of great length, that the Greek at Marathon fought *only* for his country, his hearth and his laws, while the Persian far surpassed him, because he fought for his king (those also who, according to Herodotus, were whipped into battle?), and that "a christian eye will look with far greater satisfaction and admiration on the Persians, who threw themselves out of the sinking vessel, that by their own death they might save their king, than upon Thermopylæ or Marathon." Enough! I should not have alluded to such extravagances and crudities, were not the book a very learned yet illogical apology for a doctrine which many may have supposed to be dead, and did it not occupy, in view of its preposterous theory, the first place of its class. Nor is it historically uninteresting that such a work has been written in the middle of the nineteenth century. So much is certain, that were the English government actually founded upon that hyper-absolutism, which the author considers so christian, no one would be permitted to assail its fundamental principles with that impunity which he now enjoys.

has ventured to strike them down. They appear to be rooted
in society itself, beyond the reach of government; and single
offices occasionally are called institutions, by way of flattery,
because all feel that a real institution is in dignity superior to
a single law or office, on account of its inherent principle of
self-government.

The following, then, are necessary attributes of a complete
institution, taking the term in its full modern adaptation:

A system or an organic body of laws or usages forming a
whole;

Of extensive operation, or producing widely spread effects;

Working within a certain defined sphere;

Of a high degree of independent permanency;

With an individual vitality and an organism, providing for
its own independent action, and, frequently, for its own development or expansion, or with autonomy;

And with its own officers or members, because without these
it would not be an actual system of laws, but merely a pre-
script in abeyance.

The institution is the opposite of subjective conception,
individual disposition and mere personal bias. The institution
implies organic action. In this lies, not only its capacity of
perpetuating principles and of insuring continuous, homoge-
neous and expansive action, but also its great power, its grandeur, its danger, and its mischief, according to its original
character and its inherent principle. Christ imprinted on his
church the missionary character, and from the apostles to the
servants of the gospel who lately starved near Cape Horn, the
institution of the missionary ministry has been the pioneer and
handmaid of extending civilization. But if the institution is
intrinsically bad, or contains vicious principles, it lends additional and fearful power to the evil element within it, and
gives a proportionate scope to its calamitous influence. If it
be established in a sphere in which the subjective ought to
prevail, it becomes an agent of ruin by making the objective
prevail more than is desirable, or by making the annihilation
of individuality one of its very objects. The gigantic institu-

tion of the Society of Jesus, and some of the modern Trade's Unions are impressive and amazing examples.

Whenever men allow themselves to glide into the belief that moral responsibility can be aught else than individual, and that responsibility is divisible, provided many perform but one act; whenever the esprit du corps prevails over the moral consciousness of man, which is inseperable from his individuality, the institution gives a vigor to that which is unhallowed and unattainable by the individual. The institution is, like every union of men, subject to the all-pervading, elementary law of moral reduplication, as I have called it on previous occasions, and which consists in this, that any number of united individuals, moved by the same impulse, conviction or desire, whether good or bad—whether scientific, æsthetic or ethical, patriotic or servile, self-sacrificing or self-seeking—will countenance and impel each other to far better or far worse acts, and will develop in each other the powers for the specific good or evil, in a far greater extent, than would have been possible in each separate individual. It is the law which is illustrated by the excellence of whole periods in one particular sphere; by the rapid decadence of nations when once their fall begins; by the lofty character of some times, and by the contaminating effect of indiscriminate imprisonment; by the power of example; by the silliness which at times pervades whole classes or communities; by the sublime, calm heroism on board a sinking man-of-war, and at other times by the panic of large masses. It is the universal law of mutual countenance and excitement.

If an institution is founded on a vicious principle, or if a bad impulse has seized it for a time, it will not only add to the evil force, according to the general law of moral reduplication, but lend additional strength by the force of its organization and the continuity of its action. Members of an institution will do that which, singly, they would never have dared to perpetrate. They will deny the obligation of paying what is due to widows and orphans, in cases which would have made them look upon the denial as disgraceful, had they acted in their own individual capacity. Thousands who have committed acts of crying cruelty as members of the Holy Office would not have been capable of committing them individually. The institution in these cases has the same effect which all united and continuous action has.

On the other hand, institutions have been able, for the same reason, to resist iniquitous inroads, or its members have been wrought up to a manly devotion, when the individual would not, and, often at least, could not, have resisted. In almost all cases of an invasion of rights by one of the domestic powers, we find that some institution has formed the breakwater against the rushing tide of power. There are many instances, such as the "Case of the Bishops" under James II., and the rejoicing of the better disposed Frenchmen, when the court of Paris declared itself, although in vain as it turned out, competent to judge of the spoliation which the dictator had decreed against the Orleans family, that show how instinctively men look toward institutions for support and political salvation.

I have purposely restricted my remarks on the resisting force of institutions to cases of invasion by domestic powers. When foreign invaders trample upon rights and grind down a people, something different and sharper is required to rouse them, to electrify them into united resistance. Humanity itself must be stung; an element in man's very nature must be offended, so that the most patient cannot endure the oppression any longer. We find, therefore, that innumerable popular risings against foreign despots, in antiquity and modern times, have taken place, when the insolent oppressor, having gone all lengths, at last violates a wife or a daughter. Such outrage comes home to the most torpid heart, and will not be borne by the veriest slave.

We investigate, here, the nature of the institution in general. Like everything possessing power, it may serve for weal or woe, as we have seen. Constituted evil is as much worse, as constituted good is more efficaciously good than that effected by the individual. When we know the essential nature of the

Institution, we shall be able to judge when, and where, and how it may be used beneficially. An institution is an arch: but there are arches that support bridges, and cathedrals, and hospitals; and others that support dungeons, banquet rooms of revelry, torture chambers, or spacious halls in which criminal folly enacts a melancholy farce with all the pitiful trappings of unworthy submission.

The greater or less degree in which the institutional spirit of different nations is manifested furnishes us with a striking characteristic of whole nations.   The Romans, the Nether-landers, and indeed all the Teutonic tribes, until the dire spirit of dis-individualizing centralization seized nearly all the governments of the European continent, were institutional na-tions.   The English and ourselves are still so.   The Russians and all the Sclavonic nations, the Turks and the Mongolian tribes, seem to be remarkably uninstitutional.

A similar remark naturally applies to different species of governments.   Some do not only result from a decidedly insti-tutional tendency of the people at large, but they also promote it, while there is in others an inherent antagonism to the institution.   No absolutism, whether that of one or many, brooks institutions.   Cunning monarchical absolutism, some-times, allows the forms of institutions to exist, in order to use them for its own purpose.   The reason why all absolutism is hostile to living institutions is not only because all abso-lute rulers discountenance opposition, but because there is in every despotism an ingrained incompatibility with independent action and self-government, in whatsoever narrow circle or moderate degree it may strive to maintain itself.   This is so much the case that often despots of the best intentions for the welfare of the people have been the most destructive to the remnants of former, or to the germs of future institutions, in the very proportion in which they have been gifted with bril-liant talents, activity and courage.   These served them only to press forward more vigorously and more boldly in the career of all absolutism, which consists in the absorption of individuality and institutional action, or in levelling everything which does not comport with a military uniformity, and with sweeping annihilation of diversity.

As institutions may be good or bad, so may they be favorable or unfavorable to liberty. They may indeed give to the representative of the institution great freedom, but only for the repression of general freedom. The viziership is an institution all over Asia, and has been so from remote periods, but it is an institution in the spirit of despotism, and forms an active part of the pervading system of Asiatic monarchical absolutism. The star chamber was an institution, and gave much freedom of action to its members, yet the patriots under the Stuarts made it their first business to break down this preposterous institution. When in 1660 the Danes made their king hereditary and absolute, binding him by the only oath that he should never allow his or his successors' power to be restricted, the Danish crown became undoubtedly a new institution, but assuredly not propitious to liberty. Of all the Hellenic tribes the Spartans were probably the most institutional, but they were communists, and communism is hostile to liberty. They dis-individualized the citizens, and, as a matter of course, extinguished in the same degree individual liberty, development and progress. A state in which a citizen could be punished because he had added one more to the commonly adopted number of lute strings, cannot be allowed to have been favorable to liberty.

Many of those very attributes of the institution proper, which make it so valuable in the service of liberty, constitute its inconvenience and danger when the institution is used against it. It is a bulwark, and may protect the enemy of liberty. It is like the press. Modern liberty or civilization cannot dispense with it, yet it may be used as its keenest enemy.

CHAPTER XXVI.

CIVILIZATION, so closely connected with what we love in
modern liberty, as well as progress and security, themselves
ingredients of civil liberty, stands in need of stability and
continuity, and these cannot be secured without institutions.
This is the reason why the historian, when speaking of such
organizers or refounders of their nations as Charlemagne,
Alfred, Numa, Pelayo, knows of no higher name to give them
than that of institutors.

The force of the institution in imparting stability and giving
new power to what otherwise must have swiftly passed away,
has been illustrated in our own times in mormonism. Every
observer who has gravely investigated this repulsive fraud will
agree that as for its pretensions and doctrines it must have
passed as it came, had it not been for the remarkable character which Joseph Smith possessed as an institutor.[1] Thrice
blessed is a noble idea, perpetuated in an active institution, as
charity in a hôtel-dieu; thrice cursed, a wicked idea embodied
in an institution.

---

[1] The great ability of this man seems to be peculiarly exhibited in his
mixture of truth and arrant falsehood, his uncompromising boldness and
insolence, and his organizing instituting mind. Two men have met
almost simultaneously with great success, in our own times—Joseph
Smith and Louis Napoleon. Of the two, the first seems the more clever.
What he performed he did against all probability of success, without
any assistance from tradition or prestige.

The title of institutor is coveted even by those who represent ideas the very opposite to institutions.

Louis Napoleon Bonaparte, when he inaugurated his government, dwelt on the "institutions" he had established,[1]
with pride, or a consciousness that the world prizes the
founding of good institutions as the greatest work of a statesman and a ruler.

Institutions may not have been viciously conceived, or have
grown out of a state of violence or crime, and yet they may
have become injurious in the course of time, as incompatible
with the pervading spirit of the age, or they may have become hollow, and in this latter case they are almost sure to be

---

[1] He meant, of course, the senate, legislative corps, and the council
of state. Why he calls these *new* institutions we cannot see, but he
evidently wished to indicate his own belief, or desired that others
should believe, in their permanency, as well perhaps as in their own
independent action. To those, however, who consider them as nothing
more than the pared and curtailed remnants of former institutions, who
do not see that they can enjoy any independent action of their own,
and are aware that their very existence depends upon the mere forbearance of the executive; who remember their origin by a mere decree of a dictator bound by no superior law,—to those who know with
what studied and habitual sneer "parliamentary governments" are
spoken of by the ruling party in France, all these establishments appear
in principle no more as real institutions than a tent on a stage. The
"constitution" of the present empire (Napoleon I. always spoke of *les
constitutions de l'empire*) is a close copy of the organic laws of the first
empire. Now, few of my readers, probably, are aware, that the very
name of senatus-consultum, which played so important a part in the
first empire, and by which the most violent fundamental changes were
effected, was literally smuggled in by Napoleon I. He did so on occasion of the conspiracy of Cerachi and others, when the council of state
resolved that no *law* should be demanded, because that "would lead to
discussion." The list of condemned was passed by the council of state,
upon a report of the police, not even signed, and the senate adopted and
decreed it, as a *senatus-consultum*. Memoirs of Miot de Melito, (himself a counsellor of state,) vol. i. page 360 and sequ. It hardly deserves
mention here, that Napoleon adopted the term from the Roman empire,
which was his political beau-ideal, as he did many other terms and
symbols.

injurious. Hollow institutions in the state are much like empty boxes in an ill-managed house. They are sure to be filled with litter and rubbish, and to become nuisances. But great wisdom and caution are necessary to decide whether an institution ought to be amputated or not, because it is a notable truth in politics that many important institutions and laws are chiefly efficient as preventives, not as positive agents. It is not sufficient, therefore, that at a glance we do not discover any palpable good produced by the institution, to justify us in destroying it. Antiquity is prima facie evidence in favor of an institution,[1] and must not rashly be confounded with obsoleteness; but antiquity is certainly no proof against positive and grounded arguments. On the other hand, hollow institutions have frequently the serious inconvenience of deceiving and changing the proper venue, as lawyers would express it. The form of a representative government, without the spirit, true principles and sincere guarantees of self-government in that body, or without being founded upon a candid and real representation, is worse than a government without these forms, because it eases the executive of the responsibility which without that hollow form would visibly rest on it alone.[2]

---

[1] I am aware that many persons believe now-a-days so little in this truth that not only does antiquity of itself appear to them as a proof of deficiency, but they turn their face from the whole Past, as something to be shunned, thus forgetting the continuity of society, progress and civilization. Mr. Guizot, in his lectures on the History of Representative Governments, delivered in Paris, 1820, found it necessary to warn his hearers against this horror of the past. The reader will find remarks on the impossibility of "beginning entirely anew," in my Political Ethics.

[2] Count Miot relates that when Napoleon, as consul, desired to change the entire character of the house of representatives, in order to bring it under the exclusive control of the executive, but hesitated to make an organic change by mere violence, Talleyrand at last suggested, that the other assembly had no business assigned to it; why should it not be made to sanction the measure? The history of the whole consulate, and of the early period of the empire, is a striking and continuous illustration of the assistance which a despot derives from mere forms of liberty without the reality of freedom. It would seem that Napoleon I. established

But here, again, it is necessary to observe that an institution may for a time become a mere form, and yet that very form may soon be animated again by a proper spirit. Parliament under Henry VIII. had become a subservient tool, highly noxious because it formally sanctioned many atrocious measures of the king. Yet, it was that same parliament which rose to action and importance within fifty years, and within a century and a half became the virtual seat of government and supreme power in the state. There is hardly a portion of the penal trial which has not at times and for an entire period been abused; yet the existence of this very trial, intended to rest on the principle of independence, became in a better period the starting-point of a new order of things.

We must also mention the fact that there are perennial and deciduous institutions, or institutions avowedly fit only for a preparatory state of civilization. Their office is limited in duration, like that of the deciduous teeth, which must be drawn if they do not drop of themselves, or if they resist too obstinately their perennial substitutes.

We may here close our general remarks on institutions, and, now, investigate in what the force of the institution consists, when wisely taken into the service of liberty, and inquire into the characteristics of self-government in particular.

By institutional self-government is meant that popular government which consists in a great organism of institutions or a union of harmonizing systems of laws instinct with self-government. It is essentially of a co-operative

certain forms, in conquered countries, for the very purpose of assigning the appearance of responsibility to certain bodies of the state, while he left the government absolute. It is difficult otherwise to explain the constitution which he decreed for Naples, (page 359, vol. ii. of Memoirs of Count Miot de Melito,) according to which "the national representation" was to consist of one chamber divided into five sections, namely: the clergy, nobility, proprietors, *savans*, and traders; the clergy, nobility and savans holding their places for life; the others, removable at pleasure by the government. The Roman senate, when it had become the recording body, of the imperial decrees, gave much support to the emperors, by its appearance of an ancient institution.

character, and thus the opposite to centralism. It is arti-
culated liberty, and thus the opposite to an inarticulated
government of the majority. It is of an inter-guaranteeing,
and consequently, inter-limiting character, and in this aspect the negation of absolutism. It is of a self-evolving
and genetic nature, and thus is contradistinguished from
governments founded on extra-popular principles, such as
divine right. Finally, institutional self-government is, in
the opinion of our race, and according to our experience,
the only practical self-government, or self-government carried out in the realities of life, and is thus the opposite of a
vague or theoretical liberty, which proclaims abstractions, but,
in reality, cannot disentangle itself from the despotism of
one part over another, however permanent or changing the
ruling part may be.

Institutional self-government is the political embodiment of
self-reliance and mutual acknowledgment of self-rule. It is
in this view the political realization of equality.

Institutional self-government is the only self-government
which makes it possible to unite *self*-government and self-
government.

According to the Anglican view, institutional self-government consists in the fact that all the elementary parts of the
government, as well as the highest and most powerful branches,
consist in real institutions, with all the attributes which have
been ascribed to an institution in the highest sense of the term.
It consists, farther, in the unstinted freedom and fair protection
which are granted to institutions of all sorts, commercial, religious, cultural, scientific, charitable and industrial, to germinate and to grow—provided they are moral and do not invade
the equal rights of others. It receives its aliment from a pervading spirit of self-reliance and self-respect—the real afflatus
of liberty.

It does not only require that the main functions of the
government—the legislative, the judicial, and the executive—
be clearly divided, but also that the legislature and the judiciary be bona fide institutions. The first French constituent

assembly pronounced the separation of the three powers, and was obliged to do so, since it intended to demolish the absolutism which had grown up under the Bourbons; but so long as there existed an absolute power, no matter of what name, that could dictate, liberty was not yet obtained. Indeed, it may be said that an efficient division of power cannot exist, unless the legislature and the judiciary form real institutions, in our sense of the term.

These institutions, again, consist of many minor institutions, as an organism consists of many minor ones. Our congress is a real institution, but its component parts, the senate and house of representatives, are its constituent institutions, and the whole is in close connection with other institutions, for instance the state legislatures, or depends upon others such as the common law.

Yet the self-government of our country or of England would be considered by us little more than oil floating on the surface of the water, did it consist only in a congress and state legislatures with us, and in a parliament in England. Self-government, to be of a penetrative character, requires the institutional self-government of the county or district; it requires that everything which, without general inconvenience, can be left to the circle to which it belongs, be thus left to its own management; it consists in the presenting grand jury, in the petty jury, in the fact that much which is called on the European continent the administrative branch, be left to the people. It requires, in one word, all the local appliances of government which are termed local self-government;[1] and

---

[1] T. Toulmin Smith's Local Self-government and Centralization, etc.; London, 1851.

A work which many of my readers will peruse with interest and instruction is Ferdinand Béchard's Lois Municipales des Républiques de la Swisse et des États-Unis; Paris, 1852. Mr. Béchard is also the author of a Traité de l'Administration Intérieure de la France—a work which must be welcome to every inquiring citizen, because it pictures the details of French centralization, the most consistently carried out centralization in existence.

Mr. Béchard uses repeatedly in his French work the English term Self-government.

Niebuhr says that British liberty depends at least as much on these as on parliament, and in contradistinction to them he calls the governments of the continent Staats-Regierungen, (state governments, meaning governments in which all detail is directed by the general and supreme power.)[1]

It must be in view of this local self-government, combined with parliamentary freedom, that Sir Edward Coke said of the Justice of the Peace: "It is such a form of subordinate government for the tranquillity and quiet of the realm as no part of the christian world hath the like, if the same be duly executed."[2]

Anglican self-government requires that every institution of local self-government shall have the right to pass such by-laws as it finds necessary for its own government, without obtaining the consent of any superior power, even that of the crown or parliament, and that of course such by-laws shall

---

[1] A German work, the title of which is: An Account of the Internal Administration of Great Britain, by Baron von Vincke, edited by B. G. Niebuhr; Berlin, 1815. Niebuhr, who had spent a portion of his early manhood in England, published, and probably modelled in a great measure, this work in order to influence, if possible, the Prussian government, to reorganize the state after the expulsion of the French, and to reclaim that kingdom from the centralization it had adopted in many respects from the invaders of Germany. Niebuhr was a follower and great admirer of Baron von Stein, who, when minister of Prussia, had given to the cities some degree of self-government by his Städte-Ord-nung—causing not a little umbrage to Napoleon. Niebuhr desired to give increased life to the principles contained in the Cities' Charter, when he published the work I have mentioned.

[2] Coke's Institutes, part 10, ch. xxi., Justices of the Peace. The Earl of Strafford, who, like his royal master, died so well, after, politically speaking, having lived so ill, bade his brother, on the scaffold, to take this among other messages to his eldest son: "Wish him to content himself to be a servant to his country, as a justice of the peace in his county, not aiming at higher preferment." May 12, 1641. Rushworth (who was on the scaffold,) vol. viii. p. 760. George Washington, after having aided in founding a great commonwealth, and after having been twice its chief magistrate, was a justice of the peace in his county, in which he was imitated by John Adams, and, perhaps, by other ex-presidents.

stand good in the courts of law, and shall be as binding upon every one concerned as any statute or law. I believe that it is in the Anglican system of liberty alone, that by-laws are enacted and have full force without consent of superior power. There are in other countries exceptions, but they are rare indeed, and very limited in power, while the by-law is the rule in our system. The whole subject of the by-law is characteristic and important, and stands out like the comprehensive and peculiar doctrine of the Anglican warrant. The character of self-government is moreover manifested by the fact that the right of making by-laws is not derived from any grant of superior power, but has been ever considered in the English polity as inherent in the local community—a natural right of freemen. Coke says, with reference to these laws and their force : " Of more force is the agreement of the folk and people than the grant of the king;"[1] and in another place he says: "The inhabitants of a town, without any custom, may make ordinances or by-laws for any such thing which is for the general good of the public,[2] unless indeed it be pretended by any such by-law to abridge the general liberty of the people, their inherent birthright, assured to all by the common law of the whole land, and which that common law, in its jealous regard for liberty, does not allow to be abrogated or lessened even by their own consent—much less, therefore, by the consent of their delegates in parliament."[3]

It may be added that by-law does not mean, as many suppose, additional law, law by the side of another or complementary, but it means law of the place or community, law of the bye or pye—that is, of the collection of dwellers, or of the settlement as we, in America, perhaps would naturally express it.[4]

---

[1] 8 Reports, p. 125.   [2] 5 Reports, p. 63.   [3] Ibid., p. 64.

[4] See Smith's Local Self-government, p. 230. The quotations from Coke to which the three last notes refer are likewise in Smith's work, which I recommend to every reader.

By, in by-law, is the same syllable with which the names of many English places end, such as Derby, Whitby, and is etymologically the same with the German Bauen (to build, to settle, to cultivate,) which is of the same root with the Gothic Bua and Boo, and especially the frequentative Bygga, *aedificare*. See Adelung ad verbum Bauen. It is a word which runs through all the Teutonic languages, ancient and modern.

Gradually, indeed, bye-laws came to signify laws for a limited circle, a small society, laws which any set of men have the right to pass for themselves within and under the superior law, charter, etc., which constitutes them into a society, and thus it happened that bye-law was changed into by-law, as we have by-ways, roads by the side of others. It cannot be denied that by-law at present is used in the sense of law passed by the side, as it were, of another and main law. Very few persons know of the origin, and the present sense of by-law is doubtless that of collateral, expletive or subordinate law. Such double derivations are not uncommon in our language. The scholar is probably reminded, by this note, of the term God, which we christians derive from *good*, and a better, holier derivation, as to the sense of the word, we cannot give to it; yet the historical derivation, the *verbal* etymology, if I might so say, is an entirely different one. See Jacob Grimm's German Mythology, ad verbum *Gott*. The starting-point of adoration is, with all tribes, dread, acknowledgment of superior power; then follows acknowledgment of wisdom, and last of all acknowledgment of goodness, purity, holiness.

CHAPTER XXVII.

EFFECTS AND USES OF INSTITUTIONAL SELF-DEVELOPMENT.

In order fully to appreciate institutional self-government, and not unconsciously to enjoy its blessings, as most of us enjoy the breath of life without reflecting on the organ of respiration and the atmosphere we inhale, it is necessary to present to our minds clearly and repeatedly, as we pass through life and read the history of our race, what effects it produces on the individual, on society, and on whole periods, and how it acts far beyond the limits of the country where it prevails.

The advantages of institutional liberty and organized self-government, diffused over a whole country or state, and penetrating with its quickening power all the branches of government, may be briefly summed up in the following way:

Institutional self-government trains the mind and nourishes the character for a dependence upon law and a habit of liberty, as well as of a law-abiding acknowledgment of authority. It educates for freedom. It cultivates civil dignity in all the partakers, and teaches to respect the rights of others. It has thus a gentlemanly character. It brings home palpable liberty to all, and gives a consciousness of freedom, rights and corresponding obligations such as no other system does. It is the only self-government which is a real government *of* self, as well as *by* self, and indeed is the only real self-government, of which all other governments assuming the name of self-government are but semblances, because they are at most the unrestricted rule of accidentally dominating parties, which do not even necessarily consist of the majorities. For it is a truth that what is called a majority in uninstitutional countries, which struggle nevertheless for liberty, is generally a minority, and often even a small minority.

Institutional self-government incarnates, if the expression may pass, the idea of a free country, and makes it palpable, as the jury is nobly called the country for the prisoner. It seems that as long as institutions exist in full vigor, and no actual revolution takes place, that odious and very stale part of a successful general who uses the wreaths he has gained abroad, as a means of stifling liberty at home, is unknown. Rome had her Syllas and Marius, with their long line of successors, only from the time when the institutional character of Rome had begun to fade. A French writer of ability[1] mentions as a fact worthy of note, that the Duke of Wellington never carried his ambition higher than that of a distinguished subject, although Napoleon expected the contrary; and General Scott, in his account of the offer which was made to him in Mexico, to take the reins of that country into his own hands, and rule it with his army, twice mentions the love of his country's institutions, which induced him to decline a ruler's chaplet.[2]

---

[1] Mr. Lemoisne, Wellington from a French Point of View.

[2] General Scott has given an account of this affair in some remarks he made at a public dinner at Sandusky, in the year 1852. The generals of most countries would probably charge the victorious general with *niaiserie*, for declining so tempting an offer. We delight in the dutiful and plain citizen who did not hesitate, and as the occur-rence possesses historical importance, the entire statement of the general is here given. I have it in my power to say, from the best information, that the following account is "substantially correct," and as authentic as reports of speeches can well be made :

"My friend," said General Scott, "has adverted to the proposition seen floating about in the newspapers. I have nowhere seen it correctly stated that an offer was made to me to remain in that country and govern it. The impression which generally prevails, that the proposition emanated from congress, is an erroneous one. The overture was made to me privately, by men in and out of office, of great influence— five of whom, of enormous wealth, offered to place the *bonus* of one million of dollars (mentioned below) to my credit in any bank I might name, either in New York or London. On taking possession of the city of Mexico, our system of government and police was established, which, as the inhabitants themselves confessed, gave security—for the first time perfect and absolute security—to person and property. About two-fifths of all the branches of government, including nearly a majo-

Institutional self-government is of great importance regarding the obedience of the citizen.

rity of the members of congress and the executive, were quite desirous of having that country annexed to ours. They knew that, upon the ratification of the treaty of peace, nineteen out of twenty of the persons belonging to the American army would stand disbanded, and would be absolutely free from all obligations to remain in the army another moment. It was entirely true of all the new regiments called regulars, of all the volunteers, and eight out of ten of the rank and file of the old regiments. Thirty-three and a third per cent. were to be added to the pay of the American officers and men retained as the nucleus of the Mexican army. When the war was over, the government overwhelmed me with reinforcements, after there was no possibility of fighting another battle. When the war commenced, we had but one-fourth of the force which we needed. The Mexicans knew that the men in my army would be entitled to their discharge. They supposed, if they could obtain my services, I would retain these twelve or fifteen thousand men, and that I could easily obtain one hundred thousand men from home. The hope was, that it would immediately cause annexation. They offered me one million of dollars as a bonus, with a salary of $250,000 per annum, and five responsible individuals to become security. They expected that annexation would be brought about in a few years, or, if not, that I could organize the finances, and straighten the complex affairs of that government. It was understood that nearly a majority of congress was in favor of annexation, and that it was only necessary to publish a pronunciamento to secure the object. We possessed all the fortresses, all the arms of the country, their cannon foundries and powder manufactories, and had possession of their ports of entry, and might easily have held them in our possession if this arrangement had gone into effect. A published pronunciamento would have brought congress right over to us, and, with these fifteen thousand Americans holding the fortresses of the country, all Mexico could not have disturbed us. We might have been there to this day, if it had been necessary. I loved my distant home. I was not in favor of the annexation of Mexico to my own country. Mexico has about eight millions of inhabitants, and out of these eight millions there are not more than one million who are of pure European blood. The Indians and mixed races constitute about seven millions. They are exceedingly inferior to our own. As a lover of my country, I was opposed to mixing up that race with our own. This was the first objection, on my part, to this proposition. May I plead some little love of home, which gave me the preference for the soil of my own country and its institutions? I came back to die under those institutions, and here I am. I believe I have no more to add in reply."

Obedience is one of the elements of all society, and consequently of the state. Without it political society cannot hold together. This is plain to every one. Yet there exists this great distinction, that there may be obedience, demanded on the sole ground of authority; such is the obedience expected by the parent. The authority of the parent comes from a source not within the circle of the obeyers. And there may be obedience, which has its very source within the circle of the obeyers. Such is the source of obedience due to authority in that society the component members of which live in jural relations—in one word, in the state. The freeman obeys, not because the government exists before the people and makes them, but because man is a being destined to live in a political state—because he must have laws and a government. It is his privilege, and distinguishes him from the brute creation. Yet, the government existing as a consequence of the jural nature of society and of man, it is unworthy of a freeman to obey any individual as individual, to follow his commands merely because issued by him, while the citizen of a free country acknowledges it as a prerogative to obey laws.

The obedience of a loyal free citizen is an act of self-directing compliance with a rule of action; and it becomes a triumph of reason and freedom when self-directing obedience is thus paid to laws which the obeyer considers erroneous, yet knows to be the laws of the land, rules of action legitimately prescribed by a body of which he forms a constituent part. This noble attribute of man is never politically developed except by institutions. To obey institutions of self-government has nothing galling in it on the ground of submission. We do not obey a person whom as individual we know to be no more than ourselves, but we obey the institution of which we know ourselves to be as integral a part as the superior, clothed with authority. The religious duty of obeying for conscience sake is not excluded from this obedience. On the contrary, it forms an important element. The term "law-abiding people" could never have become so favorite an expression with us, and would not be inscribed even on the banners of some who defy the law, were we not an institutional people under the authority of institutional self-government.

Rulers over thirty millions of people, like our presidents, could not be easily changed, without shock or convulsion, were not the thirty millions trained by institutional self-government, were not the ousted minority conscious that, in the spontaneous act of submitting, they obey an institution of which they form as important a portion as the ruling party, and did not their own obedience foreshadow the obedience which the others must yield, when their turn comes. The "principle of authority" has become for the time being as popular, at least as often repeated a phrase, in France, as "abiding by the law" is with us. Pamphlets are written on it, the journals descant on it. If the object of these writings is to prove that there must be authority where there is society, it would prove that the writers must consider the opinion of some communists, that all government is to be done away with, far more serious and disseminated than people at a distance can believe, to whom such absurdity appears as a mere paper and opposition fanaticism. If, however, all those discourses are intended to establish the principle of authority in politics as an independent principle, such as we find it in the church, because its institutor gave divine commandments, it would only show that the ruling party plainly desires absolutism.[1]

---

[1] There is no doubt in my mind that the institutional government is the real school of civil obedience. Whether the following remarkable passage, which I found in Baron Müffling's Memoirs of the Campaign of 1813 and 1814, edited by Col. Philip Yorke, London, 1853, must be in part explained by the general self-government of England, and by the fact that every English gentleman is accustomed to political self-government and consequently to obedience, I shall not decide, but I strongly incline to believe that we must do so. General Müffling was the Prussian officer in the staff of the Duke of Wellington, who served as an official link between the two armies. He was, therefore, in constant personal intercourse with the English commander, and had the very best opportunity of observing that which he reports.

"I observed," says General Müffling, "that the duke exercised far greater power in the army he commanded than Prince Blücher in the one

Institutional self-government distinguishes itself above all others for tenacity and a formative, assimilative and transmissible character.

Its tenacity is shown by the surviving of many institutions even in the most violent changes, although little of a self-governing character may be left in them. In no period is this truth more strikingly illustrated than in the conquest of the Roman empire by the Northern races. The Gothic sword took lands and scaled towns, but it could not scale institutions, and Theodoric assimilated his Germanic hosts to the remnants of Roman institutions, rather than the Italians to the conquerors. It has been so wherever the conqueror met with institutions and did not in turn oppose institutions of his own, as, in a great measure, the Visigoths did in Spain. The military despotism which swept over the whole continent of Europe left England unscathed; even in spite of Cromwell's military and organized absolutism, the institutions survived Cromwell's vigor and the prostitution of England under Charles II.

Lord Macaulay says that it was probably better that the English allowed Charles II. to return without insisting upon distinct and written guarantees of their liberties. This may be a disputable point, for we see that the English were after all obliged to resort to them in the Declaration of Rights and

---

committed to his care. The rules of the English service permitted the duke's suspending any officer and sending him back to England. The duke had used this power during the war in Spain, when disobedience showed itself among the higher officers. Sir Robert Wilson was an instance of this.

"Amongst all the generals, from the leaders of corps to the commanders of brigades, not one was to be found in the active army who had been known as refractory.

"It was not the custom in this army to criticize or control the commander-in-chief. Discipline was strictly enforced; every one knew his rights and his duties. The duke, in matters of service, was very short and decided. He allowed questions, but dismissed all such as were unnecessary. His detractors have accused him of being inclined to encroach on the functions of others—a charge which is at variance with my experience."

Settlement; but it will hardly be disputed that the reigns of Charles II. and James II. would have been fatal to England had she not been eminently institutional in her character.

The tenacious life of institutional liberty is proved perhaps best in times of political mediocrity and material wellbeing. Gloomy, or ardent, and bold times may try men's souls, but periods of material prosperity and public depression try a country's institutions. They are the most difficult times, and liberty is lost at least as often by stranding on pleasant shores as by wrecking on boiling breakers.

The formative character of institutional self-government is shown in such cases as the formation of the Oregon government, mentioned before. So does the extensive British empire in the East show the formative and vital character of self-government. No absolute government could have established or held such an empire at such a distance, and yet an absolute ruler would consider it indicative of feebleness and not of strength in a government, that a board of shareholders could recall a governor-general, and that a man like Sir Robert Peel, as premier, acquiesced in it.

Even the Liberians may be mentioned here. People who, while with us, belonged to a degraded class, many of whom were actual slaves, and the rest socially unfree, nevertheless have carried with them an amount of institutionalism which had percolated even down to them; and a government has been established by them which enjoys internal peace, and seems to grow in strength and character every day, at the same time that hundreds of attempts in Europe have sadly miscarried. And, again, people of the same race, but having originally lived under a government without the element of institutional self-rule—the inhabitants of St. Domingo—resemble their former masters in the rapid succession of different governments destitute of self-government and peace.

The words of Mr. Everett are doubtless true, that "the French, though excelling all other nations of the world in the art of communicating for temporary purposes with savage tribes, seem, still more than the Spaniards, to be destitute of

the august skill required to found new states. I do not know
that there is such a thing in the world as a colony of France
growing up into a prosperous commonwealth. A half a million of French peasants in Lower Canada, tenaciously adhering to the manners and customs which their fathers brought
from Normandy two centuries ago, and a third part of that
number of planters of French descent in Louisiana, are all
that is left to bear living witness to the amazing fact that not
a century ago France was the mistress of the better half of
North America."[1] Are they succeeding in establishing a
vigorous colony in Algeria? It seems not; and the question
presents itself, what is the reason of this inability of so intelligent a nation as the French to establish flourishing colonies? I believe that the chief reason is this: The French are
thoroughly wedded to centralism, and eminently uninstitutional
in their character. They want government to do everything
for them. They are peculiarly destitute of self-reliance in all
public and communal matters. They do not know self-government; they cannot impart it. Every Frenchman's mental
home is Paris, even while residing in France; as to a colonial
life, he always considers it a mere exile.[2]

The assimilative power and transmissible character of the

---

[1] Mr. Everett's Address before the New York Historical Society,
1853.

[2] There are doubtless many causes operating together, and one of these
may be that the French are not inherently fond of agriculture, as the
Germanic races are. The English are eminently so.

From the Canadian census published in 1853, the following difference
between French and the Anglo-Saxon colonists appeared: The inhabitants of Lower Canada are chiefly of French origin, and are not much
fewer in number than the Upper Canadians; the latter being 952,004,
and the former 890,261, according to the last census. But although so
close to them in point of numbers, and also in the quantity of land they
have under cultivation, the inhabitants of Lower Canada raise a much
smaller quantity of agricultural produce than the Upper Canadians obtain from the soil. With the exception of maple sugar and flax, in which
they far surpass the inhabitants of the Upper Province, they fall greatly
below them in nearly all the more valuable products.

institution are closely connected with its tenacity and formative character. Few things in all history seem to me more striking, and, if analyzed, more instructive than the fact that Great Britain, though monarchical in name, and aristocratic in many points, plants freedom wherever she sends colonies, and becomes thus the great mother of republics; while France, with all her democratic tendencies, her worship of equality and repeated proclamations of a republic, has never approached nearer to the republic than setting aside a ruling dynasty; her colonies are, politically speaking, barren dependencies. They do not bloom into empires. The colonies of Spain also teach a grave lesson on this subject.[1]

The power by which institutional self-government assimilates

---

[1] The reader has a right to ask here, why then did not the Netherlands, so institutional in their character, establish prosperous self-governments in foreign parts, as England did? I believe the answer which must be given is this:

The Netherlands lacked at home a protecting national government proper—one that could furnish them with a type of a comprehensive yet popular general government. The Netherlandish colonies always remained mere dependencies upon the executive. The Netherlanders did not plant colonial legislatures.

The Netherlands, moreover, had lapsed into a state of sejunction. The idea of their petty sovereignty was carried to the most ruinous extreme. The Greeks colonized, indeed, by dotting as it were foreign parts. The shores of the Mediterranean were sprinkled with Greek and Phœnician colonies corresponding to the ancient city-states—from which they had branched off. But a Netherlandish town could not thus have established a little colony in Java or the West Indies.

Lastly, I believe the Netherlanders did not become the disseminators of self-government, although institutional in their character, because they had no living common law to take with them, as the talent of the mother country. They had learned the civil law—at least sufficient of it to stifle farther development of common law. We know already that the Roman Law, however excellent some of its principles are, is void of the element of self-government, and, because superinduced, antagonistic to self-development of law.

Nevertheless, it is a question of interest to Americans, whether, and how far the settlers of New England were influenced by their sojourn in the republican Netherlands. I throw out the question. It deserves a thorough, yet very plain and unbiased inquiry.

22

various and originally discordant elements is forcibly shown in the United States, where every year several hundred thousand emigrants arrive from countries under different governments. The institutions of our country soon absorb and assimilate them as integral parts of our polity. In no other political system of which liberty forms any part, could this be done. Imagine an influx of foreigners in a country like France when she called herself republican, and the danger of so large a body of foreigners would soon be perceived. It would be an evil day indeed for the United States and for the emigrants, if our institutions were to be broken up and popular absolutism erected on the ruins of our institutional liberty. We, of all nations on earth, are most interested in the vigorous life and healthful development of institutional self-government. No nation has so much reason to shun mere inarticulated equality and barren centralization as ourselves.

On the other hand, it may be observed that the Turks to this day are little more than they were on the day of their conquest—isolated rulers, unassimilated and unassimilating, having for centuries been in possession of the finest country in Europe, whence in the fifteenth century our civilization received a new impulse. So unidentified are the Turks with the country or its population that the idea of their expulsion from Europe has in it nothing strange, or difficult to imagine. The reasons cannot lie in their race, for they are no longer Mongolians; they cannot lie in their religion, for Mohammedans have flourished. They have no political institutions, carrying life and action within them, nor did they find institutions, which might have absorbed the conquerors. The Byzantine empire had become a mere court government long before the Turks conquered it, and the worst court government that ever existed in Europe.[1]

---

[1] The same is said of the Manchous in China. The ruling soldier tribe has not assimilated itself with the Chinese, and the expulsion of the dynasty seems no incredible occurrence, even though the present rebellion should not be successful. In the case of China, the conquered race had

The stability obtained by an institutional government is closely connected with the tenacity which has been mentioned; but it is necessary to observe that an institutional self-government seems to be the only one which unites the two necessary elements of continuity and progression, or applicability to changing conditions. Asia, with its retrospective and traditional character, and without political mutations proper, offers the sight of stagnation. France, with her ardently prospective and intellectual character, but without political institutions proper, lacks continuity and political development. There is a succession of violent changes, which made Napoleon I. exclaim, observing the fact but not perceiving the cause, " Poor nations ! in spite of all your enlightening men,[1] of all your wisdom, you remain subject to the caprices of fashion like individuals." Now, it is pre-eminently institutional self-government which prevents the rule of political fashion, because, on the one hand, it furnishes a proper organism by which public opinion is elaborated, and may be distinguished from mere transitory general opinion,[2] from acclamation or panic; and, on the other hand, it seems to be the only government strong enough to resist momentary

---

many firmly-established laws and civil institutions, to which the conquering race continued strangers, at least so far as to remain chiefly soldiers. No reliance is weaker than that which rests mainly on the army, even if the army is in fighting order, which the Chinese is not.

[1] The word reported to have been used by Napoleon is Lumières. which may mean men who enlighten or the light which is given. The passage is found in the Mémorial de Sainte-Héléne, by Las Cases. Napoleon was speaking of the clergy, and the whole passage runs thus :

" Je ne fais rien pour le clergé qu'il ne me donne de suite sujet de m'en repentir, disait Napoléon ; peut-être qu'après moi viendront d'autres principes. Peut-être verra-t-on en France une conscription de prêtres et de religieuses, comme on y voyait de mon temps une conscription militaire. Peut-être mes casernes deviendront-elles des couvents et des séminaires. Ainsi va le monde ! Pauvres nations ! en dépit de toutes vos lumières, de toute votre sagesse, vous demeurez soumises aux caprices de la mode comme de simples individus."

[2] Public Opinion and General Opinion have been discussed in the first volume of Political Ethics.

excitement and a sweeping turn of the popular mind. Absolute popular governments are liable to be influenced by every change of general passion or desire, and monarchical concentrated absolutism is as much exposed to the mutations of passions or theóries. The difference is only that single men—ministers or rulers—may effect the sudden changes according to the views which may happen to prevail. The English government, with all its essential changes and reforms, and the lead it has taken in many of the latter, during this century, has proved itself stable and continuous in the same degree in which it is popular and institutional, compared to the chief governments of the European continent. The history of a people, longing for liberty but destitute of institutional self-government, will always present a succession of alternating tonic and clonic spasms. Many of the Italian cities in the middle ages furnish us with additional and impressive examples.

Liberty is a thing that grows, and institutions are its very garden beds. There is no liberty which as a national blessing has leaped into existence in full armor like Minerva from the head of Jove. Liberty is crescive in its nature. It takes time, and is difficult, like all noble things. Things noble are hard,[1] was the favorite saying of Socrates, and liberty is the noblest of all things. It must be defended, developed, conquered, and bled for. It can never be added, like a mere capital on a column; it must pervade the whole body. If the Emperor of China were to promulgate one of the charters of our states for his empire, it would be like hanging a gold collar around the neck of a camel.

Liberty must grow up with the whole system; therefore we must begin at once, where it does not exist, knowing that it will take time for perfection, and not indeed discard it, because it has not yet been commenced. That would be like giving up the preparation of a meal, because it has not been commenced in time. Let institutions grow, and sow them at once.

---

[1] χαλεπὰ τὰ καλά. May we not add καί καλά τὰ χαλεπά?

We see, then, how unphilosophical were the words of the present emperor of the French to the assembled bodies of state in February, 1853, when he said : " Liberty has never aided in founding a durable edifice ; liberty crowns it when it has been consolidated by time."

History denies it ; political philosophy and common sense alike contradict it.   Liberty may be planted where despotism has reigned, but it can be done only by much undoing, and breaking down ; by a great deal of rough ploughing.   We cannot prepare a people for liberty by centralized despotism, any more than we can prepare for light by destroying the means of vision.   Nowhere can liberty develop itself out of despotism.   It can only chronologically follow the rule of ab- solutism ; and if it does so, it must begin with eliminating its antagonistic government.   Every return to concentrated des- potism, therefore, creates an additional necessity of revolution, and throws an increased difficulty in the way of obtaining freedom.

CHAPTER XXVIII.

DANGERS AND INCONVENIENCES OF INSTITUTIONAL SELF-GOVERNMENT.

INSTITUTIONAL self-government has its dangers and inconveniences, as all human things have, and if its success requires the three elements necessary for all success of human action —common sense, virtue and wisdom, it must be added that, while Self-Government accepts the ancient saying: Divide and rule, in a sense different from that in which it was originally meant, the opposite is equally true: Unite and rule, as history and our own times abundantly prove.

It has been stated that nothing is more common than governments, which, fearing the united action of the nation, yet being obliged to yield in some manner to the demand for liberty, try to evade it and to deceive the people by granting provincial representations or estates. In these cases division is indeed resorted to for the greater chance of ruling the people, because when separate, they are weak, and one portion may be played off against the other, as the marines and sailors neutralize one another on board the men-of-war. In no period probably has this conduct of continental governments more strikingly shown itself than in that which began with the downfall of Napoleon, and ended with the year 1848. But it must not be forgotten that by institutional self-government a polity has been designated that comprehends institutions of self-government for all the regions of the political actions of a society, and it includes the general and national self-government as well as the minute local self-government.

The self-government of a society, be this a township or a nation, must always be adequate to its highest executive; and

(342)

when any branch is national, all the three branches must be national. The very nature of civil liberty, as we have found it, demands this. They must work abreast, like the horses of the Grecian chariot, public opinion being the charioteer. Had England, as she has now, a general executive, but not, as now, a general parliament, the self-government of the shires and towns, of courts and companies, would soon be extinguished. Had we a president of the United States and no national legislature, it is evident that either the president would be useless, and there would be no united country, or if the executive had power, there would be an end to the state self-governments, even if the president were to remain elective. Liberty requires union of the whole, whatever this whole, or Koinon, as the Greeks styled it, may be, as has been already mentioned. Wisdom, practice, political forbearance and manly independence can alone decide the proper degree of union, and the necessary balance.

One of the dangers of a strongly institutional self-government is that the tendency of localizing may prevail over the equally necessary principle of union, and that thus a disintegrating sejunction may take place, which history shows as a warning example in the United States of the Netherlands. I do not allude to their Pact of Utrecht, which furnished an inadequate government for the confederacy, and upon which the framers of our federal constitution so signally improved, after having tried a copy of it in the articles of the confederation. I refer to the Netherlandish principle, according to which every limited circle and even most towns did not only enjoy self-government, but were sovereign, and to each of which the stadtholder was obliged to take a separate oath of fidelity. The Netherlands presented the very opposite extreme of French centralism. The consequence has been that the real Netherlandish greatness lasted but a century, and in this respect may almost be compared to the brevity of Portuguese grandeur, though it resulted from the opposite cause.[1]

---

[1] We may also mention as a want of union, the fact that unanimity of

The former constitution of Hungary, according to which each comitate had the right to vote, whether it would accept or not the law passed by the diet,[1] is an instance of the ruinous effect of purely partial self-government. The nation, as nation, must participate in it; and Hungary lost her liberty, as Spain and all countries have done, which have disregarded this part of self-government.

Another danger is that with reference to the domestic government, the local self-government may impede measures of a general character. Instances and periods of long duration occur, which serve as serious and sometimes as alarming commentaries on the universal adage, that that which is everybody's business is no one's business. The roads, considered by the Romans so important that the road-law found a place on the twelve tables, and sanitary regulations frequently suffer in this way. The governments of some of our largest cities furnish us with partial yet striking illustrations.

It might be added that one of the dangers of self-government lies in this, that the importance of the institutional character may be forgotten, that the limitations may be considered as fetters, and that thus the people may come to forget that part of self-government which relates to the being governed, and only remember that part which consists in their governing. If this takes place, popular absolutism begins, and one part rules supreme over the other.

We reply to these objections that it is a characteristic of absolutism that it believes men can be ruled by formulas and systems alone. The scholar of liberty knows that important as systems and institutions, principles and bills of rights are, they still demand rational and moral beings, for which they are intended, like the revelation itself, which is for conscious man alone. Everything in this world has its dan-

---

all the states was required for all the most important measures, such as taxation and war.

[1] The author of the famous Oceana proposed a similar measure for England, as St. Just, "the most advanced" follower of Robespierre, did for France.

gers. In this lies the fearful responsibility of demagogues. "Take power, bear down limitation," is their call on the people, as it was the call of the courtiers on Louis XIV. Their advice of political intemperance resembles that which is given on the tomb of Sardanapalus, regarding bodily intemperance: "Eat, drink and lust; the rest is nothing."[1]

We must the more energetically cling to our institutional government, and the more attentively avoid extremes. At the same time the question is fair whether other systems avoid the danger or do not substitute greater evils for it; and, lastly, we must in this, as in all other cases, while honestly endeavoring to remedy or prevent evil, have an eye to the whole and see which yields the fairest results. Nothing, moreover, is more dangerous than to take single brilliant facts as representatives of systems. They prove general soundness as little as brilliant deeds necessarily prove their morality.

It is these dangers that give so great a value to constitutions, if conceived in the spirit of liberty. The office of a good constitution, besides that of pronouncing and guaranteeing the rights of the citizen, is that, as a fundamental law of the state, it so defines and limits the chief powers, that, each moving in its own orb, without jostling the others, it prevents jarring and grants harmonious protection to all the minor powers of the state.[2]

A constitution, whether it be an accumulative one, as that of Great Britain, or an enacted one, as ours, is always of great

---

[1] "The epitaph inscribed upon the tomb of Sardanapalus, 'Sardanapalus, the son of Anacyndaraxos, built Anchiola and Tarsos in one day: eat, drink and lust; the rest is nothing,' has been quoted for ages, and its antiquity is generally admitted."—Layard's Nineveh, vol. ii. p. 478.

[2] Constitutions, therefore, must not be changed too easily or too frequently; for, if a constitution be almost periodically changed, by the sovereign power of the people, it is obvious that the absolute power of the people in a degree enters as an element of government. Absolutism, therefore, is approached. Parliament is theoretically omnipotent in a political sense; the people, with us, are politically omnipotent; and if the people enact new constitutions every five or ten years, the convention sits, in reality, as an omnipotent parliament.

importance, as indeed all law is important wherever there
is human action; but, from what has been stated, it will be
readily perceived that constitutions are efficient toward the
obtaining of their main ends, the liberty of the citizen, only in
the same degree as they themselves consist of an aggregate of
institutions; as, for instance, that of the United States, which
consists of a distinct number of clearly devised and limited,
as well as life-possessing institutions, or as that of England,
which consists of the aggregate of institutions considered by
him who uses the term British Constitution, of fundamental
and vital importance. It will, moreover, have appeared that
these constitutions have a real being only if founded upon
numerous wide-spread institutions, and feeding, as it were,
upon a general institutional spirit. Without this, they will be
little more than parchment; and, important as our constitutions are, it has already been seen that the institution of the
Common Law, on which all of them are based, is still more
important. It cannot be denied that occasional jarring takes
place in a strongly institutional government. It is, as we
have called it, of a co-operative character, and all co-operation may lead to conflict. There is, however, occasional jarring of interests or powers, wherever there are general rules
of action.

This jarring of laws, and especially of institutions, so much
dreaded by the absolutists, whose beau-ideal is uncompromising and unrelieved uniformity, is very frequently the means
of development, and of that average justice which constitutes
a feature of all civil liberty. If there be anything instructive
in the history of free nations, and of high interest to the
student of civil liberty, it is these very conflicts, and the
combined results to which they have led. It must also be
remembered that liberty is life, and life is often strife, in the
social region as in that of nature. If, at times, institutions
lead to real struggles, we have to decide between all the good
of institutional liberty with this occasional inconvenience, and
absolutism with all its evils and this occasional avoidance of
conflicting interests; for even under an absolutism it is but

occasional. What domestic conflicts have there not been in the history of Russia and Turkey !

The institution unquestionably results in part from, and in turn promotes, respect for that which has been established or grown. This leads occasionally to a love of effete institutions, even to fanaticism; but fanaticism, which consists in carrying a truth or principle to undue length, irrespective of other truths and principles, equally important, besets man in all spheres. Has absolutism not its own bigotry and fanaticism ?[1]

---

[1] I have expressed my view on this subject in an address to a graduating class. I copy the passage here, because I believe the truth it contains important:

"Remember how often I have endeavored to impress upon your minds the truth, that there is no great and working idea in history, no impulse which passes on through whole masses, like a heaving wave over the sea, no yearning and endeavor which gives a marking character to a period, and no new institution or new truth, which becomes the substantial addition that a certain age adds to the stock of progressive civilization—that has not its own caricature and distorted reflection along with it. No Luther rises with heroic purpose, without being caricatured in a Carlstadt. The miracle wrought by Him, to whom it was no miracle, is mimicked in toyish marvels for easy minds. The communists are to the dignity of labor what the hideous anabaptists were to the reformation, or tyrannical hypocrites in England to the idea of British liberty in a Pym or Hampden. There was a truth of elementary importance conveyed in the saying of former ages, however irreverent it may appear to our taste, that Satan is the mimicking and grimacing clown of the Lord. I will go farther, and assert, that no great truth can be said to have fairly begun to work itself into practice, and to produce, like a vernal breath, a new growth of things, if we do not observe somewhere this historic caricature. Has christianity itself fared better ? Was the first idea, which through a series of errors led to the anchorites and pillar saints, not a true and holy one ? Does not all fanaticism consist in recklessly carrying a true idea to an extreme, irrespective of other equally true ones, which ought to be developed conjointly, and under the salutary influence of mutual modification ? There is truth in the first idea whence the communist starts, as much so as there is truth in the idea which serves as a starting-post for the advocate of the ungodly theory of divine right; but both carry out their fundamental principle to madness, and, ultimately, often run a muck in sanguinary ferocity. Do not allow your-

When an institution has become effete; when nothing but the form is left; when its life is fled—in one word, when the hull of an institution remains, and it has ceased to be a real institution, it is inconvenient, dangerous, or it may become seriously injurious. Nothing, as ·I stated before, is so convenient for despotism, as the remaining forms of an obsolete freedom, or forms of freedom purposely invented to deceive. A nobility stripped of all independence, and being nothing but a set of court retainers, the Roman senate under the emperors, the court of peers under Henry VIII., representative houses without power or free action, courts-martial dictated to by a despot, elections without freedom, are fearful engines of iniquity. They bear the responsibility, without free agency. They are in practice what syllogism is without truthfulness. But this is no reproach to the institution in general, nor any reason why we ought not to rely upon it. Many an old church has served as a den for robbers. Shall we build no churches? If the institution is effete, let it be destroyed, but do it, as Montesquieu says of laws in general, "with a trembling hand," lest you destroy what only appeared to your one-sided view as effete.

Still more vigorously must the battering-ram be directed against institutions which from the beginning have been bad, or which plainly are hostile to a new state of things. There are institutions as inconsistent with the true aim of society, though few are as monstrous, as the regularly incorporated prostitutes of ancient Geneva were. They must be razed. All historical development contains conservatism, progress and revolution, as christianity itself is most conservative and most revolutionary. The vital question is, when they are in place. And from all that has been stated, it must have appeared that the institution greatly aids in the best progress of which society is capable, that which consists in organic changes, changes

selves, then, to be misled by these distortions, or to be driven into hopeless timidity, which would end in utter irresolution, and a misconception of the firmest truths."

which lie in the very principles of continuity and conservatism themselves.

There are no countries on the European continent where such constant and vast changes are going on, in spite of all their outer revolutions, as in the United States and England, for the very reason that they are institutional governments— that there exists self-government with them ; yet they move within their institutions. This truth is symbolically exempli- fied in Westminster Abbey and the Champ-de-Mars. Century after century the former has stood, and what course of histo- rical development has flowed through it ! What representa- tive festivities, on the other hand, from the feast of the uni- versal federation of France in 1790 to the distribution of eagles to the army in May, 1852, have succeeded each other on the latter—revolutionary, conventional, republican, impe- rial, royal, imperial-restorational, again Bourbonian, Orlean- istic, socialistic, and uncrowned-imperialist and imperial—yet centralism has worked its steady dis-individualizing way through all.[1] There are " sermons in stones," and sermons in places.

---

[1] The following is taken from a late (1852) French paper. It is of sufficient symbolic interest to find a place in a note :

In 1790, on the 14th of July, the anniversary of the taking of the Bas- tile was celebrated by what was called the *Fête of the Universal Federa- tion of France.* Delegations were sent to it by every department, city, town, and village in the country, all eager to manifest their enthusiasm for the revolution of 1789. Every hundred of the National Guards was represented by six members ; and there were also six deputies from every regiment of infantry, and four for every regiment of cavalry. These "con- federates," as they were styled, were all entertained by the inhabitants of Paris, who are said to have rivalled each other in hospitality. In order to afford facilities to the immense number of spectators who were ex- pected on the *Champ-de-Mars,* over twelve thousand workmen were employed to surround it with embankments. Fears, however, being still entertained that the work would not be completed in time, all Paris turned out to assist. Men, women, and children, the National Guard, priests even, and sisters of charity, all took part in it. The Abbe Sieyes and Viscount Beauharnais were seen tugging together at the same wheel- barrow. At the entrance to the field was erected an immense triumphal arch; while in the centre was raised an altar, called the *Altar of the Country*, at which officiated Talleyrand, then Bishop of Autun. A bridge of boats was stretched across the Seine, near the *Champ-de-Mars*, where since has been erected the bridge of Jena.

In 1791, on the 18th of September, there was a splendid *Fête* for the publication of the constitution, and for receiving the oath of fidelity to it from Louis XVI.

In 1792, on the 15th of April, the *Fête of Liberty* was celebrated. The centre of attraction was an enormous car, in which was placed a statue of Liberty, holding a liberty-cap in one hand, and in the other a club. To such an extent was the principle of freedom carried on this occasion, that there was not a single policeman present to preserve order. The master of ceremonies was armed only with an ear of corn; nevertheless, there is said to have been no disorder.

In 1793, there was a *fête* in honor of the abolition of slavery. On the 10th of August of the same year, there was a *fête* for the acceptance of the constitution of 1793. The president of the convention received eighty-three commissioners from the departments; after which the registers upon which were inscribed the votes of the Primary Assemblies were brought to him, and he deposited them upon the " Altar of the Country," amid the firing of cannon, and the rejoicing of the people, who swore to defend the constitution with their lives. On the second of December following, the *Fête of Victories* took place, in celebration of the taking of Toulon. On this occasion the *Altar of the Country* was transformed, by the poet-painter David, into a temple of immortality.

In 1794, on the 21st of January, the anniversary of the death of Louis XVI. was celebrated by all the principal authorities going to the Altar of the Country, and renewing their oath of *hatred to royalty*. On the ninth of June of the same year, the *Fête of the Supreme Being* commenced at the Tuileries, and was terminated on the *Champ-de-Mars*. In the centre of the plain a " Mountain" was thrown up, surmounted by an oak. On the summit of the mountain were seated the representatives of the people; while near them were a number of young men, with drawn swords in their hands, in the act of striking a symbolical figure of the "monster fanaticism."

In 1796, on the 21st of January, the anniversary of the death of Louis XVI. was again celebrated. All the public functionaries renewed once more their oath of hatred to royalty, and the people spent the day singing the Marseillaise, *Ça ira*, and various patriotic songs. On the thirtieth of March following, the *Fête of Youth* took place, on occasion of arming all the young men over sixteen years of age; and on the thirtieth of April, on the proposition of Carnot, the *Fête of Victories* was celebrated.

In 1798, on the 20th of March, was the *Fête of the Sovereignty of the*

People. On the tenth *Vendemaire*, there was a funeral *fête* in memory of General Hoche. On the tenth *Messidor*, the *Fête of Agriculture* took place, with a great display of chariots, cattle, fruits, etc. During the five supplementary days of the revolutionary year, there was a series of *fêtes*, with an exposition of all the products of French industry, on the *Champ-de-Mars.*

In 1801 there were *fêtes* in memory of the foundation of the Republic, and in celebration of general peace, which were attended by the First Consul.

In 1804, on the 10th of November, Napoleon, then emperor, repaired to the *Champ-de-Mars*, and there received the oath of fidelity and obedience from deputations representing all the corps of the army.

In 1814, on the 7th of September, the government of the Restoration distributed colors to the National Guard of Paris. The object of this distribution was to efface, if possible, even the memory of the eagles of the empire, and of the tri colored standard of the revolution. An altar, glittering with gold and costly drapery, was erected near the military school, and in front was placed the throne occupied by Louis XVIII., who was accompanied by the Count of Artois, the Duke of Angouleme, and the Duke of Berri. Mass was celebrated by the archbishop of Paris, M. Talleyrand Perigord, uncle of the bishop of Autun, who, as we have seen, officiated at the *Fête of Federation* in 1790. The National Guards defiled before the Throne, while the band played *Vive Henry IV.* and *Charmante Gabrielle.*

In 1815, on the 1st of June, there was a *fête* in celebration of the return of the emperor. Napoleon appeared on the throne with his three brothers. A mass was performed; the constitution was acclaimed with enthusiasm; and the air was rent with cries of *Vive Napoléon!* The oath was taken with enthusiasm. Napoleon addressed the soldiers from the throne in the following words:

"Soldiers of the National Guard of Paris; soldiers of the Imperial Guard; I confide to you the imperial eagle, with the national standard. You swear to defend it with your lives, if need be, against the enemies of the country and this throne. You swear never to rally under any other banner."

During the restoration, the *Champ-de-Mars* was used chiefly for reviews of the National Guard; the most notable of which was the last one passed by Charles X., when the citizens manifested that hostility to the king which was a prelude to the revolution of 1830.

In 1837 there was a grand *fête* in honor of the marriage of the Duke of Orleans, on which occasion the crowd in the *Champ-de-Mars* was so great that twenty-four persons were suffocated or crushed to death. During most of the reign of Louis Philippe, however, the principal gatherings in the *Champ-de-Mars* were on occasion of military reviews and horse-races.

In 1848, on the 22d of May, the *Fête of Concord* was celebrated with great pomp. The *Moniteur* alluded to the occasion thus :

"This solemnity was celebrated with an eclat enhanced by the magnificent weather. Under so clear a sky, and surrounded by so many joyful countenances, how was it possible to experience any feelings but those of love, conciliation and harmony? What struck us, especially, was the attitude, so full of enthusiasm and confidence, of the vast concourse of people that crowded the *Champ-de-Mars;* cries, a thousand times repeated, of *Vive la République! Vive la République Démocratique! Vive l'Assemblée Nationale!* broke out, in formidable chorus, every instant, as if to proclaim the respect of the people for the institutions which they have adopted, and their invincible repugnance to every retrograde or reactionary idea."

To the foregoing must be added the gigantic military *fête* on the 10th of May, 1852, called the *Fête of Eagles*, that is, the distribution of eagles to all the regiments of the army. A cock had been adopted as symbol of the first republic, owing either to an etymological misconception of the word Gallia, or to an intended pun on it. The emperor adopted the Roman eagle ; the Bourbons brought back the three fleurs de lys ; and in 1830 the cock was restored. Louis Napoleon, when president for ten years, restored the imperial eagle. It must be owned the cock looked very much as our turkey would have looked had we adopted Franklin's humorous proposition of selecting our native and respectable turkey, instead of our fine native eagle.

What feast will be celebrated on the same spot next? Whatever it may be, probably it will be nothing intrinsically different from the last.

CHAPTER XXIX.

ADVANTAGES OF INSTITUTIONAL GOVERNMENT, FARTHER CONSIDERED.

THERE are some additional observations suggested by the subject of institutional self-government and by that of the institution in general, which have been deferred in order to avoid an interruption of the general argument, and to which it is necessary now to turn our attention.

It seems to me a symptomatic fact that the term People has at no period, so far as I am acquainted with the domestic history of England, become in politics a term of reproach, not even in her worst periods. On the contrary, the word People has always been surrounded with dignity, and when Chatham was called "The people's minister," it was intended by those who gave him this name as a great honor. It was far different on the continent. In French, in German and in all the continental languages with which I am acquainted, the corresponding words sank to actual terms of contempt. The word Peuple was used in France, before the first revolution, by the higher classes, in a disdainful and stigmatizing sense, and often as equivalent with canaille—that term which played so fearful a part in the sanguinary drama of the revolution, and which Napoleon purposely used, in order emphatically to express that he was or wished to be considered the man of the people, when he said somewhat soldierly : Je suis moi même sorti de la canaille.[1] In German, the words Volk and Nation

---

[1] The dictionary of the academy gives, as the last two meanings of the word Peuple—unenlightened men, and men belonging to the lowest classes. Mr. Trench in his Lessons in Proverbs, quotes the French Jesuit Bonhours, who says : Les proverbes sont les sentences du peuple,

came actually to be used as vilifying invectives, even by the lower classes themselves. The words never ceased indeed to be used in their legitimate sense, but they were vulgarly applied in the meaning which I have given. They acquired this ignominious sense, because the nobility, a very numerous class on the continent, looked with arrogance upon the people, and the people, looking up to the nobility with stolid admiration, aped the pride of that class. It is a universal law of social degradation that it consists always of a chain of degraded classes who at the same time are or try to be in turn degraders, as oppression begets the lust of oppressing in the oppressed.

On the other hand, the English word People has never acquired, not even during the English revolution, that import of political horror, which Demos had in the times of Cleon for the reflecting Athenian, or Peuple in the first French revolution. What is the cause of these remarkable facts? I can see no other than that there has always existed a high degree of institutional self-government in England—a very high degree, if we compare her to the continent. The people never ceased to respect themselves; and others never ceased to feel their partial dependence upon them. The aristocracy of England, a patrician body, far more elevated than any continental nobility, still remained connected with the people, by the fact that only one of the patrician family can enjoy the peerage.

---

et les sentences sont les proverbes des honnêtes gens. (But there are very wicked proverbs.) *Honnête* means, indeed, frequently something like the Latin *honestus*, and not exclusively our *honest*, but even with this addition the English term People could never have been contradistinguished from *honnêtes gens*. To these remarks we must add the mischievous error of giving the dignified name *the people* to *some people* gathered together in the street. We find in the French papers and other publications, at the time of the first revolution constant use of the term, in such manner, as: le peuple has hanged a baker, etc., when the murder was committed by a rabble of a few. This confusion of a few lawless people with *the* people, for whom the sovereign power was claimed, and, in turn, the arrogation of the sacred name by a few Parisians, may be observed throughout the history of the revolution.

This distinction does not, therefore, indicate a social status, inhering in the blood; for that runs in the whole family. It indicates a political position.[1]

Possibly most of my American and English readers may not perceive the whole import of these remarks, but let them live for a considerable time on the continent of Europe, and their own observations will not fail to furnish them with commentaries and full explanations of the preceding pages.

Another subject to which I desire to direct attention is Usage, which, as it has been stated, forms an important element of the institution, and, consequently, of institutional government. This is frequently not only admitted by the absolutists, but in bad faith insisted upon. Continental servilists frequently eulogize the liberty of the English, but wind up by pointing at their institutions and their widely spread usages, observing that since these are necessary and do not exist on the continent, neither can liberty exist. It is a faithless plea for servilism. An adequate reply is this : That in no sphere can we attain a given end if we do not make a beginning, and are not prepared for partial failures during that beginning. If spelling is necessary before we can attain to the skill of reading, we must not withhold the spelling-book from the learner ; and we ought never to forget the law to which I have alluded in a previous part of this work, namely, that the advancement of mankind is made possible, among other things, by the fact that when a great acquisition is once made on the

---

[1] Aristocratic as England is in many respects, it is nevertheless true that there is no nobility in the continental sense. The law knows of peers, hereditary lawgivers, but it does not know even the word nobleman. The peerage is connected with primogeniture, but there is no English nobility in the blood. The idea of maésalliance has therefore never obtained in England. There is no doubt that the little disposition of the English shown at any time to destroy the aristocracy, is in a great measure owing to this fact, as doubtless the far more judicious spirit of the English peers to yield to the people's demands, if clearly and repeatedly pronounced, has contributed much. Mr. Hallam has very correct remarks on the subject of English equality of civil rights, where he speaks of the reign of Henry III.

field of civilization, succeeding generations, or other clusters of men, are not obliged to pass through all the stages of painful struggle, or tardy experience, which may have been the share of the pioneering nation.

The third additional remark I desire to make is, that institutional and diffused self-government is peculiarly efficient in breaking those shocks which, in a centralized government, reach the farthest corners of the country, and are frequently of a ruinous tendency. This applies not only to the sphere of politics proper, but to all social spheres which more or less affect the political life of a nation. There are two similar cases in French and English history which seem to illustrate this fact with peculiar force.

Every historian admits that the well-known and infamous necklace affair contributed to hasten on the French revolution, by degrading the queen, and through her, royalty itself, in the eye of France, which then believed in her culpable participation. England was obliged to behold a far more degrading exhibition — the trial of Queen Caroline, the consort of George IV. There was no surmise about the matter. Royalty was exhibited before the nation minutely in the fullest blaze of publicity, and mixed up with an amount of immundicity the exact parallel to which it is difficult to find in history. Every civilized being seemed to be interested in the trial. The portrait of the queen and her trial were printed on kerchiefs and sold all over the continent. The trial, too, took place at a somewhat critical period in England. Yet I am not aware that it had any perceptible effect on the public affairs of England. The institutions of the country could not be affected by it, any more than high walls near muddy rivers are affected by the slime of the tides. But royalty on the continent, trying at that very time to revive absolutism founded upon divine right,[1] was damaged by the people thus seeing that the purple is too scant to cover disgrace and vulgarity.

---

[1] It was the time when Haller wrote his Restoration of Political Sciences, in which he endeavors to excel Filmer, and does not blush to

Let an American imagine what would be the inevitable consequences of local or sectional errors and excitements, of which we are never entirely free, if we did not live under a system of varied institutional self-government; each shock would be felt from one end of our country to the other with unbroken force. Had we nothing but uninstitutional Gallican universal suffrage, spreading like one undivided sea over the whole, we could not continue to be a free people, and would hardly be a united people, though not free.

A similar remark may be made with reference to that period in French history which actually obliges the historian to be at least as familiar with the long list of royal courtezans[1] as with the prime ministers. The effect of this example of the court has been most disastrous to all France. The courts of England under Charles II. and James II. were no better. The conduct of George I. and George II. added coarseness to incontinency. The English nobility followed very close in the wake of their royal masters; but with them the evil stopped. The people of England—England herself—remained comparatively untouched, and while the court plunged into vices, the people went their own way, rising and improving. Had England been an uninstitutional country, the effect must have been the same as that which ruined France.

Another observation suggested by the subject which we are discussing is, that a wide-spread and penetrating institutional

---

hold up uncompromising absolutism, although a native of Switzerland. Having secretly become a catholic, he passed into the service of the Bourbons. The student of political science, desirous of making himself acquainted with the political literature of the European continent of this period, in its whole extent, is referred to a German work of a high order, Robert von Mohl's History and Literature of the Political Sciences, 3 vols., large 8vo., Erlangen, 1855 to 1858, (containing 2052 pages.) The comprehensive erudition and liberal judgment of the author, as well as the patient research in the literature of the day and the past and of all civilized countries, make this work a storehouse of historical and critical knowledge concerning political literature, for which every scholar of this branch must feel deeply indebted to him.

[1] The very etymology, with its present meaning, is significant.

self-government has the same concentrative effect upon society which a careful and responsible occupation with one's own affairs and duties has upon the individual. This may indeed be counteracted and suspended by other and more powerful circumstances; but the natural effect of institutional self-government is, I believe, such as I have just indicated.

A large and active nation, which therefore instinctively seeks a political field of action for its energy, and which, nevertheless, is destitute of self-ruling institutions, will generally turn its attention to conquest or any other increase of territory, merely for the sake of conquest or of increased extent, until a political gluttony is produced which resembles the immoderate desire of some farmers for more land. They neglect the intensive improvement of their farm, and are known by every experienced agriculturist to be among the poorest of their class. Expansion may become desirable or necessary; but a desire of extension merely for the sake of extension is at once the most debilitating fever of a nation and the rudest of glories, in which an Attila or Timour far excels a Fabius or a Washington. So soon as a nation abandons the intensive improvement of its institutions, and directs its attention solely to foreign conquest, it enters on its downward course, and loses the influence which otherwise might have been its share. The truest, most intense, and most enduring influence a people exercises upon others is through its institutions and their progressive perfection.[1]   The sword does not plough deep.

---

[1] There are persons among us who have fallen into this error; and it will always be found that they proportionately disregard our institutions, or are not imbued with esteem for institutional government. I lately received a pamphlet in which the author wishes for a confederacy embracing America from Greenland to Cape Horn. "Universal governments" were the dream of Henry IV., and again pressed into service by Napoleon. I am not able to answer the reader, why that confederacy should comprehend America only. There is no principle or self-defining idea in the term America. America is a name. The water which surrounds it has nothing to do with principles. Water, once the Dissociabile Mare, now connects. Polynesia ought to be added, and perhaps Further Asia, and why not Hindostan? Our oath of allegiance might

This is the reason, it may be observed, why the historian, the more truly he searches for the real history of nations, and the more his mind acquires philosophical strength, becomes the more attentive to the political life manifested by the institutions of a people. It distinguishes a Niebuhr from a common narrator of Rome's many battles.[1]

On the other hand, we may observe a similar effect upon cabinets. It seems to me one of the best effects of local and national self-government, with its many elementary institutions and a national representative government, that diplomacy ceases to form the engrossing subject of statesmanship. Shrewd as English diplomacy has often proved, the history of that country, in the eighteenth century, is a totally different one from that of the other European countries in the same period. It seems as if continental statesmanship sought for objects to act on, in foreign parts, in concluding alliances and making treaties; in one word, as if diplomacy had been cultivated for the sake of diplomacy. Yet nothing is surer to lead to difficulties, to wars and suffering, than this reversed state of things.[2]

Some remarks on the undue influence of capitals in countries void of institutions would find an appropriate place here; but they are deferred until we shall have considered

---

be improved by promising to be faithful to the United States *et cetera*, as Archbishop Laud's famous oath bound the person who took it upon an Et Cetera.

[1] The same phenomenon may be observed in the more philosophical division of history. People begin to divide the history of a nation by the monarchs, or by any other labelling. When they penetrate deeper, they divide history by the rise and fall of institutions, of classes, of interests, of great ideas. To divide the history of England by George I. and George II. is about as philosophical as if a geologist were to color a chart, not according to the great layers that constitute the earth, but by indicating where the people walking upon it wear shoes or sabots, or walk barefooted.

[2] We ought to compare the repeated advice of the greatest of Americans, to beware of alliances, with the contents of such works as Raumer's Diplomatic Dispatches of the Last Century. It is for this reason that the present publicity of diplomacy has such vital importance.

somewhat more closely, the peculiar attributes of centralization, the opposite of institutional self-government.

Patience, united with energy, is as much an element of
progress and efficient action in public concerns as in private
matters.   Mr. Lamartine has feelingly said some excellent
truths on this subject, in his Counsellor for the People; but it
does not seem possible to unite the two in popular politics and
in the service of liberty, except by the self-government which
we are contemplating.   Patience, as well as desire of action,
can exist separately without an institutional government, but
in that case they are both destructive to freedom.   Activity,
without institutions, becomes a succession of unconnected
efforts; patience, without institutions that constantly incite
by self-government, and rouse as much as they form the mind,
becomes mere submission, and ends in Asiatic resignation.

It would seem, also, that by a system of institutional self-
government alone the advantage can be obtained of which
Aristotle speaks, when he says that the psephisma (the particular and detailed law) ought to be made so as to suit the
given cases by the Lesbian canon,[1] and ought to be applied so
as to fit the exact demands.

---

[1] The cyclopian walls in Greece and Italy, built before the memory
even of the ancients, and many of which still stand as firm as if raised
in recent times, have their strength in the irregularity of the component
stones, and the close fitting of one to the other, that no interstices are
left even for a blade of grass to grow.   An irregular polygonal stone
was placed first; sheets of lead were then closely fitted to the upper
and lateral surfaces.   When taken off, they served as the patterns
according to which the stones to be placed next were hewn.   It was
this sheet and this mode of proceeding which was called the Lesbian
canon or rule, while the canon or rule which the architect laid down
alike for all stones of an intended wall was called a general canon.   See
On the Cyclopian Walls, by Forchhammer, Kiel, 1847.   Now, Aristotle
compares the general law, the *nomos*, to the general canon, but the particular law, the *psephisma*, ought, as he says, to be made by the Lesbian
canon.   Ethica ad Nicomachum, 5, 14.   It is inelegant, I readily confess, to use a figure which it is necessary to explain, but I am not
acquainted with any process in modern arts similar to the one used as
an illustration by the great philosopher, except the forming of the

It is on account of the institutional character of the British polity in general and of the English constitution in particular —on account of the supremacy of the law and of the spirit of self-government which in a high degree pervades the whole polity and society of that country, that, long ago, I did not hesitate to call England a royal republic.[1] Dr. Arnold, some five years later, expressed the same idea, when in the introduction to his Roman History he styles his country "a kingly commonwealth." It will be hardly necessary to add that the British commonwealth is in many respects of a strongly patrician character, that it is occasionally aristocratic, and that the Englishman believes one of the excellencies of his polity to consist in the fact that it contains in the monarch an element of conservatism apparently high above the contending elements of progress and popular liberty.[2] What advantages and disadvantages may be wound up in this portion of her constitution, and how far the actual position of Great Britain, the state of her population and her historical development, may make it necessary, it is not our task to investigate, any

dentist's gold plate according to a mould taken from nature itself. I naturally preferred the simile of the philosopher, even with an explanatory note, to the unbidden associations which the other simile carries along with it. Nor would I withhold from my reader the pleasure we enjoy when a figure or simile is presented to us, so closely fitting the thought like the Lesbian canon, and so exact that itself amounts to the enunciation of an important truth, well *formulated*. This is the case with Aristotle's figure.

[1] In my Political Ethics, first published in 1838.

[2] I do not know that this opinion was ever more strikingly symbolized than lately, when Lord John Russell, the leader of the administration in the commons, moved an address of congratulation to the queen on the birth of a prince, and Mr. Disraeli, the leader of the opposition in the same branch, seconded the motion, while a similar motion was made in the lords by Lord Aberdeen, the premier of the administration, seconded by the Earl of Derby, the premier of the lately ousted administration, and very bitter opponent to the present ministry. What the queen is, in this respect, in England, the constitution or rather the Union is in the United States. Our feelings of loyalty centre in these, but not in our president, any more than an Englishman's loyalty finds a symbol in his prime minister.

more than to inquire whether the steady progress of England has not been toward a more and more fully developed institutional self-government and virtual republicanism, or whether the absolutists of the continent may be right as when they maintain that England is no bona fide monarchy, and by her unfortunate example is the chief cause of European unrest, by which of course the advocates of despotic power mean the popular longing for liberty.

My expression has been called " very bold." Whether it be so or not is of little importance. I have given my reason why I .have called the English polity thus, and I may be permitted to add that in doing so I meant to use no rhetorical expression, but philosophically to designate an idea, the truth of which has been ever since impressed on my mind more strongly by extended study and the ample commentaries with which the last lustres have furnished the political philosopher.

The opposite idea was expressed by a French politician of distinction, when, in writing favorably of Louis Napoleon after the vote which succeeded the second of December, but before the establishment of the imperial throne, he said : " universal suffrage is the republic."[1] It will be our duty to consider more in detail the question, whether inorganic, bare, universal suffrage, has any necessary and intrinsic connection with liberty or not, and to inquire into the consequences to which uninstitutional suffrage always leads. In this place I would only observe that if he means by republic a polity bearing within its

---

[1] Mr. Emil Girardin, who has been referred to several times. He is an unreserved writer, who knows how to express his ideas distinctly, and who is a representative of very large numbers of his countrymen. In connection with the expression of Mr. Girardin given in the text, the dictum of the Emperor Napoleon III. about the time of his elevation to the throne, may be given. He said : In crowning me, France crowns herself. The reader will find at the end of this work a similar expression of the emperor, when he opened the restored Louvre, namely, that France, in building palaces for her kings, built them to honor herself and to symbolize her unity. Unfortunately Louis XIV. sorely repented on his death-bed, his passion for building, and expressed it in warning counsel to Louis XV.

bosom civil liberty, the dictum is radically erroneous. If by republic, however, nothing is meant but a kingless state of politics, irrespective of liberty or the good government of freemen, it is not worth our while to stop for an inquiry. Nothing, indeed, is more directly antagonistic to real self-government than inorganic universal suffrage spreading over a wide dominion. I would, also allude once more to the fact that universal suffrage is, after all, a modus, and not the essence. If, however, it leads to the opposite of self-government, we have no more right to call it "the republic," nor to consider it a form of liberty, than those ancient Germans had a right to be proud of their liberty, whom unsuccessful gaming had led into slavery, if Tacitus reports the truth.

According to the French writer, the Roman republic might be said to have continued under the Cæsars, who were elected by the prætorians, and an elective monarchy would present itself as an acceptable government, while, in reality, it is one of the worst. For it possesses nearly all the evils inherent in the monarchical government, without its advantages, and all the disadvantages of a republic, vastly increased, without its advantages. History, I think, fully bears us out in this opinion, notwithstanding one authority—the only one of weight I can remember—to the contrary.[1]

---

[1] Lord Brougham, in his Political Philosophy, speaks in terms of high praise of the elective government of the former Germanic empire. Native and contemporary writers have not done so. It was only after the expulsion of the French, and when the German people instinctively longed for German unity and dignity, that, at one time, a poetic longing for the return of the medieval empire was expressed by some. If there be any German left who still desires a return to the elective empire, he must be of a very retrospective character.

CHAPTER XXX.

INSTITUTIONAL GOVERNMENT THE ONLY GOVERNMENT WHICH
PREVENTS THE GROWTH OF TOO MUCH POWER. LIBERTY,
WEALTH AND LONGEVITY OF STATES.

UNIVERSAL suffrage is power—sweeping, real power—so
vast, that even its semblance bears down everything before it.
Uninstitutional universal suffrage may be fittingly said to turn
the whole popular power and national sovereignty—the self-
sufficient source of all derivative power—into an executive,
and thus fearfully to confound sovereignty with absolute power,
absolutism with liberty.

Yet the idea of all government implies power, while that
of liberty implies check and protection. It is the necessary
harmony between these two requisites of all public vitality
and civil progress which constitutes the difficulty of establishing and maintaining liberty—a difficulty far greater than that
which a master-mind has declared the greatest, namely, the
founding of a new government.[1]

---

[1] Machiavelli—tanto nomini nullum par elogium—says in his Prince,
"But in the new government lies the greatest difficulty." This depends
upon circumstances. He undoubtedly had in mind the difficulty of
uniting Italy, or rather of eliminating so many governments and establishing one Italian state. For there has been no noble Italian, since
the times when Dante called his own Italy, Di dolor ostello, that does not
yearn for the union of his noble land, and look for the realization of his
hopes as fervently as he believes in a God. Machiavelli was one of the
foremost among these true Italians. But he had not lived through our
times. There are times when the people throw themselves into the arms
of any one that possibly may save them from impending or imaginary
shipwreck, or promises to do so. Wearied people will take a stone for a
pillow, and no persons deceive themselves so readily as the panic-stricken.
On such occasions it is easy to establish a new government, especially if

Power is necessary; an executive cannot be dispensed with; yet all power has a tendency to increase, and to clear away opposition. It would not be power if it had not this tendency. How then is liberty to be preserved? A new power may be created to check the first, like the Roman tribune; but the newly created power *is* power, and how is this in turn to be checked? Erecting one tier of power over the other affords no remedy. The chief power may thus be made to change its name or place; but the power with all its attributes is there.

Nor will it be supposed that salvation can be found in the mere veto, however multiplied. For the veto, although appearing negative with reference to that which is vetoed, nevertheless is power in itself, and to rest civil liberty upon a system of mere vetoes would indeed be expecting life, action, growth, and that which is positive, from a system of *negativism*. A government without power and inherent strength is like aught else without power, useless for action. Yet action is the object of all government. The single Polish nobleman who possessed the rakosh or veto had a very positive but a very injurious power. It was the pervading idea, in the middle ages, to protect by the requisition of unanimity of votes on all important questions. But, on the one hand, this is the principle which belonged to the disjunctive state of the middle ages, not to our broad national liberty; and, on the other hand, unanimity does not of itself insure protection or liberty. Tyranny or corruption has often been unanimous.

The only way of meeting the difficulty is to prevent the overbearing growth of any power. When grown, it is too late; and this cannot be done by putting class against class, or interest against interest. One of these must be stronger than the other, and become the absorbing one. Nor is the problem we have to solve, discord. It is harmony, peace,

---

cumbersome conscience is set aside. The reverse of Machiavelli's dictum then takes place, and the greatest difficulty lies in maintaining a government. This applies even to administrations and ministries. All is pleasant sailing at first. A new power charms like a rising sun; but the heat of noon follows upon the morning.

united yet organic action. History or speculation points to no other solution of this high problem of man, than a well-grounded and ramified system of institutions, checking and modifying one another, strong and self-ruling, with a power limited by the very principle of self-government within each, yet all united and working toward one common end, thus producing a general government of a co-operative character, and serving in many cases in which, without institutions, interests would jar with interests, as friction rollers do in machinery.

The institution is strong within its bounds, yet not feared, because necessarily bounded in its action. What can be more powerful than the king's bench in England, in each case in which it acts within its own limits. Now older than five hundred years, it has repeatedly stood up against parliament with success. Yet no one fears that its power will invade that of other institutions; nor did the people of the state of New York apprehend that the court of appeals might become an invasive power, when in its own legitimate and efficient way it lately declared the Canal Enlargement Law, which had been passed by a great majority, unconstitutional, and consequently null and void.

Seeking for liberty merely or chiefly in a vetitive power of each class or circle, interest or corporation, upon the rest, as has been often proposed, after each modern revolution,[1] would simply amount to dismembering, instead of constructing. It would produce a multitudinous antagonism, instead of a vital organism, and it would be falling back into the medieval state of narrow chartered independencies. We cannot hope for liberty in a pervading negation, but must find it in comprehensive action. All that is good or great is creative and positive. Negation cannot stand for itself, or impart life. But that negation which is necessary to check and refrain is found in the self-government of many and vigorous institutions, as they also are the only efficient preventives of

---

[1] Harris, in his Oceana, St. Just, in the first French revolution, and many former and recent writers might be mentioned,

the undue growth of power. If they are not always able to hinder it, man has no better preventive. When in the seventeenth century, the Danes threw themselves into the power of the king, making him absolute, in order to protect themselves against baronial oppression, they necessarily created a power which in turn became oppressive. The English, on the contrary, broke the power of their barons, not by raising the king, but by increasing self-government.

We find, among the characteristic distinctions between modern history and ancient,[1] the longevity of modern states, contemporaneous progress of wealth or culture and civil liberty, and the national state as contradistinguished from the ancient city-state, the only state of antiquity in which liberty existed. These are not merely facts which happen to present themselves to the historian, but they are conditions upon

---

[1] These differences between antiquity and modern times, all of which are more or less connected with christianity and the institution, are :

1. That in antiquity only one nation flourished at a time. The course of history, therefore, flows in a narrow channel, and the historian can easily arrange universal ancient history. In modern periods, many nations flourish at the same time, and their history resembles the broad Atlantic, on which they all freely meet.

2. Ancient states are short-lived; modern states have a far greater tenacity of life.

3. Ancient states, when once declining, were irretrievably lost. Their history is that of a rising curve, with its maximum and declension. Modern states have frequently shown a recuperative power. Compare present England with that of Charles II., France as it is with the times of Louis XV.

4. Ancient liberty and wealth were incompatible, at least for any length of time; modern nations may grow freer while they are growing wealthy.

5. Ancient liberty dwelt in city-states only; modern liberty requires enlarged societies—nations.

6. Ancient liberty demanded disregard of individual liberty; modern liberty is founded upon it.

7. The ancients had no international law. (Nor have the Asiatics now. The incipiency of international law is, indeed, visible with all tribes, for they are men. The Romans sent heralds to declare war, and the Greek, advised to poison his arrows, declines doing so, "for," Homer makes him say, "I fear the gods will punish me.")

which it is the modern problem to develop liberty, because they are requisites for modern civilization, and civilization is the comprehensive aim of all humanity.

We must have national states (and not city-states;) we must have national broadcast liberty (and not narrow chartered liberty;) we must have increasing wealth, for civilization is expensive; we must have liberty, and our states must endure long, to perform their great duties. All this can be effected by institutional liberty alone. It is neither affirmed that longevity alone is the object, nor that it can be obtained by institutions alone. Russia, peculiarly uninstitutional, because it unites Asiatic despotism with European bureaucracy, has lasted through long periods, even though we may consider the late celebration of its millennial existence as a great official license. All we maintain here is, that longevity, together with progressive liberty, is obtainable only by institutional liberty. England, now really a thousand years old, presents the great spectacle of an old nation advancing steadily in wealth and liberty. She is far richer than she was a century ago, and her government is of a far more popular cast. In ancient times, it was adopted as an axiom that liberty and wealth are incompatible. Modern writers, down to a very recent period, have followed the ancients. Declaimers frequently do so to this day; but they show that they do not comprehend modern liberty and civilization. Modern in-door civilization, with all her schools and charities and comforts of the masses, is incalculably dearer than ancient out-door civilization. Modern civilization requires immense production; it is highly expensive. Yet our liberty needs civilization as a basis and a prop; our progressive liberty requires progressive civilization, consequently progressive wealth—not, indeed, enormous riches in the hands of a few. Antiquity knew, and Asia possesses to this day hoarded treasures in greater number than modern Europe has ever known them.[1] We stand in need of immea-

---

[1] Indeed, the enormous treasures occasionally met with in Asia are indications of her comparative poverty.

surable wealth, but it is diffused, widely spread and widely enjoyed wealth, necessary for widely diffused and widely enjoyed culture.

To last long—to last with liberty and wealth, is the great problem to be solved by a modern state. Our destinies differ from that of brief and brilliant Greece. Let us derive all the benefit from Grecian culture and civilization—from that chosen nation, whose intellectuality and æsthetics, with christian morality, Roman legality and Teutonic individuality and independence, form the main elements of the great phenomenon we designate by the term modern civilization, without adopting her evils and errors, even as we adopt her sculpture without that religion whose very errors contributed to produce it.

24

CHAPTER XXXI.

INSECURITY OF UNINSTITUTIONAL GOVERNMENTS.   UNORGAN-
IZED INARTICULATED POPULAR POWER.

THE insecurity of concentrated governments has been discussed in a previous part of this work.   The same insecurity
exists in all governments that are not of a strongly institutional
character.   Eastern despotism is exposed to the danger of
seraglio conspiracies, as much so as the centralized governments ·
of the European continent showed their insecurity in the year
1848.   They tottered and many broke to pieces, although there
was, with very few exceptions, no ardent struggle, and nothing
that approached to a civil war.   To an observer at a distance,
it almost appeared as if those governments could be shaken by
the loud huzzaing of a crowd.   They have, indeed, recovered;
but this may be for a time only; nor will it be denied that the
lesson, even as it stands, is a pregnant one.

During all that time of angry turmoil, England and the
United States stood firm.   The government of the latter country was exposed to rude shocks indeed, at the same period;
but her institutional character protected her.   England has had
her revolution; every monarchy probably must pass through
such a period of violent change ere civil liberty can be largely
established and consciously enjoyed by the people—ere government and people fairly understand one another on the common
ground of liberty and self-government.   But no fact seems
to be so striking in the revolution of England as this, that all
her institutions of an organic character, her jury, her common
law, her representative legislature, her local self-government,
her justice of the peace, her sheriff, her coroner—all survived
domestic war and depotism, and, having done so, served as

(370)

the basis of an enlarged liberty. The reason of this broad
fact cannot be that the English revolution did not occur at
a time of bold philosophical speculation which characterized
the age of the French revolution. The English religionists
of the seventeenth century were as bold, speculative reasoners
as the French philosophers, and England's religious fanatics
were quite as fierce enemies of private property and society
as the French political fanatics were. It was, in my opinion,
pre-eminently her institutional character in general, or the
whole system of institutions and the degree of self-government contained in each, that saved each single institution,
and enabled England to weather the storm when she was
exposed to the additional great danger of a worthless general
government after the restoration. There is a tenacity of life
and a reproductive principle of vitality exhibited in the whole
seventeenth century of British history, that cannot be too
attentively examined by the candid statesmen of our family
of nations.

It may be objected to my remarks that Russia, too, has remained untouched by the attempted revolutions of the year
1848, although her government is a very centralized one.
Russia has in some respects much of an Asiatic character, and
the succession of her monarchs is marked by an almost equal
number of palace conspiracies and imperial murders or imprisonments.[1] The people, on the other hand, have not yet
been affected by the political movements of our race. There
is in politics, as in all spheres of humanity, such a thing as
being below and being above an evil. Many persons that are
free from skepticism are not above it, but the dangerous questions have never yet presented themselves; and many nations
remain quiet, while others are torn by civil wars, not because
they have reached a settled state above revolution, but because
they have not yet arrived at the period of contending elements.

Russia may be said, in one respect at least, to furnish us

---

[1] A London journal said some years ago, with great bitterness, yet
with truth : A Russian czar is a highly assassinative substance.

with the extreme opposite to self-government. "The service," that is, public service, or the being a servant of the imperial government, has been raised in that country to a real *culte*, a sort of official religion. Any infraction of justice, any hardship, any complaint is passed over with a shrug of the shoulder and the words "the service." The term Service in its present Russian adaptation is the symbol for the most consistent absolutism, the most passive bureaucracy, and a most automaton-like government set in motion by the czar, and it is thus, as it was said before, the extreme opposite to our self-government.

If concentrated governments are insecure, mere unorganized and uninstitutional popular power is no less so, and neither such power nor mere popular opposition to all government is a guarantee of liberty. The first may be the reason why all the Athenian political philosophers of mark looked from their own state of things, during and after the Peloponnesian war, with evident favor upon the Lacedæmonian government. Lacedæmon was, indeed, no home for individual liberty; but they saw in Sparta permanent institutions, and without having arrived at a perfectly clear distinction between an institutional government and one of a fluctuating absolute market majority, they may have perceived, more or less instinctively, that neither permanency nor safety is possible without an institutional system. They must have observed that there was no individual liberty in Sparta; but her institutional character may have struck them, and the contrast may have lent to that government the appearance of substantial value which it did not possess in reality. It seems otherwise difficult to explain why the most reflecting should have preferred a Lacedæmon to an Athens, even if we take into account the general view of the ancients, that individuality must be sacrificed to the state—a view of which I have spoken at the beginning of this work.

As to the second position, that the guarantee of liberty cannot be sought for in mere opposition to government or in a mere negation of power, it is only necessary to reflect that in such a state of things one of three evils must necessarily happen. Either the people are united and succeed in enfeebling or destroying the government, in which case again the new government possesses the whole sweeping power, and of course is in turn a negation of liberty; thus substituting absolutism for absolutism. Or the people are not united, do not succeed, and leave the government more powerful and despotic than before. Or a state of affairs is brought about in which all power is destroyed—political asthenia. It is a state of political disintegration, leading necessarily to general ruin, and preparing the way for a new, generally a foreign power, which then rears something fresh upon the ruins of the past—fabrics that are cemented with blood and tears.

There is no other way to escape from the appalling dilemma than to unite the people and government into one living organism, and this can only be done by a widely ramified system of sound institutions, instinct with self-government.

It is not maintained that history does not furnish us with instances of national conditions in which nothing else remained possible but a general rising against a government that had become isolated from the people; but nothing is gained if the new state of things is not founded upon institutions. This is, indeed, a difficult task; at times it would seem impossible. If so, the destruction of the whole is decreed; and its accomplishment adds another lesson to the many stored up in the book of history, that those nations who neglect to provide for institutions, and to allow them freely to grow, are walking the path of political ruin.

We are now fully able to judge how utterly mistaken those are who endeavor to press the opinion upon the people that "there are but two principles between which civilized men have to choose—Divine Right and Democratic Might." The one is as ungodly as the other. Neither is founded in justice; neither admits of liberty; both rest on the principle of absolutism. Both are theories fabricated by despotism, false in logic, unhallowed in practice, and ruinous in their progress.

Allusion has been made before to the common mistake of those men who are not bred in civil liberty, and are unacquainted with the appliances of self-government, that they believe popular power alone, uniform, sweeping and inorganic, constitutes liberty, or is all that is necessary to insure it. It is doubtless this kind of popular power which is generally called democracy in France and other countries of the continent. It confounds, as we have seen, things entirely distinct in their nature. Power is not liberty. Power is necessary for protection, and liberty consists in a great measure in the protection of certain rights and certain institutions; nevertheless, power is not liberty, and because it is power it requires limitation, or, as I have stated, it is necessary to prevent the generation of dangerous power. Of all power, however, popular power, if by this term we designate the uninstitutional sway of the multitude, is at once the most direct, because not borrowed nor theoretical, and the most deceptive, because, in reality, it is necessarily led or handled by a few or by one. The ancients knew this perfectly well, and repeatedly treated of the fact; but it is not essential that the agora, the bodily assembled multitude, have unlimited and uninstitutional power. The same defects exist and the same results are produced where, so to speak, the market extends over a whole country, and where all liberty is believed to consist in one solitary formula—universal suffrage. Many effects of the latter are, indeed, more serious.[1]

No evolution of public opinion, no debate, no gradual formation takes place. Some few prepare the measures, and Yes or No is all that can be asked or voted.

Whenever we speak of the power of the people, in an unorganized state, we cannot mean anything else but the power of the majority; and where liberty is believed to consist in the unlimited power of the people, the inevitable practical result

---

[1] Nowhere, I believe, can the views of a large class of Frenchmen on this subject, be found more distinctly enounced, than in the different works of Mr. Louis Blanc. They are many, and, in my opinion, as may be supposed, often very visionary; but Mr. Blanc is the spirited representative of that French school which believes that liberty is power, that the ouvriers are the people, that wealth consists in the largest possible amount of currency, and money is a deception, and that communism is the most perfect political phase of humanity.

is neither more nor less than the absolutism of the majority and the total want of protection of the minority.

As, however, this uninstitutional multitude has no organism, it is, as I have stated, necessarily led by a few or one, and thus we meet in history with the invariable result, that virtually one man rules where absolute power of the people is believed to exist. After a short interval, that one person openly assumes all power, sometimes observing certain forms by which the power of the people is believed to be transferred to him. The people have already been familiar with the idea of absolutism—they have been accustomed to believe that, wherever the public power resides, it is absolute and complete, so that it does not appear strange to them that the new monarch should possess the unlimited power which actually resided in the people or was considered to have belonged to them. There is but one step from the "*peuple tout-puissant*," if, indeed, it amounts to a step, to an emperor tout-puissant.[1]

It is a notable fact which, so far as I know history, has no important exception, that in all times of civil commotion in which two vast parties are arrayed against each other, the anti-institutional masses, which are erroneously yet generally called the people, are monarchical, or in favor of trusting power into the hands of one man. All dictators have become

---

[1] This, it will be observed, is very different from the English maxim, the parliament is omnipotent. Unguarded and extravagant as it is, it only means that parliament has the supreme power. But parliament itself is a vast institution, and part and parcel of a still vaster institutional system, which is pervaded by the principle of self-government. Parliament has often found that it is not omnipotent when it has attempted to break a lance with the common law. It is as unguarded a maxim as that the king can do no wrong, which is true only in a limiting sense, namely, that because *he* can do no wrong, some one else must be answerable for every act of his. Besides, there is the marginal note of James II. appended to this maxim, which never has been understood to mean what the ancient French maxim meant: In the presence of the king, the laws are silent; or what was meant by the famous "bed of justice," namely, that the personal presence of the monarch silenced all opposition, and was sufficient to ordain anything he pleased.

such by popular power, if the commotion tended to a general change of government. It was the case in Rome when Cæsar ruled. The party in the Netherlands which clamored for the return of the Stadtholder against that great citizen De Witt, and was bent on giving the largest extent of hereditary power to the house of Orange, was the popular party. Cromwell was mainly supported by the anti-institutional army and its adherents. We may go farther. The rise of the modern principate, that is, the vast increase of the power of the prince and the breaking down of the baronial power, was everywhere effected by the help of the people. We have not here to inquire, whether in many of these struggles the people did not consciously or instinctively support the prince or leader against his opponents, because the ancient institutions had become oppressive. At present, it is the fact alone which we have to consider.

Probably it was this fact, together with some other reasons, which caused Mr. Proudhon, the socialist, to utter the remarkable sentence that "no one is less democratic than the people."

The fact is certain that, merely because supreme power has been given by the people, or is pretended to have been conferred by the people, liberty is far from being insured. On the contrary, inasmuch as this theory rests on the theory of popular absolutism, it is invariably hostile to liberty, and, generally, forms the foundation of the most stringent and odious despotism. To use the words of Burke: "Law and arbitrary power are in eternal enmity. . . . It is a contradiction in terms, it is blasphemy in religion, it is wickedness in politics, to say that any man can have arbitrary power. . . We may bite our chains if we will; but we shall be made to know ourselves and be taught that man is born to be governed by law; and he that will substitute will in the place of it is an enemy to God."[1]

I add the words of one still greater, the elder Pitt, and be it remembered that he uttered them when he was an old man.

---

[1] Mr. Burke, in 1788.

"Power," said he, "without right is the most detestable object that can be offered to the human imagination; it is not only pernicious to those whom it subjects, but works its own destruction. Res detestabilis et caduca. Under the pretence of declaring law, the commons have made a law, a law for their own case, and have united in the same persons the offices of legislator, and party, and judge."[1] Frederic the Great of Prussia, perceived this clearly, for he said "he could very well understand how one man might feel a desire to make his will the law of others, but why thirty thousand or thirty millions should submit to it he could not understand." This is the saying of a monarch who probably knew or suspected as little of an institutional self-government as any one, and who continually complained of the power of parliament in changing ministers, when England was his ally.[2] But was he sincere when he wrote those words? Was he still in his period of philosophic sentiment? Did he really not see why this apparent transfer of power so often happens, or did he utter them merely as something piquant?

By whatever process this vast popular power is transferred or pretended to be transferred—for we must needs always add this qualification—is of no manner of importance with reference to liberty. Immolation brings death, though it should be self-immolation, and of the two species of political slavery,

---

[1] He spoke of Wilkes's expulsion.

[2] Raumer gives the dispatches from Mitchell, the English minister near the court of Frederic. The minister reports many complaints of the king, of this sort. But Frederic is not the only one who thus complained. General Walsh, that native Frenchman, who became minister of Spain, did the same. See Coxe's Memoirs, mentioned before. So when Russian statesmen desire to show the superiority of their government, they never fail to dwell on the low position of an English minister, inasmuch as he depends upon a parliamentary majority, or, as an English minister expressed it, must be the minister of public opinion. See Mr. Urquhart's Collection. I believe it will always be found that, where absolute governments come in contact with those of freemen, the former complain of the instability of the latter. They consider a change of ministry a revolution.

that is probably the worst which boasts of having originated
from free self-submission, such as Hobbes believed to have
been the origin of all monarchy, and of which recent history
has furnished an apparent frightful instance.

Nothing is easier than to show to an American or English
reader that the origin of power has of itself no necessary connection with liberty. What American would believe that a
particle of liberty were left him if his country were denuded of
every institution, federal or in the states, except of the president of the whole, though he alone were left to be elected
every four years by the sweeping majority of the entire country, from New York to San Francisco? Or what Englishman would continue to boast of self-government, if a civil
hurricane were to sweep from his country every institution,
common law and all, except parliament, as an "omnipotent"
body indeed?

The opposite of what we have called institutional self-
government is that liberty which Rousseau conceived of, when,
in his Social Contract, he not only assigns all power to the
majority, and almost teaches what might be called a divine
right of the majority, but declares himself against all division.
He shows a bitter animosity to the representative system. He
seeks, unconsciously to himself, for a legitimate source of public force, when he thinks he lays a foundation for liberty. In
this he may be said to be original, at least in the idea of the
permanent action of the social contract, or of the sovereignty
not only residing in the people, but continuing to act directly
and without checking institutions. For the rest, he only carried out the old French idea of unity of power, of centralization, which appeared to the French long before him, the summum bonum—not only in politics, but in all other spheres.
The works of the great Bossuet show this pervading idea, in
the sphere of theology; and numerous proofs have been given
in the course of this work, that the principle of uncompromising unity was distinctly acknowledged and almost idolized by
nearly all the leading statesmen of France from Richelieu,
through the first revolution, and continues to be so down to

the present day.[1] No one can understand the history of
France who does not remember the ardor for unconstitutional
unity of power, and what is intimately connected with it, the
idea that this all-pervading and uncompromising power must
do and provide for everything—the extinction of self-reliance.
The socialists do not differ from the imperialists; on the contrary, society is with them a unit in which the individual is
lost sight of, even in marriage and property.

Rousseau insists upon an inarticulated, unorganized, uninstitutional majority. It is a view which is shared by many
millions of people on the European continent, and has deeply
affected all the late and unsuccessful attempts at conquering
liberty. Rousseau wrote in a captivating style, and almost
always plausibly, very rarely profoundly, often with impassioned fervor. Plausibility, however, generally indicates a
fallacy, in all the higher spheres of thought and action; still
it is that which is popular with those who have had no experience to guide them; and since the theory of Rousseau has
had so decided an influence in France, and since no one can
understand the recent history of our race without having
studied the Social Contract,[2] that theory, for the sake of
brevity, may be called Rousseauism.

---

[1] One of the past statesmen of France, and renowned as a publicist,
said to me, in 1851, when we discoursed on the remarkable extinction of
former French royalty : "There is but one thing to which all Frenchmen
cling with enthusiasm, almost with fanaticism, and that is absolute unity."
Those statesmen who have not unconditionally joined this sentiment, such
as Mr. Guizot, are considered unnational.

[2] The Contract Social was the bible of the most advanced convention
men. Robespierre read it daily, and the influence of that book can be
traced throughout the revolution. Its ideas, its simplicity, and its senti-
mentality had all their effects. Indeed, we may say that two books had
a peculiar influence in the French revolution, Rousseau's Social Contract
and Plutarch's Lives, however signally they differ in character. The
translation of Plutarch by Amyot in the sixteenth century—it was the
period of Les Cents Contre Un—and subsequent ones, had a great effect
upon the ideas of a certain class of reflecting Frenchmen. We can trace
this down to the revolution, and during this struggle we find with a

We return once more to that despotism which is founded upon pre-existing popular absolutism. The processes by which the transition is effected are various. The appointment may deceptively remain in the hands of the majority, as was the case when the president of the French republic was apparently elected for ten years, after the second of December; or the prætorians may appoint the Cæsar; or there may be apparent or real acclamation for real or pretended services; or the emperor may be appointed by auction, as in the case of the emperor Didius; or the process may be a mixed one. The process is of no importance; the facts are simply these—the power thus acquired is despotic, and hostile to self-government; the power is claimed on the ground of absolute popular power; and it becomes the more uncompromising *because* it is claimed on the ground of popular power.

---

number of the leading men, a turn of ideas, a conception of republicanism formed upon their view of antiquity, and a stoicism which may be fitly called Plutarchism. It is an element in that great event. It showed itself especially with the Brissotists, the Girondists, and noble Charlotte Corday was imbued with it. A very instructive paper might be written on the influence of Plutarch on the political sentiment of the French, ever since that first translation.

CHAPTER XXXII.

IMPERATORIAL SOVEREIGNTY.

THE Cæsars of the first centuries claimed their power as bestowed upon them by the people, and went even so far as to assume the prætorians, with an accommodating and intimidated senate, as the representatives, for the time, of the people. The Cæsars never rested their power upon divine right, nor did they boldly adopt the Asiatic principle in all its nakedness, that power—the sword, the bow-string, the mere possession of power—is the only foundation of the right to wield it. The majestas populi had been transferred to the emperor.[1] Such was their theory. Julius, the first of the Cæsars, made himself sole ruler by the popular element, against the institutions of the country.

If it be observed here that these institutions had become effete, that the Roman city-government was impracticable for an extensive empire, and that the civil wars had proved how incompatible the institutions of Rome had become with the

---

[1] The idea of the populus vanished only at a late period from the Roman mind; that of liberty had passed away long before. Fronto, in a letter to Marcus Aurelius (when the prince was Cæsar,) mentions the applause which he had received from the audience for some oration which he had delivered, and then continues thus: "Quorsum hoc retuli? uti te, Domine, ita compares, ubi quid in cœtu hominum recitabis, ut scias auribus serviendum: plane non ubique et omni modo, attamen nonnunquam et aliquando. Quod ubi facies, simile facere te reputato, atque illud facitis, ubi eos qui bestias strenue interfecerint, *populo postulante* ornatis aut manumittitis, *nocentes etiam homines aut scelere damnatos, sed populo postulante conceditis. Ubique igitur populus dominatur et præpollet. Igitur ut populo gratum erit, ita facies atque ita dices.*"—Epist. ad Marc. Cæs., lib. i. epist. 1.

actual state of the people, it will be allowed—not to consider the common fact that governments or leaders first do everything to corrupt the people or plunge them into civil wars, and then, "taking advantage of their own wrong," use the corruption and bloodshed as a proof of the necessity to upset the government[1]—it will be allowed, I say, that at any rate Cæsar did not establish liberty, or claim to be the leader of a free state, and that he made his appearance at the close of a long period of freedom, marking the beginning of the most fearful decadence which stands on record; and that, unfortunately, the rulers vested with this imperatorial sovereignty[2] never prepare a better state of things with reference to civil dignity and healthful self-government. They may establish peace and police; they may silence civil war, but they also destroy those germs from which liberty might sprout forth

---

[1] Not unlike the conduct of the powers surrounding Poland, before they had sufficiently prepared her partition. The government of Poland was certainly a very defective one, but it was the climax of historical iniquity in Russia, Austria and Prussia to declare, after having used every sinister means to embroil the Polish affairs, and stir up faction, that the Poles were unfit to be a nation, and as neighbors too troublesome.

[2] The idea which I have to express, would have prompted me, and the Latin word Cæsareus would have authorized me, to use the term Cæsarean Sovereignty. It is unquestionably preferable to imperatorial sovereignty, except that the English term Cæsarean has acquired a peculiar and distinct meaning, which might even have suggested the idea of a mordant pun. I have, therefore, given up this term, although I had always used it in my lectures. It will be observed that I use the term sovereignty in this case with a meaning which corresponds to the sense in which the word sovereign continues to be used by many, designating a crowned ruler. I hope no reader will consider me so ignorant of history and political philosophy, as to think me capable of believing in the real sovereignty of an individual. If sovereignty means the self-sufficient primordial power of society, from which all other powers are derived—and unless it mean this we do not stand in need of the term—it is clear that no individual ever possessed or can possess it. On the other hand, it is not to be confounded with absolute power. My views on this important subject have been given at length in my Political Ethics, as I have said before.

at a future period. However long Napoleon I. might have reigned, his whole path must have led him farther astray from that of an Alfred, who allowed self-government to take root, and respected it where he found it. We can never arrive at the top of a steeple by descending deeper into a pit.

Whatever Cæsar's greatness may have been, he did not, at any rate, usher in a new and prosperous era, either of liberty or popular grandeur. What is the Roman empire after Cæsar? Count the good rulers, and weigh them against the unutterable wretchedness resulting from the worst of all combinations—of lust of power, voluptuousness, avarice, and cruelty—and forming a stream of increasing demoralization, which gradually swept down in its course everything noble that had remained of better times.

The Roman empire did, undoubtedly, much good, by spreading institutions which adhered to it in spite of itself, as seeds adhere to birds, and are carried to great distances; but it did this in spite, and not in consequence of the imperatorial sovereignty.

How, in view of all these facts of Roman history and of Napoleon I., the French have been able once more boastfully to return to the forms and principles of imperatorial sovereignty, and once more to confound an apparently voluntary divestment of all freedom with liberty, is difficult to be understood by any one who is accustomed to self-government. Whatever allowance we may make on the ground of vanity, both because it may please the ignorant to be called upon to vote *yes* or *no*, regarding an imperial crown, and because it may please them more to have an imperial government than one that has no such sounding name; whatever may be ascribed to military recollections—and, unfortunately, in history people only see prominent facts, as at a distance we see only the steeples of a town, and not the dark lanes and crowding misery which may be around them; whatever allowance may be made, and however well we may know that the whole could never have been effected without a wide-spread centralized govern-

ment and an enormous army[1]—it still remains surprising to us
that the French, or at least those who now govern, please
themselves in the imperatorial forms of Rome, and in presenting popular absolutism as a desirable phase of democracy. As
though Tacitus had written like a contented man, and not
with despair in his breast, breathed into many lines of his
melancholy annals!

Yet so it is. Mr. Troplong, now president of the senate,
said on a solemn occasion, after the sanguinary second of
December, when he was descanting on the services rendered
by Louis Napoleon: "The Roman democracy conquered in
Cæsar and in Augustus the era of its tardy *avènement*."[2] If
imperatorial sovereignty were to be the lasting destiny of
France, and not a phase, French history would consist of a
long royal absolutism; a short struggle for liberty, with the
long fag-end of Roman history—the *avènement* of democracy

---

[1] See paper on Elections, in the appendix.

[2] A sepulchral inscription in honor of Massaniello had an allusion
conceived in a similar spirit. I give it entire, as it probably will be interesting to many readers.

Eulogium
Thomæ Aniello de Amalfio
Cetario mox Cesareo
Honore conspicuo
qui
Oppressa patria Parthenope
cum
Suppressione nobilium
Combustione mobilium
Purgatione exulum
Extinctione vectigalium
Proregis injustitia
Liberata
Ab his qui liberavit est peringrate occisus
Ætatis suæ anno vigesimo septimo, imperii vero
Decennio
Mortuus non minus quam vivus
Triumphavit
Tantæ rei populus Neapolitanus tanquam immemor
Posuit.

in its own destroyer, the imperatorial sovereignty, but without the long period of Roman republicanism.

The same gentleman drew up the report of the senatorial committee to which had been referred the subject, whether the people should be called upon to vote Yes or No on the question: Shall the republic be changed into an empire? This extraordinary report possesses historical importance, because it is a document containing the opinion of such a body as the French senate, and the political creed of the ruling party. I shall give it, therefore, a place in the appendix. It contains the same views mentioned above, but spread over a considerable space, occasionally with surprising untenableness and inconsistency.

So little, indeed, has imperatorial sovereignty to do with liberty, that we find even the earliest Asiatics ascribing the origin of their despotic power to unanimous election. I do not allude only to the case of Daioces, related by Herodotus, but to the mythological books of Asiatic nations. The following extract from the Mongolian cosmogony, whose mythos extends over a vast part of the East, is so curious and so striking an instance of "the *avènement* of democracy"—though not a tardy one—and so clear a conception of imperatorial sovereignty without a suspicion of liberty, as a matter of course, since the whole refers to Asia, that the reader will not be dissatisfied with the extract.

"At this time (that is, after evil had made its appearance on earth) a living being appeared of great beauty and excellent aspect, and of a candid and honest soul and clear intellect. This being confirmed the righteous possessors in their property, and obliged the unrighteous possessors to give up what they had unjustly acquired. Thereupon the fields were distributed according to equal measure, and to every one was done even justice. Then all elected him for their chief, and yielded allegiance to him with these words: We elect thee for our chief, and we will never trespass thy ordinances. On account of this unanimous election, he is called in the Indian language Ma-ha-Ssamati-Radsha; in Thibetian, Mangboi-b

25

Kurbai-r Gjabbo ; and in Mongolian, Olana-ergukdeksen Cha-
gran (the many-elected Monarch.)"[1]

"In the name of the people," are the words with which
commenced the first decree of Louis Napoleon, issued after
the second of December, when he had made himself master of
France, and in which he called upon all the French to state
whether he should have unlimited power for ten years. If it
was not their will, the decree said, there was no necessity of
violence, for in that case he would resign his power. This
was naive. But theories or words proclaimed before the full
assumption of imperatorial sovereignty are of as little importance as after it. Where liberty is not a fact and a daily
recurring reality, it is not liberty. The word Libertas occurs
frequently on the coins of Nero, and still more often the sentimental words, Fides Mutua, Liberalitas Augusta, Felicitas
Publica.

Why, it may still be asked, did the Cæsars recur to the people as the source of their power, and why did the civilians say
that the emperor was legislator, and power-holder, inasmuch
as the majestas of the Roman people, who had been legislators
and power-holders, had been conferred upon him? Because,
partly, the first Cæsars, at any rate the very first, had actually ascended the steps of power with the assistance of
some popular element, cheered on somewhat like a diademed
tribune ; because there was and still is no other actual source
of power imaginable than the people, whether they positively
give it, or merely acquiesce[2] in the imperatorial power, and
because, as to the historical fact by which power in any given
case is acquired, we must never forget that the ethical element

---

[1] The History of the East Mongols, by Ssanang Ssetsen Changsaidshi,
translated into German, by I. J. Schmidt. I owe this interesting passage to my friend, the Rev. Professor J. W. Miles, who directed my
attention to the work.

[2] As the words stand above, I own, they may be variously interpreted;
but it would evidently lead me too far, were I to attempt a full statement of the sense in which I take them, which indeed I have done at
length in my Political Ethics.

and that of intellectual consistency are so inbred in man that, wherever humanity is developed, a constant desire is observable to make actions, however immoral or inconsistent, at least theoretically agree with them. No proclamation of war has ever avowed, I believe, that war was simply undertaken because he who issued the proclamation had the power and meant to use it fas aut nefas.[1] Even Attila called himself the scourge of God.

No matter what the violence of facts has been, however rudely the shocks of events have succeeded one another, the first thing that men do after these events have taken place is invariably to bring them into some theoretical consistency, and to attempt to give some reasonable account of them. This is the intellectual demand ever active in man. The other, equally active, is the ethical demand. No man, though he commanded innumerable legions, could stand up before a people and say: "I owe my crown to the murder of my mother, to the madness of the people, or to slavish place-men." To appear merely respectable in an intellectual and ethical point of view, requires some theoretical decorum. The purer the generally acknowledged code of morality, or the prevailing religion is, or the higher the general mental system which prevails at the time, the more assiduous are also those who lead the public events, to establish, however hypocritically, this apparent agreement between their acts and theory, as well as morals. It is a tribute, though impure, paid to truth and morality.

---

[1] The reader sufficiently acquainted with history will remember that the consul Manlius, when the Gallatians, a people in Asia Minor, urged that they had given no offence to the Romans, answered that they were a profligate people deserving punishment, and that some of their ancestors had, centuries before, plundered the temple of Delphi. Justin, the historian, says that the Romans assisted the Acarnanians against the Aetolians because the former had joined in the Trojan war, a thousand years before. But this principle does not act, even to a degree of caricature, in politics only. What cruelties have not been committed Pro majore Dei gloria!

CHAPTER XXXIII.

IMPERATORIAL SOVEREIGNTY, CONTINUED. ITS ORIGIN AND
CHARACTER EXAMINED.

It has been said in the preceding pages that imperatorial
sovereignty must be always the most stringent absolutism,[1]
especially when it rests theoretically on election by the whole
people, and that the transition from an uninstitutional popular
absolutism to the imperatorial sovereignty is easy and natural.
At the time of the so-called French republic of 1848, it was
a common way of expressing the idea then prevailing, to call
the people le peuple-roi (the king-people,) and an advocate,
defending certain persons before the high court of justiciary
sitting at Versailles in 1849, for having invaded the chamber
of representatives, and consequently having violated the constitution, used this remarkable expression, " the people" (con-
founding of course a set of people, a gathering of a part of
the inhabitants of a single city, with *the* people) "never violate the constitution."[2]

Where such ideas prevail, the question is not about a change
of ideas, but simply about the lodgement of power. The
minds and souls are already thoroughly familiarized with the
idea of absolutism, and destitute of the idea of self-government. This is also one of the reasons why there is so much
similarity between monarchical absolutism, such for instance

---

[1] That absolutism and imperatorial sovereignty go hand in hand, was
neatly acknowledged by an inscription over the sub-prefecture of Dun-
kerque, when the imperial couple passed it, in 1855. It was to this effect :
À l'héritier de Napoléon, la ville de Louis XIV.

[2] Mr. Michel, on the 10th of November. I quote from the French
papers, which gave detailed reports. Mr. Michel, to judge from his own
speech, seems to have been the oldest of the defending advocates.

(388)

as we see in Russia, and communism, as it was preached in France; and it explains why absolutism, having made rapid strides under the Bourbons before the first revolution, has terminated every successive revolution with a still more compressive absolutism and centralism, except indeed the revolution of 1830. This revolution was undertaken to defend parliamentary government, and may be justly called a counter-revolution on the part of the people against a revolution attempted and partially carried by the government. It explains farther how Louis Napoleon after the second of December, and later when he desired to place the crown of uncompromising absolutism on his head, could appeal to the universal suffrage of all France—he that had previously curtailed it, with the assistance of the chamber of representatives. This phenomenon, however, must be explained also by the system of centralism, which prevails in France. I shall offer a few remarks on this topic after having treated of some more details appertaining to the subject immediately in hand.

The idea of the peuple-roi (it would perhaps have been more correct to say peuple-czar) also tends to explain the otherwise inconceivable hatred against the *bourgeoisie*, by which the French understand the aggregate of those citizens who inhabit towns and live upon a small amount of property or by traffic. The communists and the French so-called democrats entertained a real hatred against the bourgeoisie; the proclamations, occasionally issued by them, openly avowed it; and the government, when it desired to establish unconditional absolutism in form as well as principle, fanned this hatred. Yet no nation can exist without this essential element of society. In reading the details of French history of the year 1848 and the next succeeding years, the idea is forced upon our mind that a vast multitude of the French were bent on establishing a real and unconditional aristocracy of the ouvrier—the workman.[1]

---

[1] This error broke forth into full blaze at the indicated time, but it had of course been long smouldering, and, as is customary, had found some fuel even in our country. In the year 1841, during the presidential canvass, a gentleman—who has since become the editor of a

If the imperatorial sovereignty is founded upon an actual process of election, whether this consist in a mere form or not, it bears down all opposition, nay all dissent, however lawful it may be, by a reference to the source of its power. It says " I am the people, and whoever dissents from me is an enemy to the people. Vox Populi vox Dei. My divine right is the voice of God, which spake in the voice of the people. The government is the true representative of the people."[1]

catholic periodical, and has probably changed his views—published a pamphlet in which he attacked individual property, and fell into the same error which is spoken of in the text above.

The author of the pamphlet, which was very widely distributed, found it of course impossible to draw the line between the workmen and those who are not "working," and I recollect that he did not even allow the superintendent of a factory to be a workman. I have treated of these subjects in detail in my Essays on Labor and Property, and believe that a Humboldt is a harder working "working man," not indeed than the poor weaver who allows himself but five hours rest in the whole twenty-four, but certainly a far harder working man than any of those physically employed persons who want to make their class a privileged order. The fact is simply this, that there is no toiling man, however laboriously employed in a physical way, that does not guide his efforts by an exertion of the brain, and no mentally employed man that is not obliged to accompany his labor by some, frequently by much physical exertion. To draw an exact line between the two, for political purposes, is impossible. All attempts at doing so are mischievous. The hands and the brain rule the world. All labor is manual and cerebral, but the proportion in which the elements combine is infinite. So soon as no cerebral labor is necessary, we substitute the animal or the machine. In reading some socialist works, one would almost suppose that men had returned to some worship of the animal element, raising pure physical exertion above all other human endeavors. Humanity does not present itself more respectably than in the industrious and intelligent artisan, but every artisan justly strives to reach that position in which he works more by the intellect than by physical exertion. He strives to be an employer. The type of a self-dependent and striving American artisan is a really noble type. The author hopes to count many an American operative among his readers; and if he be not deceived, he takes this opportunity of declaring that he believes he too has a very fair title to be called a hard-working man, without claiming any peculiar civil privileges on that account.

[1] The idea that God speaks through the voice of the people, familiar

The eight millions of votes, more or less, which elevated the present French emperor, first to the decennial presidency and then to the imperial throne, are a ready answer to all objections. If private property is confiscated by a decree; if persons are deported without trial; if the jury trial is shorn of its guarantees, the answer is always the same. The emperor is the unlimited central force of the French democracy; thus the theory goes. He is the incarnation of the popular power, and if any of the political bodies into which the imperatorial power may have subdivided itself, like a Hindoo god, should happen to indicate an opinion of its own, it is readily given to understand that the government is in fact the people. Such bodies cannot, of course, be called institutions; for they are devoid of independence and every element of self-government. The president of the French legislative corps in 1853, found it necessary, on the opening of the session, to assure his colleagues, in an official address, that their body was by no means without some importance in the political system, as many seemed to suppose.

The source of imperatorial power, however, is hardly ever what it is pretended to be, because, if the people have any power left, it is not likely that they will absolutely denude themselves of it, surely not in any modern and advanced nation. The question in these cases is not whether they love liberty, but simply whether they love power—and every one loves power. On the one hand, we have to observe that no case exists in history in which the question, whether imperatorial power shall be conferred upon an individual, is put to the peo-

_____

to the middle ages, is connected with the elections of ruder times by general acclaim. It reminds us also of the *Dieu le veut,* at Clermont, when Peter the Hermit called on the chivalry and the people to take the sign of the cross. And again it reminds us of the disastrous *decrets d'acclamation* of the first French Revolution. That the government is the true representative of the people, has been often asserted in recent times in France, and Napoleon I., in one of his addresses, delivered in the council of state, said: The government, too, is the representative of the people.—Miot de Melito, in his Memoirs.

ple, except after a successful conspiracy against the existing
powers or institutions, or a coup d'état, if the term be preferred, on the part of the imperatorial candidate; and, on the
other hand, a state of things in which so great a question is
actually left to the people is wholly unimaginable.   There may
be a so-called interregnum during the conclave, when the cardinals elect a pope, but a country cannot be imagined in a
state of perfect interregnum while the question is deciding
whether a hereditary empire shall be established.   It is idle
to feign believing that this is possible, most especially so
where the question is to be decided not by representatives,
but by universal suffrage, and that, too, in a country where
the executive power spreads over every inch of the territory,
and is characterized by the most consistent centralism.   The
two last elections of Louis Napoleon prove what is here stated.
Ministers, prefects, bishops, were openly and officially influencing the elections; not to speak of the fact that large
elections concerning persons in power, which allow to vote
only yes or no, have really little meaning, as the history of
France abundantly proves.[1]   But how elections at present
are managed in France, even when the question is not so
comprehensive, may be seen from a circular addressed by
the minister, Mr. de Morny,[2] to the prefects, previous to the
elections for the first legislative corps.   It is an official paper,
strikingly characteristic, and I shall give a place to a translation of it in the appendix.   We ought to bear in mind that
one of the heaviest charges against Mr. de Polignac, when
tried for treason, was, that he had allowed Charles X. to influence the elections.

---

[1] See the Paper on Elections, in the appendix.

[2] Mr. de Morny is the *frère adultérin* of Louis Napoleon, on the
mother's side, Queen Hortensia.   He aided his half-brother very actively
in the overthrow of the republic, and the establishment of the empire.
Mr. de Morny lost the ministry at the time when L. Bonaparte despoiled
the Orleans family of their lawful property, and, it was believed, because
the minister could not in his conscience sanction an act at once so unlawful and ungrateful.

When such a vote is put to the people under circumstances which have been indicated, the first question which presents itself, is: And what if the vote turn out No? Will the candidate, already at the head of the army, the executive, and of every other branch; whose initials are paraded everywhere, and whose portrait is in the courts of justice, some of which actually have styled themselves imperial, and who has been addressed Sire; who has an enormous civil list—will he make a polite bow, give the keys to some one else, and walk his way? And to whom was he to give the government? The question was not, as Mr. de Laroche-Jacquelin had proposed, Shall A or B rule us? Essentially this question would not have been better; but there would have been apparently some sense in it. The question simply was: Shall B rule us?—Yes or No. It is surprising that some persons can actually believe reflecting people may thus be duped.

The Cæsar always exists before the imperatorial government is acknowledged and openly established. Whether the prætorians or legions actually proclaim the Cæsar or not, it is always the army that makes him. A succeeding ballot is nothing more than a trimming belonging to more polished or more timid periods, or it may be a tribute to that civilization which does not allow armies to occupy the place they hold in barbarous or relapsing times, at least not openly so.

First to assume the power and then to direct the people to vote, whether they are satisfied with the act or not, leads psychologically to a process similar to that often pursued by Henry VIII., and according to which it became a common saying: First clap a man into prison for treason, and you will soon have abundance of testimony. It was the same in the witch-trials.

The process of election becomes peculiarly unmeaning, because the power already assumed allows no discussion. There is no free press.[1]

---

[1] When the question of the new imperial crown was before the people of France, Count Chambord, the Bourbon prince who claims the crown

Although no reliance can be placed on wide-spread elections, whose sole object is to ratify the assumption of imperatorial sovereignty, and when therefore it already dictatorially controls all affairs, it is not asserted that the dictator may not at times be supported by large masses, and possibly assume the imperatorial sovereignty with the approbation of a majority. I have repeatedly acknowledged it; but it is unquestionably true that generally in times of commotion, and especially in uninstitutional countries, minorities rule, for it is minorities that actually contend. Yet, even where this is not the case, the popularity of the Cæsar does in no way affect the question. Large, unarticulated masses are swayed by temporary opinions or passions, as much so as individuals, and it requires but a certain skill to seize upon the proper moment to receive their acclamation, if they are willing and consider themselves authorized to give away by one sudden vote, all power and liberty, not only for their own lifetime, but for future generations. In the institutional government alone, substantial public opinion can be generated and brought to light.

It sometimes happens that arbitrary power or centralism recommends itself to popular favor by showing that it intends to substitute a democratic equality for oligarchic or oppressive, unjust institutions, and the liberal principle may seem to be on the side of the levelling ruler. This was doubtless the case when in the sixteenth and seventeenth century the power of the crown made itself independent on the continent of Europe. Instead of transforming the institutions, or of substituting new ones, the governments levelled them to the ground, and that unhappy centralization was the consequence which now draws every attempt at liberty back into its vortex. At other times, monarchs or governments disguise their plans to destroy

---

of France on the principle of legitimacy, wrote a letter to his adherents, exhorting them not to vote. The leading government papers stated at the time that government would have permitted the publication of this letter, had it not attacked the principle of the people's sovereignty. The people were acknowledged sovereign, yet the government decides what the sovereign may read!

liberty in the garb of liberty itself. Thus James II. endeavored to break through the restraints of the constitution, or perhaps ultimately to establish the catholic religion in England, by proclaiming liberty of conscience for all, against the established church. Austria at one time urged measures, apparently liberal for the peasants, against the Gallician nobles. In such cases, governments are always sure to find numerous persons that do not look beyond the single measure, nor to the means by which it is carried out; yet the legality and constitutionality of these means are of great, and frequently of greater importance than the measure itself. Even historians are frequently captivated by the apparently liberal character of a single measure, forgetting that the dykes of an institutional government once being broken through, the whole country may soon be flooded by an irresistible tide of arbitrary power. We have a parallel in the criminal trial, in which the question how we arrive at the truth is of equal importance with the object of arriving at truth. Nullum bonum nisi bene.

On the other hand, all endeavors to throw more and more unarticulated power into the hands of the primary masses, to deprive a country more and more of a gradually evolving character; in one word, to introduce an ever-increasing direct, unmodified popular power, amount to an abandonment of self-government, and an approach to imperatorial sovereignty, whether there be actually a Cæsar or not—to popular absolutism, whether the absolutism remain for any length of time in the hands of a sweeping majority, subject, of course, to a skilful leader, as in Athens after the Peloponnesian war, or whether it rapidly pass over into the hands of a broadly named Cæsar. Imperatorial sovereignty may be at a certain period more plausible than the sovereignty founded upon divine right, but they are both equally hostile to self-government, and the only means to resist the inroads of power is, under the guidance of providence and a liberty-wedded people, the same means which in so many cases have withstood the inroads of the barbarians, namely, the institution—the self-sustaining and organic systems of laws.

CHAPTER XXXIV.

WE have seen in how great a degree French centralism has produced an incapacity for self-rule, according to one of the most distinguished statesmen of France herself. This centralism, in conjunction with imperatorial sovereignty, has produced some peculiar effects upon a nation so intelligent, ardent, and wedded to system as the French are. Before I conclude this treatise, therefore, I beg leave to offer a few remarks, which naturally suggest themselves, in connection with centralism and imperatorial sovereignty; both so prominent at this moment in France.

Centralism has given to Paris an importance which no capital possesses in any other country. The French themselves often say Paris is France; foreigners always say so; and to them as well as to those French people who desire to enjoy, at one round, as much as possible of all that French civilization produces, this is, doubtless, very agreeable and instructive. Paris is brilliant, as centralism frequently is; Paris naturally flatters the vanity of the French; Paris stands with many people for France, because they see nothing of France but Paris. Centralization appears most imposing in Paris—in the buildings, in demonstrations, in rapidity of execution, and in an æsthetical point of view. Upon a close examination of history, however, we shall find that it has been not only a natural effect of centralism, but an object of all absolute rulers over intelligent races, to beautify the capital and raise its activity to the highest point. The effect is remarkable. The government of King Jerome, of Westphalia—now again prince of France—was one of the most ruinous that has ever existed, and yet long after the downfall of that ephemeral kingdom, every disapproval of it was answered by a reference to the embellishment of Cassel, the capital.[1]

---

[1] There are psychological processes which indicate suspicious intentions—the adoption of a new and scientifically sounding term for an old and common offence, as Repudiation for declining to pay what is due; and of mystifying; high sounding abstractions in statesmanship. The latter is carried to a degree, in the following address of Napoleon, which is rare even in France. Louis XIV., according to the present emperor of the French, the great representative of French unity and glory, when he had ruined France by the building of Versailles, warned, on his death-bed, his successor to beware of wars and of building. There are so many points of French politics tersely put in the speech of Napoleon III., when in September of 1857 he opened the Louvre, that its record may be considered a historical document. We give it therefore entire.

The ceremony of opening the Louvre was simple but imposing. The ministers, marshals and generals, the senators and great functionaries, assembled in the hall of the Louvre. The emperor and empress arrived at two o'clock with a vast retinue. The business began by the presentation of an address to the emperor from M. Fould, briefly describing the origin and completion of a work which, begun in 1852 and finished in 1857, unites the Louvre and the Tuileries. The emperor next distributed the legion of honor to the professional men who have distinguished themselves during the erection of the building; making some commanders, some simple knights. Having distributed all the honors, the emperor delivered the following address :

" Gentlemen—I congratulate myself, with you, on the completion of the Louvre. I congratulate myself especially upon the causes which have rendered it possible. In fact, it is order, restored stability, and the ever-increasing prosperity of the country, which have enabled me to complete this national work. I call it so because the governments which have succeeded each other have made it a point to do something towards the completion of the royal dwelling commenced by Francis I. and embellished by Henry II.

" Whence this perseverance, and even this popularity, in the building of a palace ? It is because the character of a people is reflected in its institutions as in its customs, in the events that excite its enthusiasm as well as in the monuments which become the object of its chief interest. Now France, monarchical for so many centuries, which always beheld in the central power the representative of her grandeur and of her nationality, wished that the dwelling of the sovereign should be worthy of the country; and the best means of responding to that sentiment

Capital cities and residences of kings, and even of petty princes, have in this respect the same effect which single large fortunes or single busy places have on the minds of the superficial, in point of political economy. They are palpable, and strike the mind, yet they prove nothing of themselves. There is not a war, however ruinous, that does not produce gigantic gains for some bankers, contractors, and able speculators. They are often pointed out to prove that a certain war has not been fatal to general prosperity. There have never existed greater fortunes than those of some princely Roman senators,

---

was to adorn that dwelling with the different masterpieces of human intelligence.

"In the middle ages, the king dwelt in a fortress, bristling with defensive works; but soon the progress of civilization superseded battlements, and the produce of letters, of the arts and sciences, took the place of weapons of war. Thus the history of monuments has also its philosophy as well as the history of events.

"In like manner that it is remarkable that at the time of the first revolution, the committee of public welfare should have continued, without being aware of it, the work of Louis XI., of Richelieu, of Louis XIV., giving the last blow to the feudal system, and carrying out the system of unity and centralization, the constant aim of monarchy—in like manner is there not a great lesson to learn in beholding the idea of Henry IV., of Louis XIII., of Louis XIV., of Louis XV., of Louis XVI., of Napoleon, as regards the Louvre, adopted by the ephemeral power of 1848? One of the first acts, in fact, of the provisional government, was to decree the completion of the palace of our kings. So true is it that a nation draws from its antecedents, as an individual derives from his education, ideas which the passions of a moment do not succeed in destroying. When a moral impulse is the consequence of the social condition of a country, it is handed down through centuries, and through different forms of government, until the object in view is attained.

"Thus the completion of the Louvre, towards which I thank you for your co-operation, given with so much zeal and skill, is not the caprice of a moment, but is the realization of a plan conceived for the glory and kept alive by the instinct of the country for more than three hundred years."

In the evening some hundreds of persons engaged in the work—working men, artists, men of letters, journalists—were entertained at dinner by the minister of state in a gallery of the Louvre. Of course the speaking was ultra-loyal.

with their latifundia, in the very worst periods of the Roman empire, amidst universal ruin, and when the country was fast declining to that state in which the tillers of the soil abandoned their farms, because unable to pay the taxes, and in which Italy, with the utmost exertion of the government, was not able to raise an army against invading hordes.

Whenever we shall have executed our railway to the Pacific, nothing of it will be seen at one moment and by the physical eye, that differs from the rails of any other road, and the vulgar will be struck far more by a palace at Versailles, or a column of Trajan; unless, indeed, a pointing hand were hewn in granite, at San Francisco, with the words, To the Atlantic, and another at some Atlantic city, with the words, To the Pacific; and even then the grandeur of the road would not be perceived by the physical eye.[1]

We live in an age which has justly been called the age of large cities.[2] Populous cities are indispensable to civilization, and even to liberty, though I own that one of the problems we have yet to solve is, how to unite in large cities the highest degree of individual liberty and order.

But absorbing cities, cities on which monarchs are allowed to lavish millions of the national wealth, always belong to a low state of general national life, often to effete empires. The vast cities of Asia, Byzantium, imperial Rome, and many other cities prove it. On the other hand, it is an unfortunate state of things in which one city rules supreme, either by an overwhelming population, as Naples, or by concentration, as Paris. Constant changes of governments seem almost inevitable, whether they are produced by the people, as in the case of Paris, or by foreigners, as was formerly the case in Naples.

A comparison between Paris and London, in this respect, is

---

[1] No one will charge the author, he trusts, with political iconoclasm, that has read his chapter on monuments in his Political Ethics.

[2] The Age of Great Cities, or Modern Society viewed in its Relation to Intelligence, Morals and Religion, by Robert Vaughn, D.D. London, 1843.

instructive.   London, far more populous, has far less influence
than Paris ; and London, incomparably richer, is far less brilliant than Paris.   Monarchical absolutism and centralism
strike the eye and strive to do so; liberty is brilliant indeed,
but it is brilliant in history, and must be studied in her institutions.[1]

Great as the influence of Paris has been ever since the reign
of the Valois, it has steadily increased, and those who strove
for liberty were by no means behind the others in their worship of the capital.   This singular idolatry was actually acknowledged by several resolutions of the representatives of
the people, during the late republic.

The intense influence of Paris, together with the wide-spread
system of government, every single thread of which centres in
Paris, is such that, in 1848, the republic was literally telegraphed to the departments, and adopted without any resistance from any quarter, civil or military, which cannot be explained by the often avowed horror of the French at shedding
French blood, since blood was readily shed to elevate Louis
Napoleon.   The same causes made it possible for the republic,
so readily and unanimously adopted, to be with equal readiness changed by eight millions of votes into a monarchy.

It has already been admitted that centralism, by the very
fact that it concentrates great power, can produce many striking results which it is not in the power of governments on a

---

[1] This manifests itself in all spheres.   Paris leads in fashion, art,
science, language, etc.   England has her Oxford and Cambridge.

The title of Walker's Critical Pronouncing Dictionary, has these
words : "Likewise Rules to be observed by the Natives of Scotland,
Ireland and London, for avoiding their respective Peculiarities," as
indicating part of the contents.   This is strikingly English.   The pronunciation and "peculiarities" of the Parisians, even as they change
from time to time, are the very standard of French pronunciation.

Similar remarks may be made regarding the courts.   The court of
Versailles, dictated in every sphere at the time when Horace Walpole,
the whig, wrote that the English court was not fashionable, and was
considered little better than a number of Germans kept there for some
useful practical end.

different principle to exhibit. These effects please and often popularize a government; but there is another fact to be taken into consideration. Symmetry is one of the elements of humanity; systematizing is one of man's constant actions. It captivates and becomes dangerous, if other elements and activities equally important are neglected, or if it is carried into spheres in which it ought not to prevail. The regularity and consistent symmetry, together with the principle of unity, which pervade the whole French government, charm many a beholder, and afford pleasure not unlike that which many persons derive from looking at a plan of a mathematically regular city, or from gardens architectonically trimmed. But freedom is life, and wherever we find life it is marked, indeed, by agreement of principles and harmony of development, but also, by variety of form and phenomenon, and by a subordinate exactness of symmetry. The centralist, it might be said, mistakes lineal and angular exactness, formal symmetry and mathematical proportions, for harmonious evolution and profuse vitality. He prefers an angular garden of the times of Louis XIV. to an umbrageous grove.

Centralism, and the desire to bring everything under the influence of government, or to effect as far as possible everything by government, has fearfully increased from the moment that the imperatorial absolutism was declared;[1] while, at the same time, a degree of man-worship has developed itself, which makes people at a distance almost stand aghast. The same hyperbolical, and, in many cases, blasphemous flattery, which reminded the observer, in the times of Napoleon I., of imperial Rome, has been repeated since. No one who has attentively followed the events of our times stands in need of instances; they were offered by hundreds,[2] and of a character

---

[1] According to the latest news even the dead are under the control of government, not in the sense of Sidney Smith, by paying taxes, but no one can any longer be buried in Paris except by a chartered company, standing under the close inspection of the police department.

[2] Churchmen and laymen, as is well known, vie with each other on such occasions. The blasphemous flattery offered by some dignitaries

that would make the most inveterate former tory-worship of
the crowned person appear as an innocent blundering; but

---

of the church to Napoleon I. was revolting. We have seen the same
when there seemed to be a question who could bid highest in burning
incense to the present new Cæsar. The Lord's prayer was travestied.
The following "proclamation" is taken from the "Concorde de Seine et
Oise," of October, 1852, for the very reason that it is not one of the
worst:

"*Town of Sèvres. Proclamation of the Empire.*

"Inhabitants—Paris, the heart of France, acclaimed on the 10th of
May for its emperor him whose divine mission is every day revealed in
such a striking and dazzling manner. At this moment it is the whole of
France electrified which salutes her savior, the elect of God, by this new
title, which clothes him with sovereign power : ' God wills it,' is repeated
with one voice—' vox populi vox Dei.' It is the marriage of France
with the envoy of God, which is contracted in the face of the universe,
under the auspices of all the constituted bodies, and of all the people.
That union is sanctified by all the ministers of religion, and by all the
princes of the church. These addresses, these petitions, and these
speeches, which are at this moment exchanging between the chief of
the state and France, are the documents connected with that holy
union ; every one wishes to sign them, as at the church he would sign
the marriage-deed at which he is present. Inhabitants of Sèvres, as the
interpreter of your sentiments, I have prepared the deed which makes
you take part in this great national movement. Two books are opened
at the Mairie to receive your signatures : one of them will be offered in
your presence to him whom I from this day designate under the title of
emperor. Let us hope that he will deign to accede to the supplications
which I shall address to him in your name, to return to the palace of
St. Cloud through our territory, by the gate of honor which we possess.
The other book, which I shall present for the signature of the prince,
will remain in your archives as a happy souvenir of this memorable
epoch. Let all the population, without distinction, come, therefore, and
sign this document ; it sets forth that which is in your heart and in your
will."

This document is accompanied by a formal proclamation, appropriately signed—"Ménager, mayor."

Plain dealing, however, obliges us to remember, along with such
extravagances of foreigners, the repulsive flattery in which some individuals indulged when Kossuth was among us. Nor must we wholly
forget the language of certain daily journals at the time of General
Jackson's administration. But these were erratic acts of individuals,
and, however disgusting, were not officially received by government.

we cannot pass over the fact that an infatuated yet large part of a nation have for the first time in history, so far as we know, called ideas after a man of action. "Napoleonic ideas" has become a favorite expression. Not only newspapers use this term—a late one condemned free-trade because "free-trade is no Napoleonic idea"—but men whom we have been accustomed to look upon with respect[1] have fallen into this infatuation. All of us have heard of christian ethics, christian ideas and sentiments, but we have never heard of Carlovingian, Frederician, Julian, Alexandrian, Gregorian or Lutheran ideas. It is a submission to a name, an individual—and an individual, too, be it observed, who distinguished himself as a man of action, which seems to indicate a singular want of self-reliance and relf-respect.

Centralized governments can effect certain brilliant acts, but they are on this account seriously liable to fall into a method of carrying on public affairs, which, in the language of stage managers, is significantly called starring, and which has the serious inconvenience of leading popular attention from solid actions to that which dazzles, from wholesome reality to mere brilliant ideas.

The elevation of Napoleon III. may be referred in a measure to this error. Huzzaing crowds are never substantial indications of any opinion, whether the crowds are voluntary or subpœnaed. "Where are my enemies?" said Charles II. when he re-entered London and passed through the crowd of his subjects. He had enough. Prince de Ligne tells us that, when Catharine travelled through Crimea, distant populations were carried to the roadside of the imperial traveller, to wait on her, in costumes delivered to them by the government, and to personate the inhabitants of show villages which had been erected in the background. These sham villages are typical.

Still we can believe that many persons rushed to see the present emperor when he travelled through France, before he made himself emperor, because they really believed that which

---

[1] Mr. Chevalier.

had been so often repeated—that Louis Napoleon "had saved society and civilization." Now, this is exactly an idea which belongs to the order that has been indicated.

It is in the first place founded upon the belief that if civilization perishes in France, it is necessarily lost for the entire world. It would certainly produce a very serious shock; but the French idea of one leading nation is an anachronism. It belongs to ancient times; the French easily fall into this error, because Paris really leads France. Civilization, however, would not be wholly lost even for France, should Paris be destroyed; or, if it were so, what must we think of the whole country?

Secondly, those who assert that Napoleon III. saved society, mean, it must be supposed, that had he not taken the reins of absolute power, the socialists would have destroyed property, industry and individuality.

The fear which the socialists have inspired must have been very great, and doubtless the power in every individual of doing mischief is immense, compared to that of doing good. Even an insect can cause a leak to a man-of-war; but to say that a single man—such a man and by such means—has been the savior of society, is at once so monstrous an exaggeration, and such an avowal of inability to act, and want of self-reliance, that this hyperbole, if it be not altogether an error, would have led to no such results with any nation less accustomed to centralism, absolutism, and an absorbing government. These were necessary to make a nation so rapidly, and apparently with so much good-humor, bend to all the exorbitant and insulting demands of absolutism, to which, unfortunately at this moment, the French nation seems to bow with a peculiar grace.

CHAPTER XXXV.

VOX POPULI VOX DEI.

THE maxim Vox Populi Vox Dei is so closely connected with the subjects which we have been examining, and it is so often quoted on grave political occasions, that it appears to me proper to conclude this work with an inquiry into the validity of this stately saying. Its poetic boldness and epigrammatic finish, its Latin and lapidary formulation, and its apparent connection of a patriotic love of the people with religious fervor, give it an air of authority and almost of sacredness. Yet history, as well as our own times, show us that everything depends upon the question who are "the people," and that even if we have fairly ascertained the legitimate sense of this great yet abused term, we frequently find that their voice is anything rather than the voice of God.

If the term people is used for a clamoring crowd, which is not even a constituted part of an organic whole, we would be still more fatally misled by taking the clamor for the voice of the deity. We shall arrive, then, at this conclusion, that in no case can we use the maxim as a test, for, even if we call the people's voice the voice of God in those cases in which the people demand that which is right, we must first know that they do so before we could call it the voice of God. It is no guiding authority; it can sanction nothing.

" The chief priests, and the rulers, and the people," cried out all at once, " Crucify him, crucify him !"[1] Were then "the rulers and the people" not the populus? their voice was assuredly not the vox Dei in this case? If populus

---

[1] St. Luke, 23.

(405)

means the constituted people speaking through the organs and in the forms of law, the case of Socrates arises at once in our mind. It was the people of Athens, speaking by their constituted authorities, that bade him drink the hemlock ; yet it would be blasphemy to say that it was the voice of God that spoke in this case through the mouth of the Athenians. Was it the voice of the people, and, through it, the voice of God, which demanded the sway of the guillotine in the first French revolution? Or was it the voice of God which made itself heard in 1848, when all punishment of death for political offences was abolished in France? Or is it the voice of God which through " the elect one of the people" demanded the re-establishment of capital punishment for high political offences? Or is it the voice of God that used so indefinite a term in law as that of political offences?

There are, indeed, periods in history in which, centuries after, it would seem as if an impulse from on high had been given to whole masses, or to the leading minds of leading classes, in order to bring about some comprehensive changes. That remarkable age of maritime discovery which has influenced the whole succeeding history of civilization and the entire progress of our kind, would seem at first glance, and to many, even after a careful study of all its elements, to have received its motion and action from a breath not of human breathing. No person, however, living at that period would have been authorized to call the wide-spread love of maritime adventure the voice of God, merely because it was widely diffused. Impulsive movements of greater extent and intensity have been movements of error, passion, and crime. It must be observed that the thorough historian often acts in these cases as the natural philosopher who finds connection, causes and effects where former ages thought they recognized direct and detached manifestations or interpositions of a superior power, and not the greater attribute of admitting variety under eternal laws and unchanging principles.

When the whole of Europe was animated by one united longing to conquer the holy land, it appeared undoubtedly to the crusaders that the voice of the people was the voice of God. It seemed, indeed, as if an afflatus numinis breathed over the European land. Those, however, who now believe that the crusades were a great injury to Europe—and there are such—do not perceive the voice of God in this vast movement. They will perhaps maintain that it was not the people who felt this surprising impulse, but the chivalry, who by their unceasing petty feuds had developed a martial restlessness which began to lack food, and thus engaged in distant enterprises, stimulated by the highly sacerdotal character which pervaded that age. To find out, then, whether it was the vox populi, would first require to find out whether it was the vox Dei, and, consequently, we are no better off with the maxim than without it.[1]

I am under the impression that the famous maxim first came into use in the middle ages, at a contested episcopal election,[2]

---

[1] Sir Wm. Hamilton begins the third paragraph, page 770, of The Works of Thomas Reid on the Universality of the Philosophy of Common Sense, in this way:

"1.—Hesiod thus terminates his Works and Days:

$Φ_{ήμη}$ δ'οὔποτε πάμπαν ἀπόλλιται ἥι τινα πολλοὶ
Λαοὶ φημίζουσι. Θεὸς νύ τις ἐστι καὶ αμτή.

"The Word proclaimed by the concordant voice
Of mankind fails not; for in Man speaks God."

"Hence the adage?—Vox Populi, vox Dei."

It is well the learned sage added the query, for, historically at least, the V. P. V. D., certainly does not come from Hesiod.

[2] For many years I was under the impression that I had found this fact when studying the times of Abelard; but I must confess that all my attempts to recover it, when I came to write on this subject, have been fruitless. Sanderson, whom Mr. Hallam calls the most distinguished English casuist, treats of the maxim in his work De Conscientia. I copy from the London Notes and Queries, Nov. 19, 1853, the following passage, which was elicited by the preceding portion of this note:

"The earliest known instances of the use of the saying are, by William of Malmesbury, who, speaking of Odo yielding his consent to be Archbishop of Canterbury, A.D. 920, says Recogitans illud Proverbium,

when the people, by apparent acclamation, having elected one person, another aspirant believed he had a better right to the episcopate on different grounds or a different popular acclamation. That the maxim has a decidedly medieval character no one familiar with that age will doubt. The middle ages are, indeed, characterized by the fact that all Europe was parcelled out, not in states, but under a political *system* of graduated and *encapsulated* allegiance; but where this system failed to reach a sphere with its many ramifications, the same age bore a conclamatory character, especially in the earliest times. When a king was elected it was by conclamation. The earliest bishops of Rome were elected or confirmed by conclamation of the Roman people. Elections by conclamation always indicate a rude or deficiently organized state of things; and it is the same whether this want of organization be the effect of primitive rudeness or of relapse. Now the maxim we are considering has a strongly conclamatory character, and to apply it to our modern affairs is degrading rather than elevating them.

How shall we ascertain, in modern times, whether anything be the voice of the people? and next, whether that voice be the voice of God, so that it may command respect? For, unless we can do this, the whole maxim amounts to no more than a poetic sentence expressing the opinion of an individual, but no rule, no canon.

Is it unanimity that indicates the voice of the people? Unanimity in this case can mean only a very large majority. But even unanimity itself is far from indicating the voice of God. Unanimity is commanding only when it is the result of digested and organic public opinion, and even then, we know perfectly well that it may be erroneous and consequently not the voice

---

·*Vox Populi, vox Dei;*' and by Walter Reynolds, Archbishop of Canterbury, who, as we learn from Walsingham, took it as his text for the sermon which he preached when Edward III. was called to the throne, from which the people had pulled down Edward II. The reader is farther referred to Mr. G. Cornwall Lewis's Essay on the Influence of Authority in Matters of Opinion, (pp. 172, 173, and the accompanying notes,) for some interesting remarks upon it."

of God, but simply the best opinion at which erring and sinful men at the time are able to arrive.

Mr. Say informs us that when the first cotton manufactures were introduced into France, petitions from all the incorporated large towns, from merchants and silk weavers, were sent to Paris, clamoring in vehement terms against the "ungodly calico prints." Rouen, now the busiest of all the French cotton manufacturing places, was among the foremost, and the petition of the united three corporations of Amiens ended thus: "To conclude, it is enough for the eternal prohibition of the use of printed calicoes, that the whole kingdom is chilled with horror at the news of their proposed toleration. Vox populi vox Dei." This might well be considered as sufficient to prevent every reflecting man from using the maxim. We now know that the cotton tissue has become one of the greatest blessings of our race, giving comfort, health and respectability to entire masses of men formerly doomed to tatters, filth, and its fearful concomitants, typhus and vice, and we know too that cotton manufacture is one of the most lucrative branches of French industry.

Unanimity of itself proves nothing worth being proved for our purpose. In considering unanimity, the first subject that presents itself to us is that remarkable phenomenon called Fashion—a phenomenon well-nigh calculated to baffle the most searching mind, and which has never received the attention it deserves at the hands of the philosopher, in every point of view, whether psychological, moral, economical or political. Unassisted by any public power,[1] by the leading minds of the age, by religion, literature or any concerted action, it nevertheless rules with unbending authority, often in spite of health, comfort and taste, and it exacts tributes such as no sultan or legislature can levy. While it often spreads ruin among producers and consumers, it is always sure to reach the most absolute czar and subject his taste. Though the head may wear a

---

[1] It may, however, be mentioned as a historical fact, that even fashion has been shrewdly drawn within the sphere of public action and influence, by the Emperor Napoleon III., through his graceful empress.

crown, Fashion puts her shears to its hair, if she has a mind
to do so. Far more powerful than international law, which
only rules between nations, she brings innumerable nations
into one fold, and that frequently the fold of acknowledged
folly. How can we explain this stupendous phenomenon? It
is not necessary to do so here. The fact, however, must be
acknowledged. It is the most remarkable instance of unanimity, but will any one say that Fashion is a vox Dei? The
very question would be irreverent were it not candidly made
in a philosophical spirit.

Nor is the dominion of fashion restricted to dress and furniture, nor to the palate and minor intercourse. Bitter as the
remark may sound, it is nevertheless true that there are countries void of institutions, where a periodical on political fashions
might be published, with the same variety of matter as the
Petit Courrier des Dames.

There was a fearful unanimity all over Europe in the sanguinary and protracted period of witch-trials, joined in by
churchmen and laymen, protestant and catholic, Teuton, Celt,
and Sclavonic, learned and illiterate. If the fallacious and
in some respects absurd "Quod ab omnibus, semper, ubique,"
ever seemed to find an application, it was in the witch-trial
from the earliest ages of history, and in all countries down
to the time when very gradually it ceased to be ab omnibus,
semper, ubique. But was Sprenger's sad Malleus Maleficarum
on that account the voice of God?[1] What fearful fanati-

---

[1] It has been calculated that several millions of human beings have
been sacrificed by witch-trials in modern times. An article in the Westminster Review, January, 1859, shows that the belief in witches is yet
causing occasional disorder and crime in England. Indeed, if the famous
Quod omnibus, etc., could ever be applied to any subject, it is to this.
It has existed and still exists in all the corners of the earth, and with
tribes wholly insulated. There has been always whipping in the armies,
until Always ceased; there was always slavery until it ceased; a multitude of gods was always worshipped; ghosts were always believed in;
oracles were always believed in; to take interest from the borrower was
always declared a crime; it was always believed that the earth is flat or
that the sun moves; it was always believed that Jews poisoned the wells,

cisms have not swept over whole countries with deplorable unanimity ! The Romans were unanimous enough when they slaughtered the worshippers of that God whose authority is invoked to dignify the voice of men in the fallacious maxim. If the voice of the people were the voice of God, the voice of the people ought not only to be unchangeable, but there ought to be one people only. Two nations frequently clamor for war, and both, under the motto Vox populi vox Dei, draw the sword against each other.

A remarkable degree of unanimity prevails in all those periods of excited commercial speculation, such as under Law in France, the South Sea scheme in England, the railway

---

or that some general distemper whose causes could not be explained, arose from poisoned wells; people always believed that governments must answer for famines; gold was always believed to have some mysterious power, physical as well as psychological; the stars were always believed to influence the character of individuals; kings were always believed to have a peculiar healing power; it was always believed that wealth consists in money, and that therefore as one country gets rich, others must needs get poorer, or that in the same degree as one man increases his wealth so he deprives others of it; it was always believed that the security of the state requires the masses to be ground down; it was always believed that the eastern continent was all the land of the earth, and the suspicion that there might be another continent was even declared heretical; it was always believed that great cleanliness was not conducive to the health of children; it was always believed that indicted persons ought to be tortured, if they would not confess otherwise; it was always believed that persons accused of treason or witchcraft, ought not, on account of the "heinousness of their crimes," to have that protection which was granted to other indicted prisoners—until the Always and Everywhere ceased. These errors, most of which have caused commotions, risings and bloodshed, were certainly the opinion of the people; they were the opinion of our whole race, but assuredly not the vox Dei.

Wherever a Semper et ubique exists, such as it is, and if not artificially produced, there must be some adequate reason for it, but it need not be a good one, or founded in truth. When the semper et ubique is urged, in order to prove a thing, it has already ceased to be semper, etc. On the other hand, the maxim ought indeed to prevail unless there is good reason for the contrary opinion.

mania we have seen in the same country, or the commercial madness in our land some fifteen years ago.

If we carefully view the subject of unanimity, we shall find that in the cases in which vast action takes place, by impelled masses—and it is in these cases that the maxim is invoked— error is as frequently the basis as truth. It is panic, fanaticism, revenge, lust of gain, and hatred of races that produce most of the sudden and comprehensive impulses. Truth travels slowly. Indeed all essential progress is typified in the twelve humble men that followed Christ. The voice of God was not then the voice of the people. What the ancients said of the avenging gods, that they are shod with wool,[1] is true of great ideas in history. They approach softly. Great truths always dwell a long time with small minorities, and the real voice of God is often that which rises above the masses, not that which follows them.

But the difficulty of fixing the meaning of this saying is not restricted to that of ascertaining what is the voice of God. It is equally difficult to find out what is the voice of the people. If by the voice of the people be meant, as was stated before, the organically evolved opinion of a people, we do not stand in need of the saying. We know we ought to obey the laws of the land. If by the voice of the people be meant the result of universal suffrage without institutions, and especially in a large country with a powerful executive, not permitting even preparatory discussion, it is an empty phrase; it is deception, or it may be the effect of vehement yet transitory excitement, or of a political fashion. The same is true when the clamoring expression of many is taken for the voice of the whole people.[2]

In politics as in other spheres it is never the loudest who are the wisest, though they are those who are heard and whom flatterers pretend to treat as the people and as the utterers of

---

[1] Dii laneos habent pedes.

[2] The doctrine Vox Populi Vox Dei, is capable of development. In November, 1857, some female, addressing a crowd in the city of New York, said: The voice of the working men is the voice of God.

the voice of God. Governments frequently rule nations as some of the French theatres are ruled. Paid applauders, called claqueurs, force many a piece through a long series of performances, and it is these very governments of claqueurs that resort most frequently to the Vox populi vox Dei. Yet Mademoiselle Mars, one of the most distinguished French actresses that has ever played, was in the habit of saying, How much better we would play if we cared less for applause!

Another instance, showing that no dependence can be placed upon the maxim, is that of proverbs. They are doubtless the voice of the people, and many of them contain much wisdom, but there are also many in favor of our worst passions and meanest dispositions.

The following rhymes are given by Mr. Trench in his Lessons in Proverbs, as " of an old poet."

> " The people's voice the voice of God we call;
> And what are Proverbs but the people's voice?
> Coined first and current made by public choice,
> Then sure they must have weight and truth withal."[1]

A very large class of proverbs is directed against peasants and the laboring classes; against women, lawyers, physicians —indeed against all the staple topics of former satire.

Whoever wishes to give great importance to a general movement, or sincerely believes it to be truly noble, calls it the voice of God. Pope Pius IX., in his proclamation of the 30th of March, 1848, says, in speaking of the general and enthusiastic movement of the Italians for Italy and Independence: " Woe to him who does not discern the Vox Dei in this blast," etc. It cannot be supposed that the pope now considers that blast to have been the Vox Dei.

---

[1] Which might lead to this syllogism:
Vox Populi Vox Dei,
Proverbs are the voice of the people,
Hence proverbs are the voice of God;
There are many wicked proverbs,
Ergo, etc. etc.

Sometimes the maxim is doubtless used in good faith, as the French at times use, without reserve, that favorite expression of theirs : The instinct of the masses; but generally I think Vox populi vox Dei is used either hypocritically or when people have misgivings that all may not be right, pretty much in the same manner as persons say that an argument is unanswerable, when they have a strong foreboding that it may be found very answerable.

Vox populi vox Dei has never been used in France so frequently as after the second of December, yet there are unquestionably thousands in that country who would find their religious convictions much bewildered, if they were obliged to believe that it was the voice of God which spoke through ballot boxes under the menagement of the most centralized executive in existence; and that the voice of the Deity requires a thousand intrigues among men for its utterance.

The doctrine Vox populi vox Dei is essentially unrepublican, as the doctrine that the people may do what they list under the constitution, above the constitution, and against the constitution, is an open avowal of disbelief in self-government.

The true friend of freedom does not wish to be insulted by the supposition that he believes each human individual an erring man, and that nevertheless the united clamor of erring men has a character of divinity about it; nor does he desire to be told that the voice of the people, though legitimately and institutionally proclaimed and justly commanding respect and obedience, is divine on that account. He knows that the majority may err, and that he has the right and often the duty to use his whole energy to convince them of their error, and lawfully to bring about a different set of laws. The true and stanch republican wants liberty, but no deification either of himself or others; he wants a firmly built self-government and noble institutions, but no absolutism of any sort—none to practise on others, and none to be practised on himself. He is too proud for the Vox populi vox Dei. He wants no divine right of the people, for he knows very well that it means nothing but the despotic power of insinuating leaders.

He wants the real rule of the people, that is, the institutionally organized country, which distinguishes it from the mere mob. For a mob is an unorganic multitude, with a general impulse of action.[1] Woe to the country in which political hypocrisy first calls the people almighty, then teaches that the voice of the people is divine, then pretends to take a mere clamor for the true voice of the people, and lastly gets up the desired clamor. The consequences are fearful and invariably unfitting for liberty.

Whatever meaning men may choose, then, to give to Vox populi vox Dei, in other spheres, or, if applied to the long tenor of the history of a people, in active politics and in the province of practical liberty, it either implies political levity, which is one of the most mordant corrosives of liberty, or else it is a political heresy, as much so as Vox regis vox Dei would be. If it be meant to convey the idea that the people can do no wrong, it is as grievous an untruth as would be conveyed by the maxim, the king can do no wrong, if it really were meant to be taken literally.

However indistinct the meaning of the maxim may be, the idea intended to be conveyed and the imposing character of the saying, have, nevertheless, contributed to produce in some countries a general inability to remain in the opposition—that necessary element of civil liberty. A degree of shame seems there to be attached to a person that does not swim with the broad stream. No matter what flagrant contradictions may take place, or however sudden the changes may be, there seems to exist in every one a feeling of discomfort, until he has joined the general current. To differ from the dominant party or the ruling majority, appears almost like daring to contend with a deity, or a mysterious, yet irrevocable destiny. To dissent is deemed to be malcontent; it seems more than rebellious, it seems traitorous; and this feeling becomes ultimately so general, that it seizes the dissenting individuals themselves. They become ashamed, and mingle with the rest. Individuality is

---

[1] The subject of Mobs has been enlarged upon in the Political Ethics.

destroyed, manly character degenerates, and the salutary effect of parties is forfeited. He that clings to his conviction is put in ban as unnational, and as an enemy to the people. Then arises a man of personal popularity. He ruins the institutions; he bears down everything before him; yet he receives the popular acclaim, and the voice of the people being the voice of God, it is deemed equally unnational and unpatriotic to oppose him.[1]

---

[1] The Paris journal, Le Pays, informed the public at the time the present empire was established, that it had been raised to the dignity of an official paper to the imperial government. The announcement is made in that proclamatory and sententious style so much relished by the French, and in one of the paragraphs, standing by itself, it offers with a naïveté, which surpasses anything the writer can remember, this comforting assurance:

"In approaching power more closely, we shall not cease to have opinions."

The fact that it is the "journal of the empire," that the whole article is short, that every sentence seems to be well weighed by the editor, a writer of note, and that the declaration was made on a very important occasion, give to the whole a character which entitles us to take it as something more than a passing newspaper sentence.

When the maxim Vox populi vox Dei prevails, and governments change in rapid succession, it is a necessary result that there are hosts of turncoats. The French published in 1826, or thereabouts, a bitter satire on this herd of politicians, consisting of a work called Dictionnaire des Girouettes—literally translated, Dictionary of Weathercocks; but Anglicized, Dictionary of Turncoats. The names which headed the biographies in the book were succeeded by a number of symbolical weathercocks, equal to the number of political somersets of which the respective persons could boast. There was a fearful row of hieroglyphical vanes after some names. But in reading this droll and bitter account relating to a foreign nation, let us not forget St. Luke, vi. 41.

APPENDIX.

APPENDIX I.

A PAPER ON ELECTIONS, ELECTION STATISTICS AND GENERAL
VOTES OF YES OR NO.

CONSCIENTIOUS and well informed men may possibly differ in
opinion as to the question whether Cromwell was at any time the
freely accepted ruler of the English people; whether he was gladly
supported by the people at large and readily acquiesced in by a
small minority; whether he imposed himself upon the country by
the army and allayed opposition by the wisdom of his statesmanship; or whether he chiefly ruled by armed fanaticism. But it
may be asserted without hesitation, that there is neither Englishman nor American, substantially acquainted with elections, whose
judgment on this subject could be influenced in any degree, one
way or the other, were he informed that Cromwell had received
an overwhelming majority of votes all over England confirming
him in his absolutism, after he had passed his famous act of 1656,
by which he divided the British territory into twelve districts, each
presided over by a major-general with absolute power over the
inhabitants, all existing laws to the contrary notwithstanding.
There is not an American or Englishman, I think, who believes
that such a confirmatory vote could have added to his right, or
that, had such an event taken place, it could have kept Richard
Cromwell on the protectorial throne, or retarded the return of
Charles the Second, a single day. And the larger the majority for
Cromwell should have been, the more we would now consider it as
a proof of the activity exerted by the major-generals indeed, both
in pressing and compressing, but no one of us would connect it in
any way with a presumed popularity of Cromwell, or consider it
as an index of the opinion which the people at large entertained
of his repeated making and unmaking of parliaments.

A real or pretended result of such ex post facto votes may have
a certain proclamatory value; it may be convenient to point to it

(419)

and decline all farther discussion; "The People's Elect" may be a welcome formula for ribboned orators, expectant poets, or adaptive editors; but there is no intrinsic value in it. Votes of this sort have no meaning for the historian, at least so far as the subject voted on is concerned, and they have a melancholy meaning for the contemporary patriot. There seems to be a Nemesis eagerly watching these votes, and each time proving, by events succeeding shortly after, how hollow they were at the time.

An election,[1] which takes place to pass judgment on a series of acts of a person, or to decide on the adoption or rejection of a fundamental law, can have no value whatever, if the following conditions are not fulfilled :

1. The question must have been fairly before the people for a period sufficiently long to discuss the matter thoroughly, and under circumstances to allow a free discussion. Neither the police restrictions of government, nor the riotous procedures of mobs, nor the tyranny of associations ought to prevent the formation of a well-sifted and duly modified average public opinion. The liberty of the press, therefore, is a conditio sine qua non. If this be not the case, a mere general opinion of the moment, a panic on the one hand, or a maddened gratitude, for real or imaginary benefits, of a multitude excited for the day or the period, may hastily and unrighteously settle the fate of generations to come, and passion, fear or vainglory may decide that which ought to be settled by the largest and freest exchange of opinions and the broadest reciprocal modification of interests. It requires time for a great subject to present itself in all the aspects in which it ought to be viewed and examined, and for a great public opinion to form itself—the more time, the vaster the subject. All the laws regulating the formation of opinion in the individual apply with greater force to the formation of public opinion.

It is especially necessary that the army be in abeyance, as it were, with reference to all subjects and movements appertaining to the question at issue. The English law requires the removal of the garrison from every place where a common election for parliament is going on. Much more necessary is the total neu-

---

[1] There is no other term in our language, although it is obvious that these processes cannot be properly called elections. Votings would be more correct.

trality of the army in an election of the sort of which we now treat.

2. The election must be carried on by well organized election institutions, extending over small districts, because in that case alone can a really general voting be secured.

3. All elections must be superintended by election judges and officers independent of the executive or any other organized or unorganized power of government. The indecency as well as the absurdity and immorality of government recommending what is to be voted ought never to be permitted.

4. The election returns ought to be made so that they are not subject to any falsification. They must not be fingered by the government officers. This is especially important if the country labors under a stringent centralism in which every civil officer avowedly acknowledges, and is, according to command, bound to acknowledge, no principle or law above the direct command of his immediate superior; in which the host of executive, administrative, police and semi-military officers form a compact body receiving its impulse of action exclusively from one centre; in which publicity is no pervading element of acts relating to the public interest; and in which no habits have yet been formed nor customs settled concerning the whole comprehensive election business.

5. He, or that power, which passes under judgment, ought to be in a position that, should the judgment turn against him, he can be believed to abide by the judgment. If not, the whole is nothing but a farce.

6. There must be really two things to choose between. If this is not the case, the whole procedure amounts to no more than what we familiarly call "Hobson's choice," on a gigantic scale.

If there be any reader who should object to this rule that, since we speak of elections, it is evident that there must be two things at least to select from, and that therefore this rule borders on the ridiculous, I would only say that history shows people have not always adopted it. There may be something ridiculous somewhere, but it is not in the rule. It would be ridiculous to lay down the rule that, if people invite others to dinner, there ought to be something to eat, only so long as invitations to empty tables are assumed not actually to have taken place.

7. The power claiming the apparent judgment ought not to
have committed a criminal act, and then, as the law expresses it,
insist on deriving benefit from its own wrong. Nor ought he,
who pretends to present himself for judgment, stand in the position of a trustee, disputing the validity of the power by which
nevertheless he has acted, and under which he has accepted
benefits. This is a common rule in all law, because it is common
sense, and it is for the same reason a sound rule in politics.[1]

In addition to these rules, I may remind the reader of a fundamental truth concerning all elections and votes—a truth which
is simply prescribed by common sense, and yet has often been set
aside. A majority having voted for a subject is of no earthly
value, unless the subject be of such a character that there can be,
at the time, a public opinion about it. If there were, in a company of men, different opinions as to the time of the day, we cannot solve the difficulty by putting the question : "All who are in
favor of its being now six o'clock will say Aye; those who are of
the contrary opinion will say No."[2] No majority of ever so vast
a country can decide for me the chloroform question, or whether
captain Ericsson's steam generator be or be not practical. And
no majority, no matter how overwhelming, can be worth anything
if there be not, in addition to a proper apparatus of evolving
public opinion, of which we have spoken already, also one by
which the true majority can be ascertained. It is an utter and
constantly recurring error into which those that are unacquainted
with the nature and the economy of liberty fall, to believe that
what liberty requires is the ascertainment of incoherent votes on
every question sprung upon society separately and incoherently.
A French paper recently said that under certain circumstances
the emperor Napoleon the Third would put the question of war

---

[1] This has been well pointed out in the case of Louis Napoleon, by the
Hon. A. P. Butler, United States senator for South Carolina.

[2] In the time of the late French so called republic, it occurred in the little commune Saint-André (department de Nord,) that in a new church one
of three altars remained without a patron saint. There were three candidates: St. Joseph, St. Roch and St. Cecilia. The priest believed that the
question had best be left to the people. All voted, even women and children
of discretion. St. Cecilia carried the election by a majority of seventeen
votes. The old Icelanders sometimes decided by vote whether Christ or
the old gods should be worshipped.

to the universal suffrage of France. Of course I do not believe in the possibility of such an act, but I have mentioned the statement as an illustration. How can the French people at large decide on a question of war or peace, if France cannot debate the matter, cannot reflect on it? and what can a majority of votes on so grave a question mean, when the whole management of the vote, from first to last, is in the hands of that strongly concentrated government which puts the question?

I return to the seven requisites which I have pointed out.

If any one of these conditions be omitted, the whole election or voting is vitiated, and can in no way be depended upon. It will go with every experienced and truthful citizen, and pass with every serious historian, for nothing more than, possibly, for skilfully arranged deceptions of the unwary and very inexperienced. It is a question, indeed, whether these conditions can be frequently fulfilled, and whether it be possible in the nature of things to fulfil them at all, or any of them, in uninstitutional countries— in large countries enmeshed like a huge being by the close network of a bureaucratic mandarinism. They must, then, be resorted to as rarely as possible. In strictly organized police governments they have no value, except for the very purpose of deceiving, or of giving an apparently more firmly-based fulcrum for the lever of the power already existing.

Every one of my readers will agree with the necessity of the condition which has been stated as the first. There is the greatest difference between an accidental or momentary general opinion, and an organically-produced, well-settled, public opinion — the same difference which exists between a " decree of acclamation," as those decrees in the first French revolution were called, which were proposed and forthwith adopted by a burst of feeling or a clamor of passions, and an extensive law which has first been discussed and rediscussed, called for and assailed in papers, pamphlets, meetings and institutions, and then, after long and patient debate, passed through the whole sifting and purposely retarding, repetitionary and revisionary parliamentary process. Real public opinion on public matters of a truly free people under an institutional government is generally the wisest master to which the freeman can bow ; general opinion is worth nothing as a political truth. It may be correct; it may be vicious, as a thousand rumors show, and public rumor is general opinion. This subject of public and merely general opinion has been largely discussed in the Political Ethics.

When Cromwell had dissolved parliament, and even dissolved the famous council of state, in spite of Bradshaw's opposition, we are informed that addresses of gratulation and thanks reached him from all parts of England, just as they were crowded upon L. N. Bonaparte after the second of December, 1851. We cannot judge whether they expressed the opinion of the majority; for in politics, as in common life, it is the noisy that are heard and make themselves observed, while the majority and more substantial people are silent and overlooked; but, for argument's sake, we will grant that those addresses to Cromwell expressed the opinions, the views, the feelings of the majority of the nation at the moment. Even in this case they expressed nothing more than the existing general feeling, not the public opinion of England, as successive events very soon proved.

To seize upon loud and demonstrative general opinion and feeling of a part of the people while compressing the public opinion of the whole, is a frequent means of successful tyranny. It was the way the first French convention frequently managed things, and Danton knew it well. He acknowledged it.

As to the second and subsequent conditions which have been enumerated, the following observations may prove of interest. Numerous and extensive inquiries, referring to the United States as well as to Europe, and some of which I propose to give to the reader, have proved to me certain instructive facts relating to the statistics of popular elections. I do not treat in this paper of the voting in assemblies of trustees, of representatives or boards.

I must also remark that I shall always use the term election for direct elections, in which the voter votes directly upon the question at issue, and not for a person who will have the ultimate right of the direct vote; either for a person or on a measure. The election of our presidents was intended to be a double election, and in form it continues to be such; for we elect electors. But it is well known that the election has long since become virtually a direct one, so far as the individual votes express the desire of the voters, because the persons voted for as electors declare beforehand for whom they shall vote in case they are made electors, and after being elected electors they do not become members of a deliberative body in which the question of the presidential election is discussed.[1]

Where the double election is introduced as an active principle, it deprives elections of much, and often of all interest, and is frequently resorted to for this very purpose, by governments which do not feel sufficiently strong to refuse the claims of the people to a share in the government, yet desire to defeat the reality of such a share.

The following, then, are the positions which experience seems fully to bear out:

The more exclusive the privilege of voting is, the smaller is the number of qualified voters who abstain from voting; and the largest number of abstinents occurs where universal suffrage is freely left to itself, and not interfered with by the executive.

The smaller the number of qualified voters, the smaller is also the number of abstinents.

So soon as the number of qualified voters exceeds five or six hundred, the number of abstinents will be at least twenty-five per centum.

The larger the number of qualified voters, voting upon the same

---

[1] This knowledge of the vote which an elector will give does of course not affect the result. Each elector represents a majority and a minority, but his vote can only be cast for one candidate. Nevertheless, that which is called the popular vote indicates a proportion between the presidential candidates very different from that which appears from the official votes of the electors. For instance, the popular vote at the last presidential election stood:

For Pierce	.	.	.	.	.	.	1,504,471
" Scott	.	.	.	.	.	.	1,283,174
" Hale	.	.	.	.	.	.	148,851

and the votes of the electors stood

For Pierce	.	.	.	.	.	.	254
" Scott	.	.	.	.	.	.	42

So that the popular vote stood:
Pierce to Scott as 132 to 100.
But the votes of the electors:
Pierce to Scott as 605 to 100.

Such men as Benton, M'Duffie, Calhoun, Huger, Pickins, of N. Carolina, have recorded their opinion in favor of giving the election of the president to the people.

question or persons, and under one and the same electoral system, the larger is also the number of abstinents.

The larger the area over which one and the same election or voting extends, the larger is the proportion of abstainers.

When there are three fairly supported candidates, the total number of votes polled is larger than when there are but two candidates, all other things being equal.

The whole number of polled votes, compared to the number of qualified voters, does not necessarily indicate the interest a community may take in a measure or person. Whenever people feel perfectly sure of the issue, there are many who abstain because their votes will not defeat the opponent ; and many others abstain, because their candidate will be elected at any rate.

If the number of qualified voters (voting exactly upon the same question or person) exceeds several thousands, one-half of it is generally a fair number for the actual voters ; two-thirds show an animated state of things, and three-fourths are evidence of great excitement. It will be observed that the words : Voting exactly upon the same question or person—are a necessary qualification of these positions. Although an election all over England may turn upon free trade or protection, yet, if it be a parliamentary election, so that these questions appear only represented in the respective candidates, it is clear that this would not be an election extending over the area of England, in the sense in which the term is taken here, or in which we take it when we speak of our presidential election.

Voting upon men generally draws out more votes than voting upon measures themselves.

Popular votes upon measures to be expressed by *yes* or *no* are wholly fallacious, unless this vote be the last act of a long and organic process ; for instance, if a new constitution has been prepared by a variety of successive acts, and is ultimately laid before the people with the question, Will you, or will you not have it ?

Popular votes in a country with an ample bureaucracy of a centralized government, on questions concerning measures or persons in which the government takes a deep interest, and by elections the primary arrangements of which are under the direction of the government, that is, under the executive, must always be received with great suspicion. It is a fact well worthy of remembrance, that the French people have never voted *no*, when a question similar to that which was settled, as it is called, by the election of December, 1851, was placed before them. In the year 1793, in the years III., VIII. and XIII. similar appeals were made, and the answer was always *yes*, by majorities even greater than that on which Louis Napoleon Bonaparte rests his absolutism. When a senatus consùltum raised Napoleon the First to the imperial dignity, and the people were appealed to, there were in the city of Paris 70 noes and 120,947 ayes, and in all France 2,500 noes against 3,572,329 ayes. A vote of *yes* or *no* becomes especially unmeaning when the executive seizes the power by a military conspiracy, and then pretends to ask the people whether they approve of the act or not.

From the best authorities on the Athenian government, for instance Boeckh's Political Economy of Athens, and Tittman's Political Constitutions of Greece, under the head of Ostracism, we see that the common vote, polled by the Athenians, was about 5,000 (Thucydides viii. 72) out of from 20,000 to 25,000 qualified voters. Six thousand votes were considered the largest amount. They were required, therefore, for extraordinary cases, such as ostracism, or for anything that was against established law, or related to individuals only. Six thousand Athenian votes thus practically corresponded to our two-thirds of votes requisite for some peculiar cases, purposely removed beyond the pale of a simple majority, that is at least one more than one-half of the voters. Here, then, we have one-fourth of qualified voters, usually voting, although the voting took place in one and the same city by voters the great majority of whom lived in the city.

Some writers have doubted whether six thousand votes upon the whole, were necessary for ostracism and other peculiar cases, or six thousand votes in favor of the measure. I have no doubt that the first was the case. Plutarch distinctly says that one of the persons proposed was always ostracized, provided six thousand votes had been cast. (Aristides i. 7.) The same passage seems to prove that, if six thousand votes, altogether, had been cast, he who had the plurality of votes was banished; for, there were frequently several persons proposed for ostracism, or citizens knew that they were prominent, and therefore liable to fall within the ostracophory, and tried to prove that they did not possess the feared influence. Ostracism was a purely political institution, resorted to by democratic absolutism to clip prominences, and keep the hedge on a level. It was no punishment, and until Hyperbolus, a low fellow, was ostracised, it added to the reputation of a citizen.

That there were many abstainers from voting in Athens, we know from the fact that on the one hand the lexiarchi sent their toxotes before them to mark with red-powdered cords the white garments of those who tarried, so that the thirty judges, presided over by the lexiarchi, might properly fine them. In this, then, the Athenians resembled the early inhabitants of New England, who punished abstaining from voting or *neglecting to send a written vote.*[1]

On the other hand, we know that every Athenian of lawful age (viz. twenty or eighteen) received three oboli for attending a popular assembly. This reward was called ecclesiasticon.

Why there should have been at Athens so many more abstainers than generally in modern times, may be explained, probably, on the ground that many citizens were habitually absent as soldiers, and that Athens was a direct, untempered democracy. Where the democratic absolutism visibly appears every day in the market, people get tired of it. Besides, the reason which frequently induces so many of our best people to abstain from voting, the unwillingness to leave business, must have operated very strongly in Athens, when voting was so frequent and common. Let us imagine Boston or New York as an unmitigated democratic city-state, calling every other day for the meeting of the citizens; does any one believe that the most constant voters would come from the workshops and the ship-wharves rather than from the tippling shops and filthy lanes of vice?

I have stated already that I have directed my inquiries to election statistics for many years, and over a very large space. The reader will admit that I can give a few instances only.

In the year 1834, there were in France no more than 171,015 electors; yet 129,211 only were polled at the different electoral colleges, that is only 75 out of 100 qualified voters availed themselves of their privilege. So there were in 1837 in the same coun-

---

[1] See the Laws of New Plymouth, published by Authority, Boston, 1836, pp. 41 and 128.

try 198,836 qualified voters, and 151,720 votes were polled, which makes 76 of 100.

It will be remembered how small a number of citizens compared to the whole population were entitled to vote. The number of qualified voters at each electoral college was very restricted, and the voters formed a privileged class, compared to the other citizens.

The January number of the Edinburgh Review of 1852 contains a list of sixty-four English election districts, with the numbers of registered or qualified voters, and of the actually polled votes in each, at the last general election. The districts, whose qualified voters amount to less than one thousand, have been separated by me from those which possess more than one thousand. The average number of voters of the first class were 500, and 25 per centum on an average abstained from voting. The average number of qualified voters of the other class was between 2,000 and 3,000, and of them 42 per centum abstained. So that, if there be about 500 voters, only 75 in a hundred go to the poll; if there be about 2,500, only 58 in a hundred do so.

This is the more striking if it be considered that one thousand entitled voters is after all a very small number compared to those to which we are accustomed, and that far the greater part of the elections given in the mentioned table are town elections or elections with the most easily accessible polls.

After the chief part of this paper had been written, a very striking fact corroborated the results at which I had arrived. The Edinburgh Review for October, 1852, contains an article on Representative Reform, in which there is "A Table showing the Number of Counties and Boroughs in England, Wales and Scotland, in which Contested Elections have taken place in the year 1852." Where an election afterwards contested takes place, it will be allowed that generally there must be great excitement. All voters are brought up over whom the candidates or their agents have any influence. Yet it appears from this table "that the registered voters in all the contested places reached 507,192, while those who recorded their votes did not exceed 312,289, or about 60 per cent. of the whole." This is very remarkable, for out of 175 places or counties, whose elections were contested, 46 only numbered 3,000 qualified voters or more.

The whole election to which all these statistics refer was that between the adherents to the administration of Earl Derby, and those who considered it an incumbrance to the country. The contest was between Free Trade and Protection, and, I suppose, the English would plainly call it an excited election.

I pass over to instances not less striking, belonging to our own country.

According to detailed official documents, giving the number of qualified voters in every township in Massachusetts, and the number of votes actually polled during the election of the governor of that state in 1851, an election of unusual excitement, there were 182,542 persons entitled to vote, and 131,187 votes actually received. This gives less than three out of four qualified voters, or less than 75 in a hundred. If we consider that Massachusetts is no extensive country; that it is more densely peopled than France, having 127.40 inhabitants to the square mile, while France has only about 125; that the roads are good and numerous; that the people are well trained in the whole election business; and that, as it has been stated, the excitement was very great, it furnishes us with a striking piece of evidence that the electoral barometer will hardly ever rise above 75 in a hundred.[1]

There cannot be a more deeply interesting election than that which took place in the year 1851, in South Carolina, in which the palpable question was, shall or shall not the state secede from the Union? The political existence of the state formed the issue. On that occasion 42,755 votes were polled, which, taking one-fourth of

---

[1] In Letter VIII. of Silas Steadfast (believed to have been George S. Hillard,) on the proposed change of the constitution of Massachusetts, it is said: "In point of fact, no governor of Massachusetts was ever chosen by a majority *of all the existing votes.*"

In Nov. 1853, when great excitement about the new constitution existed in Massachusetts, the vote for governor (who was voted for at the same time) stood thus:

Whig	66,759
Freesoil Democrat	85,779
National Democrat	5,470
Freesoil	29,897
Scattering	224
	138,129

which resembles closely the vote of 1851.

the white population as the number of qualified voters, would show that about two-thirds only of those who had a right to vote actually did vote, or that 66 out of a hundred went to the poll.

Connecticut, a small and densely peopled state, sent, at the very excited election of 1852, about 75 or 76 out of each hundred voters to the poll. The calculation has been made from the official election returns, and taking one-fourth of the population as entitled to vote, which I have found to be the average number, where universal suffrage exists.

These instances might be greatly multiplied from statistical materials collected by me. I may only add the proportion of abstainers from our presidential elections since 1828. I have estimated the number of qualified voters by calculating, for the election year, the white population, according to the annual increments given by Mr. Kennedy, the first superintendent of the United States Census for 1850, and dividing that number by four.[1] I have called the real voters in the table *votants*, and the qualified voters simply *voters*.[2]

---

[1] In dividing by four I reduce the number of qualified voters in the United States too much, as will appear from the following table, abstracted from the American Census of 1850, and kindly furnished me by Mr. De Bow, at present superintendent of the census:

States.	Aggregate population.	Total males 20 years of age and over.	Ratio to the whole population.
Massachusetts	994,514	280,623	3.54
Rhode Island	147,545	40,563	3.63
Connecticut	370,792	104,855	3.53
Pennsylvania	2,311,786	572,284	4.04
Ohio	1,980,329	473,501	4.18

This gives an average ratio of 3.784. But this table shows the proportion of white males of twenty years and upwards, while a person acquires the right of voting with his twenty-first year only. It will be, therefore, pretty correct, if I take one-fourth of the whole white population. In several states colored persons go to the polls. If they were counted, it would reduce the proportion of actual voters to the number of qualified voters; but I am willing to take one-fourth only.

[2] I am aware that, apparently, Votare has not been used in Low Latin for voting. Du Cange says that Votum was used in the middle ages for suffrage, but Votare for Vovere, Spondere. As it is, however, no uncommon case in the English language to have a noun and an adjective which is not derived directly from the former but from an intermediate though " miss-

Years.	White population.	Number of votes cast.	Proportion of votants to voters.
1828	10,537,378	1,160,418	0.44
1832	11,169,616	1,290,468	0.46
1836	12,117,968	1,501,298	0.50
1840	14,189,895	2,402,659	0.67
1844	15,469,287	2,702,546	0.69
1848	17,154,551	2,874,712	0.67
1852	20,027,899	2,936,896	0.58

It is necessary to take into consideration that in the whole south of the United States voting is a right of a privileged class, and that the proportion of abstainers is probably much smaller than it would be otherwise.

Against this calculation, however, so uniform in England, here and in France in former times, we have the vote of seven millions and a half for Louis Bonaparte in 1852, when France was asked whether she approved of his breaking through oath and pledge, and of his proffered despotism, annihilating not only her constitution, which indeed was more than a frail one, but all the progress she had made in representative government, all her liberties, and all her civil dignity, and submitting her fortunes and all to a ruler who, never having been a soldier, tells civilized France that the history of armies is the history of nations, that responsible ministers are nothing but incumbrances, and that France desires a government which receives its whole impulse from one man.[1]

The statement which the government of the president of France officially published regarding the election which surrendered everything to the unchecked sway of the despot was thus:

Voted Yes	7,439,216
Voted No	640,737
Annulled votes	36,820
Did not vote at all	372,599
	8,489,372

ing" verb, which would be derived from the noun, did it exist, I feel sure the reader will permit me to use the term Votant, in a language in which brevity is often considered to cover logical and etymological sins.

[1] See the preamble to the constitution proclaimed by Louis Napoleon.

Whatever may be thought of the suspiciously small number of noes, I do not believe that there is a man living who knows anything of elections, and who is ready to accept the given number of abstinents as a correct statement. According to the official number, between three and four persons only in one hundred abstained from voting, or were prevented by illness, absence from home, old age, and the like, from doing so—a number utterly incredible, and which, it must be believed, would have been allowed to appear much larger had the officials who managed the business been acquainted with the usual number of abstinents. The minister of state, Mr. Persigny, stated himself, in a circular letter to the prefects at a later period, that there were about eight millions of voters in France. This agrees pretty well with the common rule of taking about one-fourth of the whole population as the number of qualified voters where universal suffrage exists. There must then have been a great deal of manipulation within that number. This is further proved when we consider that, according to the official reports of the commissioners, whom the chief of the French state sent into the departments to see who of the political prisoners might be pardoned, many thousands were actually in prison at the time of the general election. Colonel Espinasse reports that in the departments of the Lot and Garonne, and the Eastern Pyrenees, there were 30,000 affiliated socialists, and in the department of the Hérault 60,000. In three departments alone 90,000 disaffected persons. If they voted, they must have been forced by the police to vote for the coup d'état : if they did not vote, what becomes of the given number of abstinents ? But there is another fact which shows the falsification of the statement, either by actually falsifying the numbers, or by forcing people to give the desired vote, or by both.

Algeria is not so directly under the influence of the police, nor could the statment concerning that colony be so easily falsified. Accordingly we have the following : Out of 68,000 voters (the army included) 50,000 abstained ; 5,735 voted for L. N. Bonaparte, and 6,527 against him. Eighteen thousand only seem to have voted out of 68,000, not even 29 in 100.

I think this will sufficiently show how little reliance can be placed upon such a vote in a centralized country, and how futile it is to found any right or pretension upon it. Votes, without liberty of

28

the press, have no meaning; votes without liberty of the press, and with a vast standing army, itself possessing the right to vote, and considering itself above all law, have a sinister meaning; votes, without an unshackled press, with such an army, and with a compact body of officials, whose number, with those directly depending upon them, or upon government contracts, amounts to nearly a million, have no meaning, whether he who appeals to the people says that he leaves " the fate of France in the hands of the people," or not.

This paper was written, with the exception which I have mentioned, after the vote on the coup d'état had been given. Since then, the plebiscitum, making Louis Napoleon emperor, has been added.

The vote of the people on the question: Shall, or shall not, Louis Napoleon Bonaparte assume the imperial crown ? is officially stated to have been thus:

The number of electors inscribed in the departments, is	9,843,076
The number of the land and naval forces	360,352
Total of voters	10,203,428
This number is thus distributed:	
Having voted yes	7,824,189
Having voted no	253,115
Votes void on some account or other	63,326
Abstinents	2,062,798
Total	10,203,428

This shows a very different result from the vote on the coup d'état. It gives twenty-five abstinents in a hundred; but there are other points not easily understood. Of thirty-one persons, one only voted no. This is a state of harmony to which people of the Anglican race, with all their calmer temper, we venture to say, have never yet attained. It is equally inexplicable how, of a population, which, in 1851, amounted to 35,781,628, there can be, in the year 1852, as many as 10,203,428 authorized to vote, or males above twenty-one years old. The fourth part of 35,781,628 is only 8,945,407; and, if a fourth part is correct, there would be 1,258,021 unaccounted for. Nor can we forget, here, the immense number of persons, who, according to official reports, are at any given moment in the prisons of France. These, too, must be deducted.

I add, in conclusion, the statement of a Paris paper, which gives a different account, so far as that city is concerned.

In Paris, the number of abstinents were :

In 1848, for the presidential election . . 0.25

In 1851, for the ratification of the the coup d'état, and the election of the president for ten years 0.20

In 1852, for the imperial crown . . . 0.14

Only about one-half as many abstained from voting, when the empire was to be re-established, as abstained in the excited times of the republic, when there were several candidates.[1]

I do not believe that direct money-bribery exists in France to any great extent. Universal suffrage, it would seem, would preclude the possibility. But indirect bribery, by promises of promotion, or allowing shares in profitable undertakings, and, above all, intimidation, positive or indirect, I believe to have existed in the largest possible extent. We may certainly assume that every government officer, or person connected in some way with government, is worth his four or five votes at least—which he will direct as he in turn is directed to do by his superiors, or he loses his place.[2] Then, we must take into account the influence of the

---

[1] On the 10th of December, 1848, when the first French president, for four years, was voted for :

There were polled	7,327,345
Of which: For Louis Napoleon . . .	5,434,226
For General Cavaignac . . .	1,448,107
" Ledru Rollin	376,119
" Lamartine	17,910
" Changarnier	4,700
Lost Votes	12,600

France contained, in the year 1846, 35,400,486 inhabitants; consequently, in 1848, there were about 9,000,000 of authorized voters; and 7,327,345 having voted, about 80 in 100 went to the poll, according to this statement. Yet it must be supposed that the eagerness to go to the ballot-box was, in that year, much greater than after the coup d'état.

[2] The reader cannot fail to remember here the constitution proposed by Mad. de Staël for France, after the Restoration, and which was to consist of

priests in rural communities, or of the bishops in general. They
openly exerted themselves, by word and letter, in favor of the present emperor. The influence of the prefects and sub-prefects on
all occasions of election is uniform and perfectly well known,
generally quite public, and the annoyance to which a man exposes
himself by voting a ballot not agreeing with that which has been
furnished by the government, is so great that no independence
exists at French elections, except, in a limited degree, sometimes
in Paris itself, on account of its dense and large population,
although the influence of the court and government is there also
the greatest on ordinary occasions.

---

two paragraphs only, namely, of one declaring all Frenchmen to be government officers, and of another, providing that every government officer should
have a salary.

APPENDIX II.

A PAPER ON THE ABUSE OF THE PARDONING POWER.

THIS paper was originally a report. I had been appointed by a meeting of the Friends of Prison Discipline, without being present, the chairman of a committee, which was requested to report to the next meeting on "The Pardoning Privilege and its Abuse." The following was the result of this appointment. The legislature of the State of New York did me the honor of publishing it as a document; but it was printed so incorrectly, the subject is of such vital interest to a people who desire to live under the supremacy of the law, and the abuse continues in many parts of our country to so alarming an extent, that I do not hesitate here to reproduce the paper.

The pardoning privilege consists in the authority partially or wholly to remit the penalty which, in the due and regular course of justice, has been inflicted for some offence. A pardon is always an act of frustrating that common justice which has been established by law as the best means of protection; a nullification of legal justice. It is the only power in modern politics, in which the supremacy of the law is acknowledged as the primary condition of liberty, that can be compared in any degree to the veto of the ancient tribune.[1] It is an irregular power, depending upon irre-

---

[1] An inaccuracy of terms has in the case of the veto power created much confusion. The ancient tribune had the privilege of vetoing, and a so-called vetoing power being ascribed to the chief magistrate of modern constitutional states, people are apt to confound the two, and attack or defend them on common grounds. Yet the two differ materially. The Roman tribune had a complete veto. He could prohibit an entire law, or a single operation of it; he could stop the building of a public fabric, or veto an officer from doing his duty, or a general from leaving Rome for the army. But the modern veto has nothing to do with the law once passed; it amounts to

sponsible individual will.   We ought, therefore, clearly to be convinced of its necessity; and if this can be proved, we ought to inquire whether so extraordinary a power must not be guarded by
proper limitations, especially if it should be found that it is liable
to be seriously and even alarmingly abused.

In order to understand more fully the whole subject, it will not
be amiss if we endeavor to obtain a view of the origin of this
power, and to see why it is that everywhere we find it as an attribute of the chief executive power; whether this fact must be
attributed to any inherent characteristics, or to incidental circumstances.

When all government is yet mixed up with the family relations,
and the individual views of the ruler alone prevail, he pardons, as
a matter of course, whenever he sees proper and feels impelled so
to do ; but developed despotism over extensive states takes a different view.   Fear of insecurity and suspicion of disobedience to
the commands of the despot often lead the ruler to fence himself in
with a strict prohibition of applications for pardon.   That which
a wise people does for virtuous purposes by a constitution, namely,
the establishing, in calm times, of rules of action for impassioned
periods, distrusting their own power of resisting undue impulses,
and thus limiting their power, the despot does from fear of his own
weakness, and therefore limits his own absolute power that he may
not be entrapped into granting a pardon for disobedience.   Chardin[1]

------

nothing more than the withholding of one necessary ingredient to pass a
bill into a law.   In governments where the crown has the concurrent or sole
initiative, either house, whose consent is necessary in order to make a law,
may be said to have the veto power against the crown with the same propriety with which we call the power, in our president, of withholding his
approval a vetoing power.   The president can never interrupt the operation
of a law once made a law.   In the case of pardoning, however, the power
actually amounts to a tribunal veto.   There the executive, or whoever may
possess the pardoning privilege, actually stops the ordinary operation of the
law.   A man has been laboriously tried and sentenced according to the
course minutely laid down by the law, and another power steps in, not according to a prescribed course or process of law, but by a pure privilege
left to his own individual judgment, and says : I prohibit; and the due and
regular course of law is interrupted accordingly.   This *is* vetoing power in
its fullest sense.   See on the Veto, in chap. xvii. pp. 203, 204, 205, of this
work.

[1] Voyage en Perse.   London, 1686—1715.

tells us that in his time it was, in Persia, highly penal to sue for pardon for one's self or for another person; the same was a capital offence under the Roman emperors—at least under the tyrants among them, who form the great majority of the fearful list. Still it is clear that the last and highest power, the real sovereign (not only the supreme) power, must include the power of pardoning. As in Athens the assembled people had the right of remitting penalties,[1] so does the civil law acknowledge the privilege in the emperor who was supposed to be the sovereign, and acknowledged as the source of all law. Christianity confirmed these views. The mercy of the Deity is one of its chief dogmas; mercy, therefore, came also to be considered as one of the choicest attributes of the ruler, who on the one hand was held to be the vicegerent of God, and on the other, the sovereign source of law and justice; nor can it be denied that, in times when laws were yet in a very disordered state, the attribute of mercy in the ruler, and the right of pardoning flowing from it, was of great importance, and, upon the whole, probably beneficial to the people. The fact that the pardoning power necessarily originated with the sovereign power, and that the rulers were considered the sovereigns, is the reason why, when jurists came to treat of the subject, they invariably presented it as an attribute indelibly inhering in the crown. The monarch alone was considered the indisputable dispenser of pardon; and this again is the historical reason why we have always granted the pardoning privilege to the chief executive, because he stands, if any one visibly does, in the place of the monarch of other nations, forgetting that the monarch had the pardoning power not because he is the chief executive, but because he was considered the sovereign—the self-sufficient power from which all other powers flow; while with us the governor or president has but a delegated power and limited sphere of action, which by no means implies that we must necessarily or naturally delegate, along with the executive power, also the pardoning authority.

Although the pardoning power has always existed, and has been abandoned by ultra-despotism for the sake of despotism itself, yet the abuse to which it easily leads, and the apparent incongruity which it involves, have induced many men of deep reflection, in ancient as well as in modern times, to raise their voices

---

[1] Demosthenes against Timocrates.

against it : of whom we may mention Plato and Cicero[1] among the ancients, and Pastoret,[2] Servin, Filangieri, and the benevolent Beccaria among the moderns The latter, the pioneer of penal reform, and one of the benefactors of mankind, has the following remarkable passage :[3]

" As punishments become more mild, clemency and pardon are less necessary.   Happy the nation in which they will be considered as dangerous !   Clemency, which has often been deemed a sufficient substitute for every other virtue in sovereigns, should be excluded in a perfect legislation where punishments are mild, and the proceedings in criminal cases regular and expeditious.   This truth may seem cruel to those who live in countries where, from the absurdity of the laws and the severity of punishments, pardons and the clemency of the prince are necessary.   It is, indeed, one of the noblest prerogatives of the throne ; but at the same time a tacit disapprobation of the laws.   Clemency is a virtue which belongs to the legislator, and not to the executor of the laws ; a virtue which ought to shine in the code, and not in private judgment. To show mankind that crimes are sometimes pardoned, and that punishment is not a necessary consequence, is to nourish the flattering hope of impunity, and is the cause of their considering every punishment inflicted as an act of injustice and oppression.   The prince, in pardoning, gives up the public security in favor of an individual, and by ill-judged benevolence proclaims a public act of impunity.   Let, then, the legislator be tender, indulgent, and humane."

Among the truths of this passage there are some errors, the exhibition of which will at once lead us to the consideration whether the pardoning power, having already been admitted as an extraordinary and super-legal one, be necessary at all in a well and liberally constituted government, or ought to be suffered in a community which acknowledges the sovereignty of the law.   Beccaria says that clemency should be excluded in a perfect legislation, and that pardon is a tacit disapprobation of the law.   This is erroneous.   No legislation can ever be perfect in the sense in which it is taken here, namely, operating in all cases, in the same manner

---

[1] Cicero in Verrem 7.   [2] Des Lois Penales.
[3] Crimes and Punishments, chap. 46, on Pardons; English Translalation, 1807.

toward exactly the same end, for which the legislator has enacted the law; because the practical cases to which the laws apply are complex, and often involve conflicting laws; because the legislator, though he were the wisest, is but a mortal with a finite mind, who cannot foresee every combination of cases; because the changes of society, things, and relations necessarily change the effect produced by the same laws; and because the law-maker cannot otherwise than cast the rules of action, which he prescribes, in human language, which of itself is ever but an imperfect approximation to that which is to be expressed.

Laws cannot, in the very nature of things, be made abstract mathematical rules; and so long as we live on this earth, where we do not see "face to face," where mind cannot commune with mind except through signs which have their inherent imperfections, cases must frequently occur in which the strict and formal application of the law operates against essential justice, so that we shall actually come to the conclusion that, in a country in which the *sovereignty* of the laws is justly acknowledged, we stand in need of a conciliatory power to protect ourselves against a *tyranny* of the law, which would resemble the bed of Procrustes, and would sometimes sacrifice essential justice as a bleeding victim at the shrine of unconditional and inexorable law itself. It is to these cases, among others, that the adage of the jurists themselves applies : Summum jus, summa injuria. We take it then for granted on all hands, that, justice being the great end of all civil government, and law the means to obtain it, the pardoning power is necessary in order to protect the citizen against the latter, whenever, in the peculiar combination of circumstances, it militates with the true end of the state, that is, with justice itself. But it is equally true that the supremacy of the law requires that the extraordinary power of pardoning be wielded in the spirit of justice, and not according to individual bias, personal weakness, arbitrary view, or interested consideration ; a truth which is the more important in our country, because the same principles which make us bow before the law as our supreme earthly ruler, also bring the magistrate so near to the level of the citizen that he who is invested with the pardoning power is exposed to a variety of influences, individual and political, which have a powerful, and often, as practice shows, an irresistible effect, although there is no inherent connection between them and the cases to which the pardon is applied—influences, therefore, which in this respect are arbitrary or accidental. All arbitrariness, however, is odious to sterling freedom in general, and the arbitrary use of the pardoning power and its frequency produce the most disastrous consequences in particular.

It unsettles the general and firm reliance on the law, an abiding confidence in its supremacy, and a loyal love of justice.

It destroys the certainty of punishment, which is one of the most important and efficacious elements in the whole punitory scheme; and it increases the hope of impunity, already great, in the criminally disposed, according to the nature of man and the necessary deficiency even of the best contrived penal systems.

It endangers the community, since it is perfectly true what the prince of poets, in his great wisdom, has said:

> Mercy is not itself, that oft looks so;
> Pardon is still the nurse of second wo.

It interferes most effectually with the wise objects of reform which our penitentiary systems aim at; for all men, practically acquainted with their operation, are agreed that reform never fairly begins in a convict before he has calmly made up his mind to submit to the punishment, and so long as a hope of pardon leads his thoughts from the prison cell to the anticipated enjoyment of undue enlargement—a phenomenon easily to be accounted for upon psychological grounds.

It induces large numbers of well-disposed persons, male and female, from a superficial feeling of pity, to meddle with cases of which they have no detailed knowledge, and with a subject the grave importance of which has never presented itself to their minds. At times it induces persons to seek for pardons on frivolous grounds and leads communities to trifle with law, justice and government.[1]

It largely attracts to the community, in which the pardoning power is known to be abused, criminals from foreign parts where such an abuse does not exist; it imports crime.

---

[1] At the beginning of 1858 it appeared from certain documents published in California, that a petition to the governor, numerously signed by citizens of Monterey, to pardon one Jose Anastasia, under the sentence of death, claimed the pardon on the ground that Jose was the only fiddler in Monterey that understood properly to play for dancing.

It makes every sentence, not pardoned, an unjust one ; for, in matters of state, every act should be founded on right and equal justice.[1] No one, therefore, has the right, whatever his power may be, to extend a favor to one without extending it to all equally situated, and, consequently, equally entitled to the favor.   The doctrine of Dr. Paley, of "assigning capital punishment to many kinds of offences, but inflicting it only upon a few examples of each kind," which he actually calls one of the "two *methods* of administering penal *justice*," amounts to revolting monstrosity if practically viewed, and to an absurdity in a philosophical and scientific point of view.

It adds, with the very commonly annexed condition of expatriation, the flagrant abuse of saddling, in an inhuman, unchristian, and unstatesmanlike manner, neighboring communities with crime, to which the people, whose sacred and bounden duty it was to punish it, were too weak and negligent to mete out its proper reward.[2]

And it places an arbitrary power in the hands of a single individual, or several individuals, in states where all arbitrary power is disclaimed, and allows them by one irresponsible act to defeat the ends of toilsome, costly, and well-devised justice and legislation, putting the very objects of civil government to naught.

We do not theorize on this subject.   All the disastrous effects of the abuse of the pardoning power, whether inherent in the power itself, when unlimited by proper restrictions, or arising out of a state of things peculiar to ourselves, have shown themselves among us in an alarming degree, and are in many parts of the country on the increase.

[1] Lord Mansfield is reported justly to have remarked to George III., who wished to save the Rev. Dr. Dodd from the gallows, to which he had been sentenced for forgery: "If Dr. Dodd does not suffer the just sentence of the law, the Perreaus may be said to have been murdered." Holliday's Life of Lord Mansfield, London, 1797, p. 149. The Perreaus were apothecaries of very high standing, but had been hanged for forgery, in spite of the most weighty petitions.

[2] This unhallowed abuse has been raised into a law by Sir George Grey's Expatriation Law, passed in 1847, according to which convicts who behave well shall be pardoned after the lapse of two-thirds of the imprisonment to which they had been originally sentenced, *provided* they will leave the country.

For the proof of this evil state of things we appeal to every one in our whole country who has made penal matters the subject of earnest inquiry ; we appeal to the fact that, for a long series of years, the official reports of persons connected with prisons and penitentiaries, and of legislative committees, have teemed with complaints of the mischievous effects of the pardoning power; we appeal to the daily papers, near and far, and to recent occurrences in one of our most prominent states, where pardons have been granted to blood-stained criminals of the most dangerous, persevering, and resolute sort, without even the least indication of their reform, after a short time of imprisonment, which had already been substituted for capital punishment; we appeal to the statistics, whenever they have been collected, from official documents, on this melancholy subject ; and, lastly, we appeal to the presentments of grand juries in several states of our Union, in which the frequency of pardons under some governors has been called by the severe yet merited name of nuisance.

So long ago as the year 1832, Messrs. de Beaumont and de Tocqueville showed, in their work on the penitentiary system in the United States,[1] by documents and statistical tables, the frightful abuse of the pardoning power in the United States in general, and the additional abuse, naturally resulting from the circumstances, that pardon is more liberally extended to those convicts who are sentenced to a long period of imprisonment, or for life, than to less criminal persons. We refer especially to the 2d part of the 16th note of the appendix, page 232 of the translation. We are aware that in some, perhaps in many states of the Union, the pardoning power has been used more sparingly since that time; but it will be observed that there is no security against a return to the former state of things ; nor is the effect of pardoning, when it is rare, yet abused in a few glaring cases, which attract universal notice, less injurious ; for instance, when the member of a wealthy or distinguished family is pardoned, although guilty of a well-proven heinous crime, or when men are pardoned on political grounds, although they have committed infamous and revolting offences. Such cases have a peculiar tendency to loosen the necessary bonds of a law-abiding and law-relying community, which

---

[1] Translated, with many additions, by Francis Lieber, Philadelphia, 1833.

has nothing else, and is proud of having nothing else, to rely upon than the law.

Many years ago Mr. M. Carey said, in his Thoughts on Penitentiaries and Prisons : " The New York committee ascertained that there are men who make a regular trade of procuring pardons for convicts, by which they support themselves. They exert themselves to obtain signatures to recommendations to the executive authority to extend pardon to them by whom they are employed. And in this iniquitous traffic they are generally successful, through the facility with which respectable citizens lend their names, without any knowledge of the merits or demerits of the parties. Few men have the moral courage necessary to refuse their signatures when applied to by persons apparently decent and respectable, and few governors have the fortitude to refuse."

To this statement we have now to add the still more appalling fact, which we would pass over in silence if our duty permitted it, that but a short time ago the governor of a large state—a state amongst the foremost in prison discipline—was openly and widely accused of having taken money for his pardons. We have it not in our power to say whether this be true or not ; but it is obvious that a state of things which allows suspicions and charges so degrading and so ruinous to a healthy condition of public opinion, ought not to be suffered.[1] It shows that, leaving the pardoning privilege, uncontrolled in any way, to a single individual, is contrary to a substantial government of law, and hostile to a sound commonwealth.[2]

---

[1] While these sheets are passing through the press, the papers report that the governor of a large state has pardoned thirty criminals, among whom were some of the worst character, at one stroke, on leaving the gubernatorial chair. What a legacy to the people! Lord Brougham said that the only aim of counsel for the prisoner was to get him clear, no matter what the consequences might be. If all the lawyers acted on this saying, and all the executives as the mentioned governor, Justice might as well shut up her halls, and the people save the expenses which they incur for the administration of justice. It is paying too dear for a farce, which is not even entertaining.

[2] In some of the worst governments, as those of Charles II., James II., and Louis XV., pardons were sold, but not by the pardoning ruler. It was the mistresses and courtiers who carried on the infamous traffic, though the monarchs knew about it.

A very interesting paper, relating to the subject of pardon, was furnished in the year 1846 by the secretary of state, of Massachusetts, and published by the house of representatives of that commonwealth. The paper is, of itself, of much interest to every penologist ; but, when we consider that Massachusetts justly ranks amongst the best governed states of our Union, its value is much enhanced ; for we may fairly suppose that the abuse of the pardoning power exists in many of the other states in no less a degree. In many, indeed, we actually know it to exist in a far greater and more appalling degree.

From this document,[1] we have arrived at the following results :

There were imprisoned in the state of Massachusetts, from the year 1807, inclusive, to the month of February, 1847, in the state prisons, convicted, 3,850.

Of these were pardoned, before the term of imprisonment expired, 460. So that of the whole were pardoned 12 per cent., or every eighth convict.

The average time of remaining in prison (of these 460,) compared to the time of their original sentence, amounted to 65 per cent. In other words, they remained in prison but two-thirds of the time of imprisonment imposed upon them by the law of the state.

Of the 460 pardoned convicts, there had been originally sentenced to the imprisonment of ten years, or more, the number of 49. And the time which these convicts had actually remained in prison, compared to the terms of their original conviction, amounts to 60 per cent. ; so that a criminal sentenced to ten years, or more, had a better chance of having his imprisonment shortened, than those sentenced to a period less than ten years, in the proportion of about six to seven—in other words, while the less guilty was suffering a week's imprisonment, the prisoners of the darkest dye suffered six days only.

There were committed for life, by commutation of sentence, and still farther pardoned at a later period, from 1815 to 1844 inclusive, seventy-five. The average time they actually remained in prison was a fraction over seven years. So that, if we take twenty-five years as the average time of a sentence of imprisonment for life,

---

[1] House of Representatives, of Massachusetts, 1846, No. 63.

we find that they remained in prison but little over one-fourth of the time which had been allotted to them, in consequence of a first pardon, (twenty-five per cent.,) or the executive substituted seven years' imprisonment for death decreed by law. There were alto-gether, committed for life by commutation of sentence, fifteen. And, as we have seen that five of these were farther pardoned, we find that one-third of the whole were pardoned (thirty-three per cent.) It does not appear how many criminals were sentenced to death, and what proportion, therefore, had their sentences com-muted to imprisonment for life.

The abuse of pardoning in the state of Massachusetts has, how-ever, much decreased during the latter part of the period through which the mentioned report extends; for, according to a table published in the able and instructive third report of the New York Prison Association, 1847, page 41 of the report of the Prison Discipline Committee, we find that from 1835 to 1846, there was pardoned in Massachusetts one convict of 1,804; while our statement shows that in the period from 1807 to 1846 every eighth convict was pardoned.

We beg leave to copy the chief result of the table just men-tioned.[1]

---

[1] While the work was passing through the press, a document, published by the Massachusetts convention to amend the state constitution, reached the writer. It contains "A List of Pardons, Commutations and Remissions of Sentence, granted to Convicts by the Executive of the Commonwealth for the ten years including 1843 and 1852." Unfortunately this important paper, which contains the names of the persons, sentences, number of years sentenced, number of years remitted, and the crimes, does not give any clas-sifications, summings-up or comparisons with the number of sentences and unremitted punishments. It only exhibits the following recapitulation for 10 years from 1843 to 1852:

Full Pardons	36
Remissions	319
Restorations	103
Commutations	35
Total	483

This paper will doubtless be made the basis of very instructive statistical calculations, and it is greatly to be desired that other states would follow. As it is, I am incapable of giving at this moment any other information. It would require other documents, which I have not about me. My remarks

*Table showing the pardons in the following prisons in one or
several years from 1845 to 1846.*

Vermont,	one convict pardoned of	5.87 convicts.
Maine,	"	"	20.74	"
New Hampshire,	"	"	4.56	"
Connecticut,	"	"	36.50	"
Massachusetts,	"	"	18.04	"
Virginia,	"	"	33.31	"
Maryland,	"	"	41.00	"
Sing Sing,	"	"	21.25	"
Auburn,	"	"	17.83	"
Eastern Penitentiary,	"	"	20.37	"
Western Penitentiary,	"	"	6.43	"
Mississippi,	"	"	10.81	"
Kentucky,	"	"	8.50	"
District of Columbia,	"	"	87.00	"
Ohio,	"	"	11.31	"
Rhode Island,	"	"	18.00	"

If we take the above list as a fair representation of the whole
United States, we shall find that one convict of 26.33 is pardoned.
But we fear that this would not be very correct; nor must it be
believed that any average *number* fairly represents the average
mischief of the abuse of pardoning. Although there be but very
few convicts pardoned in a given community, yet incalculable mischief may be done by arbitrarily or wickedly pardoning a few prominent and deeply stained criminals, as the average temperature
of a place may turn out very fair at the end of a year, while,
nevertheless, a few blasting night-frosts may have ruined the whole
crop.

are not intended to reflect on the gentleman who has drawn up the paper;
for it appears that the convention ordered the paper on the 18th of June,
and on July 5th it was handed in. There was then no time to collect the
materials for comparisons such as I have alluded to. What is now most important to know is the sum total of what sentences for what crimes were
chiefly remitted or pardoned; for what reasons, what proportion pardons,
&c., bear to unremitted sentences; for what crimes and what duration these
sentences were inflicted; of what countries the pardoned, &c., convicts were;
and what proportion the pardoned, &c., short sentences bear to pardoned,
&c., long sentences or death.

It ought to be kept in mind that, in all calculations of probability, averages must be taken with peculiar caution in all cycles of
facts in which an exceptionally high or low state of things produces
effects of its own, differing not only in degree but also in kind from
the effects which result from the more ordinary state of things. In
these cases averages indicate very partial truth only, or cannot be
taken as an index of the desired truth at all. The effects of these
maxima or minima are not distributive, and being effects of a distinct class there are 'no facts in the opposite direction to counteract
them. This applies to moral as well as physical averages, and before we apply ourselves to averages at all we must distinctly know
whether the elements we are going to use stand in the proper
connection with the nature of the result at which we desire to
arrive.[1]

The abuse then exists, and exists in an alarming degree. How
is it to be remedied ?

In trying to answer this question, we would preface that we are
well aware that, unfortunately, the pardoning power is in almost all
states of our confederacy, determined by their constitutions, and
cannot be changed without a change of these fundamental instru-
ments. The object of the present paper, however, is not to propose any political measure. We shall treat the subject as a scientific one, and an open question, irrespective of what can or may be
done in the different states in conformity with existing fundamental
laws. It is necessary, before all, to know what is the most desira-

---

[1] A few examples may illustrate the truth too often forgotten: No farmer
can determine the fitness of a given climate for the culture of a certain
plant from the mean heat of the summer or the mean cold of the winter;
for the mean heat does not indicate whether the weather is uniform or
violently changeable; the mean interest at which money may have been
obtainable in the course of the year does not indicate the truth, unless we
know that it has not been peculiarly low at some periods and extraor-
dinarily high at others; the general criminality of a community cannot be
calculated from the percentage of crime, unless we know that there has not
been a peculiarly disturbing cause: for instance, one man who has murdered half a dozen of people in a comparatively small community; and the
mischief produced by pardons cannot be calculated by the average percentage alone, if we do not know that among these pardons there were no
some peculiarly arbitrary or peculiarly hostile to the ends of justice. A
wholesale pardon may be warranted by the truest principles, and a single
arbitrary pardon may shock the whole community.

ble object to be obtained. After this has been done, it will be proper for every one concerned to adopt that practical course which
best meets his own peculiar circumstances, and to settle how near
his own means allow him to approach the desirable end.

Many vague things have been asserted of the pardoning power
by writers otherwise distinguished for soundness of thought, because
they were unable to rid themselves of certain undefined views and
feelings concerning princes and crowns. Some have maintained
that the pardoning privilege can be justified only in the monarchy,
because the monarch combines the character of the legislator and
executive, while Montesquieu wishes to restrict the right to the
constitutional monarch alone, because he does not himself perform
the judicial functions. All these opinions appear to us unsubstan-
tial. There is nothing mysterious, nothing transcendental in the
pardoning power. The simple question for us is, Why ought it
to exist? If it ought to exist, who ought to be vested with it?
What are its abuses, and how may we protect ourselves against
them ?

We have already seen that doubtless the pardoning power ought
to exist :

That there is no inherent necessity that it ought to exist in the
executive, or in the executive alone :

That a wide-spread abuse of the pardoning power exists, and
has existed at various periods :

That the abuse of the pardoning power produces calamitous
effects :

That the executive in our country is so situated that, in the
ordinary course of things, it cannot be expected of him that he will
resist the abuse :

And that the chief abuse of the pardoning power consists in the
substitution of an arbitrary use of power or of subjective views
and individual feelings, for high, broad justice, and the unwavering
operation of the law, which ought to be freed from all arbitrariness.

We know, moreover, that all our constitutions, as well as the
laws of England, actually restrict the pardoning power in some
cases ; for instance, regarding impeachments, or fines to be paid to
private parties ; and in most of our states the executive is not invested with the right of pardoning treason, which can only be done

by the legislature.[1] In others, again, the governor has no authority to pardon capital punishment before the end of the session of that legislature which first meets after the sentence of death has been pronounced; and in other states he has only the power of respiting the capitally condemned criminal until the meeting of the legislature. It is obvious that no specific reason has induced our legislators to give the pardoning power to the executive. It was rather left where they happened to find it, or they placed it by analogy, and not in consideration of any intrinsic reasons.[2]

If it be true that pardon ought to be granted only in cases in which essential justice demands it *against* the law, or for very specific and peculiar reasons—for instance, if a convict, sentenced to a short imprisonment, is so feeble in health, that, no proper hospital existing, the incidental consequences of imprisonment would be infinitely severer than the law intended the punishment to be[3] (and

---

[1] The Constitution of the late French Republic of 1848 has this provision:

"Art. 55. He (the president of the republic) shall possess the right of pardon, but he shall not have the power to exercise the right until after he has taken the advice of the council of state. Amnesties shall only be granted by an express law. The president of the republic, the ministers, as well as all other persons condemned by the high court of justice, can only be pardoned by the national assembly."

I do not consider it desirable that the pardoning power be given or imposed upon a political body already existing for other purposes, as in this case to the council of state; but I have cited this provision to show that the French at that time did not consider the limitation of the pardoning power in the executive unfavorable to popular liberty.

[2] A remarkable proof of this fact seems to have been afforded by the late constituent assembly of the state of New York; for, so far as we are aware, there was no debate on the question whether the pardoning power ought to be left uncontrolled in the hands of the executive. We can very well imagine that, after a discussion of this subject, a majority might have decided, erroneously in our opinion, that the pardoning privilege ought to remain where it was; but we cannot imagine that a large number of men could have possibly been from the beginning so unanimous upon so important a subject, that not even a discussion was elicited, had the pardoning been made a subject of any reflection at all. This is impossible in the nature of things. Men will differ in opinion upon almost any point, and would certainly have differed upon so weighty and delicate a subject, had their minds been directed to it.

[3] We certainly think that ill health, threatening disastrous consequences, should form a ground of release in cases of comparatively short sentences,

is not this also a case of essential justice against the law ?)—or because strong suspicions of innocence have arisen after the trial, it is equally clear that pardon ought to be granted after due investigation only, and that this investigation ought to be insured by law.

The pardoning power might be transferred from the executive to the legislature, or to an assembly of judges. We are emphatically averse to either measure. The legislature is composed of members elected to represent a variety of interests and views, all of which ought to have a proportionate weight in the formation of laws; but neither the reasons why, nor the objects for which legislators are elected have any connection with deciding upon a question of pardon. If the decision were left at once to the whole assembly, it would be impossible to give that degree of attentive examination to the details of each case which its nature requires, and a party feeling would frequently warp a decision which could be justified only on the ground of the highest and of essential justice. If the case were first given to a committee (as we may imagine a standing committee of pardon), and the legislature were regularly to follow the decision of the committee, the latter step is useless; if the legislature, however, were not to follow implicitly this decision, we have the incongruities just indicated. As to the forming

---

if no good prison hospital exists. But, even where no hospital exists (which is undoubtedly a great deficiency), much caution must be exercised. An experienced and highly respectable prison physician in Massachusetts stated in his report, some years ago, that pardons on account of deficient health had a tendency to increase sickness in the prison, because many prisoners will seriously and perseveringly injure their health in the hope of obtaining thereby a pardon. A prison ought to have a hospital, and if, in spite of a good hospital, the consciousness of being imprisoned has of itself any bad consequences for the imprisoned patient, it must be taken as one of the many incidental but unavoidable consequences of all imprisonment. There are more serious consequences than this, which we are, nevertheless, unable to separate from punishment. Punishment ought always to be individual, and to strike no one but the evil doer: yet there is hardly ever an individual punished whose sentence does not at the same time entail moral or physical suffering upon others. Men are decreed to constitute societies, with concatenated weal and woe, and human judges cannot punish without indirectly inflicting suffering upon those who are unconnected with the crime, but connected with the criminal. If we were absolutely to follow out the first principle, that the offender alone should suffer, we could not punish a single convict.

a board of pardon of judges alone, we think the case would be equally incongruous. The business of the judge, his duty, and his habit of thinking, are strictly to apply the law. He is a valuable magistrate only so long as he is a faithful organ of the established law; but, in the case of pardon, the object is neither to make nor to apply a law, but to defeat its operation in a given and peculiar case.

In order to constitute a proper authority, to which the pardoning privilege can be safely intrusted, we ought to organize it so that the following points are well secured:

That a careful investigation of each case take place before pardon be granted:

That the authority be sufficiently strong to resist importunity:

That it contain a sufficient amount of knowledge of the law, its bearing, and object:

That it enjoy the full confidence of the community.

These great objects, it is believed, can be obtained by a board of pardon, consisting of a proper number of members—say nine (in the republic of Geneva it consists of this number), with one or two judges among them, to be appointed by the legislature, with a periodical partial renovation (one-third leaving every three years), and with these farther provisions:

That the board sit at certain portions of the year—say twice:

That certain and distinct grounds must be stated in every petition for pardon; and that, without them, all petitions, ever so respectably and numerously signed, be not received:

That pardon can be granted by the governor only when duly recommended by the board; and must be granted if the board recommend it a second time, after the governor has returned the recommendation with his reasons against it:

That no pardon be recommended without advertising in the county where the convict has lived previous to his imprisonment, and where he has committed his crime, that the board have in view to recommend him to pardon, and without giving proper time to act upon the advertisement:

That no pardon be granted without informing, likewise, the warden of the prison, or prisons, in which the subject of the intended pardon is, or has been, incarcerated, of the intention of the board:

That no pardon be granted without previous inquiry of the court which has sentenced the convict:

And that the reasons of the pardon, when granted, be published.

Without some such guarantees, the pardoning power will always be abused. The advertising of the intention of pardoning will not be mistaken for an extra-constitutional and illegal call upon the county to exercise functions which do not belong to it, and ought not to belong to it, as, in reality, the governor of Ohio (years ago) respited the execution of a criminal guilty of an atrocious murder, informing, at the same time, the people of the county whence the criminal came, that he was desirous of knowing whether they wished the criminal pardoned or not.[1]

Nor must it be believed that, while we recommend to inform the warden of a prisoner that his pardon is contemplated, we are desirous of countenancing a system of pardon founded upon the good conduct of the convicts in the prison. We consider such a measure inadmissible, for many reasons. It has been tried in France, on a large scale; and the effect was so bad that its own author obtained its abolition, confessing his error.[2] What we desire is, that proper information be obtained before a convict be pardoned, and that no imposition take place. It frequently happens that a pardon is obtained by persons unacquainted with the culprit, and a dangerous and infamous man is returned to a community which had the deepest interest in seeing the law take its uninterrupted course.

We think it proper that the executive, thus controlled on the one hand, and protected against importunites on the other, form a party to the pardon, because the actual release must go through his hands.

We doubt not that, if a board of pardoning were established, in a short time a series of fair principles and rules, somewhat like the rules of equity, would be settled by practice, and the pardoning would be far less exposed to arbitrary action.

Totally distinct, however, from the pardoning ought to be kept the *restitution* of a convict, when innocence has been proved after

---

[1] National Gazette, Philadelphia, October 10, 1833.

[2] De la Ville de Mirmont, Observations sur les Maisons Centrales de Detention de Paris, 1833, p. 55, and sequ.

conviction. It is a barbarous error to confound acknowledgment of wrong committed by society against an individual with the pardoning of a guilty person. Nothing can be pardoned where nothing is to be pardoned, or where the only pardoner is the convict. He is entitled to indemnity, and the process ought even to be called by a different name and differently to be provided for. Not long ago a person sentenced for forgery in England to transportation for a very long period or for life, we forget which, was pardoned after several years endurance of the sentence, because his innocence had been made patent. Some English papers justly remarked how incongruous a *pardon* is in such cases, where, in fact, the question is how a great and ruinous wrong committed by society against an individual may be repaired in some degree at least, and as far as it lies in human power. This is an important subject of its own, deserving the most serious attention of all civilized states, but does not fall within the province proper of pardoning.

FRANCIS LIEBER.

I append to this paper, besides the additional notes which the reader has seen, the following three items :

The official reports of the attorney-general of Massachusetts show that :

In 1850, prosecutions of crime cost in that state			$66,589 36
1851, " " "			71,078 18
1852, " " "			63,900 68

To this must be added the cost of the courts, detective police, rewards, penitentiaries, prison support.

When we speak of the cost of crime in general, we must not only take into account the above items, but also the waste of property by criminals, and the loss of labor, for criminals by profession do not work, therefore do not produce.

The following extract of a speech by Lord Palmerston, secretary for the home department, June 1, 1853, in the commons, is very remarkable. *C'est tout comme chez nous.* I do not mean our quakers act thus, but women inconsiderately get up petitions, and are joined by busy religionists. Lord Palmerston said :

"That would be a very great evil, were any change of the law to bring it about. But let us see how the thing would work. Even now, in cases of disputed rights of property, although it is generally matter of great scruple of conscience to depose to statements which are not consistent with truth, yet we frequently see evidence brought before courts of law not founded in fact. But in matters regarding life and liberty, I am sorry to say that benevolent individuals have very little conscience at all. (*'Hear!' and laughter.*) You may depend upon it that I have had too much experience of the truth of what I have stated. I get applications signed by great numbers of most respectable persons in favor of individuals with regard to whose guilt there can be no possible doubt, or any doubt that they have committed the most atrocious crimes. That is a matter of every-day occurrence. Not long ago, a member of the Society of Friends actually tried to bribe a witness to absent himself from the trial of a prisoner, in order to screen the man from punishment, of whose guilt no human being could doubt. If you had these second trials, you would have these pious frauds as frequently committed."

Lastly, I would put here a short newspaper paragraph—very simple yet very fearful.

" In the course of an editorial article, intended to show that it is the certainty, and not the severity, of punishment which is needed for the suppression of crime, the Pittsburg Commercial makes the following statement :—[1]

" 'In fifteen years, during which the annals of crime in this county have been stained by *more than fifty murders*, a single instance of hanging has been affirmed by the executive as the measure of extreme penalty due ; and there justice was cheated of her victim by suicide !' "

---

[1] National Intelligencer, Washington, July 12, 1853.

APPENDIX III.

A PAPER ON SUBJECTS CONNECTED WITH THE INQUISITORIAL
TRIAL AND THE LAWS OF EVIDENCE.

FEW things, in my opinion, show more distinctly the early English character than the fact that, without vindictiveness or cruelty in the national character, the penal law inflicted death with a fearful disregard of human life, while at the same time the penal trial was carried on with great regard for individual rights and for the mode of ascertaining the truth. The English were from early times a peculiarly jural nation.

Those people who have the inquisitorial trial, on the other hand, were in some instances far less sanguinary in their punishments, but perfectly regardless of the trial, or, rather, the trial seemed to have been established chiefly for the prosecuting party. It aimed at knowing the truth; the means to arrive at it were little cared about. The rights of the prosecuted person appeared in a shadowy, undefined way. And all this continues to exist in many countries.

I do not speak here of the worst countries only. I do not mean to advert to the Austrian trial, as it was before the late revolutions. I refer, for instance, to the German penal trial; and mean by it the penal trial of the countries in which the common German law prevails, as well as those where, as in Prussia, a trial by statute law is introduced. The late revolutions have changed some items. The main ideas, however, remain, in many cases, the same.

Now, when a person accustomed to a regular and well-guarded penal trial reads such works as Feuerbach's Criminal Cases, or any detailed description of a penal trial, the laxity and incongruity of the procedure strike us among other things with reference to the following points:

1. The inquiring judge, that is, the judge who has been detailed, to use a military term, to lead the whole inquiry, and who has been day after day with the prisoner, and only one witness, viz. the secretary, and whose whole skill has been exerted to bring the prisoner

(457)

to confession, or to establish the crime, is also frequently the first sentencing judge, and always very powerfully influences the sentence. If there is a separate sentencing judge, all the " acts," that is, all that has been written down, is handed over to him, and from them he frames his sentence, upon which the other judges, if there are any, vote in plenary session. As a matter of course, they cannot know much about the subject, and must be guided by the report the sentencing judge makes.

2. The inquiring judge is, in many cases, what we would consider wholly unrestricted. He takes hearsay evidence, and all sorts of evidence, if he thinks proper. He is unrestricted as to time, and an accused person may be kept for years under trial. He is allowed to resort to all kinds of tricks, in order to work upon the imagination of the prisoner; for instance, calling him up at midnight, examining him and suddenly showing a skull to him. Every worthy and puerile motive to speak the truth, and confess the offence is resorted to.

3. There is no regular indictment, nor does the accused know in his examinations what is charged against him; at least the law does not demand that he shall know it.

4. The prisoner is constantly urged to confess; the whole trial assumes the act charged against the prisoner, and treats him accordingly. Indeed it may be said that, although not avowedly, yet virtually, the inquisitorial trial assumes in a very great degree the character of an accusation which the accused has to disprove, not one which the accuser is bound to prove. In some countries and in certain cases this is positively the case. Even the French penal trial is by no means wholly free from this serious fault.

5. There is no physical torture resorted to in order " to bring out" the truth, since the positive abolition of the torture, but the moral torture which is applied is immense, and the judge is authorized by law to punish with lashes or other physical means every contradiction or lie proved from the convict's own statements. That this can easily lead to all sorts of abuses is obvious.

6. There is no cross-examination of witnesses, and no stringent law to compel witnesses in favor of the prisoner to appear before the court.

7. Court and police frightfully mingle in their functions, in the first stages of the trial.

8. There is a most sorrowful defence, cautious, fearful of offending the judges upon whom the promotion of the defensor depends, and empowered to obtain certain points further cleared up only through the court, which is the prosecuting party. Besides, the defence only begins when the whole investigation by the court is at an end, that is to say, all the "acts" are handed over to the defensor. He studies them and writes the defence, which is given along with the "acts" to the sentencing judge.

No wonder that the Germans universally called for a total change of such a trial, and, as I stated before, some very important changes have taken place.

The chief incongruity in this inquisitorial trial, however, is that it admits of half proofs, two of which amount to a whole proof, with other logical flagrancies, as well as the legal flagrancy of "deficient proof," according to which a lighter punishment, but still a punishment, is inflicted.

It is hardly conceivable how an intelligent nation, advanced in the sciences, can have continued a logical absurdity of such crying character until the most recent times, and can continue it, in some parts of the country, to this day. It is reversing the order of things, and substituting evidence, the means of arriving at the fact, which is the thing to determine the punishment, for the criminal fact.

The principle from which we start in penal law is, that crime ought to be followed by evil, as a consequence of the crime. If crimes punished themselves, we should not want judges; if judges were omniscient, we should not want trials. The object of the trial is to prove that a crime has been committed, and that it has been committed by the indicted person. This is called establishing the fact, which means proving it—reproducing it, as it were, before the eyes of the judge; in one word, convincing him of the truth of the charge, of the fact, and the fact alone—the deed can be punishable. But the idea of a fact does not admit of degrees. There may, indeed, be every possible degree of belief in a judge from the first suspicion, from surmise, doubt, and belief, to the fullest conviction; but, if he metes out his punishments accordingly, he does not punish for facts done by others, but according to the degree of belief in himself. He substitutes his own subjective belief for the objective fact. Now, there cannot be half facts, or three-fourths of facts. A man may, indeed, buy poison, to commit murder—he may add to this, the mixing of the poison with a soup ; he may add to this, the carrying of the soup to the sick-room ; and he may add to this again, the presenting of the soup to a patient, who finally consumes it ; but all these successive acts are not parts of facts. Wherever the evil-minded man stopped, it was a fact ; and, if it is punished, it is not punished as part of a crime, but the inchoate crime is a whole penal fact, and, as such, punished. Again, though four persons may, as witnesses, establish a fact, a truth, each witness does not prove, on that account, a fourth of the truth, which, like the fact, is one and indivisible. If they prove a chain which ultimately establishes a fact, they still prove but one fact, and each one proves for himself a whole truth, which, in connection with the other truths, establishes the ultimate truth.

If four not very creditable witnesses establish one fact, when I would not have believed either of them singly, because, in the assumed case, they corroborate one another, when no connivance can have taken place, they are in this case good witnesses, each one for himself, and not four witnesses, each one worth a fourth of a good witness. A thousand liars cannot, as liars, establish a truth, but they may testify under circumstances which deprive them of the character of liars, and thus be in the case good witnesses.

It is true, indeed, that man, conscious of his fallibility, and resolved severely to punish certain crimes, has laid down the rule that, to prove certain crimes in such a manner that the law shall consider them as proved, an amount of testimony shall be necessary which is not required for lighter offences. But this is only as a safeguard, so as to prevent, as far as in us lies, the unjust infliction of severe punishment. It has nothing to do with parts of truths, or parts of facts. It has nothing to do with logic. In barbarous times, however, it was actually conceived that logic itself is of a sliding character, as it were. The Ripuarian laws demanded seventy-two compurgators to absolve an incendiary, or murderer (*Leg. Ripuar.*, cap. vi. vii. and xi.) Here, the first error was to consider the accused as tainted, who must clear himself, and not as one accused, upon whom the deed must be proved. The second error was that the number of compurgators must rise to clear the tainted person, according to the *taint* (which, as yet, is nothing but accusation). The Koran prescribes, in certain cases, a number of oaths—as though each oath, even of a person unworthy of belief, contained some truth, which, by repetition, could be accumulated, and ultimately form a whole truth. Not quite dissimilar is what we read in Gregory of Tours. When the chastity of a certain queen of France was suspected, three hundred knights swore, without hesitation, that the infant prince was truly begotten by her deceased husband. As if the oath of three hundred knights could have any weight, when none of them could know the fact. But, if people once fall into the error of demanding the proof of the negative to establish innocence, instead of demanding the proof positive of the charge, they must necessarily fall into all sorts of errors. The ecclesiastical law required, in a similar manner, or still requires, seventy witnesses to prove incontinency on a cardinal; and, in Spain, as Chancellor Livingston tells us, it required more witnesses to convict a nobleman than a commoner. This is pretty much the same logic which, as Captain Wilkes tells us, induces the Fijians to put more powder into the gun if they fire at a large man.

On the other hand, the idea of punishing according to the degree of conviction in the judge, namely, lightly, if light suspicion only has been existing, more severely, if belief has been created, and so on, would not have been wholly inconsistent in ancient times, when men had not yet succeeded in strictly separating the moral law from the law of nature, and when the punishment was considered as a sort of extinction of guilt—a neutralizing agent. This is a theory which actually some modern criminalists of prominence have endeavored to revive. According to them, the fact, not the deed, is punished—society has to wipe off the criminal fact which has occurred, and the punishment is like the minus put against the plus. But Aristotle already said, even the gods cannot make undone what has been done. The punishment would resemble the penitence which in early times kings had to undergo for great national calamities. If this unphilosophical view were true, it would be difficult to show why the criminal, who has committed the deed, is the one selected to re-establish the equilibrium or for the atonement. But the common sense of mankind has been in this case, as in a thousand others, sounder than theories of unpractical thinkers.

The judge who punishes half, because the evidence has sufficed to create half a conviction only, commits the same logical fault

which a navigator would commit who has seen but dimly something
that may be a rock, and would go but half out of the way of the
danger.   I say he commits the same logical fault, although the
effects would be the reverse.

Punishment, which is the intentional infliction of some sufferance
as deserved sufferance (in which it differs from the infliction of pain
by the surgeon), requires the establishment of the deed, and this is
absolute.   The various degrees of belief in the deed are only in the
judge, not in the deed.   The deed must determine the different
degrees of infliction of pain or privation; all else is illogical.

If the reader has thought that I have dwelt too long on this
topic, he must remember that millions are to this day subject to
such legal logic as has been described.

It will be hardly necessary to refer in this place to the fact, that
although the ascertainment of truth is the main object of the trial,
it is not on that account allowed to resort to all and every means
which may bring about this end.   Sound sense and a due regard
to the rights of individuals lead men to the conviction that a fixed
law of evidence is necessary, and to prescribe rules according to
which courts shall believe facts to be established, discarding all
those means which may expose the accused to cruelty, which may
be easily abused, which in turn may deceive, and whose effects in
general would be worse than the good obtained.   Truth, established
according to those rules, is called legal truth.   There can be but
one truth, that is the conviction agreeing with fact, but truth may
be established by various means, or by means agreeing with prescribed rules.   There may be one witness who testifies that he has
seen a man doing that, which, before the court can punish it, requires two witnesses.   The judge may be thoroughly convinced that
the witness speaks the truth; yet the truth would not be legally
established—it would not be a legal truth.   This, too, may appear
unworthy of mention; but only to those who do not know how
vehemently all persons hostile to liberty declaim against the dead
letter of the law, the hollow formalism of the Anglican trial, and
how anxious they are to substitute the subjective opinion of the
judge for the positive and well-defined law.   I may put it down
here as a fact of historical interest that even so late as my early
days I heard a criminalist of some distinction regret the abolition
of "the question," *i. e.* the torture, and I speak gravely when I say

that, as times go, I should not be surprised if the re-establishment of the torture should once more be called for in some countries. Indeed, has the torture not been used ?   Mr. Gladstone's pamphlet on Neapolitan affairs tells us strange things.[1]

---

[1] It would seem that the torture actually continues to exist in some parts of Europe.   The following is taken from the London Spectator, of December 22d, 1849, which gives as its authority the well known Allgemeine Zeitung, published at Augsburg, and, consequently, not far from Switzerland.

"A strange circumstance, says the Allgemeine Zeitung, has just taken place at Herisau, the capital of Inner Appenzell, in Switzerland, showing how much, in these countries of old liberties, civilization is behindhand in some matters.   A young girl of nineteen, some months back, assassinated her rival.   Her lover was arrested with her, and, as she accused him of the crime, both were put to the torture.   The girl yielded to the pain, and confessed her crime; the young man held firm in his denial: the former was condemned to death, and on the 7th of this month was decapitated with the sword, in the market-place of Herisau.   This fact is itself a startling one, but the details are just as strange.   For two hours the woman was able to struggle against four individuals charged with the execution.   After the first hour the strength of the woman was still so great that the men were obliged to desist; the authorities were then consulted, but they declared that justice ought to follow its course.   The struggle then recommenced, with greater intensity, and despair seemed to have redoubled the woman's force.   At the end of another hour she was at last bound by the hair to a stake, and the sword of the executioner then carried the sentence into effect."

The author has touched upon the fact that, in our country, the abolition of trial by jury has been proposed, in the note appended to page 236.   The topic is one of vital importance to our entire system of government and political existence.   It is for this reason that he does not hesitate to direct the earnest student of law, and of government, to a German work of high merit —Mr. Mittermaier's Legislation and Practice, with Reference to the Penal Trial, according to their recent Development; Erlangen, 1856.   The author had not become acquainted with this important work, when the page referred to, was printing; but the testimony given by the great criminalist, of the satisfactory results derived from trial by jury, even in countries where it has been recently established, has induced the author to append this note here, rather than leave his readers unacquainted with evidence of such weight in favor of so great an institution, considered by almost all friends of liberty as one of the substantial acquisitions obtained by our progressive race.

APPENDIX IV.

MAGNA CHARTA OF KING JOHN,

FIFTEENTH DAY OF JUNE, IN THE SEVENTEENTH YEAR OF THE KING'S
REIGN, A.D. 1215.

JOHN, by the grace of God, king of England, lord of Ireland,
duke of Normandy and Aquitain, and earl of Anjou : to the archbishops, bishops, abbots, earls, barons, justiciaries of the forests,
sheriffs, governors, officers, and to all bailiffs and other of his faithful subjects, greeting. Know ye, that we, in the presence of God,
and for the health of our soul, and of the souls of our ancestors
and heirs, and to the honor of God and the exaltation of holy
church, and amendment of our kingdom, by advice of our venerable
fathers, Stephen, archbishop of Canterbury, primate of all England
and cardinal of the holy Roman church ; Henry, archbishop of
Dublin, William, bishop of London, Peter of Winchester, Jocelin,
of Bath and Glastonbury, Hugh, of Lincoln, Walter, of Worcester,
William, of Coventry, Benedict, of Rochester, bishops ; and master
Pandulph, the pope's subdeacon and ancient servant, brother Ayme-
rick, master of the temple in England, and the noble persons, William Marescall, earl of Pembroke, William, earl of Salisbury, William, earl of Warren, William, earl of Arundel, Alan de Galoway,
constable of Scotland, Warin Fitz Gerald, Peter Fitz Herbert, and
Hubert de Burghe, senechal of Poictou, Hugo de Nevill, Matthew
Fitz Herbert, Thomas Basset, Alan Basset, Philip de Albine, Robert
de Roppele, John Marescall, John Fitz Hugh, and others our liege-
men ; have, in the first place, granted to God, and by this our present charter confirmed for us and our heirs forever :

1. That the church of England shall be free, and enjoy her whole
rights and liberties inviolable. And we will have them so to be
observed ; which appears from hence that the freedom of elections,
which was reckoned most necessary for the church of England, of
our own free will and pleasure we have granted and confirmed by
our charter, and obtained the confirmation of from Pope Innocent

the Third, before the discord between us and our barons : which charter we shall observe, and do will it to be faithfully observed by our heirs forever.

II. We have also granted to all the freemen of our kingdom, for us and our heirs forever, all the underwritten liberties, to have and to hold to them and their heirs, of us and our heirs.

III. If any of our earls, or barons, or others who hold of us in chief, by military service, shall die, and at the time of his death his heir shall be of full age, and owe a relief, he shall have his inheritance by the ancient relief; that is to say, the heir or heirs of an earl, for a whole earl's barony, by a hundred pounds ; the heir or heirs of a baron, for a whole barony, by a hundred pounds ; the heir or heirs of a knight, for a whole knight's fee, by a hundred shillings at most ; and he that oweth less shall give less, according to the ancient custom of fees.

IV. But if the heir of any such shall be under age, and shall be in ward, when he comes of age he shall have his inheritance without relief or without fine.

V. The warden of the land of such heir, who shall be under age, shall take of the land of such heir only reasonable issues, reasonable customs, and reasonable services ; and that without destruction or waste of the men or things ; and if we shall commit the guardianship of those lands to the sheriff, or any other who is answerable to us for the issues of the land, and if he shall make destruction and waste upon the ward lands, we will compel him to give satisfaction, and the land shall be committed to two lawful and discreet tenants of that fee, who shall be answerable for the issues to us, or to him whom we shall assign. And if we shall give or sell the wardship of any such lands to any one, and he makes destruction or waste upon them, he shall lose the wardship, which shall be committed to two lawful and discreet tenants of that fee, who shall in like manner be answerable to us, as hath been said.

VI. But the warden, so long as he shall have the wardship of the land, shall keep up and maintain the houses, parks, warrens, ponds, mills and other things pertaining to the land, out of the issues of the same land ; and shall restore to the heir, when he comes of full age, his whole land stocked with ploughs and carriages, according as the time of wainage shall require, and the issues of the land can reasonably bear.

30

VII. Heirs shall be married without disparagement, so as that before matrimony shall be contracted those who are nearest to the heir in blood shall be made acquainted with it.

VIII. A widow, after the death of her husband, shall forthwith, and without any difficulty, have her marriage and her inheritance; nor shall she give anything for her dower or her marriage, or her inheritance, which her husband and she held at the day of his death; and she may remain in the capital messuage or mansion house of her husband, forty days after his death, within which term her dower shall be assigned.

IX. No widow shall be distrained to marry herself, so long as she has a mind to live without a husband. But yet she shall give security that she will not marry without our assent, if she holds of us, or without the consent of the lord of whom she holds, if she holds of another.

X. Neither we nor our bailiffs shall seize any land or rent for any debt, so long as there shall be chattels of the debtor's upon the premises, sufficient to pay the debt. Nor shall the sureties of the debtor be distrained, so long as the principal debtor is sufficient for the payment of the debt.

XI. And if the principal debtor fail in the payment of the debt, not having wherewithal to discharge it, then the sureties shall answer the debt; and if they will, they shall have the lands and rents of the debtor, until they shall be satisfied for the debt which they paid him; unless the principal debtor can show himself acquitted thereof, against the said sureties.

XII. If any one have borrowed anything of the Jews, more or less, and dies before the debt be satisfied, there shall be no interest paid for that debt, so long as the heir is under age, of whomsoever he may hold. And if the debt falls into our hands, we will take only the chattel mentioned in the charter or instrument.

XIII. And if any one shall die indebted to the Jews, his wife shall have her dower, and pay nothing of that debt; and if the deceased left children under age, they shall have necessaries provided for them according to the tenement (or real estate) of the deceased; and out of the residue the debt shall be paid; saving, however, the service of the lords. In like manner let it be with debts due to other persons than the Jews.

XIV. No scutage or aid shall be imposed in our kingdom, unless by the common council of our kingdom, except to redeem our person, and make our eldest son a knight, and once to marry our eldest daughter; and for this there shall only be paid a reasonable aid.

XV. In like manner it shall be concerning the aids of the city of London; and the city of London shall have all its ancient liberties and free customs, as well by land as by water.

XVI. Furthermore, we will and grant that all other cities, and boroughs, and towns, and ports, shall have all their liberties and free customs; and shall have the common council of the kingdom, concerning the assessment of their aids, except in the three cases aforesaid.

XVII. And for the assessing of scutages we shall cause to be summoned the archbishops, bishops, abbots, earls, and great barons of the realm, singly by our letters.

XVIII. And furthermore we shall cause to be summoned in general by our sheriffs and bailiffs, all others who hold of us in chief, at a certain day, that is to say, forty days before the meeting, at least, to a certain place; and in all letters of such summons we will declare the cause of the summons.

XIX. And summons being thus made, the business shall proceed on the day appointed, according to the advice of such as shall be present, although all that were summoned come not.

XX. We will not for the future grant to any one, that he may take aid from his own free tenants, unless to redeem his body, and to make his eldest son a knight and once to marry his eldest daughter; and for this there shall only be paid a reasonable aid.

XXI. No man shall be distrained to perform more service for a knight's fee, or other free tenement, than is due from thence.

XXII. Common pleas shall not follow our court, but shall be holden in some certain place. Tryals upon the writs of novel disseisin, and of mort d'ancestor, and of darreine presentment, shall be taken but in their proper counties, and after this manner: We, or if we should be out of the realm, our chief justiciary, shall send two justiciaries through every county four times a year; who with the four knights chosen out of every shire by the people, shall hold the said assizes in the county, on the day and at the place appointed.

XXIII. And if any matters cannot be determined on the day appointed to hold the assizes in each county, so many of the

knights and freeholders as have been at the assizes aforesaid shall
be appointed to decide them, as is necessary, according as there is
more or less business.

XXIV. A freeman shall not be amerced for a small fault, but
according to the degree of the fault; and for a great crime in proportion to the heinousness of it; saving to him his contenement,
and after the same manner a merchant, saving to him his merchan-
dise.

XXV. And a villain shall be amerced after the same manner,
saving to him his wainage, if he falls under our mercy; and none
of the aforesaid amerciaments shall be assessed but by the oath of
honest men of the neighborhood.

XXVI. Earls and barons shall not be amerced but by their
peers, and according to the quality of the offence.

XXVII. No ecclesiastical person shall be amerced, but according
to the proportion aforesaid, and not according to the value of his
ecclesiastical benefice.

XXVIII. Neither a town or any person, shall be distrained to
make bridges over rivers, unless that anciently and of right they
are bound to do it.

XXIX. No sheriff, constable, coroners, or other our bailiffs,
shall hold pleas of the crown.

XXX. All counties, hundreds, wapentakes and trethings shall
stand at the old ferm, without any increase, except in our demesne
lands.

XXXI. If any one that holds of us a lay fee dies, and the
sheriff or our bailiff show our letters patents of summons concerning the debt due to us from the deceased, it shall be lawful for the
sheriff or our bailiff to attach and register the chattels of the deceased found upon his lay fee, to the value of the debt, by the view
of lawful men, so as nothing be removed until our whole debt be
paid; and the rest shall be left to the executors to fulfil the will of
the deceased; and if there be nothing due from him to us, all the
chattels shall remain to the deceased, saving to his wife and children their reasonable shares.

XXXII. If any freeman dies intestate, his chattels shall be distributed by the hands of his nearest relations and friends, by the
view of the church, saving to every one his debts which the deceased owed.

XXXIII. No constable or bailiff of ours shall take corn or other chattels of any man, unless he presently gives him money for it, or hath respite of payment from the seller.

XXXIV. No constable shall distrain any knight to give money for castle guard, if he himself shall do it in his own person, or by another able man, in case he shall be hindered by any reasonable cause.

XXXV. And if we shall lead him, or if we shall send him into the army, he shall be free from castle guard for the time he shall be in the army by our command.

XXXVI. No sheriff or bailiff of ours, or any other, shall take horses or carts of any for carriage.

XXXVII. Neither shall we, or our officers, or others, take any man's timber for our castles, or other uses, unless by the consent of the owner of the timber.

XXXVIII. We will retain the lands of those that are convicted of felony but one year and a day, and then they shall be delivered to the lord of the fee.

XXXIX. All wears for the time to come shall be demolished in the rivers of Thames and Medway, and throughout all England, except upon the sea-coast.

XL. The writ which is called præcipe shall not for the future be granted to any one of any tenement whereby a free man may lose his cause.

XLI. There shall be one measure of wine and one of ale through our whole realm, and one measure of corn, that is to say, the London quarter; and one breadth of dyed cloth and russets and haberjects, that is to say, two ells within the list; and the weights shall be as the measures.

XLII. From henceforward nothing shall be given or taken for a writ of inquisition, from him that desires an inquisition of life or limb, but shall be granted gratis, and not denied.

XLIII. If any one holds of us by fee farm, or socage, or burgage, and holds lands of another by military service, we will not have the wardship of the heir or land, which belongs to another man's fee, by reason of what he holds of us by fee farm, socage, or burgage; nor will we have the wardship of the fee farm, socage, or burgage, unless the fee farm is bound to perform military service.

XLIV. We will not have the wardship of an heir, nor of any

land which he holds of another by military service, by reason of any petit-serjeanty he holds of us, as by the service of giving us arrows, daggers, or the like.

XLV. No bailiff for the future shall put any man to his law, upon his single accusation, without credible witnesses produced to prove it.

XLVI. No freeman shall be taken, or imprisoned, or disseised, or outlawed, or banished, or any ways destroyed; nor will we pass upon him, or commit him to prison, unless by the legal judgment of his peers, or unless by the law of the land.

XLVII. We will sell to no man, we will deny no man, or defer right or justice.

XLVIII. All merchants shall have safe and secure conduct to go out of and to come into England, and to stay there, and to pass, as well by land as by water, to buy and sell by the ancient and allowed customs, without any evil toll, except in time of war, or when they shall be of any nation in war with us.

XLIX. And if there shall be found any such in our land in the beginning of a war, they shall be attached, without damage to their bodies or goods, until it may be known unto us, or our chief justiciary, how our merchants be treated in the nation at war with us; and if ours be safe there, theirs shall be safe in our lands.

L. It shall be lawful for the time to come, for any one to go out of our kingdom, and return safely and securely by land or by water, saving his allegiance to us; unless in time of war, by short space, for the benefit of the kingdom, except prisoners and outlaws, according to the law of the land, and people in war with us, and merchants who shall be in such condition as is above mentioned.

LI. If any man holds of any escheat, as of the honor of Wallingford, Nottingham, Bologne, Lancaster, or of other escheats which are in our hands, and are baronies, and dies, his heir shall not give any other relief, or perform any other service to us than he would to the baron, if the barony were in possession of the baron; we will hold it after the same manner the baron held it.

LII. Those men who dwell without the forest, from henceforth shall not come before our justiciaries of the forest upon summons, but such as are impleaded or are pledges for any that were attached for something concerning the forest.

LIII. We will not make any justiciaries, constables, bailiffs or sheriffs, but what are knowing in the laws of the realm, and are disposed duly to observe it.

LIV. All barons who are founders of abbies, and have charters of the kings of England for the advowson, or are entitled to it by ancient tenure, may have the custody of them, when void, as they ought to have.

LV. All woods that have been taken into the forests, in our own time, shall forthwith be laid out again, and the like shall be done with the rivers that have been taken or fenced in by us, during our reign.

LVI. All evil customs concerning forests, warrens, and foresters warreners, sheriffs and their officers, rivers and their keepers, shall forthwith be inquired into in each county, by twelve knights of the same shire, chosen by the most creditable persons in the same county, and upon oath; and within forty days after the said inquest be utterly abolished, so as never to be restored.

LVII. We will immediately give up all hostages and engagements, delivered unto us by our English subjects as securities for their keeping the peace, and yielding us faithful service.

LVIII. We will entirely remove from our bailiwicks the relations of Gerard de Athyes, so as that for the future they shall have no bailiwick in England. We will also remove Engelard de Cygony, Andrew, Peter, and Gyon de Canceles, Gyon de Cygony, Geoffrey de Martyn and his brothers, Philip Mark and his brothers, and his nephew Geoffrey, and their whole retinue.

LIX. And as soon as peace is restored, we will send out of the kingdom all foreign soldiers, crossbowmen and stipendiaries, who are come with horses and arms, to the injury of our people.

LX. If any one hath been dispossessed or deprived by us without the legal judgment of his peers, of his lands, castles, liberties or right, we will forthwith restore them to him; and if any dispute arises upon this head, let the matter be decided by the five and twenty barons hereafter mentioned, for the preservation of the peace.

LXI. As for all those things of which any person has without the legal judgment of his peers been dispossessed or deprived, either by king Henry, our father, or our brother, king Richard, and which we have in our hands, or are possessed by others, and we are bound to warrant and make good, we shall have a respite till the term usually allowed the Croises; excepting those things about which there is a suit depending, or whereof an inquest hath been made by our order, before we undertook the crusade. But when we return from our pilgrimage, or if we do not perform it, we will immediately cause full justice to be administered therein.

LXII. The same respite we shall have for disafforesting the forests, which Henry, our father, or our brother, Richard, have afforested ; and for the wardship of lands which are in another's fee, in the same manner as we have hitherto enjoyed these wardships, by reason of a fee held of us by knight's service, and for the abbies founded in any other fee than our own, in which the lord of the fee claims a right ; and when we return from our pilgrimage, or if we should not perform it, we will immediately do full justice to all the complainants in this behalf.

LXIII. No man shall be taken or imprisoned upon the appeal of a woman, for the death of any other man than her husband.

LXIV. All unjust and illegal fines, and all amerciaments, imposed unjustly and contrary to the law of the land, shall be entirely forgiven, or else left to the decision of the five and twenty barons hereafter mentioned for the preservation of the peace, or of the major part of them, together with the foresaid Stephen, archbishop of Canterbury, if he can be present, and others whom he shall think fit to take along with him ; and if he cannot be present, the business shall nevertheless go on without him ; but so that if one or more of the five and twenty barons aforesaid be plaintiffs in the same cause, they shall be set aside as to what concerns this particular affair, and others be chosen in their room out of the said five and twenty, and sworn by the rest to decide that matter.

LXV. If we have disseised or dispossessed the Welsh of any lands, liberties, or other things, without the legal judgment of their peers, they shall be immediately restored to them. And if any dispute arises upon this head, the matter shall be determined in the Marches, by the judgment of their peers ; for tenements in England, according to the law of England ; for tenements in Wales, according to the law of Wales ; for tenements in the Marches, according to the law of the Marches ; the same shall the Welsh do to us and our subjects.

LXVI. As for all those things of which any Welshman hath, without the legal judgment of his peers, been disseised or deprived, by king Henry, our father, or our brother, king Richard, and which we either have in our hands, or others are possessed of, and we are obliged to warrant it, we shall have a respite till the time generally allowed the Croisaders ; excepting those things, about which a suit is pending, or whereof an inquest has been made by our order, before we undertook the crusade. But when we return, or if we stay at home, and do not perform our pilgrimage, we will immediately do them full justice, according to the laws of the Welsh, and of the parts aforementioned.

LXVII. We will without delay dismiss the son of Lewelin, and all the Welsh hostages, and release them from the engagements they entered into with us for the preservation of the peace.

LXVIII. We shall treat with Alexander, king of Scots, concerning the restoring of his sisters, and hostages, and rights and liberties, in the same form and manner as we shall do to the rest of our barons of England ; unless by the engagements which his father William, late king of Scots, hath entered into with us, it ought to be otherwise ; and this shall be left to the determination of his peers in our court.

LXIX. All the aforesaid customs and liberties which we have granted to be holden in our kingdom, as much as it belongs to us towards our people, all our subjects, as well clergy as laity, shall observe, as far as they are concerned, towards their dependents.

LXX. And whereas, for the honor of God and the amendment of our kingdom, and for quieting the discord that has arisen between us and our barons, we have granted all the things aforesaid ; willing to render them firm and lasting, we do give and grant our subjects the following security, namely : that the barons may choose five and twenty barons of the kingdom, whom they shall think convenient, who shall take care with all their might to hold and observe, and cause to be observed, the peace and liberties we have granted them, and by this our present charter confirmed. So as that if we, our justiciary, our bailiffs, or any of our officers, shall in any case fail in the performance of them towards any person, or shall break through any of these articles of peace and security, and the offence is notified to four barons, chosen out of the five and twenty aforementioned, the said four barons shall repair to us, or to our justiciary, if we are out of the realm, and laying open the grievance, shall petition to have it redressed without delay ; and if it is not redressed by us, or, if we should chance to be out of the realm, if it is not redressed by our justiciary within forty days, reckoning from the time it has been notified to us, or to our justiciary, if we should be out of the realm, the four barons aforesaid shall lay the cause before the rest of the five and twenty barons, and the said five and twenty barons, together with the community of the whole kingdom, shall distrein and distress us in all the ways possible ; namely, by seising our castles, lands, possessions, and in any other manner they can, till the grievance is redressed to their pleasure, saving harmless our own person, and the persons of our queen and children ; and when it is redressed, they shall obey us as before.

LXXI. And any person whatsoever in the kingdom may swear that he will obey the orders of the five and twenty barons aforesaid, in the execution of the premises, and that he will distress us jointly with them, to the utmost of his power ; and we give public and free liberty to any one that will swear to them, and never shall hinder any person from taking the same oath.

LXXII. As for all those of our subjects, who will not of their own accord swear to join the five and twenty barons in distreining and distressing us, we will issue our order to make them take the same oath as aforesaid.

LXXIII. And if any one of the five and twenty barons dies, or goes out of the kingdom, or is hindered any other way from putting the things aforesaid in execution, the rest of the said five and twenty barons may choose another in his room, at their discretion, who shall be sworn in like manner as the rest.

LXXIV. In all things that are committed to the charge of these five and twenty barons, if, when they are all assembled together, they should happen to disagree about any matter, or some of them summoned will not, or cannot come, whatever is agreed upon or enjoyned by the major part of those who are present shall be reputed as firm and valid as if all the five and twenty had given their consent ; and the foresaid five and twenty shall swear that all the premises they shall faithfully observe, and cause with all their power to be observed.

LXXV. And we will not, by ourselves or others, procure anything whereby any of these concessions and liberties be revoked or lessened ; and if any such thing be obtained, let it be null and void ; neither shall we ever make use of it, either by ourselves or any other.

LXXVI. And all the ill-will, anger and malice that hath arisen between us and our subjects of the clergy and laity, from the first breaking out of the dissension between us, we do fully remit and forgive. Moreover, all trespasses occasioned by the said dissensions, from Easter, in the sixteenth year of our reign, till the restoration of peace and tranquillity, we hereby entirely remit to all, clergy as well as laity, and as far as in us lies, do fully forgive.

LXVII. We have moreover granted them our letters patents testimonial of Stephen, lord-archbishop of Canterbury, of Henry, lord-archbishop of Dublin, and the bishops aforesaid, as also of master Pandulph, for the security and concessions aforesaid.

LXXVIII. Wherefore we will, and firmly enjoin, that the church of England be free, and that all men in our kingdom have and hold all the aforesaid liberties, rights and concessions, truly and peaceably, freely and quietly, fully and wholly, to themselves and their heirs, of us and our heirs, in all things and places forever, as is aforesaid.

LXXIX. It is also sworn, as well on our part as upon the part of the barons, that all the things aforesaid shall faithfully and sincerely be observed.

Given under our hand, in the presence of the witnesses above named, and many others, in the meadow called Runningmede, between Windelsore and Staines, the 17th day of June, in the 17th year of our reign.

[The great charter has been repeatedly amended and confirmed. I take the liberty of copying the following down to the end of page 201, from Mr. Creasy's Text-Book of the Constitution.[1]]

---

[1] The Text-Book of the Constitution, Magna Charta, The Petition of Right and the Bill of Rights, with Historical Comments and Remarks on the Present Political Emergencies, by E. S. Creasy, M. A., Barrister-at-Law, Professor of History in University College, London, &c. London, 1848. A small work of 63 pages, excellent in its kind.

Since the first edition of the Civil Liberty was issued, Mr. Creasy has published The Rise and Progress of the English Constitution, London, 1853; the third edition of which was republished, in 1856, in New York, 12mo., 350 pages. It is the best book for the student to commence the study of the British Constitution, and preparatory for Hallam's Constitutional History of England. Throughout the present work it must have appeared that a knowledge of the English Constitution and of its history, is indispensable for a correct understanding of our own, and I recommend the work of Mr. Creasy, in this point of view, to every young American student.

MAGNA CHARTA,

THE GREAT CHARTER,

(TRANSLATED AS IN THE STATUTES AT LARGE,)

MADE IN THE NINTH YEAR OF KING HENRY THE THIRD, AND CONFIRMED BY
KING EDWARD THE FIRST, IN THE FIVE AND TWENTIETH YEAR OF HIS
REIGN.

Edward, by the grace of God king of England, lord of Ireland, and duke of Guyan : to all archbishops, bishops, &c. We have seen the great charter of the lord Henry, sometimes king of England, our father, of the liberties of England, in these words :

" Henry, by the grace of God king of England, lord of Ireland, duke of Normandy and Guyan, and earl of Anjou : to all archbishops, bishops, abbots, priors, earls, barons, sheriffs, provosts, and officers, and to all bailiffs and other our faithful subjects, which shall see this present charter, greeting : Know ye, that we, unto the honor of almighty God, and for the salvation of the souls of our progenitors and successors, kings of England, to the advancement of holy church and amendment of our realm, of our mere and free will, have given and granted to all archbishops, bishops, abbots, priors, earls, barons, and to all freemen of this our realm, these liberties following, to be kept in our kingdom of England forever."

CHAPTER I.

A Confirmation of Liberties.

" First, we have granted to God, and by this our present charter have confirmed for us and our heirs forever, that the church of England shall be free, and shall have all her whole rights and liberties inviolable. We have granted, also, and given to all the freemen of our realm, for us and our heirs forever, these liberties underwritten, to have and to hold to them and their heirs, of us and our heirs forever."

CHAPTER II.

The Relief of the King's Tenant of full Age.

[Same as 2d chapter of John's Charter.]

CHAPTER III.

The Wardship of the Heir within Age. The Heir a Knight.

[Similar to 3d chapter of John's Charter.]

CHAPTER IV.

No waste shall be made by a Guardian in waste lands.

[Same as 4th chapter of John's Charter.]

CHAPTER V.

Guardians shall maintain the Inheritance of Wards. Of Bishoprics, &c.

[Similar to 5th chapter of John's Charter, with addition of like provisions against the waste of ecclesiastical possessions while in the king's hand during a vacancy in the see, &c.]

CHAPTER VI.

Heirs shall be Married without Disparagement.

[Similar to 6th chapter of John's Charter.]

CHAPTER VII.

A Widow shall have her Marriage, Inheritance and Quarantine. The King's Widow, &c.

[Similar (with additions) to the 7th and 8th chapters of John's Charter.]

CHAPTER VIII.

How Sureties shall be charged to the King.

[Same as 9th chapter of John's Charter.]

CHAPTER IX.

The Liberties of London and other Cities and Towns confirmed.

[Same as 13th chapter of John's Charter.]

CHAPTER X.

None shall distrain for more Service than is due.

[Same as 16th chapter of John's Charter.]

CHAPTER XI.

Common Pleas shall not follow the King's Court.

[Same as 17th chapter of John's Charter.]

CHAPTERS XII. & XIII.

When and before whom Assizes shall be taken.   Adjournment
for Difficulty.   Assizes of Darrein Presentment.
[Analogous to 18th and 19th chapters of John's Charter.]

CHAPTER XIV.

How Men of all sorts shall be amerced, and by whom.
[Same as 20th and 21st chapters of John's Charter.]

CHAPTERS XV. & XVI.

Making and defending of Bridges and Banks.
[Similar to 23d chapter of John's Charter.]

CHAPTER XVII.

Holding Pleas of the Crown.
[Same as 24th chapter of John's Charter.]

CHAPTER XVIII.

The King's Debtor dying, the King shall be first paid.
[Same as 26th chapter of John's Charter.]

CHAPTERS XIX., XX. & XXI.

Purveyors for a Castle.   Doing of Castle-ward.   Taking of
Horses, Carts and Woods.
[Same as 28th, 29th, 30th and 31st chapters of John's Charter.]

CHAPTER XXII.

How long Felons' Lands shall be holden by the King.
[Same as 32d chapter of John's Charter.]

CHAPTER XXIII.

In what places Wears shall be put down.
[Same as 33d chapter of John's Charter.]

CHAPTER XXIV.

In what case a Præcipe in Capite is grantable.
[Same as 14th chapter of John's Charter.]

CHAPTER XXV.
There shall be but one Measure through the Realm.
[Same as 35th chapter of John's Charter.]

CHAPTER XXVI.
Inquisition of Life and Member.
[Same as 38th chapter of John's Charter.]

CHAPTER XXVII.
Tenure of the King in Socage, and of another by Knight's Service. Petit Serjeanty.
[Same as 37th chapter of John's Charter.]

CHAPTER XXVIII.
Wager of Law shall not be without witness.
[Same as 38th chapter of John's Charter.]

CHAPTER XXIX.
None shall be condemned without Trial.   Justice shall not be sold or deferred.[1]

"No freeman shall be taken, or imprisoned, or be disseised of his freehold, or liberties, or free customs, or be outlawed or exiled, or any otherwise destroyed ; nor will we pass upon him, nor *condemn* him, but by lawful judgment of his peers, or by the law of the land.   We will sell to no man, we will not deny or *defer* to any man, either justice or right."

CHAPTER XXX.
Merchant Strangers coming into this Realm shall be well used.
[Same as 41st chapter of John's Charter.]

CHAPTER XXXI.
Tenure of a Barony coming into the King's hands by Escheat.
[Same as 43d chapter of John's Charter.]

---

[1] See 39th and 40th chapters of John's Charter.

CHAPTER XXXII.

Lands shall not be Aliened to the Prejudice of the Lord's Service [i. e. Lord of the Fee].

CHAPTER XXXIII.

Patrons of Abbeys shall have the custody of them in time of Vacation.

[Same as 46th chapter of John's Charter.]

CHAPTER XXXIV.

In what cases only a Woman shall have an Appeal of Death.

[Same as 51st chapter of John's Charter.]

CHAPTER XXXV.

At what time shall be kept a County Court, a Sheriff's Term, and a Leet.

CHAPTER XXXVI.

No Land shall be given in Mortmain.

" It shall not be lawful from henceforth to any to give his lands to any religious house, and to take the same land again to hold of the same house. Nor shall it be lawful to any house of religion to take the lands of any, and to lease the same to him of whom he received it : if any from henceforth give his lands to any religious house, and thereupon be convict, the gift shall be utterly void, and the land shall accrue to the lord of the fee."

CHAPTER XXXVII.

A Subsidy in respect of this Charter and the Charter of the Forest granted to the King.

" Escuage from henceforth shall be taken like as it was wont to be in the time of king Henry, our grandfather; reserving to all archbishops, bishops, abbots, priors, templars, hospitalers, earls, barons, and all persons, as well spiritual as temporal, all their free liberties and free customs, which they have had in time past. And all these customs and liberties aforesaid, which we have granted to be holden within this our realm, as much as appertaineth to us and our heirs, we shall observe. And all men of this our realm, as well spiritual as temporal (as much as in them is), shall observe the same against all persons in like wise. And for this our gift and grant of these liberties, and of others contained in our charter of liberties of our forest, the archbishops, bishops, abbots, priors, earls, barons, knights, freeholders, and other our subjects, have given unto us the fifteenth part of all their moveables. And we have granted unto them, for us and our heirs, that neither we nor our heirs shall procure or do anything whereby the liberties in this charter contained shall be infringed or broken. And if anything be procured by any person contrary to the premises, it shall be had of no force nor effect. These being witnesses: Lord B., archbishop of Canterbury, E., bishop of London, I., bishop of Bath, P., of Winchester, H., of Lincoln, R., of Salisbury, W., of Rochester, W., of Worcester, J., of Ely, H., of Hereford, R., of Chichester, W., of Exeter, bishops; the abbot of St. Edmonds, the abbot of St. Albans, the abbot of Bello, the abbot of St. Augustine's in Canterbury, the abbot of Evesham, the abbot of Westminster, the abbot of Bourgh St. Peter, the abbot of Reding, the abbot of Abindon, the abbot of Malmsbury, the abbot of Winchcomb, the abbot of Hyde, the abbot of Certesy, the abbot of Sherburn, the abbot of Cerne, the abbot of Abbotebir, the abbot of Middleton, the abbot of Seleby, the abbot of Cirencester; H. de Burgh, justice, H., earl of Chester and Lincoln, W., earl of Salisbury, W., earl of Warren, G. de Clare, earl of Gloucester and Hereford, W. de Ferrars, earl of Derby, W. de Mandeville, earl of Essex, H. de Bygod, earl of Norfolk, W., earl of Albemarle, H., earl of Hereford, J., constable of Chester, R. de Ros, R. Fitzwalter, R. de Vyponte, W. de Bruer, R. de Muntefichet, P. Fitzherbert, W. de Aubenie, J. Gresly, F. de Breus, J. de Monemue, J. Fitzallen, H. de Mortimer, W. de Beauchamp, W. de St. John, P. de Mauly, Brian de Lisle, Thomas de Multon, R. de Argenteyn, G. de Nevil, W. Mauduit, J. de Balun, and others."

We, ratifying and approving these gifts and grants aforesaid, confirm and make strong all the same for us and our heirs perpetually; and by the tenor of these presents do renew the same, willing and granting for us and our heirs that this charter, and all and singular its articles, forever shall be stedfastly, firmly and inviolably observed. Although some articles in the same charter contained yet hitherto peradventure have not been kept, we will

31

and, by authority royal, command from henceforth firmly they be observed. In witness whereof, we have caused these our letters patent to be made. T. Edward, our son, at Westminster, the twelfth day of October, in the twenty-fifth year of our reign.

Magna Charta, in this form, has been solemnly confirmed by our kings and parliaments upwards of thirty times; but in the twenty-fifth year of Edward I. much more than a simple confirmation of it was obtained for England. As has already been mentioned, the original charter of John forbade the levying of *escuage*, save by consent of the great council of the land; and although those important provisions were not repeated in Henry's charter, it is certain that they were respected. Henry's barons frequently refused him the subsidies which his prodigality was always demanding. Neither he nor any of his ministers seems ever to have claimed for the crown the prerogative of taxing the landholders at discretion; but the sovereign's right of levying money from his towns and cities, under the name of tallages or prises, was constantly exercised during Henry III.'s reign, and during the earlier portion of his son's. But, by the statute of Edward I. intituled *Confirmatio Chartarum*, all private property was secured from royal spoliation, and placed under the safeguard of the great council of *all* the realm. The material portions of that statute are as follows:

CONFIRMATIO CHARTARUM.

ANNO VICESIMO QUINTO EDV. I.

CAP. V.

And for so much as divers people of our realm are in fear that the aids and tasks which they have given to us beforetime, towards our wars and other business, of their own grant and good will (howsoever they were made), might turn to a bondage to them and their heirs, because they might be at another time found in the rolls, and likewise for the prises taken throughout the realm, in our name, by our ministers, we have granted for us and our heirs that we shall not draw such aids, tasks, nor prises, into a custom for anything that hath been done heretofore, be it by roll or any other precedent that may be founden.

CAP. VI.

Moreover, we have granted for us and our heirs, as well to archbishops, bishops, abbots, priors, and other folk of holy church, as also to earls, barons, and to all the commonalty of the land, that for no business from thenceforth we *shall take such manner of aids, tasks, nor prises, but by the common assent of all*[1] *the realm, and for the common* profit thereof, saving the ancient aids and prises due and accustomed.

---

[1] "Par commun assent de *tut* le roiaume." The version in our statute-book omits the important word "All."

APPENDIX V.

THE PETITION OF RIGHT.[1]

To the King's Most Excellent Majestie.

HUMBLY shew unto our Sovereign Lord the King, the Lords Spiritual and Temporal, and Commons in Parliament assembled, that whereas it is declared and enacted by a Statute, made in the tyme of the Raigne of King Edward the first, commonly called " Statutum de Tallagio non concedendo," that no Tallage or Aide should be laid or levied, by the King or his heires, in this Realme; without the good-will and assent of the Arch Bishopps, Bishopps, Earles, Barons, Knights, Burgesses and other the freemen of the cominalty of this realme; And by Authority of Parliament houlden in the five and twentieth yere of the Raigne of King Edward the third, it is declared and enacted, that from thenceforth noe person should be compelled to make any loanes to the King against his will, because such loanes were against reason, and the franchise of the land ; and by other lawes of this realme it is provided, that none should be charged by any charge or imposition, called a Benevolence, nor by such like charge, by which the Statuts before mentioned, and other the good lawes and statuts of this Realme, your Subjects have inherited this freedom, that they should not be compelled to contribute to any Tax, Tallage, Aide, or other like charge, not sett by common consent in Parliament.

Yet nevertheless of late, divers commissions, directed to sundrie commissioners in severall Counties, with instructions, have been issued, by means whereof your People have bene in divers places assembled, and required to lend certaine sommes of money unto your Majestie, and many of them upon their refusall soe to doe, have had an oath administered unto them, not warrantable by the

---

[1] This petition was drawn up by Sir Edward Coke. Coke, 207, edit. of 1697.

(484)

Lawes or Statuts of this Realme, and have been constrained to become bound to make appearance, and give attendance before your Privie Councell, and in other places; and others of them have beene therefore imprisoned, confined, and sundrie other wayes molested and disquieted : And divers other charges have bene laid and leavied upon your People in severall Counties, by Lord Lieutenants, Deputie-Lieutenants, Commissioners for musters, Justices of peace and others, by commaunde or direction from your Majestie, or your Privie-Councell, against the lawes and free customes of the realme.

And whereas alsoe by the Statute called "The greate Charter of the Liberties of England," it is declared and enacted, that noe freeman may be taken or imprisoned, or be disseised of his freehold or liberties, or his free customes, or be outlawed or exiled, or in any manner destroyed, but by the lawfull judgment of his Peeres, or by the lawe of the land.

And in the eight and twentieth yere of the reigne of King Edward the third, it was declared and ennacted by Authoritie of Parliament, that no man, of what estate or condition that he be, should be putt out of his lands or tenements, nor taken nor imprisoned, nor disherited, nor putt to death, without being brought to answer by due process of lawe.

Nevertheless against the tenour of the said Statutes, and other the good lawes and Statuts of your Realme, to that end provided, divers of your subjects have of late bene imprisoned without any cause showed; and when for their deliverance they were brought before your Justices, by your Majestie's Writ of Habeas Corpus, there to undergoe and receive, as the Court should order, and their Keepers commaunded to certify the causes of their detayner; noe cause was certified, but that they were detayned by your Majestie's special commaund, signified by the Lords of your Privie Councell, and yet were returned back to severall prisons, without being charged with any thynge to which they might make answeare according to the lawe.

And whereas of late, great companies of souldiers and marriners have bene dispersed into divers Counties of the Realme, and the inhabitants against their wills have been compelled to receive them into their houses, and there to suffer them to sojorne, against the lawes and customes of this realme, and to the great grievance and vexation of the People.

And whereas alsoe, by authority of Parliament, in the 25th yere of the raigne of King Edward III., it is declared and enacted that noe man should be forejudged of life or lymbe, against the forme of the great Charter, and the lawe of the land, and by the said great Charter, and other the Laws and Statuts of this your Realme, no man ought to be adjudged to death, but by the lawes established in this your realme, either by the customes of the same realme, or by Acts of Parliament; And whereas noe offender, of what kind soever, is exempted from the proceedings to be used, and the punishments to be inflicted by the lawes and statutes of this your realme; nevertheless of late time, divers commissions under your Majestie's Greate Seale have issued forth, by which certaine persons have been assigned and appointed commissioners, with power and authoritie to proceed within the land, according to the justice of martiall lawe, against such soulders and marriners, or other dissolute persons joining with them, as should commit any murder, robbery, felonie, meeting, or other outrage or misdemeanour, whatsoever; and by such summarie course and order as is agreeable to martiall lawe, and as is used in armies in tyme of war, to proceed to the tryal and condemnation of such offenders, and them to cause to be executed and putt to death, according to the lawe martiall.

By pretext whereof, some of your Majestie's Subjects have bene by some of the said commissioners put to death, when and where, if lawes and statuts of the land they had deserved death, by the same lawes and statuts alsoe they might, and by noe other ought, to have been judged and executed.

And alsoe sundrie grievous offenders, by colour thereof clayminge an exemption, have escaped the punishments due to them by the lawes and statuts of this your realm, by reason that divers of your officers and ministers of justice have unjustly refused or forborne to proceed against such offenders, according to the same lawes and statuts, upon pretence that the said offenders were punishable only by martiall lawe, and by authority of such commissions as aforesaid; which commissions, and all others of like nature, are wholely and directlie contrary to the said lawes and statuts of this your realme.

They doe therefore humbly pray your most excellent Majestie, That no man hereafter be compelled to make or yielde any guifte, loane, benevolence, tax, or such like charge, without common consent by Act of Parliament; and that none be called to make answeare, or take such oath, or to give attendance, or be confyned, or otherwise molested or disquieted concerning the same, or for refusal thereof : And that noe freeman, in any such manner as is before mentioned, be imprisoned or detayned : And that your Majestie would be pleased to remove the said souldiers and marriners, and that your People may not be soe burthened in the tyme to come : And that the aforesaid commissions for proceedinge by martiall lawe, may be revoaked and annulled : and that hereafter, noe commissions of like nature may issue forth to any person or persons whatsoever, to be executed as aforesaid, least by colour of them, any of your Majestie's subjects be destroyed, or putt to death, contrary to the lawes and franchise of the land.

All which they do most humbly pray of your most excellent Majestie, as their Rights and Liberties, according to the lawes and statuts of this Realme : And that your Majestie would also vouchsafe to declare, that the awardes, doeings, and proceedings, to the prejudice of your People, in any of the premisses, shall not be drawn hereafter into consequence or example : And that your Majestie would be alsoe graciously pleased, for the further comfort and safetie of your people, to declare your royal will and pleasure, That in the things aforesaid all your officers and ministers shall serve you, according to the lawes and statuts of this realme, as they tender the honour of your majestie, and the prosperity of this Kingdom.

The King's Answer to the Petition of Right.

The King willeth that Right be done, according to the laws and customs of the realme ; and that the Statutes be put in due execution, that his subjects may have no cause to complain of any wrong or oppressions, contrary to their just Rights and Liberties, to the preservation whereof he holds himself in conscience as well obliged, as of his prerogative.

Petition of both Houses to the King, on 7th day of June, 1628, *wherein a more full and satisfactory answer to the above Petition is prayed for.*

May it please your most excellent Majestie, the Lords Spiritual and Temporal, and Commons in Parliament assembled, taking in consideration that the good intelligence between your Majestie and your People, doth much depend upon your Majestie's answer upon their Petition of Right, formerly presented; with unanimous consent do now become most humble suitors unto your Majestie, that you would be pleased to give a clear and satisfactory answer thereunto in full Parliament.

To which Petition the King replied:

The answer I have already given you was made with so good deliberation, and approved by the judgments of so many wise men, that I could not have imagined but that it would have given you full satisfaction: But to avoid all ambiguous interpretations, and to show you there is no doubleness in my meaning, I am willing to pleasure you as well in words as in substance: Read your petition, and you shall have an answer that I am sure will please you.

Here the petition was read, and the following answer was returned: "Soit Droit fait comme il est desiré."   C. R.

Then said his Majesty:

This I am sure is full, yet no more than I granted you in my first answer, for the meaning of that, was to confirm your liberties, knowing according to your own protestations, that you neither mean nor can hurt my prerogative. And I assure you, my maxim is, that the People's liberties strengthen the King's Prerogative, and the King's Prerogative is to defend the People's Liberties.

You see how ready I have shown myself to satisfy your demand, so that I have done my part; wherefore if this parliament have not a happy conclusion, the sin is yours, I am free from it.

[The above is the Answer of the King in Parliament, and his Speech on that occasion, June 7th, 1628.]

APPENDIX VI.

AN ACT FOR THE BETTER SECURING THE LIBERTY OF THE
SUBJECT, AND FOR PREVENTION OF IMPRISONMENTS BEYOND
THE SEAS, COMMONLY CALLED "THE HABEAS CORPUS ACT."[1]

31 CH. 2. CH. 2, MAY, 1679.

WHEREAS great delays have been used by sheriffs, gaolers and
other officers, to whose custody any of the king's subjects have been
committed, for criminal or supposed criminal matters, in making
returns of writs of habeas corpus, to them directed, by standing out
on alias or pluries habeas corpus, and sometimes more, and by other
shifts to avoid their yielding obedience to such writs, contrary to
their duty and the known laws of the land, whereby many of the
king's subjects have been, and hereafter may be, long detained in
prison, in such cases where by law they are bailable, to their great
charge and vexation :

II. For the prevention whereof, and the more speedy relief of
all persons imprisoned for any such criminal or supposed criminal
matters ; (2) *Be it enacted, by the king's most excellent majesty,
by and with the advice and consent of the lords spiritual and
temporal, and commons in this present parliament assembled,
and by the authority thereof,* That whensoever any person or persons shall bring any *habeas corpus* directed unto any sheriff or
sheriffs, gaoler, minister, or other person whatsoever, for any person
in his or their custody, and the said writ shall be served upon the
said officer, or left at the gaol or prison with any of the under-officers, under-keepers, or deputy of the said officers or keepers, that
the said officer or officers, his or their under-officers, under-keepers
or deputies, shall within three days after the service thereof, as aforesaid (unless the commitment aforesaid were for treason or felony,
plainly and especially expressed in the warrant of commitment),

---

[1] Copied from the Statutes at Large, by Danby Pickering, Esq., edit.
1763, vol. 8, p. 432.

upon payment or tender of the charges of bringing the said prisoner, to be ascertained by the judge or court that awarded the same, and endorsed upon the said writ, not exceeding 12 pence per mile, and upon security given by his own bond to pay the charges of carrying back the prisoner, if he shall be remanded by the court or judge to which he shall be brought, according to the true intent of this present act, and that he will not make any escape by the way, make return of such writ; (3) and bring, or cause to be brought, the body of the party so committed or restrained, unto or before the lord chancellor, or lord keeper of the great seal of England, for the time being, or the judges or barons of the said court, from whence the said writ shall issue, or unto and before such other person or persons before whom the said writ is made returnable, according to the command thereof; (4) and shall then likewise certify the true causes of his detainer or imprisonment, unless the commitment of the said party be in any place beyond the distance of twenty miles from the place or places where such court or person is, or shall be residing; and if beyond the distance of 20 miles, and not above 100 miles, then within the space of ten days, and if beyond the distance of 100 miles, then within the space of 20 days after such delivery aforesaid, and not longer.

III.   And to the intent that no sheriff, gaoler or other officer may pretend ignorance of the import of any such writ; (2) Be it enacted by the authority aforesaid, that all such writs shall be marked in this manner: " Per statutum, tricesimo primo Caroli secundi Regis," and shall be signed by the person that awards the same ; (3) and if any person or persons shall be or stand committed or detained as aforesaid, for any crime, unless for felony or treason, plainly expressed in the warrant of commitment, in the vacation time and out of term it shall and may be lawful to and for the person or persons so committed or detained (other than persons convict or in execution by legal process), or any one in his or their behalf, to appeal or complain to the lord chancellor or lord keeper, or any one of his majesty's justices, either of the one bench or of the other, or the barons of the exchequer of the degree of the coif ; (4) and the said lord chancellor, lord keeper, justices or barons, or any of them, upon view of the copy or copies of the warrant or warrants of commitment and detainer, or otherwise upon oath made that such copy or copies were denied to be given by such person

or persons in whose custody the prisoner or prisoners is or are detained, are hereby authorized and required, upon request made in
writing by such person or persons, or any on his, her, or their behalf, attested and subscribed by two witnesses who were present at
the delivery of the same, to award and grant an habeas corpus,
under the seal of such court whereof he shall then be one of the
judges, (5) to be directed to the officer or officers in whose custody
the party so committed or detained shall be, returnable *immediate*
before the said lord chancellor or lord keeper, or such justice,
baron, or any other justice or baron of the degree of the coif, of
any of the said courts; (6) and upon service thereof as aforesaid,
the officer or officers, his or their under-officer or under-officers,
under-keeper or under-keepers, or their deputy, in whose custody
the party is so committed or detained, shall within the time respectively before limited, bring such prisoner or prisoners before
the said lord chancellor, or lord keeper, or such justices, barons, or
one of them, before whom the said writ is made returnable, and in
case of his absence, before any other of them, with the return of
such writ and the true causes of the commitment or detainer; (7)
and thereupon, within two days after the party shall be brought
before them, the said lord chancellor or lord keeper, or such justice
or baron before whom the prisoner shall be brought as aforesaid,
shall discharge the said prisoner from his imprisonment, taking his
or their recognizance, with one or more surety or sureties, in any
sum according to their discretions, having regard to the quality of
the prisoner and the nature of the offence, for his or their appearance in the court of king's bench the term following, or at the next
assizes, sessions, or general gaol delivery, of or for such county,
city or place where the commitment was, or where the offence was
committed, or in such other court where the said offence is properly
cognizable, as the case shall require, and then shall certify the said
writ with the return thereof, and the said recognizance or recog-
nizances into the said court where such appearance is to be made;
(8) unless it shall appear to the said lord chancellor, or lord keeper,
or justice or justices, or baron or barons, that the party so committed is detained upon a legal process, order or warrant, out of
some court that hath jurisdiction of criminal matters, or by some
warrant signed and sealed with the hand and seal of any of the
said justices or barons, or some justice or justices of the peace, for

such matters or offences for the which by the law the prisoner is not bailable.

IV. Provided always, and be it enacted, That if any person shall have wilfully neglected, by the space of two whole terms after his imprisonment, to pray a habeas corpus for his enlargement, such person so wilfully neglecting shall not have any habeas corpus to be granted in vacation time, in pursuance of this act.

V. And be it further enacted, by the authority aforesaid, That if any officer or officers, his or their under-officer or under-officers, under-keeper or under-keepers, or deputy, shall neglect or refuse to make the returns aforesaid, or to bring the body or bodies of the prisoner or prisoners according to the command of the said writ, within the respective times aforesaid, or upon demand made by the prisoner or person in his behalf, shall refuse to deliver, or within the space of six hours after demand, shall not deliver to the person so demanding, a true copy of the warrant or warrants of commit- ment and detainer of such prisoner, which he and they are hereby required to deliver accordingly; all and every the head gaolers and keepers of such person, and such other person in whose custody the prisoner shall be detained, shall for the first offence forfeit to the prisoner or party grieved the sum of £100; (2) and for the second offence the sum of £200, and shall and is hereby made in- capable to hold or execute his said office; (3) the said penalties to be recovered by the prisoner or party grieved, his executors and administrators, against such offender, his executors or adminis- trators, by any action of debt, suit, bill, plaint or information, in any of the king's courts at Westminster, wherein no essoin, protec- tion, privilege, injunction, wager of law, or stay of prosecution by " Non vult ulterius prosequi," or otherwise, shall be admitted or allowed, or any more than one imparlance; (4) and any recovery or judgment at the suit of any party grieved, shall be a sufficient conviction for the first offence ; and any after recovery or judgment at the suit of a party grieved, for any offence after the first judg- ment, shall be a sufficient conviction to bring the officers or person within the said penalty for the second offence.

VI. And for the prevention of unjust vexation by reiterated commitments for the same offence; (2) Be it enacted, by the au- thority aforesaid, That no person or persons, which shall be delivered or set at large upon any habeas corpus, shall at any time hereafter be again imprisoned or committed for the same offence, by any person or persons whatsoever, other than by the legal order and process of such court wherein he or they shall be bound by recognizance to appear, or other court having jurisdiction of the cause ; (3) and if any other person or persons shall knowingly, contrary to this act recommit or imprison, or knowingly procure or cause to be recommitted or imprisoned, for the same offence or pretended offence, any person or persons delivered or set at large as aforesaid, or be knowingly aiding or assisting therein, then he or they shall forfeit to the prisoner or party grieved, the sum of £500 ; any colorable pretence or variation in the warrant or warrants of commitment notwithstanding, to be recovered as aforesaid.

VII. Provided always, and be it further enacted, That if any person or persons shall be committed for high treason or felony, plainly and specially expressed in the warrant of commitment, upon his prayer or petition in open court, the first week of the term, or first day of the sessions of oyer and terminer or general gaol delivery, to be brought to his trial, shall not be indicted some time in the next term, sessions of oyer and terminer or general gaol delivery, after such commitment ; it shall and may be lawful to and for the judges of the court of king's bench, and justices of oyer and terminer or general gaol delivery, and they are hereby required, upon motion to them made in open court the last day of the term, sessions or gaol delivery, either by the prisoner or any one in his behalf, to set at liberty the prisoner upon bail, unless it appear to the judges and justices, upon oath made, that the witnesses for the king could not be produced the same term, sessions or general gaol delivery ; (2) and if any person or persons committed as aforesaid, upon his prayer or petition in open court the first week of the term or the first day of the sessions of oyer and terminer and general gaol delivery, to be brought to his trial, shall not be indicted and tried the second term, sessions of oyer and terminer or general gaol delivery, after his commitment, or upon his trial shall be acquitted, he shall be discharged from his imprisonment.

VIII. Provided always, That nothing in this act shall extend to discharge out of prison any person charged in debt, or other action, or with process in any civil cause, but that after he shall be discharged of his imprisonment for such his criminal offence, he shall be kept in custody according to the law for such other suit.

IX. Provided always, and be it further enacted by the authority aforesaid, That if any person or persons, subjects of this realm, shall be committed to any prison, or in custody of any officer or officers whatsoever, for any criminal or supposed criminal matter, that the said person shall not be removed from the said prison and custody, into the custody of any other officer or officers ; (2) unless it be by habeas corpus or some other legal writ ; or where the prisoner is delivered to the constable or other inferior officer, to carry such prisoner to some common gaol; (3) or where any person is sent by order of any judge of assize, or justice of the peace, to any common workhouse or house of correction ; (4) or where the prisoner is removed from one place or prison to another within the same county, in order to his or her trial or discharge in due course of law ; (5) or in case of sudden fire or infection, or other necessity ; (6) and if any person or persons shall, after such commitment aforesaid, make out and sign or countersign any warrant or warrants for such removal aforesaid, contrary to this act ; as well he that makes or signs or countersigns such warrant or warrants, as the officer or officers that obey or execute the same, shall suffer and incur the pains and forfeitures in this act before mentioned, both for the first and second offence respectively, to be recovered in manner aforesaid by the party grieved.

X. Provided also, and be it further enacted by the authority aforesaid, That it shall and may be lawful to and for any prisoner and prisoners as aforesaid, to move and obtain his or their habeas corpus, as well out of the high court of chancery or court of exchequer as out of the courts of king's bench or common pleas, or either of them ; (2) and if the said lord chancellor or lord keeper, or any judge or judges, baron or barons, for the time being, of the degree of the coif, of any of the courts aforesaid, in the vacation time, upon view of the copy or copies of the warrant or warrants of commitment or detainer, upon oath made that such copy or copies were denied as aforesaid, shall deny any writ of habeas corpus, by this act required to be granted, being moved for as aforesaid, they shall severally forfeit to the prisoner or party grieved, the sum of £500, to be recovered in manner aforesaid.

XI. And be it declared and enacted by the authority aforesaid, That an habeas corpus, according to the true intent and meaning of this act, may be directed and run into any county Palatine, the

Cinque Ports, or other privileged places within the kingdom of England, dominion of Wales, or town of Berwick upon Tweed, and the islands of Jersey or Guernsey; any law or usage to the contrary notwithstanding.

XII. And for preventing illegal imprisonments in prisons beyond the seas; (2) Be it further enacted by the authority aforesaid, That no subject of this realm, that now is or hereafter shall be an inhabitant or resiant of this kingdom of England, dominion of Wales, or town of Berwick upon Tweed, shall or may be sent prisoner into Scotland, Ireland, Jersey, Guernsey, Tangier, or into parts, garrisons, islands, or places, beyond the seas, which are or at any time hereafter shall be within or without the dominions of his majesty, his heirs or successors; (3) and that every such imprisonment is hereby enacted and adjudged to be illegal; (4) and that if any of the said subjects now is or hereafter shall be so imprisoned, every such person and persons so imprisoned, shall and may for every such imprisonment maintain, by virtue of this act, an action or actions of false imprisonment, in any of his majesty's courts of record, against the person or persons by whom he or she shall be so committed, detained, imprisoned, sent prisoner or transported, contrary to the true meaning of this act, and against all or any person or persons that shall frame, contrive, write, seal or countersign any warrant or writing for such commitment, detainer, imprisonment, or transportation, or shall be advising, aiding, or assisting in the same, or any of them; (5) and the plaintiff in every such action shall have judgment to recover his treble costs, besides damages, which damages so to be given shall not be less than £500; (6) in which action no delay, stay or stop of proceeding by rule, order or command, nor no injunction, protection or privilege whatsoever, nor any other than one imparlance, shall be allowed, excepting such rule of the court wherein such action shall depend, made in open court, as shall be thought in justice necessary for special cause to be expressed in said rule; (7) and the person or persons who shall knowingly frame, contrive, write, seal or countersign any warrant for such commitment, detainer, or transportation, or shall so commit, detain, imprison, or transport any person or persons, contrary to this act, or be any ways advising, aiding or assisting therein, being lawfully convicted thereof, shall be disabled from thenceforth to bear any office of trust or profit within the said realm of England, dominion of Wales, or town of Berwick upon Tweed, or any of the islands, territories or dominions thereunto belonging; (8) and shall incur and sustain the pains, penalties and forfeitures limited, ordained and provided in and by the statute of provision and præmunire, made in the sixteenth year of king Richard the Second; (9) and be incapable of any pardon from the king, his heirs or successors, of the said forfeitures, losses or disabilities, or any of them.

XIII. Provided always, That nothing in this act shall extend to give benefit to any person who shall by contract in writing agree with any merchant or owner of any plantation, or other person whatsoever, to be transported to any parts beyond the seas, and receive earnest upon such agreement, although that afterwards such person shall renounce such contract.

XIV. Provided always, and be it enacted, That if any person or persons lawfully convicted of any felony, shall in open court pray to be transported beyond the seas, and the court shall think fit to leave him or them in prison for that purpose, such person or persons may be transported into any parts beyond the seas; this act, or anything herein contained, to the contrary notwithstanding.

XV. Provided also, and be it enacted, That nothing herein contained shall be deemed, construed or taken to extend to the imprisonment of any person before the first day of June, one thousand six hundred and seventy-nine, or to anything advised, procured or otherwise done relating to such imprisonment; anything herein contained to the contrary notwithstanding.

XVI. Provided also, That if any person or persons at any time resiant in this realm, shall have committed any capital offence in Scotland or in Ireland, or in any of the islands or foreign plantations of the king, his heirs or successors, where he or she ought to be tried for such offence, such person or persons may be sent to such place, there to receive such trial in such manner as the same might have been used before the making of this act; anything herein contained to the contrary notwithstanding.

XVII. Provided also, and be it enacted, That no person or persons shall be sued, impleaded, molested or troubled for any of-fence against this act, unless the party offending be sued or impleaded for the same within two years at the most, after such time wherein the offence shall be committed, in case the party grieved shall not be then in prison; and if he shall be in prison, then within the space of two years after the decease of the person imprisoned, or his or her delivery out of prison, which shall first happen.

XVIII. And to the intent no person may avoid his trial at the assizes or general gaol delivery, by procuring his removal before the assizes, at such time as he cannot be brought back to receive his trial there; (2) Be it enacted, that after the assizes proclaimed for that county where the prisoner is detained, no person shall be removed from the common gaol upon any habeas corpus granted in pursuance of this act, but upon any such habeas corpus shall be brought before the judge of assize in open court, who is thereupon to do what to justice shall appertain.

XIX. Provided nevertheless, That after the assizes are ended, any person or persons detained may have his or her habeas corpus according to the direction and intention of this act.

XX. And be it also enacted by the authority aforesaid, That if any information, suit or action shall be brought or exhibited against any person or persons for any offence committed or to be committed against the form of this law, it shall be lawful for such defendants to plead the general issue, that they are not guilty or that they owe nothing, and to give such special matter in evidence to the jury that shall try the same, which matter being pleaded had been good and sufficient matter in law to have discharged the said defendant or defendants against the said information, suit or action, and the same matter shall be then as available to him or them, to all intents and purposes, as if he or they had sufficiently pleaded, set forth or alleged the same matter in bar, or discharge of such information, suit or action.

XXI. And because many times persons charged with petty treason or felony, or accessories thereunto, are committed upon suspicion only, whereupon they are bailable or not, according as the circumstances making out that suspicion are more or less weighty, which are best known to the justices of the peace that committed the persons, and have the examination before them, or to other justices of the peace in the county; (2) Be it therefore enacted, That where any person shall appear to be committed by any judge or justice of the peace, and charged as accessory before the fact to any petty treason or felony, or upon suspicion thereof, or with

32

suspicion of petty treason or felony, which petty treason or felony shall be plainly and specially expressed in the warrant of commitment, that such person shall not be removed or bailed by virtue of this act, or in any other manner than they might have been before the making of this act.

APPENDIX VII.

BILL OF RIGHTS, PASSED 1 WILLIAM AND MARY, SESS. 2,
CH. 2, 1689.

AN ACT FOR DECLARING THE RIGHTS AND LIBERTIES OF THE SUBJECT, AND
SETTLING THE SUCCESSION OF THE CROWN.

1 W. & M. 1689.

WHEREAS the lords spiritual and temporal, and commons assembled at Westminster, lawfully, fully and freely representing all the estates of the people of this realm, did, upon the thirteenth day of February, in the year of our Lord one thousand six hundred and eighty-eight, present unto their majesties then called and known by the name and style of William and Mary, prince and princess of Orange, being present in their proper persons, a certain declaration in writing, made by the said lords and commons, in the words following, viz. :

Whereas the late king James the Second, by the assistance of divers evil counsellors, judges and ministers employed by him, did endeavor to subvert and extirpate the protestant religion, and the laws and liberties of this kingdom—

1. By assuming and exercising a power of dispensing with and suspending the laws, and the execution of laws, without consent of parliament.

2. By committing and prosecuting divers worthy prelates, for humbly petitioning to be excused from concurring to the said assumed power.

3. By issuing and causing to be executed a commission under the great seal for erecting a court called the court of commissioners for ecclesiastical causes.

4. By levying money for and to the use of the crown, by pretence of prerogative, for other time and in other manner than the same was granted by parliament.

(499)

5. By raising and keeping a standing army within this kingdom in time of peace, without consent of parliament, and quartering soldiers contrary to law.

6. By causing several good subjects, being protestants, to be disarmed, at the same time when papists were both armed and employed, contrary to law.

7. By violating the freedom of election of members to serve in parliament.

8. By prosecutions in the court of king's bench, for matters and causes cognizable only in parliament; and by divers other arbitrary and illegal courses.

9. And whereas of late years, partial, corrupt and unqualified persons have been returned and served on juries in trials, and particularly divers jurors in trials for high treason, which were not freeholders.

10. And excessive bail hath been required of persons committed in criminal cases, to elude the benefit of the laws made for the liberty of the subjects.

11. And excessive fines have been imposed, and illegal and cruel punishments inflicted.

12. And several grants and promises made of fines and forfeitures, before any conviction or judgment against the persons upon whom the same were to be levied.

All which are utterly and directly contrary to the known laws and statutes, and freedom of this realm.

And whereas the said late king James the Second having abdicated the government, and the throne being thereby vacant, his highness the prince of Orange (whom it hath pleased almighty God to make the glorious instrument of delivering the kingdom from popery and arbitrary power) did (by the advice of the lords spiritual and temporal, and divers principal persons of the commons) cause letters to be written to the lords spiritual and temporal, being protestants, and other letters to the several counties, cities, universities, boroughs, and cinque-ports, for the choosing of such persons to represent them as were of right to be sent to parliament, to meet and sit at Westminster, upon the two and twentieth day of January, in this year one thousand six hundred eighty and eight, in order to such an establishment, as that their religion, laws and liberties might not again be in danger of being subverted: upon which letters, elections have been accordingly made;

And thereupon the said lords spiritual and temporal, and commons, pursuant to their respective letters and elections, being now assembled in a full and free representative of this nation, taking into their most serious consideration the best means for attaining the ends aforesaid, do, in the first place (as their ancestors in like case have usually done), for the vindicating and asserting their ancient rights and liberties, declare—

1. That the pretended power of suspending of laws, or the execution of laws, by regal authority, without consent of parliament, is illegal.

2. That the pretended power of dispensing with laws, or the execution of laws, by regal authority, as it hath been assumed and exercised of late, is illegal.

3. That the commission for erecting the late court of commissioners for ecclesiastical causes, and all other commissions and courts of like nature, are illegal and pernicious.

4. That levying money for or to the use of the crown, by pretence of prerogative, without grant of parliament, for longer time or in other manner than the same is or shall be granted, is illegal.

5. That it is the right of the subjects to petition the king, and all commitments and prosecutions for such petitioning are illegal.

6. That the raising or keeping a standing army within the kingdom in time of peace, unless it be with consent of parliament, is against law.

7. That the subjects which are protestants may have arms for their defence suitable to their conditions, and as allowed by law.

8. That election of members of parliament ought to be free.

9. That the freedom of speech, and debates or proceedings in parliament, ought not to be impeached or questioned in any court or place out of parliament.

10. That excessive bail ought not to be required, nor excessive fines imposed; nor cruel and unusual punishments inflicted.

11. That jurors ought to be duly impanelled and returned, and jurors which pass upon men in trials for high treason, ought to be freeholders.

12. That all grants and promises of fines and forfeitures of particular persons before conviction, are illegal and void.

13. And that for redress of all grievances, and for the amending, strengthening and preserving of the laws, parliaments ought to be held frequently.

And they do claim, demand and insist upon all and singular the premises, as their undoubted rights and liberties; and that no declarations, judgments, doings or proceedings, to the prejudice of the people in any of the said premises, ought in any wise to be drawn hereafter into consequence or example.

To which demand of their rights they are particularly encouraged by the declaration of his highness the prince of Orange, as being the only means for obtaining a full redress and remedy therein.

Having therefore an entire confidence, That his said highness the prince of Orange will perfect the deliverance so far advanced by him, and will still preserve them from the violation of their rights, which they have here asserted, and from all other attempts upon their religion, rights and liberties:

II. The said lords spiritual and temporal, and commons, assembled at Westminster, do resolve, That William and Mary, prince and princess of Orange, be, and be declared, king and queen of England, France and Ireland, and the dominions thereunto belonging, to hold the crown and royal dignity of the said kingdoms and dominions to them, the said prince and princess, during their lives, and the life of the survivor of them; and that the sole and full exercise of the regal power be only in, and executed by, the said prince of Orange, in the names of the said prince and princess, during their joint lives; and after their deceases, the said crown and royal dignity of the said kingdoms and dominions to be to the heirs of the body of the said princess; and for default of such issue, to the princess Anne of Denmark, and the heirs of her body; and for default of such issue, to the heirs of the body of the said prince of Orange. And the lords spiritual and temporal, and commons, do pray the said prince and princess to accept the same accordingly.

III. And that the oaths hereafter mentioned be taken by all persons of whom the oaths of allegiance and supremacy might be required by law, instead of them; and that the said oaths of allegiance and supremacy be abrogated.

I, A. B., do sincerely promise and swear, That I will be faithful and bear true allegiance to their majesties, king William and queen Mary:

So help me God.

I, A. B., do swear, That I do from my heart abhor, detest and abjure, as impious and heretical, that damnable doctrine and position, That princes excommunicated or deprived by the pope, or any authority of the see of Rome, may be deposed or murdered by their subjects, or any other whatsoever. And I do declare, That no foreign prince, person, prelate, state or potentate hath, or ought to have, any jurisdiction, power, superiority, pre-eminence or authority, ecclesiastical or spiritual, within this realm :

So help me God.

IV. Upon which their said majesties did accept the crown and royal dignity of the kingdoms of England, France and Ireland, and the dominions thereunto belonging, according to the resolution and desire of the said lords and commons contained in the said declaration.

V. And thereupon their majesties were pleased, That the said lords spiritual and temporal, and commons, being the two houses of parliament, should continue to sit, and with their majesties' royal concurrence make effectual provision for the settlement of the religion, laws and liberties of this kingdom, so that the same for the future might not be in danger again of being subverted ; to which the said lords spiritual and temporal, and commons, did agree and proceed to act accordingly.

VI. Now in pursuance of the premises, the said lords spiritual and temporal, and commons, in parliament assembled, for the ratifying, confirming and establishing the said declaration, and the articles, clauses, matters and things therein contained, by the force of a law made in due form by authority of parliament, do pray that it may be declared and enacted, That all and singular the rights and liberties asserted and claimed in the said declaration, are the true, ancient and indubitable rights and liberties of the people of this kingdom, and so shall be esteemed, allowed, adjudged, deemed and taken to be, and that all and every the particulars aforesaid shall be firmly and strictly holden and observed, as they are expressed in the said declaration ; and all officers and ministers whatsoever shall serve their majesties and their successors according to the same in all times to come.

Sections VII., VIII., IX., X., are irrelevant.

XI. All which their majesties are contented and pleased shall be declared, enacted and established by authority of this present parliament, and shall stand, remain and be the law of this realm forever; and the same are by their said majesties, by and with the advice and consent of the lords spiritual and temporal, and commons, in parliament assembled, and by the authority of the same, declared, enacted and established accordingly.

XII. And be it further declared and enacted by the authority aforesaid, That from and after this present session of parliament no dispensation by *non obstante* of or to any statute, or any part thereof, shall be allowed, but that the same shall be held void and of no effect, except a dispensation be allowed of in such statute, and except in such cases as shall be specially provided for by one or more bill or bills to be passed during this present session of parliament.

Section XIII. irrelevant.

APPENDIX VIII.

A DECLARATION BY THE REPRESENTATIVES OF THE UNITED
STATES OF AMERICA IN CONGRESS ASSEMBLED.

WHEN, in the course of human events, it becomes necessary for
one people to dissolve the political bands which have connected
them with another, and to assume, among the powers of the earth,
the separate and equal station to which the laws of nature and of
nature's God entitle them, a decent respect to the opinions of mankind requires that they should declare the causes which impel them
to the separation.

We hold these truths to be self-evident, that all men are created
equal; that they are endowed by their Creator with certain unali-
enable rights; that among these, are life, liberty, and the pursuit
of happiness. That, to secure these rights, governments are instituted among men, deriving their just powers from the consent of
the governed; that, whenever any form of government becomes
destructive of these ends, it is the right of the people to alter or
to abolish it, and to institute a new government, laying its foundation on such principles, and organizing its powers in such form as
to them shall seem most likely to effect their safety and happiness.
Prudence, indeed, will dictate that governments long established
should not be changed for light and transient causes; and, accordingly, all experience hath shown that mankind are more disposed
to suffer, while evils are sufferable, than to right themselves by
abolishing the forms to which they are accustomed. But, when a
long train of abuses and usurpations, pursuing invariably the same
object, evinces a design to reduce them under absolute despotism,
it is their right, it is their duty, to throw off such government, and
to provide new guards for their future security. Such has been
the patient sufferance of these colonies, and such is now the necessity which constrains them to alter their former systems of government. The history of the present king of Great Britain is a his-

tory of repeated injuries and usurpations, all having, in direct object, the establishment of an absolute tyranny over these States. To prove this, let facts be submitted to a candid world:

He has refused his assent to laws the most wholesome and necessary for the public good.

He has forbidden his governors to pass laws of immediate and pressing importance, unless suspended in their operation till his assent should be obtained; and, when so suspended, he has utterly neglected to attend to them.

He has refused to pass other laws for the accommodation of large districts of people, unless those people would relinquish the right of representation in the legislature; a right inestimable to them, and formidable to tyrants only.

He has called together legislative bodies at places unusual, uncomfortable, and distant from the repository of their public records, for the sole purpose of fatiguing them into compliance with his measures.

He has dissolved representative houses repeatedly, for opposing, with manly firmness, his invasions on the rights of the people.

He has refused, for a long time after such dissolutions, to cause others to be elected; whereby the legislative powers, incapable of annihilation, have returned to the people at large for their exercise; the state remaining, in the meantime, exposed to all the danger of invasion from without, and convulsions within.

He has endeavored to prevent the population of these States; for that purpose, obstructing the laws for the naturalization of foreigners; refusing to pass others to encourage their migration hither, and raising the conditions of new appropriations of lands.

He has obstructed the administration of justice, by refusing his assent to laws for establishing judiciary powers.

He has made judges dependent on his will alone, for the tenure of their offices, and the amount and payment of their salaries.

He has erected a multitude of new offices, and sent hither swarms of officers to harass our people and eat out their substance.

He has kept among us, in times of peace, standing armies, without the consent of our legislature.

He has affected to render the military independent of, and superior to, the civil power.

He has combined, with others, to subject us to a jurisdiction foreign to our constitution, and unacknowledged by our laws; giving his assent to their acts of pretended legislation :

For quartering large bodies of armed troops among us :

For protecting them, by a mock trial, from punishment, for any murders which they should commit on the inhabitants of these States :

For cutting off our trade with all parts of the world :

For imposing taxes on us without our consent :

For depriving us, in many cases, of the benefits of trial by jury :

For transporting us beyond the seas to be tried for pretended offences :

For abolishing the free system of English laws in a neighboring province, establishing therein an arbitrary government, and enlarging its boundaries, so as to render it at once an example and fit instrument for introducing the same absolute rule into these colonies :

For taking away our charters, abolishing our most valuable laws, and altering, fundamentally, the powers of our governments :

For suspending our own legislatures, and declaring themselves invested with power to legislate for us in all cases whatsoever.

He has abdicated government here, by declaring us out of his protection, and waging war against us.

He has plundered our seas, ravaged our coasts, burnt our towns, and destroyed the lives of our people.

He is, at this time, transporting large armies of foreign mercenaries to complete the works of death, desolation, and tyranny, already begun, with circumstances of cruelty and perfidy scarcely paralleled in the most barbarous ages, and totally unworthy the head of a civilized nation.

He has constrained our fellow-citizens, taken captive on the high seas, to bear arms against their country, to become the executioners of their friends and brethren, or to fall themselves by their hands.

He has excited domestic insurrection amongst us, and has endeavored to bring on the inhabitants of our frontiers, the merciless Indian savages, whose known rule of warfare is an undistinguished destruction of all ages, sexes, and conditions.

In every stage of these oppressions, we have petitioned for redress in the most humble terms ; our repeated petitions have been answered only by repeated injury. A prince, whose character is thus marked by every act which may define a tyrant, is unfit to be the ruler of a free people.

Nor have we been wanting in attention to our British brethren. We have warned them, from time to time, of attempts made by their legislature to extend an unwarrantable jurisdiction over us. We have reminded them of the circumstances of our emigration and settlement here. We have appealed to their native justice and magnanimity, and we have conjured them, by the ties of our common kindred, to disavow these usurpations, which would inevitably interrupt our connections and correspondence. They, too, have been deaf to the voice of justice and consanguinity. We must, therefore, acquiesce in the necessity which denounces our separation, and hold them, as we hold the rest of mankind, enemies in war, in peace, friends.

We, therefore, the representatives of the United States of America, in General Congress assembled, appealing to the Supreme Judge of the world for the rectitude of our intentions, do in the name, and by the authority of the good people of these colonies, solemnly publish and declare, That these United Colonies are, and of right ought to be, free and independent States ; that they are absolved from all allegiance to the British crown, and that all political connection between them and the state of Great Britain, is, and ought to be, totally dissolved ; and that, as free and independent States, they have full power to levy war, conclude peace, contract alliances, establish commerce, and to do all other acts and things which independent states may of right do. And, for the support of this declaration, with a firm reliance on the protection of Divine Providence, we mutually pledge to each other our lives, our fortunes, and our sacred honor.

The foregoing declaration was, by order of Congress, engrossed and signed by the following members.

JOHN HANCOCK.

NEW HAMPSHIRE.

Josiah Bartlett,
William Whipple,
Matthew Thornton.

MASSACHUSETTS BAY.

Samuel Adams,
John Adams,
Robert Treat Paine.
Elbridge Gerry.

RHODE ISLAND.
Stephen Hopkins,
William Ellery,

CONNECTICUT.
Roger Sherman,
Samuel Huntington,
William Williams,
Oliver Wolcott.

NEW YORK.
William Floyd,
Philip Livingston,
Francis Lewis,
Lewis Morris.

NEW JERSEY.
Richard Stockton,
John Witherspoon,
Francis Hopkinson,
John Hart,
Abraham Clark,

PENNSYLVANIA.
Robert Morris,
Benjamin Rush,
Benjamin Franklin,
John Morton,
George Clymer,
James Smith,
George Taylor,
James Wilson,
George Ross.

DELAWARE.
Cæsar Rodney,
George Read,
Thomas M'Kean.

MARYLAND.
Samuel Chase,
William Paca,
Thomas Stone,
Charles Carroll, of Carrollton.

VIRGINIA.
George Wythe,
Richard Henry Lee,
Thomas Jefferson,
Benjamin Harrison,
Thomas Nelson, Jun.,
Francis Lightfoot Lee,
Carter Braxton.

NORTH CAROLINA.
William Hooper,
Joseph Hewes,
John Penn.

SOUTH CAROLINA.
Edward Rutledge,
Thomas Hayward, Jun.,
Thomas Lynch, Jun.,
Arthur Middleton.

GEORGIA.
Button Gwinnett,
Lyman Hall,
George Walton.

Resolved, That copies of the Declaration be sent to the several assemblies, conventions, and committees, or councils of safety; and to the several commanding officers of the continental troops; that it be proclaimed in each of the United States, and at the head of the army.

APPENDIX IX.

*To all to whom these presents shall come, we, the undersigned
Delegates of the States affixed to our names, send greeting:*
Whereas the Delegates of the United States of America in con-
gress assembled, did, on the 15th day of November, in the year of
our Lord 1777, and in the second year of the Independence of
America, agree to certain articles of confederation and perpetual
union between the States of New Hampshire, Massachusetts Bay,
Rhode Island and Providence Plantations, Connecticut, New York,
New Jersey, Pennsylvania, Delaware, Maryland, Virginia, North
Carolina, South Carolina, and Georgia, in the words following,
viz :—

*Articles of Confederation and Perpetual Union between the
States of New Hampshire, Massachusetts Bay, Rhode Island
and Providence Plantations, Connecticut, New York, New
Jersey, Pennsylvania, Delaware, Maryland, Virginia, North
Carolina, South Carolina, and Georgia.*

ARTICLE I.

The style of this confederacy shall be "The United States of
America."

ARTICLE II.

Each state retains its sovereignty, freedom, and independence,
and every power, jurisdiction, and right, which is not by this confederation expressly delegated to the United States, in congress
assembled.

(510)

ARTICLE III.

The said states hereby severally enter into a firm league of friendship with each other, for their common defence, the security of their liberties, and their mutual and general welfare ; binding themselves to assist each other against all force offered to, or attacks made upon them, or any of them, on account of religion, sovereignty, trade, or any other pretence whatever.

ARTICLE IV.

The better to secure and perpetuate mutual friendship and intercourse among the people of the different states in this Union, the free inhabitants of each of these states (paupers, vagabonds, and fugitives from justice excepted) shall be entitled to all privileges and immunities of free citizens in the several states ; and the people of each state shall have free ingress and regress to and from any other state, and shall enjoy therein all the privileges of trade and commerce, subject to the same duties, impositions, and restrictions, as the inhabitants thereof respectively, provided that such restriction shall not extend so far as to prevent the removal of property imported into any state, to any other state of which the owner is an inhabitant ; provided, also, that no imposition, duties, or restriction, shall be laid by any state on the property of the United States, or either of them.

If any person guilty of, or charged with, treason, felony, or other high misdemeanor in any state shall flee from justice, and be found in any of the United States, he shall, upon demand of the governor, or executive power, of the state from which he fled, be delivered up and removed to the state having jurisdiction of his offence.

Full faith and credit shall be given in each of these states to the records, acts, and judicial proceedings, of the courts and magistrates of every other state.

ARTICLE V.

For the more convenient management of the general interests of the United States, delegates shall be annually appointed in such manner as the legislature of each state shall direct, to meet in congress on the first Monday in November in every year, with a power reserved to each state to recall its delegates, or any of them at any time within the year, and to send others in their stead for the remainder of the year.

No state shall be represented in congress by less than two, nor by more than seven members ; and no person shall be capable of being a delegate for more than three years in any term of six years ; nor shall any person, being a delegate, be capable of holding any office under the United States, for which he, or another for his benefit, receives any salary, fees, or emolument of any kind.

Each state shall maintain its own delegates in any meeting of the states, and while they act as members of the committee of the states.

In determining questions in the United States, in congress assembled, each state shall have one vote.

Freedom of speech or debate in congress shall not be impeached or questioned in any court or place out of congress, and the members of congress shall be protected in their persons from arrests and imprisonments during the time of their going to and from, and attendance on congress, except for treason, felony, or breach of the peace.

ARTICLE VI.

No state, without the consent of the United States in congress assembled, shall send any embassy to, or receive any embassy from, or enter into any conference, agreement, alliance, or treaty, with any king, prince, or state ; nor shall any person holding any office of profit or trust under the United States, or any of them, accept of any present, emolument, office, or title, of any kind whatever, from any king, prince, or foreign state ; nor shall the United States in congress assembled, or any of them, grant any title of nobility.

No two or more states shall enter into any treaty, confederation, or alliance, whatever between them, without the consent of the United States in congress assembled, specifying accurately the purposes for which the same is to be entered into, and how long it shall continue.

No state shall lay any imposts, or duties, which may interfere with any stipulations in treaties entered into by the United States in congress assembled, with any king, prince, or state, in pursuance of any treaties already proposed by congress to the courts of France or Spain.

No vessels of war shall be kept up in time of peace by any state, except such number only as shall be deemed necessary by the United States in congress assembled for the defence of such state, or its trade; nor shall any body of forces be kept up by any state in time of peace, except such number only as in the judgment of the United States in congress assembled shall be deemed requisite to garrison the forts necessary for the defence of such state; but every state shall always keep up a well-regulated and disciplined militia, sufficiently armed and accoutred, and shall provide, and have constantly ready for use in public stores, a due number of field-pieces and tents, and a proper quantity of arms, ammunition, and camp equipage.

No state shall engage in any war without the consent of the United States in congress assembled, unless such state be actually invaded by enemies, or shall have received certain advice of a resolution being formed by some nation of Indians to invade such state, and the danger is so imminent as not to admit of a delay till the United States in congress assembled can be consulted; nor shall any state grant commissions to any ships or vessels of war, nor letters of marque or reprisal, except it be after a declaration of war by the United States in congress assembled, and then only against the kingdom, or state, and the subjects thereof, against which war has been so declared, and under such regulations as shall be established by the United States in congress assembled, unless such state be infested by pirates, in which case vessels of war may be fitted out for that occasion, and kept so long as the danger shall continue, or until the United States in congress assembled shall determine otherwise.

ARTICLE VII.

When land forces are raised by any state for the common defence, all officers of, or under the rank of colonel shall be appointed by the legislature of each state respectively, by whom such forces shall be raised, or in such manner as such state shall direct, and all vacancies shall be filled up by the state which first made the appointment.

ARTICLE VIII.

All charges of war, and all other expenses that shall be incurred for the common defence or general welfare, and allowed by the United States in congress assembled, shall be defrayed out of a common treasury, which shall be supplied by the several states, in proportion to the value of all land within each state granted to, or surveyed for any person, as such land, and the buildings and improvements thereon, shall be estimated according to such mode as the United States in congress assembled shall from time to time direct and appoint. The taxes for paying that proportion shall be laid and levied by the authority and direction of the legislatures of the several states within the time agreed upon by the United States in congress assembled.

ARTICLE IX.

The United States in congress assembled shall have the sole and exclusive right and power of determining on peace and war, except in the cases mentioned in the 6th article ; of sending and receiving ambassadors ; entering into treaties and alliances, provided that no treaty of commerce shall be made whereby the legislative power of the respective states shall be restrained from imposing such imposts and duties on foreigners as their own people are subjected to, or from prohibiting the exportation or importation of any species of goods or commodities whatsoever; of establishing rules for deciding in all cases what captures on land or water shall be legal, and in what manner prizes taken by land or naval forces in the service of the United States shall be divided or appropriated; of granting letters of marque and reprisal in times of peace ; appointing courts for the trial of piracies and felonies committed on the high seas, and establishing courts for receiving and determining finally appeals in all cases of captures, provided that no member of congress shall be appointed a judge of any of the said courts.

The United States in congress assembled shall also be the last resort on appeal in all disputes and differences now subsisting, or that hereafter may arise, between two or more states, concerning boundary, jurisdiction, or any other cause whatever—which authority shall always be exercised in the manner following : Whenever the legislative or executive authority, or lawful agent, of any state in controversy with another shall present a petition to congress, stating the matter in question and praying for a hearing, notice thereof shall be given, by order of congress, to the legislative or executive authority of the other state in controversy, and a day assigned for the appearance of the parties by their lawful agents, who shall then be directed to appoint, by joint consent, commissioners or judges to constitute a court for hearing and determining the matter in question; but, if they cannot agree, congress shall name three persons out of each of the United States, and from the list of such persons each party shall alternately strike out one (the petitioners beginning,) until the number shall be reduced to thirteen; and from that number not less than seven, nor more than nine names, as congress shall direct, shall in the presence of congress be drawn out by lot, and the persons whose names shall be so drawn, or any five of them, shall be commissioners or judges, to hear and finally determine the controversy, so always as a major part of the judges who shall hear the cause shall agree in the determination; and if either party shall neglect to attend at the day appointed, without showing reasons which congress shall judge sufficient, or being present shall refuse to strike, the congress shall proceed to nominate three persons out of each state, and the secretary of congress shall strike in behalf of such party absent or refusing; and the judgment and the sentence of the court, to be appointed in the manner before prescribed, shall be final and conclusive; and if any of the parties shall refuse to submit to the authority of such court, or to appear or defend their claim or cause, the court shall, nevertheless, proceed to pronounce sentence or judgment, which shall in like manner be final and decisive—the judgment, or sentence, and other proceedings being in either case transmitted to congress, and lodged among the acts of congress for the security of the parties concerned; provided that every commissioner, before he sits in judgment, shall take an oath to be administered by one of the judges of the supreme or superior court of the state where the cause shall be tried, "well and truly to hear and determine the matter in question according to the best of his judgment, without favor, affection, or hope of reward;" provided, also, that no state shall be deprived of territory for the benefit of the United States.

All controversies concerning the private right of soil claimed under different grants of two or more states, whose jurisdictions, as they may respect such lands, and the states which passed such grants are adjusted, the said grants or either of them being at the same time claimed to have originated antecedent to such settlement of jurisdiction, shall, on the petition of either party to the Congress of the United States, be finally determined as near as may be in the same manner as is before prescribed for deciding disputes respecting territorial jurisdiction between different states.

The United States in Congress assembled shall also have the sole and exclusive right and power of regulating the alloy and value of coin struck by their own authority, or by that of the respective states—fixing the standard of weights and measures throughout the United States—regulating the trade and managing all affairs with the Indians, not members of any of the states, provided that the legislative right of any state within its own limits be not infringed or violated—establishing or regulating post-offices from one state to another, throughout all the United States, and exacting such postage on the papers passing through the same as may be requisite to defray the expenses of the said office—appointing all officers of the land forces, in the service of the United States, excepting regimental officers—appointing all the officers of the naval forces, and commissioning all officers whatever in the service of the United States—making rules for the government and regulation of the said land and naval forces, and directing their operations.

The United States, in congress assembled, shall have authority to appoint a committee, to sit in the recess of congress, to be denominated "A Committee of the States," and to consist of one delegate from each state; and to appoint such other committees and civil officers as may be necessary for managing the general affairs of the United States under their direction—to appoint one of their number to preside, provided that no person be allowed to serve in the office of president more than one year in any term of three years; to ascertain the necessary sums of money to be raised for the service of the United States, and to appropriate and apply the same for defraying the public expenses—to borrow money, or emit bills on the credit of the United States, transmitting every half year to the respective states an account of the sums of money so borrowed or emitted—to build and equip a navy—to agree upon the number of land forces, and to make requisitions from each state for its quota, in proportion to the number of white inhabitants in such state ; which requisition shall be binding, and thereupon the legislature of each state shall appoint the regimental officers, raise the men, and clothe, arm, and equip them in a soldier-like manner, at the expense of the United States ; and the officers and men so clothed, armed, and equipped shall march to the place appointed, and within the time agreed on by the United States in congress assembled : But if the United States, in congress assembled, shall, on consideration of circumstances, judge proper that any state should not raise men, or should raise a smaller number than its quota, and that any other state should raise a greater number of men than the quota thereof, such extra number shall be raised, officered, clothed, armed, and equipped in the same manner as the quota of such state, unless the legislature of such state shall judge that such extra number cannot be safely spared out of the same, in which case they shall raise, officer, clothe, arm, and equip as many of such extra number as they judge can be safely spared. And the officers and men so clothed, armed, and equipped, shall march to the place appointed, and within the time agreed on by the United States in congress assembled.

The United States in congress assembled, shall never engage in a war, nor grant letters of marque and reprisal in time of peace, nor enter into any treaties or alliances, nor coin money, nor regulate the value thereof, nor ascertain the sums and expenses necessary for the defence and welfare of the United States, or any of them, nor emit bills, nor borrow money on the credit of the United States, nor appropriate money, nor agree upon the number of vessels of war, to be built or purchased, or the number of land or sea forces to be raised, nor appoint a commander-in-chief of the army or navy, unless nine states assent to the same : nor shall a question on any other point, except for adjourning from day to day be determined, unless by the votes of a majority of the United States in congress assembled.

The congress of the United States shall have power to adjourn to any time within the year, and to any place within the United States, so that no period of adjournment be for a longer duration than the space of six months, and shall publish the journal of their proceedings monthly, except such parts thereof relating to treaties, alliances, or military operations, as in their judgment require secrecy ; and the yeas and nays of the delegates of each state on any question shall be entered on the journal, when it is desired by any delegate; and the delegates of a state, or any of them, at his or their request, shall be furnished with a transcript of the said journal, except such parts as are above excepted, to lay before the legislatures of the several states.

ARTICLE X.

The committee of the states, or any nine of them, shall be authorized to execute, in the recess of congress, such of the powers of congress as the United States in congress assembled, by the consent of nine states, shall, from time to time, think expedient to vest them with; provided that no power be delegated to the said committee, for the exercise of which, by the articles of confederation, the voice of nine states, in the congress of the United States assembled, is requisite.

ARTICLE XI.

Canada acceding to this confederation, and joining in the measures of the United States, shall be admitted into, and entitled to all the advantages of this union: but no other colony shall be admitted into the same, unless such admission be agreed to by nine states.

ARTICLE XII.

All bills of credit emitted, moneys borrowed, and debts contracted by, or under the authority of congress, before the assembling of the United States, in pursuance of the present confederation, shall be deemed and considered as a charge against the United States, for payment and satisfaction whereof the said United Slates, and the public faith are hereby solemnly pledged.

ARTICLE XIII.

Every state shall abide by the determinations of the United States in congress assembled, on all questions which by this confederation is submitted to them. And the articles of this confederation shall be inviolably observed by every state, and the union shall be perpetual; nor shall any alteration at any time hereafter be made in any of them; unless such alteration be agreed to in a congress of the United States, and be afterwards confirmed by the legislature of every state.

And whereas, it hath pleased the Great Governor of the World to incline the hearts of the legislatures we respectively represent in congress, to approve of, and to authorize us to ratify the said articles of confederation and perpetual union : Know Ye, that we the undersigned delegates, by virtue of the power and authority to us given for that purpose, do by these presents, in the name and in behalf of our respective constituents, fully and entirely ratify and confirm each and every of the said articles of confederation and perpetual union, and all and singular the matters and things therein contained : And we do further solemnly plight and engage the faith of our respective constituents, that they shall abide by the determinations of the United States in congress assembled, on all questions, which by the said confederation are submitted to them.   And that the articles thereof shall be inviolably observed by the states we respectively represent, and that the union shall be perpetual.   In witness whereof we have hereunto set our hands in congress.   Done at Philadelphia in the state of Pennsylvania, the ninth day of July in the year of our Lord 1778, and in the third year of the Independence of America.

On the part and behalf of the state of New Hampshire :

Josiah Bartlett,   John Wentworth, Jun.,
                                    Aug. 8, 1778.

On the part and behalf of the state of Massachusetts Bay :

John Hancock,   Francis Dana,
Samuel Adams,   James Lovell,
Elbridge Gerry,   Samuel Holten.

On the part and behalf of the state of Rhode Island and Providence Plantations :

William Ellery,   John Collins.
Henry Marchant,

On the part and behalf of the state of Connecticut :

Roger Sherman,   Titus Hosmer,
Samuel Huntington,   Andrew Adams.
Oliver Wolcott,

On the part and behalf of the state of New York:

Jas. Duane,
Fras. Lewis,
William Duer,
Gouvr. Morris.

On the part and behalf of the state of New Jersey, November 26, 1778:

Jno. Witherspoon,
Nathl. Scudder.

On the part and behalf of the state of Pennsylvania:

Robt. Morris,
Daniel Roberdeau,
Jona. Bayard Smith,
William Clingan,
Joseph Reed,
22d July, 1778.

On the part and behalf of the state of Delaware:

Tho. M'Kean, Feb. 12, 1779,
John Dickinson, May 5, 1779.
Nicholas Van Dyke.

On the part and behalf of the state of Maryland:

John Hanson,
   March 1, 1781.
Daniel Carroll,
   March 1, 1781.

On the part and behalf of the state of Virginia:

Richard Henry Lee,
John Banister,
Thomas Adams,
Jno. Harvie,
Francis Lightfoot Lee.

On the part and behalf of the state of North Carolina:

John Penn,
   July 21, 1778.
Corns. Harnett,
Jno. Williams.

On the part and behalf of the state of South Carolina:

Henry Laurens,
William Henry Drayton,
Jno. Mathews,
Richd. Hutson,
Thos. Hayward, Jun.

On the part and behalf of the state of Georgia:

Jno. Walton,
   24th July, 1778.
Edwd. Telfair,
Edwd. Langworthy.

APPENDIX X.

CONSTITUTION OF THE UNITED STATES OF AMERICA.

WE, the people of the United States, in order to form a more perfect Union, establish justice, insure domestic tranquillity, provide for the common defence, promote the general welfare, and secure the blessings of liberty to ourselves and our posterity, do ordain and establish this Constitution for the United States of America.

ARTICLE I.

SECTION 1. All legislative powers herein granted shall be vested in a congress of the United States, which shall consist of a senate and house of representatives.

SECTION 2. The house of representatives shall be composed of members chosen every second year by the people of the several states, and the electors in each state shall have the qualifications requisite for electors of the most numerous branch of the state legislature.

No person shall be a representative who shall not have attained to the age of twenty-five years, and been seven years a citizen of the United States, and who shall not, when elected, be an inhabitant of that state in which he shall be chosen.

Representatives and direct taxes shall be apportioned among the several states which may be included within this Union, according to their respective numbers, which shall be determined by adding to the whole number of free persons, including those bound to service for a term of years, and excluding Indians not taxed, three-fifths of all other persons. The actual enumeration shall be made within three years after the first meeting of the congress of the United States, and within every subsequent term of ten years, in such manner as they shall by law direct. The number of representatives shall not exceed one for every thirty thousand, but each

(521)

state shall have at least one representative; and until such enumeration shall be made, the state of New Hampshire shall be entitled to choose three, Massachusetts eight, Rhode Island and Providence Plantations one, Connecticut five, New York six, New Jersey four, Pennsylvania eight, Delaware one, Maryland six, Virginia ten, North Carolina five, South Carolina five, and Georgia three.

When vacancies happen in the representation from any state, the executive authority thereof shall issue writs of election to fill such vacancies.

The house of representatives shall choose their speaker, and other officers; and shall have the sole power of impeachment.

SECTION 3. The senate of the United States shall be composed of two senators from each state, chosen by the legislature thereof, for six years; and each senator shall have one vote.

Immediately after they shall be assembled in consequence of the first election, they shall be divided as equally as may be into three classes. The seats of the senators of the first class shall be vacated at the expiration of the second year, of the second class at the expiration of the fourth year, and of the third class at the expiration of the sixth year, so that one-third may be chosen every second year; and if vacancies happen by resignation, or otherwise, during the recess of the legislature of any state, the executive thereof may make temporary appointments until the next meeting of the legislature, which shall then fill such vacancies.

No person shall be a senator who shall not have attained to the age of thirty years, and been nine years a citizen of the United States, and who shall not, when elected, be an inhabitant of that State for which he shall be chosen.

The Vice-President of the United States shall be president of the senate, but shall have no vote, unless they be equally divided.

The senate shall choose their other officers, and also a president *pro tempore*, in the absence of the vice-president, or when he shall exercise the office of President of the United States.

The senate shall have the sole power to try all impeachments. When sitting for that purpose, they shall be on oath or affirmation. When the President of the United States is tried, the chief justice shall preside; and no person shall be convicted without the concurrence of two-thirds of the members present.

Judgment in case of impeachment shall not extend further than to removal from office, and disqualification to hold and enjoy any office of honor, trust, or profit, under the United States; but the party convicted shall nevertheless be liable and subject to indictment, trial, judgment, and punishment according to law.

SECTION 4. The times, places, and manner of holding elections for senators and representatives shall be prescribed in each state by the legislature thereof; but the congress may at any time by law make or alter such regulations, except as to the places of choosing senators.

The congress shall assemble at least once in every year, and such meeting shall be on the first Monday in December, unless they shall by law appoint a different day.

SECTION 5. Each house shall be the judge of the elections, returns and qualifications of its own members, and a majority of each shall constitute a quorum to do business; but a smaller number may adjourn from day to day, and may be authorized to compel the attendance of absent members, in such manner and under such penalties as each house may provide.

Each house may determine the rules of its proceedings, punish its members for disorderly behavior, and, with the concurrence of two-thirds, expel a member.

Each house shall keep a journal of its proceedings, and from time to time publish the same, excepting such parts as may in their judgment require secrecy; and the yeas and nays of the members of either house, on any question, shall, at the desire of one-fifth of those present, be entered on the journal.

Neither house, during the session of congress, shall, without the consent of the other, adjourn for more than three days, nor to any other place than that in which the two houses shall be sitting.

SECTION 6. The senators and representatives shall receive a compensation for their services, to be ascertained by law, and paid out of the treasury of the United States. They shall in all cases, except treason, felony, and breach of the peace, be privileged from arrest during their attendance at the session of their respective houses, and in going to and returning from the same; and for any speech or debate in either house, they shall not be questioned in any other place.

No senator or representative shall, during the time for which he was elected, be appointed to any civil office under the authority of the United States, which shall have been created, or the emoluments whereof shall have been increased during such time; and no person holding any office under the United States shall be a member of either house during his continuance in office.

SECTION 7. All bills for raising revenue shall originate in the house of representatives; but the senate may propose or concur with amendments as on other bills.

Every bill which shall have passed the house of representatives and the senate, shall, before it become a law, be presented to the President of the United States. If he approve, he shall sign it; but if not, he shall return it, with his objections, to that house in which it shall have originated, who shall enter the objections at large on their journal, and proceed to reconsider it. If, after such reconsideration, two-thirds of that house shall agree to pass the bill, it shall be sent, together with the objections, to the other house, by which it shall likewise be reconsidered, and if approved by two-thirds of that house, it shall become a law. But in all such cases the votes of both houses shall be determined by yeas and nays, and the names of the persons voting for and against the bill shall be entered on the journal of each house respectively. If any bill shall not be returned by the president within ten days (Sundays excepted) after it shall have been presented to him, the same shall be a law, in like manner as if he had signed it, unless the congress by their adjournment prevent its return; in which case, it shall not be a law. Every order, resolution, or vote, to which the concurrence of the senate and house of representatives may be necessary (except on a question of adjournment), shall be presented to the President of the United States; and before the same shall take effect, shall be approved by him; or, being disapproved by him, shall be repassed by two-thirds of the senate and house of representatives, according to the rules and limitations prescribed in the case of a bill.

SECTION 8. The congress shall have power

To lay and collect taxes, duties, imposts, and excises; to pay the debts and provide for the common defence and general welfare of the United States; but all duties, imposts, and excises shall be uniform throughout the United States:

To borrow money on the credit of the United States:

To regulate commerce with foreign nations, and among the several states, and with the Indian tribes:

To establish an uniform rule of naturalization, and uniform laws on the subject of bankruptcies throughout the United States:

To coin money, regulate the value thereof, and of foreign coin, and fix the standard of weights and measures :

To provide for the punishment of counterfeiting the securities and current coin of the United States:

To establish post-offices and post-roads:

To promote the progress of science and useful arts, by securing for limited times to authors and inventors the exclusive right to their respective writings and discoveries :

To constitute tribunals inferior to the supreme court:

To define and punish piracies and felonies committed on the high seas, and offences against the law of nations :

To declare war, grant letters of marque and reprisal, and make rules concerning captures on land and water :

To raise and support armies; but no appropriation of money to that use shall be for a longer term than two years :

To provide and maintain a navy :

To make rules for the government and regulation of the land and naval forces :

To provide for calling forth the militia to execute the laws of the Union, suppress insurrections, and repel invasions:

To provide for organizing, arming, and disciplining the militia, and for governing such part of them as may be employed in the service of the United States, reserving to the states respectively the appointment of the officers, and the authority of training the militia according to the discipline prescribed by congress :

To exercise exclusive legislation, in all cases whatsoever, over such district (not exceeding ten miles square) as may, by cession of particular states and the acceptance of congress, become the seat of the government of the United States, and to exercise like authority over all places purchased by the consent of the legislature of the state in which the same shall be, for the erection of forts, magazines, arsenals, dock-yards, and other needful buildings. And

To make all laws which shall be necessary and proper for carrying into execution the foregoing powers, and all other powers vested by this constitution in the government of the United States, or in any department or officer thereof.

SECTION 9. The migration or importation of such persons as any of the states now existing shall think proper to admit, shall not be prohibited by the congress prior to the year one thousand eight hundred and eight; but a tax or duty may be imposed on such importation, not exceeding ten dollars for each person.

The privilege of the writ of *habeas corpus* shall not be suspended, unless when in cases of rebellion or invasion the public safety may require it.

No bill of attainder or *ex post facto* law shall be passed.

No capitation or other direct tax shall be laid, unless in proportion to the census or enumeration hereinbefore directed to be taken.

No tax or duty shall be laid on articles exported from any state.

No preference shall be given, by any regulation of commerce or revenue, to the ports of one state over those of another; nor shall vessels bound to or from one state be obliged to enter, clear, or pay duties in another.

No money shall be drawn from the treasury, but in consequence of appropriations made by law; and a regular statement and account of the receipts and expenditures of all public money shall be published from time to time.

No title of nobility shall be granted by the United States; and no person holding any office of profit or trust under them shall, without the consent of the congress, accept of any present, emolument, office, or title of any kind whatever, from any king, prince, or foreign state.

Section 10. No state shall enter into any treaty, alliance or confederation; grant letters of marque and reprisal; coin money; emit bills of credit; make anything but gold and silver coin a tender in payment of debts; pass any bill of attainder, *ex post facto* law, or law impairing the obligation of contracts, or grant any title of nobility.

No state shall, without the consent of the congress, lay any imposts or duties on imports or exports, except what may be absolutely necessary for executing its inspection laws; and the net produce of all duties and imposts, laid by any state on imports or exports, shall be for the use of the treasury of the United States; and all such laws shall be subject to the revision and control of the congress.

No state shall, without the consent of congress, lay any duty of tonnage, keep troops or ships of war in time of peace, enter into any agreement or compact with another state, or with a foreign power, or engage in war, unless actually invaded, or in such imminent danger as will not admit of delay.

ARTICLE II.

SECTION 1. The executive power shall be vested in a president of the United States of America. He shall hold his office during the term of four years, and, together with the vice-president, chosen for the same term, be elected as follows :—

Each state shall appoint, in such manner as the legislature thereof may direct, a number of electors, equal to the whole number of senators and representatives to which the state may be entitled in the congress; but no senator or representative, or person holding an office of trust or profit under the United States, shall be appointed an elector.

[1 The electors shall meet in their respective states, and vote by ballot for two persons, of whom one at least shall not be an inhabitant of the same state with themselves. And they shall make a list of all the persons voted for, and of the number of votes for each; which list they shall sign and certify, and transmit sealed to the seat of the government of the United States, directed to the president of the senate. The president of the senate shall, in the presence of the senate and house of representatives, open all the certificates, and the votes shall then be counted. The person having the greatest number of votes shall be the president, if such number be a majority of the whole number of electors appointed; and if there be more than one who have such majority, and have an equal number of votes, then the house of representatives shall immediately choose by ballot one of them for president; and if no person have a majority, then from the five highest on the list the said house shall in like manner choose the president. But in choosing the president, the votes shall be taken by states, the representation from each state having one vote. A quorum for this purpose shall consist of a member or members from two-thirds of the states, and a majority of all the states shall be necessary to a choice. In every case, after the choice of the president, the person having the greatest number of votes of the electors shall be the vice-president. But if there should remain two or more who have equal votes, the senate shall choose from them by ballot the vice-president.]

---

1 This clause within brackets has been superseded and annulled by the 12th amendment, on pages 534–35.

The congress may determine the time of choosing the electors, and the day on which they shall give their votes; which day shall be the same throughout the United States

No person except a natural born citizen, or a citizen of the United States at the time of the adoption of this constitution, shall be eligible to the office of president; neither shall any person be eligible to that office who shall not have attained to the age of thirty-five years, and been fourteen years a resident within the United States.

In case of the removal of the president from office, or of his death, resignation, or inability to discharge the powers and duties of the said office, the same shall devolve on the vice-president, and the congress may by law provide for the case of removal, death, resignation, or inability, both of the president and vice-president, declaring what officer shall then act as president; and such officer shall act accordingly, until the disability be removed, or a president shall be elected.

The president shall, at stated times, receive for his services a compensation, which shall neither be increased nor diminished during the period for which he shall have been elected; and he shall not receive within that period any other emolument from the United States, or any of them.

Before he enter on the execution of his office, he shall take the following oath or affirmation:

"I do solemnly swear (or affirm) that I will faithfully execute the office of President of the United States, and will, to the best of my ability, preserve, protect, and defend the Constitution of the United States."

SECTION 2. The president shall be commander-in-chief of the army and navy of the United States, and of the militia of the several states, when called into the actual service of the United States; he may require the opinion, in writing, of the principal officer in each of the executive departments, upon any subject relating to the duties of their respective offices; and he shall have power to grant reprieves and pardons for offences against the United States, except in cases of impeachment.

He shall have power, by and with the advice and consent of the senate, to make treaties, provided two-thirds of the senators present concur; and he shall nominate, and by and with the advice and consent of the senate, shall appoint ambassadors, other public ministers and consuls, judges of the supreme court, and all other officers of the United States whose appointments are not herein otherwise provided for, and which shall be established by law; but the congress may by law vest the appointment of such inferior officers, as they think proper, in the president alone, in the courts of law, or in the heads of departments.

The president shall have power to fill up all vacancies that may happen during the recess of the senate, by granting commissions which shall expire at the end of their next session.

SECTION 3. He shall from time to time give to the congress information of the state of the Union, and recommend to their consideration such measures as he shall judge necessary and expedient; he may, on extraordinary occasions, convene both houses, or either of them; and in case of disagreement between them, with respect to the time of adjournment, he may adjourn them to such time as he shall think proper; he shall receive ambassadors and other public ministers; he shall take care that the laws be faithfully executed, and shall commission all the officers of the United States.

SECTION 4. The president, vice-president, and all civil officers of the United States shall be removed from office on impeachment for, and conviction of, treason, bribery, or other high crimes and misdemeanors.

ARTICLE III.

SECTION 1. The judicial power of the United States shall be vested in one supreme court, and in such inferior courts as the congress may from time to time ordain and establish. The judges, both of the supreme and inferior courts, shall hold their offices during good behavior, and shall, at stated times, receive for their services a compensation, which shall not be diminished during their continuance in office.

SECTION 2. The judicial power shall extend to all cases, in law and equity, arising under this constitution, the laws of the United States, and treaties made, or which shall be made, under their authority; to all cases affecting ambassadors, other public ministers, and consuls; to all cases of admiralty and maritime jurisdiction; to controversies, to which the United States shall be a party; to controversies between two or more states; between a state and citizens of another state ; between citizens of different states ; between citizens of the same state claiming lands under grants of different states, and between a state, or the citizens thereof, and foreign states, citizens or subjects.

In all cases affecting ambassadors, other public ministers and consuls, and those in which a state shall be party, the supreme court shall have original jurisdiction. In all the other cases before mentioned, the supreme court shall have appellate jurisdiction, both as to law and fact, with such exceptions, and under such regulations as the congress shall make.

The trial of all crimes, except in cases of impeachment, shall be by jury ; and such trial shall be held in the state where the said crimes shall have been committed ; but when not committed within any state, the trial shall be at such place or places as the congress may by law have directed.

SECTION 3. Treason against the United States shall consist only in levying war against them, or in adhering to their enemies, giving them aid and comfort. No person shall be convicted of treason unless on the testimony of two witnesses to the same overt act, or on confession in open court.

The congress shall have power to declare the punishment of treason ; but no attainder of treason shall work corruption of blood, or forfeiture except during the life of the person attainted.

ARTICLE IV.

SECTION 1. Full faith and credit shall be given in each state to the public acts, records, and judicial proceedings of every other state. And the congress may by general laws prescribe the manner in which such acts, records, and proceedings shall be proved, and the effect thereof.

SECTION 2. The citizens of each state shall be entitled to all privileges and immunities of citizens in the several states.

A person charged in any state with treason, felony, or other crime, who shall flee from justice, and be found in another state, shall, on demand of the executive authority of the state from which he fled, be delivered up, to be removed to the state having jurisdiction of the crime.

No person held to service or labor in one state, under the laws thereof, escaping into another, shall, in consequence of any law or regulation therein, be discharged from such service or labor, but

shall be delivered up on claim of the party to whom such service
or labor may be due.

SECTION 3. New states may be admitted by the congress into
this Union; but no new state shall be formed or erected within
the jurisdiction of any other state; nor any state be formed by the
junction of two or more states, or parts of states, without the consent of the legislatures of the states concerned, as well as of the
congress.

The congress shall have power to dispose of and make all needful rules and regulations respecting the territory or other property
belonging to the United States; and nothing in this constitution
shall be so construed as to prejudice any claims of the United
States, or of any particular state.

SECTION 4. The United States shall guarantee to every state in
this Union a republican form of government, and shall protect
each of them against invasion; and on application of the legislature, or of the executive (when the legislature cannot be convened),
against domestic violence.

ARTICLE V.

The congress, whenever two-thirds of both houses shall deem it
necessary, shall propose amendments to this constitution; or, on
the application of the legislatures of two-thirds of the several
states, shall call a convention for proposing amendments, which, in
either case, shall be valid to all intents and purposes, as part of
this constitution, when ratified by the legislatures of three-fourths
of the several states, or by conventions in three-fourths thereof, as
the one or the other mode of ratification may be proposed by the
congress; provided that no amendment which may be made prior
to the year one thousand eight hundred and eight, shall in any
manner affect the first and fourth clauses in the ninth section of the
first article; and that no state, without its consent, shall be deprived of its equal suffrage in the senate.

ARTICLE VI.

All debts contracted and engagements entered into, before the
adoption of this constitution, shall be as valid against the United
States, under this constitution, as under the Confederation.

This constitution, and the laws of the United States which shall be made in pursuance thereof; and all treaties made, or which shall be made, under the authority of the United States, shall be the supreme law of the land; and the judges in every state shall be bound thereby, anything in the constitution or laws of any state to the contrary notwithstanding.

The senators and representatives before mentioned, and the members of the several state legislatures, and all executive and judicial officers, both of the United States and of the several states, shall be bound by oath or affirmation to support this constitution; but no religious test shall ever be required as a qualification to any office or public trust under the United States.

ARTICLE VII.

The ratification of the conventions of nine states shall be sufficient for the establishment of this constitution between the states so ratifying the same.

Done in convention, by the unanimous consent of the states present, the seventeenth day of September, in the year of our Lord one thousand seven hundred and eighty-seven, and of the independence of the United States of America the twelfth. In witness whereof, we have hereunto subscribed our names,

GEO. WASHINGTON,
President and deputy from Virginia.

[Here follow the names of the signers from the different states. See next page for additions and amendments.]

Articles in addition to, and amendment of, the Constitution of the United States of America, proposed by Congress, and ratified by the Legislatures of the several States, pursuant to the fifth article of the original Constitution.

ARTICLE I.

Congress shall make no law respecting an establishment of religion, or prohibiting the free exercise thereof; or abridging the freedom of speech, or of the press; or the right of the people peaceably to assemble, and to petition the government for a redress of grievances.

ARTICLE II.

A well regulated militia, being necessary to the security of a free state, the right of the people to keep and bear arms shall not be infringed.

ARTICLE III.

No soldier shall, in time of peace, be quartered in any house, without the consent of the owner; nor in time of war, but in a manner to be prescribed by law.

ARTICLE IV.

The right of the people to be secure in their persons, houses, papers, and effects, against unreasonable searches and seizures, shall not be violated; and no warrants shall issue, but upon probable cause, supported by oath or affirmation, and particularly describing the place to be searched, and the persons or things to be seized.

ARTICLE V.

No person shall be held to answer for a capital, or otherwise infamous crime, unless on a presentment or indictment of a grand jury, except in cases arising in the land or naval forces, or in the militia, when in actual service in time of war or public danger; nor shall any person be subject for the same offence to be twice put in jeopardy of life or limb; nor shall be compelled, in any criminal case, to be a witness against himself; nor be deprived of life, liberty, or property, without due process of law; nor shall private property be taken for public use, without just compensation.

ARTICLE VI.

In all criminal prosecutions, the accused shall enjoy the right to a speedy and public trial, by an impartial jury of the state and district wherein the crime shall have been committed, which district shall have been previously ascertained by law, and to be informed of the nature and cause of the accusation; to be confronted with the witnesses against him ; to have compulsory process for obtaining witnesses in his favor, and to have the assistance of counsel for his defence.

ARTICLE VII.

In suits at common law, where the value in controversy shall exceed twenty dollars, the right of trial by jury shall be preserved, and no fact tried by a jury shall be otherwise re-examined in any court of the United States, than according to the rules of the common law.

ARTICLE VIII.

Excessive bail shall not be required, nor excessive fines imposed, nor cruel and unusual punishments inflicted.

ARTICLE IX.

The enumeration in the constitution of certain rights, shall not be construed to deny or disparage others retained by the people.

ARTICLE X.

The powers not delegated to the United States by the constitution, nor prohibited by it to the states, are reserved to the states respectively, or to the people.

ARTICLE XI.

The judicial power of the United States shall not be construed to extend to any suit in law or equity, commenced or prosecuted against one of the United States by citizens of another state, or by citizens or subjects of any foreign state.

ARTICLE XII.

The electors shall meet in their respective states, and vote by ballot for president and vice-president, one of whom, at least, shall not be an inhabitant of the same state with themselves; they shall name in their ballots the person voted for as president, and in distinct ballots the person voted for as vice-president; and they shall make distinct lists of all persons voted for as president, and of all persons voted for as vice-president, and of the number of votes for each, which list they shall sign and certify and transmit sealed to the seat of government of the United States, directed to the president of the senate; the president of the senate shall, in presence of the senate and house of representatives, open all the certificates and the votes shall then be counted; the person having the greatest number of votes for president, shall be the president, if such number be a majority of the whole number of electors appointed; and if no person have such majority, then from the persons having the highest numbers not exceeding three on the list of those voted for as president, the house of representatives shall choose immediately, by ballot, the president. But in choosing the president, the votes shall be taken by states, the representation from each state having one vote; a quorum for this purpose shall consist of a member, or members from two-thirds of the states, and a majority of all the states shall be necessary to a choice. And if the house of representatives shall not choose a president whenever the right of choice shall devolve upon them, before the fourth day of March next following, then the vice-president shall act as president, as in the case of the death or other constitutional disability of the president. The person having the greatest number of votes as vice-president, shall be the vice-president, if such number be a majority of the whole number of electors appointed; and if no person have a majority, then from the two highest numbers on the list the senate shall choose the vice-president; a quorum for the purpose shall consist of two-thirds of the whole number of senators, and a majority of the whole number shall be necessary to a choice. But no person constitutionally ineligible to the office of president shall be eligible to that of vice-president of the United States.

APPENDIX XI.

THE FIRST REPUBLICAN CONSTITUTION.

———

HAD the space permitted it, I would have given all the French constitutions, from the first in the first revolution, to that now called the constitution of the empire. As it is, I must restrict myself to the following selection.

I have copied the translation of the first republican constitution of France from a work by Mr. Bernard Roelker, of the New York bar, The Constitutions of France, monarchical and Republican, together with Brief Historical Remarks, relating to their Origin, and the late Orleans Dynasty, Boston, Mass. 1848.

———

DECLARATIONS OF THE RIGHTS OF MAN AND OF CITIZENS.

The French people, convinced that oblivion and contempt of the natural rights of man are the only causes of calamities in the world, has resolved to explain these sacred and inalienable rights in a solemn declaration, that all citizens, by comparing always the acts of the government with the whole social union, may never suffer themselves to be oppressed and dishonored by tyranny; that the people may always have before its eyes the fundamental pillars of its liberty and welfare, and the authorities the standard of their duties, and the legislator the object of his problem.

It accordingly makes, in the presence of the Highest Being, the following declaration of the rights of man and of the citizens.

(536)

1. The object of society is the general welfare. Government is instituted, to insure to man the free use of his natural and inalienable rights.

2. These rights are equality, liberty, security, property.

3. All men are equal by nature and before the law.

4. Law is the free and solemn proclamation of the general will; it is the same for all, be it protective or penal; it can command only what is just and beneficial to society, and prohibit only what is injurious to the same.

5. All citizens are equally admissible to all public offices. Free nations are in their elections guided by no other considerations than virtues and talents.

6. Freedom is the power, by which man can do what does not interfere with the rghts of another; its basis is nature, its standard is justice; its protection is law; its moral boundary is the maxim : *Do not unto others what you do not wish they should do unto you.*

7. The right of communicating thoughts and opinions, either through the press, or in any other manner; the right of assembling peaceably; the free exercise of religion, cannot be prohibited.

The necessity publicly to claim these rights, presupposes the actual existence of despotism, or the fresh recollection of the same.

8. Security rests on the protection given by society to each of its members, for the preservation of his person, his rights and his property.

9. Law must protect the general and the individual liberty against the oppression of those who govern.

10. No one can be accused, arrested, or kept in close custody, except in the cases specified by law, and according to the prescribed forms; every citizen who, by virtue of the law, is summoned before court or arrested, must immediately obey; every refusal shows him to be guilty.

11. Every order against a person, in cases and forms not specified by law, is arbitrary and tyrannical; the person against whom such an order should be executed by force, has the right to resist it by force.

12. Those who cause, aid in, sign, execute or cause to be executed, such arbitrary acts, are culpable, and must be punished.

13. Since every man is deemed to be innocent, until he be proved guilty, if his condemnation will necessarily lead to arrest, every severity, not required for the forthcoming of his person, is strictly prohibited.

14. Only he who has been first heard or legally summoned, can be condemned and punished, and this only by a law promulgated before the commission of the crime. A law which would punish transgressions, committed before its publication, would be tyranny; and it would be a crime to give retrospective force to law.

15. Law shall order punishments only which are unavoidably necessary; the punishments shall be suitable to the crime, and beneficial to society.

16. The right of property is that by which every citizen can enjoy his goods and his income, the fruits of his labor and industry, and dispose of them at pleasure.

17. No kind of occupation, employment and trade can be prohibited to citizens.

18. Every one may dispose of his services and time at pleasure; but he can neither sell himself nor be sold. His person is inalienable property. The law does not recognize a state of servitude; an agreement only for services rendered and a compensation for them, can exist between him who labors and him who employs him.

19. Without his consent, no one can be deprived of the least part of his property, unless it be required by a general and legally specified necessity, and then only on condition of a just and previously fixed indemnity.

20. No tax can be laid except for the common welfare. All citizens have the right to have a voice in the laying of taxes, to watch over the application of them, and to have an account rendered thereof.

21. The public support of the poor is a sacred obligation. Society takes upon itself the support of needy citizens, either by giving work to them, or by giving subsistence to those who are unable to work

22. Instruction is a want for all. Society shall further with all its power the progress of the public welfare, and regulate instruction according to the wants of all citizens.

23. Social guarantee rests on the activity of all to secure to each one the enjoyment and the preservation of his rights. This guarantee rests on the sovereignty of the people.

24. It cannot exist, if the boundaries of public administration be not definitely specified by law, and unless the responsibility of all public officers be secured.

25. Sovereignty belongs to the people. It is one and indivisible, imprescriptible and inalienable.

26. No single part of the people can exercise the power of the whole people; but every assembled section of the sovereign people enjoys the right to express its will with perfect freedom.

27. Every individual who would assume the sovereignty shall be at once condemned to death by the free men.

28. The people have the right to revise, amend, and alter their constitution. One generation cannot bind succeeding generations to its laws.

29. Every citizen has the right of taking part in the legislation, and of appointing his representatives or agents.

30. Public functions are in their nature temporary; they cannot be considered as distinctions, nor as rewards, but as obligations.

31. The offences of the representatives of the people and of its agents, shall not be unpunished. No one has the right to hold himself more inviolable than the other citizens.

32. The right of presenting petitions to the public authorities can in no case be interdicted, abolished or limited.

33. Resistance to oppression is the inference from the other rights of man.

34. It is oppression of the whole society, if but one of its members be oppressed. Oppression of every single member exists, when the whole of society is oppressed.

35. When government violates the rights of the people, insurrection of the people and of every single part of it, is the most sacred of its rights and the highest of its duties.

(Signed)   COLLOT D'HERBOIS, President.

DURAND MAILLANE, DUCOS, MÉAULLE,
CHARLES DE LA CROIX, GOSSUIN, P. A. LALOY,
                         Secrataries.

CONSTITUTION

OF THE TWENTY-FOURTH OF JUNE, 1793.

OF THE REPUBLIC.

1. The French Republic is one and indivisible.

OF THE DIVISION OF THE PEOPLE.

2. The French people is, for the purpose of exercising its sovereignty, divided into primary assemblies according to cantons.

3. For the purpose of administration and justice, it is divided into departments, districts, and municipalities.

OF THE RIGHT OF CITIZENSHIP.

4. Every man born and living in France, of twenty-one years of age, and every alien, who has attained the age of twenty-one, and has been domiciled in France one year, and lives from his labor ;

> or has acquired property ;
> or has married a French woman ;
> or has adopted a child ;
> or supports an aged man ;

and finally every alien whom the legislative body has declared as one well deserving of the human race, are admitted to exercise the rights of a French citizen.

5. The right of exercising the rights of citizen is lost :

> by being naturalized in a foreign state ;
> by accepting offices of state, or favors which do not proceed from a democratic government ;
> by being sentenced to dishonorable or corporal punishments, till reinstated in the former state.

6. The exercise of the rights of citizens is suspended :

> by being in a state of accusation ;
> by a sentence *in contumaciam,* so long as this sentence has not been rescinded.

OF THE SOVEREIGNTY OF THE PEOPLE.

7. The sovereign people embraces the whole of French citizens.

8. It chooses its deputies directly.

9. It delegates to electors the choice of administrators, public civil judges, penal judges, and judges of cassation.

10. It deliberates on laws.

OF THE PRIMARY ASSEMBLIES.

11. The primary assemblies are formed of the citizens who have resided six months in a canton.

12. They consist of no less than 200 and no more than 600 citizens, called together for the purpose of voting.

13. They are organized, after a president, secretaries and collectors of votes have been appointed.

14. They exercise their own police.

15. No one is allowed to appear there with arms.

16. The elections are made either by secret or loud voting, at the pleasure of each voter.

17. A primary meeting can in no case prescribe more than one manner of voting.

18. The collectors of votes note down the votes of those citizens who cannot write, and yet prefer to vote secretly.

19. The votes on laws are given by " Yes," and " No."

20. The elections of primary assemblies are published in the following manner :

The united citizens in the primary assembly at ——, *numbering* —— *votes, vote for, or vote against, by a majority of* ——,

OF THE NATIONAL REPRESENTATION.

21. Population is the only basis of national representation.

22. For every 40,000 individuals, one deputy is chosen.

23. Every primary assembly which is formed of from 39,000 to 41,000 individuals, chooses directly a deputy.

24. The choice is effected by an absolute majority of votes.

25. Every assembly makes an abstract of the votes, and sends a commissioner to the appointed central place of general record.

26. If at the first voting, no absolute majority be effected, a

second meeting shall be held, and those two citizens who had the most votes, shall be voted for again.

27. In case of an equal division of votes, the oldest person has the preference, no matter whether he was voted for, or whether he was chosen without it. In case of an equality of age, the casting of lots shall decide.

28. Every Frenchman, who enjoys the rights of a citizen, is eligible throughout the whole republic.

29. Every deputy belongs to the whole nation.

30. In case of non-acceptance, of abdication, or expiration of office, or of the death of a deputy, the primary assembly which had chosen him shall choose a substitute.

31. A deputy who hands in his resignation, cannot leave his post till his successor shall have been appointed.

32. The French people assembles every year on the 1st of May for election.

33. It proceeds thereto, whatever the number of citizens [present] may be, who have a right to vote.

34. Extraordinary primary meetings are held at the demand of one-fifth of the eligible citizens.

35. The meeting is, in this case, called by the municipal authority of the usual place of assembly.

36. These extraordinary meetings can transact business only when at least more than one-half of the qualified voters are present.

OF THE ELECTORAL ASSEMBLIES.

37. The citizens, united in primary assemblies, nominate in proportion of 200 citizens, (they may be present or not,) one elector; two, for from 301 to 400 ; three, for from 501 to 600.

38. The holding of election meetings, and the manner of election, are the same as in the primary meetings.

OF THE LEGISLATIVE BODY.

39. The legislative body is one, indivisible and continual.

40. Its session lasts one year.

41. It assembles on the 1st of July.

42. The national assembly cannot be organized, unless at least one more than one-half of the deputies are present.

43. The deputies can, at no time, be held answerable, accused or condemned on account of opinions uttered within the legislative body.

44. In criminal cases, they may be arrested if caught in the act; but the warrant of arrest and the warrant of committal can be issued only by the legislative body.

MODE OF PROCEDURE OF THE LEGISLATIVE BODY.

45. The sessions of the national assembly are public.

46. The debates in their sessions shall be printed.

47. It cannot deliberate, unless it consist of 200 members.

48. It cannot refuse to members the floor, in the order in which they demand the same.

49. It decides by a majority of those present.

50. Fifty members have the right to demand a call by names.

51. It has the right of censorship on the conduct of the members in its midst.

52. It exercises the power of police at the place of its sessions, and within the whole extent of its environs.

OF THE FUNCTIONS OF THE LEGISLATIVE BODY.

53. The legislative body proposes laws, and issues decrees.

54. By the general name of *law*, are understood the provisions of the legislative body which concern :

> the civil and penal legislation ;
> the general administration of revenues and of the ordinary expenditures of the republic ;
> the national domains ;
> the inscription, alloy, stamp and names of coins ;
> declaration of war ;
> every new general division of the French territory ;
> public instruction ;
> public demonstrations of honor to the memory of great men.

55. By the particular name of decrees are understood those enactments of the legislative body, which concern :

> the annual establishment of the land and marine forces ;
> the permission or refusal of the marching of foreign troops through the French territory ;

the admission of foreign vessels of war into the ports of the republic ;

the measures for the common peace and safety ;

the distribution of annual and momentary relief and of public works ;

the orders for the stamping of coins of every description ;

the unforeseen and extraordinary expenses ;

the local and particular orders for an administration, a commune, and any kind of public works ;

the defence of the territory ;

the ratification of treaties ;

the nomination and removal of the commander-in-chief of the army ;

the carrying into effect the responsibility of members of the executive council, and of public officers ;

the accusation of discovered conspiracies against the common safety of the republic ;

every alteration in the division of the French territory ;

the national rewards.

OF THE MAKING OF LAWS.

56. A notice must precede the introduction of a bill.

57. Not till after a fortnight from the giving of notice can the debate begin, and the law be temporarily accepted.

58. The proposed law is printed and sent to all the communes of the republic, under the address of, *Proposed law.*

59. If, forty days after the sending in of the proposed law, of the absolute majority of departments, one-tenth of all the primary meetings, legally assembled by the departments, have not protested, the bill is accepted and becomes a law.

60. If protest be made, the legislative body calls together the primary meetings.

ON THE SUPERSCRIPTION OF LAWS AND DECREES.

61. The laws, decrees, sentences, and all public transactions are superscribed :

In the name of the French people, in the —— year of the French Republic.

OF THE EXECUTIVE POWER.

62. There shall be an executive council, consisting of twenty-four members.

63. The electoral assembly of each department nominates a candidate. The legislative body chooses from this general list the members of the executive council.

64. It shall be renewed each half session of every legislature, in the last months of its session.

65. The executive council has the management and supervision of the general administration. Its activity is limited to the execution of laws and decrees of the legislative body.

66. It appoints, but not out of its midst, the highest agents of the general administration of the republic.

67. The legislative body establishes the number of these agents, and their business.

68. These agents form no council. They are separated one from the other, and have no relation among themselves. They exercise no personal power.

69. The executive council chooses, but not from its midst, the foreign agents of the republic.

70. It negotiates treaties.

71. The members of the executive council, are, in case of violation of duties, accused by the legislative body.

72. The executive council is responsible for the non-execution of the laws and decrees, and the abuses, of which it does not give notice.

73. It recalls and substitutes the agents at pleasure.

74. It is obliged, if possible, to inform the judicial authorities regarding them.

OF THE MUTUAL RELATIONS BETWEEN THE EXECUTIVE COUNCIL, AND THE LEGISLATIVE BODY.

75. The executive council shall have its seat near the legislative body. It shall have admittance to, and a special seat at the place of session.

76. It shall every time be heard, when it shall have to give account.

77. The legislative body shall call it into its midst, in whole or in part, when it is thought necessary.

35

OF THE ADMINISTRATIVE AUTHORITIES AND THE MUNICIPALITIES.

78. There shall be a municipal authority in each commune of the republic ; and in each district an intermediate administration ; and in each department a central administration.

79. The municipal officers are chosen by the assemblies of the commune.

80. The administrators are chosen by the electoral assemblies of the departments and of the district.

81. The municipalities and the administrative authorities are annually renewed one-half.

82. The administrative authorities and municipal officers have not a representative character. They can, in no case, limit the resolves of the legislative body, nor the execution of them.

83. The legislative body assigns the business of the municipal officers and of the administrative authorities, the rules regarding their subordination, and the punishments to which they may become liable.

84. The sessions of the municipalities and of the administrative authorities are held in public.

OF CIVIL JUSTICE.

85. The civil and penal code is the same for the whole republic.

86. No encroachment can be made upon the right of citizens, to have their matters in dispute decided on by arbitrators of their own choice.

87. The decision of these arbitrators is final, unless the citizens have reserved the right of protesting.

88. There shall be justices of the peace, chosen by the citizens of the districts, appointed by law.

89. They shall conciliate and hold court without fees.

90. Their number and extent of power shall be established by the legislative body.

91. There shall be public judges of arbitration, who are chosen by electoral assemblies.

92. Their number and districts are fixed by the legislative body.

93. They shall decide on matters in controversy, which have not been brought to a final decision by private arbitrators or by the justices of the peace.

94. They shall deliberate publicly.

They shall vote with loud voice.

They decide in the last resort on oral pleadings, or on a simple petition, without legal forms and without cost.

They shall assign the reasons of their decisions.

95. The justices of the peace and the public arbitrators are chosen annually.

OF CRIMINAL JUSTICE.

96. In criminal cases, no citizen can be put on trial, except a true bill of complaint be found by a jury, or by the legislative body.

The accused shall have advocates, either chosen by themselves, or appointed officially.

The proceedings are in public.

The state of facts and the intention are passed upon by a jury.

The punishment is executed by a criminal authority.

97. The criminal judges are chosen annually by the electoral assemblies.

OF THE COURT OF CASSATION.

98. There is a court of cassation for the whole republic.

99. This court takes no cognizance of the state of facts.

It decides on the violation of matters of form, and on transgressions expressed by law.

100. The members of this court are appointed annually through the electoral assemblies.

OF THE GENERAL TAXES.

101. No citizen is excluded from the honorable obligation to contribute towards the public expenses.

OF THE NATIONAL TREASURY.

102. The national treasury is the central point of the revenues and expenses of the republic.

103. It is managed by public accountants, whom the legislative body shall elect.

104. These agents are supervised by officers of account, whom the legislative body shall elect, but who cannot be taken from their own body: they are responsible for abuses of which they do not give legal notice to the courts.

OF THE RENDITION OF ACCOUNTS.

105. The accounts of the agents of the national treasury, and those of the administrators of public moneys are taken annually, by responsible commissioners appointed by the executive council.

106. Those persons appointed to revise the accounts are under the supervision of commissioners, who are elected by the legislative body, not out of their own number; and they are responsible for the frauds and mistakes of accounts, of which they do not give notice.

The legislative body preserves the accounts.

OF THE MILITARY FORCES OF THE REPUBLIC.

107. The general military power of the republic consists of the whole people.

108. The republic supports, also, in times of peace, a paid land and marine force.

109. All Frenchmen are soldiers; all shall be exercised in the use of arms.

110. There is no generalissimo.

111. The distinction of grade, the military marks of distinction and subordination, exist only in service and in time of its duration.

112. The general military force is used for the preservation of order and peace in the interior; it acts only on a written requisition of the constituted authorities.

113. The general military force against foreign enemies is under the command of the executive council.

114. No armed body can deliberate.

OF THE NATIONAL CONVENTION.

115. If of the absolute majority of departments, the tenth part of their regularly formed primary assemblies demand a revision of the constitution, or an alteration of some of its articles; the legislative body is obliged to call together all primary assemblies of the republic, in order to ascertain whether a national convention shall be called.

116. The national convention is formed in like manner as the legislatures, and unites in itself the highest power.

117. It is occupied, as regards the constitution, only with those subjects which caused its being called together.

OF THE RELATIONS OF THE FRENCH REPUBLIC TOWARDS FOREIGN NATIONS.

118. The French nation is the friend and natural ally of free nations.

119. It does not interfere with the affairs of government of other nations. It suffers no interference of other nations with its own.

120. It serves as a place of refuge for all who, on account of liberty, are banished from their native country.

These it refuses to deliver up to tyrants.

121. It concludes no peace with an enemy that holds possession of its territory.

OF THE GUARANTY OF RIGHTS.

122. The constitution guarantees to all Frenchmen equality, liberty, security, property, the public debt, free exercise of religion, general instruction, public assistance, absolute liberty of the press, the right of petition, the right to hold popular assemblies, and the enjoyment of all the rights of man.

123. The French republic respects loyalty, courage, age, filial love, misfortune. It places the constitution under the guaranty of all virtues.

124. The declaration of the rights of man and the constitution shall be engraven on tables, to be placed in the midst of the legislative body, and in public places.

(Signed)   COLLOT D'HERBOIS, President.

DURAND-MAILLANE, DUCOS, MÉAULLE,

CHARLES DE LA CROIX, GOSSUIN, P. A. LALOY,

Secretaries.

APPENDIX XII.

THE following is the charter of 1830, as I translated it in that
year, for a work published in Boston, under the title of Events in
Paris, during the 26th, 27th, 28th and 29th of July, translated
from the French.

This charter of August 8, 1830, is in substance the charter of
Louis XVIII. with such changes as the chambers adopted in
favor of liberty. The new articles, or the amendments of the old
ones, are printed in italics, and the old reading or suppressed
articles are given in notes, so that the paper exhibits both the
charters.

FRENCH CHARTER OF 1830.

The whole preamble of the ancient charter was suppressed, as
containing the principle of concession and *octroi* (grant), incompatible with that of the acknowledgment of national sovereignty.

The following is the substitution of the preamble :

DECLARATION OF THE CHAMBER OF DEPUTIES.

The chamber of deputies, taking into consideration the imperious necessity which results from the events of the 26th, 27th, 28th
and 29th of July, and the following days; and from the situation
in which France is placed in consequence of the violation of the
constitutional charter:

Considering, moreover, that by this violation, and the heroic resistance of the citizens of Paris, his majesty Charles X., his royal
highness Louis-Antoine, dauphin, and all the members of the senior

(550)

branch of the royal house are leaving, at this moment, the French territory—

Declares that the throne is vacant *de facto et de jure*, and that it is necessary to fill it.

The chamber of deputies declares secondly, that according to the wish, and for the interest of the French people, the preamble of the constitutional charter is suppressed, as wounding the national dignity in appearing to grant to the French rights which essentially belong to them ; and that the following articles of the same charter ought to be suppressed or modified in the following manner.

Louis Philippe, King of the French, to all to whom these presents shall come, greeting :

We have ordained and ordain, that the constitutional charter of 1814, as amended by the two chambers on the 7th August, and adopted by us on the 9th, be published anew in the following terms :

PUBLIC LAW OF THE FRENCH.

ART. 1. Frenchmen are equal before the law, whatever otherwise may be their titles or their rank.

ART. 2. They contribute in proportion to their fortunes to the charges of the state.

ART. 3. They are all equally admissible to civil and military employments.

ART. 4. Their individual liberty is equally guaranteed. No person can be either prosecuted or arrested, except in cases provided for by the law, and in the form which it prescribes.

ART. 5. Each one may profess his religion with equal liberty, and shall receive for his religious worship the same protection.

ART. 6. *The ministers of the catholic, apostolic, and Roman religion, professed by the majority of the French, and those of other christian worship, receive stipends from the public treasury.*[1]

---

[1] This article 6 is substituted for the articles 6 and 7 of the old charter, which ran thus :

6. However, the catholic, apostolic and Roman religion, is the religion of the state.

7. The ministers of the catholic, apostolic and Roman religion, and those of other christian confessions, alone receive stipends from the public treasury.

ART. 7. Frenchmen have the right of publishing and causing to
be printed their opinions, provided they conform themselves to the
laws.

The censorship can never be re-established.[1]

ART. 8. All property is inviolable, without exception of that
which is called *national,* the law making no difference between
them.

ART. 9. The state can exact the sacrifice of property for the
good of the public, legally proved, but with a previous indemnity.

ART. 10. All examination into the opinions and votes given
before the restoration are interdicted, and the same oblivion is
commanded to be adopted by the tribunals and by the citizens.

ART. 11. The conscription is abolished. The method of re-
cruiting the army for land and sea is to be determined by the law.

FORMS OF THE KING'S GOVERNMENT.

ART. 12. The person of the king is inviolable and sacred. His
ministers are responsible. To the king alone belongs executive
power.

ART. 13. The king is the supreme head of the state; commands
the forces by sea and by land; declares war, makes treaties of
peace and alliance and of commerce; he appoints to all offices in
public administration, and makes all regulations necessary for the
execution of the laws, *without ever having power either to suspend the laws themselves, or dispense with their execution.*

*Nevertheless, no foreign troops can be admitted into the ser-
vice of the state without an express law.*[2]

ART. 14. The legislative power is to be exercised collectively
by the king, the chamber of peers, and the chamber of deputies.[3]

---

[1] Article 8 of the old charter:

The French have the right to publish and to cause to be published their
opinions, conforming themselves to the laws, which shall prevent the abuse
of this liberty.

[2] Article 14 of the old charter:

The king is the supreme head of the state, commands the forces by land
and sea, declares war, makes treaties of peace, alliance and commerce, appoints to all offices of public administration, and makes rules and orders
necessary for the execution of the laws and the safety of the state.

[3] There was in article 15 of the old charter: and the chamber of deputies
of the departments. These last three words have been suppressed.

ART. 15. *The proposition of the laws belong to the king, to the chamber of peers, and to the chamber of deputies.*

Nevertheless, all the laws of taxes are to be first voted by the chamber of deputies.[1]

ART. 16. Every law to be discussed and freely voted by the majority of each of the two chambers.

ART. 17. *If a proposed law be rejected by one of the three powers, it cannot be brought forward again in the same session.*[2]

ART. 18. The king alone sanctions and promulgates the laws.

ART. 19. The civil list is to be fixed for the duration of the reign of the legislative assembly after the accession of the king.

OF THE CHAMBER OF PEERS:

ART. 20. The chamber of peers is to form an essential portion of the legislative power:

ART. 21. It is convoked by the king at the same time as the chamber of deputies. The session of one begins and ends at the same time as that of the other.

ART. 22. Any assembly of the chamber of peers, which should be held at a time which is not that of the session of the chamber of deputies, is illicit, and null of full right, *except only the case in which it is assembled as a court of justice, and then it can only exercise judicial functions.*[3]

---

[1] Art. 15 is in the place of art. 16 and 17 of the old charter, which were thus:

Art. 16. The king proposes the law.

Art. 17. The proposition of the law is carried, at the pleasure of the king, to the chamber of peers or that of the deputies, except the law of taxes, which is to be directed to the chamber of deputies.

[2] Art. 17 is substituted for articles 19, 20 and 21, suppressed as useless, after the preceding provisions. They were the following:

Art. 19. The chambers have the right to petition the king to propose a law on any subject whatever, and to indicate what seems to them proper the law ought to contain.

Art. 20. This request may be made by each of the chambers, but after having been discussed in secret committee; it is not to be sent to the other chamber, by that which proposes, until after the elapse of ten days.

Art. 21. If the proposition is adopted by the other chamber, it is to be laid before the king; if it is rejected, it cannot be presented again in the same session.

[3] This is article 26 of the old charter, augmented by this provision, which was not in the former, and the words following have been suppressed: or that it should be ordained by the king.

ART. 23. The nomination of the peers of France belongs to the king. Their number is unlimited; he can vary their dignities, and name them peers for life, or make them hereditary at his pleasure.

ART. 24. Peers can enter the chamber at twenty-five years of age, but have only a deliberative voice at the age of thirty years.

ART. 25. The chamber of peers is to be presided over by the chancellor of France ; and in his absence, by a peer named by the king.

ART. 26. The princes of blood are to be peers by right of birth. They are to take their seats immediately behind the president.[1]

ART. 27. *The sittings of the chamber of peers are public as that of the chamber of deputies.*[2]

ART. 28. The chamber of peers takes cognizance of high treason, and of attempts against the security of the state, which is to be defined by the law.

ART. 29. No peer can be arrested but by the authority of the chamber, or judged but by it in a criminal matter.

OF THE CHAMBER OF DEPUTIES.

ART. 30. The chamber of deputies will be composed of deputies elected by the electoral colleges; the organization of which is to be determined by law.[3]

ART. 31. The deputies are to be elected for five years.[4]

ART. 32. No deputy can be admitted into the chamber till he

---

[1] Art. 30 of the old charter :

The members of the royal family and the princes of the blood, are peers by the right of birth ; they sit immediately behind the president; but they have no deliberative voice before their twenty-fifth year.

Art. 31, was thus :

The princes cannot take their seat in the chamber, but by order of the king, expressed for each session by a message, under penalty of rendering everything null which has been done in their presence. Suppressed.

[2] All deliberations of the chamber of peers are secret. Art. 32 of the old charter.

[3] Art. 36 was thus :

Every department shall have the same number of deputies which it has previously had. Suppressed.

[4] Art. 37 of the old charter :

The deputies shall be elected for five years, and in such a way that the chamber is renewed each year by a fifth.

has attained the age of *thirty years, and if he does not possess the other conditions prescribed by the law*.[1]

ART. 33. If, however, there should not be in the department fifty persons of the age specified *paying the amount of taxes fixed by law*, their number shall be completed from the persons who pay the greatest amount of taxes under the amount fixed by law.[2]

ART. 34. *No person can be an elector if he is under twenty-five years of age; and if he does not possess all the other conditions determined by the law*.[3]

ART. 35. The presidents of the electoral colleges are elected by *the electors*.[4]

ART. 36. The half at least of the deputies are to be chosen from those who have their political residence in the departments.

ART. 37. The president of the chamber of deputies *is to be elected by the chamber itself at the opening of each session*.[5]

ART. 38. The sittings of the chamber are to be public, but the request *of five* members will be sufficient that it forms itself into a secret committee.

ART. 39. The chamber divides itself into *bureaux* (committees) to discuss the projects of laws, which may have been presented from the king.

---

[1] Art. 38 of the old charter:

No deputy can be admitted into the chamber if he is not forty years old, and if he does not pay direct taxes of 1000 francs.

[2] Article 39 of the old charter:

If, nevertheless, there should not be in the department fifty persons of the indicated age, paying at least 1000 francs, direct taxes, their number will be completed by those who pay the highest taxes under 1000 francs; and these may be elected concurrently with the others.

[3] Art. 40 of the old charter:

The electors who concur in electing the deputy, cannot have the right of suffrage, if they do not pay a direct tax of 300 francs; and if they are less than thirty years of age.

[4] Art. 41 of the old charter:

The presidents of the electoral colleges shall be nominated by the king, and be, by right, members of the college.

[5] Art. 43 of the old charter:

The president of the chamber of deputies is nominated by the king, from a list of five members, presented by the chamber.

[6] In consequence of the initiative, art. 46 and 47 are suppressed, which were thus:

46. No amendment can be made to a law, if it has not been proposed or

Art. 40. *No tax can be established nor imposed, if it has not been consented to by the two chambers, and sanctioned by the king.*

Art. 41. The land and house tax can only be voted for one year. The indirect taxes may be voted for many years.

Art. 42. The king convokes every year the two chambers, he prorogues them, and may dissolve that of the deputies; but in this case he must convoke a new one within the period of three months.

Art. 43. No bodily restraint can be exercised against a member of the chamber during the session, nor for six weeks which precede or follow the session.

Art. 44. No member of the chamber can be, during the session, prosecuted or arrested in a criminal matter, except taken in the act, till after the chamber has permitted his arrest.

Art. 45. Every petition to either of the chambers must be made in writing. The law interdicts its being carried in person to the bar.

OF THE MINISTERS.

Art. 46. The ministers can be members of the chamber of peers or the chamber of deputies.

They have, moreover, their entrance into either chamber, and are entitled to be heard when they demand it.

Art. 47. The chamber of deputies has the right of impeaching the ministers, or of transferring them before the chamber of peers, which alone has the right to judge them.[1]

JUDICIAL REGULATIONS.

Art. 48. All justice emanates from the king; it is administered in his name by the judges, whom he nominates, and whom he institutes.

---

consented to by the king, and if it has not been sent back and discussed by the bureaux.

47. The chamber of deputies receives all propositions of taxes; only after these have been consented to, they may be carried to the chamber of peers.

[1] Article 56 of the old charter is suppressed; it ran thus:

They cannot be accused except for treason or peculation. Particular laws will specify this kind of offences, and will determine how they are to be prosecuted.

ART. 49. The judges named by the king are immoveable.

ART. 50. The ordinary courts and tribunals existing are to be maintained, and there is to be no change but by virtue of a law.

ART. 51. The actual institution of the judges of commerce is preserved.

ART. 52. The office of justice of peace is equally preserved. The justices of peace, though named by the king, are not immoveable.

ART. 53. No one can be deprived of his natural judges.

ART. 54. There cannot, in consequence, be extraordinary committees and tribunals created, *under whatever title or denomination this ever might be.*[1]

ART. 55. The debates will be public in criminal matters, at least when the publicity will not be dangerous to order and decency, and in that case the tribunal is to declare so by a distinct judgment.

ART. 56. The institution of juries is to be preserved; the changes which a longer experience may render necessary can only be effected by a law.

ART. 57. The punishment of confiscation of goods is abolished, and cannot be re-established.

ART. 58. The king has the right to pardon and to commute the punishment.

ART. 59. The civil code, and the actual laws existing that are not contrary to the present charter, will remain in full force until they shall be legally abrogated.

PARTICULAR RIGHTS GUARANTEED BY THE STATE.

ART. 60. The military in actual service, retired officers and soldiers, widows, officers and soldiers on pension, are to preserve their grades, honors and pensions.

ART. 61. The public debt is guaranteed. Every sort of engagement made by the state with its creditors is to be inviolable.

ART. 62. The old nobility retake their titles. The new preserve theirs. The king creates nobles at his pleasure; but he only grants

---

[1] Art. 63 of the old charter:

In consequence there cannot be created extraordinary committees and tribunals. The *juridictions prevôtales*, if their re-establishment should be found necessary, are not comprised under this denomination.

to them rank and honors, without any exemption from the charges and duties of society.

ART. 63. The legion of honor is to be maintained. The king shall determine its internal regulations and the decorations.

ART. 64. The colonies are to be governed by *particular* laws.[1]

ART. 65. The king and his successors shall swear, at their accession, *in presence of the two chambers,* to observe faithfully the present constitutional charter.[2]

ART. 66. *The present charter, and the rights it consecrates, shall be intrusted to the patriotism and courage of the national guard and all the citizens.*

ART. 67. *France resumes her colors. For the future there will be no other cockade than the tri-colored cockade.*[3]

ART. 68. All the creations of peers during the reign of Charles X. are declared null and void.

Article 23 of the charter will undergo a fresh examination during the session of 1831.

ART. 69. There will be provided successively by separate laws, and that with the shortest possible delay, for the following subjects:

1. The extension of the trial by jury to offences of the press, and political offences.

2. The responsibility of ministers and the secondary agents of government.

3. The re-election of deputies appointed to public functions with salaries.

4. The annual voting of the army estimates.

5. The organization of the national guards with the intervention of the national guards in the choice of their officers.

---

[1] Art. 73 of the old charter:

The colonies will be governed by particular laws and regulations.

[2] Art. 74 of the old charter:

The king and his successors shall swear at the coronation, to observe faithfully the present constitutional charter.

[3] Arts. 75 and 76 of the old charter are suppressed; they ran thus:

75. The deputies of the departments of France who sat in the legislative body, at the last adjournment, will continue to sit in the chamber of deputies, until replaced.

76. The first renewal of the fifth of the chamber of deputies will take place the latest in the year 1816, according to the order established.

6. Provisions which insure, in a legal manner, the state of officers of each grade, by land and sea.

7. Departmental and municipal institutions founded upon an elective system.

8. Public instruction and the liberty of instruction.

9. The abolition of the double vote; the settling of the electoral conditions, and that of eligibility.

ART. 70. All laws and ordinances, inasmuch as they are contrary to the provisions adopted by the reform of the charter, are from this moment annulled and abrogated.

We give it in command to our courts and tribunals, administrative bodies, and all others, that they observe and maintain the present constitutional charter, cause it to be observed, followed and maintained, and in order to render it more known to all, they cause it to be published in all municipalities of the kingdom and everywhere, where it will be necessary, and in order that this be firm and stable for ever, we have caused our seal to be put to it.

Done at the Palais-Royal, at Paris, the 14th day of the month of August, in the year 1830.

Signed   LOUIS PHILIPPE.

By the king:

The Minister Secretary of the State for the department of the Interior.

Signed   GUIZOT.

Examined and sealed with the great seal:

The keeper of the seals, Minister Secretary of the State for the department of Justice.

Signed   DUPONT (de l'Eure).

APPENDIX XIII.

CONSTITUTION OF THE FRENCH REPUBLIC.

ADOPTED NOVEMBER, 1848.

In presence of God, and in the name of the French people, the National Assembly proclaims :

I. France has constituted herself a republic. In adopting that definite form of government, her proposed aim is to advance with greater freedom in the path of civilization and progress, to insure that the burdens and advantages of society shall be more and more equitably apportioned, to augment the comfort of every individual by the gradual reduction of the public expenses and taxes, and by the successive and constant action of her institutions and laws cause the whole body of citizens to attain, without farther commotion, a constantly increasing degree of morality, intelligence, and prosperity.

II. The French republic is democratic, one and indivisible.

III. It recognizes rights and duties anterior and superior to all positive laws.

IV. Its principles are Liberty, Equality, Fraternity.

Its basis is, Family, Labor, Property, and Public Order.

V. It respects the nationality of foreign states, as it causes its own to be respected. It undertakes no wars with a view of conquest, and never employs its power against the liberty of any people.

VI. Reciprocal duties bind the citizens to the republic and the republic to the citizens.

VII. It is the duty of the citizens to love their country, serve the republic, and defend it at the hazard of their lives; to participate in the expenses of the state, in proportion to their property; to secure to themselves, by their labor, the means of existence, and, by prudent forethought, provide resources for the future; to co-operate for the common welfare by fraternally aiding each other,

(560)

and in the preservation of general order by observing the moral and written laws which regulate society, families, and individuals.

VIII. It is the duty of the republic to protect the citizen in his person, his family, his religion, his property, and his labor, and to bring within the reach of all that education which is necessary to every man; it is also its duty, by fraternal assistance, to provide the means of existence to necessitous citizens, either by procuring employment for them, within the limits of its resources, or by giving relief to those who are unable to work and who have no relatives to help them.

For the fulfilment of all these duties, and for the guarantee of all these rights, the National Assembly, faithful to the traditions of the great Assemblies by whom the French revolution was inaugurated, decrees the constitution of the republic, as following:

CONSTITUTION.

CHAPTER I.

OF SOVEREIGNTY.

ART. 1. The sovereignty exists in the whole body of French citizens. It is inalienable and imprescriptible. No individual, no fraction of the people can arrogate to themselves its exercise.

CHAPTER II.

RIGHTS OF CITIZENS GUARANTEED BY THE CONSTITUTION.

ART. 2. No person can be arrested or detained, except as prescribed by law.

ART. 3. The dwelling of every person inhabiting the French territory is inviolable, and cannot be entered except according to the forms and in the cases provided against by law.

ART. 4. No one shall be removed from his rightful judges—no commissions or extraordinary tribunals can be created under any pretext, or by any denomination whatsoever.

ART. 5. The penalty of death for political offences is abolished.

ART. 6. Slavery cannot exist upon any French territory.

ART. 7. Every one may freely profess his own religion, and shall receive from the state equal protection in the exercise of his wor-

36

ship. The ministers of the religions at present recognized by law, as well as those which may be hereafter recognized, have the right to receive an allowance from the state.

ART. 8. Citizens have the right of associating together and assembling peaceably and unarmed, in order to petition or manifest their ideas by means of the press or otherwise. The exercise of these rights can only be limited by the rights or the liberty of others, or for the public security. The press cannot in any case be subjected to censorship.

ART. 9. Education is free. The liberty of teaching is to be exercised according to the capacity and morality determined by conditions of the laws, and under the supervision of the state. This superintendence is to be extended to all establishments of education and instruction, without any exception.

ART. 10. All citizens are equally admissible to all public employments, without other reason of preference than merit, and according to the conditions to be determined by law. All titles of nobility, all distinctions of birth, class or *caste*, are abolished forever.

ART. 11. All descriptions of property are inviolable; nevertheless, the state may demand the sacrifice of property for reasons of public utility, legally proved, and in consideration of a just and previous indemnity.

ART. 12. The confiscation of property can never be re-established.

ART. 13. The constitution guarantees to citizens the freedom of labor and of industry. Society favors and encourages the development of labor by gratuitous primary instruction, by professional education, by the equality of rights between the employer and the workman, by institutions for the deposit of savings and those of credit, by agricultural institutions; by voluntary associations, and the establishment by the state, the departments and the communes, of public works proper for the employment of unoccupied laborers. Society also will give aid to deserted children, to the sick, and to the destitute aged who are without relatives to support them.

ART. 14. The public debt is guaranteed. Every species of engagement made by the state with its creditors is inviolable.

ART. 15. All taxes are imposed for the common good. Every one is to contribute in proportion to his means and fortune.

ART. 16. No tax can be levied or collected except by virtue of the law.

ART. 17. Direct taxation is only awarded for one year. Indirect taxes may be awarded for several years.

CHAPTER III.

OF PUBLIC POWER.

ART. 18. All public powers, whatever they may be, emanate from the people. They cannot be delegated by hereditary descent.

ART. 19. The separation of powers is the first principle of a free government.

CHAPTER IV.

OF THE LEGISLATIVE POWER.

ART. 20. The French people delegate the legislative power to one sole assembly.

ART. 21. The total number of representatives of the people shall be 750, including the representatives from Algeria and the French colonies.

ART. 22. This number shall be increased to 900 for assemblies called together to revise the constitution.

ART. 23. Population is the basis for election.

ART. 24. Suffrage is direct and universal. The act of voting is by secret ballot.

ART. 25. All Frenchmen aged twenty-one, and in the enjoyment of their civil and political rights, are electors, without property qualifications of any kind.

ART. 26. All electors are eligible to be elected without reference to property qualifications or to place of abode, who are twenty-five years of age.

ART. 27. The electoral law will determine the causes which may deprive a French citizen of the right of electing or being elected. It will designate those citizens who, exercising or after having exercised official functions in a department or territory, cannot be elected there.

ART. 28. The holding of any remunerating public office is incompatible with the trust of a representative of the people. No member of the national assembly can be nominated or raised to public offices, receiving salary, the appointment to which is in the gift of the executive, during the continuance of the legislature. Exceptions to the regulations contained in the two preceding paragraphs are to be settled by the organic electoral law.

ART. 29. The conditions of the preceding articles are not applicable to assemblies elected for the revision of the constitution.

ART. 30. The elections for representatives shall be by departments, and by ballot. The electors shall vote at the chief place of their district; nevertheless the district may be, from local causes, divided into several subdivisions, under the forms and in conformity with the conditions to be determined by the electoral law.

ART. 31. The national assembly is elected for the period of three years, to be then wholly renewed. Forty-five days at least before the term of the legislature, a law shall be passed to fix the period of the new elections. If no law is passed within the time prescribed by the preceding paragraph, the electors shall have full right to assemble and vote on the thirtieth day preceding the close of the legislature. The new assembly is convoked by full right for the day following that on which the trust of the preceding assembly expires.

ART. 32. The assembly is permanent; nevertheless it may adjourn to any period which it shall determine. During the continuance of the prorogation, a commission, composed of members of committees, and twenty-five representatives appointed by the assembly, by ballot, having an absolute majority, will have the right to convoke the assembly, in cases of emergency. The president of the republic has also the right to convoke the assembly. The national assembly will determine the place where it shall hold its sessions, and will direct the number and description of the military forces which shall be appointed for its security, and have them at its order.

ART. 33. Representatives may be re-elected.

ART. 34. The members of the national assembly are the representatives, not of the department which nominates them, but of the whole of France.

ART. 35. They cannot receive imperative instructions.

ART. 36. The persons of the representatives of the people are inviolable. They cannot be pursued, accused, nor condemned, at any time, for opinions uttered within the assembly.

ART. 37. They cannot be arrested for criminal offences, excepting when taken in the very fact, nor prosecuted, until after permission granted for such purpose by the assembly. In case of an arrest in the very fact, the matter shall immediately be referred to the assembly, which shall authorize or refuse the continuation of the prosecution. The above regulation to apply also to the case of citizens imprisoned at the time of being named representatives.

ART. 38. Every representative of the people is to receive a remuneration, which he is not at liberty to renounce.

ART. 39. The sittings of the assembly are to be public. Nevertheless, the assembly may form itself into a secret committee, on the requisition of a number of representatives, as settled by the rules. Each representative has the right of initiating parliamentary measures, which he will do according to the forms determined by the regulations.

ART. 40. The presence of half the members, and also one over, is necessary to vote on any law.

ART. 41. No bill (except in cases of urgency) shall be passed till after it has undergone three readings, at intervals of not less than five days between each reading.

ART. 42. Every proposition, the object of which is to declare the urgency of a measure, must be preceded by an explanation of motives. If the assembly is of opinion to accede to the proposition, it will fix the time when the report upon the necessity of the case shall be represented. On this report, if the assembly admit the urgency of the case, it will declare it, and fix the time of the debate. If it decides against the urgency of the case, the motion will have to go through the usual course.

CHAPTER V.

OF THE EXECUTIVE POWER.

ART. 43. The French people delegates the executive power to a citizen, who shall receive the title of president of the republic.

ART. 44. The president must be born a Frenchman, thirty years of age at least, and must never have lost the quality of Frenchman.

ART. 45. The president of the republic shall be elected for four years, and shall not be eligible for re-election until after an interval of four years. Neither shall the vice-president, nor any of his relations or kindred of the president, to the sixth degree inclusive, be eligible for re-election after him, within the same interval of time.

ART. 46. The election shall take place on the second Sunday in the month of May. If, in the event of death or resignation, or from any other cause, a president be elected at any other period, his power shall expire on the second Sunday of the month of May, in the fourth year following his election. The president shall be elected by secret ballot, and by an absolute majority of votes, by the direct suffrage of all the electors of the French departments and of Algeria.

ART. 47. The records of the electoral operations shall be transmitted immediately to the national assembly, which shall determine without delay upon the validity of the election, and shall proclaim the president of the republic. If no candidate shall have obtained more than one-half of the votes given, and at the least two millions of votes, or if the conditions required by article 44 are not fulfilled, the national assembly shall elect the president of the republic by an absolute majority, and by ballot, from among the five candidates eligible who shall have obtained the greatest number of votes.

ART. 48. Before entering upon his functions, the president of the republic shall, in the presence of the assembly, take an oath of the tenor following: "In presence of God, and before the French people, represented by the national assembly, I swear to remain faithful to the democratic republic, one and indivisible, and to fulfil all the duties which the constitution imposes upon me."

ART. 49. He shall have the right of presenting bills through the ministers in the national assembly. He shall watch over and secure the execution of the laws.

ART. 50. He shall have the disposal of the armed force, without ever being allowed to command it in person.

ART. 51. He cannot cede any portion of the territory, nor dissolve or prorogue the national assembly, nor suspend the operation of the constitution and the laws.

ART. 52. He shall annually present, by a message to the national assembly, an exposition of the general state of the affairs of the republic.

ART. 53. He shall negotiate and ratify treaties. No treaty shall be definitive until after it has been approved by the national assembly.

ART. 54. He shall watch over the defence of the state, but he shall not undertake any war without the consent of the national assembly.

ART. 55. He shall possess the right of pardon; but he shall not have the power to exercise this right until after he has taken the advice of the council of state. Amnesties shall only be granted by an express law. The president of the republic, the ministers, as well as all other persons condemned by the high court of justice, can only be pardoned by the national assembly.

ART. 56. The president of the republic shall promulgate the laws in the name of the French people.

ART. 57. Laws of emergency shall be promulgated three days after, and other laws one month after their passing, counting from the day on which they were passed by the national assembly.

ART. 58. Previous to the day fixed for the promulgation, the president may, by a message assigning reasons therefor, demand a reconsideration of the law. The assembly shall then reconsider it, its resolution becomes definitive, and shall be transmitted to the president of the republic. In such a case, the promulgation shall be made within the delay allowed to laws of emergency.

ART. 59. In default of the promulgation of laws by the president, within the period fixed by the preceding articles, the president of the assembly shall provide for their due promulgation.

ART. 60. The credentials of envoys and ambassadors from foreign powers shall be addressed to the president of the republic.

ART. 61. He shall preside at all national solemnities.

ART. 62. He shall be furnished with a residence at the expense of the republic, and shall receive an allowance of six hundred thousand francs per annum.

ART. 63. He shall reside in the place in which the national assembly holds its sessions, and may not leave the continental territory of the republic without being authorized by law so to do.

ART. 64. The president of the republic shall have power to appoint and revoke the appointment of the ministers. He shall appoint and revoke, in a council of ministers, the diplomatic agents, commanders-in-chief of the armies of the republic by sea and land, prefects and the chief commandant of the national guards of the Seine, the governors of Algeria and the other colonies, the attorney-general and all other functionaries of superior rank. He shall appoint and dismiss, at the suggestion of the competent minister, according to the terms and conditions fixed by law, all other officers and functionaries of the government of secondary rank.

ART. 65. He shall have the right of suspending, for a period not exceeding three months, the agents of the executive power

elected by the people.   He shall not be able to dismiss them unless
by the advice of the council of the state.   The law will determine
the case in which agents, having been dismissed, may be declared
not to be eligible again for the same office.   Such a declaration of
ineligibility can only be pronounced by a formal judgment.

ART. 66. The number of ministers and their several powers,
duties and emoluments shall be settled by the legislative power.

ART. 67. The acts of the president, excepting those by which he
appoints or dismisses the ministers of the republic, shall be of no
effect, unless countersigned by a minister.

ART. 68. The president of the republic, the ministers, the agents,
and all the other depositaries of public authority, shall be responsible, each in so far as he is concerned, for all the acts of the
government and of the administration.   Every measure by which
the president of the republic shall dissolve or prorogue the assembly, or interpose any obstacle to the exercise of its public trust,
shall be deemed a crime of high treason.   By this sole act, the
president becomes divested of his functions, and the people are
bound not to yield obedience to him; the executive power is thereby
transferred in full authority to the national assembly.   The judges
of the high court of justice shall immediately assemble, on pain of
forfeiture of their offices.   They shall call together a jury, in some
place to be by them designated, in order to proceed to trial and
judgment upon the president and his accomplices; and they shall
themselves appoint a magistrate to be charged with the functions
of state attorney.   A law shall determine the other cases of responsibility, as well as the forms and conditions of the prosecution
of them.

ART. 69. The ministers shall have admission into the national
assembly, and shall be heard whenever they require it, and they may
also obtain the assistance of commissioners, who shall have been
appointed by a decree of the president of the republic.

ART. 70. There shall be a vice-president of the republic, to be
appointed by the national assembly, from a list of three candidates
presented by the president within the month succeeding his election.   The vice-president shall take the same oath as the president.
The vice-president shall not be appointed from among the relations
or kindred of the president to the sixth degree inclusive.   Should
the president by any cause be prevented from officiating, the vice-

president will represent him for the time being. If the presidency shall become vacant by the death of the president, his dismissal from office, or from other causes, a new election for president shall take place within a month.

CHAPTER VI.

OF THE COUNCIL OF STATE.

ART. 71. There shall be a council of state, of which the vice-president of the republic shall of right be the president.

ART. 72. The members of this council shall be appointed for six years by the national assembly. The half of this council shall be renewed in the first two months of each new legislature, by secret ballot, and by an absolute majority. They shall be indefinitely re-eligible.

ART. 73. Such of the members of the council of state, who shall have been appointed from among the members of the assembly, shall be immediately replaced as representatives of the people.

ART. 74. The members of the council of state cannot be dismissed, except by the national assembly and at the suggestion of the president.

ART. 75. The council of state shall be consulted upon all bills or laws proposed by the government, which, according to law, must be presented for their previous examination; and also upon parliamentary bills which the assembly may send to them for their examination. It shall prepare the rules of public administration, and will alone make those regulations with regard to which the national assembly have given it a special delegation. It shall exercise over the public administrations all the powers of control and of superintendence which are conferred upon it by law. The law will determine the other powers and duties of the council.

CHAPTER VII.

OF THE INTERIOR ADMINISTRATION.

ART. 76. The division of the territory into departments, arrondissements, districts and communes shall be maintained. Their present limits shall not be changed, except by law.

ART. 77. There shall be—1. In each department an administration composed of a prefect, a general council, and a council of prefecture. 2. In each arrondissement, a sub-prefect. 3. In each district, a district-council; nevertheless, only a single district-council shall be established in any city which is divided into several districts. 4. In each commune, an administration, composed of a mayor, his assistants, and a municipal council.

ART. 78. A law shall determine the composition and duties of the general councils, the district councils, and the municipal councils, as well as, also, the manner of appointing the mayors and their assistants.

ART. 79. The general councils and the municipal councils shall be elected by the direct vote of all citizens living in the department or district; each district shall elect one member of the general council; a special law shall regulate the forms of election in the department of the Seine, in the city of Paris and in cities containing a population of more than twenty thousand souls.

ART. 80. The general councils, the district councils, and the municipal councils may be dissolved by the president of the republic, with the advice of the council of state; the law will fix the period within which a new election shall be held.

CHAPTER VIII.

OF THE JUDICIARY POWER.

ART. 81. Justice shall be awarded, gratuitously, in the name of the French people. The proceedings shall be public, except in cases where publicity may be detrimental either to the public order or public morals, in which case the court shall declare the same by a formal judgment.

ART. 82. Trial by jury shall be continued in criminal cases.

ART. 83. The decision upon all political offences, and upon all offences committed by means of the press, appertains exclusively to the jury. The organic laws shall determine the tribunal and powers in relation to offences and defamation against private individuals.

ART. 84. The jury alone shall decide upon the question of damages claimed on account of offences by the press.

ART. 85. The justices of peace and their assistants, the judges of the first instance and of appeal, the members of the court of cassation and of the court of accounts, shall be appointed by the president of the republic, according to a system of candidateship on conditions which shall be regulated by the organic laws.

ART. 86. The magistrates shall be appointed by the president of the republic.

ART. 87. The judges of the first instance and of appeal, the members of the court of cassation and of the court of accounts shall be appointed for life. They shall not be dismissed or suspended, except after judgment, nor retire with a pension, except for causes, and according to proceedings appointed by law.

ART. 88. The councils of war and of revision of the armies by sea and land, the maritime tribunals, the tribunals of commerce, the *prud'hommes*, and other special tribunals, shall retain their present organization and their present functions, until the law shall decide otherwise.

ART. 89. Conflicts of privileges and duties between the administrative and the judicial authority shall be regulated by a special tribunal, composed of members of the court of cassation and of counsellors of state, to be appointed, every three years, in equal number, by the respective bodies to which they belong. This tribunal shall be presided over by the minister of justice.

ART. 90. Appeals for incompetence, or excess of power against the decrees of the court of accounts, shall be carried before the tribunal of conflictive jurisdiction.

ART. 91. A high court of justice shall decide, without appeal, demur, or recourse of annulment, in all accusations made by the national assembly against the president of the republic or the ministers. It shall likewise, in the same way, try all cases of persons accused of crimes, attempts, or plots against the internal and external safety of the state, which the assembly may have sent before it. Except in the case provided for in article 68, it shall not be called together unless by decree of the national assembly, which shall also designate the city in which the court shall hold its sittings.

ART. 92. The high court shall be composed of five judges and of thirty-six jurymen. Every year, in the first fifteen days of the month of November, the court of cassation shall appoint from among its members, by secret ballot and an absolute majority, the judges of the high court, the number to be five judges and two supplementary judges. The five judges, who are thus called upon to sit, will themselves select their president. The magistrates performing the functions of the public ministry shall be designated by

the president of the republic, and, in the event of the accusation
of the president or his ministers, by the national assembly.   The
jury, to the number of thirty-six, and four supplementary jurymen,
shall be taken from among the members of the general councils of
the departments.   Representatives of the people shall not be competent to form part of these juries.

ART. 93. When a decree of the national assembly shall have
ordered the formation of the high court of justice as also in the
cases provided for in the 68th article, on the requisition of the
president or of one of the judges, the president of the court of
appeal, and in default of that court, the president of the tribunal
of the first instance of the chief judiciary court of the department,
shall draw lots in public assembly for the name of a member of the
general council.

ART. 94. On the day appointed for the trial, if there are less than
sixty jurymen present, the number shall be filled up by supplementary jurymen, drawn by lot by the president of the high court of
justice, from among the names of the members of the general council of the department in which the court holds its sitting.

ART. 95. Those jurymen who shall not have given an adequate
excuse for absence, shall be condemned to a fine of not less than
one thousand francs, and not exceeding ten thousand, and to be
deprived of their political rights during five years at the utmost.

ART. 96. Both the accused and the public accuser shall have the
right to challenge, as in ordinary cases.

ART. 97. The verdict of the jury pronouncing the accused guilty
cannot be rendered except by a majority of two-thirds.

ART. 98. In all cases regarding the responsibility of the ministers, the national assembly may, according to the circumstances,
send the accused minister to be tried either before the high court
of justice or by the ordinary tribunals for civil indemnities (or
damages).

ART. 99. The national assembly and the president of the republic may, in all cases, transmit the examination of the acts of any
functionary (except of the president himself) to the council of state,
whose report shall be made public.

ART. 100. The president of the republic can only be brought to
trial before the high court of justice.   Except as is provided for
by article 68, he cannot be tried unless upon accusation brought

against him by the national assembly, and for crimes and misdemeanors, which shall be determined by law.

CHAPTER IX.

OF THE PUBLIC FORCES.

ART. 101. The public force is instituted for the purpose of defending the state against enemies from without, and to insure, internally, the maintenance of order, and the execution of the laws. It is composed of the national guard and of the army by sea and by land.

ART. 102. Every Frenchman, save in exceptions determined by the law, owes to his country his services in the army and in the national guard. The privilege of every citizen to free himself from personal military service shall be regulated by the law of recruitment.

ART. 103. The organization of the national guard, and the constitution of the army, shall be regulated by law.

ART. 104. The public force is essentially obedient. No armed force can deliberate.

ART. 105. The public force employed to maintain order in the interior can only act upon the requisition of the constituted authorities, according to the regulations prescribed by the legislative power.

ART. 106. A law shall determine those cases in which the state of siege shall be declared, and shall regulate the forms and determine the effects of such a measure.

ART. 107. No foreign troops can be introduced into the French territory without the previous assent of the national assembly.

CHAPTER X.

SPECIAL REGULATIONS.

ART. 108. The legion of honor is maintained; its statutes shall be revised, and made to accord with the constitution.

ART. 109. The territory of Algeria, and of the colonies, is declared to be French territory, and shall be governed by their separate laws until a special law shall place them under the provisions of the present constitution.

ART. 110. The national assembly confides the trust of this present constitution, and the rights it consecrates, to the guardianship and patriotism of every Frenchman.

CHAPTER XI.

OF THE REVISION OF THE CONSTITUTION.

Art. 111. Whenever, in the last year of a legislature, the national assembly shall have expressed the wish that the constitution should be modified, in whole or in part, this revision shall be entered upon in the following manner : The wish expressed by the assembly shall not be converted into a definitive resolution until after three successive deliberations held upon the subject, at the interval of one month between each deliberation, and the measure shall only be carried by a vote of three-fourths of the assembly. The number of votes must be five hundred at the least. The assembly for revision shall only be appointed for three months. It shall only engage in the special revision for which it has been assembled ; nevertheless, in cases of emergency, it may provide for legislative necessities.

CHAPTER XII.

TRANSITORY ARRANGEMENTS.

Art. 112. The provisions of the codes, laws, and regulations, now in force, and which are not in contradiction with the present constitution, shall remain in force until otherwise provided by law.

Art. 113. All the authorities constituted by the present laws shall continue in the exercise of their present duties until the promulgation of the organic laws which relate to them.

Art. 114. The law of judiciary organization will determine the particular mode for the appointment and first composition of the new tribunals.

Art. 115. After the vote upon the constitution, the constituent national assembly shall proceed to draw up the organic laws, which shall be determined by a special law for that purpose.

Art. 116. The first election of a president of the republic shall take place in conformity with the special law, passed by the national assembly on the 28th of October, 1848.

APPENDIX XIV.

THE PRESENT CONSTITUTION OF FRANCE.

When I wrote the article Constitution for the Encyclopædia Americana, which was before the French revolution of 1830, I classed constitutions under three general heads : 1. Those established by the sovereign power, real or so-called. These were subdivided into constitutions established by a sovereign people for their own government, as ours are; and into such as are granted, theoretically at least, by the plenary power of an absolute monarch; such as the then existing French charter was, a fundamental law called by the French octroyed. 2. Constitutions formed by contracts between nations and certain individuals whom they accept as rulers on distinct conditions. 3. Constitutions forming a compact between a number of states. The present constitution of France is not included in either of these classes. Its genesis, as the reader well knows, was that, first, an individual acquired absolute power by a conspiracy or coup d'état, then caused the people to vote whether they would grant him plenary power to prescribe a constitution; he received the power by above seven millions of votes, and issued the following document, copied from the constitution which Napoleon the First had prescribed at the beginning of this century. If, then, the reader insists upon calling this a constitution—we certainly do not call France at present a constitutional country—we may call it a constitution per saltum, for it was in former times one of the different ways of electing a pope, or the head of a great society, such as the Templars, to elect one individual with the right of appointing the chief, and this was called electing per saltum, by a leap. I also divided constitutions into cumulative constitutions, such as the constitution of England, or that of ancient Rome, and into enacted (or written) constitutions, such as ours are. The present constitution of France can again be classed neither under the one nor the other head. It may, perhaps, be called decreed, or by

(575)

any name the reader prefers. It is difficult to find an appropriate
name for a thing which is the result of a confused mixture of ideas,
of absolutism, popular sovereignty, violence, of breaking of oaths
and prescribing of others, of coup d'état, and ratification by those
whose work was destroyed by the soldiery, and by the idea of the
"incarnation" of popular absolute power in one person. Louis
Napoleon has been called the incarnation of a great principle. I
do not pretend to find a philosophical name for this product. Probably the whole constitution belongs to the "Napoleonic ideas," of
which we read so much at this moment ; or we may call it in future
an imperatorial or Cæsarean constitution.

The following, then, is the present French Constitution, as it
appeared in the official paper, the Moniteur, of January 15, 1852,
preceded by the proclamation of Louis Napoleon.

LOUIS NAPOLEON,

PRESIDENT OF THE REPUBLIC.

In the name of the French People.[1]

FRENCHMEN ! When, in my proclamation of the 2d of December,
I stated to you in all sincerity what were, according to my ideas,
the vital conditions of government in France, I had not the pretension, so common in our days, of substituting a personal theory
for the experience of ages.   On the contrary, I sought in the past
what were the best examples to follow, what men had given them,
and what benefit had resulted therefrom.

Having done so, I considered it only logical to prefer the precepts of genius to the specious doctrines of men of abstract ideas.
I took as model the political institutions which already, at the
beginning of the present century, in analogous circumstances,
strengthened society when tottering, and raised France to a high
degree of prosperity and grandeur.

I selected as model those institutions which, in place of disap-
pearing at the first breath of popular agitations, were overturned
only by all Europe being coalesced against us.

---

[1] The reader will find, on a subsequent page, that the whole of this constitution was retained under the empire with the exception of a few passages, relating to the hereditary part of the empire.

In a word, I said to myself, since France has existed for the last fifty years only in virtue of the administration, military, judicial, religious, and financial organization of the consulate and the empire, why should we not adopt likewise the political institutions of that period? As they were created by the same mind, they ought to bear in themselves the same character of nationality and practical utility.

In fact, as I stated in my proclamation, our present society, it is essential to declare, is nothing else than France regenerated by the revolution of '89 and organized by the emperor. Nothing remains of the old régime but great reminiscences and great benefits. But all that was then organized was destroyed by the revolution, and all that has been organized since the revolution, and which still exists, was done by Napoleon.

We have no longer either provinces, or *pays d'état*, or parliaments, or intendants, or farmers general, or feudal rights, or privileged classes in exclusive possession of civil and military employments, or different religious jurisdiction.

In so many things incompatible with itself had the revolution effected a radical reform, but without founding anything definitive. The first consul alone re-established the unity, the various ranks, and the veritable principles of government. They are still in vigor.

Thus, the administration of France was intrusted to prefects, sub-prefects, and mayors, who substituted unity for the commissions of the directory; and, on the contrary, the decision of business given to councils from the commune to the department. Thus, the magistracy was strengthened by the immovability of the judges, by the various ranks of the tribunals; justice was rendered more easy by the delimitation of attributions, from the justice of peace to the court of cassation. All that is still existing.

In the same way our admirable financial system, the bank of France, the establishment of budgets, the court of accounts, the organization of police, and our military regulations, date from the same period.

For fifty years it is the code Napoleon which had regulated the interests of citizens amongst themselves; and it is still the concordat which regulates the relations between the state and the church.

In fine, the greatest part of the measures which concern the pro-

37

gress of manufactures, commerce, letters, sciences, and the arts, from the regulations of the Theatre Française to those of the Institute— from the institution of the *prud'hommes* to the creation of the legion of honor, were fixed by decrees of that time.

It may then be affirmed that the framework of our social edifice is the work of the emperor, and that it has resisted his fall and three revolutions.

Why, with the same origin, should not the political institutions have the same chances of success ?

My conviction was long formed on the point, and it is on that account that I submit to your judgment the principal bases of a constitution, borrowed from that of the year 8. When approved by you, they will become the foundation of our political constitution.

Let us examine what the spirit of them is.

In our country, monarchical as it has been for eight hundred years, the central power has always gone on augmenting. The royalty destroyed the great vassals ; the revolutions themselves swept away the obstacles which opposed the rapid and uniform exercise of authority. In this country of centralization, public opinion has unceasingly attributed to the head of the government benefits as well as evils. And so, to write at the head of a charter that that chief is irresponsible, is to be against the public feeling— is to want to establish a fiction, which has three times vanished at the noise of revolutions.

The present constitution, on the contrary, declares that the chief whom you have elected is responsible before you ; and that he has always the right to appeal to your judgment, in order that, in solemn circumstances, you may continue to him your confidence, or withdraw it.

Being responsible, his action ought to be free and unshackled. Thence the obligation of his having ministers who may be the honored and puissant auxiliaries of his thought, but who no longer form a responsible council, composed of mutually responsible members, a daily obstacle to the particular impulse of the head of the state, the expression of a policy emanating from the chambers, and by that very circumstance exposed to frequent changes, which prevent all spirit of unity and all application of a regular system.

Nevertheless, the higher a man is placed the more independent he is, and the greater confidence the people have placed in him the more he has need of enlightened and conscientious councils. Thence the creation of a council of state, henceforward a veritable council of the government, first wheel in our organization, a collection of practical men, elaborating bills in special commissions, discussing them with closed doors, without oratorical ostentation in general assembly, and presenting them afterwards for acceptance to the legislative body.

Thus, the government is free in its movements and enlightened in what it does.

What is now to be the control exercised by the assemblies?

A chamber, which takes the title of legislative body, votes the laws and the taxes. It is elected by the universal suffrage, without *scrutin de liste*. The people, selecting each candidate separately, can more easily appreciate the merits of each.

The chamber is not to be any longer composed of more than about 260 members. That is a first guaranty of the calm of the deliberations, for only too often the inconsistency and ardor of passions have been seen to increase in assemblies in proportion to their number.

The report of the sittings, which is intended to inform the nation of what is going on, is no longer, as formerly, delivered to the party spirit of each journal; an official publication, drawn up by the care of the president of the chamber, will be alone permitted.

The legislative body discusses freely each law, and adopts or rejects it. But it cannot introduce all of a sudden those amendments which often disarrange the whole economy of a system and the ensemble of the original project. Still more, it does not possess that parliamentary initiative which was the source of such grave abuses, and which allowed each deputy to substitute himself at every turn for the government, by presenting projects the least carefully studied and inquired into.

The chamber being no longer in presence of the ministers, and the various bills being supported by speakers belonging to the council of state, time is not lost in vain interpellations and passionate debates, the only object of which was to overturn the ministers, in order to place others in their stead.

Thus, then, the deliberations of the legislative body will be independent, but the causes of sterile agitations will have been suppressed, and proper time and deliberation given to each modification of the law. The representatives of the nation will, in fact, maturely perform their serious functions.

Another assembly takes the name of senate. It will be composed of the elements which, throughout the whole country, create legitimate influences—an illustrious name, fortune, talent, and services rendered.

The senate is no longer, like the chamber of peers, the pale reflection of the chamber of deputies, repeating, at some days' interval, the same discussion in another tone. It is the depository of the fundamental compact, and of the liberties compatible with the constitution ; and it is only with respect to the grand principles on which our society is based that it examines all the laws, and proposes new ones to the executive power. It intervenes, whether to resolve every grave difficulty which might arise during the absence of the legislative body, or to explain the text of the constitution, or to insure what is necessary for its being acted on. It has the right to annul every arbitrary and illegal act, and, thus enjoying that consideration which belongs to a body exclusively occupied with the examination of great interests, or the application of grand principles, it occupies in the state the independent, salutary and conservative position of the ancient parliaments.

The senate will not be, like the chamber of peers, transformed into a court of justice ; it will preserve its character of supreme moderator ; for disfavor always reaches political bodies, when the sanctuary of the legislators become a criminal tribunal. The impartiality of the judge is often called in doubt, and he loses a portion of his prestige in public opinion, which sometimes goes the length of accusing him of being the instrument of passion or of hatred.

A high court of justice, chosen from amongst the higher magistrates, having for jurymen members of the councils-general throughout all France, will alone decide in cases of *attentats* against the head of the state and public safety.

The emperor used to say to the council of state : "A constitution is the work of time ; and too large a margin cannot be left to ameliorations." Consequently, the present constitution has fixed only what it was impossible to leave uncertain. It has not inclosed within an impassable circle the destinies of a great people ; it has left to change a margin sufficiently wide to allow, in great crises, other means of safety to be employed than the disastrous expedient of revolutions.

The senate can, in concert with the government, modify all that is not fundamental in the constitution; but as to the modifications effected in its primary bases, sanctioned by your suffrages, they cannot become definitive until after they have received your ratification.

Thus the people remains always master of its destiny, as nothing fundamental can be effected independently of its will.

Such are the ideas and principles which you have authorized me to carry into application. May the constitution confer on our country calm and prosperous days ! May it prevent the return of those intestine struggles, in which the victory, however legitimate it may be, is always dearly purchased ! May the sanction, which you have bestowed on my efforts, receive the benediction of heaven ! In that case, peace will be insured at home and abroad, my prayers will be granted, and my mission accomplished !

LOUIS NAPOLEON BONAPARTE.

Palace of the Tuileries, January 14, 1852.

Constitution made in virtue of the powers delegated by the French People to Louis Napoleon Bonaparte, by the vote of the 20th and 21st of December, 1851.

The president of the republic—

Considering that the French people has been called on to pronounce its opinion on the following resolution :

The people wish for the maintenance of the authority of Louis Napoleon Bonaparte, and give him the powers necessary to make a constitution, according to the bases laid down in his proclamation of the 2d December.

Considering that the bases proposed to the acceptance of the people were :

1. A responsible chief appointed for ten years.

2. Ministers dependent on the executive power alone.

3. A council of state, formed of the most distinguished men, to prepare the laws and support the discussion of them before the legislative body.

4. A legislative body, to discuss and vote the laws, elected by universal suffrage, without *scrutin de liste,* which falsifies the election.

5. A second assembly, formed of the most illustrious men of the country, as an equipoising power (*pouvoir ponderateur,*) guardian of the fundamental compact and of public liberties.

Considering that the people have replied affirmatively by seven millions five hundred thousand votes,

Promulgates the constitution, the tenor of which is as follows:

CHAPTER I.

ART. 1. The constitution admits, confirms, and guarantees the great principles proclaimed in 1789, and which are the bases of the public right of Frenchmen.

CHAPTER II.

FORMS OF THE GOVERNMENT OF THE REPUBLIC.

ART. 2. The government of the French Republic is confided for ten years to Prince Louis Napoleon Bonaparte, the actual president of the republic.

ART. 3. The president of the republic governs by means of ministers, of the council of state, of the senate, and of the legislative body.

ART. 4. The legislative power is exercised collectively by the president of the republic, the senate, and the legislative body.

CHAPTER III.

OF THE PRESIDENT OF THE REPUBLIC.

ART. 5. The president of the republic is responsible to the French people, to whom he has always the right to make an appeal.

ART. 6. The president of the republic is the chief of the state; he commands the land and sea forces, declares war, makes treaties of peace, alliance, and commerce, appoints to all employs, and makes the regulations and decrees necessary for the execution of the laws.

ART. 7. Justice is rendered in his name.

ART. 8. He alone has the initiative of laws.

ART. 9. He has the right of granting pardon.

ART. 10. He sanctions and promulgates the laws and the senatus consultum.

ART. 11. He presents every year to the senate, and to the legislative body, by a message, the state of the affairs of the republic.

ART. 12. He has the right to declare the state of siege in one or several departments, on condition of referring it to the senate within the shortest possible delay. The consequences of the state of siege are regulated by law.

ART. 13. The ministers depend only on the chief of the state—they are only responsible for the acts of the government as far as they are individually concerned in them ; there is no joint responsibility among them, and they can only be impeached by the senate.

ART. 14. The ministers, the members of the senate, of the legislative body, and of the council of state, the officers of the land and sea forces, the magistrates and public functionaries, take the following oath : *I swear obedience to the constitution and fidelity to the president.*

ART. 15. A senatus consultum fixes the sum allowed annually to the president of the republic during the whole continuance of his functions.

ART. 16. If the president of the republic dies before the expiration of his term of office, the senate is to convoke the nation, in order to proceed to a fresh election.

ART. 17. The chief of the state has the right, by a secret act deposited in the archives of the senate, to point out to the people the name of the citizens whom he recommends to the interest of France to the confidence of the people and to their suffrages.

ART. 18. Until the election of the new president of the republic, the president of the senate governs with the co-operation of the ministers in functions, who form themselves into a council of government, and deliberate by a majority of votes.

CHAPTER IV.

OF THE SENATE.

ART. 19. The number of senators shall not exceed 150; it is fixed for the first year at 80.

ART. 20. The senate is composed : 1, of cardinals, marshals, and admirals; 2, of citizens whom the president of the republic may think proper to raise to the dignity of senators.

ART. 21. The senators are appointed for life.

ART. 22. The functions of senator are gratuitous; nevertheless, the president of the republic may grant to senators, on account of services rendered, or of their position with regard to fortune, a personal donation, which cannot exceed 30,000 francs per annum.

ART. 23. The president and the vice-presidents of the senate are named by the president of the republic, and chosen from among the senators. They are appointed for one year. The salary of the president of the senate is fixed by a decree.

ART. 24. The president of the republic convokes and prorogues the senate. He fixes the duration of its sessions by a decree. The sittings of the senate are not public.

ART. 25. The senate is the guardian of the fundamental compact and of public liberties. No law can be promulgated without being submitted to it.

ART. 26. The senate may oppose the promulgation :

1. Of laws which may be contrary to, or be an attack on, the constitution, on religion, on morals, on freedom of worship, on individual liberty, on the equality of citizens in the eye of the law, on the inviolability of property, and on the principle of the immovability of the magistracy.

2. Of those which may comprise the defence of the territory.

ART. 27. The senate regulates by a senatus consultum :

1. The constitution of the colonies and of Algeria.

2. All that has not been provided for by the constitution, and which is necessary for its march.

3. The sense of the articles of the constitution which give rise to different interpretations.

ART. 28. These senatus consulta will be submitted to the sanction of the president of the republic, and promulgated by him.

ART. 29. The senate maintains or annuls all the acts which are referred to it as unconstitutional by the government, or denounced for the same cause by the petitions of citizens.

ART. 30. The senate may, in a report addressed to the president of the republic, lay down the bases of bills of great national interest.

ART. 31. It may also propose modifications in the constitution. If the proposition is adopted by the executive power, it must be stated by a senatus consultum.

ART. 32. Nevertheless, all modifications in the fundamental basis of the constitution, such as they were laid down in the proclamation of the 2d December, and adopted by the French people, shall be submitted to universal suffrage.

ART. 33. In case of the dissolution of the legislative body, and until a new convocation, the senate, on the proposition of the president of the republic, shall provide by measures of urgency for all that is necessary for the progress of the government.

CHAPTER V.

OF THE LEGISLATIVE BODY.

ART. 34. The election has for its basis the number of the population.

ART. 35. There shall be one deputy to the legislative body for every 35,000 electors.

ART. 36. The deputies are to be elected by universal suffrage, without *scrutin de liste*.

ART. 37. They will not receive any payment.

ART. 38. They are named for six years.

ART. 39. The legislative body discusses and votes bills and taxes.

ART. 40. Any amendment adopted by the committee charged to examine a bill shall be sent back without discussion to the council of state by the president of the legislative body. If the amendment is not adopted by the council of state, it cannot be submitted to the discussion of the legislative body.

ART. 41. The ordinary sessions of the legislative body last three months; its sittings are public; but, at the demand of five members, it may form itself into a secret committee.

ART. 42. The report of the sittings of the legislative body by the journals, or by any other means of publication, shall only consist in the reproduction of the minutes of the sitting, drawn up at its conclusion under the direction of the president of the legislative body.

ART. 43. The president and vice-presidents of the legislative body are named by the president of the republic for one year; they are to be chosen from among the deputies. The salary of the president of the legislative body will be fixed by a decree.

Art. 44. The ministers cannot be members of the legislative body.

Art. 45. The right of petition can only be exercised as regards the senate. No petition can be addressed to the legislative body.

Art. 46. The president of the republic convokes, adjourns, prorogues, and dissolves the legislative body. In the event of its being dissolved, the president of the republic must convoke a new one within a delay of six months.

CHAPTER VI.

OF THE COUNCIL OF STATE.

Art. 47. The number of councillors of state in ordinary service is from forty to fifty.

Art. 48. The councillors of state are named by the president of the republic, and may be dismissed by him.

Art. 49. The council of state is presded over by the president of the republic, and in his absence by the person whom he appoints as vice-president of the council of state.

Art. 50. The council of state is charged, under the direction of the president of the republic, to draw up bills and the regulations of public administration, and to solve the difficulties which may arise in administrative matters.

Art. 51. It supports, in the name of the government, the discussion of bills before the senate and legislative body. The councillors of state charged to speak in the name of the government are to be named by the president of the republic.

Art. 52. The salary of each councillor of state is 25,000 francs.

Art. 53. The ministers have rank, sitting, and deliberative votes in the council of state.

CHAPTER VII.

OF THE HIGH COURT OF JUSTICE.

Art. 54. A high court of justice shall try, without appeal, or without recourse to cassation, all persons who may be sent before it charged with crime, *attentats*, or conspiracies against the president of the republic, and against the internal and external safety of the state. It can only be formed in virtue of a decree of the president of the republic.

ART. 55. A senatus consultum will determine the organization of this high court.

CHAPTER VIII.

GENERAL AND TRANSITORY CLAUSES.

ART. 56. The provisions of the codes, laws and regulations, which are not contrary to the present constitution, remain in vigor until they shall have been legally revoked.

ART. 57. The municipal organization shall be determined by law. The mayors shall be named by the executive power, and may be chosen from those not belonging to the municipal council.

ART. 58. The present constitution will be in vigor from the day on which the great bodies of the state shall have been constituted. The decrees issued by the president of the republic, from the 2d December up to that period, shall have the force of law.

Given at the Palace of the Tuileries, this 14th day of January, 1852.

LOUIS NAPOLEON.

Sealed with the great seal.

The reader must remember that all the decrees, which were issued after the coup d'état, and before its "ratification" by the people, were considered as ratified likewise; for instance, the still existing law by which the government transports members of secret political societies, without trial, and by authority of which many other persons deemed dangerous were transported to Cayenne. The same is to be said of the stringent law of the press according to which every paper exists at the will of the government, with regulations which may become utterly ruinous for the editor and publisher. The minute regulations of the coats and trowsers of the senators and members of the legislative corps need not probably be mentioned here as organic laws; but on March 22d, 1852, appeared the following important decree :

Louis Napoleon, President of the French Republic:

Considering article 4 of the constitution, and seeing that at the moment when the senate and legislative body are about to enter on their first session, it is important to regulate their relations with the president of the republic and the council of state, and to establish, according to the constitution, the organic conditions of their works, decrees :

THIRD DIVISION.—OF THE LEGISLATIVE BODY.

CHAPTER I.

MEETING OF THE LEGISLATIVE BODY, FORMATION AND ORGANIZATION OF THE BUREAUS, AND VERIFICATION OF THE POWERS.

ART. 41. The legislative body is to meet on the day named by the decree of convocation.

ART. 42. At the opening of the first sitting the president of the legislative body, assisted by the four youngest members present, who will fill the functions of secretaries during the session, will proceed to form the assembly into seven bureaus, drawn by lot.

ART. 43. These seven bureaus, named for the whole of the session, will each be presided over by the oldest member, the youngest performing the office of secretary.

ART. 44. They will immediately proceed to the examination of the minutes of the election of the members distributed by the president of the legislative body, appointing one or several of their members to bring up a report thereof in a public sitting.

ART. 45. The assembly examines these reports; if the election be declared valid, the member when present immediately takes the oath prescribed by article 14 of the constitution; if absent, at his first appearance, after which the president of the legislative body pronounces his admission, and the deputy, who has not taken the oath within fifteen days of his election, is considered as dismissed. In case of absence the oath may be taken by writing, and in this case must be addressed by the deputy to the president of the legislative body, within the delay above mentioned.

ART. 46. After the verification of the returns, and without waiting for the decision on contested or adjourned elections, the president of the legislative body shall make known to the president of the republic that the legislative body is constituted.

CHAPTER II.

PRESENTATION, DISCUSSION, AND VOTE OF BILLS.

Art. 47. Bills presented by the president of the republic are to be presented and read to the legislative body by councillors of state appointed for that purpose, or transmitted, by order of the president of the republic, by the minister of state to the president of the legislative body, who causes them to be read at the public sitting. These bills will be printed, distributed, and placed on the order of the day of the bureaus, which will discuss them and name by ballot, and by a simple majority, a committee of seven members to report on them.

Art. 48. Any amendment arising from the initiative of one or more members, must be handed to the president, and be by him transmitted to the committee. No amendment can, however, be received after the report shall have been presented at the public sitting.

Art. 49. The authors of the amendment have a right to be heard before the committee.

Art. 50. If the amendment is adopted by the committee, it transmits the tenor of it to the president of the legislative body, who sends it to the council of state, and the report of the committee is suspended until the council of state has pronounced its opinion on it.

Art. 51. If the opinion of the council of state, transmitted to the committee through the president of the legislative body, is favorable, or a new wording proposed by the council of state be adopted by the committee, the text of the bill to be discussed in public sitting shall be modified conformably to the new wording adopted. If the opinion, on the contrary, is unfavorable, or if the new wording proposed by the council of state is not adopted by the committee, the amendment will be considered as not having been offered.

Art. 52. The report of the committee on the bill examined by it shall be read in a public sitting, and printed and distributed at least twenty-four hours before the discussion.

Art. 53. At the sitting fixed by the order of the day, the discussion shall open on the ensemble of the bill, and afterwards on the different articles or chapters, if it be a law on finance. There is never any occasion to deliberate on the question of deciding if the discussion of the articles is to be passed to, as they are successively put to the vote by the president. The vote takes place by *assis et lévé*, and if the result is doubtful, a ballot is proceeded to.

ART. 54. If any article is rejected, it is sent back to the committee for examination. Each deputy then, in the form specified in articles 48 and 49 of the present decree, presents such amendments as he pleases. Should the committee be of opinion that a new proposition ought to be made, it transmits the tenor of it to the president of the legislative body, who forwards it to the council of state. The matter is then proceeded on in conformity with articles 51, 52, and 53 of the present decree, and the public vote which then takes place is definitive.

ART. 55. After the vote on the articles, a public vote on the ensemble of the bill takes place by the absolute majority. The presence of the majority of the deputies is necessary to make the vote valid. Should less than that number be present, the vote must be recommenced. Bills of local interest are voted by *assis et lévé*, unless the ballot be called for by ten members at least.

ART. 56. The legislative body assigns no reasons for its decisions, which are expressed in the following form : "The legislative body has adopted ;" or "The legislative body has not adopted."

ART. 57. The minute of the bill adopted by the legislative body is signed by the presidents and secretaries, and deposited in the archives. A copy of the same, similarly signed, is transmitted to the president of the republic.

CHAPTER III.

MESSAGES AND PROCLAMATIONS ADDRESSED TO THE LEGISLATIVE BODY BY THE PRESIDENT OF THE REPUBLIC.

ART. 58. These are brought up and read in open sitting by the ministers or councillors of state named for that purpose. These messages or proclamations cannot be discussed or voted upon unless they contain a proposition to that effect.

ART. 59. The proclamations of the president of the republic, adjourning, proroguing, or dissolving the legislative body, are to be read in public sitting, all other business being suspended, and the members are immediately afterwards to separate.

ART. 60. The president of the legislative body announces the opening and closing of each sitting. At the end of each sitting, after having consulted the members, he names the hour of sitting for the following day, and the order of the day, which are posted up in the assembly. This order of the day is immediately forwarded to the minister of state, the president of the legislative body being responsible for all notices and communications being duly forwarded to him.

ART. 61. No member can speak without having asked and obtained leave of the president, and then only from his place.

ART. 62. The members of the council of state appointed in the name of the government to support the discussion of the laws are not subject to the formality of speaking in their turn, but whenever they require it.

ART. 63. The member called to order for having interrupted cannot be allowed to speak. If the speaker wanders from the question, the president may call him back to it. The president cannot allow any one to speak on the call to the question. If the speaker twice called to the question in the same speech shall continue to wander from it, the president consults the assembly to ascertain whether the right of speaking shall not be interdicted to the speaker for the rest of the sitting on the same question. The decision takes place by *assis et lévé* without debate.

ART. 64. The president alone calls to order the speaker who may interrupt it. The right to speak is accorded to him who, on being called to order, submits and demands to justify himself; he alone obtains the right to speak. When a speaker has been twice called to order in the same speech, the president, after having allowed him to speak to justify himself, if he demands it, consults the assembly to know if the right of speaking shall not be interdicted to the speaker for the rest of the sitting on the same question. The decision is taken by *assis et lévé* without debate.

ART. 65. All personalities and all signs of approbation or disapprobation are interdicted.

ART. 66. If a member of the legislative body disturbs order, he is called to order by name by the president; if he persists, the president orders the call to order to be inscribed in the minutes.

In case of resistance, the assembly, on the proposition of the president, pronounces, without debate exclusion from the house for a period which cannot exceed five days. The placarding of this decision in the department in which the member whom it concerns was elected may be ordered.

ART. 67. If the assembly becomes tumultuous, and if the president cannot calm it, he puts on his hat. If the disorder continues, he announces that he will suspend the sitting. If calm be not then re-established, he suspends the sitting during an hour, during which the deputies assemble in their respective bureaus. On the expiration of the hour the sitting is resumed; but, if the tumult recommences, the president breaks up the sitting and postpones it to the next day.

ART. 68. The demands for the order of the day, for priority, and for an appeal to the standing orders, have the preference over the principal question, and suspend the discussion of it. Orders of the day are never *motivés*. The previous question—that is to say, that there is no ground for deliberation—is put to the vote before the principal question. It cannot be demanded on propositions made by the president of the republic.

ART. 69. The demands for secret sittings, authorized by article 14 of the constitution, are signed by the members who make them, and placed in the hands of the president, who reads them, causes them to be executed, and mentioned in the minutes.

ART. 70. When the authorization, required by article 11 of the law of the 2d February, 1852, shall be demanded, the president shall only indicate the object of the demand, and immediately refer it to the bureaus, which shall nominate a committee to examine whether there be grounds for authorizing a prosecution.

CHAPTER IV.

MINUTES.

ART. 71. The drawing up of the minutes of the sittings is placed under the high direction of the president of the legislative body, and confided to special clerks nominated by him, and liable to dismissal by him. The minutes contain the names of the members who have spoken and the *résumé* of their opinions.

ART. 72. The minutes are signed by the president, read by one of the secretaries at the following sitting, and copied on two registers, signed also by the president.

ART. 73. The president of the legislative body regulates, by special order, the mode of communicating the minutes to the newspapers, in conformity with article 42 of the constitution.

ART. 74. Any member may, after having obtained the authorization of the assembly, cause to be printed and distributed at his own cost, the speech he may have delivered. An unauthorized printing and distribution shall be punished by a fine of from 500f. to 5,000f. against the printers, and of from 5f. to 500f. against the distributors.

We read in the Constitutionnel: "It is, as already stated, at the Tuileries, in the Salle des Maréchaux, that the sitting of the senate and legislative body on the 29th will be held. The prince-president, surrounded by his aides-de-camp, his orderly officers, his ministers, and the council of state, will be placed on a raised platform; opposite the president of the republic will be, on one side the senate, and on the other the legislative body. The prince-president will deliver a speech. A form of an oath will then be read, and each member of the senate and of the legislative body, on his name being called over, will pronounce from his place the words *Je le jure!* The clergy, the magistracy, and the diplomatic body will be represented at this solemnity. A small number of places will be reserved in an upper gallery for persons receiving invitations."

38

APPENDIX XV.

REPORT OF THE FRENCH SENATORIAL COMMITTEE ON THE
PETITIONS TO CHANGE THE REPUBLIC INTO AN EMPIRE, IN
NOVEMBER, 1852,[1] AND THE SENATUS CONSULTUM ADOPTED
IN CONFORMITY WITH IT.

MESSIEURS LES SENATEURS : France, attentive and excited, now
demands from you a great political act—to put an end to her
anxieties and to secure her future.

But this act, however serious it may be, does not meet with any
of those capital difficulties which hold in suspense the wisdom of
legislators. You know the wishes expressed by the councils general, the councils of arrondissement, and the addresses of the communes of France : wishes for stability in the government of Louis
Napoleon, and for return to a political form which has struck the
world by the majesty of its power and by the wisdom of its laws.
You have heard that immense petition of a whole people rushing
on the steps of its liberator, and those enthusiastic cries, which
we may almost call a plebiscite by anticipation, proceeding from
the hearts of thousands of agriculturists and workmen, manufac-
turers and tradesmen, Such manifestations simplify the task of
statesmen. There are circumstances in which fatal necessities prevent the firmest legislator from acting in accordance with public
opinion and with his own reason ; there are others where he requires a long consideration in order to solve questions on which
the country has not sufficiently decided. You, gentlemen, are not

---

[1] This report was read by Mr. Troplong, chairman of the committee. It
is universally ascribed to him, and Mr. Troplong is now president of the
senate. Whether this remarkable paper be considered as a political creed
or confiteor, or as a piece of attempted logic to connect certain occurrences
and account for surprising turns, or as a high state paper of singular shal-
lowness—in whatever light it may be viewed, it will be allowed on all hands
that it fully deserves preservation.

exposed either to this constraint or to this embarrassment. The national will presses and supplicates you, and your exalted experience tells you that in yielding to her entreaties you will contribute to replace France in the paths which are suitable to her interests, to her grandeur, and to the imperious necessities of her situation. All this is in fact explained by the events which take place before you.

After great political agitations, it always happens that nations throw themselves with joy into the arms of the strong man whom Providence sends to them. It was the fatigue of civil wars which made a monarch of the conqueror of Actium ; it was the horror of revolutionary excesses, as much as the glory of Marengo, which raised the imperial throne. In the midst of the recent dangers of the country, this strong man showed himself, on the 10th of December, 1848, and on the 2d of December, 1851, and France confided to him her standard, which was ready to perish. If she has declared her will to confide it to him forever in this memorable journey, which was only one suite of triumphs, it is because, by his courage and by his prudence, the man has shown himself equal to the task ; it is because, when a nation feels herself tormented by the agitations of a stormy government, a necessary reaction leads it towards him who can best secure order, stability and repose.

Louis Napoleon, therefore, is in this wonderful situation, that he alone holds in his hands these inestimable gifts. He has in the eyes of France, his immense services, the magic of his popularity, the souvenirs of his race, the imperishable remembrance of order, of organization, and of heroism, which make the hearts of all Frenchmen beat. He again revives in the eyes of Europe the greatest name of modern days, no more for the military triumphs for which his history is so rich, but for chaining down the political and social tempests, for endowing France with the conquests of peace, and for strengthening and fertilizing the good relations of states. Both at home and abroad it is to him that is attached a vast future of pacific labor and of civilization. That future must not be delivered to the chance of events and to the surprise of factions.

That is why France demands the monarchy of the emperor; that is to say, order in revolution, and rule in democracy. She wished it on the 10th December, when the artifices of an inimical constitution prevented the people from expressing their opinion. She wished it again on December 20, when the moderation of a noble character prevented its being demanded. But now the public sentiment overflows like a torrent; there are moments when enthusiasm has also the right of solving questions. For some time past visible signs announced what must be the mission of Louis Napoleon, and the foreseeing reason of statesmen put itself in accordance with the popular instinct in order to fix the character of it. After the bitter sarcasm which put the heir to a crown at the head of the republic, it was evident that France, still democratic from her habits, never ceased to be monarchical in her instincts, and that she wished for the re-establishment of the monarchy in the person of the prince who revealed himself to her as the conciliator of two ages and of two minds, the line of union of the government and of the people, the monarchical symbol of organized democracy.

At the end of the last century, the preponderance of the democratic element gave rise to a belief in speculative or ardent minds that France ought to mark the new era into which she had entered by a divorce between her government and the monarchical form. The republic was borrowed from the souvenirs of antiquity. But in France political imitations seldom succeed. Our country, although taxed with frivolity, is invincibly attached to certain national ideas and to certain traditional habits, by which it preserves the originality of which it is proud. The republic could not acclimatize itself on the French soil. It perished from its own excesses, and it only went into those excesses because it was not in the instincts of the nation. It was but an interval, brilliant abroad, and terrible at home, between two monarchies.

At that period, glory had raised to power one of those men who found dynasties and who traverse ages. It is on that new stem that France saw flourish a monarchy suitable to modern times, and which yielded to no other in its grandeur and in its power. Was it not a great lesson to see a similar fortune reserved, fifty years after, for a second trial of the republican form? Is it not a striking example of the perseverance of the French mind in things which are like the substance of her political life? Is not the proof complete and decisive?

It will be the more so, as the imperial monarchy has all the advantages of the republic without its dangers. The other monarchical régimes (the illustrious services of which we will not depreciate) have been accused of having placed the throne too far from the people, and the republic, boasting of its popular origin, skilfully entrenched itself against them in the masses, who believed themselves to be forgotten and overlooked. But the empire, stronger than the republic on democratic grounds, removes that objection. It was the government the most energetically supported, and the most deeply regretted by the people. It is the people who have again found it in their memory to oppose it to the dreams of ideaologists, and to the attempts of perturbators. On the one hand, it is the only one which can glorify itself in the right recognized by the old monarchy, "that it is to the French nation that it belongs to choose its king ;" on the other, it is the only one which has not had quarrels to settle with the people. When it disappeared in 1814, it was not by a struggle of the nation against its government. The chances of an unequal foreign war brought about that violent divorce. But the people have never ceased to see in the empire its emanation and its work ; and they placed it in their affections far above the republic—an anonymous and tumultuous government, which they remember much more by the violence of its proconsuls than by the victories which were the price of French valor.

That is why the Napoleonic monarchy absorbed the republic a first time, and must absorb it a second time. The republic is virtually in the empire, on account of the contract-like character of the institution, and of the communication and express delegation of power by the people. But the empire is superior to the republic, because it is also the monarchy ; that is to say, the government of all confided to the moderating action of one, with hereditary succession as a condition, and stability as its consequence. Monarchy has the excellent quality of yielding admirably to all the progress of civilization : by turns feudal, absolutist and mixed ; always old and always modern, it only remains to it to reopen the era of its democratic transformation, which was inaugurated by the emperor. That is what France now wishes ; it is what is asked of you by a country fatigued with utopian ideas, incredulous with respect to political abstractions, and whose genius, a union of sound sense and poesy, is so constituted that it only believes in power under the figure of a hero or a prince.

Even if the love of Frenchmen for monarchy be only a prejudice, it must be respected; a people can only be governed in accordance with its ideas.   But it must in particular be respected,
because it is inspired by the most essential wants and the most
legitimate interests of the country.

France is a great state which wishes to preserve at home and
abroad the force which a vast territory and thirty-five millions of
inhabitants give.   She is both agricultural and commercial.   Notwithstanding the fertility of her soil, she would be poor if manufactures were not to add immense personal to real capital, and if
the tastes for polite enjoyments and moderate luxury did not give
to labor an aliment always new.   But labor, in order to arrive at
the result of its enterprises, should be seconded by so many advances of funds, and such a persevering continuance of efforts, that
all success would escape it if it were interrupted or troubled by
the storms of disquieting and subversive policy.   It demands,
therefore, stability of institutions, as the source of confidence and
the mother of credit.

All these conditions of a regular and prosperous life the monarchy procures to France; any other form can only compromise
them.

Monarchy is the government of great states, to which institutions made for duration are marvellously suitable, as the most
solid foundations are required for a vast edifice.   The republic, on
the contrary, is only the government of small states, if we except
the United States of America, which, by their geographical position, form an exception to all rules, and which, besides, are only
a federation; a republic has never been able to establish itself
except in small nations, in which the embarrassments of that difficult and complicated form of government are corrected by the
small extent of territory and population.

Ancient Rome, so far from contradicting this rule, fully confirms
it.   The republic was only in the city and for the city.   Beyond it
there were only avaricious masters and oppressed subjects.   If ever
France can be said to have had a sort of neighborhood with the
republic, it was in the middle ages, when the republican spirit, extinguished from the time of the Cæsars, had become awakened in
a part of Europe; when France was only a chess-board of almost
independent provinces; and when the feudal principalities were in

all parts menaced by the communal movement. But since that movement all the interior action of France has removed her from the republican form. She, in particular, separated from it, when she gave herself a united territory and thirty-five millions of inhabitants living under the same laws, in the same country, and united by an infinite chain of dependent interests, which the same movement of circulation causes to terminate in a sole centre. Such a people is not to be shaken, as were the citizens of a single city, even if called Athens or Rome. A country which lives by its labor, and not by the labor of slaves and presents from the state, cannot be occupied with speeches of the forum, with the permanent agitation of comitia, with the anxieties of politics always in ebullition. This fever, to which democratic repúblics give the name of political life, cannot with impunity be communicated to a nation whose splendor particularly consists in the pacific development of its wealth, and in the regular and intelligent activity of its private interests.

Our fathers learned these truths in the rude school of public and private misfortunes. They compose all the interior policy of the commencement of this century.[1] Why should incorrigible innovators have in these latter times inflicted the too palpable demonstration of them upon us ? We have seen altars raised to instability and to periodical convulsions—the two plagues of the social body; we have seen laws made to reduce to solemn precepts the febrile and terrible crisis which may ruin a people ; we have seen the vessel of the state launched on an unknown sea, without a fixed point to guide itself by, without an anchor to cast out, and no one can say what would have become of the future of France, if Providence, watching over her, had not raised up the man of intrepid heart who extended his hand to her.

France, with full knowledge of what she is doing, intends to return to her natural state ; she longs to again find her real position and to resume her equilibrium. The French people, in its admirable common sense, is not so infatuated with its superior qualities that it is not aware of its weak points. It feels itself variable in its impressions, prompt to be worked on, and easy to be led away. And because it distrusts the rapidity of a first movement, it seeks

---

[1] See the speeches delivered in the Tribunal on the return to monarchy in 1804.

a fixed point in its institutions, and desires to be retained on a stable and solid basis. The French democracy has sometimes been compared to that of Athens. We have no objection to the comparison as far as politeness and elegance of mind are concerned, but we in all other respects utterly disclaim the similitude. The Greek democracies were nothing but a perpetual flux and reflux, never accepting the corrective of their levity. They were, besides, idle and grasping, living on the civic oboli and distributions of food. On the other hand, the French democracy, of a more masculine and more haughty character, does not look to the state for the care of its well-being; it depends on its own efforts for support, and most joyfully submits to the eternal law of God—daily labor. Its speculations comprise the whole world; it cultivates the earth with its free hands; it furrows the mighty deep with its vessels; it multiplies its industrial creations, engenders capital, and renders the future tributary to its able and immense combinations. When a nation thus founds its enterprises on credit and durability, when sometimes not less than half a century is necessary to it to reap the benefit of its operations, it is not the institutions of a day that can give it any hope of their success. It would be senseless if it did not desire to make the moving sphere of its interests turn round the motionless axis of a monarchy.

It is true that in France equality is an object of absolute worship, and a monarchy has, at its very first condition, the privileged existence of these grand and rare individualities which God raises above their fellows to form dynasties, and which are less human beings than the personification of a people and the concentrated radiation of a civilization. But equality, such as we conceive it in France, admits without jealousy those providential grandeurs, rendered legitimate by state reasons, below which it finds its level. At Rome and Athens equality consisted in rendering each citizen admissible to the supreme authority; and it is therefore that men considered all equality at an end when Augustus had converted the republic into a monarchy.[1] In France we considered it as saved and confirmed forever, under the reign of the emperor. The reason is, that in this country of equality there is nothing that is less supported than the government of one's equals; because equality is

---

[1] Tacitus: "Omnes, exutâ equalitate, jussa principis adspectare."— *Annal. I.* 4.

there fully satisfied in holding everything in its grasp, places, credit, wealth, and renown, and in having a wide and open road before it to arrive at everything except that extreme point of power, that inaccessible summit, which the care of the public tranquillity has placed high above all private competition. By that the democracy wonderfully agrees with the monarchy, and that union is so much the more solid that common sense unites with the habits of the people in cementing it.

But should cavilling minds, believing themselves more wise than the whole country, bring forward as an objection to the desire expressed for the hereditary empire, the inconveniences which minorities and bad princes may, at certain intervals, produce in monarchical states, we would reply that all human institutions contain within themselves certain defects and weaknesses. The monarchy has not the privilege of perfection; it has simply, for France, the merit of an incontestible superiority over the system of perpetual election, which only offers an eternal series of struggles and hazards, and which solves one difficulty only for the purpose of immediately leaving another in suspense.

Some ancient states, believing that they were improving on the monarchical system, had placed in sovereign and immoveable assemblies that element of stability which dynasties represent. But have not such assemblies also had their moments of weakness? Does not their history exhibit melancholy instances of venality or tyranny? Has not their baseness given them insolent and seditious guardians? And in the point of view of moral responsibility, which is one of the great checks on the conscience, there is not the slightest comparison between a man and an assembly. In assemblies, the responsibility of the body effaces that of the individuals; and as a collective responsibility is very nearly illusory, it comes to pass that that irresponsibility, which sometimes constitutes the force and independence of assemblies, is also the cause of their excesses. In a prince, on the contrary, the responsibility is undivided and inevitable, and presses with all its weight on the side of duty. In fine, when evil creeps into a sovereign political body, it continues there as a precedent, increases as a tradition, and the thing itself can only be kept up by keeping up the evil. On the contrary, if evil glides to the throne, it causes alarm only by temporary and intermittent perils, which are, besides, extenuated by the institutions and the modifications which are more easily effected in the case of a man than in that of an assembly. The feeble Louis XIII. was followed by the grand Louis XIV.; and, besides, Louis XIII. is, in the eyes of posterity, covered by his minister, Richelieu.

The general considerations appear to us to prove sufficiently that the national sentiment which addresses itself to you, gentlemen, as to sage mediators between the people and the prince, is neither a frivolous caprice nor a fleeting infatuation. Behind the fascination of a great name, and above the gratitude which is felt for the acts of a noble and patriotic courage, there are grand thoughts, power-ful interests, and an admirable intuitive perception of the public wants. France, gentlemen, desires to have the life of a great na-tion, and not that precarious and sickly existence which wastes away the social body. During the last four years, whilst subjected to perilous experiments, she has known how to correct by her good sense the evils of a deplorable situation. But it is necessary that such a situation should be brought to a close. Up to the present time, she had been able to find, in the midst of the tempests which assailed her, only transitory gleams of safety, on which no future prosperity could possibly be based. At present, she is about to enter the port, to found, by means of the fortunate pilot whom she greets with joy, the edifice of her prosperity on the solid ground of monarchy.

Let us now look to the details of the draft of the senatus con-sultum.

Louis Napoleon will take the name of Napoleon III. It is that name which re-echoed in the acclamations of the people; it is the name which was inscribed on the triumphal arches and trophies. We do not specially select it; we merely accept it from a natural and spontaneous election. It has, besides, that profound good sense which is always to be met with in the wonderful instincts of the people. It is a homage to Napoleon I., whom the people never forgets; and it is a pious remembrance for his youthful son, who was constitutionally proclaimed emperor of the French, and whose reign, short as it was, has not been effaced by the obscure existence of the exile. It solves for the future the question of succession, and signifies that the empire will be hereditary after Louis Napo-leon, as it has been for himself. In fine, it connects the political phase to which we owe our safety with the glorious name which was also the safety of past times.

And yet, by the side of the traditional element, contemporary events preserve their proper value and their peculiar signification. If Louis Napoleon is called on at present to resume the work of his uncle, it is not merely because he is the heir of the emperor, but because he deserves to be so ; it is on account of his devotedness to France, and of that spontaneous and personal action which has rescued the country from the horrors of anarchy. It is not sufficient for him to be the heir of the emperor; he must be again elected, for the third time, by the people. Thus the succession and the election will be in accord to double his force, the modern fact rendering the old one young and vigorous by the puissance of a reiterated consent and a second contract.

The senatus consultum next invests Louis Napoleon with the right to adopt an heir, in default of a direct successor. Adoption, which is a common right in private families, cannot be an exception in dynastic families ; for, when no natural heir exists, it is a principle in public law that the choice of the monarch belongs to the people. But that rule is that of ordinary times, and cannot suit in an absolute manner an order of things which again resumes a new course after a long interruption, and in the midst of the most extraordinary circumstances.

Louis Napoleon, the depository of the confidence of the people, charged by it to draw up a constitution, can, on infinitely stronger grounds, receive the mandate to provide for certain eventualities, and to prevent certain crises in which that constitution might perish. The strokes of nature have been often terrible in reigning families, and have set at naught the councils of wisdom. The French people will not imagine that it makes too great a sacrifice of its rights in abandoning itself once more to the prudence of the prince whom it has made the arbiter of its destinies. This provision, besides, is borrowed from the imperial constitution. The empire which revives ought not to be less powerful in its means than was the empire at its commencement. And in order to remain within the letter and the spirit of that precedent, the senatus consultum proposes to you not to admit of such adoption, except for the male descendants, natural and legitimate, of the brothers of Napoleon I. The right of unlimited adoption would be in manifest contradiction with the popular wish for the re-establishment of the empire, which is the guiding star of our deliberations. In fact, the empire is inseparable from the name of Bonaparte; and cannot be conceived without a member of that family with which the new form of the monarchy was stipulated in France. Everything ought to remain consistent in the work which we are considering.

But above that combination, solely of a political character, France places a hope which more than anything constitutes her faith in the future; and that is, that, at no distant period, a wife will take her place on the throne which is about to be raised and will give to the emperor scions worthy of his great name and of this great country. That debt was imposed on the prince on the day when the cries of "Vive l'Empereur" hailed him on his passage; and he will accept it virtually but necessarily the day when the crown will be placed on his head. For, since the empire is established with a view to the future, it ought to carry with it all the legitimate consequences which preserve that future from uncertainty and shocks.

In default of the direct line and of the adoptive line, the case of succession in the collateral line must be provided for. On that point we propose to you a clause, by which the people should confer on Louis Napoleon the right of regulating by an organic decree that order of succession in the Bonaparte family. By that means, our senatus consultum will remain more perfectly in accord with the popular wish, which in its unlimited confidence has placed in Louis Napoleon's hands the destinies of the country; it will likewise be more in conformity with the political changes which France has entered into since 2d December. The greatest political genius of Italy, in the sixteenth century, was accustomed to say, in those rare and solemn moments in which the question is to found a new state, that the will of a single man was indispensable. (1.) That is what the nation comprehended so admirably when it remitted to Louis Napoleon the task of drawing up the constitution which governs us. At present, that a capital modification is taking place in one of the very foundations of that constitution, it appears natural and logical to again confer on Louis Napoleon a portion of the constituent power, in order that, in the special point which concerns most intimately the interests of the dynasty of which the nation declares him the head, he may fix on such provisions as appear to him best appropriated to the public interest and the interest of the monarch. For his family, as well as for the country, Louis Napoleon is the man of an exceptional situation, and no fear must be entertained of adding to his power, in order that, with the assent of all, he may settle it by the authority of a single person. We, therefore, propose to you, after a conference with the organs of the government, which has led to unanimity of opinion, an article thus worded: "Art. 4. Louis Napoleon Bonaparte regulates, by an organic decree addressed to the senate and deposited in the archives, the order of succession to the throne in the Bonaparte family, in case he should not leave any di rect or adopted heir."

It is not necessary for us to say to you that in this system the formula to be submitted to the French people ought to contain an express mention of that delegation. It will be necessary, according to the constitution, that the French people be called on to declare whether it desires or not to invest Louis Napoleon with the power which we conceive ought to be conferred on him.

After having thus spoken of the succession to the imperial crown, the senatus consultum carries the attention to the condition of the family of the emperor. It divides it into two parts: 1, the imperial family, properly so called, composed of the persons who may by possibility be called to the throne, and of their descendants of both sexes; and 2, of the other members of the Bonaparte family.

The situation of the princes and princesses of the imperial family is to be regulated by senatus consulta; and they cannot marry without the emperor's consent. Art. 6 pronounces for any infraction of this regulation of public interest the penalty of losing all right to the succession, with the proviso, however, that in case of the dissolution of the marriage by the death of the wife, without issue, the right is at once recovered.

As to the other members of the Bonaparte family, who compose the civil family, it is to the emperor, and not any longer to senatus consulta, that it appertains to fix by statutes their titles and situation. It is useless to insist on this distinction, as it is explained by the difference which exists between the civil family and that uniting in itself the double character of civil family and political family.

We have also to request your special attention to the final paragraph of article six, which confers on the emperor full and entire authority over all the members of his family. These special powers are called for by the gravest considerations, and belong to the right generally instituted for reigning families. Princes are placed in so elevated a position by public right and national interest, that they are, in many respects, out of the pale of the common law. The greater their privileges are, the more their duties are immense towards the country. Montesquieu has said: " It is not for the reigning family that the order of succession is established, but because it is for the interest of the state that there should be a reigning family." They belong, therefore, to the state by stricter ties than other citizens, and on account even of their very greatness must be retained in a sort of perpetual ward-dom, under the guardianship of the emperor, the defender of their dignity, the appreciator of their actions, and serving to them as father as much as guardian, in order to preserve to the nation this patrimony in fact.

If these reasons do not apply in all their extent to the members of the private family, there are others of not less importance, which are drawn from the conjoint responsibility imposed by a name which is the property of the nation, as much as of the persons who have the honor of bearing it.

Besides, several of these persons have the privilege of being the only ones in the state that the emperor can place by adoption in the rank of the persons who may succeed to the crown. But there is no public privilege which ought not to be paid for by duties specially created to justify its necessity, and to co-operate in the object of its establishment.

There is another point which it is sufficient for us to remind you of—the maintenance of the Salic law in the imperial dynasty. In France, the Salic law is, so to speak, incorporated with the monarchy, and, although its origin goes back to the remotest periods, it has so completely penetrated into our way of thinking, and is so completely in accord with the rules of French policy, that it is inseparable from all transformations in the monarchical principle.

Finally, gentlemen, the senatus consultum provides for the case in which the throne should be vacant; "if ever the nation should be so unfortunate as to experience this affliction," (to use the language of the celebrated edict of July, 1717,) " it would be for the nation itself to repair it." Article 5 formally recognizes this fundamental, essential, and inalienable right. At the same time it provides for the means of preparing a choice worthy of the French people, by its prudence and maturity. In consequence, an organic senatus consultum, proposed to the senate by the ministers formed into a council of government, with the addition of the president of the senate, the president of the legislative body, and the president of the council of state, shall be submitted to the free acceptance of the people, and will give to France a new emperor.

Such, gentlemen, are the principal provisions of the senatus consultum, now submitted to you for consideration, and which will prepare the august contract of the nation with its chief. Should you adopt it, you will order by a concluding article, in virtue of the constitution, that the people be consulted concerning the reestablishment of the imperial dignity in the person of Louis Napoleon, with the succession of which we have just explained to you the combinations. But, gentlemen, we may affirm, whilst bending at present before a public will which only asks for an occasion to burst forth afresh, that the empire is accomplished. And that empire, the dawn of which has lighted up the path of Louis Napoleon in the departments of the south, rises over France, surrounded by the most auspicious auguries. Everywhere hope revives in men's minds ; everywhere capital, restrained by the uncertainty of the future, rushes with ardor into the channels of business ; and everywhere the national sap circulates, and vivifies to produce the most abundant fruits.

This reign, gentlemen, will not be cradled in the midst of arms and in the camp of insurgent prætorian guards. It is the work of the national feeling, most spontaneously expressed ; it has been produced in our commercial towns, in our ports, in the most peaceful centres of agriculture and manufactures, and in the midst of the joy of an affectionate people ; it will consequently be the *Empire of Peace*—that is to say, the revolution of '89, without its revolutionary ideas, religion without intolerance, equality without the follies of equality, love for the people without socialist charlatanism, and national honor without the calamities of war. Ah! if the great shade of the emperor should cast a glance at this France which he loved so much, it would thrill with joy at beholding the gloomy predictions of St. Helena, at one moment so

near being realized, totally disproved.   No ; Europe will not be
delivered up to disorder and anarchy !   No ; France will not lose
the grandeur of her institutions, and it is the ideas of Napoleon
directed towards peace by a generous-minded prince, which will be
the safeguard of civilization.

SENATUS CONSULTUM.

In the month of November, 1852, the senate adopted the following senatus consultum :

SENATUS CONSULTUM.

*Proposition to modify the Constitution, in conformity with
Articles 31 and 32.*

ART. 1. The imperial dignity is re-established.   Louis Napoleon Bonaparte is emperor, under the name of Napoleon III.

ART. 2. The imperial dignity is hereditary in the direct and legitimate issue of Louis Napoleon Bonaparte, from male to male
in the order of primogeniture, and with perpetual exclusion of
women and their descendants.

ART. 3 Louis Napoleon Bonaparte, in default of a male child,
may adopt the children and legitimate descendants in the male line
of the brothers of Napoleon I..

The forms of adoption shall be regulated by a senatus consultum.

If, after the adoption, male children of Louis Napoleon shall
be born, his adoptive sons cannot succeed him, except after his own
legitimate descendants.

The successors of Louis Napoleon, and their descendants, cannot adopt.

ART. 4. Louis Napoleon regulates, by an organic decree addressed to the senate and deposited in its archives, the order of
succession on the throne in the Bonaparte family, in case he should
not leave any direct legitimate or adopted heir.

ART. 5. In default of any legitimate or adoptive heir of Louis
Napoleon Bonaparte, and of successors in collateral line who may
derive their right from the organic decree above mentioned, a
senatus consultum, proposed to the senate by the ministers, formed
into a council of government, with the addition of the actual

presidents of the senate, the legislative corps, and of the council of state, and submitted for adoption to the people, appoints the emperor, and regulates in his family the hereditary order from male to male, to the perpetual exclusion of women and their descendants.

Until the election of the new emperor shall be consummated, the affairs of the state are governed by the actual ministers, who shall form themselves into a council of government and deliberate by a majority of votes.

ART. 6. The members of the family of Louis Napoleon eventually called to succeed him, and their descendants of both sexes, form a part of the imperial family. A senatus consultum regulates their position. They cannot marry without the authorization of the emperor. Their marriage without this authorization deprives of the right of inheritance as well him who contracts the marriage as his descendants.

Nevertheless, if there are no children of such a marriage, and the wife dies, the prince having contracted such a marriage recovers his right of inheritance.

Louis Napoleon fixes the titles and the condition of the other members of his family.

The emperor has plenary authority over all the members of his family. He regulates their duties and their obligations by statutes which have the force of laws.

ART. 7. The constitution of the 15th of January, 1852, is maintained in all those dispositions which are not contrary to the present senatus consultum; it cannot be modified except in the forms and by the means there prescribed.

ART. 8. The following proposition shall be presented for the acceptation of the people in the forms determined by the decrees of the 2d and 4th of December, 1851 :

" The people wills the re-establishment of the imperial dignity in the person of Louis Napoleon Bonaparte, with inheritance in direct legitimate or adoptive descendants, and gives him the right to regulate the order of succession to the throne in the Bonaparte family in the manner described in the senatus consultum of the 7th of November, 1852."

39

The senate adopted this senatus consultum by eighty-six votes of eighty-seven senators.

More than eight millions of people voted *yes,* according to the official publications.

"All Frenchmen of the age of twenty-one, in possession of their civil and political rights," were called upon to vote by a decree of some length, of November 7th, 1852.

The paper on elections, the first of this appendix, contains the details of this and other votes, as well as the view of the author regarding them.

In addition to the papers here given, it ought to be remembered that the senate can decree organic laws, and thus a senatus consultum has been passed, according to which the legislative corps (already so denuded of power and influence) is deprived of the right to vote on the single items of the budget. It must adopt or reject the budgets of each ministry as a whole. This means, of course, that it must adopt the whole—for government would necessarily be brought to a stop if the entire budget of a ministry were rejected; and the executive government would simply order again the soldiery to clear the legislative hall, assume the dictatorial power, and make the people rectify the coup.

APPENDIX XVI.

THE minister of the interior addressed the following circular to the prefects of the departments:

"MONSIEUR LE PREFET: You will shortly have to proceed to the elections of the legislative body. It is a grave operation, which will be either a corollary or a contradiction of the vote of the 20th December, according to the employment which you make of your legitimate influence. Bear well in mind that universal suffrage is a new and unknown element, easy for a glorious name to make the conquest of, unique in history, representing in the eyes of the populations authority and power, but very difficult to fix on secondary individualities; consequently, it is not by following former errors that you will succeed. I desire to inform you of the views of the head of the state. You perceive that the constitution has aimed at avoiding all the theatrical and dramatic part of the assemblies, by interdicting the publication of the speeches delivered; in that way the members of those assemblies, not being occupied with the effect which their words in the tribune are to produce, will think more of carrying on seriously the affairs of their country. The electoral law will pronounce on the incompatibilities. The situation of public functionaries in a political assembly is always a very delicate matter, as in voting with the government they lower their proper character, and in voting against it they weaken the principle of authority. The exclusion of functionaries, and the suppression of all indemnity, must necessarily limit, in a country where fortunes are so divided as in ours, the number of men who will be willing and able to fulfil such duties. Nevertheless, as the

(611)

government is firmly decided never to make use of corruption,
direct or indirect, and to respect the conscience of every man, the
best means of preserving to the legislative body the confidence of
the populations is to call to it men perfectly independent by their
situation and character.   When a man has made his fortune by
labor, manufactures, or agriculture, if he has been occupied in improving the position of his workmen, if he has rendered himself
popular by a noble use of his property, he is preferable to what is
conventionally called a political man, for he will bring to the preparation of the laws a practical mind, and will second the government in its work of pacification and re-edification.   As soon as
you shall have intimated to me, in the conditions indicated above,
the candidates who shall appear to you to have the most chance of
obtaining a majority of votes, the government will not hesitate to
recommend them openly to the choice of the electors.   Hitherto,
it has been the custom in France to form electoral committees
and meetings of delegates.   That system was very useful when the
vote took place *au scrutin de liste*.   The *scrutin de liste* created
such confusion, and such a necessity for coming to an understanding, that the action of a committee was indispensable; but now
these kind of meetings would be attended with no advantage, since
the election will only bear on one name; it would only have the
inconvenience of creating premature bonds, and appearances of acquired rights which would only embarrass the people, and deprive
them of all liberty.   You will, therefore, dissuade the partisans of
the government from organizing electoral committees.   Formerly,
when the suffrage was restricted, when the electoral influence was
divided among a few families, the abuse of this influence was most
shameful.   A few crosses, little merited, and a few places, could
always secure the success of an election in a small college.   It was
very natural that this abuse should cause great dissatisfaction, and
that the government should be called on to abstain from any osten-
sible interference.   Its action and its preferences were then occult,
and for that very reason compromised its dignity and its authority.
But by what favors could the government be now supposed capable
of influencing the immense body of the electors? By places? The
whole government of France has not establishments vast enough
to contain the population of one canton. By money? Without

speaking of the honorable susceptibilities of the electors, the whole public treasury would not be sufficient for such a purpose. You will remember to what the result of the efforts of the government was reduced on the 10th December, 1848, in favor of the candidate to the presidency who was then in power. With universal suffrage there is but one powerful spring, which no human hand can restrain or turn from the current in which it is directed, and that is public opinion; that imperceptible and indefinable sentiment which abandons or accompanies governments, without their being able to account for it, but which is rarely wrong in doing so; nothing escapes it, nothing is indifferent to it; it appreciates not only acts, but divines tendencies; it forgets nothing, it pardons nothing, because it has, and can have, but one moving power—the self-interest of each; it is alive to all, from the great policy which emanates from the chief of the state to the most trivial proceedings of the local authorities, and the political opinion of a department depends more than is generally believed on the spirit and conduct of its administration. For a long time past the local administrations have been subordinate to parliamentary exigencies; they occupied themselves more in pleasing some influential men in Paris than in satisfying the legitimate interests of the communes and the people. These days are happily, it may be said, at an end. Make all functionaries thoroughly understand that they must carefully occupy themselves with the interests of all, and that he who must be treated with the greatest zeal and kindness is the humblest and the weakest. The best of policies is that of kindness to persons, and facility for interests—and that functionaries shall not suppose themselves created for purposes of objection, embarrassment, and delay, when they are so for the sake of dispatch and regularity. If I attach so much importance to these details, it is because I have remarked that inferior agents often believe that they increase their importance by difficulties and embarrassments. They do not know what maledictions and unpopularity they bring down on the central government. This administrative spirit must be inflexibly modified; that depends on you; enter firmly on that path. Be assured that then, instead of seeing enemies in the government and local administration, the people will only consider them a support and help. And when afterwards you, in the name of this loyal and paternal government, recommend a candidate to the choice of the electors, they will listen to your voice and follow your counsel. All the old accusations of oppositions will fall before this new and simple line of policy, and people in France will end by understanding that order, labor, and security can only be established in a durable manner in a country under a government listened to and respected.

" Accept, &c.

" A. DE MORNY."

INDEX.

Cis-Caucasian race, 22, note.
Cities, in the Netherlands were sovereign, 173, 343; not sufficient as patria for moderns, 173, and note.
City; the ancients confound it with the state, 47 and sequ.
City-states and national states, 367 and sequ.
Civilization, law of spreading, 298.
Civil Law, influence on common law, 216.
Civil Liberty. See Liberty.
Civil List. See Taxation.
Code Napoleon and equality, essence of civilization, 19.
Codification, does not prevent interpretation, 208.
Coëtlogon, French case of opening letters, 93.
Coke, on the justice of the peace, 326, note.
Collard, Roger, on absolutism of majority, 287.
Colonization Society, 128.
Color, effect of distinction of races on American sympathy and politics, 265.
Commissions, contradistinguished from regular courts, 109.
Common law, necessary for independence of the law, 208 and sequ. Constitutes the greater portion of British constitution, 213. Compared with civil law, 214; article common law in Encyclopædia Americana, written by Judge Story, 216; American writers who take French views of liberty, and of law against it, 217.
Communion, right of, 89 and sequ. Liberty of, always abolished by absolutists, 277.
Communism, the basis of the Utopias, 46, note.
Compensation bill, intended by Romilly for accused persons not found guilty, 79.
Compurgators, 460.
Conclamation, election by, of medieval character, 408.
Confederation, articles of, and perpetual union, in full, 410 and sequ.
Confirmation of liberties, 476 and sequ.
Confirmatio Chartarum, 476 and sequ.
Confiscation, incompatible with civil liberty, 103.
Conflicts between courts and administrations, were to be decided by a

separate tribunal, according to French constitution of 1848, p. 571.
Conscience, liberty of, 99 and sequ. American court regarding it, ibid. Necessity, at present, 101. Why its full acknowledgement in England so late, 103.
Conscription in France, 122, note.
Constitutions, produced in our age, 17, 18; written and unwritten; enacted and cumulative, 166, note; of England, consists chiefly of common law, 213; what it consists of, ibid; of U. S., called atheistic, 264; of U. S., works on it, and on their government, 270, note; of United States, in full, 521 and sequ; French, of 1793, in full, 536; of the French republic, of 1848, p. 560 and sequ; of France, of 1851, p. 581.
Constitutionality, declared by supreme court, 166 and sequ.
Coode, codifying English poor law, 210, note.
Cooper, Dr. Thomas, opinion of Hamilton's parliam. logic, 195, note.
Corruption of blood, not admitted in U. S., 82; in England, 104.
Council of State, in France, 203.
Council of Trent, adopted half hour rule, 137, note.
Counsel of the prisoner, 243.
Country, necessary for moderns, instead of ancient cities, 173, and note.
Cours prévotales, abolished by charter of Louis XVIII. See Natural Courts.
Courvoisier, and Philips his counsel, 248, note.
Craik, G. L., proposed a plan of election to represent minority, 181, note.
Cranworth, Lord, on codification, 210, note; on trial by jury, 239.
Crimen exceptum, high treason, 84.
Cromwell, congratulations on dissolving parliament, 424.
Crowds, acclaiming, deceive, 403.
Crown, or principate on the continent, 51.
Crusades, in connection with the Vox populi vox Dei, 406.
Cumulative constitutions. See Enacted Constitutions.
Curtis, G. J., History of Cons. of U. S., 270, note.

208. What it consists in, ibid.
Common law, necessary for it, 208
and sequ.
Independence, Declaration of, of the
United States, in full, 505 and sequ.
Individual character and its elements,
50.
Individual property, its fullest protection an element of liberty, 103.
Individual sovereignty, 290; declared
by Lamartine, 303.
Individualism, 104, note.
Initiative, in legislation, 186.
Inorganic power of the people not
liberty, 374.
Inquisitorial trial, 221 and sequ; paper on it, 457. Influence of the
inquiring judge, ibid and sequ;
prisoner urged to confess, 458; no
cross-examination, ibid; no regular
indictment, ibid; character of court
and police, mingle, ibid; cautious
defence, 459; admits of half proofs,
ibid; illogical character of half
proofs, 460. Compurgators in Ripuarian laws, ibid. Koran, ibid.
Legal truths, 462. Torture, existed very late, 463, note.
Institute and institution, 309.
Institution, 301 and sequ. Definition
of, 304 and sequ. Grown and enacted institutions, 307; definition
by Dr. Arnold, 308; insures perpetuity, 310; must be independent, 311; alone can prevent the
growth of too much power; Greeks
had no word for it, 311. Romans
reared many institutions, 313. Old
usages called institutions, 314. Necessary attributes of an institution,
315; the opposite to subjectiveness,
ibid. Dangers, 316; tenancy, 317.
Institutional nations, 318; governments, ibid. Gives strength to error, 319; effete and hollow ones,
322; deciduous institutions, 323.
Institutional self-government, 323.
Anglican view of it, 324; its requirements, 325; its uses and efficiency with reference to liberty,
329. Obedience with reference to
institution, 332; its tenacity, 334
and sequ; its formative power,
335; its assimilative and transmissible character, 336 and sequ. Why
did the Netherlands not plant colonies which have become independencies? 337, note; its assimilative

character forcibly shown in the
United States, 338. Stability, 339.
Its dangers, 343. On conflicts, 346.
Institutions bad from beginning,
348; they protect against court
profligacy, 357; it prevents national energy from being directed
exclusively to external increase,
358. Insecurity of uninstitutional
governments, 370 and sequ. Institutions, they survive England's
revolutionary absolutism, 370; democratic inorganic masses hostile
to it, and in favor of monarchy, 375.
Institutional liberty, 304 and sequ.
Institutors, the greatest rulers are,
320.
Institutum, does not exactly correspond to our word institution, 311,
note.
Interference, French, by government,
256.
Interpretation, unavoidable, 208. Papal power against it, 209; civil law
against it, ibid. Locke against it,
210. Bavarian code, 211.

JAMES II. subverting constitution
apparently in favor of liberty, 395.
Jefferson, Manual of Parliamentary
Practice, 195.
Jeffreys, Lord, even he for allowing
counsel to prisoners, 243.
Johnson, Dr. Samuel, corn-laws, etc.,
195.
Judge-made law, 214.
Judiciary, independence of. See In-
dependence of Judiciary.
Jugements administratifs, in France,
220.
Julius Cæsar, 383.
Junkerthum, appellation of a Ger-
man party, 121.
Justice of the peace, French, 284.
Justice of the peace, English, 326.

KEEPER of the seals. See Chancel-
lor, Lord, of England.
King, Rufus, in connection with Ame-
rican free river navigation, 273.
King's Notes of the Voyage of the
Morrison, 113.
King's Bench, its power, 366.
Kingless polity, not necessarily a re-
public, 363.
Kingly commonwealth, name given by
Dr. Arnold to English polity, 361.

the introduction of publicity in the Senate of United States, by James C. Welling, 139, note.

QUARTERING of soldiers, 116 and sequ.
Queen of England, called an institution, 313.

RAIKES, CHARLES, Notes on the Northwestern Province, 131.
Rapp, General, his opinion of Napoleon, 160.
Raumer, von, Diplomatic Despatches of the Last Century, 359, note.
Rousseau hates representative government, 18; his views lead to centralized government, ibid.
Reduplication, psychical, 196; law of, 316.
Report of the French senate on the petitions to change the republic into an empire, 594.
Representative government, 168, and sequ; differs from deputative government, ibid. Derided, 18; hated by Rousseau, ibid.
Representation, basis of, 175.
Representatives must be free, 183; frequent election of them, ibid; must be protected, ibid. Free from arrest, 185. Possessing the initiative, 186. Officers of the United States cannot be members of congress, 186. Are they national, or merely for their constituents? 203.
Republic and respublica, 43.
Republic, in 1848, was telegraphed from Paris and accepted by return, 400.
République democratique et sociale, 289.
Repudiation, 106. Sir A. Alison on Repudiation, 107, and note. Repudiation has not been republican but rather monarchical, 107.
Responsible ministers, 163 and sequ.
Respublica and republic, 43.
Right, Petition of, in full, 484.
Rights, Bill of, in full, 499 and sequ.
Rights of man, 536 and sequ.
Ripuarian laws, 460.
Rivers, international question of free navigation, 272 and note; freedom of their navigation peculiar to United States, 271. Difficulty in Germany, 272; Scheldt, ibid. Magna Charta regarding rivers, ibid.

Ordinance of 1787 declaring rivers forever free, 274.
Robespierre's great speech, 280.
Roman lawyers, their definition of liberty, 26. Their dictum of the emperor's pleasure, 26 and note.
Romans did not incline to abstraction, 311 and sequ.
Romilly, Sir Samuel, his opinion on putting questions to the prisoner, 76; on absence of parliamentary practice in French revolution, 193; on ethics of lawyers, 249.
Rousseau against division of power, 155; his aversion to representative government, 287; social contract only establishes unity of power, 378. Was the text-book of leading revolutionists in France, 379.
Royal Republic, England called thus, 361.
Ruatan warrant, 180.
Ruggles, Samuel B., speech on right and duty of American Union to improve the navigable waters, 1852, and memorial of the canal board and canal commissioners, etc., 1858, p. 274.
Russell, Lord John, on definitions of liberty, 36. His History of English Government and Constitution, ibid.
Russia, insecurity of her rulers, 371.

SANDERSON, casuist, 407, note.
Sardanapalus, inscription on his tomb, 345.
Scheldt, navigation of, 272.
Schmidt, I. J., Translation of History of the East Moguls by Ssanang, etc., 386.
Scott, General, his conduct when the government of Mexico was offered, 330; his own statement, 330, note.
Secret political societies, 138.
Sejunction of the Netherlands, 343.
Self-Accusation, principle of, in China, 78.
Self-Development of law, 218 and sequ.
Self-Government, saved by England, 21; the word belongs exclusively to Anglican race, ibid; Armenian term for it, 39, note.
Self-Government, 251 and sequ. History of the term, note on 251, and sequ; is organic, 254.
Self-Government, the fittest government for man in his nobler phase,

FINIS.